Analytical
Contribution
Accounting

Recent Titles from Quorum Books

Handbook of Management Control Systems
Ahmed Belkaoui

Currency Fluctuations and the Perception of Corporate Performance:
A Communications Approach to Financial Accounting and Reporting
Loretta Graziano

International Law of Take-Overs and Mergers: United States, Canada,
and South and Central America
H. Leigh Ffrench

The Foreign Debt/National Development Conflict: External Adjustment
and Internal Disorder in the Developing Nations
Chris C. Carvounis

Effective Financial Management in Public and Nonprofit Agencies:
A Practical and Integrative Approach
Jerome B. McKinney

The Logic of Intuitive Decision Making: A Research-Based Approach
for Top Management
Weston H. Agor

International Law of Take-Overs and Mergers: The EEC, Northern Europe,
and Scandinavia
H. Leigh Ffrench

Office Information Technology: A Decision-Maker's Guide to Systems
Planning and Implementation
Randy J. Goldfield

Developing a Professional Sales Force: A Guide for Sales Trainers and
Sales Managers
David A. Stumm

A Working Guide for Directors of Not-for-Profit Organizations
Charles N. Waldo

Causation, Prediction, and Legal Analysis
Stuart S. Nagel

The Right of Privacy in the Computer Age
Warren Freedman

Information and Records Management: A Decision-Maker's Guide to
Systems Planning and Implementation
Milburn D. Smith III

Marketing and the Quality-of-Life Interface
A. Coskun Samli, editor

ANALYTICAL CONTRIBUTION ACCOUNTING

The Interface of Cost Accounting and Pricing Policy

WALTER GEORGES AND
ROBERT W. McGEE

Quorum Books

NEW YORK • WESTPORT, CONNECTICUT • LONDON

Library of Congress Cataloging-in-Publication Data

Georges, W.
　Analytical contribution accounting.

　Bibliography: p.
　Includes index.
　1. Cost accounting.　2. Pricing policy.
3. Accounting and price fluctuations.　I. McGee,
Robert W.　II. Title.
HF5686.C8G395　1987　　　658.8'16　　　86-16973
ISBN 0-89930-209-2 (lib. bdg. : alk. paper)

Library of Congress Catalog Card Number: 86-16973
ISBN: 0-89930-209-2

First published in 1987 by Quorum Books

Greenwood Press, Inc.
88 Post Road West, Westport, Connecticut 06881

Printed in the United States of America

The paper used in this book complies with the
Permanent Paper Standard issued by the National
Information Standards Organization (Z39.48-1984).

10　9　8　7　6　5　4　3　2　1

Contents

Contents

Preface

The purpose of this book is to shed new light upon the interfaces between cost accounting and pricing policy of manufacturers. The core of this study is in "management accounting," but there are also aspects of marketing management and business economics.

Considering the fact that traditional and classical "full costing" and "direct costing" are relatively inadequate for pricing purposes, we develop an accounting system in between full and direct costing. This accounting system is mainly based on the relativity of the direct cost notion. There is also considerable stress on the calculation of a set of widely differentiated "contributions." Therefore, we call this system "analytical contribution accounting (ACA)." We are confident that this accounting system is superior for pricing purposes from a theoretical as well as from a practical point of view.

This book is divided into four parts. Part I, consisting of the first four chapters, reviews some general aspects of pricing policy: pricing objectives, the determinants of pricing policy, price behavior, and pricing strategies.

Part II deals with the cost as price determinant. In the first place, the general objectives of cost accounting and some cost concepts relevant to pricing decisions are discussed (Chapter 5). Then the role of cost accounting information in determining price floors, in price differentiation, in price changes, and in cases of pricing individualized products is examined (Chapters 6 through 10).

Part III explores the cost-oriented methods of price determination. Pricing decisions based on full costing, on partial costing (both "variable" and "direct" costing), and on cost accounting methods in between full costing and partial costing are paid attention to successively (Chapters 11 through 13).

Part IV deals with the above-mentioned analytical contribution accounting system in itself and its use in price decisions. The fundamental principles and methodology of the ACA system are thoroughly discussed (Chapters 14 through 16). Then the buildup of the ACA system for pricing purposes is explained for a number of business types (Chapter 17).

Finally, a concluding chapter reviews the most essential aspects of this book.

The ultimate responsibility for this book, both content and form, lies with the authors. However, this does not mean that we do not owe much to a number of people. In the first place, we are grateful to our wives and children for their patience during the writing of this book. At the same time we apologize for the lost evenings and weekends. Special thanks go to Denise Georges for typing many versions of the manuscript. Second, we wish to thank Walter's sister Magda (Mrs. Phillips) for reading over the text and removing the grammatical and spelling mistakes. Finally, we are grateful to Mrs. Emmy Damiaens for typing and laying out the final text. She did the job cheerfully and competently.

It is really a pleasure to express our gratitude to all for their assistance.

Analytical
Contribution
Accounting

PART I

GENERAL ASPECTS OF
PRICING POLICY

1 General Considerations about Pricing Policy

It is commonplace to say that price plays an important role in a capitalistic economic system. Whereas allocation and remuneration of the production factors largely depend upon the prices of finished goods, the role of price is mainly regulating.

The macro-economic concept of price is an entity determined by a great number of individual price decisions taken in micro-economic organisms. The micro-organism under attention in this book is principally the industrial firm.

On the level of the firm, the selling price[1] is substantial because of its direct importance in the generation of trading results. This obvious importance leads to a double contradiction that cannot remain unmentioned. The former contradiction is theoretical, the latter is rather pragmatic.

In the first place, there is a gap between the economists' price theory (one of the most developed parts of economic theory) and pricing in business, which is very unsettled from a theoretical point of view.[2] This phenomenon can probably be explained by the fact that economic theory tries to explain the firm's pricing behavior on the basis of simplified deductive models. On the contrary, "real" pricing policy needs a realistic, normative approach. This allows us to doubt the significance of abstract theoretical models for tangible pricing decisions.[3]

The second contradiction applies to the firm's pricing policy. Based on the above-mentioned and other aspects, price policy could be considered one of the most important aspects of business policy in general and marketing policy in particular.[4] However, empirical evidence teaches us that pricing policy plays only a secondary role in competitive strategy.[5] An explanation of this phenomenon can be found in the fact that other elements of marketing policy can be important as well: promotions and/or advertising campaigns can boost sales more than a decrease in price; quality, design, and packing of a given product can be more important than price; psychological, ethical, legal, and other elements affect and limit pricing alternatives.

The above considerations result in the fact that little money, time, and trouble is devoted to pricing policies, which has lead to pricing decisions based on rigid, mainly cost-oriented price determination methods.[6] It is our firm conviction that the quality of marketing policy and the resulting profit figures can be improved considerably by getting away from the traditional cost-oriented pricing approach. The market factor in pricing policy must be revalued. Only then is there a real chance for pricing policy to become a full-fledged instrument of marketing policy. However, the marketing policymaker who tries to fulfill the above-mentioned idea cannot neglect the cost element in pricing.

In modern pricing policy the cost factor has more relative significance than in the traditional cost-based approach. One of the intentions of this book is to discuss the necessary principles and techniques with respect to that. Finally, it has to be said that in relation to pricing policy there is no question of the right method or the right principle. Prices are determined by a multitude of factors, some of which are imponderable and not quantifiable, so that assuming a number of general principles and techniques in function of the actual internal situation of the business and the market, a made-to-measure pricing policy must be mapped out.[7] Taking into account the dynamics of the firm and the market, it is probably helpful to carry out a price policy audit now and then.[8]

1.1 DEFINITIONS

Before beginning the discussion of pricing it seems necessary to devote a few terminological considerations to the concepts of price policy. As often is the case with concepts used in common parlance, there can be some problems when defining these concepts for scientific purposes. Quite so with the price concept.

In the first place, a number of definitions are conceivable, as the price concept can be approached from an etymological, social, juridical, or economical point of view. Naturally it is only the last modality that is relevant for our purpose. Because of the pragmatic character of this book we do not need theoretical explanations of price as explained by the relation utility—value—price as in the so-called laws of supply and demand. On the contrary, we take the individual supplier's point of view. Thus, an important problem arises: a price is always attached to a product, which, from a marketing point of view, is more than the mere material product. In addition to the material product, the firm supplies implicitly or explicitly a list of attributes or utilities inherent to the product (design, service, etc.). In a buyer's mind these material and immaterial aspects of the product form an entity. So we can agree with Stanton's definition: "price is the amount of money that is needed to acquire some combination of a product and its accompanying services."[9]

Pricing policy can be defined as the whole of economic considerations and decisions with regard to the price of supplied goods. The nuance "policy" points out that this consists of measures that can be set in a coherent whole of planning, action, and control in order to attain certain objectives.

In business literature a distinction is often made between ''asking price'' and ''selling price.'' Asking price means the price the firm desires for its product. The selling price only comes about after the buyer was confronted with the asking price. Unless explicitly mentioned, or if the context precludes misunderstanding, in this book the notion ''asking price'' is meant.

1.2 PRICING OBJECTIVES

Insofar as there is talk of a conscious pricing policy, the first problem that arises is the tracing out of pricing policy objectives.[10] As pricing policy is derived from business policy in general and marketing policy in particular, two problems arise:

a. Pricing policy objectives must be consistent with business and marketing objectives.

b. Pricing policy objectives must be consistent among themselves.

About a. It is needless to point out that the numerous theoretically conceived objectives are rather unimportant and useless. This is especially caused by the sometimes poor information about relevant costs and markets, both actual and future information. Management primarily has to think about realistic business objectives and marketing objectives consistent with them. The price-setting authority has to take these objectives and trace a pricing policy in function of them.

About b. As there are several general and marketing objectives, there can be many pricing objectives. Usually this takes the form of a main objective accompanied by a number of secondary objectives and constraints. The point is to conceive the construction of objectives such that it is a consistent and, more important, an attainable whole. This does not mean that the firm has to set a rigid and uniform pricing policy for all its products and markets.

Differentiation of objectives and policy to product groups, market segments and other criteria may be recommendable. In other words, the whole of objectives should not rigidly be fixed but it should easily be conceivable that what is a major objective for a certain market or product group may be a secondary objective for another product group or market segment.

Given a consistent and attainable whole of objectives, the next step is to determine what is a primary and what is a secondary pricing objective for each product group, market segment, and so on.[11] In a multiproduct and multimarket business one has to take into consideration the overall view of products and markets. In such firms one usually tries to realize the general pricing policy objectives with the overall pricing principles; so it is possible that the ''individual'' pricing policy (for one product, one market, etc.) is apparently conflicting with the expected policy based on general pricing objectives.[12] So it can happen that certain products are sold at a loss although the firm is adhering to a profit objective.

One can argue that this is all rather idealistic and normative. However, it is substantial to consider that selling price is only a coregulator of sales and trading results, two entities upon which several business objectives are focused. In this respect the significance of pricing policy should certainly not be exaggerated. Pricing policy is a part of marketing policy in which it can vary from a vital to a very moderate ingredient.[13]

1.2.1 Profit Objectives

1.2.1.1 Profit Maximization

In economic literature it has been pointed out abundantly that profit maximization is the theoretical basis for discussion of the objectives of the firm's pricing policy. We think, based on business as well as on marketing literature, we can say that profit maximization has to be considered unrealistic. In the cases where it is pretended that profit maximization is the main pursuit, one notices that there are a number of modifications mitigating the fundamental objective.[14] These modifications are many and varied:[15]

a. *Organizational relationships.* In the behavioral theories of the firm it is pointed that the firm has to be seen as a coalition of partners, each pursuing its own objectives. Although top management has to act in a coordinating way, generally it is such that every functional department is differentiating itself from the others and desires to keep a certain freedom of determining its own objectives, of interpreting the general business objectives and of deciding on how general objectives should be realized. This results in certain tensions and disagreements about general policy and so eventually also about pricing policy matters. The classic example is the marketing manager setting prices to maintain or increase sales or market share, although the essential objective of the firm is profit maximization.

b. *Sales objectives (amount or volume).* This modification includes considerations about market share. For this modification, see section 1.2.2.

c. *Liquidity.* R. A. Gordon mentions a certain "banker's mentality" among business managers. In some cases this mentality is so pronounced that the fear of bankruptcy or even the fear of temporary liquidity or solvency problems gets the upper hand of the "traditional" profit and market objectives.[16] Fog points out that in many firms the relationship sales-profit-liquidity is considered very important, so that the liquidity objective can become an essential secondary pricing objective and even (in periods of liquidity problems or recession) a temporary main objective.[17]

d. *Image of the firm.* Many firms, especially big ones, are very concerned about their image with the public. "Public" means here clients, competitors, employees, government, and so on. This implies that certain considerations about image can play an important role as secondary pricing objectives. Where the clients are concerned, care should be taken not to raise the price without any elucidation. If an increase in price cannot be explained by higher costs or another plausible reason, clients will interpret the price increase as mere profit motive. There can also be a reaction from the employees and, more in particular, the unions. They will eventually jump upon a price increase to extort wage and salary increases or other benefits for the employees. A very important factor is the fear of government intervention. In his pricing policy research, Fog establishes the preventive effect of the fear of government intervention in pricing policy.[18] Of the same nature is the tendency toward a "just price" or "pricing for a fair return on investment" (*cf. infra*).[19]

e. *Tax considerations*. In principle, tax considerations can influence profit maximization in two ways: heavy taxes lead to a less systematic attention to cost reduction in order to sustain more or higher tax deductibles. Insofar as the revenues are concerned, heavy taxes can have a restraining or discouraging influence. Empirical evidence, however, indicates that the influence of tax considerations in this context may not be exaggerated.[20]

f. *Meta-economical considerations*. Considerations concerning leisure time, power, prestige, and so on can also chip away at the principle of profit maximization.

g. *Continuity of business*. Survival is of substantial importance for each firm. Hence, that's why continuity is an objective every firm is (implicitly) pursuing. The notion of continuity can be interpreted in several ways. The question arises, "what will be continued?" Continuing can be related to the amount of capital invested or to the firm as an economic, social, and organizational entity (the so-called going concern).[21] It appears that continuity is a minimal objective: when profits are satisfactory and there is adequate growth the continuity objective will become a background objective. In this case continuity is automatically realized. If, on the other hand, growth is stunted and profitability is falling, the pursuit of continuity will be a more central goal.[22] Thus, continuity is a fundamental objective when the firm has to put up with problems. In our framework, market problems are most important.[23] A very substantial consideration is that continuity is mainly determined by the actual and future profit potentials of the firm. Profit maximization contributes the greatest extent to continuity, but imperfect foresight about future perspectives will probably lead to a risk-avoiding policy. When the presumed profit maximizing policy holds a chance of a considerable deterioration of the firm's position, a less profitable but safer policy will probably be chosen (*cf.* stay out pricing: a policy of moderate prices in order to avoid market entrance).[24]

h. *Growth (expansion)*. According to J. Dean, the pursuit of a specific business growth is an important pricing objective.[25] The obvious question is, what entity is meant to grow? This question cannot be answered unambiguously. Growth can be related to sales, profit, market share, and retained earnings and thus it partially coincides with other objectives. The aspiration of financial autonomy as restraining factor and a number of meta-economic objectives such as prestige, power, and "empire building" play an important role in pursuing growth. We can say that the efforts to stimulate business growth in the sense of empire building generally lead to moderate or low prices, at which, hoping for an elastic demand, one tries to increase sales. Sometimes this policy leads to the so-called profitless prosperity, an objective that is difficult to justify from a purely economic point of view.[26]

i. *Discouraging potential competition*. Especially for new, unpatented products, this consideration shall be taken into account. Hence, a low price is purposely set for such products, on the one hand to discourage competitors, on the other hand to make larger market penetration.[27]

It is self-evident that this list of modifications of the profit maximization rule is far from complete; as a matter of fact, it would be audacious to aim for completeness in this. We can say that the "profit maximization objective," under pressure of a number of modifying secondary objectives, can be translated in a simple "profit objective." This profit objective generally takes on the form of pursuing a "return on investment" or a reasonable, fair profit. These two modalities will be worked out below.

1.2.1.2 Return on Investment[28]

The R.O.I. objective was especially stressed by R. F. Lanzilotti.[29] Lanzilotti reports about the pricing objectives of 20 large American enterprises and establishes that in 10 cases R.O.I. is the primary pricing objective. Moreover, in 3 firms R.O.I. was an important secondary objective.

When pursuing a planned R.O.I., the firm's price structure is drawn up so that the overall preconceived R.O.I. is obtained. Prices of individual products and of product groups can be lower or higher than those needed to effect the premised total R.O.I. When applying the R.O.I.-based pricing, two problems arise:

a.   On what basis is the R.O.I. calculated?
b.   Which "return" is calculated?

About a. Lanzilotti points out that the value of share capital augmented with long-term debt is generally taken as the basis of calculation. If the calculation is based on fixed assets, there are a number of valuation problems. Cost, book value, replacement value, and other value measures should be weighed one against the other. In addition there is an extra complicating factor: the hardly quantifiable factor of technological progress. In contrast with the theory of business economics, which has rightly always been interested in choice of a well-justified valuation basis, practitioners show a painstaking tendency toward a consistent application of a postulated valuation concept, whatever its qualifications may be.[30]

About b. The level of the return is determined by a number of essentially marketing-oriented considerations such as:[31]

—satisfaction with a "fair" profit margin
—the "traditional" profit margin of the branch of business
—the pursuit of maintaining or increasing the actual return
—pursuit of continuity
—stable prices

The first consideration seems to be the most important.[32] The conclusion is that in big firms it is more a question of controlled profits than controlled prices. It should be pointed out besides that, resulting from the above, the calculated return should be considered as a minimum profit objective so that the actual profits exceed the "target return," unless cyclical, competitive, or structural problems would prevent this.

1.2.1.3 Fair Profits

This profit objective has already been mentioned in section 1.2.1.2. It is self-evident that the notion "fair" leads to the subjective domain. Consequently it will be essential to define what businessmen understand by "fair profit." This is rather difficult. The notion "fair" is usually not quantified and in addition is variable.[33] Moreover, the fair profit is mostly considered as a threshold, as a profit minimum. How can the notion "fair" be defined? Because the notion "fair" can vary from firm to firm and even within the same firm, the meaning of the term changes and there is a question of a so-called zonal profit objective. This is an objective situated in between a maximum and minimum level.[34] The upper limit gets essentially as much as possible near the profit maximum, the floor is made up of the equality of total cost and revenue (break-even point). In order to take a position within this zone many factors will be taken into account. All the secondary objectives ("modifications") plus a number of other factors can be taken into consideration. In that way an economic-psychological adequate and fair profit is reached. Although the economic domain is for the most part left behind here, it should be said that empirical evidence from Fog and Hague suggests that the pursuit of fair profit, however vague it may sound, is frequently used in business practice.[35] This common business practice is promoted by the fact that only a few managers reflect on their objectives and state them explicitly.

1.2.2 Market Objectives

In addition to the profit motive, business can couple its pricing policy aspirations to the market behavior. In this framework we will briefly discuss a few market objectives.

1.2.2.1 Sales Maximization

Sales maximization has only a theoretical significance as a business objective. In practice it is not maximizing sales but attaining a determined sales amount that is significant. Because in firms using a budgetary system the sales budget is in most cases the cornerstone and starting point of all other budgets, it seems that the predetermination of a sales objective is or can be important.

Apart from this consideration, many firms, especially those with a dominant or very important marketing department, are of the opinion that a sales goal is a more powerful stimulus than a predetermined profit goal. This seems plausible because, after all, a sales goal is more tangible than a profit goal, which is codetermined by partially controllable cost factors.[36]

1.2.2.2 Maintaining or Increasing Market Share

Lanzilotti's research proves that, at least in large firms, the acquisition of a certain market share is an objective just as important as the realization of a planned R.O.I. Moreover, Lanzilotti's empirical evidence suggests a certain tension between both objectives. The R.O.I. objective is first ranked as primary objective; the market share objective is mostly cited as secondary objective. In 8 of 10 cases where R.O.I. is given as the main objective, market share is the secondary objective; in six firms mentioning market share as the main objective, four assign R.O.I. as secondary objective.[37]

The pursuit of market share appears in two forms. In the first place, there is a category of firms (especially big ones) contenting themselves with maintaining their existing market share. Such firms mostly prefer other objectives (on condition that their approach is profitable) such as quality improvement, cost reduction, and so on. Such policies are inspired by considerations about competitor relations and especially about the fear of government intervention. Some firms keep their market shares constant in order to be able to act from an offensive position: an increased market share condemns them to act defensively, namely, to protect their increased market share.

Next, there is a category of firms (as a rule, smaller ones) gravitating toward increasing their market share. This policy seems to be inspired by possible profit increases and economies of scale. It is even possible that the pursuit of market share increase is so dominant that selling without or with very poor profits is found. It needs no argument that such a policy leads to the so-called profitless prosperity and creates a real danger for price wars and ruinous prices.

1.2.2.3 Various Market Objectives

The following enumeration is restricted to a few important market objectives not yet mentioned:

—When setting prices, especially for new products, the objective can be to attain the largest possible market penetration. Naturally, this is a long-term consideration: the product is meant to become of permanent importance in the market.
—Pricing can be focused on attracting, dropping, or discouraging given groups of customers or even individual clients (price discrimination, price differentation).
—Price setting can be focused on discouraging or even eliminating competitors or, on the contrary, to achieve competitive stability.

1.3 CONCLUSIONS

It was not the intention to discuss the theoretical foundations of pricing policy objectives but to describe briefly how these objectives are coming through in business practice. Insofar as the profit objective is concerned, we can conclude that pure profit maximization is almost nonexistent under the influence of one or more secondary objectives. It is more realistic to speak of the pursuit of a moderate profit.

Sometimes profit is not considered at all as a pricing objective. In that case, there are market objectives primarily expressed in terms of sales amount or market share. Here as well we do not speak of maximization because of the effect of secondary considerations. For the rest we discussed a number of modifications to the main objectives because of their important role in business practice. The most important ones were liquidity, continuity, growth, and considerations about the firm's image. Notice again that most of the secondary objectives are subjective and cannot be determined unequivocally. So we can say that quantifying does not proceed without problems and the operational character of the objectives gets pushed into a corner.

2 The Determinants of Pricing Policy

The complex character of pricing policy has already been pointed out. It is caused by the multiplicity of determinants that can lie at the root of prices. Price is the result of a decision-making process, in the course of which (from a multitude of alternatives) that price is chosen that approaches the objectives of the firm most. Which factors determine the price and thus curtail the choice of the price-setting person(s) can hardly be stated. A complete enumeration of these price-determining factors would be meaningless if not impossible. Therefore, we confine ourselves to a brief discussion of a number of relevant factors for the average practice. Notice, however, that in specific situations some factors not mentioned here can sometimes be of considerable influence.[1] The determinants in question can be grouped into two divisions, namely business internal and business external. The discussion is started with the latter division.

2.1 EXTERNAL PRICING DETERMINANTS

Above we suggested a restriction of the subject matter in question. With regard to this restriction it should be understood that general economic, ethical, and juridical price determinants stay out of consideration here. We restrict ourselves to a brief explanation of those determinants that influence the pricing methods and strategies to be discussed further on, namely, the market determinants. We made the almost classical distinction between demand factors and competitive factors.

2.1.1 Demand Factors

A capital question within the framework of pricing policy is the question of the buyer's reaction to a distinct price or price change. The firm wanting to get insight in this relation or to anticipate it will have to look deeply into the buyer's behavior, both consumers' and professional purchasers' behavior. By means of an insight in this behavior, the firm will be able to fix an accurate demand curve for a given product.

2.1.1.1 Buying Behavior

In spite of the deductive theory of consumers behavior, empirical research on buying behavior is still in its initial stages. Empirical evidence, produced by research, qualitatively very dissimilar, is contradictional and fragmented in such a manner that it is impractical for marketing purposes. Also, the theories of consumer behavior cannot be tested as to their degree of reality.

The next consideration about buying behavior concerns mainly the consumers' buying behavior. This is due to the fact that still less is known about the professional purchaser's behavior. In our opinion the difference between consumer and professional purchaser can be summed up as follows:

—On the average, the expertise of the professional purchaser with respect to the products to be bought is greater than the consumer's.

—As a rule, the professional purchaser is not swayed by prestige and other emotional considerations.

—Aspects like punctual delivery, firm quality, terms of payment, and so on play a more substantial role for the professional purchaser than for the consumer.

Taking into account these distinctions, the next discussion will deal with some interesting aspects of consumer buying behavior.

2.1.1.1.1 The Relation Price-Quality An old but still very firm idea is that "one cannot expect more than one pays for." This idea shows that the average consumer connects price with quality. Many empirical examinations have proved the soundness of this hypothesis.[2] It appears, however, that quality may not be seen as a technically determined, objective degree of use but as a subjective judgment of value concerning the degree in which the product replies to the consumer's specific needs.[3]

A few explanations that can be brought forward for the relation price-quality, are:

—The economics of well-known snob appeal (Veblen-effect).

—Because of the increasing number and complexity of products, the consumer is unable to pass a reliable judgment on quality. Consequently, he uses the price as measure of comparison.[4]

—It was established that the consumer goes through a psychological conflict caused by uncertainty. It was remarked that the consumer appeared more uncertain if, given the same article, he preferred the lower priced one to the more expensive one.[5]

2.1.1.1.2 Price Consciousness It is self-evident that the factors of price consciousness, price perception, and price sensitivity are very important in price setting. Nevertheless, there is no substantial empirical evidence about this subject. Some research indicates that:[6]

—The majority of consumers do not know at all or only know approximately ($\pm$ 5%) the price of commonly bought commodities. This directs to the thesis that the average consumer does not consider the price as a "point" but rather as a "range."[7]

—Consumers underestimate the price rather than overestimate it.

—Consumers' knowledge of price is very divergent for different articles. This knowledge does not differ with social class or age group.[8]

In view of the supposition of a relative low degree of price consciousness we could say that in an average price-setting situation extreme precision need not be strived after.

2.1.1.1.3 Price Changes The above suggests that, from a marketing point of view, one should take a critical attitude toward price changes, temporary changes as well as permanent ones. Price changes can only produce effect if the consumer knows the exact price, if he is sensitive for price changes, and if the price change exceeds a minimal order of magnitude. Thus, changing prices is not a panacea to wipe out failures in other parts of marketing policy. On the contrary, a price change by itself will not produce any effect if it is not complemented with supporting promotional actions. The above remarks, however, can be distorted substantially by such phenomena as brand loyalty, shop loyalty, and others.

2.1.1.1.4 Pricing psychology. Here we are faced with the symbolic sense consumers attach to price numbers. Van de Woestyne,[9] distinguishes between:

—"Round" prices ($1, 5, 10, 15, 20, 100). They suggest a certain generosity in buyers' and sellers' minds. At such price the former do not expect a sharp price calculation but depend on excellent quality.

—"Odd" or "charm" prices ($.95, $1.05, $1.99, etc.). These prices suggest a sharp calculation. For instance, a price of $.95 means that the seller can keep his price under the "round" price of $1 and that he explicitly does it. A price of $1.05 means that the concerning quality cannot be delivered at $1 but the seller keeps his price as near as possible to it.

Yet it is mainly an open question if the average consumer actually interprets the odd prices in such a way and if such pricing practices really are stimulating sales. Although round and charm prices are frequently used in practice, there is no unequivocal empirical evidence about consumers' response to psychological pricing.[10]

2.1.1.2 Demand Curve

One of the most important parts of price theory is the study of the relationship between demand and price. The quantitative relationship between demand and price is deductively determined by means of demand functions. In view of the pragmatic character of this book, the price theoretical aspects are neglected; yet it appears that in price theory certain ideas and notions are conceived that may be important for our further exposition.

In the first place we are concerned with the so-called price elasticity of demand. In economic theory this notion is defined as the ratio of changes in demand quantity for a product and the change in price with one unit. For practical use this interval has to be taken broader, so the notion of elasticity in question is defined as:

$$\frac{\text{proportional change in quantity of demand for product X}}{\text{proportional price change of product X}}$$

This ratio reflects quantitatively the degree of reaction of demand quantity at a given price change. It is generally accepted that demand reacts elastic upon price; in other words, that a reduction in price results in an increase of sales and vice versa. The extent to which this happens can be very divergent. In many cases and within certain limits the price does not affect demand and the case that price increases augment demand quantity is not as rare as believed (*cf.* snob appeal).

A firm confronted with an elastic demand has to take stronger account of the repercussions of price changes than firms with inelastic demand. In times of subnormal capacity usage, a price increase is not advisable in case of elastic demand and conversely.[11] Insofar as the determinants of elasticity of demand are concerned, we can essentially refer to price theory. Only the most important factor, namely, the intensity of demand (i.e., the urgency of the need for the product in question) should be looked at. The demand for urgently required products is not, or is only slighter reduced, even in the case when the buyer has the opportunity of procuring the good from other suppliers (for instance, replacement parts of machine components).

Quite another aspect, very important in the framework of this book, is the measurement of elasticity for practical pricing purposes. In this context Oxenfeldt rightly remarks that "it is essential to recognize, however, that for some products, for particular classes of customers and at certain times, similar price changes assert a far greater effect on unit sales than for other products; customers, and times."[12] The gist of this argument is the almost complete inability to determine elasticity.[13] So it is clear that price setting often is based on an intuitive and hypothetically determined measure of elasticity that results in a problematic, vague, and incomplete knowledge of the products' demand curve.[14]

2.1.2 Competitive Factors

A second important group of price determinants is the one that has to do with the reactions of cosuppliers. The price-setting firm has to look after, to analyze, and to anticipate the competitor's pricing behavior. Some important aspects of this are elucidated below.

2.1.2.1 Market Structure

Market structure is one of the most emphasized elements of price theory. For price-setting purposes, both the structure of demand and supply have to be penetrated.

The division of market structures can take place depending on numerous criteria or combinations of criteria. The most classical criterion is the number of market participants. Depending on whether one, a few, or many suppliers and buyers are operating in the market we speak respectively of a monopoly, an oligopolistic, or an atomistic market structure. In addition to the number of market participants, the market perfection or imperfection is important. We speak of a perfect market if:[15]

—The market participants behave rationally; that is, in function of the objective of profit maximization.

—The speed of reaction is immediate; in other words, there are no time lags.

—There is complete market transparency; this means that the market participants have all relevant market information at their disposal.

—There are no preferences, either from personal or from a nonpersonal kind; in other words, buyers and suppliers act as a homogeneous body and there is no question of product differentiation.

If one or more of these criteria is lacking a number of gradations of imperfect markets come about.

By combination of the criteria "number of market participants" and "market perfection" (both on the side of suppliers and buyers), a great number of market structures can be discerned. For the price-setting firm the market structure is of vital importance. It is self-evident that a monopolist has other and substantially more important potentialities of price decision making than firms in a competitive market. Yet it is important to keep in mind that the price theoretical market structures are only abstract, simplified models, hardly to be found in reality. Pricing in practice is influenced by many other factors that cannot possibly be taken into consideration in the theoretical equilibrium systems. Thus, the price-setting firm does not find much support in the solutions given by the theoretical pricing models. Besides, it has to keep an eye upon an extensive series of other factors that also can influence price determination.

Even more important than market structure in itself is the firm's own place and situation in the market. Here we can refer to the first criterion of distinction of market structures, namely, the number of buyers and suppliers involved. In general we can say that a monopolist has a stronger market position than a firm in a competitive market. This is not always true, however, because the market position is determined by a number of factors and so it can happen that a firm in competition has a stronger market position than a monopolist because of existing preferences, scarcity, or other factors. Such a competitive firm normally will then possess more price setting potentialities than the monopolist. The market transparency also seems of great importance for price setting. We can say that the less transparant the market, the greater the price setting potentialities and vice versa.

Finally, the phenomenon of market entrance can be considered. In the case the market entrance opportunities are few, the price setter only has to take into account the already existing competitors. In the other case the price setter has to consider the outside potential competitors as well. In respect to the above we speak of "closed" and "open" markets.[16] The most important impediments to market entrance are the necessary minimal initial dimension of the firm, patent protection of a product, and the already cultivated buyers' preferences for existing products.[17]

2.1.2.2 Product Differentiation and Substitution

The number of prices the price setter has to bear in mind depends upon the opportunities of substitution of his product. This is why the price setter shall not make allowance for the prices of all physically identical or similar articles. It also explains why he often keeps an eye on prices of commodities not belonging to his product category.
Examples:

—When setting the price of the Ford Escort or Sierra model, the price of Rolls Royce will not be taken into account.
—A producer of canned vegetables shall be guided by the price of frozen vegetables.

The greater the product differentiation, the smaller the direct competition among several articles from the same product group. The existence of opportunities of substitution diminishes the potentialities of autonomous price setting. Often, the price of the substitute makes the upper limit of the price of a certain product.[18] The measure to which one product is substituted with another as a result of price changes can be expressed by the so-called cross-elasticity. It can be defined as follows:

$$\frac{\text{proportional change in demand for commodity A}}{\text{proportional price change of product B}}$$

A high value of this ratio means a quick and smooth propensity to substitute; for homogeneous goods its value is evidently infinite. A low value of this ratio implies more heterogeneity; in case of a pure monopoly the limit value of O is reached.[19]

2.1.2.3 Competitive Behavior

Insofar as competition is concerned, the price setter is generally confronted with a number of questions, such as

—How does the competitor arrive at his price?
—How will the competitor react to our price change?
—Which motives will guide the competitor?

When answering the questions we can take into consideration the factors discussed above as well as a number of other factors. Some questions can be answered easily, for others one will stay in the dark. As yet the most plausible way of answering these questions consists of assuming a certain consistency in the competitor's behavior. By observing and analyzing the competitor's behavior over a longer period of time one can, to a certain extent, predict the competitor's objectives, price policy, cost structure, financial position, management abilities, and so on with a satisfactory degree of probability. Thus, one can predict and possibly anticipate competitive policies.[20] In some cases application of statistical decision theory (for instance, theory of games) may be useful in spite of the incomplete and poor information about competitors.[21]

So far, we tried to review as concisely as possible the most important external price determinants. Our starting point was an average business situation. In selected cases, however, a number of other factors, although not mentioned here, can be of particular importance. We hope that the above discussion of the extensive and heterogeneous package of determinants already has hinted at the complex character of pricing policy as well as the relative significance of the cost factor in pricing. In a second phase we shall, in the same spirit and with the same intention, give an idea of the most relevant internal selling price determinants.

2.2 INTERNAL PRICING DETERMINANTS

In general we can say that internal determinants of selling price are of a less decisive kind than the external. In this section we sum up some business internal determinants, indicating in each case how they influence the price decision process.

2.2.1 Production and Products

Pricing is, sometimes to an important extent, conditioned by the nature of the production process and the features of the goods produced.

2.2.1.1 Nature of the Production Process

The impact of the nature of the production process on price setting is indirect, it runs via the costs and the cost calculation system. In general and summarizing, the following considerations can be brought forward in this context:

—In the case of joint production, only a part of costs are caused by the individual products (or product groups). Only this part can be allocated directly.

—In the case of non–joint production, the costs can be allocated to a single product.

The more pronounced the degree of joint production, the less accurate the cost of a simple product can be calculated and thus also the selling price to attain a predetermined profitability. In the case of joint production the minimum selling prices are connected as well, thus the greater the degree of joint production the more important the effect of "calculational compensation." Besides, it should be remarked that distinction should be made between mass production and job or piece production. In the former case the selling price is mostly fixed in general while in the latter the selling price is fixed for each particular job or order.

2.2.1.2 Nature of the Product

A very important determinant of selling price and more specific of the pricing approach is the distinction between investment goods and consumer goods. The above implicitly presumes we had to do with consumer goods. Insofar as industrial goods are concerned, there is usually talk of "derived demand," that means that the goods in question are bought to produce others (machines, raw materials). So the eventual selling price will be determined by the selling potentials of the finished goods. Very important too is the role of industrial goods in the buyer's production process. Price changes will only produce little effect on sales as sales are mainly determined by the situation at the buyer's sales market. On the contrary, price changes can lead to a repartition of the market shares of investment good sellers. These considerations, however, can be distorted where there is product differentiation among goods sold.

A different matter is the situation where industrial goods account for a substantial part in the buyer's cost structure. Here, price changes of the good in question determine to a considerable extent the buyer's cost so that he will thoroughly explore the market before deciding to purchase. In this case the sales of the producer of industrial goods can to a great extent be determined by his pricing policy.

Of further influence on pricing of investment goods is the fact that acquisitions as a rule are done by professional purchasers who possibly have a more rational attitude than the common consumer. At any rate rationality is appropriate here because it often concerns large transactions both in quantity and amount or transactions with long-term repercussions.[22]

2.2.1.3 Product Life Cycle[23]

Product life cycle can be determined technically or economically. In a technical sense product life cycle can be limited by perishability of the product in question. The measure of perishability limits the price setter's choice: it ties him down to a maximum price at which buyers are still willing to accept the available supply before the product becomes unfit for use. Insofar as this restriction is concerned, it only applies to products difficult to keep fresh (horticultural and dairy products, for example). However, because of progress in preservation techniques, this aspect has become less urgent.

When the notion of perishability is used in the sense of sensitivity to fashion, we can establish that more and more goods are threatened by a limited tenability that tends to become even smaller. Especially in the case of durable goods, the lifetime plays an important role.

Price in itself is not the starting point but it will be seen in relation to the number of "performance units" the good will deliver during its (technical or economical) lifetime. So the next valuation factor can be calculated:

$$\frac{\text{Price}}{\text{Units of performance}}$$

A great factor value leaves room for a high demand price for the given product. The working expenses, the maintenance, and repair charges during the use of the durable good constitute another aspect to be considered. If their portion related to the price of the durable good is low, there will be broader price-setting potentialities. Price fixation is less flexible when the above-mentioned costs are higher than the competitor's.

2.2.1.4 Inventory Policy

Building up inventories costs money: storage charges and proper inventory charges. The former component is mainly a fixed amount, the latter usually a variable amount. Reduction of these costs can especially be achieved by increasing inventory rotation. The higher inventory rotation, the lower the relative storage charges and proper inventory charges. One of the means to affect inventory turnover is price.[24]

2.2.1.5 Activity Ratio[25]

When business capacity is fully utilized, both technically and where personnel is concerned, and one expects this situation to continue, then the interest in new, additional orders will decrease. Here the firm will normally set higher prices in relation to the expected customer's willingness to pay.

In case of subnormal capacity usage, there is an effort to increase sales. For this purpose reducing prices is an appropriate means. Where under-utilization is caused by decreased demand we can say that subnormal capacity usage coupled with elastic demand results in a tendency to establish lower prices. A special problem with subnormal capacity usage consists in the recovery of activity-independent costs ("capacity costs"). In further sections we will discuss cost accounting methods aiming at useful cost bases for price setting in order to recover costs and to realize an optimal activity ratio.

2.2.2 Some Other Determining Factors

A great number of various internal pricing policy determinants could still be mentioned. We briefly will discuss some of them in the next paragraphs.

In the first place we refer to management philosophy, business objectives, marketing, and more specific pricing objectives. Some of these aspects were discussed in Chapter 1.

Costs are or can be a very important factor in price setting. Bearing in mind the extremely controversial character of this determinant and taking account of the subject matter of this book, we refer to the next sections for the discussion of this problem.

A third factor is the firm's financial potential. It is self-evident that there is a close relationship between sales amount and volume on one side and the need of working capital on the other side. A shortage of proprietors' capital often can be covered by attracting additional short- or long-term liabilities. However, this can conflict with responsible financial management, aiming at a sound balance between proprietors' and third-party capital. But what is sound and to what extent temporary disturbances of balance can be allowed is a matter of rather differing opinions. For that reason the financial potential often is a limiting factor in pricing decisions.[26]

Last but not least there is the rank of pricing policy in the marketing mix. The selling price is an instrument of marketing policy next to quality, assortment, distribution, advertising, promotion, and so on. Most important, however, is the necessity for acting harmoniously in the same direction in such a way that the effect of one instrument supports the effect of the other and especially that no opposite results are generated.

Consistency inside the marketing mix is all the more difficult because of the many interrelations among the various subpolicies and for the reason that changes in one element of the marketing mix mostly imply changes in other marketing mix elements. So the next type of questions have to be answered:

—Advertising expenses are reduced (raised)—what about price?

—Product quality is lowered (improved)—what about price?

—Price is substantially changed—what about distribution channels?

—Price is raised (reduced)—what about advertising and promotion?[27]

It is the marketing manager's task to realize consistency among the marketing sub-policies; even more important is the carrying on of an optimal or at least the right or most indicated policy.

2.3 AVAILABILITY OF INFORMATION ABOUT PRICING DETERMINANTS

Selling price is mainly determined by market factors. In this connection the internal price determinants are valid constraints. Though the internal factors are, as a rule, less important than the external, it would testify of an uncautious policy not to consider them under the pressure of market elements or marketing people. In addition to this, there is an informational problem.

The above considerations about internal and external pricing determinants can be seen as rather idealistic; though incomplete, many often mutual variables were discussed and an almost full knowledge of them was suggested or assumed. Of course this is a gross simplification of reality. Insofar as the total needs for information are concerned, a number of requirements are needed with respect to availability, reliability, or priority. In practice it can be rather difficult to fulfill these requirements.[28]

In this era of information there is often talk of the phenomenon of "information inflation," meaning that the real problem of business information is not the shortage but rather the abundance of it. So decision making is hampered because too many alternatives have to be weighed one against another and too much information about each alternative is available. Therefore, the problem is not to increase the quantity of information but to upgrade the quality of information by properly distilling out relevant and pertinent information. Relevant and pertinent information with regard to a problem is marked by:

—necessity in the scope of problem solving;
—being unambiguous, that is, not being in contradiction with other information;
—being related, that means that the connection among relevant variables must be known and available.

So there will be a problem of dosage of information, a problem of "optimal search," that is fundamentally a problem of cost and time. This problem is all the more difficult because as a rule it is not known in advance what and how much information is needed.[29]

In the light of the above described elements we can postulate for price setting purposes that:

—It is not necessary, even if possible and practicable, that the price setter has all relevant information at his disposal to be able to make correct pricing decisions.
—As a rule, obtaining all relevant information will be impossible and impracticable because of time and cost considerations.

—The acquired relevant information has to be really and optimally applied in the price decision process.

Finally, we come back to the already mentioned qualitative aspects of information, namely, to its imperfections. These imperfections lead the price setter to an uncertain situation concerning actual and especially future situations. This can possibly be remedied by the use of models, simulation methods, or other quantitative techniques of decision making.

Other potentialities to improve the quality of information are sensitivity analysis and improvement of the management accounting system. Sensitivity analysis teaches how important adequate knowledge of a particular variable is. To that end the calculations in the framework of price decision problems are repeated several times, each time changing the magnitude of a particular variable. So it is possible to examine the impact of a change of a variable.[30]

Our contribution to the pricing decision problem can mainly be located in the domain of management accounting. In Part IV of this book we shall enunciate an appropriate method to obtain information in relation to costs in the most efficient and useful way possible in view of pricing decisions.

3 Pricing Behavior

The role of cost data in pricing varies with pricing methods, pricing objectives, pricing strategies, and with market situation. For that reason a discussion of pricing behavior is necessary to expose the need of cost information for pricing purposes.

From the firm's point of view, *grosso modo*, two ways of pricing behavior can be distinguished:

—an active pricing policy by which the firm itself sets the selling price and
—a passive pricing policy by which the firm, in accordance with certain strategies, joins existing market prices.

3.1 ACTIVE PRICING POLICY

Because of the widespread product differentiation the case of the firm able to set or to influence strongly its selling prices occurs more than that of the firm being dependent on market prices. It is self-evident that in the case of independent price setting the role of the cost factor is more important than in the case of passive pricing policy. In the event of autonomous price policy, two problems arise initially. In the first place, the question of price foundations arises: Should price fixation be dependent on costs or on market considerations? In practice the answer to this question is essentially a matter of gradation and dosage, we will see more and/and rather than or/or. In the second place, the question whether prices will be set in general or individually will be raised; in other words, will the product have only one price or more prices by function of customer, order, time, and so on. Both questions are discussed further below.

3.1.1 Cost-Oriented Pricing Policy

This policy means that the cost factor is most significant in pricing decisions. In many cases it is even so expressed that selling price is the mere addition of cost and a profit margin (the so-called cost-plus pricing).

Taking into account that the heart of this book concerns cost-oriented pricing policy, the discussion of the relative problems will not be started here. Consequently, we refer to the next parts, especially Parts III and IV.[1]

3.1.2 Market-Oriented Pricing Policy

Like the external price determinants discussed in Chapter 2, market-oriented pricing policy can be divided into pricing mainly based on demand considerations and pricing mainly taking account of competitive factors.

3.1.2.1 Demand-Oriented Pricing Policy

When discussing the price determinants, the buyer's utility estimations were pointed out. Often, the selling price can be set in function of the estimated utility the product imparts the (potential) customer. Therefore, the question that needs to be answered is how much the buyer is willing to pay for the product. Phelps and Westing point out quite rightly that this problem is probably "the most difficult and least developed of pricing."[2]

Techniques to obtain an idea of the price to be set are consumer panels, test markets, budget analyses, interviewing prospects, and other methods of marketing research out of the scope of our theme. In addition, comparisons with the price, quality, exterior, and other features of the most related substitutes can give some foundation for the price problem. In general we can say that the customer's willingness to pay a certain amount is determined by:[3]

—the prospective benefit or utility the buyer can (subjectively) or will (objectively) achieve with the concerning good;

—the comfort, delight, prestige, and esteem the product brings to the buyer himself and/or to the buyer by his environment;

—the value and availability of the product compared with value and availability of competing substitution products; and

—the buyer's knowledge of future price trends.

Depending on the knowledge and evaluation of these factors the buyer comes to a price range, a series of prices the customers would be willing to pay. In function of other external factors, especially the price sensitivity quantifiable by elasticity or cross-elasticity coefficients, the seller has to choose position within the price range.[4]

As a rule, in the case of comparatively small price sensitivity, the chosen price will be in the highest quarters of the price bracket and conversely.[5] We explicitly would like to point out that in this approach costs do not remain fully out of consideration. It is true that cost does not determine the ultimate price level, but it preserves its interest as a measure of results and as a price floor determinant.[6]

3.1.2.2 Competition-Oriented Pricing Policy

Competitive considerations were regarded as very important in the discussion of selling price determinants in chapter 2. Especially, anticipation of competitive reactions to price setting or price changing were stressed. Besides that, we can assert that competition defines the upper limit of a price setter's price discretion. The above concepts and, among others, the intensity and speed of competitive reactions to price decisions depend on the following factors:

—Number of competitors. As a rule, price increases are followed faster, the smaller the number of competitors is, and conversely. The same is valid in the case of price decreases.[7]

—Product innovation and product differentiation. The more the product is differentiated from the competitor's, the greater the price-setting latitude. The more homogeneous the product is, the less autonomous price determination can be.[8]

—Degree of understanding among competitors. This can range from a general agreement among competitors to prevent price competition or price wars, on the one hand, to the systematic use of price declines to upset or even eliminate competitors on the other.[9]

—Mutual insight in each others' cost structure.[10]

The factors mentioned above are especially applicable in the processes of price changes and fixation of the price range. The proper price will be mainly set after analysis of the competitor's reaction pattern. One can distinguish two possible reactions: the competitor has a steady price reaction policy or the competitor decides as each case arises. By means of inside information and statistical analysis of competitive behavior one should be able to solve reasonably these pricing problems.

Again, the importance of costs as a price floor should be pointed out. The above-mentioned considerations concern especially the difference between the price floor and the proper price that may be reasonably permitted on the basis of the competitive situation.[11]

3.1.3 General or Individual Pricing Policy

Irrespective of cost-oriented or market-oriented pricing policy, the question of general or individual pricing arises. General pricing means that one price is set for a product while individual pricing means that the selling price is tailored to the kind of customer, the quantity ordered, or other criteria.[12] General pricing policy is especially coupled with identical products, whereas individual pricing is the rule for individualized goods such as buildings, ships, and some machines. Therefore, general pricing is often connected with quantity production; individual pricing with piecework. That rule does not hold in all cases: goods produced in mass can have an individual price. This happens especially when the number of transactions is small but the quantity sold each time is large.[13] This is all the more valid if the buyer holds a favorable position of negotiation.

The question of general or individual pricing affects the frequency of providing cost information for pricing purposes. In the case of individual pricing, more accurate and continuous cost information is needed. In the case of general pricing, the need of cost information is rather sporadic; in this case it is connected with the frequency of price changing (for instance, the drawing up of a new price list) or the introduction of new products. The buildup of cost accounting methods will be influenced by all this. In the case of individual pricing, cost accounting methods should be conceived per transaction; in case of general pricing, a continuous cost accounting system in which the peculiarities of specific production and sales orders are leveled suffices so that the resulting cost is an "average" cost.

3.1.4 Mixed Pricing Policies

The above-mentioned methods of active pricing policy usually are not found in their pure form. In many cases active pricing policy consists of a "hybrid" in which both cost and market data are decisive.

Naturally, it cannot be denied that some firms still indulge in "price calculation" or purely base their decision on what customers are willing to pay. As a rule, however, the various factors have to be taken into consideration together. A frequently occurring method of pricing is the so-called flexible markup pricing. In this method the product's full cost is increased by a profit margin in function of anticipated reactions of customers and competitors. Combinations of individual and general pricing are frequently found too. For example, prices can be set in general but in each particular case the general price is departed from by means of allowing discounts and/or rebates.

Price setting in which a mixture of determinants plays a role is also seen in the so-called stage approach to pricing. By passing through a number of stages the pricing problem is simplified; each step involves a simplification for the next stage. At the same time the arbitrariness in the pricing procedure is reduced or mitigated. A well-known stage approach of pricing is Oxenfeldt's "multistage approach."[14] Other step-by-step approaches were premised by Stanton and Richers.[15] Characteristic of these gradual price-fixing methods is the combined use of cost, customer, and competition data.

A method by itself is the so-called P.A.P. or "product analysis pricing," a pricing method primarily based on considerations about buyer and competitor and implicitly also the cost factor.[16] Depending on the practiced price-setting method, the importance given to cost data alters. In most of the above-mentioned hybrids, except in Richers' stage approach and in the P.A.P method, cost only plays the role of price floor. The repercussion of this on the need for cost data and the inherent buildup of a cost calculation system will be discussed in Parts III and IV.

3.2 PASSIVE PRICING POLICY

For many firms the pricing autonomy is limited to a greater or lesser extent. These firms cannot carry through an independent pricing policy but are forced to conform to a given price. Two situations can be distinguished:

—either the firm links up with a given market price or
—the price-setting latitude is limited by a competitor whose prices may or may not be followed.

We continue the discussion along this vein.

3.2.1 Connection with a Given Market Price

The case in which there is a given market price fits the situations called ''perfect atomistic competition'' in price theory. The product has a market price, that is, a selling price determined by the free play of supply and demand. The supplier can either accept this price or he can refuse to sell at this price. If he attempts to sell above market price, demand falls to zero; if market price is underbid sales can, in principle, rise infinitely. In other words, there is a perfect elastic demand. Goods of which the price is determined by supply and demand are found at markets that approach the ''perfect market'' (see Chapter 2). In practice it concerns especially ores, wool, cotton, and other raw materials transacted on the exchange. To the group of products with given market price also belong these products of which the reasonableness of their price, compared with the competitor's, can be judged exactly, so that price differentiation is virtually impossible. Certain raw materials such as petroleum, petrochemicals, various qualities of steel, or standardized products such as screws, bolts, and packing materials can be included here.

It is self-evident that there is no question here of price decisions or price policy in the real sense of the word. The seller can try to adapt sales volume, he can try to find opportunities to influence the price (by means of product differentiation, for example), or he can stick closely to selling price determinants and anticipate them in order to get an insight in future price evolution.[17]

3.2.2 Price Imitation

Price imitation is a very widespread form of pricing policy and is found more or less pronounced, consciously or unconsciously, in almost every market structure.[18] It is fully emphasized here and covers all cases in which the firm directs itself toward the competitor's price without forming a clear idea of its own cost and sales situation with regard to a certain product. It can set its own selling price higher, equal, or lower than the competitor's price and subsequently carry on a coherent and consistent policy. Pricing lower than a competitor's price is frequently encountered.

The most important expression of price imitation is the price leadership system. We speak of price leadership when one producer from the industry is, silently or not, accepted as initiator of price changes.[19] Usually the price leader is the firm with a substantial market share, with a good record for pricing policy (especially where information about and insight into price setting is concerned), and with a satisfactory sense of initiative in pricing matters.[20]

Sometimes a firm can be forced to follow the price leader. This is especially the case when the price leader dominates the market and if it concerns a market of relatively homogeneous goods. In fact we are faced here with the same situation as in section 3.2.1 with the difference that price is not effected by supply and demand but fixed by a price leader. Where, in the case of price increases, there still is a certain latitude in following or not, cuts in prices compel the other firms to imitate. The element of coercion does not always play a role. Often, the cause of price imitation lies in lack of self-confidence or is even done for convenience sake.[21] Usually it is taken for granted that the competitor chosen as an example has a better knowledge of market and cost data. A number of firms are convinced that setting an optimal selling price implies thorough knowledge of many business internal and external aspects and that it is easier to follow a competitor assuming that he gathers and analyzes relevant information before setting the price, rather than gathering the information themselves. The phenomenon of price imitation has, like everything else, positive and negative sides.

The fact that it is a pricing method that costs nothing, and of which the results in many cases are very likely hardly different from results obtained by an analytical way, is certainly favorable. The fact that a substantial element of the marketing mix is handed over to competitors is negative. Aside from the fact that the competitor's decisions could be wrong, it remains to be seen whether the competitor's price is favorable or acceptable for its own firm. The competitor's business and cost structure can be totally different from the price imitator's. The product in question may be a by-product for the price leader, whereas for the price follower it is the main product and conversely. In general, and essentially, it seems advisable that price imitation only can be tolerated insofar as by-products and supplementary products are concerned. For the main product(s) the firm independently should evaluate price determinants in order to avoid being lead totally by outside influences. If not, unforeseeable and often extreme consequences in many and varied areas (sales, market share, image) will surface.

Insofar as cost information is concerned, it is as similar as joining a given market price. Cost accounting only serves the purpose of measuring the trading results.

3.3 GOVERNMENT INTERVENTION IN PRICING POLICY

The firm's freedom of movement in pricing matters can be seriously limited by government intervention. The importance of price as a marketing instrument is more far reaching than only the micro-economic aspect: it also has macro-economic consequences.[22] Price regulations can be expected to influence employment, profits, the choice of technology and input sources, product differentiation, productivity improvements, research and development efforts, and so on.[23]

Therefore, no other marketing instrument is more interfered with so much by government intervention than pricing policy. These government interventions can be widely different from country to country and are in a number of cases even organized supranationally (*cf.* OPEC countries for petroleum prices or agricultural prices in E.E.C.). The interventions of government can be direct or indirect. Below some frequently occurring interventions are listed.

a. direct interventions:
    —prior notification and approval of price increases of selected products;
    —price calculation contracts with government;
    —setting maximum or minimum prices;[24]
    —prohibition of predatory pricing;[25] and
    —prohibition or admission of the system of fixed prices for resale.

b. indirect interventions:
    —prohibition of price arrangements (*cf.* price cartels);
    —prohibition of price discrimination except maybe when it is based on cost differences; and
    —discouraging or stimulating consumption by taxes or government subsidies.

It is self-evident that these factors limit playing with the price factor in marketing strategy. As a rule, however, the firm still has at its disposal a certain price-setting latitude. It should be pointed out that government, when discussing pricing dossiers or when conducting a direct price policy, is guided mainly by the cost factor. The better a firm can document its cost, the stronger its position is in negotiations with government or in related lawsuits.

Finally, it should be noticed that government is one of the most important clients of industry. Price setting for government contracts is nearly always cost based. It is even the rule that government imposes cost-price calculation models. So government intervention is only slightly detrimental to the importance of the cost factor in pricing matters.

4 Pricing Strategies

Next to the pricing methods, pricing strategies also are important for the discussion of the significance of cost information for pricing purposes. The role and significance of costs are influenced in accordance with the firm's fundamental policy of high or low prices or its policy of changing prices frequently or keeping them constant. Of further interest is the exploitation of price differentiation. Below the main aspects of these pricing strategies are explained.

4.1 HIGH OR LOW PRICES

The price-setting firm has to make the essential choice of a relative high or low price from a commercially determined price range. The notion relative in this context means the relationship between the chosen price and the average market price for a comparable product or the costs attributable to a product unit. The choice between high or low prices has naturally to be in conformity with the overall marketing strategy and so has to support other marketing elements or has to be supported itself by the remaining marketing subpolicies. Important here are naturally also considerations about buyers and competitors.[1]

The problem of high or low prices for a product is especially of interest if there is no market price yet; in other words, in the case of new products. However, the same problem can occur for products in further stages of their life cycle.

Whatever may be the matter, the first point of attention is again the influence of price level on demand. Here, the elasticity of demand becomes of decisive importance. As a rule, at a low price a relatively larger volume can be sold. The measure to which this happens depends on the degree of elasticity. A great elasticity normally induces a policy of low prices just because in that case price decrease leads to a more than proportional increase in sales. Therefore, such a policy seems advisable for products intended for a wide circle of consumers. Because of the greater volume in the case of low prices, a decline of unit costs is a possible favorable additional effect.[2]

If, on the contrary, the product is directed more toward a limited group of customers, there is a tendency to increase prices (cf. color television in its initial stages).[3] High prices can be favorable if in the customer's mind there is a strong association between price and product quality. In that case a price increase often induces an increase in demand. From the producer's point of view a strategy of high prices can be obvious when a great demand stands face to face with limited production capacity. Initially a high price will be required; later, with increasing production capacity, the price will be reduced. A high-price policy affords the supplementary advantage that later on even radical price declines always remain commercially possible. Frequently, in case of radical price cuts, not only new groups of customers with less spending power are attracted but also new potentialities for use of the product are made available (cf. the home computer).[4] The informational basis of a policy of high or low prices especially leans on market-oriented data such as evolution of demand, price elasticity of demand, expected reactions of buyers, and competitors.

Nevertheless, this does not alter the fact that cost data are important, especially cost data at various sales volume levels as well as insight into the fixed and variable components of them. The precision and detailing of cost accounting is of more interest in case of low-price policy than in case of high-price policy. According to Dean, a policy of high prices is safer or at least seems to be so.[5] It offers more security against possible losses but, on the other hand, potential profits are sometimes set aside or an optimal activity ratio is sometimes hindered.

4.2 PERMANENT OR CHANGING PRICES

When prices are set in general the problem arises of whether selling prices should be changed frequently or whether they can be kept constant for a longer period of time. As a rule, prices should be changed when there are modifications of business internal and/or external factors such as activity ratio, cost structure, pricing objectives, demand situation, competitive behavior.[6] In practice, however, a certain inertia is observed. For a number of reasons (the most important are given special attention below) selling price is not always changed as needed so that price stability is rather the rule than the exception. So we can rightly say that price-setting frequency is relatively low.[7] In the first place, material considerations can slow down frequent price changes. Here, we think especially of firms selling on the basis of catalogs and price lists that cannot continually be changed. For that reason prices have to be kept stable over a period of time, in principle at least as long as the validity of the catalog and price list. More important, however, are market considerations. Here too, rather practical matters are taking part: for certain goods, especially daily consumption goods, the price is lodged in the consumer's minds. This makes frequent price changes, even if they are really necessary, impossible or at least hampers them.

As said before, a constant price often is experienced as a measure of constant quality. This applies especially to brand articles. The essential feature of a brand article is the continued identical quality, coupled with an equal price, even if quality change attempts are made to suggest identical quality by maintaining equal selling price. On these grounds the tendency to maintain price stability for brand articles is obvious.

A further argument against price changes is that they can disturb customers. This is not only valid for price increases but also for price reductions. Customers having bought at the former, higher price will feel cheated at a sudden price cut.[8] This applies all the more when it concerns distributors building up inventories. It should be taken into account that after a price reduction buyers often expect further price cuts and therefore delay their purchases. In the case of price increases, normally a sales volume decrease can be expected, the predictability of which depends on the measure of insight in price elasticity of demand. In general we can say that insight in price elasticity of demand is a condition *sine qua non*, if not, each price change is a blow in the dark.

Finally, competitive factors also bring about price stability, especially at oligopolistic markets. In case of price increases, the firm in question runs the risk of not being followed, which leads to sales decreases, unless the price increase is given up afterward. In the latter case the firm decidedly loses face with respect to the client. In the case of price cuts it is very likely that competitors will reduce their prices to the same extent. In the same realm we find the fear of price wars; the price deterioration coupled with it is an adequate reason for price stability unless the firm is feeling strong enough to resist.

The cost information needed in the case of constant prices differs widely from that needed with changing prices. In the latter case cost accounting has to record and point out, as soon as possible, the impact of internal origins of price changes on costs. If selling prices are kept constant, cost accounting is in charge of calculational compensation. It has to record the changes in cost structure and see to it that a risk allowance is included in selling price to compensate unexpected postponements in the firm's situation during the period the price remains constant.

4.3 FIXED OR CHANGEABLE PRICES

Closely connected with the time-related setting of prices arises the question of determining fixed prices or prices that can be changed afterward according to certain circumstances. That question exists in the case of general as well as in individual pricing policy. Of importance here is the firm's market position or negotiation position. The insertion of a clause of possible price adjustments is usually only possible if the supplying firm can assert itself against the opposing party. In any case, for long-term selling contracts, when changes in cost of labor and materials will occur almost certainly, a price adjustment clause is highly desirable. The reason for such a stipulation lies in the tendency to unload the risk of cost increases on the buyer. Naturally, this is especially applicable in times of inflation.[9]

Insofar as the impact on cost accounting is concerned we should say that the impossibility of extorting price adjustment clauses compels the firm to use cost forecasts over the period of delivery. If changeable prices are the rule, such cost forecasts are not or at least are less necessary.

4.4 PRICE DIFFERENTIATION

Differentiation is one of the most important general principles of marketing management. In this section we will demonstrate how the differentiation principle can be applied in pricing policy and what considerations are relevant to this matter. It should be understood that the problems discussed here are only applicable in the case of quantity production. In the case of piecework the prices are individualized by definition. Two cases can be distinguished:

—price differentiation with regard to the same products, or real price differentiation and

—price differentiation with regard to different but related products, or "product line pricing."

4.4.1 Real Price Differentiation

In economic and marketing literature the meaning of "price differentiation" is far from unequivocal. Leaving aside all controversies not only of commercial but also of ethical and juridical nature, the following neutral definition can be put forward: price differentiation consists of the use of different prices at the same time for identical goods, sold at the same moment and under the same circumstances without being able to motivate the price differences by parallel cost differences.[10]

Intentionally we use the notion "differentiation" instead of "discrimination" because the latter term sounds rather negative. Price discrimination measures by two standards so that in each case there is an injured and a favored party. In the case of price differentiation this does not happen, or at least it happens to a smaller extent.[11]

The business economic significance of price differentiation is uncommonly great because of its role in determining net revenue, contribution, and consequently profitability.[12]

Below we will examine the aspects to be considered when setting different prices for identical goods. Price differentiation can be based on[13] buyer's characteristics, the use of the product, buyer's location, order quantity, and the time aspect.

4.4.1.1 Based on Buyer's Characteristics

Price differentiation based on this aspect especially occurs when various categories of customers are willing to pay a different price for the same product. This willingness can be founded on different purchasing power or different appraisal of the product's utility. An important additional condition to make this form of price differentiation feasible is the possibility of separating the different groups of customers; if not, the products will be sold mutually among the groups of customers.[14]

Price differentiation can also be related to the customer's place within the branch. Since the customer's function is decisive here (he may be industrial customer, wholesaler, retailer, consumer), we speak of functional discount here. As far as obligatory or recommended prices are concerned, it is a matter of margin differentiation; when fixed prices for resale do not exist it is a matter of real price differentiation.[15]

Finally, we should not forget to mention that price differentiation is often based on the buyer's negotiation position or negotiation knowledge. It has already been pointed out that prices are often affected by negotiations, by bargaining mutually. It is perfectly thinkable then that one customer pays less for the same product than another because of his stronger negotiation position or better negotiation tactics.

4.4.1.2 Based on the Use of the Product

Price differentiation in function of the use of the product is related to what we discussed above. In this case the price differentiation is based on the different utility of the product to the customers. As an example we can take the different electricity tariffs in function of industrial or domestic consumption and different alcohol prices depending on whether the alcohol is used for the manufacture of spirits or for industrial purposes.

4.4.1.3 Based on Buyer's Location

Price differentiation in function of this aspect occurs when a product is supplied in different areas at different prices. Causes for this can be varied: it can be a means of getting additional sales, for example export prices are lower than home prices (cf. dumping);[16] it can be a means of exploiting differences in purchasing power, for example, higher prices in residential areas. The most obvious form is price differentiation arising from differences in costs of transport. The modalities to realize such a price differentiation are diverse and range from the stipulation "free domicile" via several intermediate forms as the "basing point system," and the method of freight equalization to the "free on board" clause and the stipulation "ex works."[17]

4.4.1.4 Based on Order Quantity

Price differentiation based on order quantity is the most obvious and so perhaps the most frequent. It is found in nearly every industry and in a very wide range of forms.[18]

Motives for these so-called quantity discounts are the cost-reducing effects they can bring about, for example, by putting off small orders and stimulating concentration of orders. A secondary effect can consist of a reduction of production costs because of the spreading of order-fixed costs over a larger number of products.

The quantity discounts can also be granted on other grounds: well known are additional discounts for exceeding a minimal predetermined volume of sales within a definite period (a calendar year, for instance) or for exceeding a certain sales threshold (the so-called sales bonus). Such forms of quantity discounts primarily aim to increase sales and to bind the clients (maintenance of sales).

4.4.1.5 Based on Time Considerations

We can speak of price differentiation in function of time when identical products are supplied at different prices over various periods of a larger space of time. It is clear that the price changes within a period of time due to changes in demand or costs are not what is meant here. On the contrary, a regular and systematic character of price differentiation is a necessary condition.

In many cases price differentiation in function of time is used to optimize or at least improve the activity ratio. Whenever strong fluctuations in activity ratio arise, one can try to level them out by means of price differentiation. Examples are the night tariff of electricity and the summer price of coal.

As an alternative objective, price differentiation can aim to generate additional demand. Examples of this are price reductions for afternoon performances in the theatre and cinema or winter prices of butane gas.

4.4.1.6 Role of Cost Accounting Information

Though it will be discussed in detail farther on, here the question of cost information for real price differentiation purposes can already be addressed.

When price differentiation is fully based on market considerations, cost calculations only play a minor role, namely, the one of "guard" of the price floor. When price differentiation is based on business internal considerations such as increasing or leveling the activity ratio, cost accounting has to point out the impact of costs of this ratio. For example, the cost reduction caused by leveling or increasing business acitivity should be compared with sales fluctuations. In these cases cost calculation will produce essential grounds for the need and extent of price differentiation. Cost accounting, however, has the greatest significance when price differentiation is dictated by cost considerations. The nature of cost information for this purpose and the connected buildup of cost accounting will be discussed in Parts III and IV.

4.4.2 Product Line Pricing

The master problem here is: What about the relations among prices of related products; should these prices be uniform or differentiated?

Product lines are mainly coming about because of differences in size or quantity or in quality (for example, color, packing, raw materials, etc.). Properly speaking, differences in design or finish are of concern rather than differences in quality. Yet the question remains; will the different products of a product line be sold at uniform or at differentiated prices and, if yes, how will these price differences be determined?[19]

There is a tendency toward uniform prices when the utility of the different products of a line is equal and when cost differences are not substantial. Examples of this can be shoes in different sizes, books with varying number of pages, and paint in different colors.

When utility and/or costs are different, then different prices will be set. The measures of price differentiation will be cost differences and differences in utility. Normally both differences are not proportional. In the case of discrepancy between utility and cost differences, differences in utility preponderate as determinant of price differentiation. An outstanding example of this can be seen in automobile pricing. Price differentiation among several car models is based on the buyer's willingness to pay rather than on differences in costs. For example, a price difference of $1,000 between a "standard" and a "deluxe" model can hardly be explained by cost differences alone. This tendency plays a stronger role the more the products are labeled as "quality" articles or "luxury" goods.

This fact, to some extent, confirms the classical method of cost calculation in which indirect costs are computed as a proportional supplement to direct costs. An increase of $500 of direct costs, for example, because of the use of more or better raw materials, can lead to a price increase of $2,000 only by means of the mentioned mechanism of cost calculation and profit margin addition. Another problem is the price setting of salable products of a product line. From a productive-technical point of view boosting sales of one or a few products of the product line could be tried. These products could be supplied at a relatively low price while the remaining products of the line are sold at comparatively high prices. Such a policy is meaningful only when the products of the line are mutually competitive (for example, carpets with a different pattern). If, on the contrary, there is a priori a substantial demand for certain products of a line, they can be sold at higher prices (high in the sense of more than proportional to cost differences).

The significance of cost information for product line pricing decisions is at its greatest when the differences in price are determined by cost differences. It seems, however, that the price line is mostly and mainly determined by market data. Even if that is the case, costs can naturally not be left out of view; the role of costs is then limited to the fixation of price floors.

Cost accounting also has to point out the additional costs caused by the insertion of a new product in the product line because normally these additional costs determine the necessary price difference as compared to the other products. In the case of uniform pricing, cost accounting primarily has to work out an average price floor that guarantees the coverage of the full costs of the complete product line.

4.5 SUPPLEMENTS AND SUBSTITUTES FOR PRICING POLICY

Pricing policy is only one instrument of marketing management. Therefore, it cannot be discussed isolated from other elements of marketing policy but it should be coordinated with them. The discussion of the interaction of the marketing instruments goes far beyond the boundaries of our book. In order to round off the picture of pricing policy a brief discussion will be opened on the relationship between pricing policy and some other elements of marketing policy with emphasis on support, completion, and even partial substitution of pricing policy.[20]

Closely related to pricing policy is the establishment of the terms of delivery and payment.[21] Thus, the allowance of a cash discount has the same effect as a price reduction. The terms of payment are mainly determined by the practices and customs of the industry concerned, as well as by the financial strength and negotiation position of the firm in question. Cost accounting has to point out the cost repercussions of the agreed terms of payment.

Another marketing instrument frequently used as a substitute for pricing policy is product policy.[22] When the price of a product is determined by market data, the cost has to conform to selling price. Then cost accounting has a monitoring function to avoid exceeding a definite cost level (selling price is the maximum). This is called "backward pricing." To make this possible, often the product concept has to be changed.

Another aspect of product policy, namely, product differentiation, was already discussed before and further considerations are not needed here.[23]

Advertising also can be made subservient to pricing policy.[24] The selling price can be mentioned explicitly in the advertising message. This gives certainty to both the consumer and the distributor that the product in question is sold at the same price everywhere. However, price advertising can have a very undesirable consequence especially when the producer has little hold on the distributors. Some distributors can advertise explicitly lower prices and so drag down producers and codistributors in a risky price competition or even a price war. An indirect effect of advertising on pricing policy is that it is able to establish product differentiation.

A close relationship can exist between price policy and assortment, especially when prices are determined by market data.[25] In this case the right choice of products and right composition of the assortment determine to a certain degree the firm's pricing policy. Cost accounting has to point out the product results and thus indicate to what extent the individual products contribute to the total trading results. So cost accounting provides an important foundation for product-oriented analysis of results and the possible product judgment and selection derived from it. This analysis is not directed at inserting or maintaining only profitable products in the assortment.

Frequently for commercial reasons the firm is forced to sell products yielding no profit or even involving losses.[26] This is especially the case when more products of a different kind are available for reason of demand connections (broad assortment) or when because of the canvassing effect a wide choice should be possible to the customers (deep assortment). In this case cost accounting has to provide the necessary data for calculational compensation.

A final device that directly or indirectly influences price decisions is the phenomenon of cartel formation. Unlike the above-mentioned means, formation of cartels is a means to support or even to mold pricing policy in which the price-setting firm does not remain independent but makes its pricing policy to a certain degree dependent on other firms.

Formation of cartels can be found in widely divergent forms. So the above-mentioned price leadership can be considered as a form of price cartel insofar as it is founded on explicit arrangements. Another form of price cartel is the formal agreement on guiding prices or minimum prices for a branch of industry. Important for price setting is the so-called calculation cartel in which it is agreed to use a uniform cost calculation system, possibly complemented by standard profit margins. In both cases the objective of price stability is evident.

Without thoroughly discussing and evaluating the cartel phenomenon, we nevertheless should point out that it implies a serious curtailment of the firm's pricing latitude.

At the end of Part I we want to point out again the incompleteness of the discussion of pricing policy. Such a synopsis of the substance, the objectives, the determinants, the methods, and strategies of pricing policy seemed desirable, however, before starting further considerations pertinent to the use of cost information for pricing purposes on the one hand and the repercussions of it on the buildup and design of cost accounting on the other.

We hope to have pointed out the relativity of cost data with respect to market data and other relevant data for price decisions. We also hope the reader will continue to keep this relativity in mind during the next parts so that a too simple and traditional view of pricing policy can be avoided.

PART II

COST AS PRICE DETERMINANT

In Part I some general aspects of pricing policy were discussed and consideration was given to business internal and external pricing determinants. The cost as price determinant remained for the greater part undiscussed. In this part a more thorough discussion of the cost factor in its role of selling price determinant will be set forth.

From Part I we could deduct that cost is only one of many selling price determinants. This could lead to the presumption that cost accounting and pricing policy only have a limited interface. However, many discussions, spoken and written, have been held on the subject. It is remarkable as well that the interest in this relationship, both in business literature and in practice, has been very precarious. From an external point of view, it is mainly the economic outlook that determines the interest in this matter. In times of upward movement in the business cycle there is less interest in the relationship of costs and selling price than in periods of recession and depression. From an internal business point of view the interest increases or decreases in function of specific circumstances. One can ascertain growing interest, for instance, in case of radical changes in demand and supply, introduction of new products, use of new materials or production methods, substantial changes in cost structure, and so on.

The controversial character of "costs" as determinant in pricing policy is shown clearly by the fact that opinions vary between two extremes: the almost full neglect of costs in pricing on the one hand and the opinion that costs are a preeminent price determinant. The latter thesis, however, is only propagated in rather obsolete literature. As a matter of fact, price decisions are based on considerations in between both extremes; depending on the specific case, cost information will be of greater or lesser importance. Thus, the objective of

Part II is to describe the cost factor in the above-mentioned price decision spectrum.

Normally, price determination in case of piecework, is the most cost oriented. The bid price is determined by costs plus a profit margin that is variable depending on the market situation. For generally competitive products the price is generally determined by a price leader, that is leaning on costs plus profit margin. The remaining competitors follow this price. For them costs are especially important within the scope of product comparison and product selection, in other words, for the judgment of profitability of the different products.

Insofar as products with fixed selling prices are concerned, costs determine the product's weight or quality. In fact, here we are faced with an inverted relationship between costs and selling price: starting from the selling price to the final consumer the firm's own selling price is calculated back. After having subtracted the desired profit margin the admissable product cost is obtained. Because of the inherent price rigidity, changes in production methods, raw materials, and so on should be introduced in order to resist pressure on costs. This form of pricing is called "backward pricing."

In the case of products with standardized quality and design (the so-called homogeneous goods), costs play a minor role in pricing because usually there is a set market price based on demand and supply. Costs only serve the purpose of calculating the business results and provide consequently information for the problem of product selection.

These few examples point out that the significance of costs for pricing purposes is, or can be, widely divergent according to specific circumstances. The role of costs may vary from active, really price determining, to the rather passive role of measuring the operating results. In each case, however, costs can play an important role in the determination of selling price floors. Irrespective of this, other factors that stimulate the use of costs for pricing purposes can be pointed out. In the first place we find the widespread view that cost data are known more correctly, more accurately, and more detailed than other data, especially external business price determinants. Consequently, costs are looked upon as a better point of impact for pricing purposes because more detailed information is available about costs than about such factors as demand conditions, costs of competitors, and competitive sales and price tactics. As will be shown later, this opinion can involve rather dangerous consequences. Another stimulating factor for the use of costs in pricing matters is the propitious evaluation of it by external groups such as customers, competitors, and government.

In general we can say that the role of costs in pricing is most strongly marked when differentiation of competitive products allows a certain price discretion. This product differentiation can find its origins at the moment the new product is launched as well as in its design, advertising, and other marketing instruments. Further, we can say that the significance of costs for pricing matters as a rule grows the more the concerned firm, in the range between perfect competition and monopoly, is in the monopolistic domain. In the next chapters these aspects are discussed.

In the first place we deal with the general objectives of cost accounting and the conditions and characteristics with which the costs should conform for pricing purposes. Next, some cost concepts relevant to pricing policy will be viewed. Finally, the significance of costs in several kinds of pricing situations will be discussed, namely, the determination of price floors, price differentiation, price changes, and the case of pricing individualized products.

5 General Remarks about the Relation between Cost Accounting and Pricing Policy

In this introductory chapter two subjects are touched upon, namely, the objectives of cost accounting on the one hand and the dimensions of costs on the other hand.

5.1 GENERAL OBJECTIVES OF COST ACCOUNTING

When going through the literature about cost accounting it is really striking that the same objectives of cost accounting are mentioned over again. The following classification can be set up.

5.1.1 Determination of Operating Results and Financial Position

Since the operating result over a definite period is the difference between revenues and costs of that period, the importance of cost accounting is obvious. In the scope of determining the financial position, the importance of cost accounting, in view of valuation of inventories of finished and semifinished goods and goods in process, is repeatedly pointed out. This "traditional" objective of cost accounting implies the calculation of historical and actual cost data.

5.1.2 Control of Cost and Efficiency

This aspect of cost calculation finds it origin in the so-called scientific management of Frederick Taylor. By means of a periodic comparison of actual cost with planned or standard cost, an attempt is made to judge the efficiency of the entire business or certain parts of it (divisions or departments, for example).

When the variance between actual and planned costs passes certain limits ("tol-
eration limits") a feedback process will be started to correct the course of the
business or a part of it.

5.1.3 Basis for Decision Making

For reasons such as technical progress, business growth, changing social and
economic climate, and others, business management has developed a more and
more complex character. This brings on that intuition and the so-called common
sense are insufficient guides in decision making. Adequate decision making
implies collecting and analyzing relevant and sufficiently accurate information.
Hence, the information system will have to meet requirements that are increasingly strict and varied.[1]

The question of information is not so much of a quantitative but rather of a
qualitative nature. Insofar as cost information is concerned, the cost accountant
needs to answer the following question: In view of what problem or what decision
does cost information have to be supplied? Then he has to reflect about what
cost information will be relevant. Only then can he start the rather material job
of collecting, grouping, and comparing these relevant cost data.[2]

In general we can say that cost accounting information in relation to decision
making shows the following characteristics:[3]

—Cost is not a unitary concept but takes different forms in different problems.
—The differences in costs (and in profits) rather than their absolute levels should be the
  focus of accounting analysis.
—It is therefore frequently advisable to avoid or ignore cost allocations, ascertaining
  instead specifically assignable or escapable costs.
—Whether the problem is short or long range, accounting is aided by retaining the
  distinction between "variable" and "fixed" costs and by giving attention to the behavior of the former.

Many authors explicitly mention price determination as an objective of cost
accounting.[4] From their reflections it appears, however, that pricing policy is
connected with quite a lot of other management aspects. So the question about
the relevancy of connecting cost accounting and pricing policy arises. From the
viewpoint of economic theory, of which the price determination problems traditionally constitute an important part, this question can undoubtedly be answered
affirmatively. From a management viewpoint there is less reason for such an
answer. Pricing policy is on the average not more important or unimportant than
other domains of decision making, and the role of cost accounting in it is surely
not more decisive than for other management problems.[5]

We probably have to do here with a result of the phenomenon of the sellers
market, not totally absent, and constituting in this manner an anachronism. It is

evident that the explicit mention of price policy and price determination as objective, *a fortiori* as the main objective of cost accounting, is exaggerated.

5.2 THE DIMENSIONS OF COSTS IN RELATION TO PRICING DECISIONS

It is by no means the intention to discuss in this section an exhaustive picture of the diverse cost dimensions and within each dimension to confront the different modalities. We only intend to give a brief notion of those modalities that could be important for pricing policy problems. Costs are always expressed in monetary units obtained by multiplying a certain quantity and a certain value dimension. So we have to discuss both the quantity and value dimension. In addition we will also give some reflections on the time dimension of costs.

5.2.1 The Quantity Dimension

With relation to the quantitative determination of the use of production factors, there are essentially two important systems:

1—actual quantity and
2—standard quantity.

About 1. The actual quantity of a production factor is a historical datum so that this method is of a retrospective nature. Owing to this it is clear that the actual quantity dimension is useless for pricing policy purposes.

About 2. On the basis of a production structure defined as normal and efficient, standards relating to the quantity dimension of costs can be fixed. These standards correspond to that quantity that is justified from an economic point of view, exclusive or accidental variances in the use or consumption of a particular production factor. Consequently, we say that changes in efficiency and changes in the proportions of production factors will induce changes of the standards.[6]

The advantage of using quantity standards for pricing purposes is seen especially in the speed of reporting prospective cost information to the price decision maker (at equal proportions of production factors).

For pricing policy purposes, especially when the selling price is set for a long period (long-term contracts, price lists) and there is no opportunity for price adjustments, it can even be necessary to form a picture of future proportions of production factors (for example, for the period of validity of the price list). Price setting will then be dependent on the standards corresponding with the future proportions. This is not necessary when adjustments of prices in the future are possible.

5.2.2 The Value Dimension[7]

For the value dimension of the production factors there is a multitude of possible modalities. Essentially we can distinguish three kinds:

1—cost,

2—replacement value, and

3—standard price.

About 1. The cost belongs to the same naive order of thought as the above described actual quantity. It is unnecessary to point out the historical, retrospective character of this modality and the consequently irrelevant character of this value dimension for price-setting purposes. Exception should be made for the (rather unrealistic) situation of constant future factor prices or when future price adjustments are possible.[8] It should be mentioned that this value dimension is still very usual in the business practice. Generally known and in use are the so-called FIFO and LIFO methods and a range of methods based on the arithmetic mean (weighed, progressive) of purchase prices. In each of these methods the relation to the proper acquisition price remains so that our criticism of these value dimensions holds up.

About 2. In the case of changing factor prices, the initial cost only has a historical sense. Here the so-called replacement value becomes important. A higher replacement value means a higher value of the production factors and so higher product costs; a lower replacement value points toward a lower value, by which the product costs are lower. Concerning the determination of costs on the basis of replacement value, there is an important timing problem, namely, the choice of the moment of valuation. In economic literature there is a countless number of opinions about this, going from the moment of purchase (see above 1), via the moment of sales to the future moment of replacement of the production factors. With respect to cost accounting information for pricing decisions, the next valuation moments seem relevant:

a. In principle the moment of economic exchange. Neither the moment of technical exchange (i.e., delivery) nor the moment of technical use of the production factor are relevant. The real critical moment is the moment of economic exchange, that means the moment at which the selling price is set and the price risk is passed over from the seller to the purchaser.

b. Concerning selling prices set for a longer future period, it will be necessary to approximate the expected replacement value of the product in the future period or at a future moment. The cost valuation is not to be done at current value but at a cost notion referring to a future period or moment. So a speculative element is brought into the cost calculation.[9] Contrary to that we can say that on the one hand this problem is inherent in each economic forecast and that on the other hand a large number of statistical and other forecasting techniques that are able to master the speculative element are available. For that reason the use of future replacement prices seems neither impossible nor undesirable.

About 3. The method of standard price considers the costs of used or consumed production factor at estimated prices used for a certain period. The choice of the standards can be based on purely utilitarian grounds because, essentially, it is not so important how the standards are calculated but that the chosen standards are used consistently. It is self-evident that such a standard is useless for cost valuation. It can be made useful for cost valuation by converting the standard quantity at replacement price instead of standard price. This can be easily done by setting a price index per production factor or, when the number of production factors is too extensive, per cluster of production factors with a parallel price evolution. In both cases the base of the price index is the standard price. In some cases the indexation can even be limited to the most important cost elements from which a weighed mean of prices can be calculated. By division of:

$$\frac{\text{total value at replacement price}}{\text{total value at standard price}}$$

the appropriate index number is obtained.[10] It is obvious that this index number needs adjustment in the case of relatively important changes in the price level or when real movements in the set of production factors take place. An investigation in 55 industrial firms in the United States by the National Association of Accountants (N.A.A.) delivers the following evidence:[11]

VALUE BASIS [12]	NUMBER OF FIRMS
Actual replacement price or standard price adapted to actual replacement price.	30
Future replacement price or standard price adapted to future replacement price.	6
Historical cost	12
Standard price	6
Valuation method not fixed	1
	55

Insofar as the value dimension is concerned it seems that 36 out of 55 firms follow the valuation method recommended above. Deviations from this method are motivated by such factors as inventory policy, government regulations or competitive reasons.[13]

According to Fog[14] it seems impossible to draw up such a classification. In the first place that does make sense because, according to Fog, there is little consistency in valuation practices, while in the second place there is an innumerable number of mixed methods and variants particularly based on averaged values. This can be explained in particular by considerations of inventory policy and competitive reasons that happen to be such that the valuation basis is determined by the intended pricing policy.

Both investigations suggest relatively little uniformity concerning the principles of cost valuation in practice. The valuation bases of the N.A.A. report are in closer connection with our theoretical option while Fog's investigation in Denmark rather suggests a practice based on averages. In both cases we must keep in mind that on account of considerations of inventory policy, competition, and actual or potential government intervention, many very divergent methods are practised.

5.2.3 The Time Dimension[15]

One of the most important examples of the time dimension of cost is the interest cost. The availability of producing capacity implies the presence of capital and this in its turn involves interest costs. It is not only the amount of the capital but also the duration of its availability that determines the interest costs. This duration indicates for what period the capital is withdrawn from other destinations. In fact the time dimension is concerned with a "quantity" of time and in such a way is a special case of the "quantity dimension." The effect of time even goes farther because the costs of the availability of some production factors are dependent on the time period. As an example we can consider durable capital goods.

For such goods the time dimension plays an important role because of the phenomenon of obsolescence and technical wear and tear. Other typical examples are the costs of performances of which the compensation is determined by the duration of availability such as rent and wages in case of time wages. In each of these cases the cost is determined by the time period of availability of the production factor irrespective of the intensity of use or employment. When the relation between time and cost does exist an acceleration of tempo is a benefit, a delay of tempo means a loss.

Insofar as the choice of the time basis is concerned we can refer to the discussion of the quantity dimension. Analogous to the option taken there the "actual" time is to be rejected and "standard" time has fundamentally been opted for. *Mutatis mutandis* the same considerations apply as for standard quantity.

6 Cost Concepts Relevant to Pricing Policy

During the last decennia, cost accounting has passed through a considerable evolution and as a consequence has fallen prey to a serious terminological confusion. When going through the related literature often it is difficult to find out which cost concept is used by a particular author. Furthermore, the notion "cost" is frequently used in common parlance. This additionally hampers the sharp definition of a cost notion.[1]

Our preference goes out to a broad cost concept that should be specified further for each concrete decision-making situation. For each of the decisions to make, the character of costs can be different. Consequently, an unambiguous cost concept makes little sense; it is impossible to talk about "the" cost. On the contrary, we shall employ different (of course relevant) cost concepts according to the problem to solve or the decision to make. So our option is fully typified by Clark's adage "different costs for different purposes."[2] In the following sections some cost concepts, useful for pricing decisions, will be discussed.

6.1 FIXED AND VARIABLE COSTS

Considered in relation to a measure of activity, all costs can be classified as fixed or variable. Variable costs increase or decrease in their totality if business activity increases or decreases. This cost variability can be proportional, progressive, or regressive. On the contrary, fixed costs remain equal in totality if business activity changes; they remain equal within certain limitations (the so-called relevant-range). The extent of fixed costs is especially determined by business capacity.[3]

In business practice we can frequently observe that certain costs show a "mixed" character; they are partly fixed, partly variable. A number of techniques, from the most simple rule of thumb to the more sophisticated statistical cost analyses, were developed to split up this so-called semivariable costs into their fixed and variable components so that the cost analysis is always converted to the dual basic distinction.[4]

The distinction between fixed and variable costs is very important for decision-making purposes in general and for pricing purposes in particular. Fixed and variable costs are especially important for the prospective examinations of the cost repercussions of certain decisions. Within the framework of pricing policy the repercussion of a series of alternative selling prices, combined sometimes with other marketing instruments, on sales volume and via sales volume on production volume and costs should be studied. On the other hand is the "bulk" of fixed costs that need to be recovered by sales revenues over a certain period. However, it is impossible, even in the case of full costing information, to determine which amount of fixed costs should be recovered by an individual unit of product or by a product group.[5] Yet it is possible to refine the cost calculation by further differentiating the bulk of fixed costs to certain aspects. Three criteria seem important in this context:[6]

—classification in function of imputability,[7]
—classification in function of time,[8] and
—classification in function of liquidity character.[9]

The first classification permits us to analyze fixed costs as follows:

—fixed costs attributable to product(s),
—fixed costs attributable to product group(s),
—fixed costs attributable to department(s),
—fixed costs attributable to division(s), and
—fixed costs attributable to the entire firm (i.e., undivided balance of fixed cost).

This method permits us to calculate several contributions. It is a combination of the classical full costing and partial costing. In this manner the degree to which each cost unit is contributing to the recovery of the several "hierarchical" steps of attributable fixed costs is shown, as well as the origin of profits. It is clear that in this way more information is gained from calculation, both for short- and long-term decisions.

The classification of fixed costs in function of time can lead to the next distinction:

—fixed costs directly assignable to a period of time (e.g., salaries),
—irregular, time-dependent fixed costs that therefore are merely assignable directly to more periods (e.g., costs of substantial machine repair), and

—costs resulting from one-off or irregular outlays that influence the firm's capacity for
a longer, not previously definable space of time (e.g., investment outlays).

Such a classification of fixed costs offers the possibility to determine a fixed
cost amount to be recovered period by period. Also the classification in function
of liquidity, related to the last-mentioned classification, is most important. Here
fixed costs can be subdivided into:

—fixed costs exerting impact on long-term cash expenses,
—fixed costs exerting impact on short-term cash expenses, and
—fixed costs without impact on cash expenses.

This analysis particularly aims at the security of the firm's liquidity and therefore
is important for pricing purposes, especially for setting price floors (see Chapter
7).

It is self-evident that combinations of the preceding classifications can be
useful. On the other hand, we should say that the rather extreme classifications
introduced here are probably neither workable nor necessary in practice. Therefore, the advantages of the desired cost information should be weighed against
the cost of the required calculation system.

Another decisive factor is the kinds of business problems the firm's management intends to solve with the help of information from this calculation method.
As far as pricing problems are concerned, the calculation of a set of differentiated
contributions, built up according to a combination of classification criteria of
fixed costs (to be considered in more detail later on) offers the following
advantages:

—It is less one sided in the sense that the calculation of differentiated contributions takes
into account both revenue and cost data. Pricing policy is an outstanding example of
a management field in which costs and revenues and their respective changes are central.
Therefore, contribution accounting, the contribution being the balance made by the
difference between revenues and certain costs, is an appropriate instrument to support
price decisions.
—It is broader in the sense that contribution accounting can lay the foundations of both
long- and short-term decisions; this because of the gradual absorption of fixed costs.
In such a way it combines in itself the advantages of full costing and direct costing.

6.2 DIRECT AND INDIRECT COSTS[10]

Direct costs are costs that are incurred for and are chargeable to, both in
quantity and in value, a particular product, product group, department, and so
forth. Essentially, the direct costs consist of direct wages and direct materials
but eventually other costs can be labeled as direct.

Indirect costs are those for which it is impossible to determine unambiguously for which product, product group, or department they were incurred. Classic examples are maintenance, heating, and lighting expenses of plant and office. If one intends to calculate the "full cost" of a product, many sometimes very complex problems of cost allocation arise.[11] Even in the (rather unrealistic) case of a single product firm it is often impossible to calculate precisely and accurately the full cost of a unit of product. The most usual full cost calculation methods only point out the average unit cost. The significance of such a cost amount in the scope of pricing policy is minute: it can possibly be used as a guide to fix the long-term price floor or as a point of impact for price differentiation.

An aggravating circumstance, however, is that, as already said, cost calculations for pricing purposes are mostly prospective, so that the sales volume (or production volume) on which the allocation of indirect costs is directly or indirectly based, remains an unknown quantity. Therefore, an alternative full cost should be calculated for each relevant price-volume combination so that the exactitude of average unit costs is in fact influenced by problematic anticipations of future sales and production volume.[12]

The problem of indirect costs gets even more serious in case of alternative, parallel, and joint production methods. Full costing can only exist by means of a complex process of cost allocation. In spite of the sometimes very refined allocation methods, the costs caused by a specific product are not always reached but are sometimes rather arbitrary amounts. It is self-evident that to base pricing and other decisions on such figures is irresponsible; decisions based on a defective foundation will most likely not produce the desired effect. Thus, we can conclude that for pricing purposes only the direct costs can be determined reasonably. Yet indirect costs are relevant too, namely, where the problem of recovering costs is concerned. In this connection use can be made of the approach suggested for fixed costs (classification in function of imputability, time, and/or liquidity character). This approach offers a valuable starting point to involve indirects costs in the price determination process.

6.3 HISTORICAL AND FUTURE COSTS

This subject can essentially be referred to the discussion of the dimensions of costs (see section 5.2).

Since price setting naturally refers to a future point or space of time, the relevant costs, useful for a sound pricing decision, are incontestably future (budgeted, standard) costs. For that reason, too, actual or historical cost information is useless or can at best give certain indications that should be verified critically. The simple assumption that actual or historical cost structure will recur similarly in the future should be labeled as purely speculative. If this assumption comes true, it should be labeled merely accidental. Consequently, this means that, where costs play a role in price setting, explicit approximations of future costs should be carried out, in the course of which historical and actual costs can only act as point of departure.

6.4 SHORT AND LONG-TERM COSTS

Essentially, the notions short term and long term are not chronological. In economic theory the distinction between short and long term is roughly made as follows: in the long run the firm's capacity can be fundamentally changed, in the short run merely the activity ratio at equal capacity can alter.

The distinction between short-term and long-term costs is especially founded on the adaptability of production factors to the volume and nature of the output. This adaptability can vary widely so that for pragmatic reasons an arbitrary space of time should be fixed to define unequivocally the difference between short and long term (e.g., less than one year is short, more than one year is long term).

For pricing purposes especially the short-term costs are important: pricing decisions frequently imply the weighing of short-term revenues against short-term costs. Nevertheless, the necessity for recovering total costs implies that long-term costs be considered (see section 6.8). Since long-term costs are mainly fixed and indirect, the approaches discussed in the context of fixed costs (see section 6.1) can be useful in this respect.

6.5 CASH AND NONCASH COSTS

Costs can lead to cash outlays or otherwise (*cf.* the weekly wage payments versus amortization cost). The insights of those who use this cost classification for decision-making purposes will determine the adequate limits between both concepts. In this connection we refer to the classification in function of liquidity character (see section 6.1). The consideration of this type of cost classification for pricing purposes gives information about the impact on the firm's liquidity of price decisions. This especially is of concern in setting price floors.

6.6 OPPORTUNITY COSTS

One of the chief phases of the decision-making process is the comparison of several alternatives of problem solution. In this connection a principal concept is the "opportunity cost." This is the prospective cost difference of the several alternatives against the actual, real alternative or, if the latter is lacking, the mutual cost differences among the preconceived alternatives.[13]

With reference to pricing policy the concept of opportunity cost is basic and fundamental.[14] In order to define this concept to some extent we have to start from the agreement that the firm's production factors are limited in such a way that the use of a production factor for a particular purpose prevents the use of the same factor for an other purpose. In this way bottlenecks originate. As a rule, the firm's calculation system is drawn up in such a manner that the incurred costs are inserted and allocated further to departments, products, or eventually other calculation objects. Consequently, the calculation does not point out to what degree the business results would have been changed in case of producing an other product, or product mix, with the available means of production. So traditional calculation does not furnish opportunity cost information.

This problem arises acutely in the case of full activity or even abnormal capacity usage. Then, one or more of the production factors become a bottleneck. The assessment of the product's profitability in that case implies that selling price should not only cover the variable (or direct) costs, but the contribution of a unit of bottleneck factor needed for this product should be compared with the contribution of an other product manufactured under the same circumstances. If, for example, direct labor is the bottleneck factor, the contribution per unit of bottleneck (e.g., a man hour) should be calculated. In this case the ratio is:

$$\frac{\text{total contribution of product A}}{\text{required man hours for product A}}$$

The product or order yielding the largest contribution per unit of bottleneck should normally be preferred. The above-mentioned contribution can be called "bottleneck related contribution" and is generally defined as:[15]

$$\frac{\text{unit selling price } - \text{ unit marginal cost}}{\text{use of bottleneck factor per unit}}$$

Bottleneck calculation can also be used in case of underutilization of business capacity. In this case not the production factors but market circumstances are the causal factors. As incomplete utilization of productive capacity is caused by market circumstances, sales have to be considered as bottleneck. In this connection the decisive quantity is the contribution per unit of sales (sales dollar).

In case the price setting is based on bottleneck calculation leaning on the concept of opportunity costs, the contribution per unit of bottleneck factor should be added to the unit variable costs. As a rule, here the recovery of fixed costs as well as the generation of profit are included.

6.7 TOTAL COSTS, AVERAGE COSTS, AND DIFFERENTIAL COSTS

Unit total or full costs are composed of direct costs and a fraction of indirect costs assigned to a unit of product by way of allocation with the help of distribution bases.

Full costs should be considered with great circumspection (and this not only in the context of pricing policy) because of the often rather arbitrary character of the distribution basis, so that in fact an "exact" unit full cost can never be calculated. The concepts of marginal or differential costs have to do with changes in production volume. Marginal or differential costs can be defined as changes in costs due to changes in production volume. It is self-evident that the already discussed variable costs are a plausible point of departure for the approximation of differential costs. However, variable and differential costs are not always synonymous. The salary of superintendents is a fixed cost. If because of a larger sales and production volume there is a changeover from a two-shift to a three-shift system, a new team of superintendents is needed. The salary of the new superintendents is a differential cost but does not belong to the variable costs. Generally, differential costs are very valuable information for pricing purposes (see Part III).

6.8 THE PROBLEM OF RECOVERING COSTS

It was already pointed out that most price decisions essentially are short-term decisions. As many short-term decisions, taken by themselves or in connection with other decisions, can have implications in the long run, it would be irresponsible to leave the long-term aspects without consideration.

An opinion expressed frequently in related literature considers the problem thus, that for short-term pricing decisions the variable (direct) costs offer an adequate basis so that the marginal calculation is obvious. In the case of long-term decisions, referring to the firm's continuity, the necessary recovery of total costs is pointed out so that full costing would be the evident method of calculation.[16] In our opinion, such views hold a few dangers:

—An exaggerated emphasis on the importance of variable costs for short-term pricing decisions causes a danger of possible price deterioration or at least a policy of low prices that eventually slows down or prevents the firm's long-term growth (especially in case of inelastic demand; *cf. supra*).

—Application of the classical full-costing method based on questionable or even on wrong cost allocation can lead to an inconsistent and unbalanced price structure: on the one hand, certain prices can be too high so that competitors have free play; on the other hand, certain prices can be too low so that potential profits are lost.[17]

In our opinion contribution accounting (see especially Part IV) offers a solution for this duality: for one thing the variable costs are taking part so that the calculation is usable for short-term problems. Also, fixed costs are included gradually and without making use of arbitrarily chosen distribution bases so that contribution accounting is also usable for pricing decisions with long-term impact.[18] In this context two important problems arise:

1. Which costs should be recovered within a period?
2. Which costs should be recovered per unit of product?

About 1. The cost amount assignable to a particular period (week, month, quarter, year, etc.) is not always easy to determine. For certain cost categories the amount per period can be fixed comparatively easily and unambiguously: for example, costs of raw materials, personnel costs, and such. For other cost categories the periodic amount cannot be fixed unequivocally because it depends on uncertain prospects. Examples of these are costs attached to licenses and patents, startup expenses, and costs of substantial repair and maintenance. The share of these costs to be assigned to a specific period depends on the insight into and the judgment of the future. When, for example, a plant is built, the question of the number of periods and the periodical costs that should be recharged can indeed be solved with the help of average amounts or amounts based on experience, but this does not guarantee that the decrease in value goes by as for other similar plants. Consequently, the setting of the relevant depreciation amount will always depend on the prospects and readiness to take risks. So, considered per period, only a part of total costs can be determined precisely; the determination of the other part leans on prospects and risk evaluation and therefore remains more or less uncertain.

Insofar as the imputability of costs to a period is concerned, the next distinctions can be made:

—costs directly associated with a particular period (direct period costs) and
—costs related to more periods (indirect period costs).[19]

In the first place, the direct period costs, which normally need to be recovered in the same period unless market considerations or accidental events compel one to depart from this rule, are very important for pricing purposes. Which part of indirect period costs needs to be recovered in a particular period cannot be determined unequivocally because it is a matter of judgment. Therefore, for pricing purposes, depreciation and provision amounts, relative to the indirect period costs to be recovered in a particular period, have to be premised. The difference between such planned cost amounts and the costs calculated by means of an allocation and distribution procedure is obvious; the planned cost amounts are not considered exact and incontestable but are amounts set freely and cautiously.

Price decisions are no longer founded on deliberations such as "$200,000 is allocated to this period and also must be recovered"; but the reasoning is as follows: "in this period $150,000 of direct period costs were incurred and must be recovered, besides $50,000 should be realized, appropriated for the recovery of indirect period costs."

Pricing policy based on such planned indirect period costs to recover can be

Figure 1

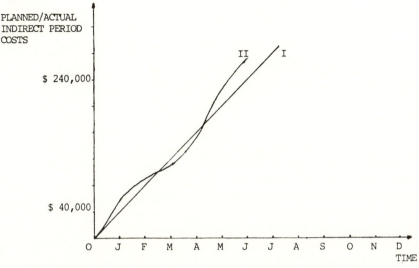

I : Line of planned recovering of indirect period costs (cumulative)
II: Hypothetical line of actual recovering of indirect period costs
    (cumulative).

more flexibly related to the ups and downs of the market than pricing policy based on average cost. At the same time there is more stress on compensation among the successive periods: business management has always in view the total indirect period costs and therefore knows at every moment which part is covered and which is the balance still to recover.

In this connection a graph conveniently can show the "recovery lines" of indirect period costs. Assumed is that the annual indirect period costs are $480,000. Sales are spread equally over the year and the recovery plan of indirect period costs is parallel (Figure 1).

If line II is above line I: more indirect costs are actually recovered than was anticipated. The situation is favorable, pricing policy may be flexible (see January, February, May, June). If line I is above line II: recovery of indirect costs is behind schedule. The situation is rather unfavorable and pricing policy should be more stringent (see March, April).

In this example the shape of line I is only determined by one factor, namely, the sales amount. In fact, before drawing line I, the determinants of the recovery of indirect period costs (e.g., seasonal factors in sales) should be analyzed. Bearing this in mind, we are convinced of the usefulness of this simple and surveyable graph with regard to the followup of indirect period costs.[20]

About 2. From the viewpoint of pricing policy the question of cost recovery per unit of product is still more important than the problem of cost recovering per period. An essential solution for this problem is easy to find: each product has to at least recover the costs caused by its production; in other words, the

costs that could be avoided by eliminating the production of the product concerned. So it concerns the direct product costs. Moreover, each particular product
has essentially to contribute to the recovery of the costs jointly caused by the
several products. Consequently, the sum of the contributions of each product
should at least be equal to the total indirect product costs: if C_j is the contribution
of the products; q_j is the sales volume of the products, and I_i is the total indirect
costs, then, in case of n products, the next condition is valid:

$$\sum_{j=1}^{n} C_j \cdot g_j \geq I_i$$

However, the problem is not solved yet; the question arises, namely, how the
bulk of indirect product costs should be spread over the several products. Because
of the indirect nature of costs this question cannot be answered unequivocally.
Nevertheless, cost accounting can, in our opinion, provide a fundamental point
of support to answer this question. The starting point of the answer is that indirect
product costs are not face to face with direct product costs but the former can
be subdivided further. The relativity of the notions direct and indirect should be
stressed here: it is perfectly thinkable that costs that cannot be assigned to a unit
of product (i.e., an indirect product cost) can be assignable to a product group
(i.e., a direct cost of this product group). Costs, indirect with regard to a product
group, can be directly related to a department. Consequently, a hierarchy of
relations can be built up in which each particular cost can be assigned as a direct
cost to a particular cost center or any other "unit of reference" (*cf.* classification
of fixed costs in function of imputability—section 6.1).[21]
    In this manner cost accounting gives the following information to aid pricing
decisions:

—how large the indirect costs are of a product group that should be carried by the totality
   of each individual product belonging to it and
—how large the direct costs are of a department that should be carried by the totality of
   product groups that are manufactured in it.

However, selling prices should not be set for product groups, departments,
and so forth but for products. How much a unit of product has to contribute to
the costs that can merely be assigned to its product group and how large the
product group's contribution should be to the costs assignable to a department—
to these questions cost accounting cannot give an answer. The determination of
the contribution each product has to yield to the recovery of indirect costs requires
a management decision. In accordance with the premised hierarchy of relations
the following calculation scheme can be used:

1. direct product costs,
2. planned contribution to recover the direct costs of the product group,
3. planned contribution to recover the direct costs of the cost center(s),
4. planned contribution to recover the direct costs of the division(s), and

5. planned contribution to recover the direct costs of the entire firm (i.e., undivided balance of indirect product costs), as well as to generate profit.

In addition to such a product-oriented hierarchy, for other purposes (e.g., price differentiation) other series can be initiated, for example:

—customer, customer group, sales area and
—unit of product, order, order group.

Normally, the distinction is usually made between direct period costs and costs allocated in the form of depreciation and provision amounts. For both, single "planned contributions" are calculated. The setting of these planned contributions is mainly based on market considerations taking into account the bearing power of the different products. Price determination based on these related direct costs seems more difficult and complex than price setting on the basis of full costing. This is indeed the case because full costing makes use of a recurrent, stereotyped allocation scheme. Yet it is just the lack of such a scheme that accounts for the advantages of the proposed method: the person responsible for price determination is continually confronted with the limited usefulness of traditional cost accounting for pricing purposes and is constantly forced to take full account of market data and the firm's objectives.

The problems of cost recovery are also influenced by the character of price determination. When a part of production is supplied at the ruling market prices, the problem may be: Which share of indirect costs should be recovered by product C if products A and B, sold at market price, have already partly contributed to recovering indirect costs? Significant for proper price setting in this case is the surplus, the balance of total costs to be recovered. In other circumstances the problem may be to what extent the minimal contribution of product C alters if the market price of product A and B changes.

If all products are sold at market price the essential information is which product or product group is most important from the point of view of recovering costs and making profit. Naturally, it is that product or product group that yields the largest contribution over its direct costs. When a bottleneck is arising in the production factors, the most important cost information for pricing purposes is the contribution per unit of bottleneck (man hour, machine hour, etc.). When the bottleneck is due to the market or marketing domain (e.g., temporary market saturation, shortage of sales representatives), the marketing efforts should be directed to that product or product group that yields the largest unit contribution (see section 6.6).

6.9 SOME TENTATIVE CONCLUSIONS

Above, a few cost concepts, one by one important for pricing matters, were discussed. From this discussion it appears that:

—Information about cost structure and cost evolution in function of sales volume (or production volume) is very important, which at the same time points out the importance of the distinction between fixed and variable costs.

—Information about costs chargeable to a particular product or product group is important, which points out the importance of the (relative) distinction between direct and indirect costs.

—The distinction between short-term and long-term cost evolution may not be lost out of sight for pricing purposes.

—For decision making in general and particularly for pricing decisions future costs are more important than historic and actual costs.

—In Part IV the system of "analytical contribution accounting" will be thoroughly discussed. In this chapter we already found some preliminary inducements and reflections on this system:

● The problem of allocation of indirect (or fixed) costs to products or product groups is apparently unsolvable. The reason for this is that the relationship between indirect costs and product is a relationship of a means opposite to an end, whereas traditional cost allocation starts from a causal connection. This misconception has lead to the fact that for more than half a century one is tinkering at full costing with all in all very poor outcome. On the contrary, contribution accounting assigns the fixed (indirect) costs in accordance with the above-mentioned means-end relationship.

● Contribution accounting ties in with the concept of opportunity costs, that, as appears, is or can be very meaningful for pricing purposes.

● Moreover, we can say that contribution accounting takes both revenues and costs into consideration. It concerns two quantities that very closely affect pricing decisions. Traditional cost accounting, especially the full-costing system, is more one-sidedly cost oriented.

7 The Role of Cost Accounting Information in Determining Price Floors

In the previous chapters the significance of costs in pricing decisions has already been toned down. However, if cost information for pricing purposes keeps any importance, it is certainly for the matter of setting price floors. On the basis of price floors, the sales department will submit price quotations taking into account the market situation and the firm's general and marketing objectives. Consequently, the present discussion of the problems of price floors finds its origin in the manifest significance of the cost factor in setting price floors.

7.1 DEFINITION OF THE PRICE FLOOR CONCEPT

In the first place it should be pointed out that because of the numerous and diverse factors influencing price floors (see *infra* section 7.2) it is impossible to give an unequivocal definition. We could paraphrase Clark and mention the adage "different price floors for different purposes." Naturally, general definitions can be given such as "the price floor is the marginal revenue under which the price may not go down." Such a definition is so general that it becomes quasi meaningless. For that reason it seems better to premise a deliberate definition in function of a concrete problem, concrete objectives, or any other concrete situation that urges us to know the minimal selling price.[1] This can only be put into effect by reviewing a number of factors affecting the price floor.

7.2 FACTORS INFLUENCING THE PRICE FLOOR

The price floor can be set either monistically or pluralistically.[2] In the former case it relates to the setting of the price floor on the basis of one particular factor of influence; in the latter case it concerns the setting of a minimum price on the ground of a simultaneous combination of two or more factors of influence. It is obvious that the pluralistic approach is more realistic and that the monistic view has to be dismissed as too simplistic.

In the next sections a number of possible factors of influence are reviewed, mentioning every time their specific role in setting price floors. Naturally, the significance of these factors is widely divergent: the factor "recovering costs" is closely connected with the firm's profit objective and consequently will be relatively important. Other factors are less important because they only indirectly influence the price floor or because of the fact that they are hardly or not controllable.

7.2.1 Recovering Costs

From the discussion of pricing objectives we learned that the profit objective is always important and in many cases even a dominant objective in the entire band of objectives. The simple truth that profit is the surplus of revenues over costs makes us realize that there is only question of profit insofar as costs are fully regained from revenues. Hence, the clear importance of cost recovery in the scope of setting of price floors: the price floor equals that selling price that, without making any operating results, recovers all costs. With this the great importance of a cost-oriented determination of price floors is evident; indeed, the employed cost concepts shall have to be chosen in such a way that full cost recovery is guaranteed. Therefore, the cost amount that can be avoided when the production of the product in question is abandoned shall generally have to be taken as price floor. It concerns the marginal costs of the product.[3]

The above is only correct in principle: by combination with factors of influence yet to be discussed, the fundamental cost concept can still be changed radically. Taking the time dimension as an example it is clear that the above is short-term oriented, for in the long run full costs need to be recovered.[4] A more thorough discussion of this and other modifications can be found in section 7.3.

7.2.2 Liquidity

Unlike the problems of recovering costs that could be reduced to the comparison of revenues and the corresponding costs, in this case it concerns the comparison of receipts and expenditures. The cash inflow is mainly determined by sales revenue; cash outflow largely depends upon costs. Therefore, between both factors of influence a certain similarity but not equality can be ascertained. A firm can only survive if it can meet its current payment obligations. In this respect price floors that only recover the variable costs are only acceptable insofar as they do not cause unsatisfactory liquidity. In this connection other sources of financing such as the possible contracting of short-term loans or the latitude of customer's credit or credit granted by suppliers should be taken into consideration. In this context the firm can eventually loose its wings by striving for preservation of its financial equilibrium. The pursuit of a decent liquidity ratio is in any case an important modification of the pure cost-oriented price floor. Taking account of the cash outlay of costs, an overhaul of price floors attuned to recovering costs to liquidity-oriented price floors can be necessary. Since cash planning forms part of financial planning, namely, the planning of short-term receipts and expenditures, the question arises as to what degree the liquidity-oriented price floors can be approximated by means of costs. This aspect is explored further in section 7.4.

7.2.3 Nature of Sales

From several sides it has been shown that market circumstances can determine the price floor to a substantial degree. It is pointed out, among other things, that the approach to price floors is entirely different, or at least should be, depending on whether it concerns normal, current sales or accidental, additional sales.[5] In this connection a frequently used approach originates from differential costing: fixed costs should be recovered by regular, current sales while the price floor of additional production and sales is made up of additional (differential) unit costs. This view is essentially right but it should be understood clearly that substantial modifications can occur in function of evolution of activity ratio, in function of potentialities of recovering full costs by current sales, or in function of objectives aimed at with additional sales.

In relation to the setting of price floors there will be a fundamental difference between additional sales with improvement of profitability in view and additional sales for reason of improvement of liquidity. In the latter case the cash character of costs shall determine the price floor (see also section 7.4).

7.2.4 Market Structure

With respect to setting of price floors, the aspect of market structure is meaningful in the sense that the price floor is important for firms with either active or passive pricing policy, acting upon markets belonging to the full range in between perfect competition and monopoly.[6] In each of these cases the question of the appropriate selling price arises, taking into account the objectives pursued.

In the case of perfect competition the imposed market price will be compared to the variable costs (short term). If the market price is greater than the variable costs it is profitable to supply as much as possible (as far as capacity limits allow) since each unit produced and sold contributes to fixed costs and results. In the case of monopoly one should start from an estimation of sales volume in function of one or more alternative selling prices. So the price floor is determined by sales volume. Essentially, the larger the sales volume the lower the price floor is. This becomes clear when the next formula of price floor is premised:

$$P_F = c_v + \frac{C_f}{x}$$

in which P_F is the price floor; c_v is the unit variable cost; C_f is fixed costs; and x is the planned sales volume.

In the short run, $P_F = c_v$; in the long run,

$$P_F = c_v + \frac{C_f}{x},$$

taking into account that P_F and x are inversely proportional.

7.2.5 Marketing Policy

Pricing policy is part of marketing policy. Pricing policy can range from a rather unimportant to a really substantial aspect of marketing management of which it should be a consistent and balanced part.

Consequently, pricing policy and thus the setting of price floors shall be influenced by the remaining marketing subpolicies in two ways:

—The implementation of marketing policy implies the origin of costs increasing directly the cost amount to be recovered and therefore exerting an influence on the cost-oriented price floor and, where these costs involve short-term cash outlays, also on liquidity-oriented price floors.

—The second aspect, however, is more important. It occurs frequently that on account of marketing considerations the cost-oriented price floor is not passed. Numerous motives can stimulate, even force, a firm to sell at prices that in no case can be related to one or another cost concept. This can happen when the firm is reacting to competitive prices or when the intention is to complete the assortment by means of broadening or deepening it ("line fillers").[7] Also, the use of "loss leaders"—delivering small orders at normal selling price in prospect of larger orders, charging no transportation costs to distant new customers in the hope they will continue to buy—are in the same order of thought.[8]

Such policies can be explained by an expected simultaneous or future reciprocation with other existing products, orders, and customers. In each of the above cases the connection among revenues is put first; the revenues of the single products are not considered separately but total revenue of total sales is put first of all. As a consequence direct costs are irrelevant and total costs should be compared to total revenues. The price floor of one specific product corresponds to the difference between the total revenue of the remaining products (orders) and total costs. If all costs are already covered by the revenues of the remaining products, the price floor of the product in question can be very low, zero, or even negative.

A well-known example in this connection is Polaroid's policy of supplying cameras below variable costs, expecting the lacking contribution can be (over) compensated for by selling more complementary photographic materials (e.g., films). Other examples are the efforts of electricity companies to sell electric household appliances nearly at cost or subsidize their purchase in order to raise the electricity consumption.[9]

7.2.6 Nature of Production Process

It is obvious that cost accounting in industrial firms will be directly influenced by the production process because cost accounting was, among other things, conceived to record costs in function of the progression of the production process. The more complex this production process, the more complex, therefore, the system of cost accounting. In this context attention is paid to an important related factor that has repercussions for the determination of selling prices, namely, the difference between single and multiple product firms.[10]

In periods of declining prices, thus in those situations where determination of price floors is most relevant, the single product firm can essentially choose between two alternatives, namely, to continue or to stop production. The multiple product firm has a range of opportunities available because of the numerous potentialities to replace or convert from one product to another.[11] Consequently, in multiple product firms an important internal competition among the several products exists in which the internal competitive status is especially influenced by the relative level of contribution, the potentialities of price compensation among products, and by whether bottlenecks are caused in production or sales.

As far as a cost-oriented approach of price floors is concerned, it should be stated that because of the existence of indirect product costs the setting of price floors is not possible or only possible to a limited extent. All this is determined by the prices, both cost and selling price, of the other products of the firm's product mix. Yet for the entire assortment a total cost amount, to be considered as a cost-oriented revenue floor for the entire assortment, can be calculated. This minimum can essentially be attained by many price combinations so that the direct significance for the real price decision is not very important.

As far as the liquidity-oriented price floors are concerned, *mutatis mutandis* the same comments can be made. In the first instance, a cost classification according to cash character is useful. Especially, costs inducing short-term cash outlays are relevant to liquidity. On the basis of this classification the single product firm can set so-called liquidity limits for different price-sales combinations. The liquidity limit indicates the sales volume that leads to recovering all costs inducing short-term outlays at the agreed selling price. In formula form:[12]

$$\text{liquidity limit} = \frac{\text{fixed costs inducing short-term cash outlays}}{\text{contribution per product}}$$

In multiple product firms the approach is rather global; the whole of pricing decisions may not influence liquidity unfavorably. Hence, no liquidity-oriented minimum price per product will be fixed but instead a minimal revenue for integral sales will be determined. It is obvious that the relevance for decision making of this approach may not be rated highly.

Finally, it should be noted that contribution accounting, by differentiating the contributions to the extreme, provides for a number of relevant data that consolidate insights into price floor decision making, especially in multiproduct firms (see Part IV).

7.2.7 Time Aspects

An important problem of pricing policy in general and the determination of price floors in particular is postulating relevant time dimensions. In this connection we currently speak of short and long term without defining clearly the import of "short" and "long." Time can generally be expressed in economic terms or in terms of calendar time. Both means of expression are not to be rejected in principle, but in the case of expressing time in economic terms there is danger of foggy and/or arbitrary definition. Therefore, the purpose is to find a method of time expression that is both economically justified and convertible into calendar time.

The feasibility of distinguishing objectively the concept of long and short term, expressed in calendar time (cf. granting of credits) and in view of determination of price floors, seems nearly impossible because, as already said, pricing decisions are rather different from firm to firm. Marshall's classical classification in "short" and "long" period is based on the feasibility to change the firm's production capacity. However, changes in production capacity can be so numerous and many sided that they may not necessarily be considered as lasting and changing substantially the entire firm. In correction of this, Raffée starts from an "existing business structure" characterized by unchanged production capacity and a standard network of market relations. On short term, both factors can change in some measure without breaking through the existing business structure. When the changes of the concerning factors are so great, the existing business structure is changed substantially and permanently.[13]

Though this distinction between short and long term is more unambiguous than Marshall's, it too remains rather vague. For example, nowhere is described when a change is serious enough to be considered as breaking through the existing business structure. A more distinctive criterion is provided by Moews, who bases the difference between short and long term on the reducibility of fixed costs.[14]

He marks off two limits: the short run, in which all production factors remain equal so that fixed costs cannot be reduced, and the long run, in which all factors are variable, and in which the totality of fixed costs can be fully reduced. In between is a range of possibilities to be labeled as "medium term." These possibilities have a more long-term character depending on the amount of fixed costs that can be reduced in the period concerned. It appears that the method of Moews is a step forward compared with the preceding methods: he does not measure the period character by the difficult to measure factor or variability but by the reducibility of fixed costs. This is relatively easy to measure but it seems desirable to include in the cost accounting system a classification of fixed costs in function of their reducibility. Again, analytical contribution accounting is the system that shows adequate flexibility to incorporate such classification.

A still more unequivocal method, and therefore preferable, is introduced by Reichmann.[15] This method starts with the available relevant information for pricing purposes. In doing so, three dimenions in which the time span can be set individually are distinguished. These three dimensions and their criteria of distinction can be reflected as follows:

—*Period:* short space of time, within which the decision maker can count in terms of certain, unambiguous expectations and constant data. The corresponding calendar time differs from firm to firm and can vary from one year to one week.

—*Planning-time fraction:* a longer period characterized by certain expectations but variability of data. The planning-time fraction comprises more periods (e.g., 6 to 12).

—*Planning time:* corresponds with the economic horizon and is marked by growing uncertainty of expectations and, naturally, data variability.

With the help of this method each individual firm can make an objective division according to calendar time. Next to static setting of price floors (i.e., per period) dynamic setting (i.e., over more periods) also can be implemented.[16]

7.2.8 Inventory Aspects

In case of unsteady or weak sales it is not always possible or desirable to contract or stop business activity. Usually only two alternatives are taken into account in the scope of setting price floors, namely, producing further or stop producing (definitely or temporarily).

A new dimension can be added when inventory building is also considered. Building inventories can be looked upon as an additional alternative next to the two already described alternatives. Market factors and inflexibility of production factors do not always permit synchronization of sales and production so that a buffer, namely, an inventory, must be inserted. The problems arising here with regard to the setting of cost-oriented price floors are of two kinds:

—How large an inventory can be built. This implies the necessity of setting a cost-optimum inventory level.

—Which are the cost repercussions. In this context the question arises to what degree the cost-oriented price floor is influenced by inventory costs.[17] Here, the problem is the estimate of future cost and sales evolution, especially in relation to the alternative selling prices and considering sales volumes. Therefore, in the cost approach of price floors actual unit costs should not only be confronted with actual selling prices but also with future selling prices.

7.2.9 Production Capacity

In this section the repercussion of capacity changes on the setting of price floors is discussed.[18] In reference to the discussion of time dimension, it is related in principle to a long-term vision.

If in the long run no profitable production can be expected, closing down production should be considered. This cessation can be:

—*Temporarily or definitely:* in case of temporary halt of production an optimum duration of it can be determined, which, on the one hand, depends on the subjective appraisal of future sales evolution and on the other hand should attempt to maximally recover the loss, by taking into account, for purposes of setting minimum prices, not only the variable product costs but also the reducible fixed costs, the costs of stoppage, the costs of being idle, and the costs of restarting the operation. In case of definitive stoppage one should start from an investment analysis leaning on the concept of opportunity costs. The decision will be based on the opportunity value of the alternative employment of capacity.

—*Completely or partly:* in case of a single product firm it naturally concerns a complete stoppage, while in the event of the multiple product firm it usually concerns a partial liquidation, for example, of a product group. Mostly no unambiguous price floor can be set but only a revenue floor, obtainable by numerous price-sales combinations, for the entire product group.

—*Abruptly or gradually:* the stoppage can happen suddenly by liquidating assets and liabilities. The liquidation can also come about gradually, for example, by adandoning replacement investments.

However, capacity increases should also be mentioned. Among other things, the bottleneck calculation based on the opportunity cost concept can give a decisive answer with respect to the direction in which the firm should be extended. The discussion of the capacity aspects is obviously peripheral to price floor decisions and belongs for the greater part to investment analysis.

7.2.10 Qualitative Aspects

The last factors to be mentioned as possible determinants of price floors consist of a number of qualitative, imponderable, and difficult to measure factors.[19] We are especially concerned here with effects due to temporal or definitive stoppage of business such as:

—loss of goodwill;
—changes in consumer preferences, for instance, the measure in which customers are going over to competitors; and
—the time of being idle will be difficult to estimate in many cases.

It is obvious that judging the calculated price floors should be done with full awareness of these and other qualitative factors.

7.3 COST-ORIENTED PRICE FLOORS

While defining the concept of price floor we pointed out its relative character. A series of factors determining price floors have been discussed and their specific effect on the setting of price floors. Naturally, it would be impossible and indeed irrelevant to discuss all thinkable combinations of factors. Therefore, the next discussion is restricted to some of the most important ones. Usually distinction is made between short- and long-term price floors, identifying short-term price floors with variable costs and long-term price floors with full costs. There is reason to point out that this rather widespread definition only is operative if market conditions, as well as inventory aspects, remain out of scope. More important are the assumptions made about the time aspect. As said before the notions short and long term are extremes, moreover, a number of medium-term situations are thinkable in which the fixed costs are partly reducible (*cf. supra*). The price floors meant here are the extremes of a broad spectrum. The intermediate field remains out of consideration. Besides, the above price floors start from the assumption of a single product firm.

The problems of calculating the product's full cost, because of the existence of indirect costs, either variable or fixed, were already discussed. Therefore, it is impossible to find an adequate cost foundation of price floors, either short term or long term. In such cases only the revenue floor, that is, the costs incurred by aggregate products over a certain time period and consequently to be recovered from revenues of that period, can be fixed. It was already pointed out that the relevance for decision making of this revenue floor is minute because it can be realized by several price-sales combinations. A special case is the differential price floor, that is, the minimum price for additional orders when total costs are already covered by normal sales. In fact, here we have to do with the phenomenon of price differentiation.[20] The same applies to different price floors for orders of varying size.

Below, the problems of short-term price floors, and more specifically the relevant costs for crucial situations, are discussed. If selling price or sales volume is decreasing to such an extent that total costs are no longer recovered by total sales revenue, the question arises as to what minimum level the price can be lowered or may fall before it is more favorable to shut down the firm temporarily, or, in the case of a multiple product firm, to suspend the production of the product. The price floor to be considered here can be labeled an "absolute" price floor.[21]

It should be noted that in the above case the opportunity to convert to another product can also be taken into consideration. This problem of conversion does not only occur in critical situations but also in the case where with a particular assortment profit is realized. It should be examined if and to what degree converting to other products would improve operating results. So the problem here is one of interfacing pricing policy and product policy. In addition to cost considerations, concerns about activity ratio and market will play a prominent role. On that account the alternative "converting" is left out and only the alternatives "continuing" or "stopping" production are further discussed.

In the case of a single product firm a general solution can be formulated as follows: production should be continued as long as revenues are higher than the costs left out in case of stopping it. These are the costs of stoppage and being idle as well as the costs of restarting operations. Therefore, the question arises about what the production costs are that are incurred additionally above the continuous capacity costs. Consequently, the first and most important question that arises is that of the variable product costs. However, variable costs can and should not always be identified with the avoidable costs of stopping the production. A share of capacity costs is absolutely fixed in function of production volume (for example, depreciation costs based on historical cost). Another share of capacity costs depends on current production and can only be omitted if the entire firm or the production of a particular product is stopped (for example, costs of heating, lighting, packing). Thus, the capacity costs being left off in case of stoppage of production are relevant for the setting of price floors. Besides that, the price floor is influenced by costs originated by temporary stoppage. These costs are of three sorts:

—costs of stoppage,
—costs of being idle, and
—costs of bringing back in operation.

The costs of stoppage are incurred by the decision to stop the production (e.g., indemnities for no longer fulfilling concluded contracts of delivery).

The costs of being idle are incurred because of the fact that during the period of stoppage the whole of production means has to be maintained. Therefore, they are composed of depreciation, repair and maintenance costs, costs of interest, costs of insurance, and so forth. The costs of reputting into operation are coupled with the putting into use again the means of production. Examples are the costs due to inefficiencies in the starting period, costs of recruitment and training of new manpower, and advertising costs. The avoidable costs (fixed) increase the price floor, the costs incurred by temporary stoppage decrease it.[22] Finally, the ultimate price floor can be calculated as follows:[23]

Premises: unit variable costs as price floor: $P_F = c_v$. In case of temporary stoppage the costs incurred by the stoppage of production should be taken into account. They are:

$$C_s = C_{sa} + C_{sb} + C_r$$

in which: C_{sa} = costs of stoppage.
C_{sb} = costs of being idle
C_r = costs of bringing back in operation.

If:　　　C_A = costs avoidable by stoppage of production,
　　　　C_F = total fixed costs,
　　　　C_V = total variable costs,
　　　　C　= total cost,

then the costs avoidable by stoppage of production amount:

$$C_A = C - C_s \text{ in which } C = C_F + C_V$$

So, the costs avoidable by stoppage of production can be expressed as follows:

$$C_A = C_F + C_V - C_s$$

Consequently, the price floor, taking account of costs of stoppage of production, is:

$$P_F = \frac{C_V}{X} + \frac{C_F - C_s}{X} \text{ (with X standing for production volume)}$$

or:

$$P_F = c_v + \frac{C_F - C_s}{X}$$

Example: A concern intends a temporary stoppage of a division manufacturing and selling product A.
The following costs were estimated:

costs of stoppage	$ 500,000
costs of being idle	$ 750,000
costs of bringing back in operation	$ 400,000
Total	$ 1,650,000

Instead of taking unit variable costs as price floor the total costs incurred by the stoppage should be taken into account.

Other cost data:	total fixed costs	$ 8,000,000
	unit variable cost	$ 20.5
Production volume :	800,000 units of A	

The costs avoidable by stoppage of production amount:

$$(\$8,000,000 + \$20.5 \times 800,000 \text{ units}) - \$ 1,650,000 = \$ 22,750,000$$

$$\text{Price floor: } \$20.5 + \frac{\$8,000,000 - \$ 1,650,000}{800,000 \text{ units}}$$

$$: \$20.5 + \frac{\$ 6,350,000}{800,000 \text{ units}}$$

$$: \$20.5 + \$ 7.94 = \$ 28.44$$

It is clear that the simplistic view that the price floor is equal to unit variable costs only holds when the algebraic sum of avoidable costs and costs originating because of temporary stoppage equals zero, so, if $C_F = C_s$. It should be remarked, however, that the above setting of the cost-oriented price floor is inaccurate to a certain degree because of the fact that some uncertain expectations have been taken into account. Indeed, unit variable costs can be calculated unequivocally, but where avoidable costs and the costs of stoppage of production are concerned, this is impossible.

The avoidable fixed costs, incurred in the period in which the product was sold at the minimum price, should be recovered by sales revenues of the same period. Conversely, the total costs of temporary stoppage should be subtracted from sales revenue of the products sold at minimum price.

Consequently, in case of high avoidable fixed costs or high costs of temporary stoppage, the calculation of price floors is hampered because of the uncertainty about the duration of business slack and the corresponding number of products sold at minimum price. Another problem arises because of the fact that both avoidable fixed costs and costs of temporary stoppage vary partly with the duration of production interruption.

In the single product firm the short-term price floor can only be set precisely or at least sufficiently accurately if, in case of temporary stoppage, only a small share of fixed costs can be reduced and the costs originating from stoppage of production are negligible. The same is valid when both costs, irrespective of their absolute amount, are approximately in the same order of magnitude. In this case the price floor approximately corresponds to the product's variable costs.

In the case of the multiple product firm the problems are more complicated. As a starting point the case of joint production can be taken because this production situation is most intricate. The principle that each particular product should recover its specific costs remains. In case of joint production that means the variable direct product costs, in other words, the variable costs incurred after the joint part of the production process is finished (after the so-called split-off point). Furthermore, each particular product should contribute to the costs incurred for maintaining the entire production.

In the case of joint production the variable costs (e.g., costs of raw materials) are for the greater part indirect product costs, so that normally no price floors per unit of product can be set. At the most the minimal amount that should be realized for the entire group of joint products can be determined. So, cost accounting data relevant for pricing purposes are:

—the amount of variable costs incurred by the joint production process and jointly to be recovered by all products and
—those variable costs originating after the split-off point as direct product costs.

In this connection a mutual dependence of the price floors of the particular joint products can be mentioned: the price floor of one product can only be calculated if the price floors (or revenues) of the other products are known.[24]

Also, in case of full activity, knowledge of price floors can be useful. Here the problem can be put as follows: what is the price floor at which it is more profitable to reduce or drop the production of a particular product and to use that free capacity for production of articles yielding a comparatively higher contribution? An approach with the help of bottleneck calculation based on opportunity costs seems obvious.[25] The relevant price floor cannot be lower than the absolute price floor since it will be composed of variable costs raised by the sacrificed contribution of the superseded product (opportunity costs). In case of a material subnormal capacity usage, when bottlenecks are impossible, the relevant price floor can be equal to the absolute price floor, since the not fully used capacity has an opportunity cost value equalling zero.

The short-term price floors can be further determined by occuring costs of setting aside production. Indeed, it may occur that certain unsalable products, jointly produced, can only be considered as trash after certain processes (stocking up, packing, transportation, etc.). The costs of these processes, called here "costs of setting aside," should be recovered by the totality of joint products, so they should be treated as costs of the joint production.

The impact on the setting of price floors can be formulated as follows: each particular product has to recover at least its variable costs incurred beyond the split-off point. Furthermore, all products have to recover jointly the indirect variable costs as well as the possible costs of setting aside. In this case unambiguous price floors cannot be fixed but only a revenue floor. In the case of parallel production it is important to ascertain that the share of direct product costs is, as a rule, much greater than in the case of joint production, since in the former method material costs and frequently labor and marketing costs are assignable to the individual products. However, there can be a lot of indirect product costs that should be recovered by the minimum selling price to secure reasonable profits.[26]

The distinction between the setting of price floors in case of joint production on the one hand and alternative or parallel production on the other is not essential but rather gradual. However, we can say that the larger the share of variable direct costs in total costs is and the smaller the share of variable indirect costs, the easier the possibilities are to determine the costs to be recovered by a particular product.

Up to now only the implications of temporary stoppage of business activities on the setting of price floors were touched. In some cases, however, the definite stoppage of business can be the only available alternative. If sales decrease, selling price diminutions or cost increases are no longer of a temporary nature but become really structural, so that even in the long run costs can no longer be recovered by revenues and the business should be closed down. In case of a multiple product firm bad prospects may only concern a segment of sales so that only the definitive stoppage of this segment has to be considered.

Consequently, the decision to liquidate the firm (segment) is in the first place based on market research. If market research points out that the further viability of the product is definitively lost, then, it should be decided if the firm (segment, product) will be liquidated abruptly or gradually.[27] If the decision is made to stop production gradually and to continue until the means of production are consumed, depreciated, reoriented, and so on, the problem of the costs to be recovered during the liquidation period arises. This can be set as follows:

—costs incurred during the liquidation period,
—liquidation revenues in case of abrupt liquidation, and
—liquidation revenues in case of selling the means of production after a period of gradual liquidation.

Therefore, an estimation should be made of the attainable liquidation revenues, the duration of the liquidation, and the volume to sell during this period. The question of to what degree the particular products or product groups should contribute was already discussed above.

7.4 LIQUIDITY-ORIENTED PRICE FLOORS

In addition to the cost-oriented price floors, liquidity-oriented price floors can be distinguished. It concerns a setting of minimum selling prices so that the firm's liquidity is not going to suffer. In the first place, the nature of liquidity-oriented price floors is discussed, next, a cost-oriented approach to this type of price floor is traced briefly.

7.4.1 General Aspects

Being profitable, which means that full costs are recovered from sales revenues, does not imply yet financial health or financial equilibrium of the firm. This can be explained by pointing out two important factors:

—*Revenues are different from cash receipts.* The mere identification of both quantities is partly incorrect. In the long run revenues approximate nearly the cash receipts but on short term this is not at all the case. Because of credits granted to customers, bad payers, and so on, a time lag can appear between revenues and the proper cash inflow.

—*Costs are different from cash expenditures.* Some costs do not involve cash outlays (e.g., depreciation costs), while other costs do (wages, materials). In the latter group, time dimension comes into play: distinction can be made between costs paid in advance (rent, insurance premium, etc.) and costs paid retrospectively. In both cases further differentiation can be made in function of time dimension, namely, the course of time between payment in advance and incurring costs on the one hand and incurring costs and their retrospective payment on the other. Here, we can essentially refer to the above discussion of time dimension in connection with price floors.

Consequently, the problem of liquidity cannot be solved by merely setting revenues against costs. This approach would be too narrow because of the fact that cash receipts and expenditures can additionally be influenced by a number of factors such as actual and future policy concerning customer credits, credits granted by suppliers, inventory turnover ratio, production time, volume of production and sales per period, liquidity reserves, and discount policy.[28]

More important, however, is the consideration that again the time aspect should be regarded. It is not a simple fact that when cash receipts are greater than cash expenditures liquidity is guaranteed. Only dispersal over a space of time of cash receipts and disbursements, taking into account the above-mentioned factors, can guarantee that in due course no solvency or liquidity problems are developing. In fact we are up against a financial problem, namely, short-term financial planning or cash planning.[29]

The question can be asked as to what extent a cost-oriented approach can contribute to this. Several authors point out the irrelevance of a cost-oriented approach to liquidity-oriented price floor.[30] Despite that the cost-oriented approach is frequently practiced. The reason for this could be attributed to the analogy with the approach of price floors attuned to recover costs. In our opinion the cost-oriented approach of liquidity-oriented price floors is unilateral, which does not preclude that this approach can produce an interesting view. This can happen by classifying costs in function of outlay character. The technical aspects of this are discussed in the next section.

7.4.2 Significance of the Cost-Oriented Approach

As said before the liquidity-oriented price floors are traditionally discussed starting from costs. More and more, however, the opinion that liquidity control should be realized within the framework of liquidity planning, taking into account all cash inflows and outflows, is rightly gaining ground.[31]

Although the above is for the most part right, we propose to make some modifications. Indeed, liquidity control neither is, nor can be an objective of cost accounting. Nevertheless, we think it can contribute seriously by setting liquidity-oriented price floors based on a subdivision of costs in function of cash outlay character. Such a price floor, it is true, will not save the firm from a possible chance of illiquidity but it does show from what price level the liquidity is influenced unfavorably.[32]

Both cost recovering and controlling liquidity are important for the firm's continuity. It is practically impossible to give priority to one or the other; both should be considered equivalent.[33] Consequently, price floors only recovering variable costs are acceptable only if no illiquidity is caused.[34] As a rule this is not the case because a share of fixed costs involve cash expenditures. Costs of renting, insurance premium, and salaries are the classic examples.

Fixed costs involving current cash outlays should be recovered by the minimum price unless the need for liquidity can be provided by other sources such as liquidity reserves and short credits. On the other hand, it should be pointed out that the need for liquidity, arising from fixed and variable costs with cash character, can be reduced by the amount of variable costs not inducing cash outlays. From a liquidity point of view the question of paramount importance is: Which costs lead to immediate cash outlays, which costs are coupled with a once-only payment either in the past or in the distant future, and which costs do not have any cash outlay character?[35]

It has occurred that because of liquidity considerations the price floors set in this manner are higher than cost-oriented price floors. However, if liquidity-oriented price floors are lower than the cost oriented, the latter are decisive; if not, the loss is increasing with each unit sold. Only exceptionally will the liquidity-oriented price floor be preferred to the cost oriented, namely, in the event of bridging short periods of acute illiquidity.

As far as the proper setting of liquidity-oriented price floors is concerned, mainly the distinction between the single and multiple product firm should be stressed.[36] Unlike the single product firm, the multiple product firm's liquidity is determined by the sum of cash receipts from the several products on the one hand and by the costs with cash character, both indirect and direct product costs, on the other.

The relevancy for pricing decisions should be determined because it apparently is impossible to set a liquidity-oriented price floor per product. Such a global approach implies that at the most an average unit revenue being valid as minimum price can be determined. The point is that the sum of contributions of the several products should be equal to the sum of fixed costs inducing short-term cash outlays. In that way a global liquidity limit can be deduced.[37]

If: s_m = sales volume of product m

    $p_m - c_m$ = contribution of product m

    C_c = fixed costs inducing short-term cash outlays.

then: $(s_1 p_1 + s_2 p_2 + \ldots + s_n p_n) = (s_1 c_1 + s_2 c_2 + \ldots + s_n c_n) + C_c$

or: $\quad s_1 (p_1 - c_1) + s_2 (p_2 - c_2) + \ldots + s_n (p_n - c_n) = C_c$

Because the equation comprises n unknowns $(s_1 \ldots s_n)$ there is no unambiguous solution for it. The liquidity limit can be obtained with numerous combinations of the quantities $s_1 \ldots s_n$.

7.5 CONCLUSIONS

Price floors are very important in the sense that they thoroughly determine business profitability and consequently business continuity.

The problems of price floors are rather complex: the definition of price floor is very relative and there is a multitude of influencing factors.

The approach to price floors was mainly put in the framework of cost recovery or liquidity maintenance. In both cases a cost-oriented approach is found most frequently. Where this is obviously for purposes of cost recovery, with maintenance of liquidity in view, it seems less appropriate. The latter should be the main objective of cash planning. In that respect the problem of price floors only plays an expedient role: the approach to price floors based on the cash outlay character of costs only points out whether sales are contributing to or are detrimental to the firm's liquidity and not if the firm is getting illiquid.

Once the significance of the cost factor is set, the most appropriate cost accounting system should be determined. Because of the fact that simultaneous subdivision of costs according to variability in function of activity ratio, assignability to cost units and classification of costs in function of outlay character is necessary, the classical methods of full and partial costing do not seem suitable. Only a system of analytical contribution accounting (see Part IV) is able to meet the above-mentioned requirements.

8 The Role of Cost Accounting Information in Price Differentiation

Part I, dealing with general aspects of pricing policy, advanced that the phenomenon of price differentiation was mainly based on market data. Especially, market segmentation (in connection with proper price differentiation) and price elasticity of demand (in connection with product line pricing) seemed substantial. Therefore, the role of costs will indeed be important though mostly second rate.

8.1 PROPER PRICE DIFFERENTIATION

We shall illustrate the significance of costs in proper price differentiation by examining successively a few forms of it and investigate the relevant cost requirements. In each case cost accounting needs to provide information about cost differences of several orders. These cost differences can be caused by differences in transportation costs, differences in direct costs of a specific order, differences in function of activity ratio, and so forth. It is obvious that the relevant cost concept will be a marginal one.[1]

In the event of spatial price differentiation, that is, price differentiation in function of the buyer's locality, cost accounting should point out transportation costs of the several sales areas. In fact, for each delivery different transportation costs are caused due to different distances between seller and buyer, even if both are established in the same area. Different transportation costs can also be caused by differences in sales volume or different transportation modalities (truck, train, ship, plane). However, as selling prices should be equal within the same sales area, the cost calculation should be conceived such that average costs per delivery in that area are provided. In the framework of the analytical contribution accounting (see Part IV) this means that next to direct costs and other planned contributions also a specific contribution to recover transportation costs should be set. In the case of price differentiation in function of order quantity (quantity discount) an interesting problem appears. The question arises as to what extent a small order comparatively costs more than a large order or how much the unit selling price of a small order should exceed that of a large order.

The problem can be solved quite easily in case of simple orders, that is, orders consisting of only one sort of product. In this case the cost amount chargeable to the order, independent of the quantity ordered, can be set rather simply. It concerns costs of invoicing, accountable processing, planning costs, costs of adjusting machines, and so on. Furthermore, costs variable in function of the number of orders and costs determined by the expected number of orders should be distinguished.

The problem is more complicated in case of compound orders, that is, orders consisting of more product sorts. Next to the direct order costs there are also costs dependent on the composition of the order. Consequently, contributions should be planned in order to recover costs variable in function of the number of orders and costs dependent on the order's composition. Price differentiation in function of time of ordering or delivering may have three objectives: lessening cost differences caused by the time factor, reducing or eliminating fluctuations in activity ratio, and finally stimulating additional needs. As far as the first objective is concerned, the cost differences between the different points in time of ordering or delivery are relevant. For the most part, they are not any problem; it is, for example, relatively easy to calculate the additional costs of a repair order (e.g., in a garage) on Sundays or public holidays. The second objective induces the comparison of the cost reductions, because of less inventory costs or on account of a possible smaller capacity with possible revenue decreases. The duration of allowing discounts plays a decisive role in it. When the third objective is considered the setting of discounts should be based on an appraisal of cost savings or an estimation of the contribution of additional sales. When judging the expediency of discounts an opinion should be expressed on their possible consequences:

—Will discounts not cause "acquired" claims?

—Can the discount allowed be justified to other customers?

Insofar as price differentiation is practiced in function of buyer's characteristics and insofar as it is based on cost differences (e.g., different cost levels in the event of selling to retailers and wholesalers), the basis of price differentiation can be found by splitting up costs according to the different customer groups.

In all forms of price differentiation, where the role of costs is minute or nonexistent, such as price differentiation in function of the product's use or the customer's bearing power, cost accounting only plays a controlling role. Cost accounting should make sure that each product not only pays back its direct costs but that the total bulk of indirect costs is recovered by total revenues.

8.2 PRODUCT LINE PRICING

Price determination for individual products from a product line can happen on the basis of either cost or market data or on a combination of both.[2]

The price differences among the several products can coincide with cost differences. In this case cost accounting should be attuned to point out these differences. When selling prices are based on market data without any relation to cost differences, cost accounting essentially should point out the total costs of the entire assortment and take care of compensation among the several products by means of adequate planned contributions. In addition to selling prices based on a different demand elasticity of the market segments or selling prices in function of the stage of the product's life cycle, three explicitly cost-oriented methods can be distinguished:[3]

—*selling prices proportionate to full costs,* so that all products yield the same (proportional) net profits. The disadvantages of this approach are obvious: deformation of unit cost (and thus selling price) because of arbitrary cost allocation on the one hand and giving no consideration to market data on the other.

—*selling prices proportional to marginal costs,* so that all products yield identical contributions. An advantage, in common with the preceding method, is its simplicity. As additional advantage the absence of arbitrary cost allocation can be mentioned. Besides that, however, remains the objection of neglecting market considerations, which leads to profit opportunities getting lost. If this method is not employed purely mechanistically, it certainly would offer advantages compared to the preceding one. Here again, the proper approach is the one based on contribution accounting because it takes into account both cost and marketing factors.

—*selling prices proportional to conversion costs,* that is, full costs decreased with costs of direct materials. So, a value added approach applies. In this approach the problems of cost allocation remain. Although profits can and may be justified by the firm's value added, the fact remains that profits are finally and predominantly determined by market opportunities. Furthermore, it can hardly be justified that the setting of the profit matter is only based on certain costs, in casu direct materials costs.[4] On these grounds we think the third method should be dismissed.

The most successful method seems to be a modified version of the second method. In this case, marginal costs are the price floor of each particular product. The real selling price is composed of marginal costs increased by a contribution margin dependent on the product's commercial potentialities. However, marketing policy should not be obsessed by contribution margin. Sometimes, for strategic reasons, certain products should be sold without regard to their contribution. Possibly a negative contribution, that is, selling price lower than marginal costs, is tolerated. Among other things, this happens in case of "line fillers," "price meeters," and "loss leaders."[5]

Fundamentally, it can be said that marketing considerations predominate over cost factors and determine the contribution. In this manner, pure cost considerations only play a secondary role.

9 The Role of Cost Accounting Information in Case of Price Changing

Price changes, both increases and decreases, can occur under various circumstances.[1] In the first place, the price change can be planned, even before the product's market introduction. The classic example of this is the planned gradual changeover from a policy of "skimming prices" followed during the market introduction to a policy of "penetration prices." Then, price changes are generally anticipations or reactions to external circumstances (demand, competition) or reactions to internal factors that are reflected in cost changes.[2] Especially the latter aspect will be discussed below.

It should be mentioned that a purely cost-oriented approach of price changes seems one sided and inadequate. It should always be verified if a cost-based price change is possible and profitable in function of the market situation. Therefore, market research always remains necessary. Where the specific role of costs in price changes is concerned, the following statements can be made:

a. It is frequently seen that cost changes are used as a means to justify price changes rather than their real basis. This is especially true in the event of price increases: in this context, referring price changes to cost increases affords an elegant and fair means of justification.[3]

b. The mechanistic view of putting a proportionate relationship between full cost and selling price seems completely abandoned today.

c. On the contrary, it has been pointed out that an approach based on marginal costs is most obvious and justifiable.[4] Indeed, when taking into consideration several alternative price changes, the selection method employed always consists of comparing, alternative by alternative, cost and revenue changes, in order to determine the consequences on operating results of the several alternatives.[5] Therefore, differential costing is very important in order to permit clear insight into cost evolution in function of sales volume.

Table 1

	Actual	Price reduction alternatives					
(in $)	situation	-5%	-10%	-15%	-20%	-25%	-40%
Unit selling price	100	95	90	85	80	75	60
Unit variable cost	50	50	50	50	50	50	50
Contribution	50	45	40	35	30	25	10
Contribution decrease	-	5	10	15	20	25	40
Required increase in sales volume	-	11.1%	25%	42.9%	66.7%	100%	400%

As example we take an intended reduction in price.[6] The measure in which such a decision may be successful especially depends on:

—the expected increase in volume and
—the cost-volume-profit relationships.

In general we can say that the larger the product's contribution percentage, the lower the required volume increase to compensate the price reduction. Consequently, the level of variable costs plays an important role. Consider the situations in Table 1.

In order to maintain the contribution, a price reduction of 5% implies a volume increase of more than 11%; a price decrease of 40% urges to a volume increase of 400%, and so on. This relationship can be reflected in diagram in such a manner that marketing management can simply compare the diverse price reduction alternatives to the necessary sales volume increases (Figure 2). In case of more radical price changes, that is, price changes entailing such volume changes that capacity repercussions occur, information about the changes in the ratio between fixed and variable costs will be necessary. This ratio is also important in order to calculate the profit repercussions. All the more so because in practice the tendency to exaggerate the impact of volume changes on unit costs is observed.[7]

As to the relationship between cost increases and price increases some general observations can be made.[8] In the first place, the impact of increases in labor costs, costs of durable and nondurable means of production, and taxes can be investigated. With regard to labor cost increases and the connected selling price increases it should be pointed out that the degree of relationship is determined by the measure to which marginal costs are changing and by the relationship between selling price and sales volume. The general tendency is that the increase of labor costs cannot be fully passed on to selling prices. Consequently, the

Figure 2

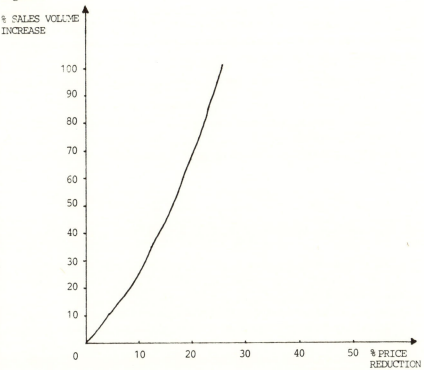

With regard to increases of costs of durable (e.g., machines) and nondurable (e.g., raw materials) production factors, we notice that a rise in variable costs usually leads to a price increase. Also, a rise in fixed costs may sometimes have the same effect.[10] In this connection the moment at which a price increase of production factors is coming through in the level of calculated costs is important. In this respect the value dimension adhered to in cost accounting plays an important role (see section 5.2.2 and *infra*).

Insofar as the role of tax increases is concerned, the following statements can be made:[11]

—An increase of indirect taxes will lead to a price increase, usually smaller than the cost increase caused by the rise in taxes.

—The relationship between increases of direct taxes and price increases is more ambiguous. Unloading the tax increases on selling prices, among others, depends on the price elasticity of demand.

Finally, the repercussion of the employed calculation method on price changes can be examined. For this purpose three cost calculation methods are distinguished: full costing allocating all costs to all products, partial costing allocating only a share of costs to all products (e.g., variable costing, direct costing), and differential costing relating certain costs to certain units of product. In this case the change in costs, because of a change in production volume, is set against the number of units of product by which the production volume has been changed $(\frac{\Delta C}{\Delta P})$. The historical full costing method always causes a time lag between cost change and change of price. The change of production factor prices shall only find expression in the full cost level after all means of production acquired before the moment of price change are used and the goods sold are made by means of production factors already changed in price. Consequently, two elements are important:

a. the availability of positive economic inventories and

b. the frequency of replacement of the means of production.

About a. Only in the absence of positive economic inventories will a price change of production factors immediately induce a change in the historic full cost of products sold.

About b. The smaller the frequency of replacement of the means of production is, dependent on volume of inventory and the pace of consumption, the larger the time lag will be. As for this, the kind of production factor is essential: the frequency of replacement is reducing and consequently the time lag is augmenting according to whether we are concerned respectively with price increases of labor, nondurable means of production, or durable means subject to wear and tear. In general we can conclude that the retarded cost change results in a retarded adjustment of selling price.[12]

Also, in the event of partial and differential cost calculation we are confronted with a time lag between changes of factor prices and connected cost and selling price changes. However, there are points of difference with full costing. In case of partial costing, the classic variable costing is taken as example here; a change of variable costs will lead to a change of the partial cost. On the contrary, a change of fixed costs is not, even with delay, expressed in the cost.

The manager is really conscious of changing fixed costs but he is lacking any exact insight into the needed change of profit margin of each particular product. Therefore, the practice of partial costing incites less than full costing to adjustment of selling prices because of changes in production factor prices. *Mutatis mutandis* the same reflections can be made when the differential costing method is in use.[13]

Two important conclusions can now be drawn:

1. The "cost price" as valuation criterion of costs should be abandoned because it causes time lags in passing on factor price changes to selling prices. This is another indication

for use of replacement value or a combined system of replacement value and standard price as a means of valuation of costs.

2. At first sight full costing seems to guarantee the process of passing on cost changes to selling price changes better than partial and differential costing methods. On the other hand, some serious drawbacks can be brought up against full costing (see above and section 11.5).

Both considerations further encourage our opinion that insofar as pricing policy is concerned, the optimal method of cost accounting combines simultaneously the advantages of both full and partial costing. It was already pointed out that contribution accounting answers to this (see especially Part IV, however).[14]

10 The Role of Cost Accounting Information in Case of Pricing Individualized Products (Job Order Costing)

An important field of application of cost-oriented pricing policy can be found in pricing piece work and selling to order. Probably, cost accounting has found its origin in this context.[1]

A basis frequently used for pricing individualized products is the predetermined full cost in which the allocation of indirect costs is based on business characteristics being assumed as "normal." By addition of a fair, realistic, or desirable net profit margin the so-called normal selling price is obtained.

Example of a minor house painting firm. Each particular order, for example, painting the outside walls and window frames of a house, is carried out according to the (potential) client's specific requirements. Since it applies to a minor firm, there is no elaborate structure of cost centers. In addition to the head of business and a bookkeeper, an "indoor service" and a "field organization" are distinguished. The former is looking after the inventory of paints and painter's tools as well as after the manufacturing of paints and the planning of the fieldwork. The costs of this "department" are not kept "by job" but are incorporated in the job's cost as a charge per gallon of paint used.

The field organization consists of a number of skilled workmen, each of whom work together with two or three apprentices. The costs of this are kept by job by means of a "performance form," on which the hours achieved job by job are completed.

The price calculation of a job is proceeding as follows:

Direct costs of the job: paint consumption   X
               field organization: rate × hours   X
               others (e.g. scaffolding rental costs, interim apprentices, sub-contracting)   X

Table 2

Fixed costs (in $)	500,000	500,000	500,000	500,000	500,000
Variable costs (in $)	500,000	1,000,000	1,500,000	2,000,000	2,500,000
Break-even sales (in $)	1,000,000	1,500,000	2,000,000	2,500,000	3,000,000
Margin on variable costs	100 %	50 %	33.3 %	25 %	20 %

Figure 3

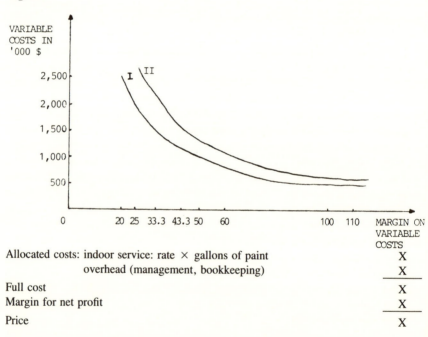

Allocated costs: indoor service: rate × gallons of paint	X
overhead (management, bookkeeping)	X
Full cost	X
Margin for net profit	X
Price	X

Calculations of the same kind are in use in minor building construction firms, in metalwork shops, contractors of electricity, roofing, plumbing jobs, and so on. As a rule, in such "cost plus pricing" situations the intended profit is calculated as a percentage of planned full order costs. Another approach consists of basing the profit margin on the cost component having the largest share of order costs.

Suppose the firm should have to recover $500,000 per period (e.g., a year). Variable costs vary with order size. This leads to the above flexible budget at break-even level. The margin is fixed on the basis of variable costs (Table 2). This can be reflected in Figure 3. Break-even line I suggests that for an order in which, for example, $1,500,000 variable costs are incorporated, a profit

Table 3

Fixed costs (in $)	500,000	500,000	500,000	500,000	500,000
Variable costs (in $)	500,000	1,000,000	1,500,000	2,000,000	2,500,000
Sales at 10 % profit objective on variable costs (in $)	1,050,000	1,600,000	2,150,000	2,700,000	3,250,000
Margin on variable costs	110 %	60 %	43.3 %	35 %	30 %

margin of at least 33.3% should be taken in order to recover total costs. It is obvious that in this manner several profit objectives can be premised. If a profit objective of 10% is chosen, the above flexible budget is relevant (Table 3).

The corresponding curve is drawn in the graph above (curve II). From this curve can be concluded that if the variable costs of a particular order amount to, for example, $1,700,000, and a profit objective of 10% on variable costs is planned, the required margin should be 39.4%. In this manner several curves corresponding with several profit objectives (in percentage of variable costs) could be drawn. If the profit margin should be applied in function of raw material costs, direct labor costs, machine costs, and so on, quite a number of alternative curves could be drawn.

The above pricing method is characterized by emphasizing cost-profit-volume relationships. It seems true, however, that sound pricing implies adequate cost estimations. For this purpose many methods are available, ranging from methods based on observation and experience to rather sophisticated mathematical methods (e.g., learning curves).

For the most part also the use of standard costs has found its origin in the scope of the need for predetermined costs.[2] The "normal" contract price calculated in this manner usually will not be equal to the selling price. The latter can be higher or lower because of external or internal business considerations. Consequently, the problem of setting an adequate price floor and price ceiling arises by which, at the same time, a latitude for price negotiations comes about.

The business externally modifying factors especially relate to the insights into the competitors' pricing behavior. In this connection one should try to see through competitors' cost structures, technological status, and activity ratio. For this purpose simulating bidding models may be useful perhaps.[3]

The question of the client's appreciation of the product should be raised. Decisive questions will be:

—How much is the customer willing to pay?

—What is the use value for the buyer?

—Where the buyer weighs "making" against "buying," at what level does the scale tip in favor of "making"?

These external considerations especially will play a role in setting price ceilings.

Where internal considerations fundamentally influencing the price floor are concerned, the actual and future activity ratio should be mentioned. However, for long-term contracts, capacity changes themselves should be taken into consideration so that in this case even certain fixed cost elements can be labeled as relevant for pricing decisions.

Dean defines the price floor by means of the concept of parity price, that is, the price resulting in the same total contribution as the contribution that could be realized by other alternative opportunities of use of the available capacity or bottleneck.[4] Consequently, price setting is determined substantially by the alternative utility of available capacity or bottleneck. So to speak, business capacity should be sold at such a price that a maximum profit is generated. So the contribution is substantial pricing information of which can be said that it is inversely proportional to the activity ratio.[5] This brings on that if unused capacity is the sole alternative, the price floor is equal to the direct costs of the job. If other alternatives causing another activity ratio are available, the concept of opportunity cost should be applied. In this case the price floor is equal to direct costs increased by the contribution given by other alternative sales.

For the sake of completeness it should be pointed that considerations about price deterioration may interfere with what is explained above, whereas in other circumstances the firm will be selling under the direct cost level in order to evade closing down the firm or to obtain a foothold in new markets.

When the selling price is coming about by means of negotiations between producer and buyer, knowledge of price floor and price ceiling is of paramount importance. It appears, as Weber suggests,[6] that an insight into the components of contribution, in the form of fixed (indirect) costs to be recovered preferentially and successively, permits a more efficacious price negotiation than if only information about the total contribution, subdivided in the indirect cost and operating results element, is available. We are convinced that the method of analytical contribution accounting is able to meet these information needs (see Part IV).

A frequently occurring aspect of job order production is its long-term character (e.g., shipbuilding, building construction). Because of this, there can be great difference between the predetermined costs and the ultimate costs of the job. So the contractor does have to bear a price risk or may negotiate price adjustments with the principal. Below some relevant problems are discussed, taking the building industry in Belgium as example:

In case of public tenders a formula of price adjustment automatically is put to work as soon as the estimate is higher than 400,000 BF (approximately $7,000). The formula of price adjustment is a stipulation by which the contractor can regularize the amount contracted for in order to take account of fluctuations in raw materials and labor costs. All other costs remain out of consideration in this official formula. If the principal is a private person or company the price adjustment clause should be explicitly stipulated in the contract; if not, the contractor cannot claim any price adjustment.[7] The formula is as follows:[8]

$$p = p \left[\left(a \times \frac{s}{S}\right) + \left(b \times \frac{i}{I}\right) + c \right] \text{ in which:}$$

the sum of the weighing coefficients equals 1

$p =$ adjusted price

$P =$ amount of the monthly debt statement

$a =$ conventional weighing coefficient reflecting the share of labor costs in the total sum contracted for (fixed at 0.4)

$b =$ conventional weighing coefficient reflecting the share of materials costs in the sum contracted for (fixed at 0.35)

$c =$ conventional weighing coefficient reflecting the share of other costs, not susceptible to adjustment (fixed at 0.25)

$S =$ conventional average hourly wages (including legal social charges) expressed in a number with three decimal places and is in force 10 calendar days before the extreme date appointed to submit the quotation

$s =$ the average hourly wages (inclusive of legal social charges) being in force the first day of the monthly period for which an adjustment is calculated

$I =$ monthly index number of the prices of building materials (published by the Department of Economic Affairs) being used in the month before the extreme date appointed to submit the quotation

$i =$ the same index number referring to the month before the initial date of the monthly period for which the adjustment is calculated.

The value of the coefficients a, b, and c is dependent on the characteristics of the job (here, building an apartment block). As coefficient "c" should be at least 20%, the price can maximally be adjusted up to 80%. Once the parameters are fixed, they cannot be changed during the execution of the job.

When the principal is a private person or company, fixing the coefficients is a matter of negotiation.

Example. (in dollars)

Principal: Department of Housing

Job: Building of an apartment block in Ghent.

Contractor: ABC Inc.

Offer for subscription: October 15, 1981.

Starting date: May 1, 1982.

Term: 550 calendar days.

Period number 10 from 2/1/83 to 2/28/83:

        cumulative amount of work in progress: $ 452,000

        cumulative up to the end of last month: $ 420,000

Amount P (value of this month's achievements):   \$ 32,000

Price adjustment:

$$p = \$ \ 32,000 \left[(0.4 \times \frac{\$9,957}{\$9,173}) + (0.35 \times \frac{\$3,189}{\$2,900}) + 0.25 \right]$$

$$= \$ \ 32,000 \left[0.43419 + 0.38438 + 0.25 \right]$$

$$= \$ \ 32,000 \ \times \ 1.06857$$
$$= \$ \ 34,194$$

Adjustment: $p - P = \$ \ 34,194 - \$ \ 32,000 = \$ \ 2,194.$

This is the amount, exclusive of V.A.T., to be invoiced for the tenth period of the building contract.

The advantages of this and similar adjustment formulae are twofold: on the one hand, the contractor does not have to bear the whole price risk and on the other hand the sometimes rather difficult problem of cost estimation can for the greater part be avoided.

PART III

COST-ORIENTED METHODS OF PRICE DETERMINATION

In Part II we attempted to elucidate the significance of costs as determinant in diverse price decision situations. It was clear that cost is only one of the numerous price determinants and frequently not the most substantial one. However, in a number of pricing decisions the cost factor seemed rather important.

The above considerations were rather fundamental, whereas the next exposition is more technical. We examine how the base price is determined, taking into account the varying relative importance of the cost factor. Several ways can be distinguished depending upon the cost concepts used.

In the first place, two extreme situations are discussed, namely, pricing based on full costing and partial costing (e.g., direct and variable costing). Next we discuss pricing decisions based on cost accounting methods in between full and partial costing.

11 Pricing Decisions Based on Full Costing

11.1 INCIDENCE OF FULL COST PRICING

Empirical research[1] points out that in business practice cost-oriented pricing is used more frequently than may appear. At the same time it seems that full cost pricing is very much in evidence, especially in oligopolistic markets.

In our opinion this exaggerated importance of full cost pricing has grown historically. Full costing found its origin in firms producing to order and according to customer's specifications (job order production). In these firms "price calculation" was practiced in the literal sense of the word. The selling price was commonly calculated by increasing the full cost of the job with a profit margin. Other stimuli for the use of full cost pricing was uniform costing, as a rule based on full costing, imposed or recommended by government or by industrial professional associations.[2] On the basis of tradition and imitation, or merely for convenience, full costing and consequently full cost pricing was disseminated widely in business practice.

The wider the application of full cost pricing in business, the less the appreciation of this method in theoretical literature. Some theorists label full cost pricing as "folklore" or even as "medieval."[3] This controversy offers the opportunity to go farther into pricing based on full costing. In this context aspects like usefulness, advantages and disadvantages, reasons for use, and shortcomings will be highlighted.

11.2 METHODOLOGY OF FULL COST PRICING

A discussion of the methodology of full cost pricing is thwarted because there is no question of "a systematic, unified body of thought."[4]

Because of a variety of interpretations of both costs and margin, the manifestations of full cost pricing are manifold. Insofar as the costs are concerned, the use of different modalities of quantity and price dimension can be pointed out: actual costs, budgeted costs, standard costs.[5] It already was mentioned that the relevant dimension should be prospective.

As to the profit margin, the diversity of possible concepts is perhaps even more extensive. The margin can be fixed in different ways in function of costs, of sales (or selling price), of a planned return on investment, and so on. The margin determined in this manner can be set (possibly determined on the ground of trade customs), in which case the term "rigid full cost pricing" is used. Sometimes the margin may be flexible, that is, different per product, product group, kind of customer, or variable over a course of time. This is called "flexible full cost pricing." Naturally, combinations of the above-mentioned cost and margin modalities lead to a great number of variants of full cost pricing.

Without regard to the concepts employed, full cost pricing always boils down to the next addition: full cost + profit margin = selling price. So the full cost is functioning as a basis of pricing decisions and frequently as absolute price floor. The selling price obtained in this manner can be actual selling price or can be an "asking price" that may be tailored after confrontation with other determinants of selling price, especially market factors.

11.3 THE PROBLEM OF COST ALLOCATION

Cost allocation, the "Achilles tendon" of full costing, is an especially acute problem in multiple product firms using full costing or related methods of cost accounting. Because single product firms are rather exceptional, and pure partial costing (direct costing or variable costing) is rather infrequent, most firms are confronted with the problem of cost allocation.[6]

Cost allocation is mainly a technical problem. The principal thing is to find a causal relationship between indirect costs and a certain "object of costing" or "cost unit," which, in the scope of our problem, is nearly always a product or product group, an order, or a job.

It is not the business economist's task to determine a set of appropriate activity units. He has to determine economically justified grounds in order to settle warranted activity units. In view of the fact that the above-mentioned causal relationship is hard to find or does not exist at all, arbitrary elements nearly always will play a role in cost allocation so that the usefulness of full costing for decision making (among other things pricing decisions) is more or less decreasing. The economic theory on cost allocation merely attempts to minimize the arbitrary elements.

11.3.1 Principles of Cost Allocation

11.3.1.1 The Principle of Accuracy

The point of accuracy is a substantial problem of cost allocation. One of the principle criticisms of the full costing opponents is the very detailed allocation of indirect costs that almost always induces a seeming accuracy. In fact we have to do with a two-sided problem: is roughly approximated allocation sufficient or should painstakingly precise allocation be employed? The solution to this problem cannot be given clearly. In our opinion there is no sense in allocating unimportant or hardly measureable cost factors, whereas substantial cost factors are allocated approximately.

Another element, perhaps the most decisive, is the objective of the calculation. For each particular decision it may be useful to wonder whether further allocation contributes to problem solving or decision making. Without being categorical, it should be said, however, that allocating costs should be justified by its utility in better decision making.[7]

11.3.1.2 The Principle of Causality[8]

The origin of costs may be ascribed to the performance of business operations. So a causal relationship can be put between achievements on the one hand and the origin of costs on the other hand. This causal relationship can be described in two ways:

a. *Cause-effect relationship.* The actual process of achievements is considered as the cause, and the effect then consists of the origin of costs directly caused by it. Naturally, this kind of causality can only be used (in view of the clause "costs caused directly") for the allocation of variable costs. A variant of this is the principle of proportionality, which presumes that costs vary proportionally to the firm's activity ratio. This is true when differential unit costs are constant and only in between definite activity limits (the so-called relevant range, see section 6.1).

b. *Objective-consequence relationship.* The business achievements are considered the objective and the consequence is that production factors should be brought into action. Consequently, this principle can be used for the allocation of indirect costs because, for the greater part, they are connected with the availability of production factors. This almost classic principle of allocation of indirect costs over units of activity (here especially products, product groups, orders, jobs) is also called the "average principle" because there is no direct relationship between indirect costs and singular achievements. There is only a connection insofar as total indirect costs of a period are put against total volume of production of that period. Consequently, nothing else but an arithmetic average amount results.

11.3.1.3 The Principle of Contribution

The allocation of indirect costs over singular cost units is based on the difference between the anticipated selling price and the unit direct costs of the particular cost units. This difference has already been defined as contribution. The principle of contribution assumes that the larger the contribution, the more the cost unit should be charged with indirect costs, and conversely. Hence, that is why this principle is also called the principle of bearing power.

It seems to us that such manner of allocation does no longer show how much a product really costs because the allocation is partially based on an external datum, namely, the selling price. Yet we already premised and will demonstrate further that the principle of contribution is useful for pricing purposes. The principle of contribution also is indispensable when it is impossible to apply the causality principle, for example, in case of joint production (see section 11.3.3).

11.3.2 Methods of Cost Allocation

For a long time the problem of cost allocation has been one of the most controversial topics of cost accounting. A fertile soil for opposite views lies in the fact that some thought they could decide undividedly upon the method of cost allocation. Actually, one realizes more and more that there is no correct method or even that there is just no method at all.[9] All this has created a number of allocation methods, ranging from rather primitive to very sophisticated, which, starting from the same indirect cost data, arrive at rather divergent full costs. Naturally, this is economic nonsense! Below, some methods are discussed concisely.

11.3.2.1 Division Calculation

This is the most simple calculation method, especially used in the single product firm with mass production. This method consists in adding up the costs incurred in a definite period and dividing the sum by the number of cost units of the same period. This quotient is called the "cost." Insofar as the calculation is carried out in terms of historical or actual cost and production data, there is the question of "naive" division calculation. It is clear that in this method the full cost increases when production volume (or any other cost unit) decreases and conversely. This is caused simply and solely by fixed costs and naturally is undesirable.

Example

Direct costs of product A:	$ 100
Total indirect costs:	$ 1,000
Production volume:	20 units
Full cost:	$ \ 100 + \dfrac{\$ \ 1{,}000}{20} = \$ \ 150$
Production volume:	10 units
Full cost:	$ \ 100 + \dfrac{\$ \ 1{,}000}{10} = \$ \ 200$
Production volume:	25 units
Full cost:	$ \ 100 + \dfrac{\$ \ 1{,}000}{25} = \$ \ 140$

It appears that a low activity ratio is attended with a high full cost and conversely. Moreover, this kind of calculation results in a historic full cost that can hardly be used as *ex ante* management information. Reformulating the above calculation method to remedy the first defect: fixed and variable costs are explicitly separated and fixed costs are allocated over a production volume taken for "normal." The concept "normal" or "standard" production level is prospective in character and is generally defined in function of business capacity and anticipations of market evolutions.[10] So, the following full cost formula can be introduced:

$$\text{Full cost} = \frac{\text{variable costs}}{\text{actual production volume}} + \frac{\text{fixed costs}}{\text{normal production volume}}$$

Suppose in the above example the normal production level is put at 20 units. Then the full cost is stabilized at:

$$\$100 + \frac{\$1,000}{20} = \$150$$

In this formula fixed costs are proportionalized. Without regard to differences between actual and normal production volume, the fixed costs account for the same amount in the full cost. Variances between actual and normal production volume lead to negative or positive volume variances that influence the operating results but do not affect the full cost. In our example:

—production volume 10 units: full cost $ 150
        : negative volume variance:
         (10-20) × $50 = − $500 (loss)
—production volume 25 units: full cost $ 150
        : positive volume variance:
         (25-20) × $50 = $250 (profit)

This formula partially remains historical: actual production volume and the corresponding variable costs are not *ex ante* quantities.

11.3.2.2 Method of Equivalency Numbers

This method is a more refined variant of the division calculation. It can be employed in multiple product firms, especially when a certain production relationship exists (e.g., same raw materials, same manufacturing process).

On this basis an index linking is made in which differences in raw materials consumption or production time are used as weighing quantities. One of the products is taken as basis and is given a certain weighing coefficient. In function of this, the weighing coefficients of the other product varieties are fixed by which, ratios, called equivalency numbers, can be calculated. These ratios are then multiplied by the production quantity of the corresponding product variety.

Then, total costs are divided by the total weighed production volume and the quotient is multiplied by the weighed production volume per variety. In this way the total costs per variety are allocated. When these costs are divided by the actual production volume, the unit cost of a particular product variety is the result.

Example. Starting from raw material X, product A is generated. Because of a different finishing process, product A comes about in four varieties, called A1, A2, A3, and A4. The total monthly costs amount to $5,000,000. From the differences in finishing time, the following equivalency numbers were derived:

Variety	Equivalency number
A1	1
A2	0.9
A3	0.8
A4	0.6

The following production volumes are given:

Variety	Volume
A1	3,000kg
A2	2,500 kg
A3	2,000 kg
A4	2,500 kg

The cost calculation follows in Table 4.

Table 4

Variety	Production Volume	Equivalency Numbers	Weighed Production Volume	Total costs (in $)	Cost per kg (in $)
A1	3,000 kg	1	3,000 kg	1,796,407	598.8
A2	2,500 kg	0.9	2,250 kg	1,347,305	538.9
A3	2,000 kg	0.8	1,600 kg	958,084	479.0
A4	2,500 kg	0.6	1,500 kg	898,204	359.3
			8,350 kg	5,000,000	

The weighed production volume is calculated by multiplying the production volume by the equivalency number. Total costs per variety are calculated by means of dividing total costs by total weighed production volume:

$$\frac{\$5,000,000}{8,350 \text{ kg}} = \$598.80239.$$

This coefficient is then multiplied by the weighed production volume of each variety.

11.3.2.3 Overhead Charge Method

The method of overhead charge is an allocation method used in the multiple product firm, more specifically in the case of heterogeneous production without any relationship among products (diversified firms). This method is based on the distinction between direct and indirect costs. Direct costs do not cause any problem, they are available per unit of product. On the contrary, indirect costs are known in total but should be allocated to product units.

This method essentially starts from the ratio between total indirect costs and total direct costs at a definite output level (in terms of a percentage, for instance). In order to calculate the unit cost, an amount of indirect costs, corresponding with the ratio between total indirect and direct costs is added to the unit direct costs. A variant of this consists of expressing total indirect costs as a percentage of a component of direct costs, such as:

—direct material cost,

—direct labor cost,

—direct machine cost,

—quantity of direct materials,

—direct man hours, and

—direct machine hours.

In each of these cases the total indirect costs are expressed in only one percentage of direct costs. This is called "singular" or "primitive" method of overhead charge.

Example
In a firm the following standards are available:
—production volume: 15,000 units
—direct materials: 0.5 kg per unit or 7,500 kg
—direct man-hours: ⅓ hour per unit or 5,000 hours
—direct machine-hours: ⅙ hour per unit or 2,500 hours.
For a certain period (e.g. month) a production volume of 10,000 units is budgeted. The corresponding costs are:
—direct material cost: $ 14,425
—direct labor cost: $ 42,310
—indirect costs: $ 153,850
—total costs: $ 210,585
In the course of this month an order of 2,000 units is coming in.
The direct costs of this order are estimated as follows:
— direct materials: $ 5,700

— direct labor: $ 8,460
— total direct costs: $ 14,160

The overhead charge can be calculated in function of:

—total direct costs, i.e. $\dfrac{\$153,850}{\$14,425 + \$42,310} = 2.71$

Full cost of the order:

$$\$14,160 + 2.71 \times \$14,160 = \$52,533.6$$

—direct materials costs, i.e. $\dfrac{\$153,850}{\$ 14,425} = 10.67$

Full cost of the order:

$$\$14,160 + 10.67 \times \$5,700 = \$74,979$$

—direct labor costs, i.e. $\dfrac{\$153,850}{\$ 42,310} = 3.64$

Full cost of the order:

$$\$14,160 + 3.64 \times \$8,460 = \$44,954.4$$

—consumption of direct $\dfrac{\$153,850}{0.5\text{kg} \times 10,000} = \$30.77$
   materials, i.e.

Full cost of the order:

$$\$14,160 + (0.5 \times 2,000 \text{ units}) \times \$30.77 = \$44,930$$

—direct labor hours, i.e. $\dfrac{\$153,850}{0.333\text{h} \times 10,000} = \$46.16$

Full cost of the order:

$$\$14,160 + (0.333 \times 2,000 \text{ units}) \times \$46.16 = \$44,902.6$$

—direct machine hours, i.e. $\dfrac{\$153,850}{0.167\text{h} \times 10,000} = \$92.13$

Full cost of the order:

$$\$14,160 + (0.167 \times 2,000 \text{ units}) \times \$92.13 = \$44,931.4$$

Because of the differences in full cost of the order it is obvious that the method described above can be criticized fundamentally. These criticisms can be summarized as follows:

a.   There is not necessarily a causal and proportional relation between the indirect costs allocated to a product and its direct costs. Of course, this may lead to a serious misrepresentation of the full cost of the product or order.

b.   This method implies that the overhead charge should be adapted in function of changes in quantity and price dimensions of the direct costs. This condition is not always fulfilled in business practice that contents itself with approximations. Irrespective of this a corrective calculation is always too late because differences are only observed at the moment of variances analysis.

Related to the preceding criticism, it is obvious that the fixation of the overhead charge should be based on future (budgeted, standard) direct and indirect costs. Especially, the objection of causality has lead to a more refined method, the so-called plural or detailed method of overhead charge. In order to put a closer

Table 5

Indirect costs		Factor	Direct labor	Direct materials	Total direct costs
Direct materials	$ 34,615	a		$ 14,425	
Machines	$ 65,385	b			$ 56,735
Personnel	$ 53,850	c	$ 42,310		

Table 6

Indirect costs		Factor	Direct hours	Direct Materials in kg	Machine hours
Direct materials	$ 34,615	a		5,000	
Machines	$ 65,385	b			1,670
Personnel	$ 53,850	c	3,333		

relation between indirect and direct costs, the indirect costs are split up, for example:

—indirect costs related to direct materials,
—indirect costs related to direct labor, and
—indirect costs related to direct machine costs.

Each of these elements of indirect costs can be related to the corresponding element of direct costs. Depending on the way of splitting up indirect costs, a number of overhead charges can be calculated. So far as a causal relationship between specific direct and indirect costs is existing, this method of calculation is more accurate.

Taking again our example, the indirect costs ($153,850) can be split up as follows:

—indirect costs caused by direct materials
  (storage, preparation): $ 34,615
—indirect costs caused by repair, depreciation,
  adjustment, etc. of machines: $ 65,385
—indirect costs caused by personnel: $ 53,850
                                     $ 153,850

The full costs of the order of 2,000 units can be calculated as shown in Table 5 (based on amounts) and Table 6 (based on quantities).

So, the following factors can be calculated:

$$a = \frac{\$ 34,615}{\$ 14,425} = 2.4 \quad b = \frac{\$ 65,385}{\$ 56,735} = 1.15 \quad c = \frac{\$ 53,850}{\$ 42,310} = 1.27$$

Full cost of the order:

$ 14,160 + 2.4 × $ 5.700 + 1.15 × $ 14,160 + 1.27 × $ 8,460 = $ 14,160 + $ 13,680 + $ 16,284 + $ 10,744.2 = $ 54,868.2

The following factors can be calculated:

$$a = \frac{\$\ 34,615}{5,000} = \$\ 6.923$$

$$b = \frac{\$\ 65,385}{1,670} = \$\ 39.15$$

$$c = \frac{\$\ 53,850}{3,333} = \$\ 16.16$$

Full cost of the order:

$ 14,160 + $ 6.923 × (0.5 × 2,000) + $ 39.15 × (0.167 × 2,000) + $ 16.16 × (0.333 × 2,000) = $ 14,160 + $ 6,923 + $ 13,076 + $ 10,762.5 = $ 44,921.5

Although the detailed method of overhead charge should lead to more accurate full costing, we can establish a substantial difference in full cost. Once more this fact points out the compelling necessity for seeking out the causal relationship between direct and indirect costs.

11.3.3 The Problem of Joint Costs

The problem of cost allocation in function of products and/or product groups narrows down to seeking out a causal relationship between the costs that should be allocated on the one hand and the product or product group on the other hand. In this context a complication can be seen in the fact that certain products are linked mutually so that so-called joint costs occur. The relation mentioned above can be of a technical or economic kind.[11]

Technical relationship is found when the manufacturing process inevitably leads to diverse products. Until the moment that these products come about, all costs are joint costs (See Figure 4).

Figure 4

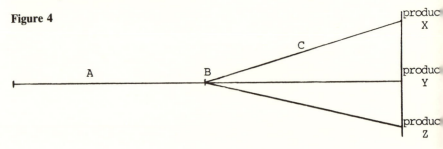

A: joint manufacturing process with joint costs
B: split-off point
C: specific manufacturing processes with specific costs

In view of the joint origin of these three products, it is impossible to argue which part of the joint costs can be assigned to each of the products X, Y, Z. Therefore, the allocation problem is essentially unsolvable here. The same remarks apply in the case of economic relations among products. This especially refers to products that are jointly sold (e.g., spoons, forks, knives, sauce ladles of a table silver assortment). The costs of design of this table silver assortment are joint costs, even if certain parts of the assortment can be sold independently.[12]

From a theoretical point of view, the problem of allocation of joint costs is unsolvable. However, the question can be raised as to how the necessary relevant cost data can be found in order to get an adequate basis for setting the sticker price or to evaluate the profitability of the products. In view of this a number of allocation methods were developed (mainly based on production volumes or sales volume or amount).[13]

Example

Joint costs:	$500,000
Direct costs: product X:	$100,000
product Y:	$150,000
product Z:	$200,000

The allocation below is based on production volumes:

Production volume of product X:	3,000 kg
Y:	2,500 kg
Z:	2,000 kg
Total production volume:	7,500 kg

Full cost of product X:

$$\$100,000 + \frac{\$500,000}{7,500 \text{ kg}} \times 3,000 \text{ kg}$$
$$= \$100,000 + \$200,000 = \$300,000$$
$$(\text{or } \$100 \text{ per kg})$$

Full cost of product Y:

$$\$150,000 + \frac{\$500,000}{7,500 \text{ kg}} \times 2,500 \text{ kg}$$
$$= \$150,000 + \$166,667 = \$316,667$$
$$(\text{or } \$126.67 \text{ per kg})$$

Full cost of product Z:

$$\$200,000 + \frac{\$500,000}{7,500 \text{ kg}} \times 2,000 \text{ kg}$$
$$= \$200,000 + \$133,333 = \$333,333$$
$$(\text{or } \$166.67 \text{ per kg})$$

Allocations based on sales volume or sales amount can be calculated in the same way but will lead to another full cost for the products X, Y, and Z. In general these methods of allocation of joint costs can be characterized as follows:

—Each method can be seen as an "artificial solution" or even only as a "rule of thumb" in the sense that one tries to solve an essentially unsolvable problem by means of more or less arbitrary relationships.

—The methods based on technical measures (e.g., caloric units, production volume) lack any economic basis.

—The frequently used methods allocated in function of the sales revenues of the joint products hold a certain extent of circle reasoning: the allocation of joint costs is done in function of the respective selling prices, whereas the fundamental objective of this allocation should be the procurement of an informational basis for selling price decisions. In this "backward costing" a functional relationship between selling price and cost is presumed. It is self-evident that such relationship is not always available. For that reason, the assumption of such relationship should be considered as a false interpretation of the principle of contribution (see above section 11.3.1.3).

Thus, the significance of the allocation of joint costs as a contribution to price decisions is almost nil. It seems that for pricing purposes other informational sources should be tapped. Bierman proves that the pricing problem in case of joint production can be solved correctly by means of marginal analysis.[14] In our opinion this is practically illusive since the price-setting authority perhaps has not all necessary information at his disposal (especially sales information). Therefore, Bierman's method is only a theoretical solution.

However, the purport of Bierman's reasoning can be useful for business practice: one can compare the total net revenues of all joint products to the total joint costs. The net revenue should be seen in this case as the difference between selling price and the direct costs of each particular product. It is that contribution that should be highlighted, namely, for diverse fixed and/or variable mixes of the joint products in question. In this application of the principle of contribution the preferable alternative is that one in which the product mix is such that the difference between revenues and costs of all products together (in other words, the sum of the contributions) is maximized. To the solution of this kind of problem, for example, linear programming may be used to find the best choice.[15]

11.3.4 Relation with and Effect on Pricing Policy

After the discussion of the allocation of indirect and joint costs, it seems appropriate to examine its significance for pricing purposes.

The economists' controversy between "marginalism" and "anti-marginalism" is also found in business economics. In this speciality the controversy between advocates of full costing and advocates of direct costing or other methods of partial costing is well known.[16]

Very often the opponents in this controversy put the problem of the costing method as a black and white problem, thereby losing sight of a variety of grey tones. Adherence to such extreme points of view can be explained, for the greater part, by neglecting the time aspects (short versus long term) and the firm's position (price maker or price taker). It is obvious that under such circumstances the dispute becomes relatively sterile.

In the long run, both direct and indirect costs should be recovered by sales revenues.[17] Starting from the pursuit of the firm's continuity there can reasonably be no objection to this principle. However, the question of whether the necessity of recovering full costs also implies cost allocation can be raised. In our opinion the answer should be negative. Allocation leads to an average or deformed cost because activity units frequently are more or less arbitrary.

A more justified practice consists in ensuring the recovery of indirect costs, without any allocation, by means of differentiation of the product's gross profit margin based on the contribution. This method will be enunciated thoroughly in Part IV. In this method the principle of contribution (see section 11.3.1.3) is applied. In that manner price setting is approached from an appropriate "mix" of commercial and calculational determinants. Besides, not only is each product taken in focus, but also its relationship to other products of the sales mix is explored. For short-term pricing decisions the marginal approach combined with application of the contribution principle unconditionally is the obvious method. A contribution-oriented pricing policy leaves room for commercial and other considerations and therefore shall make a more realistic and flexible pricing policy feasible. Because of the potential danger of price deterioration, also the short-term recovery of indirect costs should be kept in mind. However, the opinion that, aside from some precisely defined exceptions, the selling price should in each particular case at least be equal to the full cost is not only economically wrong but leads to such a rigid pricing policy that the firm runs the risk of pricing itself out.[18]

In any case there is a dualism between the largely unwarranted allocation of costs on the one hand and the inevitable fact that indirect costs should be recovered. Above we already mentioned that both aspects should not always be considered indissolubly. Fog points out, based on empirical evidence, that he cannot establish unequivocally whether allocation leads to better price setting. In general Fog observes that cost allocation leads to a more cost-conscious but a rather rigid price setting. We could call this "risk avoiding" pricing policy. In case of pricing based on direct costing, combined perhaps with contribution analysis, the price setter has a greater freedom of movement and is more inclined to bear in mind extra-calculational factors (e.g., market factors). This approach is more dynamic and flexible but also more risk bearing. Essentially, both methods can lead to an optimum price, but the marginal approach is potentially the most appropriate.[19] This is true in the case of both price taking and price making.[20] To this can be added that as the exactitude with which the full cost can be calculated decreases, the significance of the marginal approach for pricing purposes grows. So, full costing can only be a valid cost accounting system if the cost structure of the firm is relatively simple. If not, partial costing methods should be used.[21]

The greatest degree of complexity of cost structure is found in firms with joint production resulting in a joint cost pattern. With regard to joint costs only the aggregate costs are positively known. For the reasons mentioned above, cost allocation is tampering with the real cost picture. In this way the total cost is the floor for the total sales revenue. In order to maintain the overall profitability, price decreases should be balanced out by price increases. This can be realized most adequately by using the product's contribution. In any case the whole of joint production should always be taken into consideration.[22] Shillinglaw writes: "Pricing is a fascinating, frustrating topic, as well as a most difficult art. And costs for pricing? Well, there are as many viewpoints on this as there are viewers."[23] The last part of this assertion is especially true in respect to cost allocation. Our opinion is clear: cost allocation should be minimalized. We clearly give preference to the marginal approach, especially that approach based on contribution analysis. We think this is the most clean and most informative calculation for pricing purposes. How this method should be realized in practice will be discussed further (Part IV).

11.4 USE AND ADVANTAGES OF PRICING POLICY BASED ON FULL COSTING

Essentially here, we discuss the use and the advantages of "rigid" full cost pricing. The disadvantages as well as the confrontation with more flexible versions of full cost pricing are discussed in the following section.

11.4.1 Simplicity and Quickness

Both are obvious advantages of pricing based on full costing. Both are realized because the one-off prescription of the cost calculation and margin determination procedures reduces the price decision into an uncomplicated and routine occupation.

11.4.2 Security

Price setting by adding a profit margin to the full cost certainly leads to a sense of security because profit making is ensured, so to speak. This contrasts with the more analytical, market-oriented pricing methods, which always include, in function of imponderable market factors, a more or less important factor of uncertainty. Because, as a rule, full cost pricing leads to a certain price stability, volume changes caused by price changes should not be feared as much, which simplifies production planning. Besides, avoiding frequent price changes prevents displeasure on the part of the customers. In this way some business internal procedures are simplified (e.g., planning) and the market factor "customers" becomes more consistent. This too may reduce uncertainty.[24]

11.4.3 Competitive Stability

It was already pointed out that full cost based pricing leads toward price rigidity. The fact that the full cost is frequently used as price floor also contributes to a greater resistance to price declines so that phenomena like price deterioration and price wars are avoided or at least reduced. This applies with greater force when the various firms operating at the same market are characterized by an almost parallel cost structure.[25]

11.4.4 Ethical Aspects

It is frequently emphasized, especially by business men, that price setting based on full cost increased with a profit margin that is considered "justified" and "normal," leads to a selling price that is favorable for both the seller and the customer. The seller succeeds in recovering his costs, while the customer pays a "justified" price. In this circumstance the realization of a maximal profit margin is forgone purposely, yet full cost is raised with a profit margin regarded as "right," "just," or "fair."[26]

It should also be pointed out that government often prefers such a way of price setting because it is favorable for the seller on the one hand while the buyer is not exploited on the other hand. As a secondary effect the possible smaller propensity to inflation as a result of this pricing method should be mentioned.[27]

11.4.5 Informational Aspects

The most fundamental explanation of the manifold use of full cost pricing is probably the chronic lack of information, especially market information, in many firms. The average firm is confronted with a lack of market information because of insufficient familiarity with market research methods, because market research is too expensive, or also because of a pronounced market intransparency.[28] The only information on which its pricing decisions are based is its vague, inaccurate, for the greater part intuitive market knowledge, which is only significant in the case of well-defined, greatly transparent markets, which have become rather exceptional. The firm confronted with such market uncertainty, as a rule, goes to work as follows:[29] the available information (cost information) is observed; this information is highlighted and the information more difficult to obtain or

Figure 5

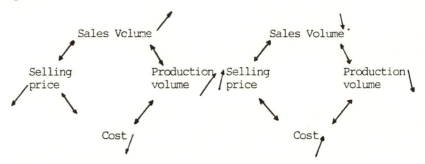

not available (systematic market information) is ignored. This means that cost information takes the place of market information. Indeed, market information should be taken into consideration first when setting the workable price and the corresponding sales volume. However, for want of something better (i.e., price-volume relationship) costs are highlighted because they are available and can be calculated with greater precision than price-volume relationships.

11.5 DISADVANTAGES AND DEFECTS OF PRICING POLICY BASED ON FULL COSTING

The fact that full cost–oriented pricing is still much in evidence in business practice does not alter the fact that this method shows a number of disadvantages and defects neutralizing at least the advantages and laying the foundation of other pricing methods. The most essential disadvantages and defects are briefly discussed below, distinguishing between defects related to costs and to defects with respect to the profit margin.

11.5.1 Disadvantages with Reference to the Costs

A number of disadvantages inherent to full costing were already discussed above. Here, they will be discussed concisely. Other disadvantages will be studied more thoroughly.

11.5.1.1 Circle Reasoning

Repeatedly it was pointed out that full cost pricing contains to a certain extent circle reasoning. This way of reasoning can be summarized as follows: the cost determines the selling price; however, the cost itself is determined by the sales (or production) volume which is dependent on the selling price.[30] Schematically this is represented in Figure 5.

The bilateral influence—cost and selling price on the one hand and selling price (via activity ratio) and cost on the other hand—greatly restricts the utility of full

Table 7

Production/Sales Volume (units)	Total Fixed Costs (in $)	Unit Fixed Costs (in $)	Unit Variable Costs (in $)	Full Cost (in $)
700	11,000	15.71	12	27.71
800	11,000	13.75	12	25.75
900	11,000	12.22	12	24.22
1,000	11,000	11	12	23

costing for pricing purposes. This disadvantage can partly be eliminated by using the concept of standard full cost, in which indirect costs, irrespective of the actual activity ratio, are allocated in function of a hypothetical activity ratio, considered as "normal."

Example. Presume the cost structure in Table 7. When the selling price is based on full costing, it increases when sales volume is decreasing (and conversely) in such a way that one is pulled into a vicious circle. This vicious circle can be broken by relating fixed costs and standard production volume. So the following cost formula is worked out (see also section 11.3.2.1):

$$\text{Full cost} = \frac{\text{Variable cost}}{\text{actual production volume}} + \frac{\text{Fixed cost}}{\text{standard production volume}}$$

Presuming that the standard production volume is 850 units, the full cost amounts:

$$\$ 12 + \frac{\$ 11{,}000}{850 \text{ units}} = \$ 24.94$$

At other activity ratios (within a relevant range) we arrive at the same cost every time, so that the effect of activity ratio fluctuations on full cost (and thus on selling price) is neutralized. Naturally the "circle effect" exerts its influence at the strongest in these "cost plus pricing" versions in which the margin is expressed in function of costs or of a well-defined return on investment.

11.5.1.2 Wrong Cost Concept

There are two main reasons why the full cost may be considered as an improper cost concept for pricing purposes. In the first place, it is important to have an insight into the evolution of sales volume in function of diverse price alternatives. In view of the measurement of operating results, on which the choice of a particular alternative is ultimately based, it is necessary to gain an insight into the cost structure, which brings to the foreground the importance and necessity of knowledge of cost variability in function of sales volume. The vicious circle concept explains that full costing is useless as measuring-instrument of cost differences. The adequate cost concept for this purpose should be a marginal concept.[31]

The second case in which the full cost can be labeled as a wrong concept is rather potential and is also in force in the case of pricing based on marginal costing. This case relates to the choice of an adequate cost dimension, both for quantity and value. In Chapter 5 we already advocated which modalities should be taken into consideration for pricing purposes; the problem narrows down to the fact that actual and *a fortiori* historical cost data should be avoided and that the only useful cost dimension should be prospective. On these grounds only cost valuation based on standard or replacement value is considered appropriate for pricing purposes[32] and becomes more necessary the more the factor prices are subject to fluctuations.

11.5.1.3 Arbitrary Cost Allocation

Insofar as this negative aspect is concerned we can confine ourselves to a brief summary. In section 11.3 the inability of calculating the correct full cost was already pointed out. This weakness of full costing is weighing heavier the more the manufacturing process becomes complex or the more the number of products increases. In the sphere of pricing this naturally has some substantial repercussions:

—The choice of an (arbitrary) activity unit is almost always production oriented, in other words, the choice is made in function of the production situation (e.g., technical data), without taking into account the commercial factors. On the other hand, cost allocation directly influences the full cost and consequently the selling price. Thus, the selling price is mainly determined by internal business technical factors.

—On the grounds of the above and bearing in mind the reality of very divergent commercial potentialities, it should be said that allocation of indirect costs may lead to perilous errors: reckoning with their commercial potentialities some products are burdened too heavy, others too light, so that sales can be directed in the wrong way, which may result in incomplete recovery of indirect costs. In other words, though production and sales are apparently evolving favorably, the accounting period concerned is closed with a negative balance, which is probably for the greater part caused by wrong cost allocation. Therefore, using the full cost for pricing purposes, especially as price floor, is dangerous. From this it appears that the already mentioned advantage "security" is rather illusive and that reality may bring surprises, which, moreover, are only detected afterward.

—Full costing essentially leads to a rigid pricing policy. This was mentioned before as an advantage, but there are also negative aspects. Thus, it can be favorable, at least under certain circumstances, to sell at a price that does not recover the full costs but only direct costs. In that manner, the activity ratio, for instance, can be improved. It is obvious that such policy cannot be pursued continuously and that in principle, in view of the danger of price deterioration, market segregation should be a fact. In Part IV we will prove that in these circumstances and where cost information is used in the price decision process, analytical contribution accounting offers the best basis for that kind of pricing decision.

11.5.2 Disadvantages and Defects with Reference to the Margin

11.5.2.1 Insufficient Basis for Determination, Change, and Differentiation of the Margin

Each selling price is an entity that should simultaneously conform to both internal and external business requirements. The internal business requirements especially apply to cost recovery, return on investment, profits, and so on and therefore determine the desirable. On the contrary, external business elements especially determine what is or shall be attainable under the influence of market data.

It is obvious that "naive" application of full cost pricing, and this only in the best conditions, meets the mentioned internal business considerations, while the simultaneous realization of external business considerations is left to chance.[33] Indeed, the setting of the profit margin on the basis of costs guarantees the recovering of costs; margin setting based on sales amount or selling prices or on capital invested, respectively, yields a desired sales profitability and capital productiveness. Therefore, changes of the margin will only take place in absolute amount (and perhaps also proportionally) where the basis of computation is changed, without taking account of the commercial reality. Insofar as the merely commercially determined margin differentiation is concerned, it can be said that neither costs nor sales or capital invested are able to offer any suitable basis. This consideration leads to a last handicap of full cost pricing, namely, that the market factor is not considered.

11.5.2.2 Neglecting the Market Element

This disadvantage is the most substantial of all the above and besides is at the same time a direct consequence as well as a synthesis of them. As a matter of fact, neglecting demand and competitive factors is the most frequently cited disadvantage of the rigorous application of full cost pricing.[34]

In order to prevent and remedy this kind of one-sided pricing policy, a variant of full cost pricing, more dynamic and flexible, is frequently recommended. In this variant both cost and market factors are taken into consideration in order to set an attainable selling price. This pricing method is usually called "flexible full cost pricing" or "flexible markup method."[35] The latter name suggests that the margin will be adapted to market circumstances. However, this can also happen with respect to the cost component.

In general it can be said that this more flexible method of pricing is not a unified, unequivocal technique but takes different forms in different situations or firms. As a consequence there is all but consensus of opinion concerning the incidence of flexible full costing in practice. According to some, flexible full cost pricing is rarely found; others think it is the most outstanding pricing method.[36]

As said before, how one is generally going to proceed when applying flexible markup pricing cannot be laid out unequivocally. Because this method is partially market oriented, much depends on the degree of market transparency and the eventuality of market research. Market intransparency and lack of market research will lead to rigid full cost pricing. When the market can be examined to a certain degree and one is additionally relying on the experience and intuition of the marketing personnel, then forms of "trial-and-error pricing" or "intuitive pricing" are under discussion.[37]

As the market becomes more and more transparent or as more refined market research methods become available, then the use of the veritable flexible full cost pricing becomes possible. The broader market information, historical, actual, as well as prospective, then leads to a number of commercial considerations, forming part of the overall marketing mix that may give rise to cost and margin adjustments. Starting from a certain full cost plus margin (possibly at several relevant activity ratios), the following considerations may lead to adjustment of margin (and/or costs):

—comparison with the competitors' costs. In principle, cost parallelism does not lead to price changes. If competitive costs are significantly higher or lower, price increases or decreases should be considered.

—the situation of the backlog of unfilled orders. If obtaining orders is rather difficult, a price decrease can be the obvious curative means. In the reverse case a price increase could be advisable (a form of demarketing). This price change naturally should be coupled with considerations about actual and potential market share and activity ratio. Also, the competitive prices can have a stimulating or prohibitive effect in this respect.

—as, in general, competitors will be confronted with the same cost increases, an increase in factor prices can be an ideal opportunity to raise prices. In case the actual selling prices are not considered as "generous" by the clients, the price increase will be accepted more readily. Besides, such practice stands or falls with the other market characteristics (e.g., the ease of obtaining orders).

—the fact that the own selling prices are above the competitive, though costs are hardly recovered, can be an indication of inefficient manufacturing and organization. In this case a cost reduction program should be elaborated.

—when the complete production can be sold at prices yielding a substantial profit, expansion may be considered.

—a distinct seasonal demand may be smoothed out by "anti-cyclical" pricing: relatively lower prices outside the season, higher prices within the season.

—if the clients' behavior, especially with regard to the selling price, can be determined positively (e.g., elasticity of demand), this factor should be directly involved in setting prices.

—if possible, the competitive behavior with regard to the selling price should be quantified: reaction upon price decreases or increases (e.g., Chance of reaction? What kind of reaction? In what measure?).

Based on the above and many other considerations the rigidly set desirable full cost based price shall be adjusted into an attainable selling price of which the connection with the full cost is more or less detached. Perhaps one shall sell under the full cost.

A still more extreme method of flexible full cost pricing consists of taking into consideration market factors at first and from these an attainable selling price is set. Afterward this selling price is compared to the full cost. This is called "backward pricing," in which cost calculation only plays the rather passive role of measure of operating results.

A concise evaluation of flexible full cost pricing can be worded as follows: flexible full cost pricing can hardly be seen as a separate method of pricing. Its manifestations are too heterogeneous. Where the cost factor has the upper hand over market factors, the difference with rigid full cost pricing will be rather gradual: by taking account, in a limited or defective measure of market factors, the price determination is somewhat mitigated. When market factors predominate, one can hardly speak of a cost-oriented pricing approach. Here, the role of costs is merely passive: measure of results and possibly absolute or flexible price floor. In both cases the risk is run of being market oriented in an extravagant measure. This is at least as dangerous as being excessively cost oriented in pricing decisions.

11.6 GENERAL REVIEW

In the above an evolution was outlined of the application of full costing for pricing purposes. This evolution is characterized by the following stages:

rigid full cost printing

↓

cost-oriented flexible full cost pricing

↓

market-oriented flexible full cost pricing

↓

backward pricing

↓

The use of these methods was especially elucidated in function of the degree of market transparency and the facilities of market research.

Where price determination is cost oriented, the danger lies in wrong cost calculation, especially arbitrary cost allocation, and in rigid pricing policy due to mechanistic techniques proceeding from taking insufficient account of the market element, by definition a dynamic element.

When price setting is market oriented, the danger lies in wrong interpretation of market research data, and aside from that, especially in a one-sided market-oriented approach, in which internal business factors are looked upon as mere dependent variables.

Both full cost–based pricing methods can be justified intrinsically, yet the manner and the circumstances in which they are used may potentially lead to real dangers. A more justified pricing method, in which the advantages of both are brought together while their disadvantages are for the greater part eliminated, is based on analytical contribution accounting. In this "golden mean" method an attempt is made to bring together harmoniously both cost and market information (see Part IV).

12 Pricing Decisions Based on Partial Costing

By "partial costs" is meant the part of costs that is directly assignable to a product or that varies in function of production or sales volume. Thus, it concerns the concepts of "direct" and "variable" costs, of which may be said, because of their greatly parallel character, that for our purpose they can be taken into consideration simultaneously. *Mutatis mutandis*, the same applies to the corresponding concepts of indirect and fixed costs.

12.1 INCIDENCE OF PARTIAL COST PRICING

In contrast with full cost pricing the idea of pricing based on partial costing is closely linked to the economic theory of marginal analysis.[1] Indeed, in marginal theory the selling price is explained from demand and supply factors, which are quantified, respectively, in marginal revenues and marginal costs. Also, partial cost–based pricing is started from a marginal cost concept, which is set against market factors. As the significance of the market element is growing with regard to the cost factor, likewise is the affinity with flexible full cost pricing. According to Machlup the full cost principle is rather frequently given up in favor of market considerations, even if they cannot be quantified accurately.[2] On the opposite, other authors maintain that partial cost pricing is found less frequently because the necessary quantitative market information is lacking.[3] According to these authors, the use of partial cost–based pricing is retricted to "emergency calculations" in periods of business depressions and as bases of the selling price of by-products, rubbish, accidental orders, and the like.[4]

12.2 METHODOLOGY OF PARTIAL COST PRICING

The most simple manner of partial cost pricing can be described as follows:

$$\frac{\text{partial cost } + \text{ margin in order to recover fixed (indirect) costs and to gain profit}}{\text{selling price}}$$

or: partial cost $\times$ markup factor $=$ selling price.

In this view, both the mentioned margin and markup factor normally are determined on the basis of market elements. Here again, diverse possibilities of interpretation should be pointed out in function of:

—the definition of partial costs;
—the margin or markup factor concept; and
—the choice of cost dimensions.

Consequently, partial cost pricing is not an unequivocal, clearcut management instrument.[5] It should even be pointed out, at least in the opinion of many businessmen, the full cost notion is favored over partial costing, this insofar as the systematics are concerned. Really, it could be said that full costing is characterized by an apparent systematic cost allocation system, while in partial costing the cost elements not absorbed in the cost remain as an undifferentiated whole.

Naturally, the latter procedure is less elegant than the former.[6] Again, the "golden mean" lies in analytical contribution accounting (see Part IV) in which direct costs on the one hand and a limited but justified allocation of indirect costs on the other hand are stressed.

12.3 USE AND ADVANTAGES OF PRICING POLICY BASED ON PARTIAL COSTING

12.3.1 Improvement of Activity Ratio

One of the most frequently mentioned advantages of pricing based on partial costing is the comparatively better use of business capacity.[7] Partial calculation as an "emergency calculation" in times of business depression was already pointed out. Though not necessarily in the context of depression or recession "improvement of activity ratio" generally means leveling up the actual activity ratio considered as too low to an activity ratio thought ideal, normal, or desirable.

As partial costing is confined to the "relevant" costs, that is, the costs which will vary in function of a decision to be taken, partial cost pricing contributes more to the attainment of a desirable activity ratio. So, a cost-minimal activity ratio can be calculated. Thus, it could be said that by means of marginal calculation a well-grounded opinion can be expressed on:

a. the desirability/eventuality of accepting accidental orders.
   Example. A firm working at full capacity can produce 10,000 units per month.

Table 8

	Total (in $)	Per unit (in $)
Sales : 6,000 units at $ 20	120,000	20
Cost of goods sold : - variable : 6,000 units at $ 12 - fixed	72,000 36,000	12 6
Gross profit	12,000	2
Distribution and selling costs - variable (transportation) - fixed	1,200 2,400	0.2 0.4
Net operating result	8,400	1.4

In view of the market conditions, the actual production volume comes to 6,000 units. At a selling price of $20, the operating results can be calculated as shown in Table 8. A mail order house proposes to buy 2,000 units at $16 and is willing to pay the transportation costs. At first the firm is not inclined to accept terms because full production costs ($12 + $6 = $18) are not recovered. However, at the insistence of the marketing manager, the cost accountant makes the (differential) calculation illustrated in Table 9. As differential revenue amounts to $32,000 and differential costs are $24,000, the differential (additional) profit amounts to $8,000. Consequently, accepting the incidental order improves the activity ratio and profitability of the firm in spite of the apparent insufficient recovering of full production costs.

b. selection of orders in the event of approaching the maximum activity level. Bottleneck calculation may be applied successfully here.
   Example. When a firm finds that its capacity to perform certain functions is fully utilized, it must find some way of rationing the available capacity among alternative uses. This requires a decision criterion and measures of the relative desirability of the various possible uses of the capacity (i.e. contribution). In a firm three products are manufactured (See Table 10). If there is no scarce production factor and the turnover rate is left out of consideration, production of B should be maximized. If raw materials or direct labor are the bottlenecks, the "contribution per unit of scarce factor" should be calculated previously (See Table 11).
   If raw materials are the scarce factors, manufacturing B should be preferred (0.4 > $ 0.25 > $ 0.16). If direct labor is the scarce factor, production of A should be maximized ($ 0.2 > $ 0.13 > $ 0.06).
   By means of a flexible pricing policy and the resulting repercussions on activity

Table 9

	Without additional order (in $)	Difference (in $)	With additional order (in $)
Sales	120,000	2,000 x $ 16 = 32,000	152,000
Variable production cost	72,000	2,000 x $ 12 = 24,000	96,000
Variable selling cost	1,200		1,200
Total variable cost	73,200	24,000	97,200
Contribution	46,800	8,000	54,800
Fixed production cost	36,000		36,000
Fixed selling cost	2,400		2,400
Total fixed cost	38,400		38,400
Net operating result	8,400	8,000	16,400

Table 10

Products	A	B	C
Selling Price	$ 12	$ 20	$ 10
Raw materials ($ 1 per unit)	$ 8	$ 10	$ 6
Direct labor ($ 0.2 per minute)	$ 2	$ 6	$ 3
Contribution	$ 2	$ 4	$ 1
Contribution percentage	16.6 %	20 %	10 %

ratio, partial cost pricing offers potentialities to maximize contribution or, in case of very low activity ratio due to market factors, to limit or even to minimize losses.[8]

12.3.2 Adequate Calculation of Operating Results

It is generally accepted that the contribution as a product-wise measure of results has a greater exploratory and decisive value than the net-profit concept

Table 11

Products	A	B	C
Raw materials (contribution units)	$\frac{\$\ 2}{8} = \$\ 0.25$	$\frac{\$\ 4}{10} = \$\ 0.4$	$\frac{\$\ 1}{6} = \$\ 0.16$
Direct labor (contribution minutes)	$\frac{\$\ 2}{10} = \$\ 0.2$	$\frac{\$\ 4}{30} = \$\ 0.13$	$\frac{\$\ 1}{15} = \$\ 0.06$

arising from full costing. Moreover, the former can be calculated more easily and more accurately than the latter, which may be distorted by sometimes extreme cost allocation.[9]

Therefore, the contribution as measure of results may be a basis of the buildup of the assortment (in principle commercial aspects will be more decisive, however) and in this capacity may lead to stop production and sale of certain products or admit new products into the assortment. In principle those products with the relatively most favorable contribution should be stressed, which leads to optimum operating results.

12.3.3 Right Cost Concept

This advantage was already pointed out so that the following consideration can be handled briefly.[10] Since the direct costs are meant here, we may say that:

—The allocation of costs to units of product does not involve any problem.
—Because direct costs are controllable at the same time, these costs can be adjusted or changed, among other things by means of a cost reduction program, which is a direct way to improve the firm's competitive position. This originates from the fact that the firm's prices can only become noncompetitive as a consequence of exorbitant direct costs, which can in principle be remedied on short term. This significantly contrasts with indirect costs, which have for the greater part a long-term character and consequently can hardly be controlled.
—(Price setting) managers, insufficiently or not at all acquainted with cost accounting techniques, will label partial costing information as more clear and understandable than full cost information obtained by means of allocation of indirect costs.
—As a rule, forecasting direct costs is much easier than forecasting certain indirect cost elements. These forecasts are, as stated before, very important for pricing purposes.

12.3.4 More Flexible Pricing Policy

One of the advantages of full cost pricing is price stability. This advantage should be specified more and toned down further here. It is a matter of fact that frequently price stability is a disguise for rigid, uniform pricing, although a more differentiated and flexible approach could improve substantially the firm's profits. Many prices, obtained by means of partial costing would probably be rejected as uneconomic when comparing them with the full cost of the products in question.

According to the marginal view, the total costs should not be recovered transaction by transaction but the whole of fixed (indirect) costs should be recovered by the revenues of the entire assortment, after which the operating result is left as a balance. Consequently, it is perfectly thinkable that on the basis of partial costing, sales transactions, of which the selling price is set in between the full and partial cost, are contracted and carried out. Naturally, this view endows the price-setting authority with substantial latitude, which allows him to act more flexibly and perhaps more aggressively. In that manner he may sell more selectively: from a package of orders (products) he may prefer the ones that, relatively, yield the most substantial contribution, which normally tends to improve both activity ratio and operating results.[11]

12.4 DISADVANTAGES AND DEFECTS OF PRICING POLICY BASED ON PARTIAL COSTING

12.4.1 Lack of Price Stability

Changing prices is a matter of dosage: in the case of full cost pricing, price stability was considered as an advantage; in the contrary, partial cost–based pricing was recommended as a means to improve the activity ratio and profitability. In the latter case, however, there can be adverse effects of insufficient price stability. Flexible pricing policy does not mean that each change of either internal or external business elements should be answered by a price change. On the contrary, there are certain limits beyond which price changes can be labeled as unsuitable. These limits are attached to market structure (e.g., price leadership in oligopolistic markets), costs of changing prices (e.g., drawing up new price lists), customers (e.g., relation between price and quality), and so on. If the advantages of a sound pricing policy have to be maintained, partial cost–based pricing should bear these factors in mind.

12.4.2 Lack of Market Information

It was already pointed out that rigid full cost pricing can be considered as a protecting reflex caused by lack of market information. The selling price based on a ''sure'' cost is preferred to a selling price based on inaccurate and doubtful market data. It is clear that partial costing–oriented pricing implies thorough knowledge of market characteristics. The interval from partial cost data to the eventual selling price is longer than the one from full cost to selling price, so that in the former case a better compass and proper direction arrows are required. These can be found in market research, that is, information about competitors and customers and for preference objective, quantitative imformation. Therefore, in case of market intransparency, pricing on the basis of partial costing seems fundamentally wrong.

12.4.3 Problematic Cost Recovering

Closely linked to the two shortcomings mentioned above, a third, rather fundamental handicap should be pointed out, namely, the danger of recovering insufficiently costs (see also section 6.8).

In fact we are dealing here with the problem of the price floor, which has already been discussed in Chapter 7. So, we can confine ourselves to the essentials. The risk is incurred that by means of forceful market-oriented pricing, in which, because of sharp competition, an indulgent attitude toward clients and competitors is adopted, sight may be lost of the recovery of fixed (indirect) costs. Such policy may probably be justified on short term (e.g., in function of the activity ratio) but it may be very dangerous in the long run because of the risk of price war or price deterioration.[12]

This is so if profits are only realized if fixed (indirect) costs of a certain period are recovered. Though this does not mean that profits should be made transaction by transaction, the total sales volume should be sold at such a price that full costs are recovered. For this purpose partial cost–based pricing does not provide much guidance, and on the other hand, full cost–based pricing is not desirable.

Again, we think we can premise that analytical contribution accounting, in which fixed (indirect) costs are partially incorporated in relevant costs, is able to offer the better cost information.

12.4.4 Liquidity Problems

In the case of partial cost–based pricing the danger of tight liquidity is evident. As a matter of fact, each method of cost based pricing may cause liquidity problems, because costs are expressed on a transaction basis and not on outlay basis. This is especially true in case of partial costing, just because not all costs are incorporated here. In order to remedy this, all out-of-pocket costs should be compiled and it should be the goal that total sales revenues of a certain period of time at least reach the level of total out-of-pocket costs of the same period.[13] In our opinion, also for this purpose, analytical contribution accounting may be helpful. By accumulating direct costs, in principle having a "cash" character, and indirect costs subdivided in function of cash character, it may be relatively easy to determine, both per product unit and in total, which should be the selling price or sales revenue required in order to safeguard liquidity (see Part IV).

12.5 GENERAL REVIEW

Our final appraisal of pricing based on partial costing can be recapitulated as carefully balanced and measured. Pricing on the basis of partial costing is both in method and use much more flexible than full cost pricing. The principal reason for this is the use of direct (variable) costs as selling price basis. As a result the cost repercussions of pricing decisions can be observed better and may lead to better activity ratio, more flexible pricing policy, better cost control, and, as ultimate outcome of this improvement, even optimalization of operating results. Naturally, a certain minimal level of market information is a *"conditio sine qua non."* As for commercial reasons one is inclined to lose sight of fixed (indirect) cost, the most substantial danger seems to be the risk of insufficient recovery of costs.

It is self-evident that selling below full cost may be justified accidentally, yet the propensity to continual application of this principle may lead to disastrous consequences. Our overall impression is favorable. Yet it should be clearly said that pricing based on partial costing should not be applied mechanically but with deliberation, both in calculational and in commercial respect.

Once again, we would like to state that the difficulty of insufficient recovery of costs is eliminated if pricing decisions are based on information proceeding from analytical contribution accounting (see Part IV).

13 Pricing Decisions Based on Cost Accounting Methods in between Full Costing and Partial Costing

It is not at all our intention to go extensively into the controversy between advocates of full costing and partial costing. The aims of this chapter are rather limited: in light of the considerations in the two preceding chapters, we will consider here pricing policy based on intermediate forms of cost accounting.

Both full costing and partial costing can be considered as extreme methods of cost accounting.[1] Both methods and their corresponding pricing policies form the poles of the following spectrum:

$$\text{FULL} \quad \longleftarrow \hspace{2cm} \longrightarrow \quad \begin{array}{c} \text{VARIABLE} \\ \text{DIRECT} \end{array} \quad \text{COSTING}$$
$$\text{COSTING}$$

The interval between these poles is filled with variants and mixed forms of calculation from which we decided in favor of analytical contribution accounting.[2] The reasons for this choice have already been suggested above and will be discussed more formally in Part IV.

In this chapter (see section 13.3) the basic principles of analytical contribution accounting are briefly described. This should be considered as a preamble to Part IV, which is entirely devoted to this accounting method and its applicability in pricing matters. Prior to this, however, two other intermediate cost accounting methods and their pricing implications are discussed, namely, pricing based on the normal costing principle and conversion cost pricing.

13.1 PRICING BASED ON THE NORMAL COSTING PRINCIPLE

13.1.1 Origin and Definition

The founder of the normal costing principle, P.W.S Andrews,[3] arrived at his concept starting from a number of shortcomings of the full cost and marginal cost approach to pricing decisions. Insofar as the marginal pricing theory is concerned, Andrews points out the substantial discrepancy between theory and practice.[4] Furthermore, the theory of monopolistic competition explains the price formation starting from the long-run cost evolution and the short-term demand situation. Andrews adopts the explanation of price setting based on costs and demand but thinks that it should be approached in light of short-term costs and long-term market situation.[5]

Andrew's criticism of full costing can be summed up as follows: costs play a decisive role in pricing in such a way that other important factors such as demand and competition are largely neglected.[6] In reaction to this Andrews puts his normal costing principle, which in fact includes a method of setting the selling price. This selling price is composed of: budgeted average direct production costs plus flexible gross margin ("costing margin").[7] Being given the prices of the direct production factors, Andrews properly observes that direct product costs are constant. So the determination of the costing margin, which at the same time is substantial for the determination of the selling price, is emphasized.

13.1.2 Pricing on the Basis of the Normal Costing Principle

In Andrews' normal costing theory and where pricing matters are concerned, the margin problems predominate over the costing problems. Therefore, below a brief discussion is devoted to the considerations on which the margin is based. It should be said, to begin with, that the normal costing theory should explicitly be located in industrial firms and is not consumer oriented.

As a rule, the industrial firm's customers are wholesalers, retailers, or other industrial firms, in other words, customers characterized by a higher degree of rational market behavior than consumers. Consequently, differences in selling price can only be maintained when they are clearly tied to cost differences.[8]

Pricing policy based on the normal costing principle starts with the following principles:

—The selling price should be able to recover average costs as well as a normal profit margin.
—Each selling price exceeding a certain limit endangers the market share.

The former principle seems rather obvious, the latter, however, should be explained more fully.

Andrews points out that in the long run each supplier will have to be content with a selling price equivalent to normal average unit costs including a fair amount of profit. Each selling price difference that cannot be warranted by cost differences will lead to a shrinking market share. Consequently, a cautious policy, sacrificing short-term advantages to a more stable price and production policy that offers more guarantee in respect to safety and continuity, is advised. In the normal costing theory the selling price norm lies outside the firm, namely, in demand and competitive conditions. In this connection Andrews strongly underlines the importance of potential competition.[9] This is found in the form of converting production processes, assortment enlargement, and so on, which possibly may be realized within a short period of time. This means that potential competition becomes an important part of pricing decisions. As a rule it should be impossible to pursue a pricing policy resulting in more than normal profits. In this case the market share would shrink by the mechanism of market entrance. From all this results that the selling price approximates the normal cost.

In all respects, Andrews' pricing method has one advantage over the classical full cost pricing, namely, that more attention is given to market factors. Yet in our opinion there are a number of shortcomings:

—Bearing in mind market factors presupposes market information. A fruitful application of Andrews' pricing method presumes transparent markets. If this is not available, market research about cross elasticities, actual and potential competition, and so forth should be possible. In many cases both requirements are not met so that Andrews' method is demoted to an ordinary rule of thumb.[10]

—As already mentioned, Andrews intended to offer an alternative to the (in his opinion) unrealistic theory of monopolistic competition (see section 13.1.1). He only partly succeeded in it: Andrews' theory is nothing more than a system of rather general rules in which the market element is mentioned fragmentarily. The clause "fragmentarily" means that in our opinion the element "potential competition" is stressed too much. Although substantial, this factor is only one of the many pricing decision variables.

Andrews' normal costing theory is a typical example of a pricing method situated in between "full cost pricing" and "partial cost pricing."

In technical sense we still have to do with a "cost plus" approach, in the economic sense we find some characteristics of marginal reasoning in the determination of the flexible "costing margin." This margin is not only different from kind of product to kind of product but also in function of changing demand and competitive conditions.

Potentially, this method offers a maximum of guarantees of both cost recovery and commercial attainability. The lack of market information may be a serious obstacle, however. Within the scope of an appropriate pricing policy this lack of market information should be compensated by more adequate business internal information, notably by calculation data, which make a flexible pricing policy possible and guarantee the recovering of costs. One such method will be introduced in Part IV.

13.2 CONVERSION COST PRICING

This pricing method, also called "production value added pricing"[11] is a good example of a method in between full cost pricing and partial cost pricing.

Again we have to do with a pricing method existing in several variants. The most frequently used variant is full cost plus profit margin in function of those costs that correspond with or approximate the firm's value added. Generally, the total costs reduced by material costs are used as approximation of the value added. Variants of this method of setting prices may be:

—calculation of a differentiated profit margin based on direct material costs on the one hand and direct labor cost (or any other direct cost) on the other hand. The indirect costs are left out of consideration.[12]

In formula form: $P = M (1 + m_1) + L (1 + m_2)$
in which: P = selling price
$\qquad\qquad m_1, m_2$ = differentiated profit margins (in %)
$\qquad\qquad M$: direct material costs
$\qquad\qquad L$: direct labor costs
—total costs are seen as the sum of total labor and material costs
$\quad$ In formula form:[13] $P = a \cdot r \cdot L + b \cdot M$
in which: a = factor by which direct labor costs are converted into total labor costs.
$\qquad\qquad$ = reciprocal of the percentage of total labor costs in the firm's value added. This is the sales revenue minus the value of all cost factors obtained from outside. This factor represents the profit margin.
$\qquad\quad b$ = factor by which direct material costs are converted into total material costs.

The selling price P has the character of a price floor. According to Hapgood, this method stand or falls with an adequate calculation of the factors $a, b,$ and r. Normally, this should happen on the basis of periodical technical-economic analysis of the relevant data.[14]

In general, conversion cost pricing arises from the assumed necessity of determining the profit on the basis of the firm's value added. An advantage may be the contribution of this pricing method to a better activity ratio. Unlike the case discussed in the context of partial costing, it does not concern problems of subnormal capacity usage but rather problems of full capacity or even abnormal capacity usage. This is founded on the view that the conversion costs are a more or less accurate indication of the firm's activity ratio. As profits are determined in function of conversion costs, the products making great demands on business capacity have to bear greater profit margins (in absolute terms). In that manner the salesmix can be oriented so as to phase out abnormal capacity usage.[15] It should be pointed out, however, that this method makes abstraction of the capital invested in the diverse components of business capacity.

Still other defects of conversion cost pricing can be mentioned. In the first place, it should be pointed out that taking the firm's value added as the only measure of its social and economical significance should be labeled as narrow and one sided.[16]

In the second place, the inconsistent and different handling of material cost

Figure 6

	A	B	C	D
Gross revenue of the period	X	X	X	X
Less: direct distribution costs of the products	X	X	X	X
Net revenue	X	X	X	X
Less : direct production costs of the products	X	X	X	X
Contribution of the products after the direct product costs	X	X	X	X
Less : direct production costs of the product group		X		
Contribution of the products and product group after direct product costs	X	X		X
Less : direct costs of manufacturing departments : Dept. 1		X		
Dept. 2		X		
Dept. 3		X		
Less : direct costs of auxiliary departments : Dept. 10		X		
Dept. 11		X		
Less : direct administrative expenses		X		
Less: direct distribution and selling costs		X		
Operating Results of the Period		X		

on the one hand and other costs (e.g., labor costs) on the other hand should be pointed out. In our opinion this difference cannot be justified. Strictly speaking, workers, machines, and so on are production factors obtained from outside the firm.

Finally, it should be said that demand and competitive factors are for the greater part left out of consideration so that this method should be labeled as highly mechanical with all annexed negative phenomena from a marketing point of view.

The above-mentioned critical items perhaps for the greater part explain the scanty application and adverse attitude toward this pricing method from the side of trade and industry.[17]

13.3 ANALYTICAL CONTRIBUTION ACCOUNTING AS MIXED CALCULATION METHOD

Above, several times we referred to analytical contribution accounting as an adequate calculation method for pricing purposes. In part IV this method of

Figure 7

	A	B	C	D
Gross revenue of the period	X	X	X	X
Less : variable direct distribution costs of the products	X	X	X	X
Net revenue	X	X	X	X
Less : variable direct production costs of the products	X	X	X	X
Contribution of the products after variable product costs	X	X	X	X
Less : variable direct production costs of the product group		X		
Contribution of the products and product group after variable direct production and distribution costs	X		X	X
Less : variable direct costs of production departments: Dept. 1		X		
Dept. 2		X		
Dept. 3		X		
Less : variable direct costs of auxiliary departments: Dept. 10		X		
Dept. 11		X		
Less :variable direct administrative expenses		X		
Less : variable direct distribution costs		X		
Contribution after total cost involving short term cash outlays		X		
Less : fixed costs without cash character		X		
Operating Results of the period		X		

calculation and especially its application in pricing policy will be discussed in depth. In this section, some introductory considerations will be made about the origin and basic principle of ACA.

Under the name of "Einzelkosten und Deckungsbeitragsrechnung" analytical contribution accounting has been developed especially in Western Germany. The German economist Paul Riebel was one of the most prominent pioneers.[18] Riebel is starting from the concept "Einzelkosten," which is defined as directly apportionable costs. However, the concept "Einzelkosten" is enlarged: it does not only apply to the allocation of costs to "product units" (this is the classical view); on the contrary, Riebel says that on each level of the production process there are costs directly apportionable to cost centers but not to a product or product group or that are directly apportionable to auxiliary departments and not to principal departments and conversely.

Consequently, on each level of the production process there are direct costs that can no longer be considered as direct on the next level nearer to the ultimate unit. In the second place, distinction is made between fixed and variable costs and insofar fixed costs are concerned a division is made in function of cash outlay character. Dependent on the decision or problem involved the most appropriate cost concept should be used and put against revenues.[19] In this manner a ''contribution'' is calculated. By contribution is understood the difference between revenue and certain costs, dependent on the relevant option.[20] Some important contributions much in evidence are:

revenue—variable costs
revenue—direct costs
revenue—variable direct costs
revenue—out-of-pocket costs

As Rieble does not give a uniform scheme of calculation, we reproduce two typical examples of the calculation of operating results.[21] (See Figures 6 and 7). In both figures four products are concerned (A,B,C,D) from which B and C form a product group.

Riebel points out that contribution accounting may lead to an indulgent pricing policy, which gives occasion to incomplete recovering of costs. In order to prevent this, Riebel recommends periodically planning minimum contributions in light of a planned recovery of indirect costs and of net profit objectives (cf. section 6.8)

By means of analysis of variances between actual and planned cost recovering, the overall profitability of the firm is controlled. It is left to the responsible marketing/sales manager to determine by means of what orders, products, product groups, and by what customers or customer groups he intends to realize the required cost recovery.[22] Consequently, pricing policy may be more flexible and adaptive than, for instance, full cost–oriented pricing.[23]

PART IV

ANALYTICAL CONTRIBUTION ACCOUNTING AND PRICING POLICY

We have repeatedly pointed out that ACA is a versatile and adequate calculation method for pricing purposes. At the same time we underlined that this method is preferable insofar as pricing decisions are concerned. The following aspects of ACA were already mentioned:

—The bulk of fixed costs is differentiated and fixed (indirect) costs are partially incorporated in relevant costs (see Part II, sections 6.1 and 6.2 and Chapter 10; Part III section 12.4.3).

—It is a "golden mean" method in which direct costs on the one hand and a limited but justified allocation of indirect costs on the other hand are stressed. Consequently, differentiated contributions can be calculated (see Part II, sections 6.1 and 7.2.6; Part III, section 12.2).

—It is a "golden mean" method in which both cost and market information are brought together harmoniously. It takes into account revenue as well as cost data. Besides, the focus is on each product separately but also considers its relationship with other products of the sales mix (see Part II, sections 6.1, 6.9, and 8.2; Part III, sections 11.3.4 and 11.6).

—It is useful for both long- and short-term pricing decisions (see Part II, sections 6.1, 6.4, and 6.7).

—It contributes to avoiding liquidity problems by accumulating direct costs and indirect costs subdivided in function of cash character (see Part II, sections 6.1, 6.5, 7.4.1, and 7.4.2; Part III, section 12.4.4).

—It is an accounting method connected to the concept of opportunity costs (sacrificed contribution of the superseded product) (see Part II, sections 6.9 and 7.3).

—By means of simultaneous subdivision of costs according to variability in function of activity ratio, assignability to cost units, classification of costs in function of outlay character, and imputing costs to a period of time, the problem of insufficient recovery of costs can be neglected. ACA offers the potentiality of insight in fixed (indirect) costs to be recovered preferentially and successively (see Part II, sections 6.7, 7.5, and Chapter 10; Part III, section 12.5).

—It makes feasible a more realistic and flexible pricing policy and lays the adequate foundation for price differentiation (see Part III, sections 11.3.4 and 11.5.1.3).

—Finally, a brief discussion was devoted to the origins and basic principles of ACA. Two simple calculation models were represented (see Part III, section 13.3).

As a matter of fact, each pricing method may be considered as a manner in which quantitative information is compiled and processed for pricing purposes. Just like each problem of selection, the choice of the pricing method is a problem of optimization, in which the selling price is the unity to optimize, being given information about demand, competition, and costs. Which one of these factors will carry the most weight depends on the circumstances (market, kind of product) and cannot be determined once and for all. In the scope of our book the cost aspects will be stressed. Consequently, it concerns a submodel, namely, the role of cost accounting information, as a component of the entire price decision model.

Because of restrictions of time and money, the optimum pricing method is found quite rarely. The advantages of a better pricing method should be weighed against time and costs of the method in question. Among other things this approach explains the frequent occurrence of far from optimum methods as cost plus pricing in most of its variants or price imitation, which is often based on tradition, love of ease, and so on. Below, we aspire to justify ACA in light of the above-mentioned conditions. Also, the fundamental principles and the buildup of ACA will be discussed. Last but not least, pricing decisions by means of ACA will be explained more fully.

14 Motives for the Choice of Analytical Contribution Accounting (ACA)

The purpose of this chapter is to justify ACA versus full costing and partial costing. Therefore, it should be demonstrated that ACA, at least potentially, leads to optimal or better selling prices than those based on full or partial costing.

The more or less limited significance of cost accounting for pricing purposes has already been pointed out. This limited significance is especially due to the fact that the cost factor is only one of the possible many determinants of pricing policy. Add to this that the significance of full costs has strongly decreased because of the frequent incidence of joint production and the annexed problems of allocating fixed costs. In spite of these restrictions the cost factor remains substantial, especially where the following situations are concerned:

—indication of the costs to be recovered in all and per unit of product,

—furnishing the foundations underlying product line pricing and certain forms of price differentiation,

—indication of price floors, and

—determination of the sticker price.

It has already been pointed out that the traditional full costing method is not able to offer much relevant information for these purposes. Because of proportionalizing and allocating indirect costs, the provided information becomes problematic and untransparent. In reaction to this, allocation of fixed and indirect costs was abandoned and these costs were removed to the income statement. Only the direct (variable) costs are considered as regular cost elements. This has led to the origin of diverse forms of partial costing, of which direct costing is the most important. For pricing and other decision-making purposes, the weakness lies in the fact that indirect costs are set "in bulk," without any differentiation, against direct costs, which may be a profound simplification (cf. problems of cost recovering).

ACA is an intermediate method: according to certain principles the bulk of indirect costs is spread over various objects.[1] We shall prove that this approach allows better insight into cost recovery and profitability of the particular products.

The above considerations may be condensed in the following pricing dilemma: on the one hand, costs cannot be allocated unarbitrarily to product units; on the other hand, the firm should recover its full costs, which implies the need of full cost information. Then rises the important question: What amount of indirect costs should be recovered per unit of product sold? In our opinion this question cannot be answered unequivocally but requires a management decision in the course of which two principles may be taken into account:[2]

—*principle of equality*: this is an arbitrary method by which an equal amount of indirect costs is allocated to each unit of product. It is this principle that is commonly used in traditional full costing.

—*principle of "ability to bear"*: the costs to be recovered per unit are determined by the commercial potentialities of the product in question. In this manner, we deal with compensation in the sense that products with a considerable commercial status will have to bear a comparatively greater portion of indirect costs than products with a weaker market status.

We certainly prefer the principle of "ability to bear" to the principle of equality because consistent application of the former implies that in addition to costs, demand factors and competitors' reactions should be taken into account. So, the three essential components of the pricing decision model are considered.[3] In order to clear the way for the above-mentioned compensation, the concept of "contribution" should be defined in more detail.

Contribution is usually defined as the difference between sales and direct costs or, on a unitary basis, as the difference between selling price and direct product costs. So, the contribution coincides with the margin wanted for recovering indirect costs and for realization of net profits.[4]

The limitation of this definition lies in the fact that the distinction between direct and indirect costs is considered an absolute distinction. In other words, there is only one meaning, namely, direct or indirect with respect to one particular product. On the contrary, the relative distinction between direct and indirect costs should be stressed here. Direct or indirect costs can also be examined with reference to cost centers, product groups, periods of time, customer groups, channels of distribution, sales area, and a number of other "units of reference."[5] Each of these particular units of reference offers the possibility to calculate a contribution that may be very meaningful for pricing decision purposes. In function of the objectives of ACA (e.g., pricing) it will be of vital importance to select a series of units of reference to which costs should be imputed. These aspects will be treated further.

In summary ACA can be compared with full costing and partial costing as follows:

—Indirect costs are neither set in bulk against direct costs nor are they proportionalized. Resting on the principle of ability to bear and on the relativity of the distinction between direct and indirect costs, the indirect costs are assigned to those units of reference in which they are incurred. How this is carried out will be discussed in the next chapters.

—The principle of ability to bear compels us to take market factors into consideration. An optimum selling price can be deduced from any kind of cost concept. For that purpose demand and competitive factors should also be considered. Thus, the potentialities of recovering indirect costs are determined by examination of alternative price/sales combinations or in function of competitive reactions to a premised selling price. In a number of cases adequate market research will be required. In this connection it is important to consider the role of costs in pricing decisions as only a partial one.

—The relative distinction between direct and indirect costs opens a number of valuable perspectives for pricing policy. Direct and indirect costs in function of products, periods of time, and outlay character are very interesting. This will be discussed further.

In conclusion, how costs will be recovered will no longer be decided by the cost accountant but by the one who is responsible for price setting. Since mechanistic pricing policy is completely abandoned here, the pricing authority should have given up traditional cost accounting methods.

15 Fundamental Principles of Analytical Contribution Accounting

Before discussing the technical aspects of ACA it is necessary to throw some light on the fundamentals of it.

In the preceding chapter we pointed out that the classical distinction between direct and indirect costs is made in function of assignability to a cost unit. This view was labeled as too narrow. On the contrary, the relativity of this cost distinction and at the same time other units of reference to which costs can be allocated directly should be highlighted. For instance, the distinction between direct and indirect costs of a cost center could be made. The direct costs of the cost center may be direct or indirect product costs; both may be fixed or variable. The indirect costs of a cost center are caused by several cost centers. They may be direct, relating to a certain other cost center (e.g., auxiliary department). They may also be direct in relation to a group of cost centers. In that way a hierarchy of units of reference (e.g., cost centers) can be conceived in which each cost element is only allocated to that unit in which it still can be discerned as direct cost. The costs, allocated in that manner to a certain stage of the hierarchy of units of reference, are indirect with respect to the other stages.

In the same way hierarchies of units of reference may be created with reference to cost units, commercial segments, and so forth.

Example
—with respect to cost units (furniture industry):
1. total production   —furniture   —highest stage
2. segment of production —seat furniture
3. product group   —chairs
4. kind of product   —chairs model K
5. unit of product   —chair K no. 20   —lowest stage

—with respect to commercial data (e.g. in food industry):
1. customers   —retailers, wholesalers, industry
2. customer group   —retailers
3. individual customer   —Mr. X, retailer

As already mentioned each unit of reference may be subdivided. Especially, the division in fixed and variable costs is important. Also, this cost distinction is relative. Classically, it is a matter of variability in function of production volume. However, variability can also be considered from the point of view of sales and size of order. Such divisions may be very relevant for pricing purposes. Insofar as the problems of recovering of costs are concerned, the problem of assignability of fixed costs to certain periods of time arises (see also Part II, section 6.8). In this connection, a hierarchy of periods of time could be constructed that may look as follows:

—year
—quarter
—month

Taking the month as example, three kinds of fixed costs can be distinguished:

—direct period costs, usually involving outlays in the same period (e.g., salaries, monthly rent)
—indirect period costs, directly attributable to a known number of periods. They are indirect with regard to a particular month, yet direct with respect to a quarter, a year, or possibly a longer period of time (e.g., holiday allowance, maintenance costs).
—indirect period costs to be assigned to a previously unknown number of periods. They usually relate to one-off or irregular costs, producing effect over a longer period of time, unknown in advance (e.g., costs of substantial repair and maintenance, costs attached to brevets).

So it needs no explaining that insofar as recovering of costs is concerned, the outlay character of costs also may be substantial. Both kinds of indirect period costs may not be allocated unarbitrarily to particular subperiods irrespective of allocating them proportional to time, to production volume, or to one or another combined ratio of allocation. Such allocations are merely arbitrary and do not teach anything about periodical requirements of cost recovering.

For pricing purposes this problem can be bypassed by premising "planned contributions" to indirect period costs. These can have the character of a provision if activities precede the payment or of a depreciation if the payment is prior to the performance. In summary the following principles are in force:

—The relativity of the distinction between direct and indirect costs on the one hand and between fixed and variable costs on the other hand is highlighted, including all the consequences resulting from it.

—All costs are recorded as direct costs in such a way that they are assigned to the lowest possible stage of a hierarchy of units of reference where they still can be considered as direct costs of that stage.

—Indirect costs are no longer allocated to cost centers and/or cost units.

—All costs that cannot be assigned to a period of time are incorporated in "planned contributions" in view of recovering full costs.

—Per unit of reference a distinction among costs with short-term outlay character, long-run outlay character, or without cash character may be relevant for many decision problems. Of course, this distinction, in function of outlay character, can be differentiated and refined further.

16 Methodology of Analytical Contribution Accounting

After the discussion of some fundamentals of ACA, we will now pay attention to the technical aspects of it. In the first place, the general methodological problems of ACA will be explained, next the buildup of ACA for pricing purposes will be introduced.

16.1 GENERAL ASPECTS

In the ACA system distinction should be made between the basic calculation and a number of specialized cost calculations (cf. different costs for different purposes). The basic calculation serves as foundation. Therefore, it should be designed in such a way that the necessary differentiated cost data are provided on behalf of special cost calculations conceived in function of specific decision-making cases. Out of these special cost calculations an ordered whole of relevant contributions will be distilled starting from the differentiated cost data of the basic calculation.

In the scope of our book, emphasis is put on the buildup of the basic calculation in order to deduce from the specialized cost calculations contributions relevant for pricing purposes.[1] Thus, the basic calculation is a universally usable grouping of relative direct costs. Its components can be combined in several ways. By that, a number of calculations, drafted with certain decision-making problems in view, can be built up.

The basic calculation is an accounting system in which costs, classified by type, cost centers, and cost units are found in combination. As it contains total costs of a financial period (e.g., month, quarter, year) it may be seen as an expression of full costing. As already mentioned, we are leaning on the principle of relative assignability of costs in such a way that costs, classified by type, are allocated to those cost centers, cost units, or other units of reference to which they are directly assignable. In this manner, a part of the costs can be found in cost center accounts and other costs are found in cost units or other units of reference so that the basic calculation, seen from the individual units of reference, is an orderly construction of partial calculations. These characteristics really point to the fact that ACA is an accounting method in between full costing and partial costing (cf. Part III, Chapter 13).

Insofar as there is no transfer of cost centers to cost units, the basic calculation is in principle identical to the traditional cost calculation. However, the basic calculation is different from the traditional cost calculation in two ways, namely:

—The costs, classified by type, are assigned to a number of cost categories.
—The costing objective is less unambiguous; possible costing objectives that may occur are: cost centers, cost units (traditional costing objectives) but also customer groups, distribution channels, and sales area can be mentioned as (marketing oriented) costing objectives.

When problems of assignability arise, for example, when a certain type of cost can be equally assigned to more units of reference, a number of unequivocal principles of allotment should be made out previously. In other words, those principles should be chosen so as to assign a certain type of cost to only one of the possible units of reference. Assignment to other units of reference should be done by means of memorandum entries (i.e., not based on books).

With respect to both above-mentioned differences the following questions arise:

1. To which categories should the diverse types of cost be differentiated and how should these cost categories be detailed?
2. According to which criteria should the units of reference be classified?

About 1. The division of types of costs in so-called cost categories depends on the objectives of cost accounting. The important objectives are fixation of operating results and financial position, efficiency control, and providing bases for decision making. As already mentioned (see Part II, Chapter 6) cost categories relevant for these purposes may be the categories in function of:

—imputability to a period of time (month, quarter, year)
—the outlay character of costs, and
—a number of cost-influencing factors.

It depends on business structure and the specific objectives of cost accounting to which of these cost categories the costs, classified by type, will be differentiated.

In its turn each cost category can be analysed further. When an analysis in function of outlay character is the aim, distinction can be made in the first place between costs with outlay character or those without. In function of the frequency of outlays the "cash" costs can be subdivided further in:

—costs causing short-term payments (raw materials, salaries) and
—costs causing long-term cash outlays (depreciations, accrued liabilities).

As a rule, the latter group is composed of indirect period costs, which are allocated to a period by means of planned contributions.

If required, the analysis according to frequency of outlays could be executed more accurately and more formally. The first-mentioned group should be subdivided in direct and indirect period costs. First of all, the concepts "short period" and "long period" should be defined. Insofar as indirect period costs with short-term outlay character are concerned, consideration could be given to further differentiation taking into account the circumstances that these costs can be assigned to a clearcut, superior period of time. This is, for example, the case with holiday allowances and annual merit bonus, in contrast to advertising expenses and repair and maintenance costs. It should be pointed out that the division according to outlay character and to imputability in function of periods of time partly fall together.

Another important criterion in order to subdivide cost categories is the one in which cost categories are taken in function of certain factors influencing costs. Especially, the phenomenon of cost variability is meant here. The relative character of this subdivision has already been mentioned (see Part II, section 6.1). Usually, the variability of costs is expressed in terms of production volume or sales volume. Further division could be made in costs varying promptly ("automatically"), costs varying after a certain course of time, and costs not at all varying with production volume or sales volume. In case of variability in function of sales volume, distinction can be made between variability in function of sales amount and variability in function of different factors such as sales volume, number of orders, and size of order.

Also, in case of variability in function of production volume, further refining subdivisions can be introduced. In spite of these further refinements, business management should be selective and content itself with the strictly essential and above all useful subdivisions. Figure 8 gives a plausible and attainable example of differentiation of costs, classified by type, to cost categories, and gives an idea of the accounting procedure of the basic calculation. This is elaborated further in Table 12.

Primarily, costs are subdivided in function of imputability to periods; next, the costs are subdivided according to outlay character, while the direct period costs are subdivided further in function of cost variability. It is obvious that this order is not unique but may vary from firm to firm. Also, the measure of detailing

Figure 8

SCHEDULE 1.

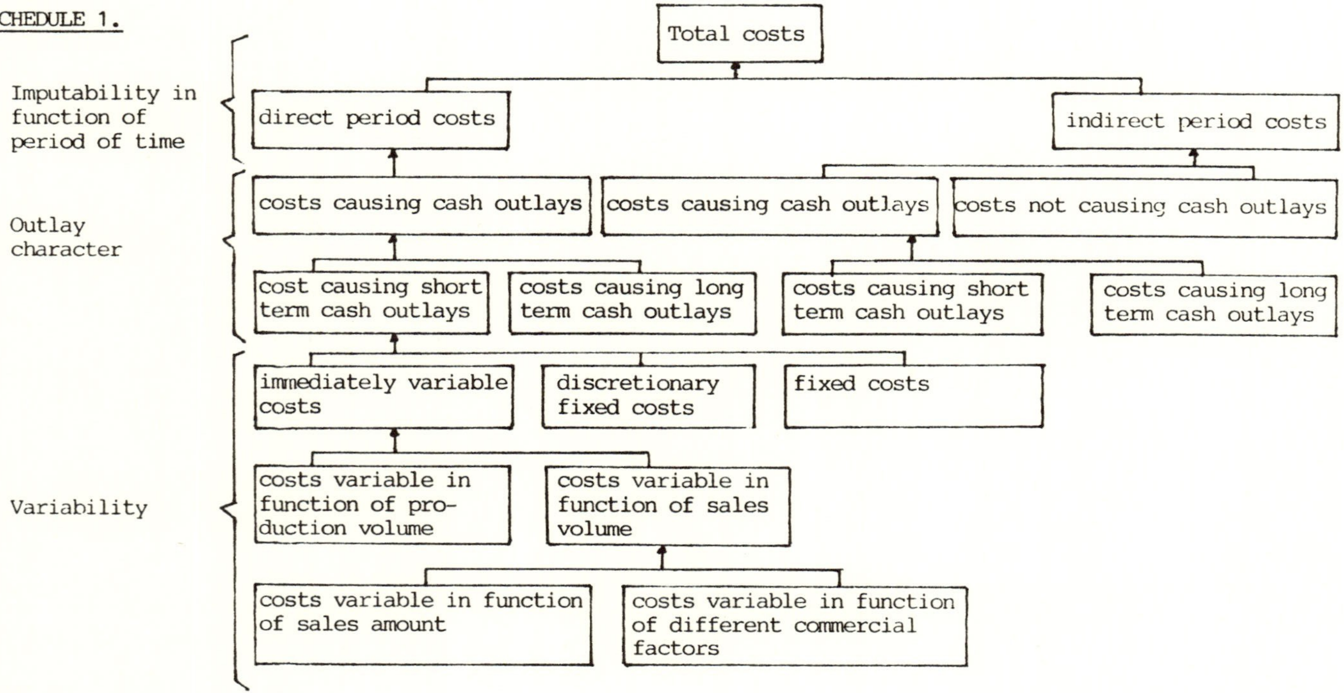

Imputability in function of period of time
Outlay character
Variability
Total costs
direct period costs
indirect period costs
costs causing cash outlays
costs causing cash outlays
costs not causing cash outlays
cost causing short term cash outlays
costs causing long term cash outlays
costs causing short term cash outlays
costs causing long term cash outlays
immediately variable costs
discretionary fixed costs
fixed costs
costs variable in function of production volume
costs variable in function of sales volume
costs variable in function of sales amount
costs variable in function of different commercial factors

Table 12

SCHEDULE II : MODEL OF BASIC CALCULATION

COSTS CLASSIFIED BY TYPE SUBDIVIDED IN COST CATEGORIES / COST CENTERS AND COST UNITS	COST CENTERS				COSTS UNITS			Total
	Service Centers	Overhead Centers	Autonomous Centers	Manufacturing Centers	A	B	C	
I. Direct Period Costs.								
A. Costs variable in function of sales volume								
a. costs variable in function of sales amount								
b. costs variable in function of different commercial factors								
B. Costs variable in function of production volume.								
C. Promptly variable costs								
D. Costs varying after a certain course of time								
E. Fixed costs								
F. Costs causing short term cash outlays								
G. Costs causing long term cash outlays								
H. Costs causing cash outlays								
I. Direct period costs	$\Sigma 1$	$\Sigma 1$	$\Sigma 1$	$\Sigma 1$	$\Sigma 1$	$\Sigma 1$	$\Sigma 1$	$\Sigma 1$
II. Indirect Period Costs								
A. Costs causing short term cash outlays								
B. Costs causing long term cash outlays								
C. Costs causing cash outlays								
D. Costs not causing cash outlays								
E. Indirect period costs	$\Sigma 2$	$\Sigma 2$	$\Sigma 2$	$\Sigma 2$	$\Sigma 2$	$\Sigma 2$	$\Sigma 2$	$\Sigma 2$
Total costs	$\Sigma 1 + \Sigma 2$	$\Sigma 1 + \Sigma 2$	$\Sigma 1 + \Sigma 2$	$\Sigma 1 + \Sigma 2$	$\Sigma 1 + \Sigma 2$	$\Sigma 1 + \Sigma 2$	$\Sigma 1 + \Sigma 2$	$\Sigma 1 + \Sigma 2$

should be determined deliberately. Again, the structure of business and the most important objectives of cost calculation shall be decisive.

About 2. Next to the choice of the cost categories, an option should be taken with respect to the units of reference to which the costs, classified by type, should be assigned. Again, the business structure and the objectives of the calculation are the relevant criteria.

Two groups of units of reference are essential, namely, units of reference in the domain of production and in the sphere of sales. Production-oriented units of reference consist of cost centers and cost units. The sales-oriented units of reference may be numerous and should especially be in function of the most important marketing-oriented objectives of calculation. In this context units of reference being much in evidence are customer groups, channels of distribution, and sales area. The units of reference can be grouped in function of an existing hierarchy of responsibility centers. This will especially happen when management control is the primary objective of cost accounting.

For planning and decision-making purposes the hierarchy of units of reference is especially built up in function of the flow of production and marketing achievements. This is rather easy when the manufacturing and marketing (sales) departments concerned with a particular product or product group are clearly differentiated from product (group) to product (group). The conception of a hierarchy of units of reference is more complex when production departments and marketing (sales) departments are intertwined (e.g., joint products).

The more complex the business organization, the more hierarchies of units of reference can and possibly will have to be built up. In such event it is essential to choose the adequate units of reference and their hierarchy correctly. This will vary from decision to decision. However, this problem may be relatively easy to solve because it concerns classifying in a different way the figures available from the basic calculation.[2] Figure 9 may illustrate this. In Figure 9 P_a, P_b, and P_c represent manufacturing centers; S_a and S_b are sales departments; ah 1, ah 2, bh 1, bh 2 are purchased, directly salable articles while a_1, a_2, a_3, b_1, and b_2 are self-manufactured products.

In this rather simple example the hierarchy of units of reference can be built in two ways; a) with primarily the sales relationship in mind and then the production process b) with first the production process in mind and next the sales relationship (see Figure 10). From this a hierarchy of units of reference can be gathered, as shown in Figure 11.

The hierarchy of assigning costs follows very conscientiously the flow of production and marketing performances, except manufacturing center P_c and general manufacturing and marketing management. In this structure, primarily oriented to sales relationship, the manufacturing center P_c and the general manufacturing management are working for both product groups and at the same time also for both selling groups. Consequently, the relative costs are not assignable directly and therefore are incorporated into the top level of our hierarchy, which is besides the most general level (see Figure 12).

Figure 9

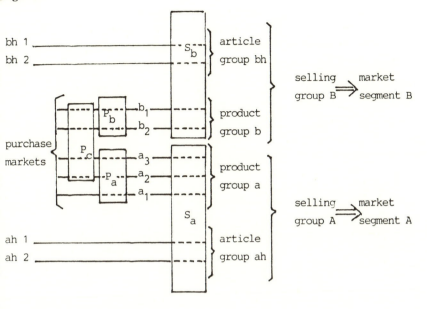

From version 1 as well as from version 2 a hierarchy of units of reference can be distilled. By way of example version 2 is worked out further (Figure 13).

In this case, the costs of department P_c are assignable. The ultimate choice of the system is mainly determined by the objectives of cost calculation. Also, the extent to which the costs are measurable, which, among others, depends on the firm's structure, is influencing the degree to which costs can be differentiated. Another aspect is that each unit of reference connected with sales revenue offers the opportunity to calculate specific relevant contributions.

Below, we examine how the basic calculation should be built up and which requirements it should meet in view of pricing decisions.

16.2 INFORMATION OUTPUT OF A PRICING POLICY– ORIENTED ACA SYSTEM

16.2.1 General Remarks

Above, the fundamentals of the basic calculation underlying ACA have been discussed. How these considerations should be adapted for pricing purposes will

Figure 10

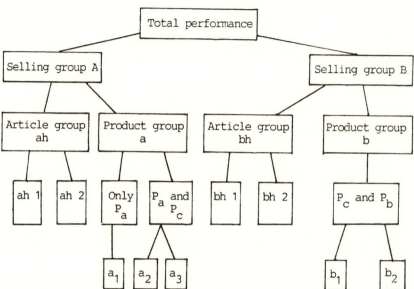

be examined farther on. The following problem may be stated: How should the ACA system be conceived in order to provide adequate information for pricing purposes?[3]

Part II shows that in view of pricing decisions the following cost information is or may be relevant:

—total period costs

—direct product costs

—indirect product costs

—cost variability in function of sales volume

—avoidable costs

—outlay character of costs

—various cost determinants

Part III pointed out that the classical full costing and partial costing methods are not able to furnish simultaneously these cost data.

Figure 11

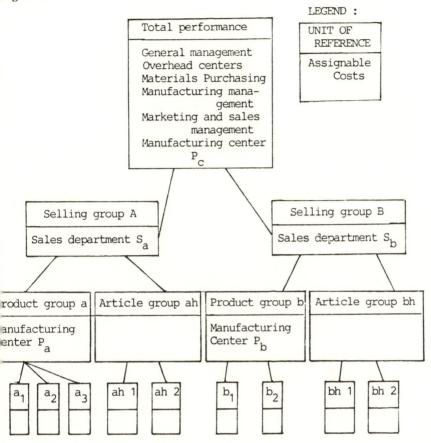

Below, a calculation method by which the needs of cost information for pricing purposes are met will be elucidated and worked out. To that end, the cost elements mentioned above will be discussed further.

16.2.2 Total Period Costs

In view of business continuity and in this way fitting in our "going concern" vision, all costs chargeable to a definite period of time should be recovered in the same period. However, the determination of that cost amount is not so simple (see Part II, section 6.8). Some types of costs may be assigned unequivocally to a definite space of time (e.g. month, quarter, semester, year). Examples are raw materials costs, salaries, and costs of consumption of current.

Other types of costs cannot be assigned unambiguously to a period because

Figure 12

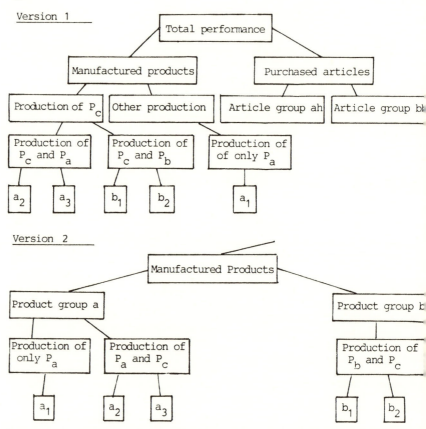

these cost amounts depend on uncertain anticipations and insights into the future. Especially, those costs that are paid once only but influence several periods are difficult in this respect. Examples are costs of brevets and licences and startup expenses. In the classical full costing method these cost elements are incorporated in the cost rather arbitrarily. What amount should be taken into consideration as "period cost" depends on managerial judgment of the future and readiness to take risks. A vivid example of this kind of reasoning can be found when fixing allowances for doubtful accounts. So, it seems that the total period costs can only partially be fixed exactly, while the allocation of the other part is based on more or less uncertain anticipations. Consequently, the distinction between direct and indirect period costs will be very important for pricing purposes.

Direct period costs are the first consideration: they are known unequivocally and normally (marketing considerations may be a reason for deviation) should be recovered in the same period. What amount of indirect period costs should be recovered in a certain period is a matter of judgment. For pricing purposes "planned cover margins," which may have the character of depreciation or

Figure 13

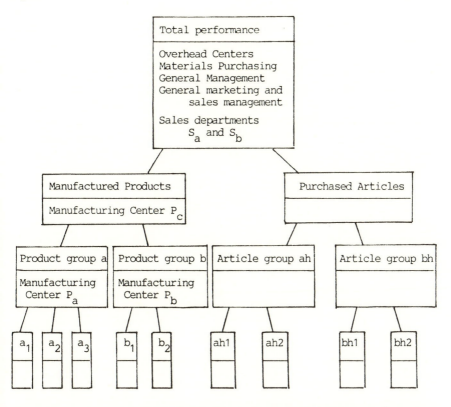

provision amounts and which specify the amount of indirect period costs that are planned to be recovered in the next period, are determined.

This cover margin is not fixed arbitrarily as is the case in traditional full costing but is the result of a well-considered management decision. Such procedure may take into consideration more flexible market characteristics, marketing policies, and, if necessary, compensation of the amount to be recovered among the successive periods.

16.2.3 Direct Product Costs

Normally, the selling price is set per unit of product. Consequently, the cost unit of a cost accounting system conceived for pricing purposes should be the product unit. The most important question will be: What amount of costs is directly caused by a unit of product? So the question of direct product costs is the concern. It has already been said that from the selling price at least the direct product costs should be recovered (see Part II, section 6.8).

16.2.4 Indirect Product Costs

Next to its direct costs, each particular product normally should contribute to recovery of indirect product costs (see Part II, section 6.8). In our opinion, a weak point of partial costing is that the indirect costs are put in bulk against direct product costs. Starting from the relativity of the distinction between direct and indirect costs, we think it may be necessary to differentiate further this bulk of indirect costs without making use of any arbitrary activity unit. This will improve the insight into the structure of indirect costs and consequently will simplify their recovery. The method to realize this is the already-discussed assignment of costs to a hierarchy of units of reference (see section 16.1 and also Part II, section 6.8).

For pricing purposes, the following hierarchy is essential:

—total production

—segment of production

—product group

—product

In accordance with this hierarchy of units of reference the following scheme can be deduced:

1. direct product costs,

2. planned cover margin in order to recover the direct costs of the product group,

3. planned cover margin in order to recover the direct costs of a segment of production, and

4. planned cover margin in order to recover the direct costs of the total production (i.e., undivided balance of indirect product costs) and in order to realize profits.

This scheme suggests several price floor levels. In the long run total costs have to be recovered but for short-term pricing decisions this scheme allows the serious consideration of market and marketing elements as well as the "ability to bear" of the different products.

16.2.5 Cost Variability in Function of Sales Volume

The relative character of the distinction between fixed and variable costs has already been mentioned. For pricing purposes, variability in function of sales volume is more relevant than cost variability in function of production volume. Consequently, pricing policy–oriented cost accounting should point out the former kind of cost variability.

16.2.6 Avoidable Costs

When a business is shut down, entirely or partially, definitively or temporarily, a part of capacity costs (indirect product costs) are omitted. With a view to the determination of price floors and the recovery of costs the portion of the costs being left out in relation to total capacity costs should be reported (see Part II, section 7.3).

16.2.7 Outlay Character of Costs

The problem of price floors can also be studied from a financial (liquidity) point of view. Consequently, pricing policy implies knowledge of costs in function of their outlay character. In this connection the following classification is important:

—costs directly involving cash outlays

—costs involving cash outlays in another period of time than the period in which they are incurred, and

—costs involving no cash outlays.

This classification was already discussed in Part II, sections 6.1 and 7.4.

16.2.8 Various Cost Determinants

For pricing purposes a thorough knowledge of certain cost determinants is important. Therefore, cost accounting should meet the need for deeper insight into certain relevant cost determinants. This information will be especially important with a view to price differentiation, particularly in the case of cost-oriented price differentiation.

Above, we stressed imputability and outlay character of costs. In this section cost differences will be highlighted.

For example, how much is the cost difference of two or more products from the same product group? What are the reasons of this cost difference? These cost differences possible may lead to differences in selling price, so that we get in the sphere of price differentiation.

It has already been pointed out that price differentiation (including product line pricing) is for the greater part determined by market considerations. However, also in this case cost information remains important, for example, to answer the question of the most favorable product or order in relation to the cost differences or the question of the extent of price differences in relation to cost differences (see also Part II, Chapter 8).

16.3 DESIGN OF A PRICING POLICY–ORIENTED ACA SYSTEM

Above, the desirable informational output of a pricing policy–oriented ACA system has been discussed. Below, a related aspect will be examined, namely, the diverse aspects modeling cost accounting so that it would be able to provide the required information for pricing purposes in the most adequate way. In this connection, a number of fundamental options should be taken.

16.3.1 Cost Dimensions

Cost accounting should make available the bases for setting actual and future selling prices. These selling prices should not only safeguard the financial and material survival of the business but should also be in conformity with market circumstances.[4] Therefore an adequate, deliberate choice of value and quantity dimensions of costs is important. The modalities relating to this have already been discussed in Part II, section 5.2. In the framework of ACA the options taken in this chapter remain so that we can refer to that part of our book.

16.3.2 Objectives of the Cost Accounting System

The objectives of cost accounting have already been discussed in Part II, section 5.1. A technical problem originating from that is how the costing system should be conceived in order to contribute simultaneously to the attainment of the diverse objectives of cost accounting.

What requirements cost accounting is supposed to meet for pricing purposes has already been pointed out. Actually, cost accounting should also meet any other objectives so that the next question is evident: In a multipurpose cost accounting system, which are the points of difference and which are the common points with respect to the diverse objectives of it?

The objectives of cost accounting have already been grouped in three series, namely:

a. determination of operating results and financial position,

b. control of cost and efficiency, and

c. basis for decision making.

About a. The principal characteristic of cost accounting, seen in the context of determination of operating results and financial position, is that it is to a greater or lesser extent regulated. As the method of determination of results and financial position may have consequences extending outside the firm (dividend, tax assessment, statistics), in a number of countries compulsory or recommended uniform costing procedures are in use.

The design of such chart of accounts corresponds with the current accounting principles of the country in question and consequently is rather formalized insofar as design, choice of cost dimensions, and definition of the cost concept are concerned. Generally, such a chart of accounts applies to a minimal obligatory costing method that may additionally be changed in function of the firm's characteristics and needs. Therefore, the difference with a pricing policy–oriented cost accounting procedure is that the latter is perfectly free and in function of the firm's pricing policy needs, while a financial statements–oriented cost-accounting is for the greater part regulated both in structure and in operation.

About b. The most substantial distinction between pricing policy–oriented cost accounting and control–oriented cost accounting lies in the costing object. For pricing purposes the cost unit may be the product unit, product group, or order. For control purposes, organizational units or processes are the typical cost units (e.g., production department or production process). A second difference has to do with the external business orientation (i.e., market orientation) of pricing–oriented cost accounting. Control–oriented cost accounting has an internal business scope. A third difference has to do with the cost amount that should be considered. In view of recovering costs, pricing policy–oriented cost accounting normally should take total costs into consideration, while for control purposes only controllable costs should be considered.

About c. Characteristic of many business decisions is the question of additional or canceled costs. It is equally important to have at your disposal information about the outlay character of costs. Information about the product's contribution to the recovering of indirect costs may be relevant.

As seems from the above, the requirements posed to cost accounting are very divergent. As a tool that should be adapted to the use that will be made of it, cost accounting should be conceived in such a way as to answer the above objectives simultaneously. Opposite to that can be said that the more cost accounting is designed universally, the less it will be adapted to provide relevant cost information for specific purposes. This does not mean, however, that for each objective a special calculation is required, not even when the frequency of the decision in question is high. A substantial part of the cost information relevant for a variety of cost accounting objectives is overlapping so that here the basis will have to be found for what we have been calling the "basic calculation". Consequently, it is appropriate to start from such a basic calculation and next to it, to design separate calculations, not based on books, providing information for specific less-frequent decisions.

The basic calculation is a continuous calculation in which those elements that are essential for all or at least the most important or most frequent cost accounting objectives, are incorporated. So it forms the basis of the separate cost calculations, conceived in function of specific decision making. In the basic calculation a primary registration takes place by which the costs, classified by type, are assigned to an appropriate structure of units of reference (products, product groups, cost centers). Thus, the basic calculation proves a polyvalent whole of cost data, applicable for a multitude of divergent objectives by means of the above-mentioned separate specific calculation. The measure to which the basic calculation should be attuned to specific pricing policy–oriented calculations (ACA) largely depends upon the comparative importance of pricing policy.

It is obvious that this adaptation needs to be very rigorous if the firm is a so-called price taker, if market prices are unassailable data, or if the frequency of price setting is very low. On the contrary, in case of "price making," especially if the frequency of price setting is high or also in case of selling individualized products, the connection of the basic calculation to specific pricing-oriented calculations should be closer. In this case the basic calculation should be designed as product and/or order oriented.

16.3.3 Required Correctness and Accuracy of the System

The notion "correctness" can be defined unequivocally: something is right or wrong. Cost accounting can be labeled as correct if the cost amounts pointed out completely correspond with the actual causal and objective-consequence relationships. By accuracy is understood the measure of approximation of a certain quantity. Somebody's age can be expressed in terms of years, months, days, hours, minutes, seconds. Naturally, the age only expressed in years is adequate for most purposes. So when we say that Mr. X is 45 years old, then our assertion indeed is correct but inaccurate. Below, we will examine which requirements on the subject of correctness and accuracy should be posed to pricing-oriented cost accounting.

Above, the causes of incorrect cost calculation have been repeatedly pointed out. Incorrect cost accounting originates from errors against logic, for example, proportioning fixed costs and allocating indirect costs by means of arbitrary activity ratios. Yet the influence of correctness of cost information is substantial for decision-making purposes in general and especially for pricing purposes.

Inaccurate cost information may be caused by diverse reasons. The pursuit of more accuracy should at least be compensated by the greater utility of the cost data involved. Insofar as cost accounting is concerned, the following kinds of inaccuracy can be distinguished:[5]

1. unavoidable inaccuracies
   —because of impossibility of quantity determination of certain cost factors
   —because of impossibility of valuation of certain cost factors
2. avoidable inaccuracies
   —consciously accepted inaccuracies leaning on economic considerations:
      desist from accurate quantity registration
      desist from accurate valuation
      desist from correct cost allocation
   —human errors, committed consciously or not, in the sphere of cost registration and cost allocation.

Although cost information for pricing purposes should be correct, a certain measure of inaccuracy need not have weighty consequences. The question of accurate cost accounting is a matter of proportions and possibilities. The most perfect cost calculation is not the one with the greatest accuracy but the one with an economically limited accuracy.[6]

The advantages of greater accuracy should be compared to the additional costs caused by it. As the significance of cost information for pricing purposes increases, the advantages of greater accuracy will become more important. The requirements of accuracy of cost information shall have to be leveled up in case of active pricing policy and when the market price is near the cost-based price floor.[7]

In general it can be said that in difficult periods the accuracy of cost accounting should be greater than in prosperous times. As a rule, this does not hold for all cost factors but only for the relevant costs, namely, those that have to do with a critical situation. For example, in case of liquidity disturbances, the classification of costs according to outlay character shall have to be paid attention to closely.

The pursuit of accuracy in cost accounting may not degenerate into "seeming accuracy." Among other things, this is found when the full cost is calculated to several decimal places while certain components of cost are only known approximately or while the costing system shows structural defects.

16.3.4 Quickness and Flexibility of the System

Quickness and flexibility are not synonymous. For example, the costing process may be able to provide very quickly all kinds of relevant cost data but still remain rigid and immobile.

In the first place, pricing policy requires cost accounting to be flexible, that is, to have the ability to adapt easily to changing problems and situations. The measure of adaptability required depends on the significance of cost accounting for pricing decisions. Quick and flexible cost information is less important in the case of selling prices yielding ample profits. On the contrary, in the case of active cost-oriented pricing policy or when profit margins are rather scanty, quick and flexible cost reporting is required.

Also, the kind of selling price plays a part. In case of individualized pricing (e.g., piece work) quick and flexible cost accounting is a must. When selling prices are set for a long period (e.g., branded mass products), then quickness and flexibility are less essential than accuracy and correct estimation of future evolutions.

Also, market structures play a role: in the case of frequent price changes at purchase markets, cost calculation should be able to adapt quickly. The same applies to sales: where a steady price policy prevails, quickness and flexibility of cost information are less urgent than where a rather precarious price policy exists.

16.3.5 Appropriate Classification and Registration of Costs

16.3.5.1 Classification and Registration of Costs According to Their Nature

As a rule, all costs incurred are incorporated in the costing process through a classification of costs by type. This primary recording of costs has been discussed sufficiently above so that we can confine ourselves to the pricing implications. For pricing purposes an extreme differentiation of costs, classified by type, is recommended and even required. Normally, far-reaching analysis of costs, classified by type, does not cause substantial additional costs, especially not when these additional costs are connected with the additional information that can be gathered from a strongly differentiated costing system. Moreover, advanced analysis of costs classified by type has the advantage that "pure" types of costs are available. This means that the content of each type of cost is fixed unequivocally. The more costs are analysed, the more pure they become regarding content. It is obvious that the impact of cost information is thus increased significantly.

16.3.5.2 Classification and Registration of Costs According to Particular Characteristics

As a rule, the classical allocation of costs, starting from costs classified by type to cost centers and finally to cost units is insufficient for pricing purposes. The analysis of costs to certain particular characteristics may increase strongly the exploratory significance of cost accounting. So the same cost amount should be assigned to more particular characteristics, for example:

1. Starting from the payroll, the periodical wages and salaries should be recorded not only on the relevant cost account (classified by type) but also as:
   —variable or fixed production cost
   —incurred in cost center A
   —for product X, and that
   —have a short-term character.
2. Consumable supplies (e.g., fuel, lubricating and cleaning materials) may be recorded:
   —on the cost center account of the department in which they are consumed,
   —in function of variability with production volume, or
   —in function of outlay character.
3. Depreciation of a "single purpose machine" may be recorded:
   —on the relevant cost account (classified by type),
   —as direct product cost of product X,
   —fixed cost in function of production volume, or
   —noncash cost.

From these examples it appears that the mere classification of costs by type is insufficient and that for pricing and other decision-making purposes registration to other characteristics is highly desirable. For pricing purposes the most essential characteristics are:

—certain units of reference,

—certain cost determinants, and

—cash character of costs.

16.3.5.2.1 According to Specified Units of Reference   Units of reference are units to which costs classified by type may be assigned directly. These units of reference may be products, product groups, departments, orders, customers or customer groups, sales area, and many others.

It has already been pointed out that for pricing purposes product-oriented units of reference are most appropriate. It has also been mentioned that costs should be assigned to the lowest possible level of the hierarchy, at which they still can be considered as direct costs. As a rule, this assignment does not make any special problem. However, it may happen that the used method of assignment is getting complex and detailed. Our principles about accuracy in mind, the assignment of certain negligible cost elements can be abandoned. The latter cost elements can be treated then as indirect costs.

In the scope of a product-oriented hierarchy of units of reference, for example, in the case of parallel or alternative production, costs of material consumption can be assigned to each particular product, costs of machines and tools can be assigned to particular kinds of products, costs of production planning are direct in relation to product groups, and so on. In view of this, insight into the conduct of manufacturing processes is necessary.

In order to know, for example, variable direct product costs, there are two possible ways. One can start from the product unit and try to determine the volume of material consumption, labor time, and so forth used for this unit of product. In the case of similar products one can calculate the total variable direct product cost of a period and divide this amount by the number of units produced in the same period. Sometimes specific orders or orders classified by size/class may be relevant units of reference for pricing purposes. This arises, for example, if selling prices are differentiated in function of size of order. In this case, the costs directly assignable to orders or size/class of orders should be highlighted. For other kinds of price differentiation direct cost information about sales areas, customer groups, and channels of distribution may be relevant. For pricing purposes cost information about departments (i.e., cost centers) is only of secondary significance, namely, insofar as this cost classification is an intermediary in order to permit assignment of costs to product groups. So the costs of a manufacturing department are directly assignable with respect to the total production volume of this department.[8]

16.3.5.2.2 According to Certain Cost Determinants   Traditionally, cost variability is always seen in function of the activity ratio and distinction is made between fixed and variable costs. The relativity of this cost distinction has already been pointed out.

As the cost accounting system in question is attuned to pricing decisions and consequently is product oriented, we can confine ourselves to express the activity ratio in terms of periodic production volume. In this respect, a more or less substantial part of costs do not cause any problem. They change proportionally with production volume (cf. raw materials) or remain constant irrespective of production volume (e.g., plant depreciation). In order to determine the measure of cost variability, for many types of costs the period of time considered plays an important role. For pricing purposes, the period of time taken as basis should be dependent on the frequency of price setting. When selling prices are set for a comparatively short period of time, many types of costs, variable in the long run, should be considered as fixed in relation to the production volume. Many types of costs, however, are semivariable, that is, costs remaining partly fixed within a period but in part varying with the volume of activity. By means of technical and/or statistical analysis (e.g., high point, low point method; method of least squares) these costs should be split up into their fixed and variable components.

In this connection, wages and salaries are particularly problematic. Generally, they are labeled as variable costs. As a matter of fact, as one frequently desires to express wages and salaries as a fixed amount per unit of product, the above statement is self-evident. It should be pointed out, however, that wages and salaries may show certain characteristics of fixed costs. When the activity ratio is decreasing, the number of employees cannot be reduced immediately and simply (among others, because of legal regulations). In such cases the sum of wages and salaries remains almost stable irrespective of the smaller production volume. This arises in full in case of time-based wages and salaries.

Frequently, the actual amount of wages and salaries are dependent on the expected production volume rather than on actual production volume. This happens when the potential of personnel is actually increased in view of an expected volume of activity. The relative costs of personnel are ''capacity costs'' so that it would not be meaningful to assign them directly to units of product. Consequently, there is a relationship between assignability and variability of these costs: if wages and salaries are varying in proportion to production volume, then the cost amount caused by a particular unit of product and thus assignable to it is known. If wages and salaries have the character of ''capacity costs,'' there is no causal relationship between unit of product and wages and salaries. In this case wages and salaries are joint costs and consequently should be considered as indirect product costs.

Finally, it should be pointed that many types of costs are only fixed within a certain range of activity ratios (the so-called relevant range). This is a question of ''step costs.''[9] For pricing purposes it is essential to know from what level of production the phenomenon of step costs is arising. For example, the price floors set are only valid within the relevant range. Out of this range other price floors should be premised. *Mutatis mutandis*, all above considerations remain in force insofar as cost variability in function of sales volume is concerned. Also, order quantity (or other elements) can play a decisive role in cost variability and thus be meaningful for price differentiation in function of size of order (or other elements).

16.3.5.2.3 According to liquidity character   The problem of splitting up costs according to their outlay character is especially a matter of subdividing costs, classified by type. For example, costs classified by type may be subdivided into:

—costs with short-term outlay character,

—costs with long-term outlay character, and

—noncash costs.

Certain costs (e.g., wages and salaries) are always out-of-pocket costs; other costs correspond with outlays in the past (e.g., depreciation) or with future outlays (e.g., substantial maintenance). Other costs do not cause cash outlays (e.g., interest on capital invested). This classification of costs may be especially important for the purpose of setting liquidity-oriented price floors (see also Part II, section 7.4).

17 Pricing Policy–Oriented Calculation Models

From the preceding chapters it will be clear that there can be no question of the ACA system. In each kind of firm another cost accounting structure will be required (e.g., the cost accounting structure will be different for a mass production business versus a piecework business). Consequently, the buildup of the ACA system for pricing purposes will be discussed for a number of business types,[1] including:

—the single product firm,

—the firm with alternating production, and

—the firm with joint production.

17.1 BUILDUP AND USE OF A CALCULATION MODEL IN A SINGLE PRODUCT FIRM

In the single product firm the relations are simple so that all costs can be directly assigned to the product in question. Problems may arise when the measure of cost variability in function of production or sales volume is different.

17.1.1 Description of the Example

We are starting with a business that, on the basis of raw materials A and B, is manufacturing in mass product Y. This firm can further be characterized as follows:

Table 13

Raw material A	$ 65,810
Raw material B	$ 32,175
Transport costs for raw materials	$ 8,775
Wages	$ 28,125
Salaries	$ 12,000
Costs of power supply	$ 29,250
Depreciation of machines	$ 27,500
Depreciation of business premises	$ 3,750
Repair and maintenance of machines	$ 7,310
Calculational interest (9 % at capital employed)	$ 24,860
Consumable supplies and sundries	$ 8,750
Total costs	$ 248,305

—The machinery has an economic working life of 10 years, irrespective of the activity ratio.

—The maintenance and repair expenses of this machinery is independent of activity ratio.

—For the business premises an economic working life of 50 years is taken into consideration.

—The firm puts to work 8 employees: 2 foremen, 3 salesmen, and 3 clerks. They earn a fixed salary and also have regular employment.

—Twenty-five workers are employed: 17 are unskilled and do production work. This group of workers can be layed off and hired again in function of activity ratio. Eight workers are employed as chauffeur, packer, warehouseman, maintenance mechanic, and so on. This group cannot be layed off in case of declining activity ratio.

At a monthly production volume of 4,000 units of Y, the costs incurred are shown in Table 13.

This cost indicates the long-term price floor. It includes, however, very heterogeneous cost elements: fixed and variable costs, costs with or without outlay character. The significance of this average full cost is limited and only serves as point of support in order to set a cost-recovering selling price. For the rest it is unsuited for other pricing purposes. These purposes may be in the sphere of liquidity control (liquidity-oriented price floor), price changes in function of fluctuations in the activity ratio, and so forth.

17.1.2 Division in Cost Categories

Based on the above, the total costs can be divided in function of the measure of variability as follows:

—*variable costs*: costs of raw materials A and B as well as transport costs for raw materials.

—*fixed costs*: salaries, depreciations of machines and business premises, costs of machine repair and maintenance, calculational interest, and finally, consumable supplies and sundries.

—*semivariable costs*: wages and costs of power supply.

Analysis of the wages points out that $18,750 can be labeled as variable cost. The balance ($9,375) is pure time wage and consequently a fixed cost. Insofar as the costs of power supply are concerned, one part has to do with heating and lighting. This part is fixed and amounts to $8,770. The balance are energy costs of the production process itself and consequently variable with production volume. It amounts to $20,480.

Analysis of the total costs according to outlay character leads to the following division:

—*costs involving current outlays*: costs of raw materials A and B, transport costs for raw materials, wages, salaries, costs of power supply, repair and maintenance of machines, and, finally, consumable supplies and sundries.

—*costs not involving outlays*: depreciation of machines and business premises.

The calculational interest consists partially of cash outlays (interest paid for the use of borrowed money). The balance relates to interest of proprietors' equity and consequently does not involve cash outlays. It is assumed that 9% has to be paid for the use of all external liabilities ($160,000), that is, $14,400. The balance of $10,460 does not involve cash outlays. The above division in cost categories can be reflected in Table 14.

17.1.3 Use of These Cost Data for Pricing Purposes

It is obvious that the above cost chart has a greater informative significance for pricing and other decision-making purposes than the initial cost chart. Almost without complications, several price floors can be calculated from it.

With a production volume of 4,000 units, the variable costs amount to $145,990, that is, $36.5 per unit. This is the "absolute" price floor. In case of subnormal capacity usage this is at the same time the price floor for additional orders. This minimum selling price can only be operative if sufficient liquidity reserves are available in order to recover the fixed costs involving current outlays. If not, this part of the costs (i.e., sum II-A) should be recovered from current

Table 14

I. Variable costs (involving current cash outlays) :		
Costs of raw material A	$ 65,810	
Costs of raw material B	$ 32,175	
Transport costs for raw materials	$ 8,775	
Part of wages	$ 18,750	
Part of costs of power supply	$ 20,480	
Total I		$ 145,990
II. Fixed costs :		
A. Involving current cash outlays :		
Part of wages	$ 9,375	
Salaries	$ 12,000	
Part of costs of power supply	$ 8,770	
Repair and maintenance of machines	$ 7,310	
Interest external liabilities	$ 14,400	
Consumable supplies and sundries	$ 8,750	
Total A	$ 60,605	
B. Not involving cash outlays :		
Depreciation of machines	$ 27,500	
Depreciation of business premises	$ 3,750	
Interest proprietors' equity	$ 10,460	
Total B	$ 41,710	
Total II		$ 102,315
Total costs		$ 248,305

sales. This part of the costs amounts to $60,605 or, on the basis of 4,000 units of Y, $15.15 per unit. Consequently, the liquidity-oriented price floor amounts to $36.5 + $15.15 = $51.65.

The above scheme permits the determination of the average full cost at several production volumes. At a production volume of 3,000 units the average full cost amounts to:

$$\$36.5 + \frac{\$102,315}{3,000 \text{ units}} = \$70.60$$

Given that a price increase from $80 to $100 is considered and that one is estimating that this would be attended by a sales decrease from 4,000 units to 3,000 units, the distinction between fixed and variable costs offers sound judgment. With the help of the analytical cost chart the following computation can be made:

Contribution in case of alternative 1 ($80):

$$(\$80 - \$36.5) \times 4,000 \text{ units} = \$174,000$$

Contribution in case of alternative 2 ($100):

$$(\$100 - \$36.5) \times 3,000 \text{ units} = \$190,500$$

A price increase to $100 does increase the contribution with $16,500. Consequently, from a business economic point of view, alternative 2 should be chosen.

When a maximum activity ratio is the aim, the question may be asked which price concession (with respect to the actual price of $80) would promote this goal. When a producing capacity of 4,500 units is supposed, the following computation can be made:

$$(P - \$36.5) \times 4,500 \text{ units} = (\$80 - \$36.5) \times 4,000 \text{ units}$$

$$P = \$36.5 + \frac{\$43.5 \times 4,000 \text{ units}}{4,500 \text{ units}}$$

$$P = \$36.5 + \$38.66 = \$75.16$$

An increase of production volume up to 4,500 units is only interesting if a minimum selling price of $75.16 can be obtained. In case of full capacity, the minimum selling price to be obtained in order to recover costs can be calculated as follows:

$$P = \$36.5 + \frac{\$102,315}{4,500 \text{ units}} = \$59.24$$

Supposing that long-term contracts of sale (monthly 2,500 units) at a fixed selling price of $70 are available, the minimum selling price of the remaining production can be calculated as follows:

2,500 units sold at $70 yield a contribution of:

$$2,500 \ (\$70 - \$36.50) = \$83,750$$

In the long run, the monthly cost amount to be recovered minimally is:

$$\$102,315 - \$83,750 = \$18,565$$

At full capacity, this amount should be earned by means of selling 4,500 units − 2,500 units = 2,000 units, that is,

$$\frac{\$18,565}{2,000 \text{ units}} = \$9.28 \text{ per unit.}$$

Consequently, the price floor of the remaining sales should be:

$$\$36.5 + \$9.28 = \$45.78$$

If only 1,000 units can be sold additionally each month, the minimum selling price should be:

$$\$36.5 + \$18.56 = \$55.06$$

Because of weak market circumstances, it may occur that the total costs are not recovered. Suppose that 1,500 units can be sold at $60 and that 1,000 units can be sold monthly at $54. For the latter orders, however, the firm has to bear the transport costs to the amount of $5,800. It is also assumed that no liquidity reserves are available. In this situation, in addition to the variable costs the fixed costs involving current cash outlays ($60,605) should be recovered. The first group of orders (1,500 units) yield a unit contribution of $60 − $36.5 = $23.5 or $35,250 in all.

The second category of orders causes the following additional costs:

1,000 units × $ 36.5   = $ 36,500 (variable production costs)

                                 + $ 5,800 (transport costs)

                                     $ 42,300

The sales revenue amounts to: 1,000 units × $54 = $54,000, so that a contribution of $11,700 is made to the fixed costs involving current cash outlays. So, from $60,605 to be recovered monthly, $35,250 + $11,700 = $46,950 actually is recovered. Nat-

Table 15

MONTH	SALES VO-LUME (UNITS)	PRODUC-TION VO-LUME (UNITS)	INVEN-TORY (UNITS)	NEW SALES VOLUME (UNITS)	NEW INVEN-TORY (UNITS)
January	1,700	4,500	2,800	1,700	2,800
February	2,400	4,500	4,900	2,400	4,900
March	2,800	4,500	6,600	2,800	6,600
April	4,000	4,500	7,100	8,000	3,100
May	5,300	4,500	6,300	5,000	2,600
June	7,200	4,500	3,600	5,500	1,600
July	7,000	4,500	1,100	5,000	1,100
August	4,800	4,500	800	4,800	800
September	4,700	4,500	600	4,700	600
October	3,400	3,800	1,000	3,400	1,000
November	3,000	2,500	500	3,000	500
December	3,000	2,500	–	3,000	–
TOTAL	49,300	49,300		49,300	

urally, this is insufficient. Only by means of granting larger credits, price increases, and increases of sales volumes can this situation be remedied. Even rolling off transport costs on the customers is insufficient to straighten out the tight liquidity position.

We could also suppose that our model firm is characterized by seasonal sales. This leads to the situation depicted in Table 15.

In the peak season, monthly sales exceed the producing capacity of 4,500 units. The adjustment of production volume to sales volume is realized by inventory building. Next to the interest expense there is an additional cost of $0.9 monthly. By means of price differentiation one can try to decrease the inventory. Market analysis shows that a special discount of 5% (selling price $70) in April is expected to cause a movement of a part of sales for the summer months to April. This movement is reported in the above table (see columns 5 and 6). Through comparison of column 6 and column 4, it can be seen that the inventory of April is 4,000 units lower, in May 3,700 units, and in June 2,000 units lower than the inventory without price differentiation (on the whole the inventory has decreased by 9,700 units). This means a saving in inventory expenses to the amount of 9,700 units x $0.9 = $8,730. The savings in interest expenses can be calculated as follows:

$$\text{Interest saving} = \begin{array}{l}\text{accelerated} \\ \text{sales volume}\end{array} \times \begin{array}{l}\text{differentiated} \\ \text{selling price}\end{array} \times \frac{\text{rate of interest}}{100} \times \frac{\text{number of months}}{12}$$

Comparison of column 2 with column 5 shows the accelerated sales volume:

July	2,000 units	3 months earlier
June	1,700 units	2 months earlier
May	300 units	1 month earlier

Consequently, the net saving of interest expenses is:

$$2,000 \text{ units} \times \$ \ 66.5 \times \frac{9}{100} \times \frac{3}{12} = \$ \ 2,992.5$$

$$1,700 \text{ units} \times \$ \ 66.5 \times \frac{9}{100} \times \frac{2}{12} = \$ \ 1,695.75$$

$$300 \text{ units} \times \$ \ 66.5 \times \frac{9}{100} \times \frac{1}{12} = \underline{\$ \ \ \ 149.62}$$

$$\$ \ 4,837.87$$

The total saving of costs amounts to:

$$\$ \ 8,730 + \$ \ 4,837.87 = \$ \ 13,567.87$$

On the other hand, there is a sales decrease of 8,000 units × $ 3.5 = $ 28,000. The conclusion is that allowing a special temporary discount of 5% does not pay.

With these examples we think we have shown how an adequate division of costs according to variability and cash outlay character may improve and facilitate price decision making.

17.2 BUILDUP AND USE OF A CALCULATION MODEL IN A FIRM WITH ALTERNATING PRODUCTION

17.2.1 Description of the Example

A furniture business is manufacturing seven kinds of products spread over three product groups, notably:

—two kinds of big furniture (A1 and A2),

—three kinds of small furniture (B1, B2, and B3), and

—two kinds of seating furniture (C1 and C2).

The following departments exist:

—manufacturing of components: the timber, being purchased in several sorts, is sawed and manufactured into components, destined for further assembly

—manufacturing of big furniture

—manufacturing of small furniture

—manufacturing of seating furniture

—finishing department: a number of finishing processes performed for all kinds of product are brought together here.

—accounting and management

—sales department

The products manufactured are standardized and are produced and sold in only one design.

The business structure shown in Figure 14 may be deduced.

Volumes that have been sold during the latest trading period are shown in Table 16.

Table 17 shows costs incurred during the same period. These costs can be specified as follows:

—Raw materials: are assignable to each kind of product and proportional to production volumes.

—Services: a part of these costs is fixed (e.g., insurance premiums, a part of energy expenses); the other part is proportional to production volumes.

—Wages: since the department ''Big Furniture'' is employing skilled and specialized labor, wages are fixed. In the department ''Small Furniture,'' mainly unskilled laborers are employed. Here, wages have to be looked upon as proportional to production volumes.

—Salaries are fixed costs.

—Commissions: sales are conducted by sales representatives. Their commission amounts to 4% of sales.

—Depreciation: linear.

—Miscellaneous costs: semivariable in respect of production volumes.

All costs, with the exception of depreciations, have short-term (i.e., immediate) cash outlay repercussions.

For pricing purposes the costing object is the cost unit. In this firm there are three levels: kind of product, product group, and total production. Raw material costs, wages, and the other variable costs are assignable to the kinds of product.

Figure 14

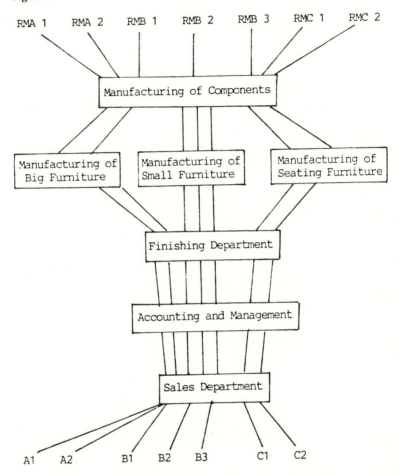

RMA 1 - RMC 2 : raw materials
A1 - A2 : big furniture
B1 - B2 - B3 : small furniture
C1 - C2 : seating furniture

Table 16

Kind of Product	Sales Volume
A1	375
A2	500
B1	1,500
B2	1,000
B3	1,750
C1	800
C2	1,500

Table 17

Type of cost	Amount
Raw materials	$ 350,000
Rendering of services	$ 105,000
Wages	$ 366,667
Salaries	$ 106,061
Commissions	$ 52,438
Depreciation of machines	$ 84,000
Depreciation of business premises	$ 7,000
Miscellaneous costs	$ 66,664
Total costs	$ 1,137,830

Fixed costs are not assignable to the level "kind of product" but insofar as they are incurred in departments being operative within a product group, they can be assigned to that product group. For example, the wages of the department "Big Furniture" are direct costs of the product group A. The commissions require special attention: this type of cost is independent of production volumes, yet depends on selling price and sales volume.

As ACA exactly intends to determine the basis of selling prices, the commissions form a disturbing factor. Therefore, they are excluded from the following calculation. Consequently, the selling prices determined in this manner are net prices, to which the commission should be added proportionally afterward.

On the basis of the principles discussed in the preceding chapter the following cost statements can be drawn up:

—a statement of costs, classified by type and cost units. The costs, classified by type, are subdivided in relevant cost categories. (See Table 18).

—a statement in function of costs units, on the basis of direct costs and subdivided in relevant cost categories. (See Table 19).

Table 18

COSTS CLASSIFIED BY TYPE AND CATEGORY (in $) / COST UNITS	TOTAL COSTS	PRODUCT A 1	PRODUCT A 2	PRODUCT GROUP A BIG FURNITURE	PRODUCT B 1	PRODUCT B 2	PRODUCT B 3	PRODUCT GROUP B SMALL FURNITURE	PRODUCT C 1	PRODUCT C 2	PRODUCT GROUP C SEATING FURNITURE	TOTAL PRODUCTION
I. Variable costs (with outlay character)												
1. Raw materials	350,000	70,000	41,000		42,000	40,000	25,000		75,000	57,000		
2. Services	70,000	9,000	8,000		7,000	6,000	5,000		15,000	20,000		
3. Wages	205,000	-	-		51,000	34,000	30,000		50,000	40,000		
4. Miscellaneous costs	41,360	7,000	4,660		4,500	4,200	3,900		9,000	8,100		
Total I	666,360	86,000	53,660		104,500	84,200	63,900		149,000	125,100		
II. Fixed costs												
A. With outlay character												
1. Services	35,000			3,300				3,600			3,500	24,600
2. Wages	161,667			32,117								129,550
3. Salaries	106,061			10,603				9,000			11,000	75,458
4. Miscellaneous	25,304			1,500				2,800			2,500	18,504
Total A	328,032			47,520				15,400			17,000	248,112
B. Without outlay character												
1. Depreciation of machines	84,000			20,000				13,000			16,500	34,500
2. Depreciation of business premises	7,000											7,000
Total B	91,000			20,000				13,000			16,500	41,500
Total II	419,032			67,520				28,400			33,500	289,612
TOTAL COSTS	1,085,392	86,000	53,660	67,520	104,500	84,200	63,900	28,400	149,000	125,100	33,500	289,612

Table 19

COST UNIT STATEMENT (in $)

Direct product costs (with outlay character)		DIRECT COSTS OF THE PRODUCT GROUPS			DIRECT COSTS OF TOTAL PRODUCTION		
		With outlay character	Without outlay character	Total	With outlay character	Without outlay character	Total
A1	86,000	47,520	20,000	67,520			
A2	53,660						
B1	104,500	15,400	13,000	28,400	248,112	41,500	289,612
B2	84,200						
B3	63,900						
C1	149,000	17,000	16,500	33,500			
C2	125,100						
Total	666,360	79,920	49,500	129,420	248,112	41,500	289,612

Table 20

Kind of Product	Direct product cost (in $)	Production volumes (units)	Price floor (in $)
A1	86,000	375	229.33
A2	53,660	500	107.32
B1	104,500	1,500	69.67
B2	84,200	1,000	84.20
B3	63,900	1,750	36.51
C1	149,000	800	186.25
C2	125,100	1,500	83.40

Here, the sum totals of the above-mentioned cost statement are summarized by cost category.

17.2.2 Information for Pricing Purposes

In the first place, the diverse price floors are discussed. From a business economic point of view the short-term price floors fall together with the direct product costs. As there are no direct fixed costs, these price floors can be calculated easily: the direct product costs should be divided by the respective production volumes, as shown in Table 20.

It should be repeated that the price floors are net prices, to which the 4% commission should be added. For example, the real gross price floor for product A1 amounts to $238.50.

When determining the long-term price floors the question arises how (in function of the kinds of product) the indirect costs will be recovered. Indeed, in the long run each kind of product has not only to recover its direct product cost but also should contribute to the recovery of the direct costs of its product group and to the direct costs of total production. For example, products A1 and A2 have to recover jointly $67,520 direct costs of product group A and besides should contribute to cover $289,612, an amount that can only be assigned to the total production.

From a liquidity point of view, in addition to the variable costs, the fixed costs involving cash outlays should be taken into account. In that way the products A1 and A2 have to recover jointly $47,520 cash costs of product group A and they should contribute to recover $248,112 cash costs of total production. The same reasoning can be made for the products B1, B2, B3, and C1, C2.

Insofar as the problems of price floors are concerned the above "cost unit statement" turns out to be very exploratory. For other pricing decisions, next to pure cost data also revenue data and other market information will be taken into consideration.

Table 21

Kind of products and product groups	Sales volume (units)	Selling price (in $)	Sales (in $)
A1	375	520	195,000
A2	500	310	155,000
Product group A			350,000
B1	1,500	99	148,500
B2	1,000	129	129,000
B3	1,750	65	113,750
Product group B			391,250
C1	800	339	271,200
C2	1,500	199	298,500
Product group C			569,700
Total			1,310,950

In this firm, sales are composed as presented in Table 21.

Comparison between sales and costs shows that each product yields more than its direct costs. The same applies for the product groups. Also, the confrontation of total sales with total costs gives positive results, notably:

Sales	$ 1,310,950
Total Costs	$ 1,085,392
Result	$ 225,558

Table 22 gives a clear idea of the origin of this result (gradual cost recovery). Table 23 is made similarly on the basis of liquidity character of costs. This table points out the surplus/deficit with regard to current outlays. The information may give direction to pricing policy in firms with a tight liquidity position (step-by-step recovery of costs involving cash outlays).

The table "Gradual Cost Recovery" shows the origin of the result. Among other things one can ascertain that products C1 and C2 yield the absolute highest contribution and thus are the most important products of this firm. However, in order to know the most favorable kind of product, the unit contribution should be considered. These contributions are calculated in Table 24. Products A1 and

Table 22

GRADUAL COST RECOVERY

KINDS OF PRODUCT/ PRODUCT GROUPS	SALES (in $)	DIRECT PRODUCT COSTS (in $)	CONTRIBUTION PER KIND OF PRODUCT (in $)	DIRECT COSTS OF THE PRODUCT GROUPS (in $)	CONTRIBUTION OF PRODUCT GROUPS (in $)	DIRECT COSTS OF TOTAL PRODUCTION (in $)	RESULT (in $)
A1	195,000	86,000	109,000				
A2	155,000	53,660	101,340				
Product group A	350,000	139,660	210,340	67,520	142,820		
B1	148,500	104,500	44,000				
B2	129,000	84,200	44,800				
B3	113,750	63,900	49,850				
Product group B	391,250	252,600	138,650	28,400	110,250		
C1	271,200	149,000	122,200				
C2	298,500	125,100	173,400				
Product group C	569,700	274,100	295,600	33,500	262,100		
TOTALS	1,310,950	666,360	644,590	129,420	515,170	289,612	225,558

Table 23

STEP BY STEP RECOVERY OF COSTS INVOLVING CASH OUTLAYS

KIND OF PRODUCT / PRODUCT GROUP	SALES (in $)	DIRECT PRODUCT COSTS (INVOLVING CASH OUTLAYS) (in $)	CONTRIBUTION PER KIND OF PRODUCT (in $)	DIRECT COSTS OF THE PRODUCT GROUPS (INVOLVING CASH OUTLAYS) (in $)	CONTRIBUTION OF PRODUCT GROUPS (in $)	DIRECT COSTS OF TOTAL PRODUCTION (INVOLVING CASH OUTLAYS) (in $)	SURPLUS/DEFICIT (in $)
A1	195,000	86,000	109,000				
A2	155,000	53,660	101,340				
Product group A	350,000	139,660	210,340	47,520	162,820		
B1	148,500	104,500	44,000				
B2	129,000	84,200	44,800				
B3	113,750	63,900	49,850				
Product group B	391,250	252,600	138,650	15,400	123,250		
C1	271,200	149,000	122,200				
C2	298,500	125,100	173,400				
Product group C	569,700	274,100	295,600	17,000	278,600		
TOTAL	1,310,950	666,360	644,590	79,920	564,670	248,112	316,558

Table 24

PRO- DUCT	DIRECT PRODUCT COSTS (in $)	SALES VOLUME (units)	SELLING PRICE (in $)	DIRECT COSTS PER UNIT OF PRODUCT (in $)	UNIT CONTRIBU- TION (in $)	CONTRIBU- TION PER SALES DOLLAR (in $)
A1	86,000	375	520	229.33	290.67	0.56
A2	53,660	500	310	107.32	202.68	0.65
B1	104,500	1,500	99	69.67	29.33	0.30
B2	84,200	1,000	129	84.20	44.80	0.35
B3	63,900	1,750	65	36.51	28.49	0.44
C1	149,000	800	339	186.25	152.75	0.45
C2	125,100	1,500	199	83.40	115.60	0.58

A2 are most profitable, followed by product group C, and, finally, group B. However, because the diverse kinds of product cause different costs and generate different revenues, one should not be obsessed too much by the unit contribution. Therefore, it is better to calculate the "contribution per unit of bottleneck factor."

If, for example, the sales potentialities form the bottleneck, then the contribution per sales dollar is decisive (see last column). According to this criterion product A2 is the most profitable, followed by C2 and A1, respectively. Within product group B, the product B3 is most profitable.

In quite a number of cases the limiting factor is internal, for example, availability of manpower (man hours), raw materials (units, kilograms), machine capacity (machine hours). At a given market price, in these cases preferably those products that yield the largest contribution per unit of scarce factor will be sold. If the firm is able to conduct an active and autonomous pricing policy, then it will raise the price of those products which make great demands on the scarce factors. The example below will illustrate this. For the sake of simplicity all products are manufactured from the same raw material. This raw material is only available in the measure to which the firm is committed to the production/ sales volumes of the last period (cf. *supra*). In Table 25, the contribution per dollar of raw material consumption is calculated. Compared with the contribution per sales dollar, the order of the products is mixed together. According to the criterion "contribution per $ of raw material consumption," product C2 should be preferred, followed by A2 and B3 respectively.

Suppose that market research indicates that it is impossible to sell more of products C2, A2, and B3 but that the sales of the other products can be extended further. If in this assumption more raw materials would be available, the firm will only manufacture and sell the products A1, B2, and B1 when these products yield at least the same contribution as product C1 per dollar of raw material consumption, namely, $1.63. For the products A1, B2, and B1 this becomes a price increase.

Table 25

PRODUCTS	RAW MATERIAL COST PER KIND OF PRODUCT (in $)	CONTRIBUTION PER KIND OF PRODUCT (in $)	CONTRIBUTION PER $ OF RAW MATERIAL CONSUMPTION (in $)
A1	70,000	109,000	1.56
A2	41,000	101,340	2.47
B1	42,000	44,000	1.05
B2	40,000	44,800	1.12
B3	25,000	49,850	1.99
C1	75,000	122,200	1.63
C2	57,000	173,400	3.04

If, for example, product B2 should have to yield a unit contribution of $60 (instead of $44.80), this should have to lead to a price increase of $129 to $144.2, at equal direct product costs. Our purpose is to show that ACA can be a meaningful and useful instrument for pricing purposes.

In our example we are only concerned with standardized products. It may happen, however, that more individualized products should have to be manufactured. In this event, cost variability in function of order size plays an important role for pricing purposes. In the case that the firm is manufacturing only to order, even if the products remain standardized, in between two orders the machinery will have to be converted and adjusted. So, irrespective of order size, additional costs are incurred. These costs are assignable to the particular order and should be regained from the revenue of that order.

Suppose that adjusting the machines in order to manufacture product A1 brings on a cost of $1,500. Consequently, each order of product A1 should yield $1,500 additionally. The absolute price floor of an order of 100 units of A1 is no longer $22,933 but $22,933 + $1,500 = $24,433.

In fact we are close to price differentiation here. Indeed, the required price floors could be differentiated in function of certain premised order-size classes. In general it can be said that the more the firm is taking into account customers' specifications, the more the product becomes differentiated and the less the market will provide a starting point for pricing purposes. Especially in these cases price setting will be more and more cost oriented.

17.3 BUILDUP AND USE OF A CALCULATION MODEL IN A FIRM WITH JOINT PRODUCTION

Joint production is characterized by a high measure of product connection. By that, not only fixed costs but also large parts of variable costs have to be

Figure 15

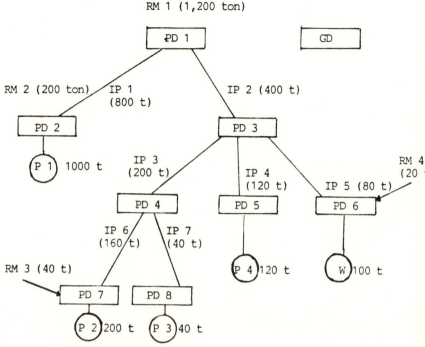

PD 1-8 : manufacturing departments   IP 1-7 : intermediate products
GD   : general department   P 1- 4 : finished products
RM 1-4 : raw materials   W   : waste product

looked upon as indirect product costs. Below is illustrated how in a joint production firm ACA may be built up and used for pricing purposes.

17.3.1 Description of the Example

The manufacturing process of our model firm is represented in Figure 15. The
quantitative proportions are fixed. The quantities mentioned in the scheme refer
to full utilization of the productive capacity. P 2 is the main product. All the
other products can be characterized more or less as secondary products. IP 5
cannot be finished to a salable product and besides is pollutive. In department
PD 6 it is worked up into a harmless waste product W by mixing it with RM
4. The intermediate products IP 4 and IP 6 have a market and therefore can also
be sold directly. The costs, divided according to cost centers and according to
variability in function of the activity ratio, are given in Table 26 (in dollars). In
this example the classification of costs according to outlay character is abandoned.
Naturally, this classification keeps its usefulness but is omitted for ease of survey.

Table 26

Dept.	Variable Costs	Fixed Costs	Total Costs
G.D.	–	12,000	12,000
PD 1	385,000	36,000	421,000
PD 2	60,000	25,000	85,000
PD 3	30,000	35,000	65,000
PD 4	22,000	27,000	49,000
PD 5	–	15,000	15,000
PD 6	6,000	7,000	13,000
PD 7	145,000	95,000	240,000
PD 8	6,000	8,000	14,000
TOTAL	654,000	260,000	914,000

The cost of raw materials form part of the variable costs of the manufacturing departments in which they are consumed:

In: PD 1: RM 1: 1,200 t x $ 300 = $ 360,000
PD 2: RM 2: 300 t x $ 230 = $ 46,000
PD 6: RM 4:   20 t x $ 300 = $ 6,000
PD 7: RM 3:   40 t x $ 2,400 = $ 96,000

17.3.2 Use of These Cost Data for Pricing Purposes

The above cost table is only a starting point. Indeed, for pricing purposes costs should be brought into relation with products. As direct product costs can only be taken into account the costs of those departments that are involved in the manufacturing of only one product. For example, the costs of PD 2 (inclusive RM 2) are direct costs of product P 1. In Table 27 the direct product costs are pointed out.

This table provides adequate information for setting price floors. Because, aside from intermediate product IP 5, no transforming costs are incurred, one will only be willing to incur additional costs for a particular product unless these costs can be paid back by sales revenues of the product in question. If the joint costs are recovered by the other products, the long-range price floor equals the unit total direct product costs (see table, column 8). Naturally, these amounts are only valid in case of full capacity usage. As fixed and variable costs are calculated separately, the unit total direct product costs at other activity ratios can be calculated easily. For example, at 75% capacity usage, the production

Table 27

Product	Quantity	Total Variable Direct Product Costs (in $)	Total Fixed Direct Product Costs (in $)	Total Direct Product Costs (in $)	Unit Variable Direct Prod. Costs (in $)	Unit Fixed Direct Prod. Costs (based on full capacity usage) (in $)	Total Direct Prod. Costs (on basis of full capacity usage) (in $)
1	2	3	4	5	6	7	8
P 1	1,000	60,000	25,000	85,000	60	25	85
P 2	200	145,000	95,000	240,000	725	475	1,200
P 3	40	6,000	8,000	14,000	150	200	350
P 4	120	----	15,000	15,000	----	125	125
TOTAL	-----	211,000	143,000	354,000	----	----	-----

of P2 come to 150 tons. The fixed direct costs should be spread over this volume and thus amount to $\dfrac{\$95,000}{150\ t} = \$633.33$ per ton.

Consequently, the long-term price floor stands at:

$$\$725 + \$633.33 = \$1,358.33$$

Equally important is the short-term price floor. It can also be derived from the above table. Even if the variable joint costs are recovered by the other products, an intermediate product will only be converted into a finished product if the variable conversion costs can be recovered by revenues (see table, column 6).

Insofar as waste product W is concerned, a special situation arises. The costs, assignable to department PD 6, in which IP 5 is transformed into W, are inevitable. Indeed, IP 5 originates from the manufacturing of other intermediate products (in PD 3), from which the products P 2, P 3, and P 4 are manufactured further. These costs have to be incurred, regardless of whether W is sold. Because in this firm the expulsion of waste product W does not cause additional costs, the price floor of W equals zero. If one would succeed in selling IP 5, the transformation costs could be saved. Then, the price floor of IP 5 is negative. Each ton of IP 5, which should not have to be transformed, leads to a cost saving in the amount of $\dfrac{\$6,000}{100\ t} = \$60$ (see cost center table). If the volume of IP 5 could be sold completely, department PD 6 could be closed down entirely. In this case the fixed costs, at least partially, are omitted. If the total fixed costs of department PD 6 could be omitted, the absolute price floor of IP 5 is:

$$\$60 - \frac{\$7,000}{100\ t} = -\ \$130\ \text{per ton.}$$

The price floors calculated above are only valid if the joint costs are already recovered by the other products. This is true both for long-term and short-term price floors. In the former case, next to the total direct product costs to the amount of $354,000, still $560,000 of joint costs have to be recovered. In the latter case, next to the variable direct product costs in the amount of $211,000 a further amount of $443,000 of variable joint costs has to be recovered.

The question arises as to which criteria should be applied in order to spread the joint costs over the particular products. The joint costs are partially caused by the complete production. Another part, however, is caused only by a certain part of the production. According to this a "hierarchy" of units of reference, namely, products and product groups, can be built up. In this hierarchy the cost elements should be assigned to the lowest possible stage, to which they still can be assigned directly. This is carried out in Table 28, which illustrates direct product costs and direct costs of the product groups, classified in variable and total costs (in $). From this table it can be deduced that P2 and P3, next to their respective direct costs, should still recover at short notice $22,000 jointly assignable variable costs (variable costs of PD 4; see table, column 5). In the long run P2 and P3 should recover their total jointly assignable costs to the amount of $49,000. In the same way the products P2, P3, and P4 should recover $36,000 at short notice and $78,000 in the long run (see table, columns 7 and 8). Here the costs of PD 3 and PD 6 are concerned. The costs of PD 6 are caused by the conversion of IP 5. This intermediate product comes about in department PD 5 together with the manufacturing of IP 3 and IP 4. In this manner the costs of both PD 3 and PD 6 can be labeled as direct costs of the product groups P2P3P4.

When the columns of the above table are cumulated, the minimum required sales revenues of the products and product groups are obtained. This calculation [minimal sales revenues of the products and product groups (in $)] is made in Table 29.

From this table, among other things, it seems that in the long run product P2 should at least yield $240,000, that the product group P2P3 should at least yield $303,000, that product group P2P3P4 should at least bring in $396,000, and, finally, that $914,000 should be recovered altogether. As costs are split up into fixed and variable, the minimum revenues at other activity ratios can be calculated easily.

As already mentioned, the classification of costs according to outlay character is left out of consideration. The same analysis, as well as the calculation of liquidity-oriented price floors can be executed in the same manner as above.

It should be pointed out (cf. Part IV, Chapter 16) that cost accounting in itself is not able to settle how the joint costs should be recovered by the particular products. For example, product group P2P3 should recover $49,000. Which part of it has to be brought in [by P2 and P3 respectively] should not be decided by the cost accountant but by marketing and sales management (cf. principle of "ability to bear").

The above analysis is completely based on cost accounting data. When also marketing and sales data, such as sales revenues, sales volume, and selling prices are taken into consideration, pricing decisions can be studied further.

If one or a few products are sold at a fixed price or at market price, then the required contribution and price floors of the other products can be set more concretely. If for example, product P 1 is sold at a fixed price of $250 per ton and if the market price of the main product P 2 amounts to $3,200 per ton, the following calculation can be made: at full capacity usage, product P 2 yields $640,000. In the first place this sales revenue will be used in order to recover the direct product costs of P 2 ($240,000); further, all direct costs of product

Table 28

Prod.	Volume (tons)	Direct Product Costs		Direct Costs of Product Group P2P3		Direct Costs of Product Group P2P3P4		Direct Costs of Total Production	
		Variable	Total	Variable	Total	Variable	Total	Variable	Total
1	2	3	4	5	6	7	8	9	10
P 1	1,000	60,000	85,000					385,000	433,000
P 2	200	145,000	240,000	22,000	49,000				
P 3	40	6,000	14,000			36,000	78,000		
P 4	120	---	15,000						

195

Table 29

Prod.	Volume	Minimum Revenue of the Products		Minimum Revenue of Product Group P2P3		Minimum Revenue of Product Group P2P3P4		Total Minimum Sales Revenue	
		Short Term	Long Term	Short Term	Long Term	Short Term	Long Term	Short Term	Long Term
1	2	3	4	5	6	7	8	9	10
P 1	1,000	60,000	85,000						
P 2	200	145,000	240,000						
				173,000	303,000				
P 3	40	6,000	14,000						
P 4	120	---	15,000			209,000	396,000	654,000	914,000

Table 30

Product	Price per ton (in $)	Volume (in ton)	Sales (in $)	Contribution over variable product costs (in $)
1	2	3	4	5
P 1	170	1,000	170,000	110,000
P 3	320	40	12,800	6,800
P 4	160	120	19,200	19,200
Total	–	–	202,000	136,000

group P2P3 are recovered ($49,000); next, the direct costs of product group P2P3P4 are fully recovered ($78,000). Finally, an amount of $273,000 is yielded, contributing to the recovery of the direct costs of total production. Product P 1 brings in $250,000. In the first place, this amount should be used to recover the direct cost of P 1 ($85,000), next, $165,000 is contributed to the recovery of the direct costs of total production (indivisible balance).

Both products already provide full recovery of costs; also, a profit is made. As things are, this means that the price floors of P 3 and P 4 are equal to their direct product costs:

for P 3: $14,000: 40 t = $350 per ton
for P 4: $15,000: 120 t = $125 per ton

In another situation the following selling prices are given:

P 1: $170
P 3: $320
P 4: $160

The selling price of the main product is at the same moment and probably only for a short period of time at high pressure. In view of full capacity usage the preservation of the firm's market share is pursued.

Considering the short-term character of this situation the fixed costs can be left out of consideration. The question is: Taking into account the above market data, what should be the price floor of product P 2? The products P 1, P 3, and P 4 yield sales and contributions shown in Table 30. Consequently, the main product P 2 should minimally recover the following costs:

1. variable direct costs of P 2 $ 145,000
2. variable costs of product group P2P3
   not recovered by product P 3: $ 22,000 − $ 6,800 = $ 15,200
3. variable cost of product group P2P3P4 not
   recovered by P 3 and P 4: $ 36,000 − $ 19,200 = $ 16,800

4. variable costs of total production not recovered
   by P 1, P 3, and P 4: $ 385,000 $-$ $ 110,000$ $= \dfrac{\$\ 275{,}000}{}$

                                                Total $ 452,000

Therefore, P 2 should yield at least \$452,000. This amount can also be calculated by subtracting the aggregate sales revenue from total variable cost: \$654,000 $-$ \$202,000 = \$452,000. So, the price floor of product P 2 amounts to:

$$\frac{\$452{,}000}{200\ t} = \$2{,}260 \text{ per ton}$$

Suppose that a part of intermediate product IP6 could be sold directly. Then, the question is at what price per ton IP6 should at least be sold when P 2 is sold at \$3,200 per ton. The production scheme points out that 160 t IP6 leads to 200 t of P 2 or, from 1 t of IP6, 1.25 t of P 2 can be manufactured. Consequently, each ton of IP6 that is sold leads to a sales decrease of \$3,200 x 1,25 = \$4,000. On the other hand, however, the variable costs of department PD7 will decrease to the amount of:

$$\frac{\$145{,}000}{160\ t} = \$906.25 \text{ per ton.}$$

So the price floor of IP6 is: \$4,000 $-$ \$906.25 = \$3,093.75.

Supposing that the market price of product P 4 amounts to \$400. A customer is willing to buy large volumes of IP 4 at \$300. Is this proposition profitable? If the volumes produced of IP4 are sold partly there is no cost reduction in department PD5. Indeed, all costs of this department are fixed (namely, \$15,000). The offer is only favorable if on the one hand the customer is pledging himself to buy the total production of IP 4 and on the other hand if because of closing down department PD5 all fixed costs of this department are omitted. So a cost reduction of $\dfrac{\$15{,}000}{120\ t}$ = \$125 per ton IP4 is realized versus a revenue decrease of \$400 $-$ \$300 = \$100 per ton.

The above examples may suffice to show that the combination of costs and market data may provide decisive answers to pricing problems.

17.3.3 Some Remarks in the Case of Variable Quantitative Proportions

In the above examples fixed quantitative proportions were presumed. In case of variable quantitative proportions the following specific characteristics apply:

—In principle, the proportions are selected such that the total contribution is maximized.
—The limiting condition for the above rule is the absorption capacity of the market.

—In principle, these proportions will only be changed under the idea that the prices of certain products can be raised to such degree that the lost sales are compensated for by other products.

Example. In a firm 200 tons of raw materials are used for manufacturing the products X and Y. It is supposed that the total costs amount to $500,000 and that they are independent of the quantitative proportions between X and Y. The production volumes can be varied to such an extent that at most 120 t X and 80 t Y and minimally 100 t X and 100 t Y can be manufactured. The market price of X amounts to $4,000 per ton; this of product Y amounts to $3,200 per ton. Under these circumstances one naturally attempts to produce as much as possible of product X. In that case the following sales revenues are realized:

$$
\begin{array}{llll}
\text{product X:} & 120 \text{ t} \times \$ \ 4,000 & = & \$ \ 480,000 \\
\text{product Y:} & \ \ 80 \text{ t} \times \$ \ 3,200 & = & \$ \ 256,000 \\
\\
\text{total sales} & & & \$ \ 736,000
\end{array}
$$

An increase in the demand for product Y can only be met by sacrificing production of X in favor of product Y. One will only turn to this change of production mix if the sales decrease can be met by increasing the selling prices of X and/or Y. If the selling price of X remains constant, the selling price of product Y should rise to a sufficient degree: 100 t of X yield: 100 t x $4,000 = $400,000; thus 100 t of Y should yield minimally $736,000 − $400,000 = $336,000, which averages out at $3,360 per ton (always in the supposition that costs remain equal).

Normally, a change in quantitative proportions is accompanied by a change in the costs of production. If in the above example a changeover from a 120/80 proportion to a 100/100 proportion is coupled with a cost reduction of $10,000, the price floor of product Y may be reduced by $\dfrac{\$10,000}{100 \text{ t}} = \$100$. Then, the price floor of product Y amounts to

$$
\$3,360 - \$100 = \$3,260.
$$

General Conclusions

In the light of the discussion of costs as price determinant, a rundown of some important cost-oriented methods of price setting was given. For several reasons the ACA system was preferred to full costing and partial costing methods. This cost accounting system was discussed in general and also in function of its role in pricing policy. For each management decision in which cost data play a role, either directly or indirectly, cost accounting should point out adequate cost information. More than once we mentioned that for these purposes there is no "all-around," uniform cost concept. Consequently, the vision of costs should be broader and should link up with Clark's principle of "different costs of different purposes." One of the main problems of this book consists in defining what should be understood by "different costs" for pricing purposes. Perhaps there is not a single decision problem about which the views are so different. In summary the solution of this problem coincides with answering the two following questions:[1]

1. What cost information is needed for pricing purposes?
2. What cost accounting system is able to provide this information in an adequate way?

The first question was answered thoroughly in Part II. It should especially be borne in mind that the importance of cost information may vary from nearly unimportant to all important, this in function of market structure, kind of product, business objective, price setting frequency, pricing strategy, and so on.

The second question was answered in Part III and Part IV of this book. Naturally, the nature and framework of a pricing policy–oriented cost accounting system is closely connected with the above-mentioned variable importance of cost information for pricing purposes. For multiple product firms, for example, the cost accounting system should be very flexible. The same applies for firms being confronted with strongly fluctuating market data or with a high frequency of price changes.

Insofar as the cost accounting system is concerned the direct cost can be regarded as hardly problematic compared with indirect costs. In view of cost recovery the main problem of building up a pricing-oriented cost accounting system lies in an adequate treatment of indirect costs. In this connection it has been pointed out that full costing, by means of unadapted and arbitrary allocation of indirect costs, leads to irrelevant cost data, which suggest a deceptive accuracy besides. In many forms of partial costing, the indirect costs, yet being relevant for a number of pricing decisions, are left out of consideration.

The better solution was found in the ACA system. In this cost accounting method the indirect costs are taken into account and are assigned to one or more hierarchies of units of reference. In this manner ACA is a synthesis of pure full costing and partial costing. By differentiating the indirect costs, a number of contributions, being relevant for short-term or long-term pricing decisions, can be calculated.[2] So, an important step forward is made in the problems of cost recovery.

An important criticism of cost-oriented pricing lies in disregarding market factors. When applying ACA the real pricing decisions and as a consequence cost recovery are left to the price setter. As contrasted with the traditional cost-oriented pricing methods, the role of cost accounting is reduced here to the essence, namely, providing adequate cost information on behalf of the price setter. Whether the information provided is used and how it is used are not the cost accountant's responsibilities but should be determined by the price setter who is responsible for the use and interpretation of the cost information.

Another and related characteristic, by which the adequacy of pricing-oriented cost information can be judged, is the flexibility of it. As mentioned above the required flexibility of cost information depends on many factors. In general terms can be said that cost accounting should be able to provide information for pricing purposes either ad hoc or continuously. The kind of pricing decision and pricing situation plays a substantial role.

At given market prices, cost accounting should provide periodically cost data in order to judge the profitability of the products in question. In principle, in this case ad hoc information suffices. However, the periodicity of this cost information should be based on the frequency of market price changes or on changes of certain cost elements. In case of price imitation the same applies. It should be noticed that in these cases cost accounting especially plays a role as a means of calculating operating results. With a view to profit maximization (or minimizing losses), analysis and judgment of contributions may lead to sales mix changes.

In case of active pricing policy, the nature of the products and market data also play a role. In case of standardized mass products, especially insofar as branded goods or products sold by means of catalog are concerned, selling prices sometimes are kept constant for a longer period of time. Consequently, the frequency of setting prices may be very low so that ad hoc cost information is sufficient. In case of individualized products (piecework) the situation is completely different. In this case selling prices have to be set permanently, either per unit of product or per order. Consequently, the pricing-oriented cost accounting system should provide cost information on a permanent basis.

Another important factor is the measure of stability of the cost elements. In firms characterized by little technological changes or changes in personnel, for example, the need for a permanent cost accounting system is less than in firms where the opposite occurs.

Considering the multitude of factors influencing both cost calculation and pricing policy, the pricing-oriented cost accounting system should be multiple purpose. This implies a strongly differentiated cost accounting system: several unequivocal and clearcut cost distinctions should be used simultaneously. To these characteristics, the ACA-system advocated in this book, answers better than the more classic full costing and partial costing methods.

Notes

CHAPTER 1

1. The notions "price" and "selling price" are here considered as synonyms. In the same sense the words pricing policy, price setting, and so on are used instead of selling price policy, selling price setting, and so forth.

2. See DAVIES (J.) & HUGHES (S.). Pricing in Practice. London, Heinemann, 1975, pp. 45–94.

3. VAN ACKER (J.). Bewuste Commerciële Beleidsvoering. Ghent, Seminarie voor Produktiviteitsstudie en Onderzoek, 1968. p. 359.

4. VAN ACKER (J.), op. cit., p. 358 labels pricing policy as a capital key of the marketing management piano. See also: STANTON (W.J.). Fundamentals of Marketing. New York, McGraw-Hill, 1981, pp. 221–222. BURT (D.M.) & BOYETT (J.E.). Reduction in Selling Price after the Introduction of Competition. Journal of Marketing Research, May 1979, who state at p. 275: "Price is one of the most important and least understood factors of marketing." MASON (R.S.). Price Competition in Industrial Markets. Industrial Marketing Management, October 1974, pp. 275–284. GUILTINAN (J.P.). Risk-Aversive Pricing Policies: Problems and Alternatives. Journal of Marketing, January 1976, p. 15.

5. See BRUHN (J.). Preispolitik: der falsche Fetisch. Marketing Journal, No. 6, 1973, pp. 512–513. UDELL (J.). How Important Is Pricing in Competitive Strategy? Journal of Marketing, March 1964, pp. 44–48. Similar research in the Netherlands shows the same tendency; see: VERKUIL (J.). Prijsbeleid, achtergebleven gebied van de marketing. Tijdschrift voor Marketing. March 1970, pp. 73–77, especially table p. 74 and comment pp. 73–74.

6. See in this connection: OXENFELDT (A.). Executive Action in Marketing. Belmont, Wadsworth, 1966, pp. 238–239. PHELPS (D.) & WESTING (H.). Marketing Management. Homewood, Ill., Irwin, 1968, p. 299. STURDIVANT (F.) & Others. Managerial Analysis in Marketing. Glenview, Scott, Foreman & Co., 1970, p. 437.

7. See UHL (K.). What You Should Know about Pricing. Industrial Marketing, March 1962, pp. 90–92.

8. For a discussion of price policy audit, see KARGER (T.) & THOMPSON (G.). Pricing Policies and Practices. Conference Board Business Record, September 1957, p. 442.

9. STANTON (W.J.), op. cit., p. 224.

10. Pricing policy objectives are discussed in general in: GABOR (A.). Pricing: Principles and Practice. London, Heinemann, 1977, pp. 16–25. BELL (M.L.). Marketing Concepts and Strategy. Boston, Houghton Mifflin Co., 1979, pp. 397–399. DAVIES (J.) & HUGHES (S.), op. cit., pp. 2–11. RADEMAKER (B.). Industriële marketing voor strategisch beleid. Deventer, Kluwer, 1981, pp. 143–157. STANTON (W.J.), op. cit., pp. 225–228. LEEFLANG (P.S.H.) & BEUKENKAMP (P.A.). Probleemgebied Marketing. Een management benadering. Leiden, H.E. Stenfert-Kroese B.V., 1981, pp. 568–572. McCARTHY (E.J.). Basic Marketing: A Managerial Approach. Homewood, Ill., Irwin, 1978, pp. 479–483.

11. Pricing policy objectives will also vary in function of the stages of product life cycle. These problems are not considered here.

12. See SPENCER (M.). Managerial Economics. Homewood, Ill., Irwin, 1968, p. 294. LANZILOTTI (R.). Pricing Objectives in Large Companies. Consulted in: MULVIHILL (D.) & PARANKA (S.), eds. Price Policies and Practices: A Source Book in Readings. New York, J. Wiley & Sons, 1967, p. 82.

13. See notes 1 and 2, Chapter 1.

14. The same conclusion based on empirical evidence, is found in: FOG (B.) Industrial Pricing Policies. Amsterdam, North-Holland Publishing Co., 1960, p. 32. HAGUE (D.C.). Pricing in Business. London, G. Allen & Unwin Ltd., 1971, pp. 80–85.

15. For modifications a-b-c-d-e: see FOG (B.), op. cit., pp. 32–38.

16. GORDON (R.). Short-Period Price Determination in Theory and Practice. American Economic Review. June 1948, p. 271.

17. FOG (B.), op. cit., pp. 34–35.

18. Ibid., pp. 35–36.

19. LANZILOTTI (R.), op. cit., pp. 79–80.

20. See HAGUE (D.), op. cit., p. 61.

21. WYTZES (H.). Ondernemingsgroei en ondernemingsstrategie. Haarlem, De Erven F. Bohn N.V., 1967, p. 21.

22. See ANKUM (L.). Prijsinflatie, kostprijsberekening en winstbepaling. Leiden, H.E. Stenfert Kroese N.V., 1969, pp. 76–77.

23. This is expressed clearly in the empirical evidence about pricing policy in the western Canadian garment industry. See LAZER (W.). Price Determination in the Western Canadian Garment Industry. The Journal of Industrial Economics, March 1957, pp. 124–136, especially pp. 125–126.

24. See RUTTEN (F.). Prijsvorming in de industrie. Leiden, H.E. Stenfert Kroese N.V., 1965, pp. 15–16.

25. DEAN (J.). Managerial Economics. Englewood Cliffs, N.J., Prentice-Hall, 1956, p. 399.

26. McCARTHY (E.J.), op. cit., p. 482.

27. See especially DEAN (J.), op. cit., pp. 419–424, where he is weighing "penetration price" against "skimming price."

28. In the next pages indicated as R.O.I.

29. LANZILOTTI (R.), op. cit., pp. 63–83; see also: KAMERSCHEN (D.R.). The Return of Target Pricing? Journal of Business, No. 2, 1975, pp. 242–252.

30. See HAGUE (D.), op. cit., pp. 59–60.

31. LANZILOTTI (R.), op. cit., p. 73.

32. See section 1.2.1.3.

33. LYNN (R.). Price Policies and Marketing Management. Homewood, Ill., Irwin, 1967, p. 100.

34. BIDLINGMAIER (J.). Die Ziele der Unternehmer. Zeitschrift für Betriebswirtschaft, September 1963, p. 522.

35. See FOG (B.), op. cit., p. 31, and HAGUE (D.), op. cit., p. 82.

36. FOG (B.), op. cit., pp. 33–34.

37. LANZILOTTI (R.), op. cit., pp. 65–67.

CHAPTER 2

1. In marketing literature a number of pricing policy checklists are published. They can be very useful in the context of price policy audits. Most of the checklists are partial but sometimes exclusively concerned with price determinants. For example: HUEGY (H.). Price Decisions and Marketing Policies. Consulted in: MULVIHILL (D.) & PARANKA (S.). Price Policies and Practices. New York, J. Wiley & Sons, 1967, pp. 11–14. BACKMAN (J.). Price Practices and Price Policies. New York, Ronald Press, 1953, pp. 59–60. POTH (L.). Checkliste für preispolitische Entscheidungen. Absatzwirtschaft, November 1970, pp. 39–45. McRAE (T.). Analytical Management. London, Wiley Interscience, 1970, pp. 290–292. HAGUE (D.C.). Pricing in Business. London, G. Allen & Unwin, 1971, pp. 39–44.

2. See, for example: TULL (D.), BORING (R.) & GONSIOR (M.). The Relationship of Price and Imputed Quality. Consulted in: TAYLOR (B.) & WILLS (G.). Pricing Strategy. London, Staples Press, 1969, pp. 44–49. OLANDER (F.). The Influence of Price on the Consumer Evaluation of Products and Purchases. Consulted in: TAYLOR (B.) & WILLS (G.), op. cit., pp. 50–69. SHAPIRO (B.). The Psychology of Pricing. Harvard Business Review, July-August 1968, pp. 14–16. MASSEY (M.). Consumer Reactions to Price-Quality Relations: An Exploratory Study. Houston Business Review, Summer 1963, pp. 25–48. STAFFORD (J.) & ENIS (B.). The Price-Quality Relationship: An Extension. Journal of Marketing Research, August 1968, pp. 331–334. STANTON (W.J.). Fundamentals of Marketing. New York, McGraw-Hill, 1981, p. 222. JOLSON (M.A.). Marketing Management, New York, Macmillan, 1978, pp. 470–472. GABOR (A.). Pricing: Principles and Practice. London, Heinemann, 1977, pp. 192–210, plus lengthy literature references. The positive causal relationship between price and quality is questioned by: MORRIS (R.) & BRONSON (C.). The Chaos of Competition Indicated by Consumer Reports. Journal of Marketing, July 1969, pp. 26–34. REISZ (P.C.). A Major Price-Perceived Quality Study Re-examined. Journal of Marketing Research, May 1980, pp. 259–262, points out the methodological weakness of much of the research about the price-quality relationship.

3. This applies especially to consumers; industrial buyers often consider quality as a quantifiable concept.

4. See, for example: GABOR (A.) & GRANGER (C.). The Attitude of Consumer to Price. Consulted in: TAYLOR (B.) & WILLS (G.), op. cit., pp. 132–146.

5. See LEAVITT (H.). Experimental Findings about the Meaning of Price. Consulted in: TAYLOR (B.) & WILLS (G.), op. cit., pp. 37–43.

6. See: GABOR (A.) & GRANGER (C.). Price Consciousness of Consumers. Consulted in: TAYLOR (B.) & WILLS (G.), op. cit., pp. 5–25. ADAM (D.). Consumer Reactions to Price. Consulted in: TAYLOR (B.) & WILLS (G.), op. cit., pp. 75–88. GUTJAHR (G.). Wie preistolerant ist der Verbraucher? Marketing Journal, No. 6, 1976, pp. 530–532. DELLA BITTA (A.J.), MONROE (K.B.) & McGINNIS (J.M.). Consumer Perceptions of Comparative Price Advertisements. Journal of Marketing Research, November 1981, pp. 416–427. MONROE (K.B.), DELLA BITTA (A.J.) & DOWNEY (S.L.). Contextual Influences on Subjective Price Perceptions. Journal of Business Research, December 1977, pp. 277–291. WILLENBORG (J.F.) & PITTS (R.E.). Perceived Situational Effects on Price Sensitivity. Journal of Business Research, March 1977, pp. 27–38. STERN (H.W.). Markte oder Preis: Entscheidingskriterium der Verbraucher. Der Markenartikel, No. 3, 1981, pp. 138–150 (market consciousness is greater than price consciousness). LEEFLANG (P.S.H.) & BEUKENKAMP (P.A). Probleemgebied marketing: een managementbenadering. Leiden, H.E. Stenfert-Kroese B.V., 1981, pp. 573–576.

7. See STOETZEL (J.). Psychological and Sociological Aspects of Price. Consulted in: TAYLOR (B.) & WILLS (G.), op. cit., pp. 70–74. VERHULP (J.). Prijsacceptatie. Bedrijskunde, No. 1, 1978, pp. 60–64.

8. ALLEN (B.H.) & LAMBERT (D.R.). Searching for the Best Price: An Experimental Look at Consumer Research Effort. Journal of the Academy of Marketing Science, Fall 1978, pp. 245–257. GOLDMAN (A.). Consumer Knowledge of Food Prices as an Indicator of Shopping Effectiveness. Journal of Marketing, October 1977, pp. 67–75, claims that price consciousness is inversely proportional to income bracket.

9. VAN DE WOESTIJNE (W.). Prijspolitiek van de producent. Economisch-Statistische Berichten, 21 November 1956, pp. 1026–1027. LAMBIN (J.). La decision commerciale face a l'incertain. Leuven, Vander, 1965, pp. 70–72, where a frequency table is given of the last digit of price numbers.

10. McCARTHY (E.J.). Basic Marketing: A Managerial Approach. Homewood, Ill., Irwin, 1978, p. 518. STANTON (W.J.), op. cit., pp. 263–264. BELL (M.L.). Marketing Concepts and Strategy. Boston, Houghton-Mifflin, 1979, pp. 422–423. KOTLER (P.). Principles of Marketing. Englewood Cliffs, N.J., Prentice-Hall, 1980, pp. 409–410. See also the conclusion about ''charm pricing'' of DEAN (J.). Managerial Economics. Englewood Cliffs, N.J., Prentice-Hall, 1956, pp. 490–491.

11. For a thorough discussion of these problems: SCHOBER (A.). Produktions—und Nachfrageelastizität als Determinanten der Preispolitik. Frankfurt, F. Nowack Verlag, 1962, p. 109.

12. OXENFELDT (A.). Executive Action in Marketing. Belmont, Wadsworth, 1966, p. 258.

13. See, however, SIMON (H.). Dynamics of Price Elasticity and Brand Life Cycle: An Empirical Study. Journal of Marketing Research, November 1979, pp. 439–452.

14. This is proved by empirical evidence: FOG (B.). Industrial Pricing Policies. Amsterdam, North Holland Publishing, 1960, pp. 48–49. Haynes touches on that in his inquiry in 88 small firms not a trace was to be found of some quantitative approach of elasticity. See: HAYNES (W.). Pricing Decisions in Small Business. Lexington, University of Kentucky Press, 1962, p. 44.

15. See GUTENBERG (E.). Grundlagen der Betriebswirtschaftslehre. Band II. Der Absatz. Berlin, Springer Verlag, 1962, p. 166. MOLLER (H.). Kalkulation, Absatzpolitick und Preisbildung. Tübingen, J.C.B. Mohr (Paul Siebeck), 1962, p. 44. HARTMANN (B.). Preisbildung und Preispolitik. Stuttgart C.E. Poeschel Verlag, 1963, p. 55.

16. JACOB (H.). Preispolitik. Weisbaden, Th. Gabler Verlag, 1963, p. 37.

17. For further comments about market entrance as price determinant: see HARPER (D.). Price Policy and Procedure. New York, Harcourt, Brace & World, 1966, pp. 76–77. HEFLEBOWER (B.). Some Observations on Industrial Prices. Journal of Business, July 1954, pp. 187–195. JACOB (H.), op. cit., pp. 36–37.

18. DEAN (J.), op. cit., pp. 409–410.

19. For an example of the impact of product differentiation and product substitution on pricing policy, see: LAZER (W.). Price determination in the Western Canadian Garment Industry. Journal of Industrial Economics, March 1957, pp. 135–136.

20. STANTON (W.J.), op. cit., p. 230.

21. OXENFELDT (A.),op. cit., p. 263, points out quite rightly that quantitative techniques at their actual stage of development have only a limited significance for practically resolving problems of a competitive nature.

22. For a more detailed discussion of these aspects, see HARPER (D.), op. cit., pp. 42–49.

23. Here, the technical life cycle is discussed. Furthermore, there is an extensive literature about the relationship between "financial" and "commercial" life cycles and pricing policy. See: LEEFLANG (P.S.H.) & BEUKENKAMP (P.A.), op. cit., pp. 311–341. RADEMAKER (B.). Industriële Marketing voor Strategisch Beleid. Deventer, Kluwer, 1981, pp. 81–91. MATHIEU (G.). Lebenszyklen als Entscheidingshilfe. Marketing Journal, No. 2, 1978, pp. 122–128. DEAN (J.). Pricing Policies for New Products. Harvard Business Review, November-December 1976, pp. 141–150. SIZER (J.). Pricing Policy in Inflation: A Management Accountant's Perspective. Accounting and Business Research, Spring 1976, pp. 107–109. SIMON (H.). Preisstrategie und Markenlebenszyklus. Der Markenartikel, No. 8, 1980, pp. 410–416.

24. For a practical example, see HAGUE (D.), op. cit., p. 181.

25. For a general discussion of the relation: activity ratio-cost-selling price, see: TUCKER (S.A.). Profit Planning Decisions with the Break-Even System. Aldershot, Gower, 1981, pp. 121–124. CLARKE (F.H.), DARROUGH (M.N.) & HEINEKE (J.M.). Optimal Pricing Policy in the Presence of Experience Effects. Journal of Business, October 1982, pp. 517–530. WILLEMS (A.D.). Het prijselement in de industriële marketing. Tijdschrift voor Marketing, October 1980, pp. 10–13. DOLAN (R.J.) & JEULAND (A.P.). Experience Curve and Dynamic Demand Models: Implications for Pricing Strategies. Journal of Marketing, Winter 1981, pp. 52–62.

26. JACOB (H.), op. cit., p. 56.

27. See also: HARPER (D.), op. cit., pp. 37–40. PHELPS (D.) & WESTING (J.). Marketing Management. Homewood, Ill., Irwin, 1968, pp. 315–316. FARRIS (P.W.) & REIBSTEIN (D.J.). How Prices, Ad Expenditures and Profits are Linked. Harvard Business Review, November-December 1979, p. 173–184.

28. See McRAE (T.), op. cit., p. 292.

29. HAGUE (D.), op. cit., pp. 95–96.

30. Ibid., pp. 260–261.

CHAPTER 3

1. Some elegant discussions of cost-oriented pricing can be found in: LEEFLANG (P.S.H.) & BEUKENKAMP (P.A.). Probleemgebied marketing. Een management benadering. Leiden, H.E. Stenfert-Kroese B.V., 1981, pp. 595–598. KOTLER (P.). Principles of Marketing. Englewood Cliffs, N.J., Prentice-Hall, 1980, pp. 402–405. GABOR (A.). Pricing. Principles and Practice. London, Heinemann, 1977, pp. 49–69. DAVIES (J.) & HUGHES (S.). Pricing in Practice. London, Heinemann, 1975, pp. 27–44. OXENFELDT (A.R.). The Computation of Costs for Price Decisions. Industrial Marketing Management, No. 2, 1977, pp. 83–90.

2. PHELPS (D.) & WESTING (J.). Marketing Management. Homewood, Ill., Irwin, 1968, p. 321.

3. See HUBNER (T.). Marketing Factors in Fixing Prices. AICA Cost Bulletin, May 1960, p. 19.

4. For a price-setting problem with accent on positioning within a price range, see OLMI (A.). Bedrijf en bedrijfseconoom. Alphen a/d Rijn, N.V. Samsom, 1970. pp. 58–67.

5. See, for example: VAN ACKER (J.). Bewuste commerciële beleidsvoering. Ghent, Seminarie voor Produktiviteitsstudie en Onderzoek, 1968, p. 383.

6. Some thorough discussions of demand-oriented pricing can be found in: McCARTHY (E.J.). Basic Marketing: A Managerial Emphasis. Homewood, Ill., Irwin, 1978, pp. 516–519. LEEFLANG (P.S.H.) & BEUKENKAMP (P.A.), op. cit., pp. 598–602. GABOR, (A.), op. cit., pp. 179–191. JOLSON (M.A.). Marketing Management. New York, Macmillan, 1978, pp. 474–475. MONROE (K.B.). Pricing: Making Profitable Decisions. New York, McGraw-Hill, 1979, pp. 17–48; SHAPIRO (B.P.) & JACKSON (B.B.). Industrial Pricing to Meet Customers' Needs. Harvard Business Review, November-December 1978, pp. 119–127. THOMPSON (H.A.). The Use of Customer Attitude Assessment in Pricing. Industrial Marketing Management, June 1975, pp. 107–111. PATRICK (K.J.) & COAKER (J.W.). The Importance of Price as a Choice Criterion for Industrial Purchasing Decisions. Industrial Marketing Management, No. 3, 1976, pp. 281–293. JAIN (S.C.) & LARIC (M.V.). A Framework for Strategic Pricing. Industrial Marketing Management, January 1979, pp. 75–80. WAGNER (W.B.). Changing Industrial Buyer-Seller Pricing Concern. Industrial Marketing Management, April 1981, pp. 109–117.

7. STIGLER (G.). The Kinky Oligopoly Demand Curve and Rigid Prices. Journal of Political Economy, October 1947, p. 444.

8. PHELPS (D.) & WESTING (J.), op. cit., p. 313.

9. See: COTTA (A.). Politique de prix et strategie d'entreprise. Concurrence, fourth trimester, 1971, pp. 13–14. LIPPMAN (S.). Optimal Pricing to Retard Entry. Review of Economic Studies, July 1980, pp. 723–731. SIMON (H.). Preispolitik bei ertwartetem Konkurenzeintritt. Zeitschrift für Betriebswirtschaft, December 1977, pp. 745–766.

10. BATES (J.) & PARKINSON (J.). Business Economics. Oxford, Basil Blackwell, 1971, p. 173.

11. For a discussion of competition-oriented pricing policy, see: LEEFLANG (P.S.H.) & BEUKENKAMP (P.A.), op. cit., 593–595, KOTLER (P.), op. cit., pp. 408–409.

12. For a discussion of advantages and disadvantages of general and individual pricing policy, see: PHELPS (D.) & WESTING (J.), op. cit., pp. 362–363.

13. Ibid., p. 363.

14. First published in: OXENFELDT (A.). Multi-stage Approach to Pricing. Harvard Business Review, July-August 1960, pp. 125–133.

15. See STANTON (W.J.). Fundamentals of Marketing. New York, McGraw-Hill, 1981, p. 228. RICHERS (R.). Eine Strategie der Preisbestimmung für die Unternehmung. Kostenrechnungspraxis, October 1967, pp. 195–206.

16. An ample discussion of this pricing method can be found in: BROWN (W.) & JAQUES (E.). Product Analysis Pricing. London, Heinemann, 1964, p. 148. A brief discussion and evaluation in: SIMONS (L.). Product Analysis Pricing. Consulted in: TAYLOR (B.) & WILLS (G.). Pricing Strategy. London, Staples Press, 1969, pp. 334–345.

17. For the last-mentioned aspects, see LYNN (R.). Price Policies and Marketing Management. Homewood, Ill., Irwin, 1967, pp. 116–118.

18. FOG (B.). Industrial Pricing Policies. Amsterdam, North-Holland Publishing, 1960, p. 136.

19. VAN ACKER (J.), op. cit., p. 378.

20. Ibid., p. 379. DEAN (J.). Managerial Economics. Englewood Cliffs, N.J., Prentice-Hall, 1956, p. 434.

21. OXENFELDT (A.). Industrial Pricing and Market Practices. New York, Prentice-Hall, 1951, p. 297, where an American metal producer interprets his behavior as follows: "We follow the prices set by the bigger companies because it is the custom of the industry. We have always done it . . . I think they know what they are doing; they probably know what their costs are a lot better than I do. . . . I must confess that our costs are very sketchy."

22. Government intervention in pricing is really a subject apart. General considerations can be found in: MITCHELL (J.). Price Determination and Prices Policy. London, G. Allen & Unwin, 1978, pp. 36–45. DAVIES (J.) & HUGHES (S.), op. cit., pp. 126–150. COWAN (T.). Price Control Decisions—The Realistic Approach. Accountancy, February 1976, pp. 64–68. SIZER (J.). Pricing Policy in Inflation: A Management Accountant's Perspective. Accounting and Business Research, Spring 1976, p. 114 and following. SIMON (D.S.). The Effect of a Price Code on Company Profits in a Period of Inflation. Accountancy and Business Research, Autumn 1977, pp. 295–299.

23. DE BONDT (R.). Industrial Economic Aspects of Belgian Price Regulation. Tijdschrift voor Economie en Management, No. 2, 1978, p. 250.

24. REYNOLDS (A.). A Kind Word for "Cream Skimming." Harvard Business Review, November-December 1974, pp. 113–120.

25. DEARDEN (J.). Taming Predatory Pricing. Financial Executive, January 1983, pp. 38–44.

CHAPTER 4

1. For a brief but sound discussion of high and low prices with the help of many examples, see: LYNN (R.). Price Policies and Marketing Management. Homewood, Ill., Irwin, 1967, pp. 130–142. See also: GARRISON (R.). Managerial Accounting. Plano, Texas, Business Publications, 1982, pp. 497–498.

2. See DEARDEN (J.). Taming Predatory Pricing. Financial Executive, January 1983, pp. 38–44.

3. See: DEAN (J.). Managerial Economics. Englewood Cliffs, N.J., Prentice-Hall, 1956, p. 419. REYNOLDS (A.) A Kind Word for "Cream Skimming." Harvard Business Review, November-December 1974, pp. 113–120.

4. KAPLAN (A.), DIRLAM (J.) & LANZILOTTI (R.). Pricing in Big Business. Washington, D.C., Brookings Institution, 1958, p. 100.

5. DEAN (J.), op. cit., p. 420.

6. For a more thorough discussion of the reasons for price changes, see: LYNN (R.), op. cit., pp. 178–185. PHELPS (D.) & WESTING (J.). Marketing Management. Homewood, Ill., Irwin, 1968, pp. 358–359. STRAUCH (P.) & NOUGAREDE (G.). L'innovation et les prix. Concurrence, first trimester, 1972, pp. 49–61. KOTLER (P.). Principles of Marketing. Englewood Cliffs, N.J., Prentice-Hall, 1980, pp. 412–415. ARNOLD (J.). An Approach to Pricing and Output Decisions When Prices Are Changing. Journal of Business Finance and Accounting, No. 4, 1977, pp. 383–406. EDEN (B.). Towards a Theory of Competitive Price Adjustments. Review of Economic Studies, April 1981, pp. 199–216.

7. VAN ACKER (J.). Bewuste Commerciële Beleidsvoering. Ghent, Seminarie voor Produktiviteitsstudie en Onderzoek, 1968, p. 358.

8. MELLEROWICZ (K.). Preis-, Kosten-, und Produktgestaltung als Mittel der Absatzpolitik. Der Markenartikel, 1959, p. 479.

9. For a discussion of advantages and disadvantages of fixed prices, see PHELPS (D.) & WESTING (J.), op. cit., p. 361. See also: SHESHINSKY (E.) & WEISS (Y.). Inflation and Cost of Price Adjustments. Review of Economic Studies, June 1977, pp. 287–303. GEE (K.G.). A Note on Cost Escalation Clauses. Journal of Business Finance and Accounting, No. 3, 1979, pp. 339–346.

10. WITLOX (H.). Compositie rond de commerciële voorkeursbehandeling. Maandschrift Economie, May 1960, p. 457.

11. Criticisms of price differentiation can be found in: ibid., pp. 474–475. DEAN (J.), op. cit., pp. 508–510. MARTIN (J.). Justifying Price Differentials. Management Accounting, November 1965, p. 56. Verkaufen Sie mehr durch Preisdifferenzierung. Absatzwirtschaft, December 1972, pp. 48–56. BLATTBERG (R.C.), EPPEN (G.D.) & LIEBERMANN (J.). A Theoretical and Empirical Evaluation of Price Deals for Consumer Nondurables. Journal of Marketing, Winter 1981, pp. 116–129. CHIANG (R.) & SPATT (C.S.). Imperfect Price Discrimination and Welfare. Review of Economic Studies, April 1982, pp. 155–181. WIESMETH (H.). Price Discrimination Based on Imperfect Information: Necessary and Sufficient Conditions. Review of Economic Studies, July 1982, pp. 391–402.

12. See VAN ACKER (J.), op. cit., pp. 396–397.

13. An extended enumeration is mentioned by: COLBERG (M.), FORBUSH (D.) & WHITAKER (G.) Business Economics. Homewood, Ill., Irwin, 1970, pp. 369–372, and Verkaufen Sie mehr, op. cit., pp. 48–49 (table).

14. Further comments about this market segmentation can be found in: DEAN (J.), op. cit., pp. 512–515; this segmentation can sometimes take rather surprising forms. See, for example: WISE (G.L.). Differential Pricing and Treatment by New Car Salesmen: The Effect of the Prospect's Race, Sex and Dress. Journal of Business, April 1974, pp. 218–230.

15. VAN ACKER (J.), op. cit., pp. 398–399.

16. An investigation in 120 British industrial firms states that 69% of them practice

export price discrimination. See: PIERCY (N.). British Export Market Selection and Pricing. Industrial Marketing Management, October 1981, pp. 287–297.

17. The discussion of these "geographic price policies" exceeds the framework of this book. For further information, see: STANTON (W.). Fundamentals of Marketing. New York, McGraw-Hill, 1981, pp. 259–260. McCARTHY (E.). Basic Marketing: A Managerial Approach. Homewood, Ill., Irwin, 1978, pp. 497–501. HARPER (D.). Price Policy and Procedure. New York, Harcourt, Brace & World, 1966, pp. 203–220. LYNN (R.), op. cit., pp. 206–209. DEAN (J.), op. cit., pp. 541–548. PHELPS (D.) & WESTING (J.), op. cit., pp. 400–407.

18. See GABOR (A.). Pricing, Principles and Practice. London, Heinemann, 1977, pp. 81–84.

19. More information about product line pricing can be found in: McCARTHY (E.) op. cit., pp. 519–520. GABOR (A.), op. cit., pp. 143–151. BELL (M.L.). Marketing Concepts and Strategy. Boston, Houghton-Mifflin, 1979, pp. 410–411. MONROE (K.B.). Pricing: Making Profitable Decisions. New York, McGraw-Hill, 1979, pp. 141–153. KOTLER (P.), op. cit., pp. 416–417. MONROE (K.B.) & ZOLTNERS (A.A.). Pricing the Product Line during Periods of Scarcity. Journal of Marketing, Summer 1979, pp. 49–59.

20. Some general aspects are discussed in: WAGNER (W.B.). Changing Industrial Buyer-Seller Pricing Concern. Industrial Marketing Management, April 1981, pp. 109–117.

21. MELLEROWICZ (K.). Untermehmenspolitik, Band II. Freiburg im Breisgau, Rudolf Haufe Verlag, 1963, pp. 71–73.

22. An ample discussion of the relation product policy–price policy can be found in MELLEROWICZ (K.). Preis-, Kosten-, und Produktgestaltung als Mittel der Absatzpolitik, op. cit. pp. 477–482.

23. See, however: SHAKED (A.) & SUTTON (J.). Relaxing Price Competition through Product Differentiation. Review of Economic Studies, January 1982, pp. 3–13.

24. Some important considerations about this can be found in: LEVY (J.) & DE BISSY (R.). La formation des prix dans l'enterprise. Organisation Gestion de l'Entreprise, February 1972, pp. 45–47. BELL (M.L.), op. cit., pp. 426–428. METWALLY (M.M.) & DAVY (G.M.). Advertising—Price Competition and Market Stability. Industrial Marketing Management, No. 3, 1977, pp. 237–240. FARRIS (P.W.) & REIBSTEIN (D.J.). How Prices, Ad Expenditures and Profits Are Linked. Harvard Business Review, November-December 1979, pp. 173–184.

25. A detailed discussion of this relationship can be found in: SANDIG (C.). Betriebswirtschaftspolitik. Stuttgart, C.E. Poeschel Verlag, 1966, pp. 215–219 and p. 245.

26. DEAN (J.), op. cit., p. 484.

CHAPTER 5

1. See also: HEINZELBECKER (K.). Marketing—Informationssysteme heute. Marketing Journal, No. 2, 1978, pp. 133–138.

2. DE LEMBRE (E.), GEORGES (W.), PAEMELEIRE (R.) & VAN GEYT (E.). Analytisch boekhouden en Kostencalculatie. Brussels, C.E.D. Samsom, 1982, p. 31.

3. EARLEY (J.). Recent Developments in Cost Accounting and the Marginal Analysis. Journal of Political Economy, June 1955, p. 230.

4. See, for instance: VANDER SCHROEFF (H.J.). Kosten en kostprijs. Deel I.

Amsterdam, N.V. Kosmos, 1970, pp. 38–42. MATZ (A.) & CURRY (D.). Cost Accounting. Cincinnati, South-Western, 1972, p. 41. MOEWS (D.). Zur Aussagefähigkeit neuerer Kostenrechnungsverfahren. Berlin, Duncker & Humblot, 1969, pp. 36–37 and 42–45. MELLEROWICZ (K.). Kosten und Kostenrechnung. Berlin, W. de Gruyter, 1958, pp. 56–58. THOMPSON MONTGOMERY (A.). Managerial Accounting Information. Reading, Penn., Addison-Wesley, 1979, pp. 257–264. MORSE (W.J.). Cost Accounting. Reading, Penn., Addison-Wesley, 1981, pp. 274–280. EILER (K.G.), GOLETZ (W.K.) & KEEGAN (D.P.) Is Your Cost Accounting Up to Date? Harvard Business Review, July-August 1982, p. 134. WOLF (W.G.). Developing a Cost System for Today's Decision Making. Management Accounting, December 1982, pp. 20–21. WIJNBERG (H.E.). Direct Costing en bijdragecalculatie I. Tijdschrift Financieel Management, No. 2, 1982, pp. 76–77.

5. See VERBURG (P.). De betekenis van de kosteninformatie voor de besluitvorming. Leiden, H.E. Stenfert-Kroese, 1966, p. 14.

6. For a more detailed discussion of the quantity dimension, see: VAN DER SCHROEFF (H.J.), op. cit., pp. 96–108; applied to raw materials, pp. 148–152; applied to labor costs, pp. 302–306.

7. There is at present a very extensive literature about the value dimension of costs as part of the broader subject "inflation accounting." Considerations in connection with pricing policy can be found in: VAN DER SCHROEFF (H.J.), op. cit., pp. 84–96. KAPLAN (R.S.). Advanced Management Accounting. Englewood Cliffs, N.J., Prentice-Hall, 1982, pp. 233–235. BOURN (M.), STONEY (P.J.M.) & WYNN (R.F.). Price Indices for Current Cost Accounting. Journal of Business Finance and Accounting, No. 3, 1976, pp. 149–172. DEAN (J.) How to Price during Inflation. European Journal of Marketing, Vol. 13, 1979, pp. 213–227. WEBSTER (F.E.), LARGAY III (J.A.) & STICKNEY (C.P.). The Impact of Inflation Accounting for Marketing Decisions. Journal of Marketing, Fall 1980, pp. 9–17. VAN DER ZIJPP (I.). Herwaarderingen in Kostencalculatie. Maandblad voor Bedrijfsadministratie en Organisatie, March 1982, pp. 80–82. ARNOLD (J.). An Approach to Pricing and Output Decisions When Prices Are Changing. Journal of Business Finance and Accounting, No. 4, 1977, pp. 383–406.

8. See, for instance: ALLEN (B.), TATHEM (R.) & LAMBERT (D.). Flexible Pricing Strategies for High Inflation Periods. Industrial Marketing Management, No. 4, 1976, pp. 243–248. SHESHINSKY (E.) & WEISS (Y.). Inflation and Cost of Price Adjustments. Review of Economic Studies, June 1977, pp. 287–303. GEE (K.G.). A Note on Cost Escalation Clauses. Journal of Business Finance and Accounting, No. 3, 1979, p. 339–346. DOLAN (R.J.). Pricing Strategies That Adjust to Inflation. Industrial Marketing Management, July 1981, pp. 151–156.

9. VAN DER SCHROEFF (H.J.), op. cit., pp. 15–16.

10. For an example, see ibid., op. cit., p. 94.

11. N.A.A. Product Costs for Pricing Purposes. Research Report No. 14, New York, N.A.A., 1953, p. 16.

12. The valuation moment is not specified, however.

13. N.A.A., op. cit., p. 19.

14. FOG (B.) Industrial Pricing Policies. Amsterdam, North-Holland, 1960, pp. 64–68.

15. See especially VAN DER SCHROEFF (H.J.), op. cit., pp. 82–83 and pp. 109–111.

CHAPTER 6

1. Valuable discussions of cost concepts in relation to pricing policy can be found in: HEITGER (L.E.) & MATULICH (S.). Managerial Accounting. New York, McGraw-Hill, 1982, pp. 26–92. MOST (K.) & LEWIS (R.J.) Cost Accounting. Columbus, Ohio, Grid, 1982, pp. 63–92. GARRISON (R.H.). Managerial Accounting. Plano, Texas, Business Publication, 1982, pp. 27–60. MONROE (K.B.). Pricing: Making Profitable Decisions. New York, McGraw-Hill, 1979, pp. 51–59. PAEMELEIRE (R.), GEORGES (W.) & VAN GEYT (E.). Kostencalculatie en beleidsbeslissingen. Brussels, CED-Samsom, 1983, pp. 91–98. KAPLAN (R.S.). Advanced Management Accounting. Englewood Cliffs, N.J., Prentice-Hall, 1982, pp. 23–40. OXENFELDT (A.). The Computation of Costs for Price Decisions. Industrial Marketing Management, No. 2, 1977, pp. 83–90.

2. See CLARK (J.). Studies in the Economics of Overhead Costs. Chicago, University of Chicago Press, 1950, p. 175 and passim.

3. The difference between fixed and variable costs sometimes happens to be rather tricky; see: WHITING (E.). Fixed/Variable Cost: Beware! Accountancy, May 1981, pp. 74–78.

4. Such techniques are discussed in most books about cost accounting. Some methods used in practice are set out in: N.A.A. Separating and Using Costs as Fixed and Variable. New York, N.A.A., Accounting Practice Report No. 10, 1960.

5. See: HAGUE (D.C). Pricing in Business. London, G. Allen & Unwin, 1971, p. 164.

6. An important view about these three criteria can be found in: UNTERGUGGEN-BERGER (S.). Cybernetica en Direct Costing. Leiden, H.E. Stenfert-Kroese B.V., 1973, pp. 85–92.

7. See especially: AGHTE (K.). Stufenweise Fixkostendeckung im System des Direct Costing. Zeitschrift für Betriebswirtschaft, July 1959, pp. 406–409.

8. RIEBEL (P.). Einzelkosten- und Deckungsbeitragsrechnung. Opladen, Westdeutscher Verlag, 1982, pp. 38–39.

9. See AGHTE (K.), op. cit., pp. 410–411, and RIEBEL (P.), op. cit., p. 39.

10. Sometimes, the concepts "unique" costs and "joint" costs are used instead of direct and indirect costs. See: DEARDEN (J.). Taming Predatory Pricing. Financial Executive, January 1983, pp. 38–44.

11. See, for example: BLANCHARD (G.A.) & CHOW (C.W.). Allocating Indirect Costs for Improved Management Performance. Management Accounting, March 1983, pp. 38–40.

12. See, for example: LADD (D.R.). The Role of Costs in Pricing Decisions. Hamilton, Ontario, Society of Industrial and Cost Accountants of Canada, 1965, p. 29.

13. The meaning of the concept "opportunity costs" is not fixed unequivocally but varies in function of the firm's objectives. In the case of profit maximization the opportunity costs are measured as the lost profit of the best of all alternatives being omitted. The definition of opportunity costs in case of a band of objectives can be very problematic. See with regard to this: UNTERGUGGENBERGER (S.), op. cit., pp. 77–79.

14. See FISHER (L.). Industrial Marketing. London, Business Books, 1969, p. 206. OXENFELDT (A.) & BAXTER (W.). Approaches to Pricing: Economist versus Accountant. Consulted in: TAYLOR (B.) & WILLS (G.). Pricing Strategy. London, Staples

Press, 1969, pp. 401–418. HORNGREN (C.T.) Introduction to Management Accounting. London, Prentice-Hall International, 1981, pp. 118–120. VAN HELLEMAN (J.). Inhoud en toepassing van het "opportunity cost" begrip. Rotterdam, Erasmus Universiteit, s.d., s.p. MACKEY (J.T.). Allocating Opportunity Cost. Management Accounting, March 1983, pp. 33–37.

15. RIEBEL (P.), op. cit., p. 52.
16. See N.A.A. Product Costs for Pricing Purposes. New York, N.A.A., 1953, pp. 46–53. SLOT (R.). Kostenvariabiliteit en variable kostencalculatie. Leiden, H.E. Stenfert-Kroese N.V., 1962, p. 150.
17. See also: MARTIN (J.R.). Multiproduct Profit Analyses: Contribution Margin vs. Gross Profit. Cost and Management, September-October 1982, pp. 22–27.
18. See also UNTERGUGGENBERGER (S.), op. cit., p. 94.
19. See also RIEBEL (P.), op. cit., pp. 38–39.
20. See also PAEMELEIRE (R.), GEORGES (W.) & VAN GEYT (E.), op. cit., pp. 116–117.
21. RIEBEL (P.), op. cit., p. 37.

CHAPTER 7

1. Definitions of price floors are discussed by: RAFFEE (H.). Kurzfristige Preisuntergrenzen als betriebswirtschaftliches Problem. Köln, Westdeutscher Verlag, 1961, pp. 12–15. REICHMANN (T.). Kosten und Preisgrenzen. Weisbaden, Th. Gabler Verlag, 1973, p. 11. TETTERO (J.H.J.P.). Bodemprijzen en levensmiddelen. Markeur, June-July 1982, pp. 14–16.
2. RAFFEE (H.), op. cit., p. 59.
3. For an evaluation of this monistic view, see ibid., pp. 60–62.
4. See BICKEL (G.). Die Preisuntergrenze unter besonderen Berück-sichtigung der Sorge um die Liquidität. Zeitschrift für Betriebswirtschaft, August 1966, p. 527–543.
5. See KILGER (W.). Flexible Plankostenrechnung. Köln, Westdeutscher Verlag, 1970, pp. 677–683. PACK (L.). Zum Problem statischer und dynamischer Preisuntergrenzen. Consulted in: KOCH (H.). Zur Theorie des Absatzes. Weisbaden, Th. Gabler Verlag, 1973, p. 304.
6. See PACK (L.), op. cit., pp. 353–362, and RAFFEE (H.), op. cit., pp. 113–133.
7. DEAN (J.). Managerial Economics. Englewood Cliffs, N.J., Prentice-Hall, 1956, pp. 484–485.
8. RAFFEE (H.), op. cit., pp. 134–135.
9. See, for example: VAN ACKER (J.). Bewuste Commerciële Beleidsvoering. Ghent, Seminarie voor Produktiviteitsstudie en Onderzoek, 1968, p. 391.
10. See REICHMANN (T.), op. cit., pp. 16–25.
11. HAX (H.). Preisuntergrenzen im Ein- und Mehrproduktbetrieb. Zeitschrift für handelswissenschaftliche Forschung, August-September 1961, pp. 424–425.
12. See UNTERGUGGENBERGER (S.). Cybernetica en Direct Costing, Leiden, H.E. Stenfert-Kroese, 1973, p. 129.
13. RAFFEE (H.), op. cit., pp. 36–37.
14. MOEWS (D.). Zur Ausagefähigkeit neueren Kostenrechnungsverfahren. Berlin, Duncker & Humblot, 1969, pp. 72–73.
15. REICHMANN (T.), op. cit., pp. 35–36.

16. See LANGEN (T.). Dynamische Preisuntergrenzen. Zeitschrift für betriebswirtschaftliche Forschung, 1966, pp. 649–659. PACK (L.), op. cit., pp. 301–379.

17. The impact of inventory policy on cost-oriented price floors is thoroughly discussed in: RAFFEE (H.), op. cit., pp. 101–113. MOEWS (D.), op. cit., pp. 79–84. REICHMANN (T.), op. cit., pp. 54–62 and 98–103.

18. This problem is thoroughly discussed by: RAFFEE (H.), op. cit., pp. 74–79. SCHMIDT (R.). Aspekte zur Bestimmung finanzwirtschaftlicher Preisuntergrenzen. Betriebswirtschaftliche Forschung und Praxis, 1965, pp. 284–289. ENGELEITER (H.). Die Bestimmung der Preisuntergrenze als investitions-theoretisches Problem. Betriebswirtschaftliche Forschung und Praxis, No. 10, 1965, pp. 572–581. KILGER (W.), op. cit., pp. 683–688. PACK (L.), op. cit., pp. 351–376. REICHMANN (T.), op. cit., pp. 20–25 and passim. KÖHLER (R.) & STÖLZEL (A.). Nutzen Sie Ihr Rechnungswesen für die Preispolitik. Marketing Journal, No. 5, 1976, p. 492.

19. See especially: SCHNEIDER (G.). Fixkosten und Kalkulation im Konkurrenzkampf. Berlin, E. Schmidt Verlag, 1967, p. 83.

20. RAFFEE (H.), op. cit., p. 73.

21. DEARDEN (J.). Taming Predatory Pricing. Financial Executive, January 1983, pp. 39–41.

22. Temporary stoppage of business can also generate revenues such as interest on finances out of use, revenues from selling patents, and so on; see: SCHNEIDER (G.), op. cit., p. 82.

23. ENGELEITER (H.), op. cit., pp. 569–570.

24. RAFFEE (H.), op. cit., p. 99.

25. REICHMANN (T.), op. cit., p. 73, and KRUSCHWITZ (L.). Die Kalkulation von Kuppelprodukten. Kostenrechnungspraxis, October 1973, pp. 219–230.

26. RAFFEE (H.), op. cit., p. 98.

27. For a thorough discussion, see REICHMANN (T.), op. cit., pp. 62–69.

28. RAFFEE (H.), op. cit., pp. 163–167 and pp. 173–174.

29. Ibid., p. 178.

30. See LANGEN (W.), op. cit., pp. 650–651; BICKEL (G.), op. cit., p. 540; and KILGER (W.), op. cit., pp. 674–676.

31. See for this view: BICKEL (G.), op. cit., pp. 527–543; KILGER (W.), op. cit., pp. 674–675; MOEWS (D.), op. cit., pp. 84–85; and REICHMANN (T.), op. cit., pp. 24–25.

32. RAFFEE (H.), op. cit., p. 174.

33. BICKEL (G.), op. cit., p. 542.

34. See, however: TUCKER (S.). Profit Planning Decisions with the Break-Even System. Aldershot, England, Gower, 1981, pp. 111–112.

35. For a corresponding cost classification, see RAFFEE (H.), op. cit., pp. 156–161.

36. UNTERGUGGENBERGER (S.),op. cit., pp. 129–131.

37. Ibid., p. 130.

CHAPTER 8

1. KÖHLER (R.) & STÖLZEL (A.). Nutzen Sie Ihr Rechnungswesen für die Preispolitik. Marketing Journal, No. 5, 1976, p. 490.

2. See, for example: TUCKER (S.A.). Profit Planning Decisions with the Break-Even Analysis. Aldershot, England, Gower, 1981, pp. 136–147. GABOR (A.). Pricing:

Principles and Practice. London, Heinemann, 1977, pp. 143–151. MONROE (K.B.) & ZOLTNERS (A.A.). Pricing the Product Line during Periods of Scarcity. Journal of Marketing, Summer 1979, pp. 49–59.
3. DEAN (J.). Managerial Economics. Englewood Cliffs, N.J., Prentice-Hall, 1956, pp. 472–477.
4. Pricing based on conversion costs is discussed more in detail section 13.2.
5. See DEAN (J.), op. cit., p. 484. VAN ACKER (J.E.). Bewuste Commerciële Beleidsvoering. Ghent, Seminarie voor Produktiviteitsstudie en Onderzoek, 1968, p. 390.

CHAPTER 9

1. See KOTLER (P.). Principles of Marketing. Englewood Cliffs, N.J., Prentice-Hall, 1980, pp. 412–415.
2. See for this: SIMMONDS (K.). Strategic Management Accounting for Pricing: A Case Example. Accounting and Business Research, Summer 1982, pp. 206–214.
3. LYNN (R.A.). Price Policies and Marketing Management. Homewood, Ill., Irwin, 1967, pp. 179–180.
4. See, for example, DICKEY (R.). Accountants' Cost Handbook. New York, Ronald Press, 1967, pp. 19–31.
5. See TUCKER (S.A.). Profit Planning Decisions with the Break-Even System. Aldershot, England, Gower, 1981, pp. 124–127.
6. See: PAMELEIRE (R.), GEORGES (W.) & VAN GEYT (E.). Kostencalculatie en besleidsbeslissingen. Brussels, CED-Samsom, 1983, pp. 102–103.
7. See for this: GRIFFIN (C.E.). When Is Price Reduction Profitable? Harvard Business Review, September-October 1960, pp. 126–127.
8. See especially ANKUM (L.A.). Prijsinflatie, kostprijsberekening en winstbepaling. Leiden, H.E. Stenfert-Kroese N.V., 1971, pp. 67–69 and pp. 133–138.
9. Ibid., p. 70.
10. FOG (B.). Industrial Pricing Policies. Amsterdam, North-Holland, 1960, pp. 115–116.
11. ANKUM (L.A.), op. cit., pp. 94–95.
12. Ibid., pp. 129–134.
13. For the relationship method of calculation–selling price change, see ibid., pp. 133–137.
14. Though not explicitly, this method of calculation is suggested by ibid., pp. 136–137.

CHAPTER 10

1. This subject still remains substantial in cost and management accounting literature, for example, BATTY (J.). Advanced Cost Accounting. Estover, Macdonald & Evans, 1978, pp. 113–134. MORSE (W.J.). Cost Accounting. Reading, Penn., Addison-Wesley, 1981, pp. 54–99. GARRISON (R.H.). Managerial Accounting. Plano, Texas, Business Publications, 1982, pp. 61–110.
2. See, for examples: PETERS (C.L.). Keeping Competitive in Pricing Defense Contracts. N.A.A. Bulletin, April 1964, pp. 27–33. ROWLANDS (J.J.). Formula Elements of Incentive Contracts. Management Accounting, April 1967, pp. 30–37. YOUNG

(S.L.). The Need for Should-Cost Estimating: Pricing in Aerospace. Management Accounting, November 1968, pp. 38–42.

3. See, for example: SEWALL (M.A.). A Decision Calculus Model for Contract Bidding. Journal of Marketing, October 1976, pp. 92–98.

4. See DEAN (J.). Managerial Economics. Englewood Cliffs, N.J., Prentice-Hall, 1956, p. 492.

5. See, for example: BLOM (F.W.C.). Grenskostenrekening en Direct Costing. Alphen aan den Rijn, N. Samsom N.V., 1969, p. 19.

6. WEBER (H.K.). Fixe und variabele Kosten. Göttingen, Verlag Otto Schwey, 1972, p. 47.

7. GEE (K.G.). A Note on Cost Escalation Clauses. Journal of Business Finance and Accounting, No. 3, 1979, pp. 339–346.

8. NATIONALE MAATSCHAPPIJ VOOR DE HUISVESTING. Tweede deel van het bijzonder bestek NM/B 82 of "Type bestek." Brussels, 1982, pp. 5–6.

CHAPTER 11

1. See, for instance: N.A.A. Product Costs for Pricing Purposes. New York, N.A.A., 1953. KAPLAN (A.D.), DIRLAM (J.B.) & LANZILOTTI (R.F.). Pricing in Big Business. Washington, D.C., Brookings Institution, 1958. FOG (B.). Industrial Pricing Policies. Amsterdam, North-Holland, 1960. BARBACK (R.N.). The Pricing of Manufacturers. London, Macmillan, 1964. HAGUE (D.C). Pricing in Business. London, G. Allen & Unwin, 1971. GORDON (L.A.). The Pricing Decision. New York, N.A.A., 1981.

2. See, for example: RIEBEL (P.). Einzelkosten- und Deckungsbeitragsrechnung. Opladen, Westdeutscher Verlag, 1982, pp. 208–209.

3. See, for example: DHALLA (N.K.). A Guide to New Product Development. Phase 5—Pricing. Canadian Business, April 1964, p. 85.

4. See HALDI (J.). Pricing Behavior: Economic Theory and Business Practice. Current Economic Thought, November 1958, p. 58. MORSE (W.J.). Cost Accounting. Reading, Penn., Addison-Wesley, 1981, pp. 191–197.

5. See, among others, DEAN (J.). Managerial Economics. Englewood Cliffs, N.J., Prentice-Hall, 1956, p. 445. LAIMON (S.). Cost Analysis and Pricing Policies. Cost and Management, September 1961, p. 362.

6. General discussions can be found in: BATTY (J.). Advanced Cost Accounting. Estover, Macdonald & Evans, 1978, pp. 173–195. HEITGER (L.E.) & MATULICH (S.). Managerial Accounting. New York, McGraw-Hill, 1982, pp. 107–133. MORSE (W.J.), op. cit., pp. 100–139.

7. VAN DER SCHROEFF (H.J.). Kosten en Kostprijs. Volume II, Antwerp, Kosmos, 1970, pp. 260–262.

8. See, for instance: VORMBAUM (H.). Kalkulationsarten und Kalkulationsverfahren. Stuttgart, C.E. Poeschel Verlag, 1966. pp. 13–16.

9. See WEBER (H.). Die Verrechnung des Fixkostenblocks in der Produktkalkulation. Kostenrechnungspraxis, August/September 1970, p. 154. RIEBEL (P.), op. cit., p. 57.

10. For definitions of the concept "normal production," see: LANG (T.). Cost Accountants Handbook. New York, Ronald Press, 1954, pp. 1069–1070. DICKEY (R.). Accountants' Cost Handbook. New York, Ronald Press, 1967, pp. 102–103.

11. See VAN DER SCHROEFF (H.J.) Kosten en Kostprijs. Volume I, Antwerp, Kosmos, 1970, p. 69.

12. See VAN DE WOESTIJNE (W.J.). Enkele bedrijfseconomische aspecten van prijstheorie en prijspolitiek. Maandblad Economie, June/July 1965, pp. 507–508.

13. See, for example: BATTY (J.), op. cit., pp. 99–112. KILLOUGH (L.N.) & LEININGER (W.E.). Cost Accounting for Managerial Decision Making. Encino, Calif., Dickenson, 1977, pp. 105–110. GANGOLLY (J.). On Joint Cost Allocation: Independent Cost Proportional Scheme (ICPS) and Its Properties. Journal of Accounting Research, Autumn 1981, pp. 299–312.

14. See BIERMAN (H.). Topics in Cost Accounting and Decisions. New York, McGraw-Hill, 1963, pp. 65–67.

15. See GOODALE (D.). Joint Cost Allocation and Management Decisions. Cost and Management, July/August 1961, pp. 300–308. MATZ (A.) & CURRY (O.). Cost Accounting: Planning and Control. Cincinnati, South-Western, 1972, pp. 712–713.

16. See, for instance: ANTHONY (R.N.) & WELSCH (G.A.). Fundamentals of Management Accounting. Homewood, Ill., Irwin, 1977, pp. 42–49. MONROE (K.B.). Pricing: Making Profitable Decisions. New York, McGraw-Hill, 1979, pp. 90–102. STANTON (W.J.). Fundamentals of Marketing. New York, McGraw-Hill, 1981, pp. 235–239. KAPLAN (R.S.). Advanced Management Accounting. Englewood Cliffs, N.J., Prentice-Hall, 1982, pp. 226–230.

17. See, for example: N.A.A., op. cit., p. 39. BURGERT (R.). Enkele beschouwingen over kosteninformatie ten behoeve van het bedrijfsbeleid. De Economist, March/April 1967, p. 165.

18. See, for instance: TIMMONS (D.). Product Costing for a Meat Packer. N.A.A. Bulletin, March 1961, pp. 81–82.

19. FOG (B.), op. cit., pp. 93–94.

20. See, for example: SHILLINGLAW (G.). Overhead in Costing and Competitive Pricing. Cost and Management, December 1961, pp. 512–515. N.A.A. Accounting for Costs of Capacity. New York, N.A.A., 1963, pp. 60–61.

21. BURGERT (R.), op. cit., p. 179.

22. N.A.A. Costing Joint Products. New York, N.A.A., 1957, pp. 48–49.

23. SHILLINGLAW (G.), op. cit., p. 512.

24. WILES (P.T.). Price, Cost and Output. Oxford, Basil Blackwell, 1961, p. 47.

25. See DEVINE (C.T.). Cost Accounting and Pricing Policies. Consulted in: THOMAS (W.E.). Studies in Cost Accounting, Budgeting and Control. Cincinnati, South-Western, 1960, p. 360. LAIMON (S.), op. cit., p. 363. McRAE (I.W.). Analytical Management. New York, Wiley Interscience, 1970, pp. 275–276.

26. See OXENFELDT (A.R.) & BAXTER (W.). Approaches to Pricing: Economist versus Accountant. Consulted in: TAYLOR (B.) & WILLS (G.). Pricing Strategy. London, Staples Press, 1969, p. 403. FOG (B.), op. cit., pp. 112–115. LAIMON (S.), op. cit., p. 362. HARPER (W.M.). The Pitfalls in Fixing Prices. Accountancy, January 1972, p. 62.

27. LAIMON (S.), op. cit., p. 363.

28. Ibid. JACOB (H.). Preispolitik. Wiesbaden, Gabler Verlag, 1963, p. 106. GIBSON (J.L.) & HAYNES (W.W.). Accounting in Small Business Decisions. Lexington, University of Kentucky Press, 1963, pp. 67–68.

29. HAGUE (D.C.), op. cit., p. 156.

30. See, for example, McCARTHY (E.J.). Basic Marketing: A Managerial Approach. Homewood, Ill., Irwin, 1978, p. 510.

31. SIZER (J.). The Accountant's Contribution to the Pricing Problem. Consulted in: TAYLOR (W.) & WILLS (G.), op. cit., p. 382. DEAN (J.), op. cit., p. 451. SPENCER M.H.). Managerial Economics. Homewood, Ill., Irwin, 1968, pp. 296–297. Mc-CARTHY (E.J.), op. cit., p. 511.

32. See DEAN (J.), op. cit., p. 451. OXENFELDT (A.R.) & BAXTER (W.), op. cit., p. 402. MANTELL (L.H.) & SING (F.P.). Economics for Business Decisions. New York, McGraw-Hill, 1972, p. 242.

33. See, for example, MARTIN (J.R.). Multiproduct Profit Analysis: Contribution Margin vs. Gross Profit. Cost and Management, September/October 1982, pp. 22–27.

34. See, among others: DEAN (J.), op. cit., p. 451. BACKER (M.). The Importance of Costs in Pricing Decisions. Consulted in: MARTING (E.). Creative Pricing. New York, American Management Association, 1968, p. 57. SKINNER (R.C.). The Determination of Selling Prices. Journal of Industrial Economics, July 1970, p. 201. FISHER (L.). Industrial Marketing. London, Business Books, 1969, p. 210. McCARTHY (E.J.), op. cit., pp. 513–514. FINKENRATH (R.). So finden Sie den richtigen Marktpreis. Marketing Journal, No. 6, 1967, pp. 534–538.

35. For the former denomination, see: FOG (B.), op. cit., p. 102. For the latter, see: OXENFELDT (A.R.). Pricing for Marketing Executives. Belmont, Adsworth, 1966, p. 70.

36. According to FOG (B.), op. cit., and HAYNES (W.W.), op. cit., flexible full cost pricing is much in evidence. According to SPENCER (M.H.), op. cit., pp. 297–298, flexible full cost pricing is not a common pricing practice.

37. This pricing method is described by FOG (B.), op. cit., p. 102.

CHAPTER 12

1. MAY (R.). Cost and Value in Pricing Policy. Consulted in: LOCK (D.) & TAVERNIER (G.). Director's Guide to Management Techniques. London, Gower Press, 1970, p. 81. WIJNBERG (H.E.). Direct Costing en Bijdragecalculatie I. Tijdschrift Financieel Management, No. 2, 1982, p. 77.

2. MACHLUP (F.). Marginal Analysis and Empirical Research. American Economic Review, September 1946, pp. 545–547.

3. SIZER (J.). The Accountant's Contribution to the Pricing Decision. Consulted in: TAYLOR (B.) & WILLS (G.). Pricing Strategy. London, Staples Press, 1969, pp. 398–399. HOWE (M.). Marginal Analysis in Accounting. Yorkshire Bulletin of Economic and Social Research, November 1962, p. 89.

4. See LEHMANN (M.R.). Die Problematik der Preispolitik auf Grenzkosten- und auf Vollkosten-Basis. Zeitschrift für Betriebswirtschaft, 1950, pp. 335–336. SOLMS (W.). Wählerisch selektieren. Marktpreisorientierte Kalkulationsverfahren helfen werten. Absatzwirtschaft, March 1970, pp. 27–29.

5. MORSE (W.J.). Cost Accounting. Reading, Penn., Addison-Wesley, 1981, pp. 276–280.

6. See, for instance HOWE (M.), op. cit., pp. 88–89.

7. SIZER (J.), op. cit., p. 384. KNUTZEN (K.K.). Using Direct Costing Information for Pricing. N.A.A. Bulletin, August 1962, p. 47. BACKER (M.) & JACOBSEN (L.E.).

Cost Accounting: A Managerial Approach. New York, McGraw-Hill, 1964, pp. 520–521. FISHER (L.). Industrial Marketing. London, Business Books, 1969, p. 228.

8. Mit der Grenzkostenrechnung aus der Absatzklemme. Absatzwirtschaft, May 1972, p. 40.

9. ANTHONY (R.N.) & WELSCH (G.A.). Fundamentals of Management Accounting. Homewood, Ill., Irwin, 1977, pp. 49–50. KLEIN (D.J.) & HADAD (N.E.). Direct Costing Is Alive and Well, and Doing Nicely, Thank You. Cost and Management, May/June 1982, pp. 46–47.

10. See Part II, Chapter 6. See also OXENFELDT (A.R.). The Computation of Costs for Price Decisions, Industrial Marketing Management, No. 2, 1977, pp. 83–90.

11. See, among others: Mit der Grenzkostenrechnung, op. cit., p. 40. MANTELL (L.H.) & SING (F.P.). Economics for Business Decisions. New York, McGraw-Hill, 1972, pp. 246–247. SOLMS (H.), op. cit., pp. 32–33.

12. See Mit der Grenzkostenrechnung, op. cit., p. 41, and BACKER (M.) & JACOBSEN (L.E.), op. cit., p. 520.

13. See Mit der Grenzkostenrechnung, op. cit., p. 41.

CHAPTER 13

1. See PHELPS (D.M.) & WESTING (J.H.). Marketing Management. Homewood, Ill., Irwin, 1968, p. 323.

2. See, for example, BURGERT (R.) Enkele beschouwingen over kosteninformatie ten behoeve van het bedrijfsbeleid. De Economist, March-April 1967, pp. 187–188. MONROE (K.B.). Pricing: Making Profitable Decisions. New York, McGraw-Hill, 1979, pp. 60–76.

3. See ANDREWS (P.W.S.). Manufacturing Business. London, Macmillan, 1959, pp. 145–204.

4. ANDRIESSEN (J.E.). De ontwikkeling van de moderne prijstheorie. Leiden, H.E. Stenfert Kroese N.V., 1961, p. 170.

5. Ibid., p. 171.

6. See BRUNNER (E.). Competition and the Theory of the Firm. Economia Internazionale, November 1952, p. 731.

7. BRUNNER (E.) op. cit., August 1952, p. 521.

8. ANDREWS (P.W.S.), op. cit., p. 184.

9. Ibid., pp. 148–157.

10. Ibid., pp. 113–180.

11. See HAPGOOD (R.). A New Approach to Profitable Pricing. Consulted in: TAYLOR (B.) & WILLS (G.) Pricing Strategy. London, Staples Press, 1969, pp. 346–355.

12. See WRIGHT (W.). Direct Costs Are Better for Pricing. N.A.A. Bulletin, April 1960, pp. 22–25.

13. See HAPGOOD (R.), op. cit., p. 349. Also, WIJNBERG (H.E.). Het onderscheid vaste en variable kosten: opgepast! Tijdschrift Financieel Management, No. 6, 1982, p. 81.

14. See HAPGOOD (R.), op. cit., p. 350.

15. ROSELL (J.H.) & FRASURE (W.W.). Managerial Accounting. Columbus, Ohio, Charles E. Merill, 1964, p. 511.

16. DEAN (J.). Managerial Economics. Englewood Cliffs, N.J., Prentice-Hall, 1956, p. 475.

17. See BACKER (M.) & JACOBSEN (L.E.). Cost Accounting: A Managerial Approach. New York, McGraw-Hill, 1964, p. 517.

18. See RIEBEL (P.). Einzelkosten- und Deckungsbeitragsrechnung. Opladen, Westdeutscher Verlag, 1982, pp. 35–59.

19. BERRY (L.E.). Deciding on Discretionary Costs: A Cost-Benefit Approach. Cost and Management, July-August 1982, pp. 38–41.

20. RIEBEL (P.), op. cit., p. 46. WIJNBERG (H.E.). Direct Costing en Bijdragecalculatie II. Tijdschrift Financieel Management, No. 3, 1982, pp. 77–79; GARRISON (R.H.) Managerial Accounting. Plano, Texas, Business Publications, 1982, pp. 237–286.

21. MELLEROWICZ (K.) Neutzeitliche Kalkulationsverfahren. Freiburg im Breisgau, R. Haufe Verlag, 1966, p. 145.

22. AICPA. Cost Analysis for Pricing and Distribution Policies. New York, AICPA, 1965, pp. 8–10.

23. RIEBEL (P.), op. cit., p. 64.

CHAPTER 14

1. See DAUMLER (K.D.). Stufenweise Fixkostendeckung. Buchfürung— Bilanz. Kostenrechnung, No. 4, 1982, pp. 120–121.

2. See RIEBEL (P.). Kosten und Preise. Opladen, Westduetscher Verlag, 1972, p. 58.

3. BERRY (L.E.). Deciding on Discretionary Costs: A Cost-Benefit Approach. Cost and Management, July-August 1982, pp. 38–41.

4. This narrow vision is widespread in American cost accounting and marketing literature. The three following examples are chosen from the very extensive literature about pricing policy: HARPER (D.V.). Price Policy and Procedure. New York, Harcourt, Brace and World, 1966, pp. 58–59. LOWELL (S.B.). Pricing Problems and Methods. Management Accounting, March 1967, p. 27. MONROE (K.B.). Pricing: Making Profitable Decisions. New York, McGraw-Hill, 1979, pp. 60–76.

5. See HEINZE (E.). Organisieren Sie Ihren Verkauf als Profit-Center. Marketing Journal, No. 2, 1979, p. 130. RIEBEL (P.). Einzelkosten- und Deckungsbeitragsrechnung. Opladen, Westdeutscher Verlag, 1982, pp. 36–39.

CHAPTER 16

1. See also: RIEBEL (P.). Einzelkosten- und Deckungsbeitragsrechnung. Wiesbaden, Gabler Verlag, 1982, pp. 259–266. BECKER (H.D.). Die Anforderungen der Preispolitik an die Gestaltung der Kostenrechnung. Frankfurt, 1962, pp. 98–104. GRETZ (W.). Richtige Preise durch marktgerechte Angebotskalkulation. Buchfürung-Bilanz-Kostenrechnung, No. 19, 1982, pp. 663–672. MOSSMAN (F.H.), CRISSY (W.J.E.) & FISHER (P.M.). Financial Dimensions of Marketing Management. New York, J. Wiley & Sons, 1978, pp. 25–51. MONROE (K.B.) Pricing: Making Profitable Decisions. New York, McGraw-Hill, 1979, pp. 60–76.

2. RIEBEL (P.), op. cit., pp. 158–165.

3. See also GAYDOUL (P.), HORVATH (P.) & SCHAFER (H.T.). Deckungsbeitragsrechnung. Wiesbaden, Gabler Verlag, 1976, pp. 103–122. BECKER (H.D.), op. cit., pp. 99–101.

4. See especially WEBSTER (F.E.), LARGAY III (J.A.) & STICKNEY (C.P.). The Impact of Inflation Accounting on Marketing Decisions. Journal of Marketing, Fall 1980, pp. 9–17. BECKER (H.D.), op. cit., p. 105. VAN DER ZIJPP (I.). Herwaarderingen in kostencalculaties. Maandblad voor Bedrijfsadministratie en Organisatie, March 1982, pp. 80–82.

5. See RIEBEL (P.), op. cit., pp. 26–29. BECKER (H.D.), op. cit., pp. 118–119.

6. See SCHMALENBACH (E.). Kostenrechnung und Preispolitik. Köln, Westdeutscher Verlag, 1963, p. 24.

7. BLASER (P.). Sichering des Deckungsbeitragsvolumens bei Preissenkungen. Buchführung-Bilanz-Kostenrechnung, No. 15, 1982, pp. 517–520. BECKER (H.D.), op. cit., p. 119.

8. HEINZE (E.). Organisieren Sie Ihren Verkauf als Profit-Center. Marketing Journal, No. 2, 1979, p. 130. BECKER (H.D.), op. cit., p. 125.

9. See N.A.A. Direct Costing. New York, N.A.A., 1971, p. 10. SCHLAMENBACH (E.), op. cit., p. 57. BECKER (H.D.), op. cit., p. 129.

CHAPTER 17

1. See also BECKER (H.D.). Die Anforderungen der Preispolitik an die Gestaltung der Kostenrechnung. Frankfurt, 1962, pp. 130–173.

GENERAL CONCLUSIONS

1. See also: HAGUE (D.C.). Pricing in Business. London, G. Allen & Unwin, 1971, pp. 158–164 and p. 168.

2. UNTERGUGGENBERGER (S.). Cybernetica en Direct Costing. Leiden, H.E. Stenfert Kroese B.V., 1972, pp. 85–92.

Bibliography

BOOKS

A.I.C.P.A. Cost Analysis for Pricing and Distribution Policies. New York, American Institute of Certified Public Accountants, 1965, p. 138.

ALPERT (M.I.). Pricing Decisions. Glenview, Scott, Foresman, 1975, p. 145.

ANDREWS (P.W.S.). Manufacturing Business. London, Macmillan, 1959, p. 308.

ANDREWS (P.W.S.) & BRUNNER (E.). Studies in Pricing. London, Macmillan, 1975, p. 176.

ANDRIESSEN (J.E.). De ontwikkeling van de moderne prijstheorie. Leiden, H.E. Stenfert-Kroese N.V., 1965, p. 285.

ANKUM (L.A.). Prijsinflatie, Kostprijsberekening en Winstbepaling. Leiden, H.E. Stengert-Kroese N.V., 1971, p. 301.

ANSON (C.J.). Profit from Figures: A Manager's Guide to Statistical Methods. London, McGraw-Hill, 1971, p. 273.

ANTHONY (R.N.). Management Accounting: Text and Cases. Homewood, Ill., Irwin, 1970, p. 790.

ANTHONY (R.N.) & WELSCH (G.A.). Fundamentals of Management Accounting. Homewood, Ill., Irwin, 1977, p. 748.

ARNOLD (J.). Pricing and Output Decisions. London, Haymarket, 1973, p. 181.

AUBERT-KRIER (J.) & RIO (E.Y.) & VAILHEN (C.A.). Gestion de l'Entreprise. II—Activités et politiques. Paris, P.U.F., 1971, p. 572.

BACKER (M.) & JACOBSEN (L.E.). Cost Accounting: A Managerial Approach. New York, McGraw-Hill, 1964, p. 678.

BACKMAN (J.), Ed. Price Practices and Price Policies: Selected Writings. New York, Ronald Press, 1953, p. 660.

BARBACK (R.H.). The Pricing of Manufacturers. London, Macmillan, 1964, p. 174.

BATES (J.) & PARKINSON (J.R.). Business Economics. Oxford, Basil Blackwell, 1971, p. 316.

BATTY (J.). Advanced Cost Accountancy. Estover, Macdonald & Evans, 1978, p. 496.

BATTY (J.). Managerial Standard Costing. London, Macdonald & Evans, 1970, p. 221.

BECKER (H.D.). Die Anforderungen der Preispolitik an die Gestaltung der Kosten-rechnung. Frankfurt am Main, Dissertation, 1962, p. 183.

BELL (M.L.). Marketing Concepts and Strategy. Boston, Houghton Mifflin, 1979, p. 595.

BENSTON (G.J.), Ed. Contemporary Cost Accounting and Control. Boston, C.B.I. Publishing, 1977, p. 493.

BERGFELD (A.J.), EARLEY (J.S.) & KNOBLOCH (W.R.). Pricing for Profit and Growth. Englewood Cliffs, N.J., Prentice-Hall, 1962, p. 128.

BIERMAN (H.). Topics in Cost Accounting and Decisions. New York, McGraw-Hill, 1963, p. 210.

BIERMAN (H.) & DYCKMAN (T.R.). Managerial Cost Accounting. New York, Mac-millan, 1976, p. 573.

BILSEN (R.) & Van WATERSCHOOT (W.). Marketingbeleid: theorie en praktijk. Deurne, M.I.M., 1981.

BLOM (F.W.C.). Grenskostenrekening en Direct Costing. Bewerking van: "A Report on Marginal Costing." Alphen a/d Rijn, N. Samsom N.V., 1969, p. 128.

BOER (G.). Direct Cost and Contribution Accounting. New York, J. Wiley & Sons, 1974, p. 246.

BORD (P.) & BRUEL (O.). Fixation du prix de vente des produits industriels. Paris, Les Editions d'Organisation, 1972, p. 176.

BOURGOIGNIE (T.). La Réglementation des Prix en Belgique. Leuven, Vander, 1973, p. 239.

BRIGHAM (E.F.), PAPPAS (J.L.) & HIRSCHEY (M.). Managerial Economics. Tokyo, Holt Saunders, 1983, p. 628.

BROWN (G.). Prix de revient, prix de vente et contrôle d'exploitation dans l'entreprise moyenne. Paris, Entreprise moderne d'édition, 1973, p. 191.

BROWN (W.) & JAQUES (E.). Product Analysis Pricing. London, Heinemann, Ltd., 1964, p. 148.

BURGERT (R.). Enkele beschouwingen over kosteninformatie ten behoeve van het be-drijfsbeleid. Haarlem, De Erven F. Bohn N.V., 1967, p. 28.

BURKE (W.L.) & SMYTH (E.B.). Accounting for Management: Cost Analysis, Plan-ning, Control and Decision-Making. Sydney, Law Book, 1966, p. 514.

BUSKIRK (R.H.). Principles of Marketing: The Management View. New York, Holt, Rinehart & Winston, 1970, p. 605.

CHEVALIER (M.). Fixation des prix et stratégie marketing. Paris, Dalloz Gestion, 1977, p. 180.

CLARK (J.M.). Studies in the Economics of Overhead Costs. Chicago, University of Chicago Press, 1950, p. 502.

CLUGSTON (R.). Estimating Manufacturing Costs. London, Gower Press, 1971, p. 201.

COLBERG (M.R.) & FORBUSH (D.R.) & WHITAKER (G.R.). Business Economics: Principles and Cases. Homewood, Ill., Irwin, 1970, p. 601.

CORAM (T.C.) & HILL (R.W.). New Ideas in Industrial Marketing. London, Staples Press, 1970, p. 319.

CORCORAN (A.W.). Costs: Accounting, Analysis and Control. New York, John Wiley & Sons, 1978, p. 786.

DAVIDSON (S.) & WEIL (R.L.). Handbook of Cost Accounting. New York, McGraw-Hill, 1978.

DAVIES (J.) & HUGHES (S.). Pricing in Practice. London, Heinemann, 1975, p. 154.

DEAN (J.). Managerial Economics. Englewood Cliffs, N.J., Prentice-Hall, 1956, p. 621.

DE BODT (G.). Direct Costing Profit Planning. Paris, Dunod, 1974, p. 314.

DE BODT (J.P.). La Formation des Prix. Analyse des rapports entre la théorie économique et la politique industrielle. Bruxelles, Les Editions De Visscher, 1955, p. 217.

DE COSTER (D.), RAMANATHAN (K.V.) & SUNDEM (G.L.). Accounting for Managerial Decision Making. Los Angeles, Melville, 1974, p. 462.

DE LEMBRE (E.), GEORGES (W.), PAEMELEIRE (R.) & VAN GEYT (E.). Analytisch Boekhouden en Kostencalculatie. Brussels, CED Samsom, 1982, p. 654.

DICKEY (R.I.). Accountants Cost Handbook. New York, Ronald Press, 1967.

DIEDERICH (H.). Allegmeine Betriebswirtschaftslehre II. Stuttgart, Verlag W. Kohlhammer, 1972, p. 217.

DODGE (R.). Industrial Marketing. New York, McGraw-Hill, 1970, p. 467.

DORFMAN (R.). Prices and Markets. Englewood Cliffs, N.J., Prentice-Hall, 1967, p. 151.

DUDICK (T.S.). Profile for Profitability: Using Cost Control and Profitability Analysis. New York, J. Wiley & Sons, 1972, p. 253.

EASTON (A.). Complex Managerial Decisions Involving Multiple Objectives. New York, J. Wiley & Sons, 1973, p. 421.

FASZLER (K.), REHKUGLER (H.) & WEGENAST (C.). Kostenrechnungslexikon. München, Verlag Moderne Industrie, 1971, p. 512.

FEMGEN (J.M.). Accounting for Managerial Analysis. Homewood, Ill., Irwin, 1976, p. 627.

FISHER (L.). Industrial Marketing. London, Business Books, 1969, p. 268.

FITZPATRICK (A.A.). Pricing Methods of Industry. Boulder, Colo., Pruett Press, 1964, p. 156.

FOG (B.). Industrial Pricing Policies. Amsterdam, North-Holland, 1960, p. 224.

FOSTER (D.). Managing for Profit. London, Longman, 1972, p. 307.

FRÖHLICH (K.G.). Preispolitik und Kalkulation im Buchverlag. Stuttgart, C.E. Poeschel Verlag, 1964, p. 129.

GABOR (A.). Pricing: Principles and Practice. London, Heinemann, 1977, p. 212.

GARRISON (R.H.). Managerial Accounting. Plano, Texas, Business Publications, 1982, p. 799.

GAYDOUL (P.), HORVATH (P.) & SCHÄFER (H.T.). Deckungsbeitragsrechnung. Wiesbaden, Gabler Verlag, 1976, p. 178.

GEORGES (W.). Differentiële en marginale kostenbeschouwingen in de bedrijfseconomie. Ghent, Licentiaatsverhandeling, 1970, p. 150.

GIBSON (J.L.) & HAYNES (W.W.). Accounting in Small Business Decisions. Lexington, University of Kentucky Press, 1963, p. 133.

GILCHRIST (R.R.). Managing for Profit: The Added Value Concept. London, G. Allen & Unwin, 1971, p. 165.

GILLESPIE (C.). Standard and Direct Costing. Englewood Cliffs, N.J., Prentice-Hall, 1962, p. 337.

GOODMAN (S.R.). Techniques of Profitability Analysis. New York, Wiley Interscience, 1970, p. 219.

GORDON (L.A.). The Pricing Decision. New York, N.A.A., 1981, p. 52.

GUTENBERG (E.). Grundlagen der Betriebswirtschaftslehre. Erster Band: Die Produktion. Berlin, Springer Verlag, 1968, p. 505.

GUTENBERG (E.). Grundlagen der Betriebswirtschaftslehre. Zweiter Band: Der Absatz. Berlin, Springer Verlag, 1962, p. 481.

HAGUE (D.C.). Managerial Economics: Analysis for Business Decisions. London, Longman, 1979, p. 356.

HAGUE (D.C.). Pricing in Business. London, G. Allen & Unwin, 1971, p. 336.

HANTKE (H.). Moderne Verfahren der Kostenrechnung II. Bonn, W. Stollfuss Verlag, 1974, p. 170.

HARLAN (N.E.), CHRISTENSON (C.J.) & VANCIL (R.F.). Managerial Economics. Homewood, Ill., Irwin, 1971, p. 679.

HARPER (D.). Price Policy and Procedure. New York, Harcourt, Brace & World, 1966, p. 308.

HARTMAN (B.). Preisbildung und Preispolitik. Stuttgart, C.E. Poeschel Verlag, 1963, p. 81.

HAYNES (W.W.). Managerial Economics: Analysis and Cases. Homewood, Ill., Dorsey Press, 1969, p. 726.

HAYNES (W.W.). Pricing Decisions in Small Business. Lexington, University of Kentucky Press, 1962, p. 107.

HAYNES (W.W.), COYNE (T.J.) & OSBORNE (D.K.). Readings in Managerial Economics. Dallas, Business Publications, 1973, p. 438.

HEERTJE (A.). Enkele aspecten van de prijsvorming van consumptiegoederen op monopolistische en oligopolistische markten. Leiden, H.E. Stenfert-Kroese N.V., 1960, p. 111.

HEIDINGSFIELD (M.S.). Changing Patterns in Marketing: A Study in Strategy. Boston, Allyn and Bacon, 1968, p. 167.

HEITGER (L.E.) & MATULICH (S.). Managerial Accounting. New York, McGraw-Hill, 1982, p. 824.

HOLLOWAY (R.J.) & HANCOCK (R.S.). Marketing in a Changing Environment. New York, J. Wiley & Sons, 1968, p. 352.

HORNGREN (C.T.) Cost Accounting: A Managerial Emphasis. Englewood Cliffs, N.J., Prentice-Hall, 1977, p. 934.

HORNGREN (C.T.). Introduction to Management Accounting. London, Prentice-Hall International, 1981, p. 638.

HUDSON (C.L.). The Marketing-Sales Operation. London, Staples Press, 1970, p. 512.

JACOB (H.). Preispolitik. Wiesbaden, Gabler Verlag, 1963, p. 271.

JOLSON (M.A.). Marketing Management. New York, Macmillan, 1978, p. 628.

KAPLAN (A.D.H.), DIRLAM (J.B.) & LANZILOTTI (R.F.). Pricing in Big Business. Washington, D.C., Brookings Institution, 1958, p. 344.

KAPLAN (R.S.). Advanced Management Accounting. Englewood Cliffs, N.J., Prentice-Hall, 1982, p. 655.

KELLER (I.W.) & FERRARA (W.L.). Management Accounting for Profit Control. San Francisco, McGraw-Hill, 1977. p. 744.

KELLEY (E.J.). Marketing Planning and Competitive Strategy. Englewood Cliffs, N.J., Prentice-Hall, 1972, p. 132.

KERBY (J.K.). Essentials of Marketing Management. Cincinnati, South-Western, 1970, p. 696.

KILGER (W.). Flexible Plankostenrechnung. Köln, Westdeutscher Verlag, 1970, p. 770.

KILLOUGH (L.N.) & LEININGER (W.E.). Cost Accounting for Managerial Decision Making. Enrico, Dickenson, 1977, p. 426.

KING (W.R.). Marketing Management Information Systems. New York, Mason-Charter, 1977, p. 213.

KOCH (H.). Zur Theorie des Absatzes. Wiesbaden, Th. Gabler Verlag, 1973, p. 393.

KOHL (M.). The Role of Accounting in Pricing. New York, Columbia Graduate School of Business. Doctoral Dissertation, 1954, p. 315.

KOOLSCHIJN (J.) & WIJNBERG (H.E.). Kostencalculatie en waarderingsproblemen. Alphen a/d Rijn, Samsom, Uitgeverij N.V., 1972, p. 401.

KORN (S.W.) & BOYD (T.). Accounting for Management Planning and Decision Making. New York, J. Wiley & Sons, 1969, p. 745.

KOTLER (P.). Marketing Management: Analysis, Planning and Control. Englewood Cliffs, N.J., Prentice-Hall, 1980, p. 722.

KOTLER (P.). Principles of Marketing. Englewood Cliffs, N.J., Prentice-Hall, 1980, p. 684.

KURZ (I.). Das Wesen der verschiedenen Fixkostentheorieën und ihre Verwertungsmöglichkeiten für die betriebliche Preispolitik. Berlin, Duncker & Humblot, 1969, p. 220.

LADD (D.R.). The Role of Costs in Pricing Decisions. Hamilton, Ontario, Society of Industrial and Cost Accountants of Canada, 1965, p. 50.

LAMBIN (J.J.). La décision commerciale face à l'incertain. Paris, Dunod, 1965, p. 420.

LANG (T.), Ed. Cost Accountants' Handbook. New York, Ronald Press, 1954, p. 1482.

LANGE (M.). Preisbildung bei neuen Produkten. Berlin, Duncker & Humblot, 1972, p. 199.

LANZILOTTI (R.F.) & PARRISH (G.O.). Pricing, Production, and Marketing Policies of Small Manufacturers. Pullman, Washington State University Press, 1964, p. 81.

LARGAY III (J.A.) & LIVINGSTONE (J.L.). Accounting for Changing Prices. New York, Wiley/Hamilton, 1976, p. 303.

LAWRENCE (F.C.) & HUMPHREYS (E.N.). Marginal Costing. London, Macdonald & Evans, 1967, p. 113.

LAYER (M.). Möglichkeiten und Grenzen der Anwendbarkeit der Deckungsbeitragsrechnung im Rechnungswesen der Unternehmung. Berlin, E. Schmidt Verlag, 1967, p. 226.

LEEFLANG (P.S.H.) & BEUKENKAMP (P.A.). Probleemgebied marketing. Een management benadering. Leiden, H.E. Stenfert-Kroese B.V., 1981, p. 981.

LERE (J.C.). Pricing Techniques for the Financial Executive. New York, J. Wiley & Sons, 1974, p. 195.

LEVY (M.). Stratégie des prix de vente. Paris, Ed. Nathan-Entreprise, 1974, p. 111.

LOCK (D.) & TAVERNIER (G.), Eds. Director's Guide to Management Techniques. London, Gower Press, 1970, p. 422.

LOUDERBACK III (J.G.) & DOMINIAK (G.F.). Managerial Accounting. Belmont, Wadsworth, 1978, p. 652.

LYNN (R.A.). Marketing Principles and Market Action. New York, McGraw-Hill, 1969, p. 290.

LYNN (R.A.). Price Policies and Marketing Management. Homewood, Ill., Irwin, 1967, p. 331.

MANTELL (L.H.) & SING (F.P.). Economics for Business Decisions. New York, McGraw-Hill, 1972, p. 460.

MARTING (E.). Creative Pricing. New York, American Management Association, 1968, p. 224.

MATZ (A.) & CURRY (O.J.). Cost Accounting. Cincinnati, South-Western, 1972, p. 863.

MAXWELL (W.D.). Price Theory and Applications in Business Administration. Englewood Cliffs, N.J., Prentice-Hall, 1970, p. 270.

McCARTHY (E.J.). Basic Marketing: A Managerial Approach. Homewood, Ill., Irwin, 1978, p. 767.

McKENNA (J.P.). The Logic of Price. Hinsdale, Dryden Press, 1973. p. 297.

McNEILL (T.F.) & CLARK (D.S.). Cost Estimating and Contract Pricing. New York, American Elsevier, 1966, p. 514.

McRAE (T.W.). Analytical Management. London, Wiley Interscience, 1970, p. 580.

MEARNS (I.). Fundamentals of Cost and Management Accounting. London, Longman, 1981, p. 319.

MELLEROWICZ (K.). Kosten und Kostenrechnung I. Theorie der Kosten. Berlin, Walter de Gruyter, 1958, p. 530.

MELLEROWICZ (K.). Neuzeitliche Kalkulationsverfahren. Freiburg im Breisgau, Rudolf Haufe Verlag, 1966, p. 239.

MELLEROWICZ (K.). Unternehmenspolitik. Band II. Freiburg im Breisgau, R. Haufe Verlag, 1963, p. 603.

MEREDITH (G.G.). Profit-Volume Decisions: A Manual for Managerial Planning and Control. New York, Harper & Row, 1969, p. 140.

MITCHELL (J.). Price Determination and Prices Policy. London, George Allen & Unwin, 1978, p. 215.

MOERLAND (P.W.). Prijsgedrag in theorie in praktijk. Rotterdam, Erasmus University-Report 7809/A, 1978.

MOEWS (D.). Zur Aussagefähigkeit neuerer Kostenrechnungsverfahren. Berlin, Duncker & Humblot, 1969, p. 216.

MÖLLER (H.). Kalkulation, Absatzpolitik und Preisbildung. Tübingen, J.C.B. Mohr (P. Siebeck), 1962, p. 222.

MONROE (K.B.). Pricing: Making Profitable Decisions. New York, McGraw-Hill, 1979, p. 286.

MOORE (C.L.) & JAEDICKE (R.K.). Managerial Accounting. Cincinnati, South-Western, 1972, p. 707.

MORSE (W.J.). Cost Accounting. Reading, Penn., Addison-Wesley, 1981, p. 824.

MOSSMAN (F.H.), CRISSY (W.J.E.) & FISCHER (P.M.). Financial Dimensions of Marketing Management. New York, J. Wiley & Sons, 1978, p. 170.

MOST (K.S.) & LEWIS (R.J.). Cost Accounting. Columbus, Ohio, Grid, 1982, p. 606.

MULDER (K.J.). Kosten en prijzen. Leiden, H.E. Stenfert-Kroese N.V., 1971, p. 23.

MULLER (J.C.). Recherche d'une méthode rationelle de détermination de prix sur la base des coûts. Paris, Editions Cujas, 1966, p. 430.

MULVIHILL (D.F.) & PARANKA (S.). Price Policies and Practices: A Source Book in Readings. New York, John Wiley & Sons, 1967, p. 333.

MUNZEL (G.). Die fixen Kosten in der Kostenträgerrechnung. Wiesbaden, Gabler Verlag, 1966, p. 301.

N.A.A. Accounting for Costs of Capacity. New York, N.A.A., 1963, p. 63.

N.A.A. Analysis of Non-manufacturing Costs for Managerial Decisions. New York, N.A.A., 1970, p. 96.

N.A.A. Costing Joint Products. New York, N.A.A., 1957, p. 54.

N.A.A. Current Application of Direct Costing. New York, N.A.A., 1961, p. 107.

N.A.A. Direct Costing. New York, N.A.A., 1971, p. 56.

N.A.A. Product Costs for Pricing Purposes. Research Report No. 24. New York, N.A.A., 1953, p. 60.

N.A.A. Separating and Using Costs as Fixed and Variable. New York, N.A.A., 1960, p. 39.

NACHTKAMP (H.H.). Der kurzfristige optimale Angebotspreis der Unternehmung bei Vollkostenkalkulation und unsicheren Erwartungen. Tübingen, J.C.B. Mohr (P. Siebeck), 1969, p. 339.

NAGTEGAAL (H.). Der Verkaufspreis in der Industrie. Wiesbaden, Gabler Verlag, 1974, p. 233.

NELSON (J.R.). Marginal Cost Pricing in Practice. Englewood Cliffs, N.J., Prentice-Hall, 1964, p. 266.

NEUNER (J.J.W.) & FRUMER (S.). Cost Accounting: Principles and Practice. Homewood, Ill., Irwin, 1967, p. 844.

N.I.C.B. Decision Making in Marketing. New York, National Industrial Conference Board, 1971, p. 103.

N.M.H. Tweede deel van het bijzonder bestek NM/B 82 "Type bestek." Brussels, Nationale Maatschappij voor de Huisvesting, 1982, p. 18.

OLMI (A.). Bedrijf en Bedrijfseconoom. Brussels, N. Samsom N.V., 1970, p. 155.

OWLER (L.W.J.) & BROWN (J.L.). Wheldon's Cost Accounting and Costing Methods. London, Macdonald & Evans, 1970, p. 688.

OXENFELDT (A.R.). Executive Action in Marketing. Belmont, Wadsworth, 1966, p. 817.

OXENFELDT (A.R.). Industrial Pricing and Market Practices. New York, Prentice-Hall, 1951, p. 602.

OXENFELDT (A.R.). Pricing for Marketing Executives. Belmont, Wadsworth, 1966, p. 90.

OXENFELDT (A.R.). Pricing Strategies. New York, Amacom, 1975, p. 255.

OXENFELDT (A.R.)., MILLER (D.), SHUCHMAN (A.) & WINICK (C.). Insights into Pricing. Belmont, Wadsworth, 1965, p. 124.

PAEMELEIRE (R.), GEORGES (W.) & VAN GEYT (E.). Kostencalculatie en beleidsbeslissingen. Brussels, C.E.D. Samsom, 1983, p. 348.

PALDA (K.S.). Pricing Decisions and Marketing Policy. Englewood Cliffs, N.J., Prentice-Hall, 1971, p. 116.

PALDA (K.S.). Readings in Managerial Economics. Englewood Cliffs, N.J., Prentice-Hall, 1973, p. 320.

PHELPS (D.M.) & WESTING (H.). Marketing Management. Homewood, Ill., Irwin, 1968, p. 925.

PHILLIPS (A.) & WILLIAMSON (O.E.), Eds. Prices: Issues in Theory, Practice and Public Policy. Philadelphia, University of Pennsylvania Press, 1967, p. 253.

RADEMAKER (B.). Industriële marketing voor strategisch beleid. Deventer, Kluwer, 1981, p. 392.

RAFFEE (H.). Kurzfristige Preisuntergrenzen als betriebswirtschaftliches Problem. Köln, Westdeutscher Verlag, 1961, p. 203.

RAPPAPORT (A.), Ed. Information for Decision Making. Englewood Cliffs, N.J., Prentice-Hall, 1982, p. 412.

REICHMANN (T.). Kosten und Preisgrenzen. Wiesbaden, Betriebswirtschaftlicher Verlag Gabler, 1973, p. 144.

RIEBEL (P.). Einselkosten- und Deckungsbeitragsrechnung. Opladen, Westdeutscher Verlag, 1982, p. 549.

RIEBEL (P.). Kosten und Preise. Opladen, Westedeutscher Verlag, 1972, p. 119.

ROBINSON (R.D.). International Business Management: A Guide to Decision Making. New York, Holt, Rinehart & Winston, 1973.

ROSELL (J.H.) & FRASURE (W.W.). Managerial Accounting. Columbus, Ohio, Charles E. Merill, 1964, p. 614.

ROSEN (L.S.), Ed. Topics in Managerial Accounting. Toronto, McGraw-Hill Ryerson, 1974, p. 412.

ROWE (D.) & ALEXANDER (I.). Selling Industrial Products. London, Hutchinson, 1968, p. 159.

RUTTEN (F.W.). Prijsvorming in de Industrie. Leiden, H.E. Stenfert-Kroese N.V., 1965, p. 200.

SANDIG (C.). Betriebwirtschaftspolitik. Stuttgart, Poeschel Verlag, 1966, p. 307.

SCHMALENBACH (E.). Kostenrechnung und Preispolitik. Köln, Westdeutscher Verlag, 1963, p. 530.

SCHNEIDER (G.). Fixkosten und Kalkulation im Konkurrenzkampf. Berlin, E. Schmidt Verlag, 1967, p. 100.

SCHOBER (A.). Produktions—und Nachfrageelastizität als Determinanten der Preispolitik. Frankfurt a/Main, Franz Nowack Verlag, 1962, p. 109.

SHILLINGLAW (G.). Cost Accounting: Analysis and Control. Homewood, Ill., Irwin, 1972, p. 789.

SIEGELMAN (L.) & SPENCER (M.H.). Managerial Economics: Decision Making and Forward Planning. Homewood, Ill., Irwin, 1960, p. 445.

SIMON (H.). Preismanagement. Wiesbaden, Gabler Verlag, 1980, p. 483.

SIMON (L.S.) & FREIMER (M.). Analytical Marketing. New York, Harcourt, Brace & World, 1970, p. 346.

SIMON (S.R.). Managing Marketing Profitability. New York, American Management Association, 1969, p. 219.

SIZER (J.). Kosteninformatie in het bedrijfsbeleid. Antwerpen/Utrecht, Het Spectrum B.V., 1970, p. 350.

SLOT (R.). Kostenberekening en Prijspolitiek. Leiden, H.E. Stenfert-Kroese N.V., 1966, p. 30.

SLOT (R.). Kostenvariabiliteit en variabele kostencalculatie. Leiden, H.E. Stenfert-Kroese N.V., 1962, p. 215.

SPENCER (M.H.). Managerial Economics: Text, Problems and Short Cases. Homewood, Ill., Irwin, 1968, p. 515.

STANTON (W.J.). Fundamentals of Marketing. New York, McGraw-Hill, 1981, p. 604.

STAR (S.H.), DAVIS (N.J.), LOVELOCK (C.H.) & SHAPIRO (B.P.). Problems in Marketing. New York, McGraw-Hill, 1977, p. 851.

STIGLER (G.L.). The Theory of Price. New York, Macmillan, 1966, p. 355.

STILL (R.) & CUNDIFF (E.W.). Essentials of Marketing. Englewood Cliffs, N.J., Prentice-Hall, 1966, p. 186.

STURDIVANT (F.). Managerial Analysis in Marketing. Glenview, Scott, Foresman, 1970, p. 756.

TAYLOR (B.) & WILLS (G.). Pricing Strategy. London, Staples Press, 1969, p. 566.

THOMAS (W.E.). Readings in Cost Accounting, Budgeting and Control. Cincinnati, South-Western, 1960, p. 833.

THOMPSON MONTGOMERY (A.). Managerial Accounting Information. Reading, Penn., Addison-Wesley, 1979, p. 750.

TRIOLAIRE (G.). Coût de la distribution et formation des prix. Paris, Sirey, 1965, p. 174.

TUCKER (S.A.). Pricing for Higher Profit. New York, McGraw-Hill, 1966, p. 294.

TUCKER (S.A.). Profit Planning Decisions with the Break-Even System. Aldershot, England, Gower, 1981, p. 213.

TURVEY (R.). Optimal Pricing and Investment in Electricity Supply. London, G. Allen & Unwin, 1968, p. 124.

UNTERGUGGENBERGER (S.). Cybernetica en Direct Costing. Leiden H.E. Stenfert-Kroese, 1973, p. 242.

VAN ACKER (J.E.). Bewuste Commerciële Beleidsvoering. Alphen a/d Rijn, N. Samsom N.V., 1968, p. 463.

VAN DER SCHROEFF (H.J.). Kosten en Kostprijs. Part I, p. 362; Part II, p. 402. Antwerp, N.V. Uitgeversmij. Kosmos, 1970.

VAN DER ZIJPP (I.). Opbrengsten, Kosten en winsten. Leiden H.E. Stenfert-Kroese N.V, 1971, p. 398.

VAN DE WOESTIJNE (W.J.). Economie en organisatie voor de manager. Deventer, Kluwer/NIVE, 1972, p. 217.

VAN EUNEN (E.A.) & HOLZHAUER (F.F.O.). Marketing Handboek. Leiden, Stenfert-Kroese, 1982, p. 714.

VAN HELLEMAN (J.). Inhoud en toepassing van het "Opportunity Cost"—begrip. Rotterdam, Erasmus University, n.d.

VERBURG (P.). De betekenis van de kosteninformatie voor de besluitvorming. Leiden, H.E. Stenfert-Kroese N.V., 1966, p. 242.

VERNON (I.R.) & LAMB (C.W.), Eds. The Pricing Function: A Pragmatic Approach. Toronto, Lexington, 1976, p. 298.

VORMBAUM (H.). Differenzierte Preise. Köln, Westdeutscher Verlag, 1960, p. 291.

VORMBAUM (H.). Kalkulationsarten und Kalkulationsverfahren. Stuttgart, C.E. Poeschel Verlag, 1966, p. 114.

WALKER (C.J.). Principles of Cost Accounting. London, Macdonald & Evans, 1970, p. 368.

WALLEY (B.H.). How to Apply Strategy in Profit Planning. London, Business Books, 1971, p. 306.

WATSON (D.S.), Ed. Price Theory in Action: A Book of Readings. Boston, Houghton Mifflin, 1965, p. 355.

WEBER (H.K.). Fixe und variable Kosten. Göttingen, Verlag Otto Schwarz. 1972, p. 86.

WEBER (K.). Amerikanisches Direct Costing. Stuttgart, Verlag Paul Haupt, 1970, p. 138.

WEILENMANN (P.) & NÜSSELER (A.). Planungsrechnung in der Unternehmung. Stuttgart, C.E. Poeschel Verlag, 1971, p. 240.

WENTZ (W.B.) & EYRICH (G.I.). Marketing: Theory and Application. New York, Harcourt, Brace & World, 1970, p. 689.

WILES (P.J.D.). Price, Cost and Output. Oxford, Basil Blackwell, 1961, p. 313.

WRIGHT (W.). Direct Standard Costs for Decision Making and Control. New York, McGraw-Hill, 1962, p. 221.

WYTZES (H.C.). Ondernemingsgroei en Ondernemingsstrategie. Haarlem, De Erven F. Bohn N.V., 1967, p. 279.

ZOBER (M.). Principles of Marketing. Boston, Allyn & Bacon, 1971, p. 626.

JOURNAL ARTICLES

ABEL (R.). The Role of Costs and Cost Accounting in Price Determination. Management Accounting, April 1978, pp. 29–32.

AGTHE (K.). Stufenweise Fixkostendeckung im System des Direct Costing. Zeitschrift für Betriebswirtschaft, July 1959, pp. 404–418.

AGTHE (K.). Zur stufenweisen Fixkostendeckung. Zeitschrift für Betriebswirtschaft, December 1959, pp. 742–748.

ALLEN (B.H.) & LAMBERT (D.R.). Searching for the Best Price: An Experimental Look at Consumer Research Effort. Journal of the Academy of Marketing Science, Fall 1978, pp. 245–257.

ALLEN (B.H.), TATHEM (R.L.) & LAMBERT (D.R.). Flexible Pricing Strategies for High Inflation Periods. Industrial Marketing Management, No. 4, 1976, pp. 243–248.

ALLEN (C.B.). Price Analysis for Recommendations to Management. N.A.A. Bulletin, July 1960, pp. 71–80.

ALLYN (R.G.). Some Economic and Accounting Observations on the Utility of Costs for Pricing. N.A.A. Bulletin, July 1959, pp. 5–10.

AMEY (L.). On Opportunity Cost and Decision Making. Accountancy, July 1968, pp. 442–451.

ANDERSON (J.E.). How to Price for Maximum Profits. Management Methods, November 1958, pp. 37–40, 88.

ANTHONY (R.N.). A Case for Historical Costs. Harvard Business Review, November-December 1976, pp. 69–79.

ANTHONY (R.N.). What Should "Cost" Mean? Harvard Business Review, May-June 1970, pp. 121–131.

ARNOLD (J.). An Approach to Pricing and Output Decisions When Prices Are Changing. Journal of Business Finance & Accounting, No. 4, 1977, pp. 383–406.

ARNOLD (J.A.). On the Problem of Interim Pricing Decisions. Accounting and Business Research, No. 10, Spring 1973, pp. 83–91.

ARNSTEIN (W.E.). Price Changes and Profitability. Management Accounting, May 1970, p. 17–18.

BACKER (M.). Flexible Costs for Pricing Decisions. N.A.A. Bulletin, May 1961, pp. 55–66.

BAXTER (W.T.) & OXENFELDT (A.R.). Costing and Pricing: The Cost Accountant versus the Economist. Business Horizons, Winter 1961, pp. 77–90.

BEISZNER (H.). Ketzerische Gedanken zur Preisbildung und Preispolitik. Kostenrechnungspraxis, August 1964, pp. 167–171.

BERRY (L.E.). Deciding on Discretionary Costs: A Cost-Benefit Approach. Cost and Management, July-August 1982, pp. 38–41.

BESTE (T.). Möglichkeiten und Grezen der Preispolitik in der Unternehmung. Zeitschrift für betriebswirtschaftliche Forschung, 1964, pp. 122–144.

BETHOUART (A.). L'Incertitude du prix de revient. Management International Review, January 1971, pp. 95–111.

BICKEL (G.). Die Preisuntergrenze unter besonderer Berücksichtigung der Sorge um die Liquidität. Zeitschrift für Betriebswirtschaft, August 1966, pp. 527–543.

BIDLINGMAIER (J.). Die Ziele der Unternehmer. Ein Beitrag zur Theorie des Unternehmerverhaltens. Zeitschrift für Betriebswirtschaft, July-August 1963, pp. 409–422; September 1963, pp. 519–530.

BLANCHARD (G.A.) & CHOW (C.W.). Allocating Indirect Costs for Improved Management Performance. Management Accounting, March 1983, pp. 38–41.

BLÄSER (P.). Sicherung der Deckungsbeitragsvolumens bei Preissenkungen. Buchführung-Bilanz-Kostenrechnung, No. 15, 1982, pp. 517–520.

BLATTBERG (R.C.), EPPEN (G.D.) & LIEBERMAN (J.). A Theoretical and Empirical Evaluation of Price Deals for Consumer Nondurables. Journal of Marketing, Winter 1981, pp. 116–129.

BLOIS (K.J.). The Pricing of Supplies by Large Customers. Journal of Business Finance & Accounting, No.3, 1978, pp. 367–379.

BLOOD (W.I.). Basic Analysis for Product-Pricing and Marketing Purposes. N.A.A. Bulletin, July 1962, pp. 47–55.

BOITEUX (M.). Marginal Cost Pricing. Revue Française de l'Energie, December 1956, pp. 113–117.

BOUDON (A.).La formation du prix dans le secteur textile. Revue Française du Marketing, No. 3, 1979, pp. 73–102.

BOURGOIGNIE (T.). La réglementation des prix en Belgique. Economisch en Sociaal Tijdschrift, August 1973, pp. 387–400.

BOURN (M.), STONEY (P.J.M.) & WYNN (R.F.). Price Indices for Current Cost Acounting. Journal of Business Finance & Accounting, No. 3, 1976, pp. 149–172.

BRICKSONS (W.B.) Price Fixing conspiracies: Their Long Term Impact. Journal of Industrial Economics, March 1976, pp. 189–202.

BRIESE (P.M.). Informationen aus der Kostenrechnung für den Entscheidungsprozess der Unternehmung. Kostenrechnungspraxis, April-May 1971, pp. 81–91.

BROOKS (D.G.). Cost-Oriented Pricing: A Realistic Solution to a Complicated Problem. Journal of Marketing, April 1975, pp. 72–74.

BROSTER (E.J.). The Dynamics of Marginal Costing. The Accountant, 1970, pp. 451–454.

BROSTER (E.J.). Rational Price Fixing. (1. The Marginal Cost). Certified Accountants Journal, September 1971, pp. 447–450.

BROSTER (E.J.). Rational Price Fixing (2. The Factor of Market Competition). Certified Accountants Journal, October 1971, pp. 517–520.

BROSTER (E.J.). Rational Price Fixing (3. The Pricing Formula in Theory and Practice). Certified Accountants Journal, November 1971, pp. 579–586.

BROWN (F.E.) & OXENFELDT (A.R.). Should Prices Depend on Costs? M.S.U. Business Topics, Autumn 1968, pp. 73–77.

BRUHN (J.). Preispolitik: der falsche Fetisch. Marketing Journal, No. 6, 1973, pp. 512–513.

BRUNNER (E.). Competition and the Theory of the Firm. Economia Internazionale, August 1952, pp. 509–526; November 1952, pp. 727–747.

BUDDE (K.H.). Die Problematik der Preisbildung auf der Grundlage von Voll- und Teilkosten. Kostenrechnungspraxis, December 1971, pp. 253–257.

BURGERT (R.). Enkele beschouwingen over kosteninformatie ten behoeve van het bedrijfsbeleid. De Economist, March-April 1967, pp. 161–188.

BURGESS (A.R.). The Modelling of Business Profitability: A New Approach. Strategic Management Journal, January-March 1982, pp. 53–65.

BURKART (A.J.). Some Managerial Influences on a Firm's Pricing Policy. Journal of Industrial Economics, July 1969, pp. 180–187.

BURROWS (C.A.). Management and Financial Accounting: A Case for Separate Systems. Cost and Management, January-February 1974, pp. 6–12.

BURT (D.N.) & BOYETT (J.E.). Reduction in Selling Price after the Introduction of Competition. Journal of Marketing Research, May 1979, pp. 275–279.

CARROLL (J.). Accountants and Marketing. The Australian Accountant, February 1969, pp. 76–78.

CHIANG (R.) & SPATT (C.S.). Imperfect Price Discrimination and Welfare. Review of Economic Studies, April 1982, pp. 155–181.

CLARKE (F.H.), DARROUGH (M.N.) & HEINEKE (J.M.). Optimal Pricing Policy in the Presence of Experience Effects. Journal of Business, October 1982, pp. 517–530.

CLARKE (J.). Pricing: The Incredible Three-Headed Monster. Accountancy, November 1981, pp. 79–80.

CLAY (M.). Contribution Theory in Practice. The Accountant, August 9, 1973, pp. 183–186.

COCKS (D.L.) & VIRTS (J.R.). Pricing Behavior of the Ethical Pharmaceutical Industry. Journal of Business, July 1974, pp. 349–362.

COLANTONI (C.S.), MANES (R.P.) & WHINSTON (A.). Programming, Profit Rates and Pricing Decisions. The Accounting Review, 1969, pp. 467–481.

CORDES (W.). Kostenentwicklung und Preispolitik in der Eisen- und Stahlindustrie. Zeitschrift für betriebswirtschaftliche Forschung, April 1969, pp. 225–240.

CORDES (W.). Preispolitik zur Erzielung optimaler Beschäftigung. Zeitschrift für betriebswirtschaftliche Forschung, 1964. pp. 145–157.

CORDIER (J.). Le "coût marginal" dans les petites et moyennes entreprises. Travail et Méthodes, October 1972, pp. 3–7.

CORR (A.V.). The Role of Cost in Pricing. Management Accounting, November 1974, pp. 15–18.

COTTA (A.). Politique des prix et stratégie d'entreprise. Concurrence, No. 4, 1971, pp. 6–16.

COWAN (T.). Price Control Decisions—The Realistic Approach. Accountancy, February 1976, pp. 64–68.

CUTLER (G.). Developing the Selling Price. Management Accounting, August 1971, pp. 41–42.

DANERT (G.). Preispolitik bei Voll- und Ueberbeschäftigung. Zeitschrift für betriebswirtschaftliche Forschung, 1964, pp. 158–167.

DANIEL (D.R.). Management Information Crisis. Harvard Business Review, September-October 1961, pp. 111–121.

DARDEN (B.R.). An Operational Approach to Product Pricing. Journal of Marketing, April 1968, pp. 29–33.

DÄUMLER (K.D.). Stufenweise Fixkostendeckungsrechnung. Buchführung Bilanz Kostenrechnung, No. 4, 1982, pp. 117–128.

DEAN (J.). How to Price during Inflation. European Journal of Marketing. Vol. 13, 1979, pp. 213–227.

DEAN (J.). Pricing Policies for New Products. Harvard Business Review, November-December 1976, pp. 141–150.

DEAN (J.). Retrospective Commentary on Pricing Policies for New Products. Harvard Business Review, November-December 1976, pp. 151–153.

DEARDEN (J.). Taming Predatory Pricing. Financial Executive, January 1983, pp. 38–44.

DE BONDT (R.). Industrial Economic Aspects of Belgian Price Regulation. Tijdschrift voor Economie en Management, No. 2, 1978, pp. 249–264.

DE COORDE (F.) & REYNS (C.). Accountancy versus Management. Economisch en Sociaal Tijdschrift, June 1973, pp. 277–286.

DE JONG (G.). Het prijsbeleid in historisch perspectief. De Accountant-Adviseur, September 1973, pp. 174–178.

DELLA BITTA (A.J.), MONROE (K.B.) & McGINNIS (J.M.). Consumer Perceptions of Comparative Price Advertisements. Journal of Marketing Research, November 1981, pp. 416–427.

DENYER (J.C.). Pricing Policies. Accountants Review, September 1974, pp. 201–208.

DE SALVIA (D.N.). An Application of Peak-Load Pricing. The Journal of Business, October 1969, pp. 458–476.

DE WILDE (C.B.) & VAN HEUZEN (P.R.). Prijszetting op basis van marginale of integrale calculatie. Naschrift door A. Nouwens. Maandschrift Economie, April 1956, pp. 335–347.

DEYHLE (A.). Grenz- oder relative Einzelkosten? Zeitschrift für Betriebswirtschaft, January 1962, pp. 61–64.

DHALLA (A.). A Guide to New Product Development: Phase 5—Pricing. Canadian Business, April 1964, p. 85.

DHALLA (N.K.). The Art of Product Pricing. Management Review, June 1964, pp. 63–66.

Die Gemeinkosten in der Preiskalkulation. Kostenrechnungspraxis, May 1959, pp. 113–116.

DILLER (H.). Die Preispolitik als Wettbewerbswaffe in der Marktwirtschaft. Der Markenartikel, March 1983, pp. 104–117.

DOLAN (R.J.). Pricing Strategies That Adjust to Inflation. Industrial Marketing Management, July 1981, pp. 151–156.

DOLAN (R.J.) & JEULAND (A.P.). Experience Curves and Dynamic Demand Models: Implications for Optimal Pricing Strategies. Journal of Marketing, Winter 1981, pp. 52–62.

DRIAY (P.). Determination des prix de vente: des calculs et un choix économique. Travail et Méthodes, December 1970, pp. 3–8.

DRIAY (P.). Détermination des prix de vente. Travail et Méthodes, January 1971, pp. 11–18.

DRIAY (P.). Détermination des prix de vente. Travail et Méthodes, April 1971, pp. 13–18.

DUCK (R.E.V.). The Use of Management Accounting Techniques in Industry. The Journal of Management Studies, October 1971, pp. 355–361.

DUDICK (T.S.). Alternative Costing Methods for Reporting and Pricing Purposes. The Journal of Accountancy, October 1969, pp. 49–54.

DUN (L.C.). Managerial Uses of Direct Costing. The Australian Accountant, December 1970, pp. 517–520.

DUVENECK (D.). Steuerung und Entscheidung mit den richtigen Daten: Direct Costing. Betriebswirtschaftliche Forschung and Praxis, February 1973, pp. 87–100.

EARLEY (J.S.). Recent Developments in Cost Accounting and the "Marginal Analysis." The Journal of Political Economy, June 1955, pp. 227–242.

ECKSTEIN (O.) & FROMM (G.). The Price Equation. American Economic Review, December 1968, pp. 1159–1183.

EDELMAN (F.). Art and Science of Competitive Bidding. Harvard Business Review, July-August 1965, pp. 53–66.

EDEN (B.). Toward a Theory of Competitive Price Adjustments. Review of Economic Studies, April 1981, pp. 199–216.

EDWARDS (R.S.). The Pricing of Manufactured Products. Economica, August 1952, pp. 298–307.

EILER (R.G.), GOLETZ (W.K.) & KEEGAN (D.P.). Is Your Cost Accounting Up to Date? Harvard Business Review, July-August 1982, pp. 133–139.

ENGELEITER (H.J.). Die Bestimmung der Preisuntergrenze als investitionstheoretisches Problem. Betriebswirtschaftliche Forschung und Praxis, No. 10, 1965, pp. 566–581.

FARRIS (P.W.) & REIBSTEIN (D.J.). How Prices, Ad Expenditures, and Profits Are Linked. Harvard Business Review, November-December 1979, pp. 173–184.

FASE (M.M.G.). Over prijstheorie en derzelver nut. Economisch-Statistische Berichten, September 23, 1970, pp. 915–918.

FEKRAT (A.). The Conceptual Foundations of Absorption Costing. The Accounting Review, April 1972, pp. 351–355.

FERNER (W.). Grenzkostenrechnung als Instrument der Unternhmensplanung. Betriebswirtschaftliche Forschung und Praxis, No. 6, 1974, pp. 530–542.

FERRARA (W.L.). Are Direct Costs Relevant Costs? The Journal of Accountancy, August 1961, pp. 61–62.

FINKENRATH (R.). So finden Sie den richtigen Marktpreis. Marketing Journal, No. 6, 1976, pp. 534–538.

FOGG (C.D.) & KOHNKEN (K.H.). Price-Cost Planning. Journal of Marketing, April 1978, pp. 97–106.

FOX (H.W.). Different Costs for Different Purposes. Cost and Management, March 1965, pp. 110–118.

FOXALL (G.). A Descriptive Theory of Pricing for Marketing. European Journal of Marketing, Autumn 1972, pp. 190–194.

FRYE (D.J.). Combined Costing Method: Absorption and Direct. Management Accounting, January 1971, pp. 18–20.

GANGOLLY (J.S.). On Joint Cost Allocation: Independent Cost Proportional Scheme (ICPS) and Its Properties. Journal of Accounting Research, Autumn 1981, pp. 299–312.

GASKINS (D.W.). Dynamic Limit Pricing: Optimal Pricing under Threat of Entry. Journal of Economic Theory, September 1971, pp. 306–322.

GEE (K.G.). A Note on Cost Escalation Clauses. Journal of Business Finance & Accounting, No. 3, 1979, pp. 339–346.

GEERTMAN (J.A.). Enkele beschouwingen bij prijs- en rabattenpolitiek. Synopsis, October 1966, pp. 25–32.

GERGELY (I.). Die Deckungsbeitragsrechnung als Grundlage von Preiskakulation im Machinenbau. Kostenrechnungspraxis, June 1966, pp. 101–110.

GIANESSI (E.). Der Kreislauf zwischen Kosten und Preisen als bestimmender Factor der Gleichgewichtsbedingungen im System der Unternehmung. Zeitschrift für handelswissenschaftliche Forschung, December 1958, pp. 613–649.

GIBSON (J.L). Accounting in the Decision-Making Process: Some Empirical Evidence. The Accounting Review, July 1963, pp. 492–500.

GILLILAND (C.E.). Bases for Responsible Decisions in Business. The Economic and Business Bulletin, Autumn 1968, pp. 27–32.

GLOTIN (G.). Prix de Revient et prix de vente des produits proposés à l'exportation. Travail et Méthodes, June-July 1968, pp. 53–56.

GLUTH (H.). Vertriebsleiter zwischen Kosten- und Marktpreis. Kostenrechnungspraxis, August 1963, pp. 157–161.

GOLDMAN (A.). Consumer Knowledge of Food Prices as an Indicator of Shopping Effectiveness. Journal of Marketing, October 1977, pp. 67–75.

GOODALE (D.). Joint Cost Allocation and Managerial Decisions. Cost and Management, July-August 1961, pp. 300–308.

GORDON (R.A.). Short-Period Price Determination in Theory and Practice. American Economic Review, June 1948, pp. 265–288.

GRAY (S.F.). The Practical Application of Cost and Price Theory. A.I.C.A. Cost Bulletin, May 1960, pp. 25–33.

GREEN (P.E.). La fixation d'un prix de vente d'une matière plastique sur la base d'une théorie de la décision. Revue Française du Marketing, No.1, 1970, pp. 14–22.

GREER (H.C.). Cost Factors in Price-Making. Harvard Business Review, September-October 1952, pp. 127–136.

GREER (H.C.). Cost Factors in Price-Marketing. Harvard Business Review, July-August 1952, pp. 33–45.

GRETZ (W.). Praxis der kombinierten Deckungsbeitrags-/Vollkostenkalkulation. Buchfürung Bilanz Kostenrechnung, No. 21, 1982, pp. 753–760.

GRETZ (W.). Richtige Preise durch marktgerechte Angebotskalkulation. Buchführung Bilanz Kostenrechnung, No. 19, 1982, pp. 663–680.

GRIECO (V.A.). Cost Levels Required for Product Pricing, Cost Records or Profit Plan? Management International Review, No. 2–3, 1970, pp. 119–126.

GRIFFIN (C.E.). When Is Price Reduction Profitable? Harvard Business Review, September-October 1960, pp. 125–132.

GROOT (A.M.). Is hernieuwde bezinning op de juistheid van de kostprijsberekening noodzakelijk? Maandblad voor Accountancy en Bedrijfshuishoudkunde, July 1959, pp. 290–299.

GUILTINAN (J.P.). Risk-Aversive Pricing Policies: Problems and Alternatives. Journal of Marketing, January 1976, pp. 10–15.

GUTJAHR (G.). Wie preistolerant ist der Verbraucher? Marketing Journal, No. 6, 1976, pp. 530–532.

HALDI (J.). Pricing Behavior: Economic Theory and Business Practice. Current Economic Comment, November 1958, pp. 55–66.

HALL (O.L.). Mark-Up Based on Assets Employed. Management Accounting, February 1971, pp. 48–49, 52.

HAMPEL (R.E.). Pricing Policies and Profitability. Management Accounting, July 1977, pp. 53–56.

HANSMANN (K.W.). Gewinnmaximale Preispolitik bei multipel variierbarer Betriebsgrösze. Zeitschrift für Betriebswirtschaft, December 1973, pp. 869–880.

HARPER (W.M.). A case study on pricing. Accountancy, July 1972, pp. 84–90.

HARPER (W.M.). The Pitfalls in Fixing Prices. Accountancy, March 1972, pp. 61–63.

HARPER (W.M.). Principles of Contribution Pricing. Accountancy, March 1972, pp. 60–65.

HART (H.). A Review of Some Recent Major Develpments in the Management Accounting Field. Accounting and Business Research, Spring 1981, pp. 99–115.

HARTOGENSIS (A.M.). The Art and Practice of Pricing. N.A.A. Bulletin, March 1958, pp. 63–74.

HAWKINS (E.R.). Price Policies and Theory. The Journal of Marketing, January 1954, pp. 233–240.

HAX (H.). Preisuntergrenzen im Ein- und Mehrproduktbetrieb. Zeitschrift für handelswissenschaftliche Forschung, August-September 1961, pp. 424–449.

HAYNES (W.W.). Pricing in Small Firms. Southern Economic Journal, April 1964, pp. 315–324.

HEERTJE (A.). Marginalisme. De Economist, October 1963, pp. 663–669.

HEFLEBOWER (R.B.). Some Observations on Industrial Prices. The Journal of Business, July 1954, pp. 187–195.

HEINEN (E.). Das Vollkostendenken und das Teilkostendenken. Kostenrechnungspraxis, November 1959, pp. 275–278.

HEINEN (E.). Entwickelungstendenzen in der Entscheidungsorientierten Betriebswirtschaftslehre. Die Unternehmung, No. 2, 1971, pp. 89–99.

HEINEN (E.). Kosteninformation und Preispolitik bei Auftragsfertigung. Kostenrechnungspraxis, April 1975, pp. 55–62.

HEINZE (E.). Organisieren Sie Ihren Verkauf als Profit-Center. Marketing Journal, No. 2, 1979, pp. 127–134.

HEINZELBECKER (K.). Marketing—Informationssysteme heute. Marketing Journal, No. 2, 1978, pp. 133–138.

HENZEL (F.). Kalkulatorische Fehler in ihrer Wirkung auf das Preisniveau. Kostenrechnungspraxis, June 1964, pp. 101–108.

HENZEL (F.). Vollkostenrechnung mit gesonderten Fixkostenbeiträgen. Zeitschrift für Betriebswirtschaft, August 1967, pp. 485–502.

HORNGREN (C.T.). & SORTER (G.H.). An Evaluation of Some Criticisms of Relevant Costing. The Accounting Review, April 1964, pp. 417–421.

HOWE (M.). Marginal Analysis in Accounting. Yorkshire Bulletin of Economic and Social Research, November 1962, pp. 81–89.

HUBNER (T.J.). Marketing Factors in Fixing Prices. A.I.C.A. Cost Bulletin, May 1960, pp. 18–23.

HUCH (B.). Die Kalkulation von Kuppelprodukten. Kostenrechnungspraxis, February-March 1973, pp. 5–12.

HUDIG (J.). A Flexible Pricing Formula. N.A.A. Bulletin, July 1962, pp. 71–76.

HUMMEL (S.). Fixe und variabele Kosten. Zwei haufig miszverstandene Grundbegriffe der Kostenrechnung. Kostenrechnungspraxis, April 1975, pp. 63–74.

IBIELSKI (D.) & HERZKE (K.). Hilfe für zielorientierte Unternehmungsführung, Marketing Journal, No. 2, 1978, pp. 118–121.

JACKSON (B.B.). Manage Risk in Industrial Pricing. Harvard Business Review, July-August 1980, pp. 121–133.

JAIN (S.C.) & LARIC (M.V.). A Framework for Strategic Industrial Pricing. Industrial Marketing Management, January 1979, pp. 75–80.

JOYCE (J.E.). The Overhead Mystique. Management Accounting, November 1968, pp. 43–46.

KALLIMANIS (W.S.). Product Contribution Analysis for Multi-Product Pricing. Management Accounting, July 1968, pp. 3–11.

KAMERSCHEN (D.R.). The Return of Target Pricing? Journal of Business, No. 2, 1975, pp. 242–252.

KAY (J.A.). Uncertainty, Congestion and Peak Load Pricing. Review of Economic Studies, October 1979, pp. 601–610.

KELLEY (E.W.). Marketing Cost Analysis—The Accountant's Most Neglected Opportunity. N.A.A. Bulletin, July 1960, pp. 11–21.

KERN (W.). Kalkulation mit Opportunitätskosten. Zeitschrift für Betriebswirtschaft, March 1965, pp. 133–147.

KLEIN (D.J.) & HADAD (N.E.). Direct Costing Is Alive and Well, and Doing Nicely, Thank You. Cost and Management, May-June 1982, pp. 46–51.

KNOX (R.L.). Competitive Oligopolistic Pricing. Journal of Marketing, July 1968, pp. 47–51.

KNUTZEN (K.K.). Using Direct Cost Information for Pricing. N.A.A. Bulletin, August 1962, pp. 39–47.

KÖHLER (R.) & STÖLZEL (A.). Nutzen Sie Ihr Rechnungswesen für die Preispolitik. Marketing Journal, No. 5, 1976, pp. 485–492.

Kostenrechnung und Preisbildung. Kostenrechnungspraxis, October 1964, pp. 237–240.

KRUSCHWITZ (L.). Die Kalkulation van Kuppelprodukten. Kostenrechnungspraxis, October 1973, pp. 219–230.

KUHLMEIJER (H.J.). Pricing—Its Place in the Marketing Mix: Major Problem Areas and Approaches. Marketing Forum, July-August 1971, pp. 25–28.

LACOSTE (W.) & SCHERESCHEWSKY (D.). Ermittlung Leistungsgerechter Angebotspreise. Kostenrechnungspraxis, April 1969, pp. 61–68.

LADO (L.). Kosten- und Gewinnrechnung. Accountancy en Bedrijfskunde, No. 4, 1977, pp. 33–50.

LAFFER (K.). A Note on Some Marginalist and Other Explanations of Full Cost Price Theory. The Economic Record, May 1953, pp. 51–62.

LAIMON (S.). Cost Analysis and Pricing Policies. Cost and Management, September 1961, pp. 360–375.

LANGDON (W.E.). Accounting for Changing Prices—The Basic Issues. Cost and Managment, July-August 1976, pp. 56–59.

LANGEN (H.). Dynamische Preisuntergrenzen. Zeitschrift für betriebswirtschaftliche Forschung, 1966, pp. 649–659.

LANGHOLM (O.). Cost Structure and Costing Method: An Empirical Study. Journal of Accounting Research, Autumn 1965, pp. 218–227.

LANGHOLM (O.) Industrial Pricing: The Theoretical Basis. Swedish Journal of Economics, June 1968, pp. 65–93.

LAZER (W.). Price Determination in the Western Canadian Garment Industry. The Journal of Industrial Economics, March 1957, pp. 124–136.

LEBEDEL (C.). La politique des prix en économie socialiste. Concurence, No. 1, 1972, pp. 39–47.

LEHMANN (M.R.). Die Problematik der Preispolitik auf Grenzkosten—und auf Vollkosten-Basis. Zeitschrift für Betriebswirtschaft, 1950. pp. 332–338.

LEVY (J.) & BISSY (R.). La formation des prix dans l'entreprise. Organisation Gestion de l'Entreprise, February 1972, pp. 37–47.

LIEFFERINK (B.). Maximumprijzen. Ars Aequi, No. 1, 1980, pp. 2–12.

LIPPMAN (S.A.). Optimal Pricing to Retard Entry. Review of Economic Studies, July 1980, pp. 723–731.

LITTLECHILD (S.C.). Marginal Cost Pricing with Joint Costs. The Economic Journal, June 1970, pp. 323–331.

LOHFERT (C.). Ermittlung der Preisuntergrenzen durch Analyse der beschaftigungsabhängigen Deckungsveränderung im Gemeinkostenergebnis. Kostenrechnungspraxis, April 1967, pp. 51–59.

LOHFERT (C.) Preisuntergrenzenbestimmung durch Analyse der Deckungsveränderung. Kostenrechnungspraxis, August 1967, pp. 155–158.

LOHFERT (C.). Statistische Methode zur Fixkostenbestimmung und Preisuntergrenzenermittlung. Kostenrechnungspraxis, December 1967, pp. 257–264.

LORCH (F.). Vollkostenrechnung mit gesonderten Fixkostenbeiträgen. Eine weitere Stellungnahme zu dem von Prof. dr. F. Henzel vorgeschlagenen Kalkulationsschema. Zeitschrift für Betriebswirtschaft, March 1968, pp. 208-210.

LOUCHEZ (A.) & SOUTH (J.R.). Fixation de prix industriels dans une multinationale. Revue Française du Marketing, No. 4, 1980, pp. 51–63.

LOWELL (S.B.). Pricing Policies and Methods. Management Accounting, March 1967, pp. 23–28.

LUCAS (A.) & GEOFFROY (M.). Rigidité des prix: l'exemple de l'indistrie automobile. Concurrence, No. 4, 1971, pp. 17–25.

MACHLUP (F.). Marginal Analysis and Empirical Research. American Economic Review, September 1946, pp. 519–554.

MACKEY (J.T.). Allocating Opportunity Costs. Management Accounting, March 1983, pp. 33–37.

MAINGAUD (P.). La Comptabilité, outil interne d'analyse des prix de revient. Revue Française de Comptabilité, October 1973, pp. 425–429.

MÄNNEL (W.). Kann die Vollkostenrechnung durch den Ausweiss "gesonderter Fixkostenbeiträge" gerettet werden? Zeitschrift für Betriebswirtschaft, December 1967, pp. 759–782.

MÄNNEL (W.). Preiskalkulation auf Vollkostenbasis oder nach den Grundsätzen der Deckungsbeitragsrechnung? Der Betrieb, No. 12, 1981, pp. 593–599.

MARQUEZ (V.O.). Direct Costing from the Marketing Point of View. Cost and Management, June 1963, pp. 342–349.

MARTIN (J.E.). Justifying Price Differentials. Management Accounting, November 1965, pp. 56–62.

MARTIN (J.R.). Multiproduct Profit Analysis: Contribution Margin vs. Gross Profit. Cost and Management, September-October 1982, pp. 22–27.

MASON (R.S.). Price Competition in Industrial Markets. Industrial Marketing Management, October 1974, pp. 275–284.

MASSEY (M.). Consumer Reactions to Price-Quality Relations: An Exploratory Study. Houston Business Review, Summer 1963, pp. 25–48.

MATHIEU (G.). Lebenszyklen als Entscheidungshilfe. Marketing Journal, No. 2, 1978, pp. 122–128.

McANLY (H.T.). Some Fundamentals of Costs for Pricing. N.A.C.A. Bulletin, January 1956, pp. 606–610.

McCOLL (G.D.). Pricing for Profit and Continuity. The Australian Accountant, 1970, pp. 143–146.

McDONALD (M.J.). Profit-Volume and Net Profit Percentages Computed on Cost. Management Accounting, June 1968, pp. 46–50.

McFETRIDGE (D.G.). The Determinants of Pricing Behavior: A Study of the Canadian Cotton Textile Industry. Journal of Industrial Economics, December 1973, pp. 141–152.

McKEAN (J.R.). A Note on Administered Prices with Fluctuating Demand. Journal of Financial and Quantitative Analysis, March 1969, pp. 15–23.

MELLEROWICZ (K.). Preis-, Kosten- und Produktgestaltung als Mittel der Absatzpolitik. Der Markenartikel, 1959, pp. 465–483.

METWALLY (M.M.) & DAVY (G.M.). Advertising—Price Competition and Market Stability. Industrial Marketing Management, No. 3, 1977, pp. 237–240.

MICHEL (H.). Grenzkalkulation in der Praxis. Kostenrechnungspraxis, June 1960, pp. 107–112.

MINNICH (C.J.). Estimating and Costing Variable Order Quantities for Fair Pricing and Profitability. Cost and Management, October 1962, pp. 414–424.

MISSET (H.A.J.F.). Het productengedrag en het marginalisme. De Economist, September-October 1966, pp. 485–512.

Mit der Grenzkostenrechnung aus der Absatzklemme. Absatzwirtschaft, May 1978, pp. 38–41.

MIZOGUCHI (K.). Direct Costing und Preisbestimmung. Zeitschrift für betriebswirtschaftliche Forschung, No. 2–3, 1969, pp. 123–130.

MOERLAND (P.W.). Prijsgedrag in theorie en praktijk. Bedrijfskunde, No. 4, 1979, pp. 324–327.

MONROE (K.) & DELLA BITTA (A.). Models for Pricing Decisions. Journal of Marketing Research, August 1978, pp. 413–428.

MONROE (K.B.), DELLA BITTA (A.J.) & DOWNEY (S.L.). Contextual Influences on Subjective Price Perceptions. Journal of Business Research, December 1977, pp. 277–291.

MONROE (K.B.) & ZOLTNERS (A.A.). Pricing the Product Line during Periods of Scarcity. Journal of Marketing, Summer 1979, pp. 49–59.

MORGENROTH (W.M.). A Method for Understanding Price Determinants. Journal of Marketing Research, August 1964, pp. 17–26.

MORRIS (P.F.). Widget Pricing. Management Accounting, December 1969, pp. 12–14.

MORRIS (R.) & BRONSON (C.). The Chaos of Competition Indicated by Consumer Reports. Journal of Marketing, July 1969, pp. 26–34.

MOSSMAN (F.H.), FISCHER (P.M.) & CRISSY (W.J.E.). New Approaches to Analyzing Marketing Profitability. Journal of Marketing, April 1974, pp. 43–48.

MOSSMAN (F.H.) & WORELL (M.L.). Analytical Methods of Measuring Marketing Profitability: A Matrix Approach. Business Topics, Autumn 1966, pp. 35–45.

NAGTEGAAL (H.). Plädoyer für einen Preis-Manager. Marketing Journal, No. 5, 1973, pp. 390–395.

NECKEBROEK (M.). Direct Costing. Accountancy en Bedrijfskunde, No. 6, 1976, pp. 49–66.

NEWMAN (L.E.). Diseases That Make Whole Industries Sick. Harvard Business Review, March-April 1961, pp. 87–92.

NOUWENS (A.). Kostprijs en Verkoopprijs. Maandschrift Economie, April 1954, pp. 318–332.

OXENFELDT (A.R.). The Computation of Costs for Price Decisions. Industrial Marketing Management, No. 2, 1977, pp. 83–90.

OXENFELDT (A.R.). A Decision-Making Structure for Price Decisions. Journal of Marketing, January 1973, pp. 48–53.

OXENFELDT (A.R.). The Differential Method of Pricing. European Journal of Marketing, Vol. 18, 1979, pp. 199–212.

OXENFELDT (A.R.). Multi-Stage Approach to Pricing. Harvard Business Review, July-August 1960, pp. 125–133.

OXENFELDT (A.R.). Product Line Pricing. Harvard Business Review, July-August 1966, pp. 137–144.

PASS (C.). Pricing Policies and Market Strategy: An Empirical Note. European Journal of Marketing, Autumn 1971, pp. 94–98.

PATRICK (K.J.) & COAKER (J.W.). The Importance of Price as a Choice Criterion for Industrial Purchasing Decisions. Industrial Marketing Management, No. 3, 1976, pp. 281–293.

PATTON (D.R.). The Accountant's Contribution to Pricing Policy. Cost and Management, November 1960, pp. 387–399.

PEARCE (I.F.). A Study in Price Policy. Economica, May 1956, pp. 114–127.

PETER (E.). Betriebliche Preispolitik. Kostenrechnungspraxis, June 1974, pp. 129–132.

PETERS (C.L.). Keeping Competitive in Pricing Defense Contracts. N.A.A. Bulletin, April 1964, pp. 27–33.

PETERSON (W.H.). Divergent Views on Pricing Policy. Harvard Business Review, March-April 1963, pp. 20–30, 172–173.

PIERCY (N.). British Export Market Selection and Pricing. Industrial Marketing Management, October 1981, pp. 287–297.

POMPAN (J.M.). Direct and Absorption Costing in One System. N.A.A. Bulletin, March 1959, pp. 5–18.

POTH (L.G.). Checkliste für preispolitische Entscheidungen. Absatzwirtschaft, November 1970, pp. 39–45.

REICHMANN (T.). Die Berechnung von Preisuntergrenzen unter Berücksichtigung der zeitlichen Fixkostenstrucktur. Kostenrechnungspraxis, February 1974, pp. 21–26.

RENTMEESTERS (F.). Mathematische Aaanbiedingsprijsmodellen. Kwartaalschrift Wetenschappelijk Onderwijs Limburg, No. 1, 1973, pp. 5–28.

REYNOLDS (A.). A Kind Word for "Cream Skimming." Harvard Business Review, November-December 1974, pp. 113–120.

RICHERS (R.). Eine Strategie der Preisbestimmung für die Unternehmung. Kostenrechnungspraxis, October 1967, pp. 195–206.

RICKEN (H.) & MICHEL (H.). Kostenplanung als Grundlage der Verkaufspolitik. Kostenrechnungspraxis, September 1959, pp. 209–214.

RIEBEL (P.). Das Rechnen mit Einzelkosten und Deckungsbeiträgen. Zeitschrift für handelswissenschaftliche Forschung, May 1959, pp. 213–238.

RIEBEL (P.). Die Preiskalkulation auf Gundlage von "Selbstkosten" oder von Relativen Einzelkosten und Deckungsbeiträgen. Zeitschrift für betriebswirtschaftliche Forschung, 1964, pp. 549–612.

RIEBEL (P.). Systemimmanente und anwendungsbedingte Gefahren von Differenzkosten- und Deckungsbeitragsrechnungen. Betriebswirtschaftliche Forschung und Praxis, No. 6, 1974, pp. 493–529.

RIESZ (P.C.). A Major Price-Perceived Quality Study Re-examined. Journal of Marketing Research, May 1980, pp. 259–262.

RILEY (W.J.). Financial Responsibility and Sales Prices. Management Accounting, September 1967, pp. 55–62.

ROWLANDS (J.J.). Formula Elements of Incentive Contracts. Management Accounting, April 1967, pp. 30–37.

RUTENBERG (D.P.). Three Pricing Policies for a Multi-Product Multi-National Company. Management Science, April 1971, pp. 451–461.

SCHAFFNER (H.). Die Deckungsbeitragsrechnung als Instrument der unternehmerischen Betriebsdisposition und Preispolitik. Die Unternehmung, July 1964, pp. 82–96.

SCHICK (A.). Die Bedeutung des betrieblichen Informationsniveaus für die Verwendung von Teilkostenmethoden. Die Unternehmung, No. 3, 1972, pp. 155–164.

SCHLOSSER (J.H.). Helping Management Choose Between Direct and Absorption Costing. N.A.A. Bulletin, November 1963, pp. 47–54.

SCHMIDT (R.B.). Aspekte zur Bestimmung finanzwirtschaftlicher Preisuntergrenzen. Betriebswirtschaftliche Forschung und Praxis, 1965, pp. 275–289.

SCHNEIDER (L.J.). Calculating Price Determining Factors—A Procedure. N.A.A. Bulletin, December 1961, pp. 83–88.

SCHNUTENHAUS (O.R.). Preisanpassung an die Kosten oder Kostenanpassung an die Preise? Der Markenartikel, October 1956, pp. 534–549.

SCHOLTZ (H.D.). Wer Preise macht, musz rechnen können. Absatzwirtschaft, March 1970, pp. 35–38.

SCHULTZ (R.S.). Profit, Prices and Excess Capacity. Harvard Business Review, July-August 1963, pp. 68–81.

SEED (A.H.). A Flexible Cost Basis for Pricing. N.A.A. Bulletin, September 1957, pp. 5–12.

SELCHERT (F.W.). Der Absatz in kostentheoretischer Sicht. Ein Beitrag zur Kombination der absatzpolitischen Instrumente. Zeitschrift für Betriebswirtschaft, 1971, pp. 235–256.

SEWALL (M.A.). A Decision Calculus Model for Contract Bidding. Journal of Marketing, October 1976, pp. 92–98.

SHAKED (A.) & SUTTON (J.). Relaxing Price Competition through Product Differentiation. Review of Economic Studies, January 1982, pp. 3–13.

SHAPIRO (B.). The Psychology of Pricing. Harvard Business Review, July-August 1968, pp. 14–16.

SHAPIRO (B.P.) & JACKSON (B.B). Industrial Pricing to Meet Customer Needs. Harvard Business Review, November-December 1978, pp. 119–127.

SHEARER (L.L.). Direct Costing for Sales Pricing and Profit Planning. Management Accounting, July 1967, pp. 17–23.

SHESHINSKI (E.) & WEISS (Y.). Inflation and Cost of Price Adjustments. The Review of Economic Studies, June 1977, pp. 287–303.

SHILLINGLAW (G.). The Concept of Attributable Cost. The Journal of Accounting Research, Spring 1963, pp. 73—85.

SHILLINGLAW (G.). Overhead in Costing and Competitive Pricing. Cost and Management, December 1961, pp. 508–515.

SIEGFRIED (J.J.) & WHEELER (E.H.). Cost Efficiency and Monopoly Power: A Survey. Quarterly Review of Economics and Business, Spring 1981, pp. 25–46.

SILBERSTON (A.). Surveys of Applied Economics: Price Behaviour of Firms. The Economic Journal, September 1976, pp. 511–582.

SIMMONDS (K.). Strategic Management for Pricing: A Case Example. Accounting and Business Research, Summer 1982, pp. 206–214.

SIMON (D.S.). The Effect of a Price on Company Profits in a Period of Inflation. Accounting and Business Research, Autumn 1977, pp. 295–299.

SIMON (G.). Das Rechnen mit Teilkosten im Klein- und Mittelbetrieb. Kostenrechnungspraxis, December 1968, pp. 255–264.

SIMON (H.). Dynamics of Price Elasticity and Brand Life Cycles: An Empirical Study. Journal of Marketing Research, November 1979, pp. 439–452.

SIMON (H.). Preispolitik bei erwartetem Konkurrenzeintritt. Zeitschrift für Betriebswirtschaft, December 1977, pp. 745–746.

SIMON (H.). Preisstrategie und Markenlebenszyklus. Der Markenartikel, No. 8, 1980, pp. 410–416.

SIMONS (L.). The Accountant's Contribution to the Pricing Decision. The Journal of Mangement Studies, February 1967, p. 95.

SIZER (J.). The Accountant's Contribution to the Pricing Decision. The Journal of Management Studies, May 1968, pp. 129–149.

SIZER (J.). Accountants, Product Managers, and Selling Price Decisions in Multi-Consumer Product Firms. Journal of Business Finance, Spring 1972, pp. 70–85.

SIZER (J.). Accounting Information for Marketing Management. Accountant, January 16, 1975, pp. 67–70.

SIZER (J.). Pricing Policy in Inflation: A Management Accountant's Perspective. Accounting and Business Research, Spring 1976, pp. 107–124.

SKINNER (R.C.). The Determination of Selling Prices. The Journal of Industrial Economics, July 1970, pp. 201–217.

SLEETH (I.N.). The Accountant's Contribution to Profitability. The Accountant, August 27, 1970, pp. 266–268.

SLOT (R.). Is de integrale calculatie "economic nonsense"? Maandblad voor Bedrijfsadministratie en Organisatie, May 1966, pp. 176–177.

SLOT (R.). Nog eens de gevaren van de leer der marginale kostprijscalculatie. De Economist, February 1966, pp. 107–117.

SMITTEN (L.J.). Direct Costing and Its Significance in Marketing. The Canadian Chartered Accountant, December 1961, pp. 561–567.

SOLMS (H.). Wählerisch selektieren. Marktpreisorientierte Kalkulationsverfahren helfen weiter. Absatzwirtschaft, March 1970, pp. 27–33.

STAFFORD (J.) & ENIS (B.). The Price-Quality Relationship: An Extension. Journal of Marketing Research, August 1968, pp. 331–334.

STARREVELD (R.W.). Boekbespreking: "De betekenis van de kosteninformatie voor de besluitvorming" door P. Verburg. Maandschrift voor Accountancy en Bedrijfshuishoudkunde, February 1967, pp. 63–65.

STEPHENSON (P.R.), CRON (W.L.) & FRAZIER (G.L.). Delegating Pricing Authority to the Sales Force: The Effects on Sales and Profit Performance. Journal of Marketing, Spring 1979, pp. 21–28.

STERN (H.W.). Markte oder Preis: Entscheidungskriterium der Verbraucher. Der Markenartikel, No. 3, 1981, pp. 138–150.

STEWART (W.J.). Price Fixing Policy and Direct Costing. A.I.C.A. Cost Bulletin, May 1960, pp. 4–16.

STIGLER (G.J.). The Kinky Oligopoly Demand Curve and Rigid Prices. The Journal of Political Economy, October 1947, pp. 432–449.

STOBAUGH (R.B.) & TOWNSEND (P.L.). Price Forecasting and Strategic Planning: The Case of Petrochemicals. Journal of Marketing Research, February 1975, pp. 19–29.

STRAUCH (P.) & NOUGAREDE (G.). L'innovation et les prix. Concurrence, No. 1, 1972, pp. 49–61.

STURMEY (S.G.). Cost Curves and Pricing in Aircraft Production. The Economic Journal, December 1964, pp. 954–982.

SUPE (H.D.). Die Andebotskalkulation. Baumarkt, April 1969, pp. 739–744.

SWOBODA (P.). Die Kostenbewertung in Kostenrechnungen, die der betrieblichen Preispolitik oder der staatlichen Preisfestzetzung dienen. Zeitschrift für betriebwirtschaftliche Forschung, June 1973, pp. 353–367.

TETTERO (J.H.J.P.). Bodemprijzen en levensmiddelen. Markeur, June-July 1982, pp. 14–16.

THOMAS (J.). Price-Production Decisions with Deterministic Demand. Management Science, July 1970, pp. 747–750.

THOMPSON (H.A.). The Use of Customer Attitude Assessment in Pricing. Industrial Marketing Management, June 1975, pp. 107–111.

TIMMONS (D.F.). Product Costing for a Meat Packer. N.A.A. Bulletin, March 1961, pp. 77–82.

TRECHSEL (F.). Das betriebliche Rechnungswesen als Führungsmittel. Gewerbliche Rundschau, March 1968, pp. 38–49.

TURVEY (R.). Marginal Cost. The Economic Journal, June 1969, pp. 282–299.

TUTHILL (W.C.). Marginal Income as a Factor in Pricing. N.A.A. Bulletin, July 1962, pp. 63–70.

UDELL (J.G.). How Important Is Pricing in Competitive Strategy? Journal of Marketing, January 1964, pp. 44–48.

UHL (K.). What You Should Know about Pricing. Industrial Marketing, March 1962, pp. 90–92.

UNTERGUGGENBERGER (S.) Die kybernetische Function des Deckungsbeitrages. Maandblad voor Accountancy en Bedrijfshuishoudkunde, December 1971, pp. 454–461.

UNTERGUGGENBERGER (S.) Die stufenweise Fixkostendeckung. Kostenrechnungspraxis, April 1975, pp. 75–78.

VAN DER ZIJPP (I.) De principes van het afzet- en prijsbeleid: een pleidooi voor een herorientatie in de literatuur. Maandblad voor Accountancy en Bedrijfshuishoudkunde, January 1977, pp. 2–20.

VAN DER ZIJPP (I.) Herwaarderingen in kostencalculaties. Maandblad voor Bedrijfsadministratie en Organisatie, March 1982, pp. 80–82.

VAN DER ZIJPP (I.) Kostencalculatie en Prijsbeleid. Ekonomie, April 1970, pp. 365–384.

VAN DE WOESTIJNE (W.J.). Enkele bedrijfseconomische aspecten van prijstheorie en prijspolitiek. Maandschrift Economie, July 1965, pp. 504–515.

VAN DE WOESTIJNE (W.J.). Kosten, Prijzen en Assortiment. Maandblad voor Accountancy en Bedrijfshuishoudkunde, January 1967, pp. 4–28.

VAN DE WOESTIJNE (W.J.). Prijsverstarring en merkartikel. Een bijdrage tot de theorie en praktijk van de bepaling van de verkoopprijs. Economisch-Statistische Berichten, March 7, 1956, pp. 196–200.

VAN DE WOESTIJNE (W.J.). Prijspolitiek van de producent. Economisch- Statistische Berichten, November 21, 1956, pp. 1026–1028.

VAN HELDEN (G.J.). Prijszetting. De prijs als marktinstrument. Maandblad Bedrijfadministratie en Organisatie, June 1974, pp. 212–215.

VAN HELDEN (G.J.). Prijszetting. Economisch-Statistische Berichten, October 6, 1976, pp. 963–969.

VAN HELDEN (G.J.). & REUIJL (J.C.). "Competitive Bidding" als voorbeeld van beslissen onder risico. Maandblad voor Bedrijfsadministratie en Organisatie, January, 1975, pp. 6–13.

VERHULP (J.). Prijsacceptatie. Bedrijfskunde, No. 1, 1978, pp. 60–64.

Verkaufen Sie mehr durch Preisdifferenzierung. Absatzwirtschaft, December 1972, pp. 48–56.

VERKUIL (J.M.). Prijsbeleid, achtergebleven gebied van de marketing. Tijdschrift voor Marketing, March 1970, pp. 73–77.

VON PETERSDORFF-CAMPEN (W.). Die Ermittlung von Preisuntergrenzen unter Berücksichtigung der Möglichkeiten alternativer Kapazitätsauslastung in Mehrproduktbetrieben. Zeitschrift für Betriebswirtschaft, July 1968, pp. 553–560.

VORMBAUM (H.). Die Zielsetzung der beschäftigungsbezogenen Absatzpolitik erwerbswirtschaftlich orientierter Betriebe. Zeitschrift für handelswissenschaftliche Forschung, December 1959, pp. 624–636.

WAGNER (W.B.). Changing Industrial Buyer-Selling Pricing Concern. Industrial Marketing Management, April 1981, pp. 109–117.

WALKER (A.W.). How to Price Industrial Products. Harvard Business Review, September-October 1967, pp. 125–132.

WANTY (J.). Recherche d'un programme "optimum" de production et de vente. Organisation Scientifique, No. 8–9, 1966, pp. 214–217.

WARSHAW (M.R.). Pricing to Gain Wholesalers' Selling Support. Journal of Marketing, July 1962, pp. 50–54.

WEBER (H.). Die Verrechnung des Fixkostenblocks in der Produktkalkulation. Kostenrechnungspraxis, August-September 1970, pp. 153–158.

WEBSTER (F.E.), LARGAY III (J.A.) & STICKNEY (C.P.). The Impact of Inflation Accounting on Marketing Decisions. Journal of Marketing, Fall 1980, pp. 9–17.

WEISS (E.L.S.). Costing and Pricing in a Time of Inflation. The Accountant, November 1971, pp. 650–652.

WEMELSFELDER (J.). Het "nut" van de prijstheorie. Economisch-Statistische Berichten, March 4, 1970, pp. 252–255; March 11, 1970, pp. 275–278.

WENTZ (T.E.). Realism in Pricing Analyses. Journal of Marketing, April 1966, pp. 19–26.

WESTERMANN (H.). Probleme des kalkulatorischen Ausgleichs. Kostenrechnungspraxis, December 1974, pp. 247–250.

WESTFIELD (F.M.). Practicing Marginal-Cost Pricing—A Review. The Journal of Business, January 1966, pp. 67–73.

WESTON (J.F.). The Myths and Realities of Corporate Pricing. Fortune, April 1972, p. 85.

WESTON (J.F.). Pricing Behavior of Large Firms. Western Economic Journal, March 1972, pp. 1–18.

WHITIN (T.M.). Output Dimensions and Their Implications for Cost and Price Analysis. The Journal of Business, April 1972, pp. 305–315.

WHITING (E.). Fixed/Variable Cost: Beware! Accountancy, May 1981, pp. 74–78.

WIESMETH (H.). Price Discrimination Based on Imperfect Information: Necessary and Sufficient Conditions. Review of Economic Studies, July 1982, pp. 391–402.

WIJNBERG (H.E.). Direct Costing en bijdragecalculatie I. Tijdschrift Financieel Management, No. 2, 1982, pp. 75–78.

WIJNBERG (H.E.). Direct Costing en bijdragecalculatie II. Tijdschrift Financieel Management, No. 3, 1982, pp. 77–79.

WIJNBERG (H.E.). Het onderscheid vaste en variable kosten: opgepast! Tijdschrift Financieel Management, No. 6, 1982, pp. 81–89.

WILKES (F.M.) & HARRISON (R.). Classical Pricing Rules, Cost-Plus Pricing and the Capacity Constrained Firm. Journal of Business Finance and Accounting, Spring 1975, pp. 19–37.

WILLEMS (A.D.). Het prijselement in de industriële marketing. Tijdschrift voor Marketing. October 1980, pp. 10–13.

WILLENBORG (J.F.) & PITTS (R.E.). Perceived Situational Effects on Price Sensitivity. Journal of Business Research, March 1977, pp. 27–38.

WILLIAMS (T.H.) & GRIFFIN (C.H.). Matrix Theory and Cost Allocation. The Accounting Review, July 1964, pp. 671–678.

WINER (L.). A Profit-Oriented Decision System. Journal of Marketing, April 1966, pp. 38–44.

WISE (G.L.). Differential Pricing and Treatment by New Car Salesmen: The Effect of the Prospect's Race, Sex and Dress. Journal of Business, April 1974, pp. 218–230.

WITLOX (H.). Compositie rond de commerciële voorkeursbehandeling. Prijsdifferentiatie of prijsdiscriminatie. Maandschrift Economie, May 1960, pp. 457–475.

WOLF (W.G.). Developing a Cost System for Today's Decision Making. Management Accounting, December 1982, pp. 19–23.

WRIGHT (F.K.). Marginal Cost and Pricing. The Australian Accountant, August 1956, pp. 323–330.

WRIGHT (W.). Direct Costs Are Better for Pricing. N.A.A. Bulletin, April 1960, pp. 17–26.

WRIGHT (W.R.). Pricing with Direct Costs. The Controller, March 1956, pp. 112–115.

WRINCH (R.P.). Less Guesswork in Sales Price Determination. The Accountant, August 3, 1968, pp. 138–142.

YANCE (J.V.). A Model of Price Flexibility. American Economic Review, June 1960, pp. 401–418.

YOUNG (S.L.). The Need for Should-Cost Estimating/Pricing in Aerospace. Management Accounting, November 1968, pp. 38–42.

ZEITEL (G.). Zusatzkosten und betriebliche Preispolitik. Zeitschrift für Betriebswirtschaft, September 1961, pp. 531–539.

Index

ABOUT THE AUTHORS

WALTER GEORGES is a full time lecturer in Accounting at the Institute for Business Management, Ghent, and is a Consultant in Cost Accounting, Financial Analysis, and Budgeting. He has written 6 books and more than 30 articles on accounting, and won the prize for the best Master's Dissertation in Business Economics.

ROBERT W. MCGEE is Associate Professor of Accounting at Seton Hall University, New Jersey, and has a consulting practice in the New York area. He is a CPA, Certified Management Accountant, Certified Internal Auditor, Chartered Bank Auditor, Certified Systems Professional, and Certified Cost Analyst. He is a contributing editor to two United States accounting journals, and a British accounting journal. He has authored, or coauthored 26 books and over 100 articles. For three consecutive years, he won the Faculty Merit Award at Seton Hall University for excellence in teaching, research, and service.

Week by Week

Plans for Observing and Recording Young Children

Barbara Nilsen, Ed. D.

Broome Community College

Delmar Publishers

I(T)P® **International Thomson Publishing**

Albany • Bonn • Boston • Cincinnati • Detroit • London • Madrid
Melbourne • Mexico City • New York • Pacific Grove • Paris • San Francisco
Singapore • Tokyo • Toronto • Washington

NOTICE TO THE READER

Cover design: Brucie Rosch

Delmar Staff:

Senior Editor: Jay S. Whitney
Associate Editor: Erin J. O'Connor
Project Editor: Timothy Coleman
Index prepared by Andrea J. Anesi

Production Coordinator: Sandra Woods
Art and Design Coordinator: Carol Keohane
Editorial Assistant: Glenna Stanfield

COPYRIGHT © 1997
By Barbara Nilsen, Ed.D.

The ITP logo is a trademark under license.

Printed in the United States of America

For more information, contact:

Delmar Publishers
3 Columbia Circle, Box 15015
Albany, New York 12212-5015

International Thomson Publishing Europe
Berkshire House
168-173 High Holborn
London, WC1V 7AA
England

Thomas Nelson Australia
102 Dodds Street
South Melbourne 3205
Victoria, Australia

Nelson Canada
1120 Birchmont Road
Scarborough, Ontario
Canada M1K 5G4

International Thomson Editores
Campos Eliseos 385, Piso 7
Col Polonco
11560 Mexico D F Mexico

International Thomson Publishing GmbH
Konigswinterer Str. 418
53227 Bonn
Germany

International Thomson Publishing Asia
221 Henderson Road
#05 - 10 Henderson Building
Singapore 0315

International Thomson Publishing Japan
Kyowa Building, 3F
2-2-1 Hirakawa-cho
Chiyoda-ku, Tokoyo 102
Japan

4 5 6 7 8 9 10 XXX 02 01 00 99 98

Library of Congress Cataloging-in-Publication Data

Nilsen, Barbara.
    Week by week : plans for observing and recording young children's development / Barbara Nilsen.
      p.   cm.
    Includes bibliographical references and index.
    ISBN 0-8273-7646-4
      1. Behavioral assessment of children.   2. Observation (Psychology)
    3. Observation (Educational method)   4. Child development.
    I. Title
    BF722.N53   1996
    370.15—dc20   96-12008
                                                                          CIP

Contents..

CHAPTER 10   USING WORK SAMPLES TO LOOK AT CREATIVITY 195

CHAPTER 11   USING MEDIA TO LOOK AT SOCIODRAMATIC PLAY 218

**CHAPTER 14 USING PORTFOLIOS TO CONFERENCE WITH PARENTS
AND LOOKING AT THE CHILD'S INTERACTIONS WITH ADULTS**..............**278**

Preface ....

"I don't have time to write it down!" is the lament of busy teachers of young children. They know that recording what they observe is important in assessing and evaluating each child's development, but the priority is meeting the many needs of young children.

It can be accomplished, with many benefits, by using *Week by Week*, a systematic plan for documenting children's behavior. *Week by Week* is written as a text for observation methods but can be used by practicum students in field placements and by teachers in the classroom.

Various methods of recording are featured in each chapter along with principles of child development and appropriate practice. Weekly assignments are manageable, planned to be comprehensive in observing all areas of development several times over the course of a year, and fairly distributed so that each child is observed in all areas as well as the focus of several individual observations.

The appendixes give the details of the overall plan, so the reader can see a display of its coverage. Assignments for weeks 15 through 40 are included so the book is not just a 14-week text but a resource book for the practicing teacher. Recording forms are included in Appendix D with perforations for ease of use. These are designed to be duplicated, but a clean copy should be retained for future use.

Each chapter includes vignettes from the author's experiences, topics in the form of essays or editorials to broaden the reader's viewpoint, and sections addressing special populations and a listing of helping professionals who the teacher can enlist. Key terms are highlighted in bold type the first time they are discussed and are defined in the glossary at the end of the text. Exercises are included throughout so the reader is interactive with the text, setting the stage for the discussion that follows. Readers are encouraged to write their "answers" on a separate sheet of paper and actively participate.

This text is dedicated to the busy hands and minds and caring hearts of all who work with young children. They bear the worthy name: Teacher.

Acknowledgments...

Week by Week could not have been written without the encouragement and support of the Delmar team: Jay Whitney, who shared my vision and made it come true; Glenna Stanfield and Erin O'Connor, who were always there to answer my questions and listen to my ideas; Tim Coleman, for the technical support in writing; and the team, who took rough drawings, inconsistencies, and pages of drafts and produced this text. To all of you, I express my appreciation.

The next group who deserves to be recognized for their part in this book is my fan club: my husband, helpmate, and friend, Ole, who was my "wife" for a year; my children, who cheered me on; my friends Carol and Jane, who read pages and pages of rough draft; my many other friends and colleagues, who encouraged me and promised to buy the book; and my students, big and small, who gave me the inspiration and some of the stories to tell.

Lastly, I thank the following reviewers for their good advice to make the text clear and useable:

Rosemary Cameron
College of St. Rose
Albany, New York

Sandra Enders
San Antonia College
San Antonio, Texas

Berta Harris
San Diego City College
San Diego, California

Jann James
Troy State University
Goshen, Alabama

Mary Kasindorf
CLASP Children's Center
Great Neck, New York

Diane M. Kohl
The University of Georgia
Athens, Georgia.

To all those who assisted in this project, I now ask, "What to do with it?" After reading the book, you will know what this means.

Introduction: Getting Started

IN THIS INTRODUCTION ···

- ✔ Week-by-Week Plan
- ✔ Topics in Observation: The Ecological View of the Child
- ✔ Why Observe?
- ✔ Why Write It Down?
- ✔ Building a Portfolio
- ✔ A Word About Confidentiality
- ✔ Now You Can Get Started

···

WEEK-BY-WEEK PLAN

Exercise: How long do these big projects take? What steps lead to completion of the projects?

Conception to birth
Earning a college degree
Losing 25 pounds
Crocheting a bedspread

Some of those projects take months, some take years, and some take a lifetime. Each one begins with a plan with small steps along the way, leading to the completion of the project. None of them can happen overnight. Some may even seem impossible; however, when broken down into manageable steps, planned, and worked on over a period of time, they can be accomplished. Eventually, the desired goal will be reached.

Teachers of young children *know* they should be keeping written records on each child's behavior for many good reasons, but there is one seemingly insurmountable obstacle: time. This book

begins with the premise that writing down observations of children's activities is the preferred method of assessing and documenting children's development.

"But I don't have time!" Every busy adult working with children has said it. The priority is to applaud the climb to the top of the ladder, redirect that arm ready to throw a block, or give a thoughtful response to a parent as she hurriedly says on her way out, "He's running a little fever and had a touch of diarrhea this morning, but he says he feels fine." The role of the teacher is to provide physical and psychological safety and intellectual challenge to each child. The teacher also strives to maximize the teachable moment and expand on the child's interests and conversations.

Those two assumptions—accurate record keeping and responsiveness to the needs of each child—seem incompatible. Time and attention for record keeping is minimal. Teachers who know they should be making written records are caught in a bind, Figure I.1. They recognize the importance of

1

Figure I.1 The teacher plans to observe.

keeping accurate records on which to base evaluations or plan individualized curriculum. The difficulty, and for some the impossibility, is doing that while interacting with the children.

Major accomplishments require time and planning. A meaningful portfolio of a child's development and work is not gathered in a few days. Authentic assessment is achieved when each child's development is observed and documented objectively and periodically. The results then can be used to help the child move to the next developmental level. To accomplish this desirable goal, the task must be broken down into manageable segments, planned and executed in a systematic manner. Doris Bergen (1993/94) says "Developing a systematic way of evaluating every child's performance and carefully recording assessment results is a crucial component of authentic assessment" (p. 102). Newman and Roskos (1993) point out "Programs need to *build in* the means and opportunities for all caregivers to watch and record what young children do in some systematic way over time" (p. 22). Benjamin (1994) suggests scattering observation chairs in strategic places around the room in preplanning and organizing for successful recording of observations. Skills, tools, materials, help, and dedication to the plan are needed to build a systematic portfolio demonstrating a child's development.

Week by Week is designed to be used one week at a time by the teacher in the classroom. When the word *teacher* is used, it refers to the recorder who is documenting the child's behavior. It may be the early childhood student in a practicum experience, caregiver in a child care setting, or teacher in a classroom setting. All are in the *teacher* role and will be called by that worthy name in this text. The teacher using the *Week by*

Week system will gain skill in using various methods of recording observations and will be reviewing child development and good teaching practices. These are not separate but are dependent on each other. The *Week by Week* system will enable the teacher to document important information about each child, useable, accurate, and objective information.

Time? When is there time to write? A developmentally appropriate classroom for young children dedicates blocks of time to children's choice of activities. These are self-initiated, with materials and equipment available on shelves the children can reach themselves. Whole-group activities are limited to very short periods, if included at all. That leaves the teacher with time, once the environment is prepared, to observe, make notes, and even closely follow and document a child's play. If there is no time for this, the teacher should look at the environment, the schedule, the ratio of children to adults, the curriculum, and the teaching practices. Perhaps there is work to be done in those areas before observation techniques can be implemented.

Each chapter contains elements to acquaint the teacher with various observation methods, and child development stages. Chapters are interspersed with anecdotes. A feature of each chapter is a discussion of a topic relating to observation. Observation adaptations for special populations are suggested. Weekly assignments lead the observer through an organized, methodical collection of documents to build a portfolio of the child's developmental progress throughout the year.

Exercises

Scattered throughout the book are interactive sections inviting the reader to answer a question or formulate a list. Readers should write their "answers" on a separate sheet of paper. These exercises are designed to introduce a concept that is applied in the following portion of the text. These are designed to be fun with a purpose, so the reader is encouraged to complete them as they appear.

Using the...

Exercise: How many ways can you cook a chicken?

You probably could think of at least ten, maybe twenty, or more. What determines the method chosen? It is a personal choice but is strongly influenced by the desired outcome. If you want crispy chicken, you fry it. If you want low-calorie chicken, you remove the skin and avoid rich sauces. Different results are obtained by different methods, affected by your skill as a cook.

Just as a cooking method is chosen for the desired outcome, the observation and recording methods are chosen to document certain developmental areas. There are many different ways to record in an early childhood setting, each with its purpose, technique, advantages, and disadvantages. Each chapter presents a method, gives examples, and offers suggestions for its use. They correspond with the particular developmental area they can document efficiently. Characteristics of the method are outlined, such as its ability to preserve raw data and eliminate bias. Exercises, such as the two already presented, are interspersed within the text. These invite readers to interact with the subject, focus their thinking, or practice the methods of recording.

Topics in Observation

There are subjects related to observing and recording children's development. They are intended to help the reader gain a broad understanding of a specific topic in teaching, learning, or authentic assessment. These essays offer a deeper consideration of a certain aspect of the field of observing and recording. The first one appears on the following page.

Looking at...

The radiologist shows the X-ray of a broken bone to the parents of the crying child. They look at it but may not *see it as the radiologist does*. Without specialized knowledge, they all look at the same visual image but understand it at a different level.

The teacher needs the knowledge base of child development. Without it, behavior is observed, seen but not recognized for its importance. For that reason, each chapter includes an overview of a developmental area discussing influences, milestones, terminology, and key theories. There is an emphasis on observable skills and behaviors that demonstrate progress. Developmentally appropriate practices are suggested to help foster that development.

* *

IT HAPPENED TO ME: Why Doesn't Johnny Paint?

* *

Early in my preschool teaching career, a mother asked me after class, "Why doesn't my Johnny ever paint? He never has any paintings to bring home." I thought, "Of course he paints! Every one paints at the easel. There are always children on both sides for more than an hour every day. We use gallons of paint and reams of paper every year. Of course, he paints!" I started watching Johnny closely. Sure enough, he never chose easel painting. Even more revealing from my closer observation was how little I knew about what Johnny ever did. He was one of those children who did not draw attention to himself by negative behavior. He played and followed the rules of the classroom. At the end of the day I had no idea what Johnny, and many others like him, had done.

I was teaching a college course in observation techniques but struggling to apply the methods in my own classroom. There were mounds of checklists, one for each child, index cards, and note pads all over the room. When I tried to write a daily journal or mark a checklist, I could not remember children like Johnny. They flowed along, never doing anything "noteworthy." This plagued me until I realized I had to have a plan. I went looking for one but had no success. After calculating the weeks in the school year, what I wanted to know, and the appropriate method to record it, I had a systematic plan. That plan, refined through many years of teaching and research, is presented in this book.

Vignettes of my classroom experiences are scattered throughout the book. These anecdotes illustrate points about child development from children I have known and mistakes I have made that have taught me what *not* to do. Some are observations my college students have written. Others are humorous stories related to me. All are stories, incredible, yet true. There are millions that "got away" because I never wrote them down. Many of these are remembered because after reflection on the real meaning of the incident, they taught me a lesson. Why is it that we often learn best from our mistakes? Many events became more important than I thought they were at the time. I hope you will begin to collect your own stories that have taught you lessons about teaching and life.

* *

TOPICS IN OBSERVATION: The Ecological View of the Child

The scientist looks through the microscope, closely examining a slide, measuring what she sees against what she knows about this organism. She then examines the tissue sample from which it came, then the animal from which the tissue came. The animal has known characteristics because of its species. These characteristics have been affected by food, water, and air, which have been influenced by greater forces of nature or human interventions, such as pollution or protective laws. Government policies determine these interventions based on the national and world situation. In other words, the whole world contributes to what the scientist sees on the slide.

A teacher observes a small segment of a child's behavior, such as how the child holds the scissors to cut. This is reflected against what the teacher knows about stages of normal small muscle development. The teacher recognizes the family influences on the child, both biologically and socially. How are her other small muscle skills and large muscle skills? Has she been allowed to use scissors at home? The family's situation in the community is appraised, along with the political and economic influences. Does this family value independence in a child, or are they so stressed over not having enough food that providing opportunities to write and draw are not a priority? Did this family just emigrate to this country after months of nomadic life? National and world conditions have influenced the life of this family and ultimately the development of the child. Historical events in distant lands and another time have brought the child to this point in time.

The ecological view of the child takes steps backward to visualize a broader view than just cutting with scissors, Figure I.2. This ecological view of development gives the observer multiple perspectives on the child, looking at the big picture.

Scientists do not jump to conclusions based on one view through the microscope. The same is true when observing a child's behavior or skill, frozen in time on a particular day. Other developmental areas overlap to influence that observation. What is observed must be considered in context of the whole child—this child in particular and added to the body of knowledge about children, families, and the society around them. For more on the ecological view of the child, read Bronfenbrenner's *The Ecology of Human Development* (1979).

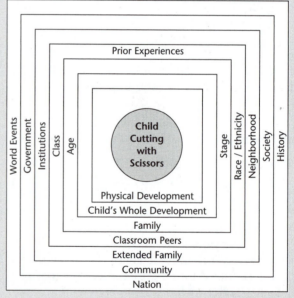

Figure I.2 The Ecological View of the Child from the Teacher's Viewpoint

Special Populations

Every child is unique, as different from each other as observers are. There are sometimes special considerations when observing the widely diverse populations in today's early childhood programs. At the risk of reinforcing stereotypes, this section is included to suggest insight relevant to the developmental area or the observation and recording process. It is a reminder that all children are children first, with circumstances that cannot be ignored. Recognizing their individuality influences the responses of thoughtful practitioners.

Helping Professionals

When working with children and families, teachers are often the resource or intermediary between people who need specialized advice and services and the professionals and agencies. This section is included in each chapter to acquaint the reader with the terminology of specialists to whom the teacher may refer the family. Each program should have a list of specific referral agencies and professionals from which the family can select, with guidance from the people they trust.

Resources

Resources listing helpful books and articles on selected topics are included at the end of the chapters.

Week-by-Week Assignments

The monumental task of documenting every child in the class becomes a series of small weekly assignments, using the methods learned in each chapter to observe the developmental area that has been reviewed. *Week by Week* is a systematic plan to gather documentation on each child, in every developmental area, over a period of time, using a variety of recording methods. Some methods record small, specific bits of information on all the children in the class. Other methods focus on one child, gathering detailed information. The *Week by Week* plan usually gathers both kinds of information each week, rotating developmental areas and individual children. Over the span of 14 weeks, every child is recorded, in every developmental area, and is the focus of at least three detailed recordings. The developmental area, method of recording, and selection of focus children are planned systematically to give every child a fair representation rather than depending on attention-getting behaviors as the documentation cue.

The instructions for using the recording method are included, along with the form on which to write the information. With each weekly assignment is a section, What to Do with It. This suggests where to file the information and how to use this information for useful purposes. Included in this section are suggestions on how to communicate to the parents, and the child, if appropriate, what has been observed. It always is suggested to use the observations as the basis for making decisions about the child, and a way to individualize the curriculum.

Some open-ended questions each week guide the teacher's inward examination in a Reflective Journal. The journal is personal, for the recorder, and not meant to be a part of the child's record.

In 14 weeks, the methods are presented and practiced. All developmental areas are observed at least once. In real life, the areas must be revisited repeatedly to accomplish the objective of seeing change over time. An overview of the 40-week plan is in Appendix A. Care has been taken to observe each child equally, in all developmental areas, using a variety of methods. (See Appendix C for a summary of individual observations on each child by group.) The weekly assignments for the rest of the year are included in Appendix B; this book can be a manual for use in an early childhood program throughout the year. Adaptations for class size and situation are explained.

That is how this book is arranged. It is meant to be a weekly plan for recording observations of each child's development. The outcome of the plan is a meaningful, comprehensive portfolio. What are the benefits of observation? Why should they be recorded or written down? What is a portfolio? Here is the basis for this whole effort.

WHY OBSERVE?

Exercise: Observe (or imagine) these things:

- a clock
- inside your refrigerator
- a traffic light

Exactly what do you see? What does this mean? What will you do?

Write down on a separate sheet of paper what decisions you might make based on these "observations."

The word *observe* brings to mind the action of looking, seeing, not participating but as an outsider viewing the action. Most **observing** done in any context is just the first step. It is taking in information. This stage is the most important, the evaluation and selection of a course of action. The clock is observed, usually not to admire the design, but to determine the time. Looking inside the refrigerator may indicate a trip to the store is needed or the source of a foul odor should be investigated. The traffic light is a lovely shade of green, but its meaning is more important. Observation of the light produces action: Go!

Every observation, everything perceived by the senses, is not just observed but interpreted for meaning. A decision is made to do nothing or to act. The observation may be so insignificant that it is sensed but not acted upon. Later it might prove to be important, like the traffic light that was green but the car in the cross street came through the intersection anyway. When filling out the accident report, these details are important ones.

Figure I.3 Close observation of routine events helps the teacher evaluate and make decisions.

When a teacher observes a child, information is collected and measured against a whole body of knowledge about child development in general and that child in particular. It is used to make decisions about the next actions. Someone has estimated a teacher makes thousands of decisions in a day. They are all based on observations evaluated for meaning and most appropriate response.

The types of decisions the teacher makes are based on observation, Figure I.4.

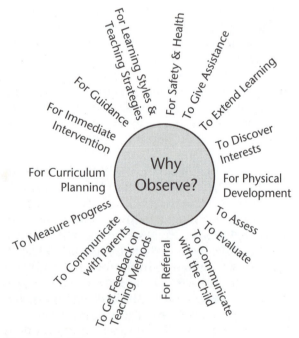

Figure I.4 Why observe?

Assistance

Observation may indicate that help is needed. A child is observed preparing to paint at the easel for the first time. The teacher walks over and shows the child where the apron is and how to put it on. He touches the brush to the edge of the paint container to show how to reduce the drips.

Extend Learning

Teaching is building bridges, facilitating connections between the new information and the old. The teacher expands the learning opportunity by suggesting and planning for related experiences. The teacher mentions to the child at the easel that watercolor paints also are available on the art shelf whenever she would like to use them.

Discover Interests

Recognizing, remembering, and relating to a person's interests raises self-esteem. It also is another way of building bridges from interests to needs, and from home to school, and making the curriculum relevant. The theme of animals (in the beginning stages of drawing recognizable objects) emerges in the painting. The observer remembers the home visit when this child showed a menagerie of pets, potential classroom visitors!

Learning Styles and Teaching Strategies

Teachers develop different strategies as they watch children's responses. By observing the painter, learning styles are indicated that will work better for her, maybe verbal directions, being shown, or trial and error. Reflective observation of the student's learning process leads the teacher to adapt teaching strategies to the child's styles and needs.

Guidance

Prevention is always better than remedy. From observations, potential problems can be averted. The painter's brush is approaching the wall. The teacher says, "We paint on paper," guiding the brush back to the paper on the easel.

Immediate Intervention

Safety is always of utmost importance. Careful observation, leading to immediate intervention, keeps children safe. A child waiting to paint is observed trying to wrestle the brush away from the painter. With angry looks and harsh words, she is trying to gain control of the painting area. The teacher rushes over and intervenes before the painter is knocked aside or a brush is poked into someone's eye.

Physical Health

A trained eye can spot symptoms of illness to expedite a rapid response and diagnosis of the ill child, which can protect the physical health of others too. The teacher notices a few small, red spots behind the painter's ear. She casually pats the child's arm and feels bumps beneath the skin. These observations, along with the knowledge that the child's brother had chicken pox two weeks ago, prompts the teacher's decision to isolate the child and call the child's family to take the child home. When the child returns to school, a painting reveals the child's thinking about chicken pox, Figure I.5.

Assessment

Assessment is the process of documenting a child's skills and development. Information is gathered to measure the child's development against accepted stages or set of norms of development. It measures where the child is at this point and indicates what stage comes next. Assessment may take

Figure I.5 Observing children's work as well as the child as she works give valuable information.

many forms but the premise here is that observation is the best method. It alerts the observer to unusually delayed or accelerated development. The painter paints first with the right hand then switches to the left and back again. The observer assesses the lack of "handedness" at this point in the child's development. Alphabet letters emerge from the painter's strokes as the observer watches. Ah hah!

Evaluation

Evaluation is the next step of decision making. Woodward (1993) uses the following definition:

Evaluation is the collection and analysis of data, from a variety of sources and perspectives, which will contribute to:

- making judgments of merit and worth
- making decisions about future planning
- informing learning (p. 2).

The observer of the painter judges that this child is in the Preschematic Stage, beginning to represent thought. She can make a circle and controlled straight lines, and has a positive mood at the time of the painting. The teacher may decide to read a story about sick children, or bring out the skeleton for the science area to give ideas about anatomy. She can file a copy of this drawing in the child's portfolio to make later comparisons.

Curriculum Planning

There is no need to teach lessons already learned. Through observations, teachers can recognize that teachable moment, that budding interest, that blossoming skill. Providing materials, activities, and opportunities to build on that observed development capitalize on it. From observing that painting, it is decided this is a good time to bring out the alphabet magnets, because the child has shown a beginning awareness in her painting. She invites the painter to play with them.

Measure Progress

By relating observations with knowledge of development, progress is recognized and measured. Over time, it has been observed that the painter moved from experimenting with line and color to the beginning of representing objects. A smiling face with dots is vaguely recognizable. She proclaims this is a picture of her brother who is just getting over the chicken pox. The teacher can see her control of small muscles and low frustration level when the paint does not behave in the way the painter thinks it should. The child's social world is portrayed in the pictures she paints. Many areas of development can be observed in this one activity.

Communication with Parents

Reporting observations not only informs parents of the event but gives many other messages:

- My child is under a watchful eye.
- This teacher sees important development in my child's actions, rather than giving me a test score I do not understand.
- I am being included in the world this person and my child share.

Unfortunately, many children and parents have come to only expect to hear bad reports. Phone calls and notes from school bring a sense of dread. Historically, they told of misdeeds, failure to perform to expectations, or commands to act in a different way. Discussing the observations from the portfolio with the child's parents will give positive, substantive information about the child's progress, compared only to their previous work, not anyone else's. Observation gives descriptive accounts of the child's behavior and skill from the point of view of achievement rather than deficit. Observations are shared with parents in formal and informal ways.

The paintings in the child's portfolio previously were scribbles, then pages filled with lines and deliberate designs. The teacher and child show her parents the collection in the portfolio. The parents realize the teacher *knows* their child and sees their child's work from a different point of view.

Communication about the child with families with home languages other than English takes some extra consideration. Through an interpreter, at a home visit perhaps, it should be learned what language the family prefers, both for speaking and for written communication. The teacher will learn also what the family values and will incorporate it into planning for the child and the classroom.

Woodward (1993) gives several suggestions to help with two-way communication. An older, more English-proficient child could act as interpreter. Using older children as interpreters is possible only if it is not offensive to the family for a child to be in such an important position. A tape recorder could be used to send messages between home and school along with the written versions (p. 45).

Communication with the Child

Every child deserves to hear objective descriptions of their efforts. Too often, the observation is

not discussed with the person it affects most, the child. Often the child can give the reason or explanation in a way that makes sense if only someone asked them. That is the basis for Piaget's cognitive questioning method (Piaget & Inhelder, 1969), to delve more deeply into children's wrong answers. In that way, their thinking processes are explored, rather than just evaluating the result or answer. Woodward (1993) calls this "negotiated evaluation." This process involves discussing observations with the child, and also the parents.

The teacher says to the painter, "You have worked hard on that painting. You used red, and blue, and yellow, and made straight lines and curved lines. Let's compare this picture to one you painted a month ago. What do you see that is the same or different?"

Referral

As teachers observe, certain behaviors, actions, skills, or lack of them, will send an alert to examine a developmental area more closely. It may warrant the discussion of the concern first with the parent, other professionals within the agency, and perhaps a suggested referral to the parent for closer examination. The referral may be for further evaluation in areas such as hearing, speech, physical, or cognitive development. Parental involvement and decision-making in the referral process are the pivotal factors. They are recognized and deferred to as the authority over the child. There may be situations where it is necessary to report suspicions of abuse. Empathy and consideration are important skills for the teacher in all these circumstances.

From the child's paintings, a concern is raised over the subjects or approach. Conclusions are not made lightly, but supplemented with other observations to suggest that a referral may be necessary.

Get Feedback on Teaching Methods

By observing and recording, the teacher's effectiveness can be measured. The interest children have in the planned activities indicates to the teacher if the activities are appropriate. Activities that are not challenging or are too difficult will be avoided or abandoned by the child. By closely observing what keeps them involved, the observer can learn what skills the child is working on and then modify activities to meet those needs.

This type of observation is active research, constantly accumulating data to analyze for its meaning. Yetta Goodman (Goodman, et al., 1989) says this "kid watching" is "teachers who interact with students and who monitor class activities in order to understand more about teaching and learning, mostly learning" (p. 8).

By observing the painter, the teacher sees that the painter is limited by the art supply choices the teacher has provided. A decision is made to offer more choices and other media for this child to explore. Upon reflection, the teacher discovers a lack of knowledge about art stages and decides to research the topic.

WHY WRITE IT DOWN?

Exercise: Using a separate sheet of paper, list the kinds of writing you do in a day. Jot down the reason for each.

"I'll remember this and write it down later." Everyone has said that and then did not write it down. It is lost with all the other details of life that intercede and blur the image, blotting out the details and erasing the exact words. **Recording** is used here to refer to a written account or notation of what has been observed. What are the reasons for writing down what has been seen? See Figure I.6.

To Remember

Even if a grocery list, Figure I.7, is left home on the refrigerator door, because it was written down, it is retained. Many students copy their notes over or condense them as a study technique. There is a connection between writing and memory. The

Grocery List

eggs	*vegetable soup*
milk	*toothpicks*
chocolate chips	*paper towels*

banking

dry cleaning

birthday card for Louise

Figure I.7 Write to remember.

words that are written form a visual and kinetic connection in the brain assist memory and recall even when the visual cues are not present.

To Compare

A child's height is measured with a line on the wall and it is surprising a few months later how much the child has grown without anyone realizing it. If that mark had not been made, the change would not have been noticed. Children are expected to change, so a mark of comparison is needed. Relying on the memory of the child one, three, or six months ago is inaccurate and unreliable. By writing observations down, teachers have tangible comparison points. Portfolios, collections of the child's work, and written observations are becoming an accepted method of documenting the child's progress. Written observations that are thorough, objective, regular, and done in the natural classroom environment are accurate measures of the child's progress.

To Amplify Later

Sometimes there is no time to write the whole incident. A few strategic notes written at the time, and dated, can be just enough to jog the memory for a longer, more complete narrative.

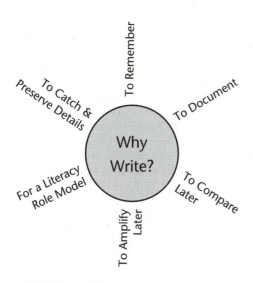

Figure I.6 Why write?

The teacher was showing a new song chart and had just said, "I need all your eyes up here." Andrew asked "What's sixteen plus sixteen?" A puzzled look came over her face, followed immediately by one of irritation for the interruption. He repeated his question louder. "Thirty-two, now let's look at this new song chart." Andrew replied "Oh, you want all thirty-two eyes looking at the chart."

This tells us about Andrew's thinking, his beginning understanding of math concepts and caused the teacher to vow to listen more closely to children's questions. This is a wonderful incident to relay to Andrew's parents to demonstrate his thinking and his humor, Figure I.8.

To Catch and Preserve Details

The fine details that are unimportant now, but may be important later, can best be preserved by writing them down. These details can give clues to trends or correlations that are not seen at the time. Upon closer examination and comparisons later, they gain significance. For example, keeping some data on where and how long each child spends in certain areas of free choice gives much information about the child. Without some method of tracking, there is no way to recall details like this that can yield important information.

For a Literacy Role Model

Literacy is an important concept to teach young children. The importance of the written word is emphasized when children see the usefulness and practical applications by their role models, the adults in their lives. When an adult writes something down a child often asks "What are you doing?" A reply such as "I'm writing this

Figure I.9 Teachers become role models for the children on the importance of literacy.

down so I won't forget" is laying literacy foundations for the child, Figure I.9. It shows that writing is a way to help memory, what is written is constant, and stirs the desire to want to write himself. Accessible materials encourage him to do that, Figure I.10.

Dramatic Play Area—paper and pencil next to the play phone, sheets cut for grocery lists attached to a pad on the play refrigerator, calendars on which children can write important events to remember

Block Area— paper, markers, tape for signs on buildings

Large Motor— paper, markers, tape for signs signifying what the climber is today (a rocket ship, a house on fire, Jenny's house)

Sand/Water—paper and pencil nearby to write down a mark at what sinks or floats, draw pictures of what has been found hidden in the sand; paper to list who is waiting for a turn

Cubbies—paper and pencil to list what children say they want to do outside today to decide which toys to load in the wagon

Group Area—chart paper, markers to take surveys of favorite things, lists of things to remember contributed by the group, safety rules

Figure I.8 Busy teachers jot short notes to amplify later.

Figure I.10 A Literacy-Rich Environment

To Document

Reliable research demands hard data. It is necessary to preserve in writing what has been observed to substantiate it. Recording methods that include facts rather than inferences along with date and time of the recording are essential to meaningful documentation. The details must be preserved to see progress, trends, and correlations.

It is especially critical if a child discloses an incident of abuse. The reports must be accurate and show the child was not led or influenced for the disclosure to be supportable evidence. One would like to never deal with this. but, for the protection of the child, it is important not to jeopardize the testimony by negligence or inaccuracy.

BUILDING A PORTFOLIO

The systematic gathering of information about the child is **portfolio** assessment. Portfolios are more than a scrapbook or folder full of unrelated pieces of paper. Pierson and Beck (1993) point out that "an unstructured collection provides no data for analysis or comparison...to become a viable alternative to conventional testing, it must be rigorous" (p. 30). Portfolios are collections of materials useful for authentic assessment says Grace and Shores (1991) because they gather data to

- measure multiple dimensions
- illustrate learning as an ongoing process
- use for instructional improvement
- be gathered in a natural setting with a variety of the child's natural responses
- share with parents
- use methods that are free of cultural or gender bias

Portfolios can be a valid, reliable replacement for standardized testing. Organizations like the National Association for the Education of Young Children (NAEYC) and National Association of Early Childhood specialists in State Departments of Education (NAECS/SDE) "object to the overuse, misuse, and abuse of formal, standardized testing, epitomized by standardized achievement tests that are unrelated to the ongoing activities of the classrooms" (Hills, 1992, p. 44). They take the position of calling for more authentic assessment methods that provide documentation gathered from multiple sources, over a period of time in the child's natural environment. The *Week by Week* systematic plan for portfolio building will enable the user to gather data to meet the need of authentic assessment in a manageable way. It meets the guidelines for appropriate assessment for planning instruction and communicating with parents, identifying children with special needs, and for program evaluation and accountability. For a full discussion of these guidelines see *Reaching Potentials: Appropriate Curriculum and Assessment for Young Children* (Bredekamp, et al., 1992, pp. 22–26).

Boehm and Weinberg (1987) remind readers of the valuable work of many social scientists, sociologists, and anthropologists who have gathered observational field data. An ecological view is studying in naturalistic settings not in the traditional control experimental atmosphere. An early childhood setting is not a controlled laboratory but an environment that is just a part of the child's larger realm.

Much has been written in the last ten years concerning portfolio building. The lack of a systematic way of gathering that information, using a variety of methods, has led to this book. The purpose of the methods, rationale, instruction, and child development is to come to *know the whole child*. By knowing, then reflecting on this knowing, the teacher can really plan and assess learning and progress.

What's in a Portfolio?

A portfolio is contained in an individual folder for each child in the class, Figure I.11. Eventually, it may hold many pieces of the child's work, teachers' observations, photos, videos, or tapes; so, it should be expandable. All the portfolios should be stored in a locked file cabinet or file box. This ensures it is accessible only to authorized people, including the staff working with the child and the director. The portfolio is available to the parents, upon request, and to the child.

The systematic plan to build the portfolio gathers information from multiple sources:

- The child contributes work samples such as drawings, art work, and samples of writing and language. Media such as audio and video tape and photographs also can be included. The portfolio is a book about the child so, from a very early age, the child has a voice in the included works.
- Parents, who are the true authority on the child, because they know the child better than anyone, submit information to the portfolio on forms and written comments.

INPUT:

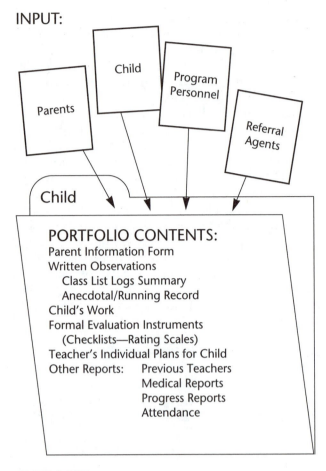

PURPOSES:
Hold information about the child
Document child's development
Periodically review progress

Plan individually for child
Hold examples of child's work
Share with parents, child, teaching team

Figure I.11 Portfolios

- Teachers, who see the child regularly, submit formal observations using a variety of methods to best record different kinds of data in the most objective styles. Informal observations are included as important events worthy of remembering for a variety of reasons.
- Staff in the program who have contact with the child may write a submission for the portfolio. The cook, the bus driver, the nurse, all see the child from a different perspective in different settings and have information to contribute.
- Previous teachers' records may be passed on in the portfolio.
- Referral agents may include reports or suggestions for working with the child in the portfolio.

The portfolio includes documentation of all developmental areas for helping, measuring, and reporting the child's progress. Documentation is arranged chronologically and in developmental areas, and logged in on an overview sheet so that contents are noted. Because of the completeness and intimacy of a portfolio, its contents must be protected from unauthorized viewers. NAEYC's *Code of Ethical Conduct* (Feeney, et al., 1992) under the section on Ethical Responsibilities to Families reads:

> P-2.8—We shall develop written policies for the protection of confidentiality and the disclosure of children's records. The policy documents shall be made available to all program personnel and families. Disclosure of children's records beyond family members, program personnel, and consultants having an obligation of confidentiality shall require familiar consent (except in cases of abuse or neglect).
>
> P-2.9—We shall maintain confidentiality and shall respect the family's right to privacy, refraining from disclosure of confidential information and intrusion into family life. However, when we are concerned about a child's welfare, it is permissible to reveal confidential information to agencies and individuals who may be able to act in the child's interest. (p. 7)

Parents have a right to see and control school records under the Family Educational Rights and Privacy Act (Buckley Amendment) passed by Congress in 1974. In the basic belief that early childhood programs are in partnership with parents, the records are subject to their inspection. The systematic plan of gathering information has nothing to hide for it seeks to provide objective, descriptive documentation.

Parent handbooks should inform parents their child's portfolio is open to them any time. They usually have final determination of it at the end of the year, whether it will go to the next teacher, on to the public school, or taken home. The school should obtain written permission before releasing any portfolio document to others: The exceptions are school officials with a legitimate educational interest, officials for use in audit or accreditation associations (with names deleted). In emergencies, the information is used to protect the health of the individual (Berger, 1991, p. 390).

What Is *Not* in the Portfolio?

If there are any suspected, but as yet unsubstantiated, concerns about possible child abuse, those records should be kept in a confidential file, separate from the child's records. Any Anecdotal Recordings that document a possible disclosure of child abuse should be placed in this confidential file. A copy of the filed child abuse reporting form and notations tracking the action should also be retained there.

The teacher's Reflective Journal is the writer's private property not to be kept with children's records, but preferably kept at home.

A WORD ABOUT CONFIDENTIALITY

Writing enhances memory. That point has been strongly emphasized as the reason for writing observations. It is also true that what is remembered is discussed. As one becomes a better observer and recorder, it will also be only natural that conversations will be full of anecdotes. Cute stories, interesting quotes, and even concerns and "inside" information are on the observer's mind and, sometimes, lips. These should be related to parents using tact and much deliberation about how it will be received. Occasionally, what the teacher thinks is a triumph the parent may see as otherwise because of a different perspective or value.

Talking about the child in front of the child should be done with consideration. Sometimes children want privacy and a sense of being a person apart from the parent. The teacher could ask the child, "May I tell your parents about how long you painted today as we show them the painting?" Sometimes the child needs to hear their accomplishments related to their parents. Misdeeds or concerns, however, must be done in private away from the child and other parents, of course.

Discussions outside the classroom with friends, or one's own family demands discretion. Sometimes stories are related for illustration, but should never include children's names. Complaining, rejecting, or criticizing children or families is unprofessional. Professional behavior is guided by judgment, kindness, and most of all, respect for an individual's privacy.

NOW YOU CAN GET STARTED

You will need a new file folder for each child in your class, plus a few extras for new children through the year. Write names on tabs, last name first, and place in alphabetical order. Place in the file any information supplied by the parents.

A Portfolio Overview Sheet (found in Appendix D) is a summary of all the recordings in the portfolio so the reader can see at a glance what is contained there, a type of table of contents. Duplicate one form for each student: place one in each student's portfolio.

This chapter sets the stage, gives you the background, and acquaints you with the format of the book. The next steps are yours. Complete the exercises and adapt the assignments for your particular group of children. At the end of 14 weeks, you will have accumulated sizable portfolios on each child, with documentation in each developmental area. If you continue the assignments throughout the year, you will see the progress they make, and become a better observer, recorder, and teacher.

REFERENCES

Each chapter includes references used in the chapter.

Benjamin, A. (1994). Observations in early childhood classrooms: Advice from the field. *Young Children 49*, (6).

Bergen, D. (1993/94). Authentic performance assessments. *Childhood Education 70*, (2), 102.

Berger, E. (1991). *Parents as partners in education: The school and home working together*. New York: Macmillan Publishing Co.

Boehm, A. E. & Weinberg, R. A. (1987). *The classroom observer: Developing observation skills in early childhood settings*. New York: Teachers College Press.

Bredekamp, S. & Rosegrant, T. (1992). *Reaching potentials: Appropriate curriculum and assessment for young children*. Washington: National Association for the Education of Young Children.

Bronfenbrenner, U. (1979). *The ecology of human development*. Cambridge, MA: Harvard University Press.

Feeney. S. & Kipnis, K. (1992). *Code of ethical conduct*. Washington, DC: National Association for the Education of Young Children.

Goodman, Y. M. (1989). Evaluation of students. In K. S. Goodman, Y. M. Goodman, & W. J. Hood (Eds.), *The Whole Language Evaluation Book*. Portsmouth, NH: Heinemann.

Grace, C. & Shores, E. (1991). *The portfolio and its use: Developmentally appropriate assessment of young children*. Little Rock, AR: Southern Association of Children Under Six.

Hills, T. (1992) Reaching potentials through appropriate assessment. In S. Bredekamp & T. Rosegrant (Eds.) *Reaching potentials: Appropriate curriculum and assessment for young children*. Washington: National Association for the Education of Young Children.

Newman, S. B. & Roskos, K. A. (1993). *Language and literacy learning in the early years: An integrated approach*. New York: Harcourt Brace Janovich.

Piaget, J. & Inhelder, B. (1969). *The psychology of the child. New York: Basic Books.*

Pierson, C. A. & Beck, S. (1993). Performance assessment: The realities that will influence the rewards. *Childhood Education 70,* (1) 30.

Woodward, H. (1993). *Negotiated evaluation: Involving children and parents in the process.* Portsmouth, NH: Heinemann.

RESOURCES

Bredekamp, S. & Rosegrant, T. (1992). *Reaching potentials: Appropriate curriculum and assessment for young children. Washington: National Association for the Education of Young Children.*

Grace, C. & Shores, E. (1991). *The portfolio and its use: Developmentally appropriate assessment of young children.* Little Rock, AR: Southern Association of Children Under Six.

Using the Class List Log to Look at Separation and Adjustment

IN THIS CHAPTER •

✔ Using the Class List Log

✔ Topics in Observation: Why Not Use a Diary or Daily Journal?

✔ Using the Reflective Journal

✔ Looking at Separation and Adjustment

✔ Special Populations and Separation Adjustment

✔ Helping Professionals for Separation and Adjustment Concerns

• •

USING THE CLASS LIST LOG

Exercise: Make a list of all the people you have had contact with today. Note what color shirt each person was wearing.

Some assumptions can be made about the list in the preceding exercise. It may be difficult to list every person one is with but easy to remember more significant people. It also may be difficult to remember the color of the shirt each person wore, especially casual contacts. It would have been easier if one knew at the beginning of the day what the assignment was and noted it as it occurred. At the end of the day, or after the fact, recall is more accurate concerning some people and some facts than others. Memory might fail regarding others who demanded no attention and received none.

The teacher's clearest recollection at the end of the day is usually of those children who did memorable things. The memory might be a child splashing paint across the room or one singing every song from the latest Disney movie. Children who cause no trouble or draw attention

to themselves might not be remembered at the end of the day.

A method is needed to guide the teacher to record information about every child in the class. The same category of information should be recorded on every child in the group on the same day: It is more equitable to standardize the criteria and collect data on all the children in the group. Memory cannot be trusted for accuracy or remembering each child.

The **Class List Log** is a method or format to record one or more short, specific pieces of information about each child present on that day. It is designed to be quick and easy (something every teacher is looking for). However, it provides information on every child in the group. It records facts that may be interpreted later or incorporated into another type of developmental comparison over time. The Class List Log criterion is determined in advance and is the same for each child, Figure 1.1.

Blank forms are made by alphabetically arranging the first names of the children. This arrangement allows for the quickest way to find the space to jot a note. There is a line at the top for the date.

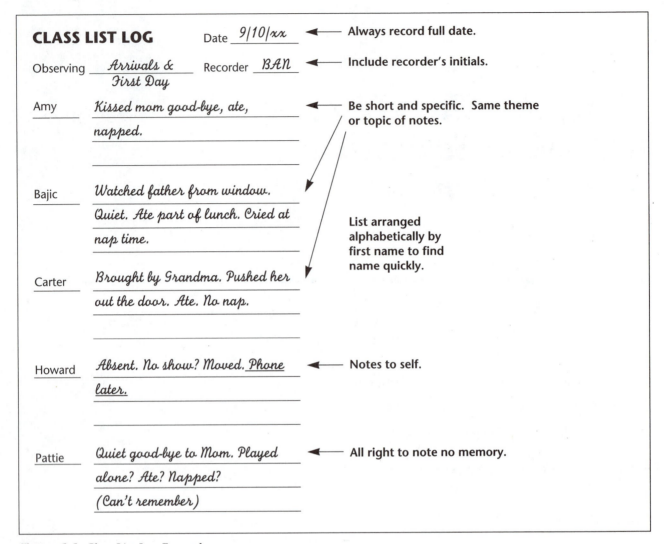

CLASS LIST LOG   Date _9/10/xx_ ◄—— **Always record full date.**

Observing _Arrivals &_   Recorder _BAN_ ◄—— **Include recorder's initials.**
First Day

Amy   _Kissed mom good-bye, ate,_ ◄—— **Be short and specific. Same theme**
napped.   **or topic of notes.**

Bajic   _Watched father from window._
Quiet. Ate part of lunch. Cried at   **List arranged**
nap time.   **alphabetically by**
   first name to find

Carter   _Brought by Grandma. Pushed her_   **name quickly.**
out the door. Ate. No nap.

Howard   _Absent. No show? Moved. Phone_ ◄—— **Notes to self.**
later.

Pattie   _Quiet good-bye to Mom. Played_ ◄—— **All right to note no memory.**
alone? Ate? Napped?
(Can't remember)

Figure 1.1   Class List Log Example

Using a date stamp is a good routine to follow. This assures the date is on every recording, including the year. Leave as much space between names as possible. Two forms may be made vertically on one page and kept on hand for various purposes. Bits of information then can be copied over or cut apart and stapled into each child's file. (Blank Class List Logs are provided in Appendix D.)

Computer-generated mailing labels with first names in alphabetical order can easily be peeled and attached to a page in each child's portfolio. The names could be typed or hand written and copied on sheets of mailing labels. The availability of the Class List Log form is essential to its usefulness.

While actively engaged in play or work, the recorder uses the Class List Log to record information on one skill or behavior on each child in the group. This provides a natural information-gathering process. For example, cutting could be observed by placing children's scissors on a table with interesting papers to cut, such as gift wrap, wallpaper samples, or comics. The observer sits nearby with a Class List Log and makes notes as each child works in that area. Large motor skills can be observed easily as children go through a maze that includes climbing, balancing, throwing, jumping, and crawling skills. It is important to date every observation, including the year.

Exercise: Mark the following *Yes* or *No* for suitability of Class List Log criteria.

- ❑ has toileting accidents
- ❑ is able to cut
- ❑ listens to story
- ❑ pours own juice, usually without spilling
- ❑ sleeps at rest time
- ❑ considerate of others' feelings

❑ can pedal a tricycle
❑ understands concepts of front/back, up/down, loud/soft
❑ uses words to resolve conflicts
❑ follows classroom rules

Now go back to the list and record in which setting or activity this most easily could be observed for every child in the group in one class session. If that is difficult, then that skill or behavior probably is not suitable for a Class List Log.

Uses

The Class List Log might be used to take attendance or to make notes on one behavior for a specific purpose. For example:

- separation from parent
- large motor: specific skills such as climbing, standing on one leg for 5 seconds, walking the length of the balance beam, alternating feet coming down stairs, or hopping
- small motor: cutting with scissors, printing first name, rolling a ball, folding a napkin or paper in half, or putting together an eight-piece puzzle
- language: reciting nursery rhymes; responding to vocabulary of over, under, small, bigger, biggest
- literacy: looking at book from front to back, "reading" pictures
- math: rote counting, using one-to-one correspondence
- science: placing items in sequence, sorting items by color or size
- art: paintings lines, circles, human figures, alphabet letters (Use Class List Log at the easel to tally each time a child chooses to paint in a week.)
- blocks and dramatic play: noting level of play, role in dramatic play, or type of constructions made

Advantages

The Class List Log is an efficient recording method because it:

- is quick and easy
- records specific information on every child in the group
- gives specific, dated, brief, factual information
- can be transferred to other forms of recording as base information
- can be used later for comparison

Disadvantages

The Class List Log may not be desirable because:

- the form becomes outdated as children enter or leave group
- rewriting is time-consuming
- limited information or data is recorded
- it must be repeated to be valuable for comparison

Avoid the Pitfalls

The recorder should remember to:

- Always date each entry. A stamp dater is great
- Include the time of day, if pertinent
- Select an observable criterion
- Write short, factual notes

What to Do with This Information

A few words of summary are jotted on the Portfolio Overview Sheet with the recorder's name and date, Figure 1.2. If bits of data are on mailing labels, these are attached to a page in each child's portfolio with the date. Class List Log sheets can be cut apart and each child's portion stapled, taped, or pasted on a sheet in the portfolio. Later, observations in this category will be added to this page.

If the program uses a developmental checklist, the bits of information can be transferred to the checklist category in the child's portfolio, with the date and specifics. For example, Class List Log information gathered on cutting may be transferred to a developmental checklist on small muscle development.

Information gathered with the Class List Log could be shared with the parent verbally at the end of the day. "Today, Aillio used the scissors to cut up the funny papers. He worked hard at cutting along the lines." A written happy note, Figure 1.3,

SEPARATIONS AND ADJUSTMENT		
Documentation	Recorder	Date
CL Arrival, cried then OK	BAN	9/7
CL Arrival, depart OK	BAN	2/14
CL Organizes, anticipates	MS	4/5
RR Typical arrival	BAN	5/9

Figure 1.2 Portfolio Overview Sheet Example

could be sent home informing parents, "Today, Aillio worked hard at cutting."

If a skill below the expected level of development at this age or stage is observed, a curriculum plan is implemented to address this area. This gives the child the opportunity to practice and advance the skill.

The Class List Log is an effective method to use in the first week of school to record observations. This method recognizes the teacher's first priority is making relationships with the child and parents. The observations of separations and first impressions are important ones to record, however, providing an understanding of the foundations and outward manifestations of attachment and separation. The Class List Log provides a quick, easy format on which to record first observations without consuming much of the recorder's time.

Figure 1.3 Happy notes are a method of communicating with parents.

TOPICS IN OBSERVATION: Why Not Use a Diary or Daily Journal?

Exercise: Write a diary entry for yesterday on a separate piece of paper (for your eyes only).

Many people working with children know they should write about the children. Many even have written diligently in a notebook or in each child's file every day. The difficulty comes when this type of record keeping is considered in light of objectivity and comprehensiveness across the developmental areas.

An entry in a **diary** written at the end of the day is likely to omit details in sequence, Figure 1.4. Exact conversations and movements, which give so much important information to the assessment of children's development, are forgotten. At the end of the day, the strongest memories are those frustrations and difficulties. When it comes to remembering what each child did, the few who were the most difficult are most vividly recalled. Some are remembered at the end of the day because of an unexpectedly advanced skill or a novel, cute incident. The problem occurs when trying to remember the children in the middle. Those are the children who cause no trouble, who quietly abide by the rules, float through the day, doing nothing out of the ordinary to attract attention. Informal diary writing leaves those children out day after day after day.

This same difficulty occurs when writing in

each child's page in a notebook. At the end of the day, try as one might, some children are not memorable. How can a teacher say to a parent, "I don't know what your child did today. I can't remember a thing." So instead, general comments are made, not based on hard data. The child is cheated out of being the focus of the observer's attention. It is not out of malice but because of the unsystematic way this type of recording is done. There is no hard data. Observations are written from memory, after the event.

The other shortcoming of the diary as an observational method is its subjectivity. People have used diaries traditionally for writing their innermost thoughts and feelings. **Subjective** recordings are those that are influenced by state of mind, point of view, or inferences into the meaning of events. The opposite is **objective** recordings, which are detached, impersonal, unprejudiced, recording facts rather than feelings and generalities. For the purpose of fair assessment and documentation of each child's development in all areas, objective methods should be used. The goal is an objective measurement system for each child. Diary entries do not help the teacher meet that goal.

Analyze your diary entry written in the preceding exercise. Can you separate the objective and subjective parts?

9/10	The First Day! It's a large class with many more boys than girls. They're going to give me a run for my money! They seem to have adjusted well for the first day ☺ and are eager to learn the routines, especially to explore the classroom. Carter was already in the Teacher's Cupboard. Said "What else ya got in here? Can I have that?" He's so cute. I'm especially interested in who makes friends . Today Jeff, Pia, Maurice, Jan & Chanique played together. I think this clearly will help me be a better observer. I'm so tired!
9/20	Day 2: I found out today that I need to find ways to separate Scott & Jeff together they're dynamite! They had me so busy doing damage control I can't remember what the other children did. Oh yes, Casper left to visit another class for 45 min. before I realized he was gone!
12/3	Wow has it been that long since I last wrote. I have parent conferences in two weeks. I better start better record keeping!

Figure 1.4 This diary example was written at the end of the day. It was difficult to remember details about every child.

Exercise: Mark these phrases *S* for subjective or *O* for objective.

❑ jumped from 18 inches
❑ very smart
❑ nice boy
❑ grabbed toy and said, "Mine!"
❑ doing fine
❑ she's a challenge
❑ polite
❑ counted to 8
❑ recognized nametag
❑ called someone a bad name
❑ clapped to "Bingo" song
❑ enjoyed music time

Check yourself: OSSOSSSOOSOS

USING THE REFLECTIVE JOURNAL

Exercise: Which of the following things would you rather discover yourself rather than have someone else tell you?

❑ You have bad breath.
❑ You are unzipped or unbuttoned.
❑ You have food stuck between your teeth.
❑ You are prejudiced against something.
❑ You are acting unprofessionally.

The **Reflective Journal** can help to discover things others might know but would rather not tell because the receiver of the information would be offended or embarrassed, or would deny it or perhaps act in defiance rather than remedy the situation. **Reflection,** thinking about the child, the day, yourself, or your teaching, is important. Airasian (1991) calls this beginning-of-the-year reflection, "sizing up," those informal first impressions that tend to become permanent generalizations of perceptions that are accurate very often. This kind of judgment is only natural. An awareness of the possible self-fulfilling prophecy of these assessments limits their usefulness. They may result in subjective interpretation of behaviors based on a small sample of information (jumping to conclusions) rather than accumulating factual information and coming to informed judgments. Awareness of biases of all kinds, and how easily they can creep into assessments, is an important factor in these "sizing up" observations. The teacher's reflections in a private diary or journal, rather than as a part of the child's record, is more appropriate. These first impressions form the basis of hypotheses that more formal information-gathering will either prove or disprove. The professional relies on objective rather than subjective recordings but professional judgments are important. They are based on knowledge and experience, but authentic assessment depends on more objective data-gathering methods.

The Reflective Journal is like looking into a mirror, Figure 1.5:

- External view—When looking into a mirror, the viewpoint is from the outside, as others see the person. The Reflective journal is an opportunity to explore the view that others see and compare it to the inner, deeper meaning. It helps the observer see as others see.
- Quick check—Often the mirror is used for a quick, overall glance to see that clothes, hair, and makeup are satisfactory. A Reflective Journal can be a place for a cursory overview of performance,

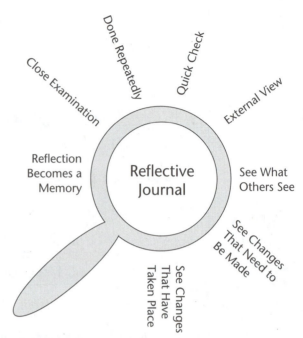

Figure 1.5 The Reflective Journal is like a mirror.

feelings, or events of the day without getting into deep analysis.
- See changes—Changes in appearance are identified by looking in the mirror. Grey hairs (or disappearing ones) or extra pounds are noticed visually when reflected in the mirror. The Reflective Journal can help the writer notice changes about thinking and attitudes.
- Close examination—The mirror can be used for a concentrated examination of a certain area. It may be a changing spot on the skin, clothing alignment, or a new wrinkle that has appeared overnight. The Reflective Journal can be a private place to self-examine a troublesome area. It may be premature or too private to discuss with someone else. An attitude toward a child or coworker, a creeping doubt about one's ability or a prejudice that has come into one's consciousness can be closely examined in a journal.
- Make changes—When a look in the mirror shows something is askew, missing, or undone, the resultant action is an adjustment to correct the problem. Reaction to visions in the mirror is one of the purposes of looking. Writing in a Reflective Journal raises issues that call for change and presents the opportunity to resolve to take action. The Reflective Journal becomes an agent of change.
- Done repeatedly—Glances in the mirror are done many times a day, sometimes using substitutes such as windows in storefronts to re-

examine certain areas. The Reflective Journal brings the teacher to inward examination again and again, whether in writing or in thinking.

- Reflection becomes a memory—The vision in the mirror is remembered. Looking internally through a Reflective Journal to examine values, beliefs, and feelings also forms memories. Those become as real as physical experiences. Reflection is more than daydreaming. It can be a life-changing experience.

Exercise: Try some Reflective Journal writing:

When I enter a new place for the first time I feel…

Writing about myself is…

An area I would like to explore about myself is my…

I chose to work with children because…

What Is Its Purpose?

Just like a personal diary, the teacher's Reflective Journal is a place to express emotions, make judgments, and form hypotheses, Figure 1.6. It is not a

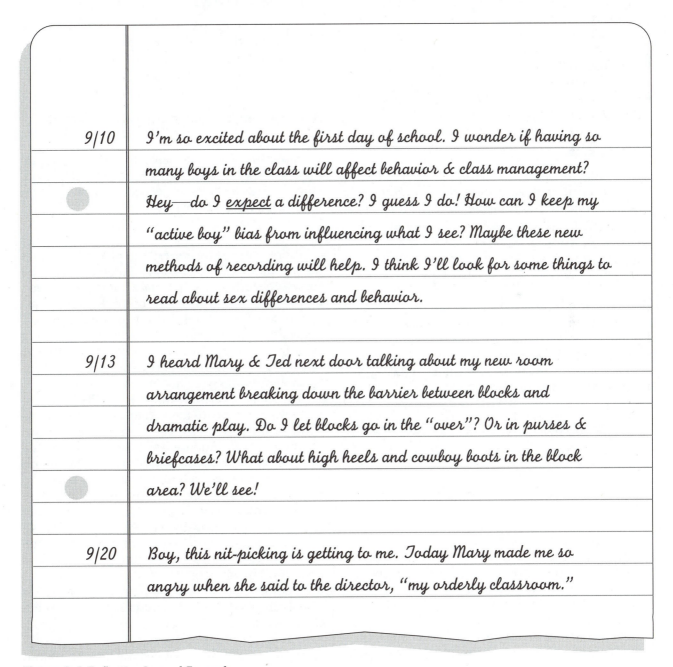

9/10 I'm so excited about the first day of school. I wonder if having so many boys in the class will affect behavior & class management? Hey—do I *expect* a difference? I guess I do! How can I keep my "active boy" bias from influencing what I see? Maybe these new methods of recording will help. I think I'll look for some things to read about sex differences and behavior.

9/13 I heard Mary & Ted next door talking about my new room arrangement breaking down the barrier between blocks and dramatic play. Do I let blocks go in the "over"? Or in purses & briefcases? What about high heels and cowboy boots in the block area? We'll see!

9/20 Boy, this nit-picking is getting to me. Today Mary made me so angry when she said to the director, "my orderly classroom."

Figure 1.6 Reflective Journal Example

part of the child's file but the personal property of the writer, providing a healthy outlet for emotions. This type of recording must be kept separate from the assessments of the development of the child. For privacy, it must be kept at home, away from the work site.

Uses

The Reflective Journal is useful

- to express emotions or questions, to let off "steam," anger, frustration, elation; to express worry concerning a child, a coworker, a parent, a supervisor, or self
- for self-examination of attitudes, biases, or prejudices
- to pose theories about a child's behavior that are from intuition
- to explore remedies, strategies, advantages, and disadvantages of possible solutions

Advantages

- an outlet for emotions
- process writing to work through theories and to clarify and expand thinking
- becomes a record of professional development

Disadvantages

It is not useful for assessing children's development because it is:

- written after the event when facts are lost.
- highly inferential and emotionally based.
- not comprehensive in recording information remembered on each and every child, only those who stand out.

What to Do with the Reflective Journal

Because of the confidential, subjective nature, it must be

- kept secure and private, away from the work place.
- used as an emotional release that may not be possible in any other form.
- used to take a measurement of your personal and professional development in working with children and their families and coworkers.
- used to explore questions, develop theories, and examine biases.
- reviewed at intervals to examine changes in thinking and attitudes, and measure professional development.

Pitfalls to Avoid

The Reflective Journal is very personal. It is important to maintain trust that what is written there will not be read by anyone. Keep it at home. Get in the habit of writing in it every week. Go beyond the guided questions and use it to vent your feelings, questions, ideas, and theories. Keep it safe.

LOOKING AT SEPARATION AND ADJUSTMENT

A smooth transition from home to school at the beginning of the year or as a child enters a program provides for the child's immediate comfort and contributes to later success.

Attachment's Relationship to Separation

Exercise: Using a separate sheet of paper, make a list of objects that are important to you. How did they become so valued? How would you feel if they were destroyed in a fire, lost, or stolen?

People form **attachments** to objects and other people for a variety of reasons. An object might be something attained after hard work and much preparation. It may be a gift received as an expression of love. Sometimes the longer an item is possessed, the more valuable it becomes. Strong attachment or value makes it hard to part with that object or person. Familiarity provides comfort. Separation brings a feeling of loss.

The infant's relationship with adults begins at birth when needs are met, Figure 1.7. This attachment to the parent emerges from built-in survival techniques and responses. In the early weeks, the provider of those needs is irrelevant to the infant, as long as the needs are met. The infant begins to focus on the face, voice, and smells of those close to him, and begins to form mental images of those who hold him. Bowlby (1969), Yarrow (1964), Shaffer and Emerson (1964), and Ainsworth et al. (1978) have all done important studies of this process of attachment. These studies are the basis for guiding expectations and practices. The professional caregiver's role is to build the child's bond to the parent as the primary adult and to the caregiver as a trustworthy substitute.

In the first few weeks of life, the infant responds to and attends to any nearby person, parent, or

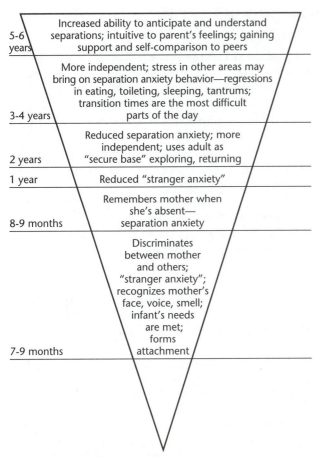

5-6 years	Increased ability to anticipate and understand separations; intuitive to parent's feelings; gaining support and self-comparison to peers
3-4 years	More independent; stress in other areas may bring on separation anxiety behavior—regressions in eating, toileting, sleeping, tantrums; transition times are the most difficult parts of the day
2 years	Reduced separation anxiety; more independent; uses adult as "secure base" exploring, returning
1 year	Reduced "stranger anxiety"
8-9 months	Remembers mother when she's absent— separation anxiety
7-9 months	Discriminates between mother and others; "stranger anxiety"; recognizes mother's face, voice, smell; infant's needs are met; forms attachment

Figure 1.7 Development of Independence—Separation and Adjustment to Out-of-Home Experiences

caregiver. This is the survival instinct: Without adult provision of needs, the infant could not live.

Between eight weeks and six months, the infant begins to discriminate between familiar people, such as parents, and unfamiliar people. The child is more responsive, and smiles and vocalizes more to familiar people than to unfamiliar people. There are implications for infants entering child care prior to six months old. As the infant is beginning to differentiate between self and significant others, the primary caregivers should be consistent people who are responsive to the infant's needs. Infants may exhibit **stranger anxiety** as they are increasingly aware of the difference between close family and other people. However, Shaffer and Emerson (1964) found that most infants are capable of forming a number of attachments at the same time. The role of the caregiver is to keep the infant primarily attached to the parents. This can be done by providing reminders of the parents. Images (photographs), voices (tapes), and smells (belongings) surrounding the child during the day at the center will help to maintain that attachment during the

family's absence. This gives assurance to parent and child that their bond is the primary one. The caregiver maintains that bond during their hours away from each other.

The infant and toddler maintain contact or stay near the attached person by creeping, walking, and following those important people. The child uses vocal signals, cooing, crying, and eventually words to maintain contact. Older infants and toddlers begin to anticipate the coming separation. This may happen when they see their coat and diaper bag, being readied by the caregiver at the end of the day, or when they see the parent. This is what is called **separation anxiety.** This is a normal part of development but is distressing to all involved. The intensity of this stage is dependent on many factors: attachment to the parents, temperament of the child, and experiences with consistent responsive caregivers. It can be minimized by establishing those **good-bye rituals** that Balaban (1987) speaks about in a very helpful book on this subject, *Learning to Say Good-bye.* She advises parents to establish a good-bye routine that is consistent every time they part, Figure 1.8. It serves as a dependable signal that leads the child to trust that the parent will return, even though parting may be full of tears and anger.

The toddler or preschooler engages in forming relationships with the attachment figures, learning how to get parents and caregivers to change their behavior to conform to child's wishes. Preschoolers still experience separation anxiety because they now realize their power to manipulate others to meet their desires. They may not want the parent to have a life outside of their realm. Life in group care is different from life at home. Adjusting to discontinuity between home and the center may be

Figure 1.8 Good-bye rituals help the child and the parent with the transition and separation.

stressful. The child learns to use separation anxiety as a tool to receive special attention and special promises. It often results in a relaxation of standards of behavior. The parent may feel guilt or ambivalence for leaving. The caregiver's responsibility is to help the child cope and empower the parent to leave without guilt or losing a battle. Good-bye routines, once established, work very well at helping to ease tension.

Why all the attention to this area? Research has indicated some serious long-term consequences from separations of parents and children. Bjorklund and Bjorklund (1992) summarized the attachment research of Bowlby; 1969; and Ainsworth, et al., 1978; and others to suggest that securely attached children:

- are more independent (than unattached children)
- have a more positive self-image
- engage in positive social interactions with peers
- have fewer behavioral problems
- are able to negotiate in conflicts
- score higher in IQ and standardized tests
- are more socially competent, self-directed, and attentive at age 35
- are more curious, flexible, and persistent
- have better impulse control (pp. 321–323)

With important outcomes associated with attachment, giving attention and developing strategies to assist in this important developmental area is critical.

Preparation for Good Beginnings

Exercise: Using a separate sheet of paper, list important "first" events in a lifetime (such as birth, first step, first tooth, first date).

Beginnings are memorable events. They are celebrated with much thought, preparation, and anticipation. Photographs, videos, and certificates are concrete remembrances of the occasion. Memories are recited in detailed stories of the process. Lengthy discussions relate what went well and reflect on what did not and how it could have been done differently.

Beginning a new school year, entrance to a new child care center, and even the beginning of every day, is an important event. These beginnings are worthy of careful preparations, thoughtful processes, and detailed recording. Making smooth transitions into the program, whether for the first time

ever or the first time that day, begins long before the parent and child come through the door.

Important Information Gathering Prior to the First Day. Every program has its own information-gathering form for facts about the child from the parents. The type of program, the objectives, and state regulations prescribe the type of information gathered on this form. A copy is placed in the child's portfolio for the teacher's reference. The original is kept in the program office.

Exercise: On a separate sheet of paper, make a list of information you think should be included on a parent information form.

Refer to the parent information form, Figure 1.9, and see how many pieces of information you thought of and which ones you feel are the highest priority.

Parents are the most important source of information for assessing the child's development. By requesting developmental information, the program is recognizing the parents as the child's first teachers, the ones who know the child best. In special education programs where children have been formally evaluated, Bloch (1987) stresses the importance of collaboration with families as information gatherers. She makes the point that "a radical rethinking of the way professionals work with parents and families is required" (p. 4). Bloch's parent assessment component, Figure 1.10, in the Five P's Parent Professional PreSchool Performance Profile program, teaches them to:

- learn to observe their child's behavior
- systematically collect data about their child's performance at home
- understand early childhood development
- acquire rating skills
- recognize behaviors that interfere with learning
- share and compare assessments with the school
- develop more realistic expectations for their child (p. 5)

Many questionnaires have been developed for parents to assess their own child's development, used as a screening device to identify those children who may have developmental delays. The *Ages and Stages Questionnaires System* (Bricker, 1995) is an especially easy tool to use, along with home visits. It has a few selected questions in developmental areas at eleven intervals between four months and four years of age.

FAMILY, HEALTH, AND DEVELOPMENT FORM

FAMILY HISTORY

Child's Name:

Phone: _____   Birthdate: _____

Address: _____   Zip Code _____

Other members of the household (Include ages for siblings)

Name: _____   Relationship: _____   Age: _____

Name: _____   Relationship: _____   Age: _____

Name: _____   Relationship: _____   Age: _____

HEALTH HISTORY

Type of Birth: _____   Was the child preterm? _____

Does your child have a history of the following:

Frequent colds: _____   Frequent Diarrhea: _____   Asthma: _____   Nosebleeds: _____

Ear Infections: _____   Stomach Aches: _____   Seizures: _____   Headaches: _____

Urinary Infections: _____   Please indicate what brings on the above conditions if you know. _____

_____

_____

What illness has your child had? At what age?

Chicken Pox: _____   Scarlet Fever: _____   Hepatitis: _____   Diabetes: _____   Mumps: _____

Measles: _____   Other: _____

Does your child vomit easily? _____   Does your child run high fevers easily? _____

Has your child had any serious accidents? If so, please explain: _____

_____

Does your child have allergies? _____   If so, how are they manifested?

Asthma: _____   Hay Fever: _____   Hives: _____   Other: _____

What causes the allergy? _____

Does your child have any food allergies? _____

Does your child receive any medication regularly? _____

Do you have any concerns in these areas: Speech: _____   Physical: _____   Hearing: _____

Is your child covered by health insurance? _____

If so, what company? _____   Insurance #: _____

DEVELOPMENTAL HISTORY

Please answer to the best of your memory!

Age at which child: crept _____   sat alone _____   walked alone _____

named simple objects _____   spoke in sentences _____   slept through the night _____

dress self _____   undress self _____   began toilet training _____

Words child uses for urination and bowel movements _____

Are there any eating problems? _____

If the family vegetarian? _____   Are there dietary restrictions? _____

How would you describe your child's personality? _____

Are there other daytime child care arrangements during hours when the child does not attend this Center? _____

Have there been any recent family changes about which we should be aware? _____

Has your child had group play experience and for how long? _____

_____

How does your child cope with separation? _____

What do you find best comforts your child? _____

How does your child respond to other children? _____

Does your child have any special fears that you are aware of? _____

How does your child show stress and what do you do to relieve it? _____

Do you have any concerns about your child's development? _____

Is there any other information about your child you feel it is necessary for us to know? _____

_____

Figure 1.9 Parental Information Form (Reproduced with permission, BC Center, Broome Community College, Binghamton, NY)

The Five P's Parent Data Questionnaire
SOCIAL DEVELOPMENT

Emerging Self   N   S   Y

DS   1.   Uses personal pronouns (I, me) when viewing image in mirror or picture

DS   2.   Seems to understand what behaviors are right or wrong

DS   3.   Attempts to complete task despite previous failure

DS   4.   Demonstrates ability to react and recover from anger or disappointment within a reasonable amount of time

DS   5.   Controls unacceptable impulsive behaviors (e.g., hitting other children; eating everything in sight)

DS   6.   States and carries out own ideas about play activities

DS   7.   Tells age on request

DS   8.   Self-regulates in a socially accepted manner (e.g., conforms to established classroom or home routines and rules)

DS   9.   Seems to understand family relationships (i.e., identifies members other than parents and own position)

IB   10.   Unaware of dangerous situations

IB   11.   Only pursues activities chosen by self

IB   12.   Has frequent temper tantrums

IB   13.   Overreacts to changes/disappointments (e.g., cries, screams, throws objects)

IB   14.   Asks for help when not really needed

Relationships to Adults

DS   1.   Seeks individual time or play activity with significant adult

DS   2.   Follows simple directions from familiar adults

DS   3.   Expresses affection toward familiar adults

DS   4.   Accepts limits from familiar adults

DS   5.   Cooperates with requests from familiar adults

DS   6.   Modifies behavior to please significant adults

DS   7.   Demonstrates empathy toward mood of significant adults

DS   8.   Demonstrates increasing ability to explain own feelings to caregiver

DS   9.   Negotiates compromises with significant adults

IB   10.   Clings excessively to primary caregiver

IB   11.   Demands excessive attention from primary caregiver

IB   12.   Appears unaffected by primary caregiver's disapproval

IB   13.   Indiscriminately shows all adults affection

IB   14.   Disregards limits or rules set by adult authority

Relationship to Children

DS   1.   Imitates behavior of another child

DS   2.   Physically interacts with other children (e.g., builds with blocks together; hands toys back and forth)

DS   3.   Engages in simple pretend play with another child

DS   4.   Takes turns with other children

DS   5.   Begins to share toys with other children

DS   6.   Asks and waits for permission to use toy of another child

DS   7.   Chooses and maintains a friendship

DS   8.   Comforts or helps a child in distress

DS   9.   Negotiates compromises with other children

IB   10.   Shows little or no interest in children

IB   11.   Disrupts or destroys another child's play activities

IB   12.   Shows difficulty playing unless child sets own rules

IB   13.   Actively resists group activities

(DS) refers to Developmental Skills; (IB) referes to Interfering Behaviors

Comments:
Is there anything else you would like to share with us about your child's strengths and needs in this area?

Figure 1.10 The Five P's Parent Data Questionnaire (Reproduced with the permission of Variety Pre-Schooler's Workshop, Syosset, New York. Copyright ©1992 Variety Pre-Schooler's Workshop.)

Parents should be consulted concerning their goals for the child and expectations of the program. This can be done in an informal conversation, a more formal interview, or in a questionnaire. McAfee and Leong (1994) recommend these procedures for eliciting information from parents:

- Have several ways for parents to get information to you.
- Help parents know what information would be helpful.
- Use sensitive and respectful discussion, interview, and question-asking techniques.
- Make communication with parents a two-way process.
- Let parents know how information will be used (p. 73).

Personal Meetings. Building a relationship with the child and the parents begins before the first day at school. This can be done in a variety of ways, depending on the program, the timing, and the age of the child.

Exercise: Check the ways you get acquainted with someone:

- ❑ phone conversations
- ❑ reading a questionnaire they have answered
- ❑ visiting one another's home
- ❑ introductions
- ❑ work on a task together
- ❑ have a common interest

Home Visits. One of the best ways to get to know the child in the family context is to make a home visit. This can be used to fill out the necessary paperwork and begin to establish a bond with the child in the child's surroundings. A home visit is not to inspect or to judge but to better understand the family situation. It is usually done in pairs, by the people who will be directly interacting with the child. It often helps to bring an activity or some piece of the school's equipment along, such as a toy or a book. Parents and children would be interested in an album of photographs of school activities and people. It is important to provide time for the parent and child to ask questions and tell stories of their family. The visitors will not only talk but listen.

This is a friendly, short visit to get acquainted. It can determine the parent's needs of assistance from the program. Parents can ask questions or express concerns they may have. They could both explore ways in which they can be involved in the life of the program. A home visit can be an excellent opportunity to explain the typical arrival and departure procedures. It informs the parents and the child of the daily schedule, and what they should provide, Figure 1.11.

The visitor talks and begins to make friends with the child by smiling and making gestures of friendship without overpowering or demanding their participation. The family watches the developing relationship. Reactions may vary depending on their knowledge and trust of the program and feelings about the impending separation. Some visitors take a photograph of the family that will greet them on the first day. Giving the child a photograph of the teachers will begin the acquaintance on a visual level also. Of course, notes about the visit are written and placed in the class or program's file and are confidential, open only to those directly responsible for the child, including the parents. (See the resources list at the end of this chapter for more information about home visits.)

Visit to the School or Center. Another effective way to become acquainted is for the parents to bring the child to visit the center by appointment, so they receive individual attention. After-hours seems to work best. A typical day's routine is reviewed, from arrival through departure. They can take a tour of the center to see the rooms and areas the child will be using. The child can play and become familiar with the room and equipment. This is easier without the distraction of other children and the impending separation from

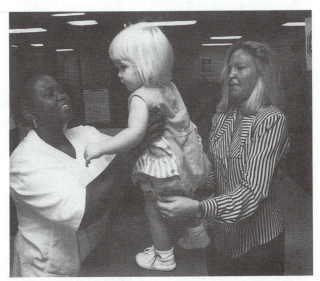

Figure 1.11 A home visit is a way to establish a relationship between the teacher, the child, and the family.

the parent. A nutritional snack time with the visitors sets a social atmosphere. An unhurried visit can help the child adjust to the environment. The child forms a visual image of the center and begins to build positive images of herself at play there. This also builds the relationship of trust with the parents. They see this is a good place for the child, and parents experience the center's willingness to be a part of the support system to their family.

Formal Parent Orientation. Many centers have a "parents only" orientation where staff is introduced, policies are reviewed, and relationships between the parents and the center are established. Food, adult chairs, and friendly greetings set the tone of partnership and cooperation. Providing child care will not only assist more parents to attend but be one of the first signs that this is a parent-friendly place.

A tour of the center and a short video or slide presentation showing the "action" of the program help establish a positive atmosphere. Parents' questions and concerns are anticipated in a short, reassuring presentation. The staff communicates the recognition of the needs of parents and the dedication of the program to cooperate and accommodate as much as possible. Humor, understanding, and active listening are characteristics that will make this step in the transition smoother. Individual relationship-building between parent and staff at this orientation helps alleviate the anxiety for the parent, the child, and the staff. This is useful not only on the first day, but throughout the year, as situations develop that no one can foresee right now. An opportunity for individual questions or even anonymous questions will help to provide an open forum.

Working with Parents for Great Beginnings

Exercise: Think about the necessary foundations or building blocks of parent-teacher relationships. Write the characteristics in the blocks in Figure 1.12.

Building blocks help the child adjust to a new environment; they are necessities in growth and development. Qualities such as trust, open communication, respect, a friendly face, approachability, kindness, and understanding might appear in the blocks. The partnership of parents and teachers gives the child the confidence that needs will be met by trustworthy adults. When there are barriers

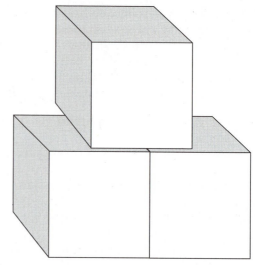

Figure 1.12 Building Blocks of Parent-Teacher Relationships. Fill in the skills, qualities, and activities that will build a strong relationship.

such as jealousy, fear, or differences in value systems that are not addressed, it is more difficult for the child to adjust to and develop in that environment. Open communication between parents and program personnel is an important process.

If it is the beginning of the school year and all children are entering for the first time, a staggered first day, or first week, may be possible: Half, or a portion, of the children attend one day or one morning with the other portion coming on a second day or in the afternoon. The rationale is that children are learning the routine and adjusting to the setting in small groups. This allows the staff to closely observe and interact with fewer children, forming friendships with them. Staff also can anticipate if there may be a separation stage to work through and begin to consult with parents about strategies.

Every child should be greeted as they arrive. The greeter or door person sets the mood for the day, letting the child know he is important. The smile communicates acceptance and friendship. Greeting the child by name, and commenting on an event in the day that he particularly will enjoy, helps to prepare him for a good day ahead. This cannot be stated emphatically enough. Every child should be greeted and made to feel welcome!

Exercise: A parent brings his child to your program for the first time. He gets the child interested in the water table then walks over to you and says, "I'm just going to slip out so he won't cause a scene." What would you say?

Parents should be encouraged to establish a good-bye routine, stay for a while, and leave firmly. This allows the child to slowly adjust and not feel rushed or rejected. The child can anticipate the parent's departure by dependable cues. Caution should be taken that the child not manipulate the parent into "one more kiss, one more hug, one more...." Sneaking out is discouraged no matter how much the parent sees it as an easier way. For the child, this builds mistrust and a fear that every time he gets involved in play or turns his back, the parent will leave. Parents witness the staff's concern for the child and are assured that the needed comfort is given. The staff assists the parent in involving the child in the routines and activities of the classroom. A phone call to the parent later to say the child is no longer crying will alleviate the anxiety. Feldman (1995) recommends a reminder poster for parents in the hallway "Did you remember to kiss me? Hug me? Say goodbye to me? Tell me you'll be back?" (p. 34)

Separation Anxiety and Difficulties

Exercise: Describe an incident of separation difficulty you have witnessed.

As parents consider leaving their child in someone else's care, there are psychological issues for all concerned: the parents, the child, and the caregiver. It is important to know about how a child develops attachments and separations' possible effects on those attachments. There are strategies for helping the child and the parent cope with the trauma of separation that reinforce the primary parent-child relationship.

Exercise: Describe what feelings each of these people might have upon the first day of school or care in a new program: the parent, the child, and the teacher or caregiver.

Separation Anxiety Behavior. A child in the midst of a "separation anxiety attack" may display out-of-control behavior. It is embarrassing for the parent, who is fearful that the teacher will judge the child or the family in a negative way. It is difficult for the caregiver to address the emotional needs of an unfamiliar child. The parent and many other children and parents as well may be looking on. It is equally difficult for the child who is distressed and out of control, needing someone to help. These extreme moments call for calm reassurance that the parent will return at the end of the day. An established good-bye routine such as "kiss, kiss, hug, nose rub, bye-bye" and a prompt departure helps the child anticipate the parent's departure and come to rely on the parent's return.

The distressed child, of course, should receive holding and comforting as long as necessary to help overcome the feeling of abandonment. Often the child rejects any physical contact or comforting from this new adult. The teacher respects that but shows reliability of care and interest in the child's difficult moment. The teacher offers choices of activities that may be of interest to the child. The child may be kicking and screaming. This should be ignored if it is hurting no one, or gently restrained if it is aimed at the caregiver, other children, or furniture. Removal of the child from the curious stares of other children prevents embarrassment and copycat behavior from others.

Verbal and body language convey understanding for the feelings of loneliness and anger. Reassurances are given that the parent will return. The teacher communicates the desire to help the child gain control and have a safe, happy time while she is here. Reading a book, singing a song, rocking, or stroking the back sometimes help soothe those feelings. Continued violent reactions call for patience, tolerance, and endurance. They will eventually subside. Sometimes the most effective caregiver action is just quiet acceptance of the strong emotions without overtures to distract the child. Each child has individual behavior patterns to be learned. The caregiver seeks the most effective relaxation techniques for each child. The child builds trust in the parent's return and learns coping mechanisms.

Exercise: What would you say to this child? See Figure 1.13.

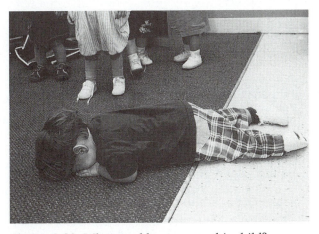

Figure 1.13 What would you say to this child?

Difficulties with separation may not always appear at the beginning of the year, the beginning of the day, or in a violent emotional outburst. It is just as important for the teacher to respond promptly to more subtle separation behavior. They can take many forms: difficulties in eating, sleeping, toileting, learning, or social difficulties.

Eating. For the infant, refusal to take nourishment is an immediate danger signal. Teachers can try various positions of holding during feeding, and even blocking the infant's view of the caregiver. Communication with the parent about feeding routines ahead of time, and even a phone call to verify and seek advice, may be helpful. A joint effort of parent and caregiver should make this difficulty short-lived. Continued difficulty may need the involvement of the pediatrician and other support personnel.

For toddlers and preschoolers, eating away from home may be distressing, perceived as a betrayal of that very personal time with close family members.

A relaxed environment without pressure from caregivers, along with familiar foods and utensils, will help ease this time. It usually is just a matter of days until children adjust and join in the sociability of mealtime and look forward to it with enthusiasm. If a child is crying at mealtime, refusing food day after day, or indicating by behaviors that this is a stressful time, it demands attention. Parent-caregiver communication, sometimes with a referral agent, such as the director, and the pediatrician, can usually work this through.

IT HAPPENED TO ME:
Wrapped in Love

I was visiting in an infant room and saw a baby about 6 months old wrapped in a large red shawl while the caregiver fed him. She later explained he was having difficulty adjusting and would not eat at the center. Through trial and error she and his mother came up with the idea of bringing in something of the mother's from home. Wrapped in his mother's shawl, he was wrapped in the essence of her love and security. Now he could eat.

Sleeping. Environmental changes can affect sleep, so children in new places may have difficulty resting. Other children's schedules and sleep patterns may keep the child from sleeping. The new environment, governed by licensing regulations, may add to the child's difficulty in adjustment to sleeping away from home. The caregiver gathers information from the parent on the child's sleep patterns. Upon each day's arrival, parents give information about last night's sleep. Everything possible is done to make the environment conducive to the child's relaxation. Music, favorite toys, books, or a blanket help with sleep routines and should be individual choices for children. Children having adjustment problems to center care may have continued sleep disturbances. Again, the close observation and responsiveness of the caregiver to the individual child's needs will help. Communication with the parent for understanding and accommodating the child's needs to the center's practices also helps, Figure 1.14. Sleep deprivation might result in the child's irritable behavior and increased anxiety for the adults.

Making notes on the child's sleepy times of day, indicators of sleep needs, techniques that relax the child, positions of sleep, and toys or physical items normally taken to bed are important pieces of information for the child's file. Sharing and exchanging information such as this with parents will help the child's adjustment to sleeping away from home. It assists substitute caregivers in meeting the child's needs when the regular teacher is absent.

Toileting. For two-year-olds, managing toilet needs on their own is a big accomplishment but not without its relapses for a variety of reasons. Adjustment to a new place may upset that delicate balance. The child is curious and may frequently

Figure 1.14 Parents and teachers need to communicate about children's routines.

use the child-sized toilet as a novelty. The new stimulating environment full of active play areas and new playmates may result in forgetfulness or inattention to toileting cues, leading to accidents. A matter-of-fact attitude by caregivers, along with a change into familiar clothing after a toileting accident, usually is all that is necessary to help the child cope with these events.

Some children, however, have a delicate emotional response to new places, making it difficult to eliminate in this new surrounding. A child may hold the genitals, lay over a chair until the urge passes, or even cry from a severe stomachache. It is up to the teacher to be a detective, interpreting these subtle clues. Once the cause is determined, appropriate action can be taken. Again, communication with the parents about the child's patterns, times, and physical cues is an important part of making the child comfortable. Parents taking the child into the bathroom and talking about using it should be part of the first visit or first day at the center. Continued disruption in toileting may cause bladder infections or constipation and other disorders. A daily, unobtrusive observation of the child's toileting behavior is also a part of the record keeping procedure. Any extraordinary behavior should be noted factually and shared at the end of the day with the parent, away from the presence of the child.

Participation. The child who is experiencing separation difficulties may not be able to attend to the learning activities that are planned. He may have difficulty making choices or staying with a task. Transitions from one area to another or interacting positively with other children may precipitate crying or tantrums. After a normal adjustment period, if this behavior is observed, it should be recorded. Reference to it later will indicate the stages the child has gone through in the separation process.

Social Interactions. When a child is in emotional turmoil, it may affect the child's outward behavior to others. The child may cling to one caregiver, transferring parental attachment to another adult. That is a healthy **coping mechanism** in an infant and toddler and, temporarily, for the preschooler. A branching out of friendships and social contacts is expected after a time. Some interventions may be necessary if that is not observed.

Children who are experiencing separation difficulties may be socially withdrawn. The group situation may be overwhelming. The child just needs some time to watch and see how other children are

handling it. A sensitive caregiver will allow the child this luxury of watching, along with an occasional commentary on what the other children are doing. The child is invited to join the play. The caregiver will also be familiar with the stages of play and have realistic expectations for the child's positive social interactions. Communication with parents to know the child's social history will also help to better understand the child's reactions. It would be helpful to know the positive or negative experiences the child has had with siblings and other children who are the same age.

Acting Out As a Symptom of Separation Anxiety. For some children, the new environment is so stimulating that their self-control is not strong enough to govern their behavior. The child may be unaccustomed to so many playmates and play areas. Inappropriate and unsafe actions may erupt, which might result in rejection by other children. The teacher redirects or restricts behavior. The staggered first day can help to ease this transition. For the child entering the program once it has already begun, it may be overwhelming. Other children are already established in routines and have formed friendships. The teacher coaches the new child through routines and introduces expectations in various areas to help the child adjust.

The child comes into a new situation, not knowing the rules and the people; she feels rejected and abandoned by the parent. When the teacher places herself in those little sneakers, it will help to ease the child through these first days.

Later-Developing Adjustment Problems. Sometimes part way through the day or the year, a child who appeared adjusted to school, begins to display some difficulties: Crying at the parent's leaving, inability to eat, sleep, play, all can happen at any time. What is going on? It may be the aging process. As the child develops, thinking changes. They may be passing into a new stage. That happy baby who held out her arms wide to the caregiver is now burying her head in her dad's coat. She may be the toddler who takes one look at the caregiver, looks at mom, and kicks and shrieks as her coat is removed. The child grabs it back, latches onto her mom's pocketbook strap like it is a life preserver and will not let go. It may be that child who came happily each day with a smile and a picture she drew for the teacher who now says "I don't like it here. I wanna go home."

The child is going through a new phase and the best defense is that close communication and understanding between parent and caregiver. It is helpful to have a talk, outside of the child's hearing, about the change. This may reveal some unusual events at home that are manifested in behaviors of insecurity and separation anxiety. Together, some ideas can be generated about how to help everyone cope with changes or troubled times.

• •

IT HAPPENED TO ME:
Mid-September Reflection

• •

We had gotten through those first days and weeks. All those plans for smooth transitions seem to have paid off. Each child came ready to play and said good-bye to parents willingly. They had fallen into the routine of the day. Today during free play, I could move from area to area, observe their play, comment on their actions, add a prop here and there, and enjoy their absorption with activities of their choosing.

Then I heard a noise, a long sucking in of air with a quiet sort of high-pitched wail. Where did it come from? I looked around the room. Children were climbing and sliding and going in and out the door on the climber, which was their spaceship today. A boy was sitting at the table in the dramatic play area with a police hat on. He was packing a lunch pail with dishes and silverware, talking to another boy who was stirring "soup." Several children were in the block area piling blocks, laying out carpet squares, and standing up farm animals. Sand box players were pouring, shoveling, and digging for shells they found hidden there. Two children at the easel, a boy on one side and a girl on the other, were busily making lines and circles. There it was again! I looked around again. Same scene as before but now I could locate the source of the sound. It seemed to be coming from the boy at the easel. As I looked closer, he stared at his paper as his hands moved methodically up and down. He watched the paint as it dripped from the brush, then I heard the sound again and saw his face muscles tense into a frozen stare.

I walked over and placed my hand on his shoulder. The dam broke. He let out all those sobs he had been trying to hold in! He was missing his mom and had tried to hide it for an hour but just could not hold it in any

longer. Were there signs I could have seen before it got to this point? Are there others who were feeling this internal sadness, holding it in reign but inwardly hurting? Was I being smug and self-congratulating without really addressing the issue of separation with those who were least capable of coping with it—the children? I vowed to be a more empathetic observer and to use more touch as a message to each child that I am here to support and comfort if they need me. Tomorrow I'll read *Are You My Mother?* by Eastman to stimulate some discussion about separation and the ever-returning parent.

• •

Departures and Good-byes

Just as beginnings are important, so are endings.

Exercise: Using a separate sheet of paper, make a list of ending celebrations, rituals, or customs.

Bringing closure to a letter, a day, or a life has emotional importance. It closes the circle. Planning for the end of the day is an important part of curriculum as well. It helps to have the child's belongings all in one place, like the cubbie or a mailbox system, so there is no last-minute hunt for paintings or library books. When dismissal time is the same for everyone, some programs have closing circles, hand squeeze, or recall and review of the day. Ellen Booth Church (1994) suggests a group song, musical hugs, and remembering favorite things.

If children leave at different but predictable times, it is up to the teacher to give the child a cue that the departure time is approaching so the child can bring closure to the activity and mentally prepare for the change. When the parent's pick-up unpredictably, the teacher can help the child cope with the change by assisting in the closing of the activity and engaging the parent in conversation so the child can work independently to prepare to leave.

A good-bye party for a child who is moving or leaving the program helps recognize the child for the contribution she made to the class. Classmates can present physical reminders of her friends there. Though it is a sad occasion, it can be a part of learning to say good-bye. By attempting to remain in contact, a sense of the larger community is felt with her as a link to the next city, state, or country. This helps both the child leaving and those remaining.

At the end of the year, a child-centered farewell celebration (as opposed to cap-and-gown commencement for preschoolers) can be planned. This is also a time for remembering (part of the cognitive process); expressing positive feelings for one another (social and emotional development); and drawing, dictating, or writing the remembrances (literacy and art activities).

Planning for departures as well as arrivals is an important part of the teacher's responsibilities and also can be opportunities to observe. How does the child organize for the end of the day? What is the child's response to the cue of the approaching end to an activity? How does the child greet the parent at the end of the day? These are possible Class List Log criterion.

SPECIAL POPULATIONS AND SEPARATION AND ADJUSTMENT

Children with special needs and children from nonmainstream cultures or who may not speak English are entering programs nationwide. The practitioner has the responsibility to be prepared to help these children make the transition into the program as stress-free as possible. Prior knowledge of the child, no matter what the situation, helps this process. Specific knowledge of these special populations is imperative. Research, parent and professionals providing information, and extra observation and patience will be required.

Children with Special Needs

The Americans with Disabilities Act of 1990 (P.L. 101-336) protects against discrimination based on a person's disability. Children with disabilities must be admitted into settings that have been adapted to accommodate them. When children with special needs are integrated into a group, it is important to have knowledge and information concerning the handicapping condition and this child's situation in particular before the first day they come to school. This can be obtained from the parent questionnaire, a home visit, or the child's report from helping professionals if the parents have given permission for its release. Karnes (1992) says, "When parents are concerned that others may not accept their child, or that he will not do well, the child may pick up on these anxious feelings and have an even more difficult time separating." This child will have the same need for

the feeling of security and trust that the setting and people will be able to care for him.

For children with visual impairments, tape recordings about the routines and what to expect from a typical day would be helpful. If the child is hearing-impaired, this could be done through a picture album. The caregivers should become familiar with the language the child will be using to communicate. Knowledge of a child's physical impairments will help modify the setting to be more accessible. Of course, the building already meets the guidelines for accessibility under the Americans with Disabilities Act (P.L. 101-336). Modifications may need to be made within the classroom arrangement and in the thinking and approach of the staff. Any modifications for the child preferably are made before the child enters the program. Emotional or behavioral disabilities should be understood thoroughly by conferences with the parents and helping professionals so that the teachers are prepared and react in a consistent way.

Diverse Cultures

The attachment between parent and child varies for different cultures. For some, the infant never is physically apart from an adult, being held, carried, or touched almost constantly. For these children, the physical and emotional separation needs special attention. For other cultures, children are expected to become independent very quickly so any expectation of separation anxiety is not understood or tolerated. An awareness of cultural parenting styles and the attachment and separation practices will help the teacher adjust expectations and actions.

For the child who is non-English speaking, it is most helpful if the teacher learns a few of the most important words such as greetings, routines like "Eat," "Toilet," "Mother returning soon," and "I can help you." This can be accomplished by asking the parent, working through an interpreter, or researching translations at the library. The child will need time and an environment that is child-centered. When the environment is restricted by teacher's directions, and highly emphasizes following directions, the non-English speaking child will have difficulty adjusting. Play is a universal language and once the child feels comfortable, the lure of play will help her feel more comfortable.

Special populations and the needs of each child as an individual necessitate preparation, understanding, and careful observation skills.

HELPING PROFESSIONALS FOR SEPARATION AND ADJUSTMENT CONCERNS

If a child is having separation or classroom adjustment problems beyond his ability to cope, it may be necessary to consult helping professionals. After consultations with parents and the director or program personnel, outside professionals who may help are the:

pediatrician—physician specifically trained to care for the health and well-being of children

child psychologist—conducts screenings for diagnosis and treatment of children with emotional, behavioral, or developmental problems

child psychiatrist—provides counseling or consultative services to individuals or families who may be experiencing problems

play therapist—child psychologist who uses play to diagnose and treat children who may be withdrawn, nonverbal, or traumatized

Week 1, Assignment A

CLASS LIST LOG—SEPARATION AND ADJUSTMENT

Photocopy the Class List Log found in Appendix D. Alphabetize the class by first names down the left side. Make a supply of these partially completed Class List Log forms.

Fill out the heading of one Class List Log form. Observe the group this week. Make short, descriptive notes about each one's arrival at school, noting how each child is separating from family member.

What to Do with It

Summarize or jot notes in each child's portfolio overview under this section, Figure 1.15. A blank portfolio overview appears in Appendix D.

If further action is needed, write a note here and follow it up. Come back later and write the result.

Share your observations with the parents and the child, if appropriate. For example: "Mrs. Jones, the way you are helping Joshua become accustomed to being here has given me ideas to share with other parents. I was observing yesterday and saw some of the things you did to make him feel comfortable here and confident of your return before you left. He had a wonderful day and I believe it was because of that."

Completed Class List Logs contain information on all the children in the class, so it is not appropriate to file them in a child's portfolio. Establish a class file that will hold those recordings that contain information on all the children. (Other methods of this type are explained later in this book.) This is the teacher's and the program's property and should be stored separately from the portfolios to protect confidentiality.

File Week 1, Assignment A, in the class file.

SEPARATIONS AND ADJUSTMENT		
Documentation	Recorder	Date
CL Arrival, cried then OK	BAN	9/7
CL Arrival OK, depart OK	BAN	2/14
CL Organizes, anticipates	MS	4/5
RR Typical arrival	BAN	5/9

Figure 1.15 Portfolio Overview Example

Week 1, Assignment B

WORK SAMPLES FOR ALL

This week encourage each child to draw or decorate the cover (one panel) of his or her own portfolio. This is a good one-on-one activity to help you get acquainted with each child. Write the date in the corner. Explain to the child, if the child is old enough to understand, that this is a place where you, the teacher, will be collecting writing about the child at school and some artwork throughout the year. Invite the child to add samples of their work to the portfolio. You will show them the file at times throughout the year.

If the child wants to fill the folder with work, you might want to establish separate work sample folders that are accessible to each child. The children can store their own work.

Week 1, Assignment C

REFLECTIVE JOURNAL

Respond to the following in your Reflective Journal, kept in a private file at home.

As I approach this year, my life seems…

This year I hope that…

When I walk into a place I have never been before I feel…

Maybe a child feels…

The one different approach I will try this year will be…

I wonder…

REFERENCES

Ainsworth, M., Blehar, M., Waters, E., & Wall, S. (1978). *Patterns of attachment.* Hillsdale, NJ: Lawrence Erlbaum Associates.

Airasian, P. W. (1991). *Classroom assessment.* New York: McGraw-Hill, Inc.

Balaban, N. (1987). *Learning to say good-bye: Starting school and other early childhood separations.* New York: New American Library.

Bjorklund, D. F. & Bjorklund, B. R. (1992). *Looking at children: An introduction to child development.* Pacific Grove, CA: Brooks/Cole Publishing Co.

Bloch, J. S. (1987). *The five P's manual.* Syosset, NY: Variety Pre-Schooler's Workshop.

Bowlby, J. (1969). *Attachment.* New York: Basic Books.

Bricker, (1995). *ASQ Questionnaire System.* Baltimore MD: Paul H. Brooks Pub.

Church, E. B. (1994). So many ways to say good-bye. *Early Childhood Today, 8* (8), 65.

Eastman, P. D. (1988). *Are you my mother?* New York: Random House.

Feldman, J. (1995). *Transition time: Let's do something different!* Beltsville, MD: Gryphon House.

Johnson, L. & Mermen, J. (1994). Easing children's entry to school: Home visits help. *Young children, 49* (6), 62–68.

Karnes, M. (1992). Children with disabilities. *Pre-K Today, 7* (1), 67.

McAfee, O. & Leong, D. (1994). *Assessing and guiding young children's development and learning.* Boston: Allyn and Bacon.

Shaffer, H. & Emerson, P. E. (1964). The development of social attachments in infancy. *Monographs of the Society for Child Development, 29,* (3), serial No. 94.

Yarrow, L. J. (1964). Separation from parents during early childhood. In M. L. Hoffman & L. W. Hoffman (Eds.) *Review of child development research, Vol. I.* New York: Russell Sage Foundation.

RESOURCES

Balaban, N. (1987). *Learning to say good-bye: Starting school and other early childhood separations.* New York: New American Library.

Brodkin, A. (1994). She cries when I leave." *Early Childhood Today, 9* (1), 38–39.

Church, E. B. Separation: Helping kids and families through the transition. (1992). *Pre-K Today, 7* (1), 62–78.

Johnson, L. & Mermen, J. (1994). Easing children's entry to school: Home visits help. *Young Children, 49* (4), 62–68.

CHAPTER 2

Using Anecdotal Recordings to Look at Self-Care

IN THIS CHAPTER . . . .

✔ Using the Anecdotal Recording

✔ Topics in Observation: Using All of Our Senses

✔ Looking at Self-Care Skills

✔ Special Populations and Self-Care Skills

✔ Helping Professionals for Self-Care Skills

USING THE ANECDOTAL RECORDING

Maralyce went into the bathroom in the three-year-old classroom. After considerable time, she could be heard screaming and crying. The teacher rushed to the door to find Maralyce standing by the toilet, pants around ankles, trying to adjust streams of toilet paper to cover the seat. Every time she put one strip on, another would slide off. The teacher asked "What's wrong, Maralyce? Why are you crying?" Maralyce sobbed, "Mommy said I can't go potty 'til I cover the seat, and it won't stay on." The teacher went and quickly got tape and gave it to Maralyce. She taped the paper on the seat, sat down quickly, and let out a "Wooo!" (The teacher saw the still-developing coordination of a three-year-old in conflict with a parental expectation. She was inclined to say, "You don't need that paper. The seat is clean." However, she wanted Maralyce to have a way to do it herself.)

There are incidents that need to be remembered exactly as they happened. They tell a story that lets the reader see, hear, and feel as if he were

there. It contains a factual account of an incident that may be typical or out of the ordinary. The incident, however, is best remembered in its entirety. The most factual recording method is **Anecdotal Recording.** It can be used to:

• portray an incident that indicates a child's development in a specific area
• record a humorous incident to share with parents
• preserve the details of a curious incident for later reflection
• record the exact details of a child's disclosure of an incidence of abuse
• exemplify a child's typical behavior
• record the details of an incident that is totally foreign to the child's typical behavior

The Anecdotal Recording is a narrative account of an incident that may be a few seconds or several minutes in length. The Anecdotal Recording recounts the event telling the reader when, where, who, and what. It does not answer the question *why* in the body of the recording. That conclusion or inference is separated from the recording.

Every newspaper reporter, police officer, and insurance claims adjuster knows that facts written on the scene or very shortly thereafter are the most accurate. When an event occurs that is important to remember, a few notes are jotted down to refer to later. If an interesting conversation is happening, it is recorded word for word. It is written, as much as possible, as it is happening, Figure 2.1. By the end of the day, the notes are amplified and rewritten into a full account while the details are still fresh. It can be written on regular lined paper. It helps to fold the paper in half vertically and write on the left side so explanatory comments can be written in the right-hand column. In this way, comments of the recorder are placed separately from the recording. The reader then knows the difference between the actual recounting of the incident and the writer's conclusions. It also is possible

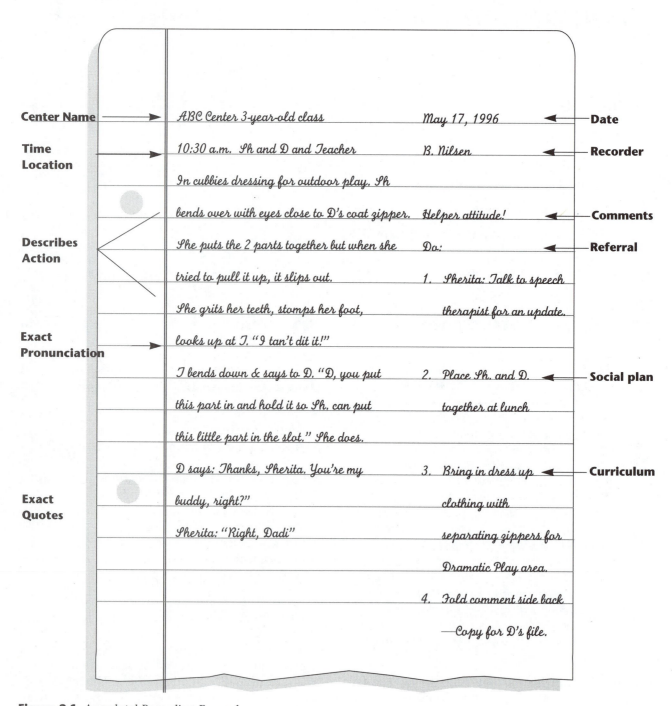

Figure 2.1 Anecdotal Recording Example

to fold the paper so the comments are not visible. Another reader can then draw independent conclusions about the incident.

Bentzen (1993) calls this an **open method,** a narrative that preserves the details so that different interpretations can be made, determined by the reader's focus. The reader receives a mental picture of that event by reading the words.

An Anecdotal Recording is a written replay of an incident. Separate from that account, the reader will make inferences. Inferences or evaluations may differ, depending on the role of the observer. Davi's parent might infer he is not getting proper attention from the teacher. Another child's parent might wonder why this helpless child is in such an advanced class, demanding time from the teacher. Another teacher might deduce that this child needs some instruction in self-care skills. The speech pathologist might be overjoyed to hear Sherita express herself in nearly recognizable words. The teacher might write a comment to the side, "Sherita is the youngest in her family so seldom has a chance to be the helper. Davi has often excluded Sherita from play so this may be the beginning of a friendship." All people read the same account, but their inferences are different because of their perspectives.

Many people use the term *Anecdotal Recording* when what actually has been written is a diary account, Figure 2.2. This type of recording is true, but it is not factual. It summarizes actions, draws conclusions, and leaves out information that could be useful. The anecdotal recording relates

body positions—"bent over, eyes closed"
actions—"puts two parts together," "slips out"

reactions—"grits teeth," "stomps foot," "looks up"
exact words—"Davi, you hold this," "Thanks Sherita"
inflection and pronunciation—"I tan't dit it"

The reader "sees" the incident. She "hears" the conversation along with emphasis as it was spoken. Then more accurate and individual judgments based on the reader's perspective are made.

Uses

Anecdotal Recordings can be

- used for preserving details about any developmental skill, behavior, or incident for later judgments and reflection
- given to other people for their independent evaluation
- used as an accurate, detailed recording method in suspicion or disclosure of child abuse

Exercise: What advantages and disadvantages do you see in using an Anecdotal Recording?

Read those that follow and see if you agree.

Advantages

Anecdotal Recordings

- need no special forms.
- are preserved facts and details for any reader to draw conclusions.

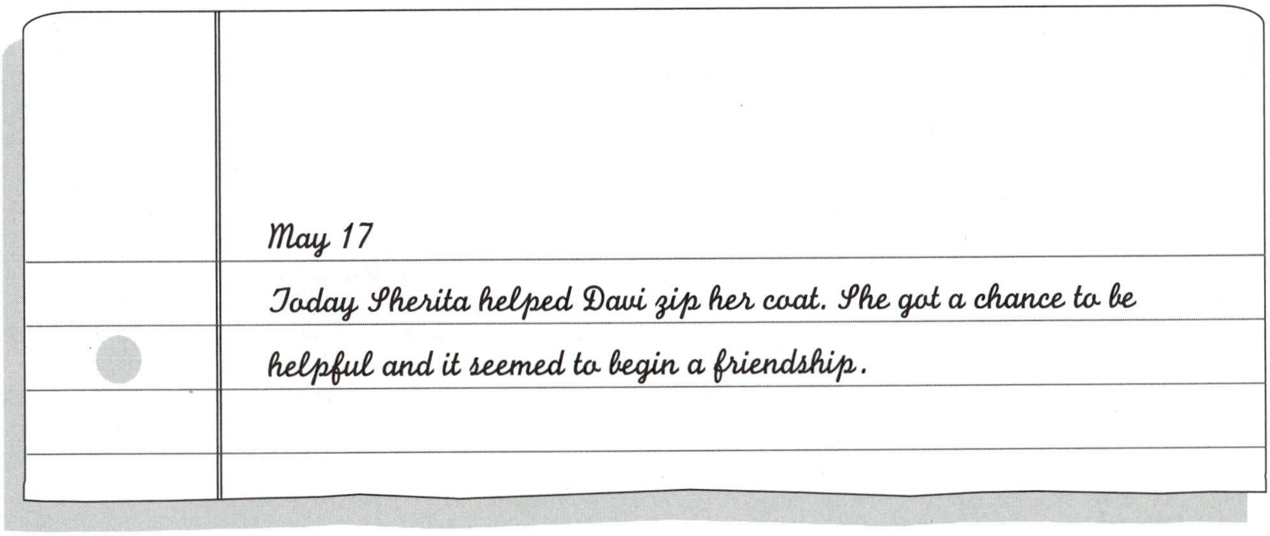

May 17

Today Sherita helped Davi zip her coat. She got a chance to be helpful and it seemed to begin a friendship.

Figure 2.2 Diary Example

- give a short, contextual account of an incident.
- give the reader a "sense of being there."
- separate judgments or inferences from details of incident.
- are easy for the reader to interpret according to purpose.

Disadvantages

Shortcomings of Anecdotal Recordings are:

- choosing which incidents to record gives the writer selectivity that may influence positive or negative collections
- intense writing to capture all details, quotes, body movements
- diverts attention from interactions with children
- can only focus on a few minutes of action
- can only focus on one or two children at a time

What to Do with This Information

An Anecdotal Recording preserves specific information that can be used in many ways. It contributes to the overall assessment and evaluation of the child when combined with other information-gathering resources. It is stored in the child's portfolio, Figure 2.3.

Child's Portfolio. If the incident captured in an Anecdotal Recording involves more than one child, it can be copied and the names of other children blocked out to place in more than one file. Block out names other than the child of this portfolio. The previous incident could be placed in Sherita's file with Davi's name blocked out. It could be copied for Davi's file with Sherita's name blocked out. In this particular incident, blocking the name may not be necessary but it does establish a practice of confidentiality. Sometimes it is unpredictable what judgments the reader will make about the other children involved. The teacher's copy in the class file preserves all names for reference.

SELF-CARE		
Documentation	Recorder	Date
CL ate, toilet, no nap	BAN	9/14
AR Initiates Pickup	MS	3/15

Figure 2.3 Overview Sheet Example

In the portfolio, this Anecdotal Recording will serve as documentation for judgments made about the child: "Sherita is using words in conversations now (language development) and even helping other children (social development)."

This recording can be compared to earlier incidents: "Compare anecdotal record of 2/13 to those of 9/27, 10/14, and 12/20 to see the progress Sherita has made."

Curriculum Planning. Class activity ideas come from close observations: "I think I'll bring in some clothes with separating zippers for the dramatic play area to give all the children some practice. That sequined vest I got at a garage sale will be a hit."

It can be the basis for making an individual plan: "Sherita is beginning to play near other children. Strategies: Model play and sharing behaviors, connect Sherita with Davi in a cooperative activity, read a book to small group including Sherita, and initiate playmate discussion."

The recorder may decide to further investigate or question a concern: "Listen more closely to Sherita's language and ask the speech pathologist if this is age-appropriate."

Other Teachers on the Team. The recording may be read by others on the team to gather their opinions on the meaning of the incident: "Does this incident seem like unusual behavior for Davi from what you've been seeing?" Seeking the advice of colleagues not responsible for the child is also a way to gain the perspective of an uninvolved professional. Of course, the names would all be blocked out. Without parental written permission, records are not shown to anyone outside the team.

Sharing with Parents. Giving the parents a copy of the incident provides them with a glimpse into the child's day: "Here's a little incident I wrote down today about Davi getting some help getting ready for outside play. I know you've been working on her manners. She spontaneously said, "Thank you" and invited the other child to be her friend."

Actions or behavior are recorded descriptively as a way to explain development to the parents: "Sherita initiated helping another child today for the first time. I thought you'd like to read about it. We'll be working on helping her develop more ways to play cooperatively."

Factual examples illustrate the teacher's assessment or concern to the parents: "Sherita's language seems to be at a younger stage. Here are some examples I tape recorded. Maybe you'd like to take these to talk with the speech pathologist and see if a full evaluation is recommended."

Conferring with Helping Professionals. Upon permission from the parents, Anecdotal Recordings can be read by helping professionals. This allows people such as the speech and language pathologist, child psychologist, art teacher, and social worker to draw their own conclusions. They evaluate the incident based on their specialized knowledge and area of expertise: "The strategies you've been working on with Sherita in therapy seem to be working. Here's an incident in which she helped another child. What do you think we should do next?"

Talking with the Child. The child can give insight into an incident and also should be aware of the recorder's interest and writing about her actions: "Davi, I wrote down about how Sherita helped you with your jacket today. Then you invited her to be your buddy." The child may respond with an explanation or further conversation.

Evidence to Child Protective Services. An Anecdotal Recording is acceptable evidence to document a child abuse disclosure. When a child reveals information that may indicate abuse, it is important to accurately write down how the disclosure came about. The record must contain exact questions and comments of the adult and the child. Behavior or visual indicators may raise suspicions of abuse. The Anecdotal Recording preserves details and factual descriptions without conclusions or judgments.

Pitfalls to Avoid

Random selection of children to write about in an anecdotal format presents the same problem as diary entries. There is usually some child who is performing attention-getting behavior. Others would never have a focused anecdotal record in their file. They are placid, follow the rules, and rarely draw attention to themselves.

This is overcome by the *Week by Week* portfolio plan. It specifies a few children a week as the focus of in-depth recordings. These children are not selected randomly but from a planned numbering system from the alphabetical Class List Log. In addition, the developmental area to be observed is suggested so that the selection of what and when to write about is more objective and documentation is collected in all developmental areas. With the *Week by Week* plan, information is gathered on all the children every week in a different developmental area. In addition to that, a more focused observation and recording is done on a specified group of children. Over the course of a year, using the *Week*

by Week plan, each developmental area is revisited at least three times for each child. Also, each child is the focus of at least three Anecdotal Recordings. Appendix A contains the full *Week by Week* plan. Appendix C illustrates how the *Week by Week* plan documents the developmental areas for each child in the class.

The most difficult part of Anecdotal Recording is just writing factually. Those little inferences, explanations, reasons, feelings, and biases just slip in. The recorder constantly needs to test if the reader will "see it in the mind." If it is not describing an event exactly as it occurred then the writer is summarizing and it ceases to be an accurate recording. It requires the recorder to stretch vocabulary to describe actions in noninferential, nonjudgmental terms.

"zipped Davi's jacket," not "helped"

"jumped and fell," not "clumsy"

"gave a piece of Play Doh" not "shared"

"eyes widened, mouth open," not "looked surprised"

Exercise 1: Mark the following sentences *Yes* if they fit the criteria for Anecdotal Recording or *No* if they are inferences, explanations, or not exact quotes.

❑ a. Tara ran over to the cubbie area.
❑ b. She had on a short shirt and wanted to get her jacket.
❑ c. Stacey asked her, "Why do you want your jacket on?
❑ d. She said her stomach was cold.
❑ e. Tara shrugged her shoulders.
❑ f. Stacey went over and zipped the jacket for Tara.
❑ g. Tara thanked her.

Answers:

a. Yes. It tells where she went and how she went there.
b. No. How does the reader know what she wanted? Just describe what is visible: "She had on a short shirt. She got her jacket from the hook."
c. Yes. These were the exact words.
d. No. This is not a direct quote. Instead, write, "Tara said, 'My belly is cold.'
e. Yes. Body motion is described.
f. Yes. Action is described.
g. No. This is not a direct quote. Instead, Tara said, "Thank you, my dear."

Exercise 2: Make a list of descriptive, but noninferential, nonjudgmental words to use in place

Figure 2.4 Examine this photograph and write an imaginary Anecdotal Record.

of these to give the reader more information about the nature of how the action was carried out:

> stood
> walked
> said
> cried
> laughed

Exercise 3: Look at Figure 2.4. Write an imaginary Anecdotal Recording as if you were there. Remember the technique: description and quotes.

Exercise 4: Watch a person performing a routine task, such as walking to and turning on a light, getting something from a purse, or coming into a room and finding a seat. Write an Anecdotal Recording so the reader can mentally visualize exactly the motions of that person. Have someone else read it to determine if it is descriptive and not inferential.

LOOKING AT SELF-CARE SKILLS

Exercise: On a separate sheet of paper, list the things you do for yourself that give you pride, for example, changing a tire, programming the video-cassette recorder, cruising the Internet.

"I can do it myself!" Those words spoken, sometimes defiantly, stand as a declaration of independence or a statement proclaiming a milestone accomplishment. Why are a child's **self-care** (sometimes called self-help) skills important, other than to free the adult from tasks previously done for the child? The accomplishment of taking care of one's own needs is a progression throughout childhood. It can be viewed as **development**, moving from simple to complex tasks, in an orderly predictable sequence yet at an individual rate for each person. The sequences of self-care skills incorporate many other components of developmental areas and contribute to self-worth and competency. The observer can assess, facilitate, and celebrate those accomplishments, Figure 2.6.

The self-care skills are closely allied to the areas that are affected by separation anxiety. This is probably because they are the tasks a parent does for a child. These are the most tenuous when the parent is no longer present. For the youngest child, they are the basis of survival and comfort. They become common elements in different environments for the older child. They are actions that are expected responsibilities of the caregiver, routines that can be sources of observation and assessment of development, and the basis for curricula planning.

Development of Self-Care Skills

The word *development* is an important one to understand. It is more than just change. The changes are:

- orderly—occur in a sequence or series
- directional—show some kind of accumulation or organization of components; each change in a sequence builds on the results of preceding changes

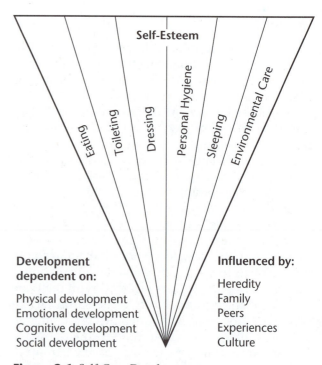

Figure 2.6 Self-Care Development

TOPICS IN OBSERVATION: Using All Our Senses

Exercise: Using a separate piece of paper, make a list of what you can observe about a child from senses other than seeing:

hearing,
smelling,
touching, and
tasting.

The word *observe* is understood to use sight as the primary source of taking in information; however, all senses are receptors of information on which to base decisions. As observers of young children, all senses can be used to assess and evaluate the child.

Seeing

Visually, information is gathered on the child's physical appearance; size; attributes, such as hair, coloring, features, facial expressions; coordination; actions; location in the room; and choices of activities. From all those visual cues, **inferences** are made regarding the child, Figure 2.5.

Hearing

The adult attunes to the message being communicated, from the first "coos" to intricate stories recounted with sound effects and voice. Many areas of development can be assessed from listening.

Emotional state—laughter, crying, whining, teasing, anger, silence

Cognitive development—vocabulary, content, grammar, problem-solving strategies, humor, storybook characters

Physical development—formation of teeth, tongue, and jaw

Health—nasal or bronchial congestion, wheezing, possible hearing difficulties affecting speech, digestive sounds

Family—home language, activities, siblings, other family members, other significant people in the child's life, television and video usage

Visual Cues	Inferences
Height, weight, body proportions, coordination, glasses, brace on leg, hearing aid	Physical growth and development, health, developmental delays, physical limitations
Skin color, hair color, eye shape	Racial or ethnic group, health, cosmetic use
Clothing, hairstyle, hygiene	Socioeconomic level, parental style and care
Activity level	Emotional state, health factors
Facial expressions and body language	Emotional states, attention, interest
Playmates, interactions	Social stage, personality, sexual preference of playmates, aggressiveness
Approach to play, work, other people	Self-esteem, learning style, cognitive level and style
Mannerisms	Role models—parents, TV characters, other children
Evidence of injury	Accident, surgery, abuse

Figure 2.5 Visual cues may lead one to make inferences about a child.

Sociability—play stage, themes, playmates, leadership

Touching

Some information may not be apparent to sight or sound. The reaction to an adult's soft touch might seem unusual, giving rise to conjecture about the origin of that response.

Muscle tone—firm muscle tissue, eating disorders, and some diseases

Illness—fever, rashes, cold, clammy skin

TOPICS IN OBSERVATION: continued

Stress—tension in the body, trembling, goosebumps

Injury—swelling, reaction to touch indicating a tenderness

Response to touch—cuddly, withdrawal, rigid

Smelling

The most obvious information gathered by smelling is that a diaper change is needed. In a one-year-old, that observation is common and demands a standard response. In a six-year-old that observation, of course, also calls for the action of cleaning up, but it is noteworthy and a red flag for other assessments. Smelling gives the keen observer clues about:

Hygiene—cleanliness, tooth decay, bed wetting

Illness—respiratory infections, diseases such as diabetes that may give off a sweet odor

Home odors—smoking, seasonings, animals, perfume

Safety—ingestion of a poisonous substance

Tasting

Taste probably would not be used to gather information on the child.

The "Sixth Sense"

The observer's instinct, or "gut" feeling should receive attention. Sometimes there is something about a child sensed not by eyes, ears, nose, or touch but by a feeling. Professionals must rely on substantive information but often have a heightened awareness. This is not to be used as a measurement but as an indicator that further hard evidence needs to be gathered. The observer makes a closer investigation with detailed documentation for later analysis. This may involve other professionals, with the permission of the parents, such as a social worker, health coordinator, psychologist, or speech therapist.

The keen observer uses all senses to gather information. The knowledge of child development is applied, using multiple methods of documentation of the observations. All of this information-gathering is used to benefit the child and the program.

- stable—effects do not disappear in a short time. (Fischer, 1984, p. 3)

This diagram of development, the inverted triangle, illustrates the expanding nature of development, Figure 2.7. It is used throughout the book to illustrate the expansion of skills and knowledge that begins in a limited, crude way but broadens and builds upon prior experiences.

Each self-care skill meets that definition of development. Babies suck before they chew, eat with their fingers before they use a spoon, spoon before fork, fork before knife, knife before melon baller. This series always follows this progression because it depends on physical growth and development and builds on the skills and experience with the preceding attainment. The skills do not appear then disappear. They last a lifetime unless some trauma or drastic event interrupts or prevents the accomplishment of the task.

The reason for knowing the progression of self-care skills is the same as it is for every other area of development. Watching for the first time is a reassurance that development is taking place. It is a milestone, a marker. The first time the baby reaches out to hold her own bottle or takes the spoon and feeds herself is a momentous occasion. It demonstrates an increasing self-responsibility that is an indicator of maturity. Besides recognizing the mas-

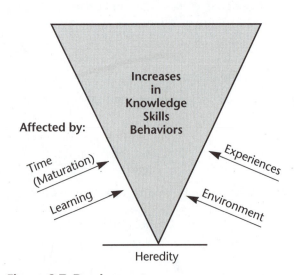

Figure 2.7 Development

tery of a new skill, the adult then provides practice and more opportunities for the child to perform that task independently. The caregiver will also be looking to the next task in the progression and providing experiences for the child to attempt that task.

Once the child has mastered the spoon, the parent introduces a little fork and demonstrates the stabbing motion that differentiates a fork from a spoon. This is planning curriculum based on developmental level. The caregiver sees that one child is ready for this at 10 months. Another is still working on the spoon at 12 months. This is individualizing the curriculum, developmental education. Parents and teachers do it all the time without realizing it.

Self-Care and Autonomy

Exercise: At what point did you feel independent of your parents? List the milestones toward that accomplishment.

Autonomy, the process of governing oneself and providing for one's own needs, is the goal of childhood. For twentieth-century children, that seems to be a very long process. The human infant is born totally helpless but by 1½ years, they are mobile and wanting to do more things for themselves. Caregivers still need to be protective and restrictive while allowing the child opportunities to begin to be more independent. Erikson (1963) describes this conflict as Autonomy vs. Shame and Doubt. Children who have had no experience of success in becoming independent have a fundamental lack of confidence in their own self-worth. In *Miseducation: Preschoolers at Risk,* David Elkind (1987) gives the practical advice "children are just learning these skills, so it is important not to force them... The important thing, as I have tried to suggest, is to find a healthy middle ground between doing everything for children and doing nothing for them and expecting them to cope with the adult-sized world" (p. 111).

Self-Care Skills in the Curriculum

By observing with the developmental progression in mind, observations become assessments and tools for planning curriculum. The area of self-care is not always recognized as a curriculum. It is taken for granted, probably because it develops so naturally. Self-care skills are recognized as a very important part of the curriculum for children with special needs (Hallahan, Kauffman, 1986). Upon consideration, taking care of one's own body functions involves many areas of development and

contributes not only to physical but emotional well-being. Both large and small muscle strength and coordination are necessary for these tasks. A great many thinking processes are involved in each skill, beginning with body awareness of the cues of hunger, tiredness, need to eliminate, and feeling cold or hot. The connections between past experiences build and form new thinking patterns.

Certainly self-care skills are necessary for social acceptance. It is part of that whole realm of manners and out-in-public actions. These are learned by observing and imitating role models and from direct instruction. The learning depends on the child's desire to be accepted and liked. There is a feeling of accomplishment and increased self-esteem when one can do something independently, without assistance. Following surgery or an illness, people report how good it feels just to be able to brush their own teeth or go up a few steps. Those actions become so natural, done without thinking or appreciating their complexity. In childhood, they are skills to learn, moving from basic to complex levels.

Individual differences are significant in self-care skills. Predictability of body rhythmicity is seen dramatically in the Thomas and Chess (1977, 1980) longitudinal studies. The studies indicated that feeding, elimination, and sleeping patterns at 2 months were consistent or at least similar at 10 years old. In addition to physical differences, social, racial, and cultural influences as well as birth order may affect self-care development. Marci Hanson (1992) warns, "Expectations for children concerning feeding, sleeping and speaking, as well as the use of discipline, to mention only a few may vary widely across cultural groups" (p. 13). The book reviews many different cultural beliefs important for teachers to know. Information on the child's self-care skills can be gathered from parents as well as observed in the natural routines of the day in the group setting. Figure 2.8, Ireton (1995), is a checklist that could be used to assess self-help skills with the ages at which these normally occur. These are part of the developmental process so the observer realizes that each child attains these milestones in an individual timetable.

Self-Care Skills

Self-care skills are points of observing and recording used to recognize milestones, plot and share progress, and plan curriculum, Figure 2.9.

Eating. In infancy, the adult is the source of nourishment to the child, whether by breast or by bottle. The infant depends on the adult to provide the acceptable food at regular times and as the

SELF-HELP
Includes eating, dressing, bathing, toileting, independence, and responsibility

Age 1-2
- Removes socks.   12m
- Lifts a cup to mouth and drinks.   12m
- Feeds self with a spoon.   15m
- Hands empty dish to adult.   15m
- Ⓟ Remembers where things are kept in the house. 15m
- Uses a small pail or other container for carrying things. Or used to.   15m
- Tries to put on shoes. Or puts them on.   15m
- Climbs on chair, stool, or box to reach things.   15m
- Eats with a fork.   18m
- Eats with a spoon with little spilling.   21m
- Takes off shoes and socks.   21m
- Unzips zippers.   21m

Age 2-3
- Ⓟ Wipes up spills, using cloth or sponge.   2-0
- Ⓟ Takes off unbuttoned shirt/blouse without help. 2-0
- Ⓟ Opens door by turning knob and pulling.   2-0
- Ⓟ Washes and dries hands.   2-6
- Ⓟ Goes around the house independently; requires little supervision.   2-6
- Ⓟ Washes self in bathtub—may need a little help.   2-6

Ages 3-4
- Puts a shirt/blouse or jacket without help.   3-0
- Toilet trained for urine control and bowel movements.   3-0, 2-6
- Ⓟ Brushes teeth without help.   3-0
- Ⓟ Takes responsibility for self in eating, dressing, and washing—but may need a little help.   3-3
- Ⓟ Undresses completely without help.   3-6, 3-0
- Ⓟ Washes face without help.   3-9, 3-3
- Ⓟ Notices when shirt/blouse or pants are inside-out and turns them right-side-out.   3-9
- Ⓟ Dresses and undresses without help, except for tying shoelaces.   3-9, 3-6
- Ⓟ Stays dry all night.   4-3, 3-3

Age 4-5
- Uses table knife for spreading.   4-3
- Buttons one or more buttons.   4-3
- Ⓟ Usually looks both ways when crossing streets.   4-6
- Buttons a shirt, blouse, or coat, having all the buttons in the correct holes.   5-0, 4-3
- Goes to the toilet without help; wipes self, flushes toilet, and washes hands.   5-0, 4-3
- Takes care of personal belongings.   5-3, 4-6

Age 5-6
- Puts shoes on the correct feet.   5-0
- Ⓟ Pours self a drink.   5-0
- Ⓟ Pours dry cereal and milk into a bowl without spilling.   5-3

OTHER SKILLS
- _____
- _____
- _____

PROBLEMS
- Immature; acts much younger than age.
- Disorganized; messy, careless, irresponsible.
- Can't sit still; may be hyperactive
- Passive; seldom shows initiative
- Lacks self-confidence; says "I'm dumb," etc.

Figure 2.8 Self-Help Milestones. Ireton, H. *Child Development Inventory Teacher's Observation Guide*, © 1995. Reprinted by permission of Behavior Science Systems, Minneapolis, MN.

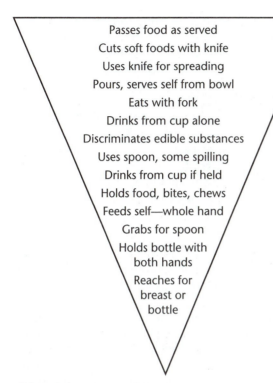

Passes food as served
Cuts soft foods with knife
Uses knife for spreading
Pours, serves self from bowl
Eats with fork
Drinks from cup alone
Discriminates edible substances
Uses spoon, some spilling
Drinks from cup if held
Holds food, bites, chews
Feeds self—whole hand
Grabs for spoon
Holds bottle with both hands
Reaches for breast or bottle

Figure 2.9 Eating Skills

infant gives signals of hunger. Reflex actions of rooting (turning toward the cheek that is touched) and sucking once the nipple is felt on the lips are built-in muscle responses. They enable the infant to receive nourishment. By three or four months, the baby will begin to recognize the breast or bottle, reach for it, and hold it firmly to get it all. In another month, the baby begins to push it away when full. By six months, the pincer grasp of thumb and forefinger enables the baby to indiscriminately pick up small food items (and fuzz balls) and get them into the mouth. This means the caregiver must give extra caution to the cleanliness of the environment. The caregiver must be vigilant regarding small ingestible and undigestible items. Soon the caregiver will begin to give the baby the opportunity to eat small bits of appropriate food items while the child is securely strapped in a high chair or infant seat.

In the second year, the child begins to assert independence by grabbing the spoon, the bottle, or the cracker. He now has the small motor skills to get them to his mouth fairly accurately and teeth to chew. Three and four year olds gain skill at using utensils: spoon first, then the fork, then the knife. They should be given the opportunity to practice under supervision, Figure 2.10. Gentle reminders and pointers for using the silverware effectively are given. They can efficiently pour, if the pitcher is lightweight and clear, so they can

see the liquid approaching the spout. It helps if the glass or paper cup has a fill line for a visual cue to stop pouring. It helps to place the glass on a tray to catch "over pours" until control is gained.

By late four and early five years, children have the physical mobility and manual dexterity to help themselves to food as it is passed. They love to assist in preparation of peeling foods with proper utensils and supervision. They can set the table, fold napkins, clear the table, and be quite helpful in the whole mealtime routine.

Learning and language connected with eating begins with the recognition of food sources, such as the breast or bottle. Accompanying vocabulary is built as the caregiver says, "Here comes the baba, baby hungry?" As the creeper finds tidbits, her ability to discriminate between food and nonfood items is not developed, possibly placing her in danger.

By one year she begins to display likes and dislikes of foods by their appearance or a single taste. As language explodes in the second year, she can recognize and name many foods. The sorting skills of the three- and four-year-old transfer into food groups. It begins with likes and dislikes. Eventually, she can classify meat, vegetables, fruits, drinks, and breads. She is learning the names for the individual items based on visual and aromatic cues.

Exercise: What table rules did you learn as a child? How did you learn them?

The social-emotional aspects of eating are lessons that are learned early. The aura of mealtime lasts a lifetime. It may be a relaxed, social gathering, or a tense, emotion-laden time of restrictions and prohibitions. Adults are responsible for the physical environment of cleanliness, safety, appropriateness of menu, cognitive con-

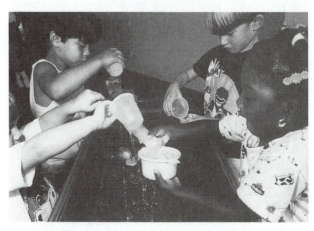

Figure 2.10 Pouring takes physical skills, concentration, and patience.

Figure 2.11 Eating is a social event in which many lessons may be learned.

nections, and language and vocabulary expansion. They are modeling social graces and providing an emotional atmosphere where psychological safety and individualism are recognized, Figure 2.11.

When children sit at a table that fits them and participate to their ability with the preparation, serving, and feeding of the meal, it builds the feeling of competency. The interaction with peers and adults in pleasant conversation teaches many social lessons. Verna Hildebrand (1990) admonishes teachers:

> You wouldn't tell your coteacher to eat sweet potatoes because you like them. You wouldn't tell a coteacher to eat more mashed potatoes or squash, or not to drink more milk, so you shouldn't tell children that. The amount required and the kind of foods liked are very personal tastes (p. 136).

Children learn they are trusted when they are given autonomy over choices among healthy foods. By participating in the food preparation, serving, and self-feeding they feel competent. When they interact with others during mealtime, they learn skills that they will be using around the table the rest of their life. Because eating disorders are beginning as early as three and four, close attention should be given to mealtimes and the emotions involved.

IT HAPPENED TO ME:
Bad Example

I was observing in a child care center at morning snack time. Some of the children had been doing puzzles and playing with Play Doh at the table while others had been painting, stacking with blocks, shoveling sand, and looking at books. The teacher rattled a box of Coco Puffs and the children came running to sit at the table. She stood behind each child, scooped up a handful of cereal from the box and placed it on the bare table in front of each one. She poured juice from a can into paper cups and set them in front of each child. She said, "OK, eat, and no spilling." She stepped away from the table and ate a candy bar from her pocket.

Exercise: The preceding is a true Anecdotal Recording, unfortunately! What was wrong with the teacher's practices?

Toileting. Control of body eliminations is truly an illustration of development: from no control with only reflex actions, through the steps dependent on physical growth, to a complex set of controls and releases dependent on many other factors, Figure 2.12.

Of course, the infant has no control over body eliminations so the adult performs all necessary tasks of absorbing, catching, cleaning, and rediapering. This routine function, like any other done with an infant, is not without its effect on the infant's cognitive, language, and social-emotional realm.

Adults give many messages to the infant during diapering, such as messages about safety, gentleness, hygiene, acceptance of body elimination, and sexual attitudes. When a caregiver expresses unpleasantness at the task, the infant confuses the message. He does not know it is the task, and not him, that is the cause of the unpleasant facial expressions and expressive language.

Exercise: Ask a parent to recount a toilet-training story (everyone has at least one), and write it down as it is told. Use the criteria for an Anecdotal Recording.

Usually children are well into the second year before they begin to recognize the body signals of an impending bowel movement and, even later, the need to urinate. The physical growth of muscles is occurring, along with the mental attention to body signals. Unfortunately, it is at a time when there is a strong desire to gain more control of the world. In this battle to control the body, the child and the adult are often at opposite poles, making toilet training a chore many adults dread. The struggle can be eased by recognizing the turmoil going on inside the

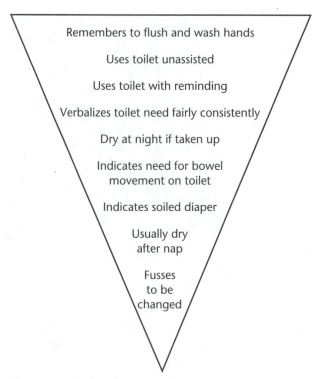

Remembers to flush and wash hands

Uses toilet unassisted

Uses toilet with reminding

Verbalizes toilet need fairly consistently

Dry at night if taken up

Indicates need for bowel
movement on toilet

Indicates soiled diaper

Usually dry
after nap

Fusses
to be
changed

Figure 2.12 Toileting Development

child. She is given control, since the adult cannot control it anyway. Psaltis and Stonehouse (1990) give the strong warning, "As in other areas of care, *there is no place in learning self toileting for shaming, embarrassing, or making a toddler feel guilty*" (p. 83, italics in original work). Curriculum for this area is in environment preparation, positive role models, and sometimes direct instruction.

Environment. The adult's role is to provide an environment that encourages the desired action: potty chair, steps to the toilet, child-sized toilet seat, books, pictures, pleasant room decor. The bathroom often is overlooked as a place where learning occurs. Interesting pictures at the side and back of the toilet give "goers" thought-provoking visual aids. Of course, visual reminders of hand washing will link toileting with personal hygiene.

Exercise: Toileting is an emotionally charged subject for child and adult. Finish these reflective questions:

The most uncomfortable part for me about working with children surrounding toileting is...
I think it is because...
Maybe it would be better if I...

Role Models. Toileting is sometimes aided by the social aspect in group care because of the child's natural imitative nature. When one child

uses the toilet, others will want to do it also. When a child is praised for potty use, it is likely to occur again and again and eventually become a routine.

Direct Instruction. Some children may need to be taught proper use of the toilet and toilet paper. This is best accomplished on an anatomically correct doll. Teachers should avoid performing this task on a child in an enclosed bathroom stall. For children still needing assistance, stalls are without doors or the task is done with the door propped open. This is a precaution to possible child abuse allegations.

As the child is expanding her vocabulary, a consideration of which words to use for body elimination functions should be explored so that parents and teachers attain consistency. This also gives a positive rather than negative connotation to the function. The struggle over toilet training is an emotionally and culturally sensitive topic that is enhanced by the caregiver's partnership with the parents and the child. Hanson (1992) gives the reminder that "in the United States, toilet training between the child's second and third birthday is a common practice and is highly valued by many families. However, this practice may be viewed by many other cultural groups as unnecessary and too early" (p. 13).

• •

IT HAPPENED TO ME:
Am I Clean?

• •

This happened to a friend of mine. In a four-year-old class, a child had gone to the bathroom while they were having snack. She waddled back from the bathroom with her pants around her ankles, bent over, looking through her legs yelled, "Am I clean?" "Yes, you're clean. Good job wiping," said the teacher matter-of-factly. The girl returned to the bathroom, dressed, washed hands, and returned to snack.

• •

Exercise: What does that tell you about the child's stage of development? Home influence? The teacher?

Dressing. It is always easier to knock down a building than to build it, delete a page of type than to write it, criticize than to praise. So it is with dressing—the first step in self-care is taking clothing off. Parents have all experienced, at least once, the shock of a stark-naked child appearing when they were just fully clothed a few minutes ago. Dressing is a developmental progression of skills, Figure 2.13.

Children can be given the power to take off the articles of clothing they can manage. By the time they are two or three years old, they can take off their shoes at nap time, their hat after coming in from outside play, and all their clothes at bath time. They should do what they can do. By selecting clothing that children can manage themselves, such as boxer pants, the child finds the task much easier. It is easier than a one-piece jumpsuit or buttons up the back of a dress.

Exercise: Make a list of clothing fasteners that are difficult even for adults. How could it have been designed differently?

Teachers can add play items with buttons, snaps, zippers, and ties to the curriculum to encourage practice of those skills. It is always amazing how a child can squeeze into a leotard and tutu over a pair of jeans and a sweatshirt and sneakers. If they want it on, they will find a way. Inviting dress-up props stimulate interest and practice skills, Figure 2.14.

When helping a child after toileting or getting ready to go outside, the child should be assisted

Figure 2.14 Dress-up clothes give practice in buttoning, zipping, and tying.

with what they cannot do and encouraged to do what they can. The adult can pull up the pants and let the child pull up the suspenders. The teacher can start the separating zipper and let her finish it, or finish tying the bow after she has crossed the ties.

"Never do for a children what they can do for themselves."

Personal Hygiene. Body cleanliness and care of the infant is, of course, the sole responsibility of the adult, Figure 2.15. It is a physical function performed which is building associations in the infant between certain events. "They change my diaper and wash my body and hands." "They set me in the high chair, wash my hands, then give me food." "They take me away from the table and wash my face and hands." In the first year, these associations are being made. In the second year when the child gains mobility and small muscle control, she can go to the sink, which is adapted so she can reach it, and wash her hands. She is taught to do this after going to the toilet or wiping her nose, or before eating. She can manage to turn on the water, wash, dry, and go on with play. In the fourth and fifth years, small muscle control is more developed. The child can now efficiently handle combing hair, brushing teeth, and bathing in the tub with supervision.

Recognition of the need for washing is a difficult lesson for young children to learn because of the "invisible" germs. They are concrete thinkers. When they look at their hands and see no dirt, they find it incomprehensible that they should wash, especially if they did it once today already. It is the social acceptance and cognitive bridging that reinforce the personal hygiene habits until the

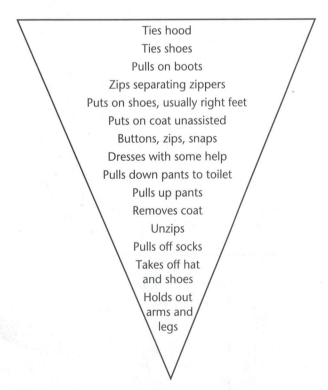

Ties hood

Ties shoes

Pulls on boots

Zips separating zippers

Puts on shoes, usually right feet

Puts on coat unassisted

Buttons, zips, snaps

Dresses with some help

Pulls down pants to toilet

Pulls up pants

Removes coat

Unzips

Pulls off socks

Takes off hat and shoes

Holds out arms and legs

Figure 2.13 Dressing Development

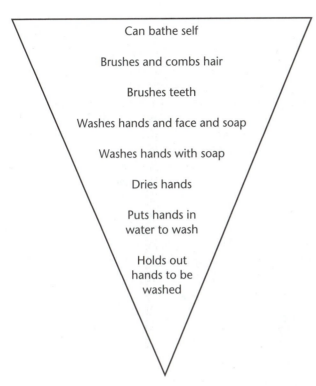

Figure 2.15 Personal Hygiene Skill Development

child is into the elementary school years when microscopic particles are understood.

Sleeping. Sleep needs and patterns are individual but follow a developmental pattern. Individual differences are seen in the amount of sleep children need, how they get to sleep, how soundly they sleep, and their usual waking-up routines.

Children in group care tend to be overstimulated because of many available playmates and play things. It is lessened by stress reduction throughout the day and by planning for smooth transitions, and alternating active and quiet activity choices. Prior to nap time, consistent routines, such as mealtime, teeth brushing, and music listening or a story, help to prepare the children for sleep. Attention is given to the program schedule and environment to allow for resting and sleeping time on self-demand. Sleeping arrangements often are strictly mandated by state regulations for safety and supervision. The National Association for the Education of Young Children's (NAEYC) *Developmentally Appropriate Practice* (Bredekamp, et al., 1987) mandates "Children have their own cribs, bedding, feeding utensils, clothing, diapers, pacifiers, and other special comforting objects. Infant's names are used to label every personal item" (p. 36). Individual programs develop routines of backrubs, soft music, and quiet play preceding rest times to help children relax and

sleep if they need to, Figure 2.16. Allowances are made for those children who are no longer taking naps to look quietly at books in the napping area or to play in a quiet learning center.

Individual children have sleep patterns such as sleeping position or what soothes them into sleep. They may require possessions nearby to fall asleep. By noting a reduction in sleep times, modifications are made for the child who no longer requires a nap. Communication of daily sleep patterns between home and school assists both family and center in meeting the needs of the child.

Parent and staff daily reports are used in most centers to convey this type of information at arrival and departure times. Sharing "what works" benefits the child at home and at the center.

Self-Care in the Classroom

Caring for the classroom environment is another area of development.

Exercise: Observe the room you are in. What are the items in the room or the arrangement that encourages self-care? (Example: Wastebasket is available).

Some observable signs of a child's participation in classroom self-care are:

- selects toys for play
- puts a toy back in its place

Figure 2.16 Allowances should be made for children's individual sleeping patterns.

- plays actively without adult leadership
- follows classroom routines
- cleans up spills
- helps prepare for activity
- can carry breakable objects
- performs "job chart" tasks
- demonstrates safety awareness
- assists another child to do a task

With "Home Alone" and its sequels in mind, many have visions of the immense capacities of a child's competency. On the other hand, there have been newspaper horror stories of children left alone at a very young age. Some of these children are caring for even younger siblings and often there are tragedies. This self-care concept is not to hurry the child along to independence before he is ready. It allows him the freedom and responsibili- ty for self-care. This is done in small, manageable steps that build confidence and competency. They eventually form the ability to make safe self-care decisions. The age at which a child can be allowed to play unattended in a room at home, go down the street alone, and eventually stay at home alone for a short time varies with the individual child. It also is affected by the home setting, the neighbor- hood, and prior experiences. There should be a his- tory of smaller, successful instances of self-care. Parents are in the business of working themselves out of a job and building into the child the com- petencies for self-care. It is done one day at a time.

Many classrooms and home environments use job charts for daily responsibilities. This is an orga- nized way to ensure care of the environment. It also teaches that each one must do a part for the good of the group, Figure 2.17.

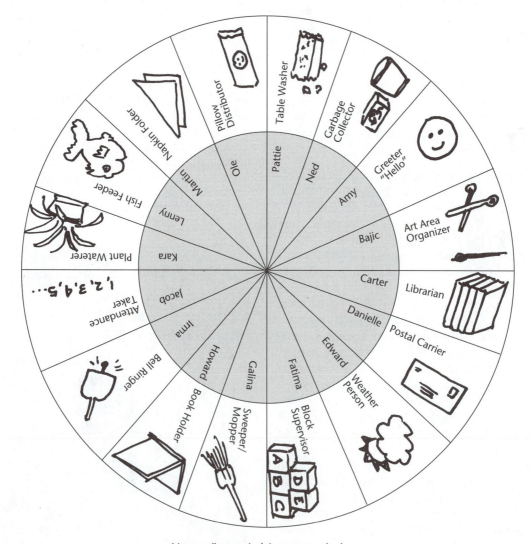

Names (inner circle) move each day.

Figure 2.17 Job Chart. (Reprinted with permission from Carol Fuller, Conklin Presbyterian Preschool, Conklin, NY.)

In the classroom as well, children become competent in self-care as they learn the routines. They can meet realistic expectations for cleaning up after themselves and should be given responsibilities for themselves and others. There are children who are so averse to cleaning up that they are reluctant to play with anything so they do not have to put anything away. Clean up time is easier with the aid of effective transitions. These begin with a warning time that playtime is almost over, which helps to prepare children to end play and begin to pick up. Little ritual songs or signals, such as music or a bell, work better than an adult yelling "Pick up time!" See Figure 2.18.

Adults can make pick-up time fun by using child-sized brooms, small vacuum cleaners, and toy trucks to transport toys back to their places that clearly are labeled. This reinforces the group participation in taking care of the classroom and initiates the concept of environmental responsibility. Ruth Charney in *Teaching Children to Care* (1991) suggests some excellent strategies with a list of questions teachers can use.

T: Who can show us a careful and safe way to put all the blocks away in their container?

T: Who can show us what to do while waiting for the container?

T: Who can show us how they would pass the container when they are done?

T: What's another way we could put away the pattern blocks when lots of people are using them? (Someone gets all the circles, someone else will get the squares...) (p. 296)

If the Child Is Having Difficulty. The teacher begins with a closer examination of the environment. Modifications are made to help the child, such as low close hooks, reduced lighting in the nap area, or steps up to the changing table or toilet. If the environment is appropriate, the expectations for the child may not be reasonable. Other areas of the child's development are considered (language, cognitive, small muscle). Are these self-care expectations realistic? After this, a talk with the parents is the next step to find out if they can give advice, insight, or assistance.

The teacher should be aware of the parents' expectations for the child at home, how the child does these things at home, and what may be the reason for this inability here. More time may be all that is needed.

The Importance of Self-Care. Children who can care for their own bodies are physically and psychologically strong. It is a progression. It may have relapses, need reminders, and result in frustration. Parents sometimes wonder if their child will be graduating from high school in diapers, sucking on a bottle, with zippers unzipped. That rarely happens; they do learn it along the way. The adult's role is consideration of the environment, realistic expectations, positive role models, and direct, specific instructions. Children then develop these self-care skills that allow them to be independent and socially accepted.

SPECIAL POPULATIONS AND SELF-CARE SKILLS

It has already been mentioned that cultural differences are seen most in the area of self-care skills. The caregiver needs to be sensitive to different attitudes and practices. This can be done through home visits, research, parent questionnaires, and gaining information from watching the child and parent together. Adjustment of routines for these differences is the appropriate action, rather than forcing the child to conform. Communication and coordination between school and home must occur for the benefit of the child.

Children with special needs, as previously mentioned, need to be allowed to do all they can for themselves. It may mean that some modifications are made to the environment and expectations. All children have the need to feel competent and responsible.

Pick up, pick up.

Everybody do your share.

Pick up, pick up.

Pick up everywhere.

To the traditional "Today Is Monday" tune:

It's time to pick up.

It's time to pick up,

Mary's picking up blocks.

Jack's sweeping sand.

Tania's finishing her painting.

Soon it will be snack.

Figure 2.18 Pick-up songs help make an orderly environment everyone's responsibility.

HELPING PROFESSIONALS FOR SELF-CARE SKILLS

Other professionals may be consulted depending on the area of difficulty, such as a

pediatrician—for a thorough physical checkup to rule out any possible physical reasons for difficulties

social worker—for advice on family and center practices and expectations

occupational therapist—to examine more closely fine muscle skills involved in self-care

child psychologist—to explore the child's attitudes and reasons for refusing to care for herself

Week 2

NOTE FOR ADJUSTING WEEK-BY-WEEK PLAN TO YOUR CLASS

Each week's assignments will include recordings on the whole class and on individual children. In our effort to record fairly and equally, divide the class into four groups by taking one of the Class List Log forms and dividing it as equally as you can into four groups: groups A, B, C, and D. These children will be in these recording groups for the rest of the year, so keep this as your master group plan.

When the weekly assignment is to observe each child in group A (or B, C, or D) use the Class List Log of the children in that group to determine how many children you must observe each day.

(In this way you can factor in short weeks and so on.) Write those names on the calendar. For example, if you had 16 children in your class, group A will have child 1, 2, 3, and 4. On Monday, child 1 will be the focus of the recording; on Tuesday, child 2, and so on. If you had 23 in your class, group A will have child 1, 2, 3, 4, 5, and 6. You may decide that on Tuesday and Wednesday you will focus on child 2 in the morning and child 3 in the afternoon for the assignment. The following week, the assignment for individual recordings probably will be group B, so you would focus on each of the children in the next group, one or two per day.

Week 2, Assignment A

ANECDOTAL RECORDING— SELF-CARE FOR GROUP A

Select each of the children in group A. On Monday, while working with the children through the day, focus attention skills displayed by child 1 during eating, dressing, toileting, taking care of themselves, or taking care of the room. Jot notes. Later in the day, on the left-hand column of a sheet of paper, write an Anecdotal Recording as an illustration of child 1's self-care skills. Remember to just be a detail writer, including actions and exact quotes to give the reader the feeling of being there. On Tuesday, repeat the assignment for child 2, Wednesday for child 3, and so on. In the right-hand column, make notes about what this self-care incident shows about the child's physical, cognitive, language, and social-emotional development. In the right column, you make comments such as, "This is the first time she's done this by herself. She was so proud" or "This is unusual for him," or "I wonder if she would have done this if she hadn't felt me watching her."

What to Do with It

On each child's portfolio overview sheet, note that the Anecdotal Record is being included that documents an aspect of self-care, along with your name and date, Figure 2.19.

Share the incident with parents and the child, if it is appropriate. For example: "I was observing Boneva today and noticed how well she's handling the butter knife for spreading and even cutting up her potato into small pieces. That's quite an advanced skill."

SELF–CARE		
Documentation	Recorder	Date
CL ate, toilet, no nap	*BAN*	*9/14*
AR Initiates pickup	*MS*	*3/15*

Figure 2.19 Portfolio Overview Example

File the recording in the child's portfolio.

If a concern arises during the observation, speak with your supervisor then possibly discuss it with the parent to decide on a course of action.

Note and follow through, writing down the results.

Plan specific curriculum activities to practice the accomplished skill and next-level skills, and give experiences to develop with help.

Week 2, Assignment B

CLASS LIST LOG—SELF-CARE FOR ALL

Take a Class List Log form and divide the writing spaces vertically to record eating, toileting, dressing, personal hygiene, sleeping, and classroom self-care. Review the developmental milestones for the age of the children in your class and observe this week, noting the degree of self-care each child exhibits in these areas. Be sure you are allowing each child to do for themselves what they can do.

What to Do with It

In each child's portfolio overview sheet, note the date of the Class List Log, the self-care level observed, and the recorder's name (yours). File the completed Class List Log in your class file. You will refer to it again later in the year.

Make a note if further action is indicated and follow through on further observation. Discuss with the teaching team, your supervisor, or the child's parents.

Week 2, Assignment C

REFLECTIVE JOURNAL

Respond to the following in your Reflective Journal, kept in a private file at home.

I need to be giving children more opportunities for self-care. I think I'll...

I find myself doing more for _____ than the other children. The reasons for this may be...

When I'm trying to do something and someone tries to help me, it makes me...

These are the things I can do for myself that make me feel competent:

REFERENCES

Bentzen, W. (1997). *Seeing young children: A guide to observing and recording behavior.* Albany: Delmar Publishers.

Bergen, D. (1994). *Assessment methods for infants and toddlers.* New York: Teachers College Press.

Bredekamp, S. (1987). *Developmentally appropriate practice in early childhood programs serving children from birth through age 8.* Washington, DC: National Association for the Education of Young Children.

Charney, R. S. (1991). *Teaching children to care: Management in the responsive classroom.* Greenfield, MA: Northeast Foundation for Children.

Elkind. D. (1987). *Miseducation: Preschoolers at risk.* New York: Alfred A. Knopf.

Erikson, E. (1963). *Childhood and society* (2nd ed.) New York: Norton.

Feldman, J. (1995). Transition *time: Let's do something different.* Beltsville, MD: Gryphon House.

Fischer, K. W. & Lazerson, A. (1984). *Human development: From conception through adolescence.* New York: W. H. Freeman and Co. p. 3.

Hallahan, D. P. & Kauffman, J. M. (1986). *Exceptional children: An introduction to special education.* Englewood Cliffs, NJ: Prentice-Hall, Inc.

Hanson, M. J. (1992). Ethnic, cultural, and language diversity in intervention settings in Lynch, E. W. & Hanson, M. J. Developing cross-cultural competence: A guide for working with young children and their families. Baltimore: Paul H. Brookes Publishing Co.

Harms, T. & Clifford, R. M. (1980). *Early childhood environment rating scale.* New York: Teachers College Press.

Hildebrand, V. (1990). *Guiding young children.* New York: Macmillan Publishing Co.

Ireton, H. R. (1995). *Teacher's observation guide.* Minneapolis, MN: Behavioral Science Systems.

Psaltis, M. & Stonehouse, A. (1990). Toddler-centered routines in Stonehouse, A. *Trusting toddlers: Planning for one- to three-year-olds in child care centers.* St. Paul, MN: Toys 'n Things Press.

Thomas, A. & Chess, S. (1977). *Temperament and development.* New York: Brunner/Mazel.

Thomas, A. & Chess, S. (1980). *The dynamics of psychological development.* New York; Brunner/Mazel.

Warren, J. (1991). *Piggyback songs for school.* Everett, WA: Warren Publishing Co.

RESOURCES

Feldman, J. (1995). *Transition time: Let's do something different!* Beltsville, MD: Gryphon House.

Hanson, M. J. (1992). Ethnic, cultural, and language diversity in intervention settings in Lynch, E. W., & Hanson, M. J. *Developing cross-cultural competence: A guide for working with young children and their families.* Baltimore: Paul H. Brookes Publishing Co.

Psaltis, M. & Stonehouse, A. (1990). Toddler-centered routines in Stonehouse, A. *Trusting Toddlers: Planning for one- to three-year-olds in child care centers.* St. Paul, MN: Toys 'n Things Press.

CHAPTER 3

Using Checklists to Look at Physical Development

IN THIS CHAPTER

✔ Using the Checklist

✔ Topics in Observation: Your Frame of Reference

✔ Looking at Physical Development

✔ Special Populations and Physical Development

✔ Helping Professionals for Physical Development Concerns

USING THE CHECKLIST

Exercise: Complete this Checklist.

❑ I read Chapters 1 and 2.
❑ I completed each exercise in Chapters 1 and 2.
❑ I enjoyed writing in my Reflective Journal.
❑ I underlined key passages.
❑ I know the definition of *development*.

A **Checklist** is a predetermined list of criteria against which the recorder answers *yes* or *no.* In Checklist ratings, the recorder reads the criterion, decides on an answer, and makes a checkmark as an indication of an affirmative answer. Some of the preceding criterion are observable while others are judgmental or inferential. Mark those with a *J.* The third and fifth items are not observable.

Bentzen (1993) describes Checklists as a **closed method** because no raw data or evidence is recorded, just the decision (inference) of the recorder about the criterion. Checklists are highly selective, only giving the recorder the opportunity to record a decision concerning the criterion. That does not mean it is not useful or accurate, but the reader has

no raw data or details to check the recorder's decision. This is a characteristic of Checklist recording.

A valid child development Checklist records the attainment of accepted developmental milestones of knowledge, behavior, and skills. All Checklists depend on the familiarity of the observer with the criteria and ability to assess the criteria accurately. Therefore, the criteria should be clearly observable, leaving little room for subjective judgments. If not, two raters may see the same child performing a skill, yet rate the skill differently. Checklists' criteria should be closely examined for appropriateness to the population it is assessing and the developmental sequence of the criterion. Many programs and teachers design their own Checklists to fit the goals and objectives of the program and the population the program serves.

The developmental sequence of a Checklist makes it a forecaster or predictor of the skills or behaviors that will appear next. In this way, they help the teacher to individualize the curriculum by suggesting what experiences to provide in the next stage. For example:

☒ Child sits unassisted.

☒ Child creeps.
❑ Child pulls to a standing position.
❑ Child walks holding onto furniture.
❑ Child walks alone.

By seeing that the next stage is pulling to a standing position, the teacher will provide an environment that stimulates pulling up to a standing position, such as stable furniture and interesting things to look at above the creeping level. The teacher may plan activities in which the child is lifted to a standing position and supported for short periods of time.

Each criterion should measure the presence or absence of the knowledge, behavior, or skill. Checklists sometimes contain criterion that ask the recorder to judge or summarize groups of actions. For example, a Checklist item on small muscle skills may list:

❑ Coordinated eye/hand movements.

The teacher observed the child putting puzzle pieces into the correct holes. The meaning or summary of that skill could be inferred as "coordinated eye/hand movements." This type of criterion leaves much room for interpretation and the greater chance that it is subjective rather than factual, objective recording. Valid Checklists list specific knowledge, behaviors, and skills, in developmental sequence, that describe exactly a movement, skill, or behavior. This leaves the recorder only to answer the basic question, "Is the child doing that or not?"

Exercise: Mark the following Checklist items *O* for observed, or *I* for interpreted.

❑ 1. Can sit unassisted for 2 minutes
❑ 2. Uses pincer grasp to pick up small objects
❑ 3. Enjoys pulling self up on furniture
❑ 4. Able to do most small muscle skills
❑ 5. Can walk 6 feet on a 4-inch balance beam.
❑ 6. Can cut
❑ 7. Moves gracefully
❑ 8. Increasing strength and dexterity
❑ 9. Gives little attention to small muscle activities
❑ 10. Balances on one foot for 5 seconds.

Check yourself:

1. O—The position is observable, and time is measured.
2. O—How the child picks up the object is observed.
3. I—If the child enjoys it or not is interpreted by observing behavior and forming a conclusion. If the criteria were "Pulls self up on furniture," it would be O.
4. I—What are *most small muscle tasks?* It is not clear what they are, and if they are observed or not.
5. O—The length and width of board is a precise measurement, and action is observable.
6. I—The criteria is too broad. More accurate criteria is "Can cut a straight line" or "Can cut a curved line."
7. I—The observer has much latitude in deciding if the movement is "graceful. "An observable criteria is "Moves without bumping into objects in the room" or "Moves to rhythm of music."
8. I—Increasing from what? This is not measurable. An observable criteria is "Can suspend body weight on bars for 10 seconds" or "Can catch an 8-inch ball from 10 feet."
9. I—Judgment of the observer is recorded rather than observed behavior. An observable criteria is "Spends ____ minutes on small muscle activity."
10. O—Position and time measurement is specific. This is an objective criteria.

If Checklists were used for every increment, in every skill or behavior, in every developmental area, the Checklist would be unwieldy. Well-constructed Checklists are specific and limited to observable milestones. They are used with other methods of recording to document the specifics of observations.

The Checklist is reused periodically to measure the progress along the developmental continuum. If progress is not indicated by observing criterion farther along the scale, the teacher takes a closer look to be sure the data is correct. The Checklist may indicate significant lags that need to be addressed. A discussion is held with the parents, possibly referring them to helping professionals for a full evaluation. The decision may be made just to wait and watch for another period to see if the skills develop.

A Checklist is an effective tool to share with parents. It shows expected developmental progression and the level attained within those expectations. It indicates the dates of the observations and how much progress has taken place over that time. It may reveal accelerated or delayed development in specific areas, showing the child's strengths or areas yet to be developed. The Checklist becomes a permanent part of the child's portfolio or file.

Checklists, their content or format, can be varied to meet the needs of the recorder or program.

Some recorders recommend that different colored pens be used for each rating period. Many observers and Checklists are entering the technological age with computer scanning and analysis.

There are limitations to the usefulness of the Checklist:

1. It does not preserve the details of a conversation where vocabulary, tone of voice, and exact words give the essence of the exchange.

2. The observer sees behaviors and skills and makes a decision as to the presence or absence of the criteria. Once the checkmark or indication is made, there is no further notation about the event. Occasionally, a question or challenge of a notation may occur, such as a parent asking, "What do you mean? 'Builds complex block structures' Like what? Give me an example." It may have been checked on a day when the child built a replica of the Taj Mahal but the details are only in the recorder's memory, which may be overloaded with the activities of many children and the passing of time. The details have not been recorded. All the recorder did

was check, "yes" to the criterion that the child builds complex block structures. Modifications can be made to preserve more details, at least enough to jog the memory, such as Beaty's (1994) evidence column in *Observing Development of the Young Child.*

3. The observer's decision may be influenced by personal biases. The Checklist provides no way for the reader to form an independent opinion. The reader has to trust the recorder's judgment. This shortcoming of Checklists can be overcome by having various individuals recording with the Checklist. This gives more than one person's opinion on the decision of the criteria.

Exercise: You and another person, using the Beaty Large and Small Motor Checklist, observe the same child and independently mark the Checklist. Compare your ratings.

4. Because of its lack of detail, the Checklist is not a method that is reliable for documentation of suspected child abuse.

Item	Evidence	Date
5. Large Motor Development		
❑ Walks down steps alternating feet		
❑ Runs with control over speed and direction		
❑ Jumps over obstacle, landing on two feet		
❑ Hops forward on one foot		
❑ Climbs up and down, climbing equipment with ease		
❑ Moves legs/feet in rhythm to beat		
❑ Claps hands in rhythm to beat		
❑ Beats drum, alternating hands in rhythm to beat		

Figure 3.1 Large Motor Checklist (Courtesy of Beaty, J. *Observing Development of the Young Child,* © 1994, p. 161. Reprinted by permission of Prentice Hall, Upper Saddle River, NJ.)

Item	Evidence	Date
6. Small Motor Development		
❑ Shows hand preference (which is _____)		
❑ Turns with hand easily (knobs, lids, eggbeaters)		
❑ Pours liquid into glass without spilling		
❑ Unfastens/fastens zippers, buttons, Velcro tabs		
❑ Picks up and inserts objects with ease		
❑ Uses drawing/writing tools with control		
❑ Uses scissors with control		
❑ Pounds in nails with control		

Figure 3.2 Small Motor Checklist (Courtesy of Beaty, J. *Observing Development of the Young Child,* © 1994, p. 189. Reprinted by permission of Prentice Hall, Upper Saddle River, NJ.)

Uses

The Checklist method of recording
- records the presence or absence of pre-determined criterion
- shows the sequence of developmental progress
- measures progress
- can be used as a screening for developmental lags
- can be used as a curriculum planning tool for individualizing the curriculum

Advantages

The Checklist is
- time- and labor-efficient
- Comprehensive (It may cover many developmental areas in one Checklist.)
- documentation of development
- individual documentation on each child
- a clear illustration of the developmental continuum

Disadvantages

The Checklist
- loses the details of events
- may be biased by the recorder
- depends on the criteria to be clearly observable
- may have many items to check, making it time-consuming

What to Do with It

Programs usually purchase or develop a Checklist to match program goals and the age range of the children in the program or class. An individual Checklist is kept in each child's portfolio or file. Periodically, the recorder reexamines each developmental area. It is objective only as long as the Checklist closely describes exact observable behavior rather than vague generalizations that may be interpreted many ways.

The parents have access to this portfolio and the Checklist. It is a good tool to show parents the developmental sequence and the documentation of the accomplishments of their child. Focusing on the accomplishments, rather than the areas yet to be attained, is a positive way of evaluating a child's development.

Some Examples of Checklists

Observing Development of the Young Child, is by J. Beaty (Macmillan Publishing Company, 1994). It is a Checklist with evidence column for three- to six-year-olds with ascending criteria in all developmental areas. Child development and curriculum planning resources.

The *Brigance Diagnostic Inventory of Early Development* is by A. H. Brigance (Curriculum Associates, Inc., 1991). It is a comprehensive Checklist to assess development and diagnose developmental delay.

The *Child Development Inventory (CDI)* is by H. Ireton (Behavior Science Systems, 1992). It is a Parent Checklist for ages six months to six years to measure development and identify potential problems for further assessment.

The *Denver Developmental Screening Test II (DDST-II)* is by W. Frankenburg, et al. (Denver Developmental Materials, Inc., 1990). It is a range of criterion over four domains: social-emotional, fine motor, gross motor, and language. Can be used for screening at-risk children.

The *Child Observation Record (COR)* is by High/Scope Press (1987). It is an ascending Checklist for cognitive, movement, and social-emotional development.

The Work Sampling System is by S. Meisels, et al. (Rebus Planning Associates, 1994). It has Checklist components in personal and social development, language and literacy, mathematical and scientific thinking, social studies, the arts, and physical development. It assesses children's skills, knowledge, behavior, and accomplishments.

Developmental Profiles: Pre-birth Through Eight is by K. E. Allen and L. Marotz (Delmar Publishers, 1994). One-page-for-one-year developmental Checklists give the milestones for that year. The text provides more specific information, learning activities, and developmental alerts.

Personal Factors That Affect Observation. Adults may have their own situations that have nothing to do with the child but may affect the observer enough to interfere with objective recording:

Health—headache, awaiting test results, impending surgery, pregnancy, or premenstrual syndrome

Stress—financial, personal, or workplace tension

Outside pressure—gathering evidence to document a decision or a referral

The observer's consciousness is raised on these issues through reflection. By selecting objective observation methods, communicating and sharing observations and inferences with coworkers and parents, these biases can be minimized.

TOPICS IN OBSERVATION: Your Frame of Reference

Everyone looks at the world through a unique **frame of reference**. That frame of reference can be compared to a picture frame to help understand the concept.

A frame is the boundary or outer limits around a picture. The frame around the perimeter of a piece of glass sets the boundaries all around and limits vision beyond. Each person's understanding or "vision" is limited by boundaries different from every other person. The frame of reference is formed from past experiences but is very influential in viewing the present and the future. For the teacher, the frame of reference must be considered when observing children because it determines how the child is viewed. Some experiences that form the frame of reference follow.

Childhood. Each person's childhood is unique, even for children born in the same family, even for twins. Birth order, health, dynamics of personality in interactions with family members, inborn characteristics, and family environment all have an effect on childhood. When observing a child, adults subconsciously reflect on their own childhoods. These are factors in limiting how the adult sees the child. They unconsciously ask themselves, "How is this child like me or different from me as a child? What advantages or disadvantages does this child have that might influence the child in a different way from my own childhood? Can I even relate to the situation of this child because of the kind of childhood I have had?"

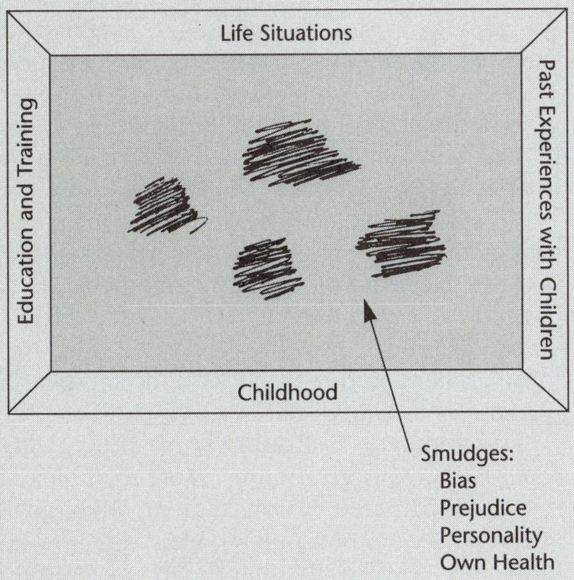

Education and Training. The educational level and philosophies learned affect the teacher's perceptions and judgments of the child being viewed. From a psychological background, the viewer may look for the meaning behind the behavior. From a psychosocial background, the viewer may look for conflict between biological and social demands at each maturational stage. From a behaviorist background, the viewer might look for the stimulus and responses reinforced in the behavior.

Past Experiences with Children. Many people working with children have a long history. They may be parents and grandparents or started out their career caring for younger siblings, babysitting as a teenager and now caring for extended family members. The past is the keyhole through which the present is viewed. This observed behavior may trigger memories and situations from the past and send up a warning signal, while other observers ignore the same action or regard it as insignificant. What is seen is always reflected back to what has been experienced in the past. Those new to the profession with little experience are going to see behaviors and incidents differently from those with much experience.

Own Learning Styles. With the advent of more knowledge of individual learning styles, it becomes clearer that a teacher's learning style is as important as the student's. Depending on the acute sensory reception, the observer will absorb information in different ways:

Auditory learner—from language and sounds the child makes

Visual learner—from actions, scenes, pictures of the child's behavior

Tactile learner—from touching the child

Figure 3.3 Frame of Reference

TOPICS IN OBSERVATION: continued

Values. Society has influenced each person differently in the formation of values and viewpoints. The societal influences of socioeconomic level, race, ethnicity, and gender enter into the observation framework. There is little control over the formation until an awareness is raised.

Smudges on the Looking Glass

The frame of reference is the perimeter but the viewing is done through the glass. There may be smudges on the glass. Those smudges are **biases** that keep the observer from seeing the child objectively.

Biases For or Against the Child. Individual biases and prejudices are human factors that may interfere with a clear view of the child. Those biases may be positive, causing a child's needs to be overlooked because of personal feelings that get in the way. Strengths of the child may be overlooked because of a prejudice or bias that will negatively affect objective observation. Some might be:

Sex—may prefer boys or girls better
Hair color—may love or hate redheads
Racial or ethnic—stereotypic beliefs
Economic or social status—rich or poor may interfere with how the child is perceived
Personality clashes—may love or hate children who are whiny, mischievous, active, sassy, bold, shy
Prior contact with the family—older child was in the class
Physical attributes—beauty, handicaps, weight
Hearsay—teacher talk has formed an opinion

All of these—the framework, the biases, and the daily situation—influence observation. Because observation is subjective, many criticize it as untrustworthy for evaluation. Many prefer standardized tests as more objective measuring tools. Testing will be discussed in a later section. These warnings of influences on observations are discussed here as a prelude to offer evidence for the necessity of carefully choosing recording methods. When limitations are recognized, efforts can be made to overcome the possible negative influences. "Forewarned is forearmed" as the saying goes. "We do, because we know." Some recording methods can be biased. Some days might not be good ones to gather information and make decisions. The professional acts ethically.

LOOKING AT PHYSICAL DEVELOPMENT

Exercise: Using a separate sheet of paper, list five phrases to describe your body.

Read the chapter, then return to your descriptions and mark them *G* for growth areas and *D* for development areas.

Bodies change. They grow and develop. What is the difference? **Growth** refers to changes in size, *quantitative* change, those changes that can be measured in increasing numbers such as height, weight, head circumference, and teeth.

- Most infants range in length from 18 to 21 inches at birth and are expected to grow longer and taller.
- By 36 months, the toddler has molars and a total of 20 "baby" teeth and is expected to grow more.
- The average five-year-old weighs 38 to 45 pounds and is expected to increase in weight as they grow older.

There are norms, or averages, established by statistical analysis of large groups of people. These are the established ranges for average growth at specific ages. Tables like these can alert observers to significant variations that warrant further investigation for the cause.

Other changes can be measured in numbers that are not physical. Vocabulary also "grows" because it can be measured in numbers. The toddler has a vocabulary of 50 to 300 words. The attention span is growing. It can be measured in minutes (sometimes seconds) and is expected to increase as the child matures.

Development is also change, but *qualitative change,* increasingly better, more complex, and more coordinated. Development, like growth, occurs in sequential, predictable stages, yet is different for every individual based on several factors. Physical development, both large and small muscle coordination begins with reflex actions to rudimentary then fundamental movement quality

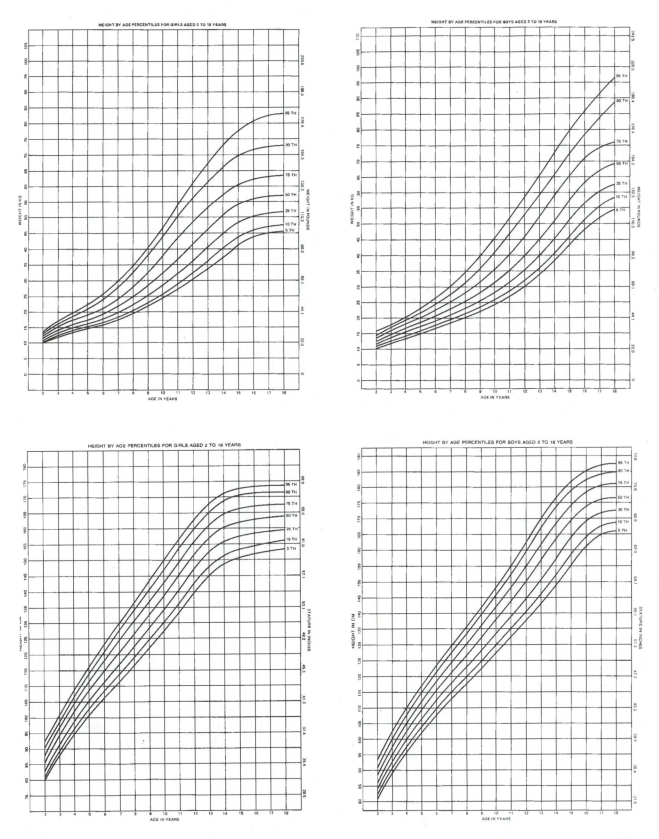

Figure 3.4 Height and Weight Charts. (Courtesy of Marotz, L. R., Rush, J. M., & Cross, M. Z., 1989, pp. 406–503. *Health, Safety, and Nutrition for the Young Child, 2nd edition.* Albany, NY: Delmar Publishers. Reprinted with permission.)

Large, Gross, or Locomotor   Small, Fine, or Manipulative

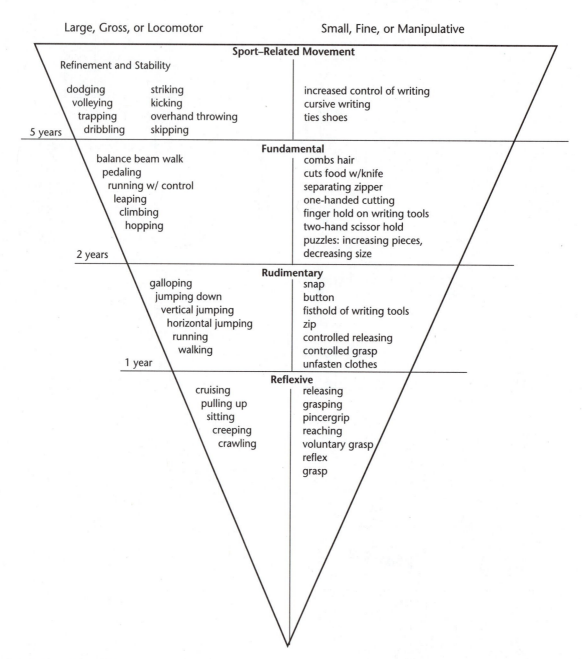

Figure 3.5 Muscle and Motor Development

during the preschool years. It forms the basis for refinements that are used in all active sports.

Exercise: List all the factors you can think of that affect physical development.

Now read on and see how many correlate to your list.

Many factors affect growth and development:

- Genetics determines thousands of characteristics of growth and development, such as body size, sex, and coloring.

- Prenatal care, including the mother's nutrition and physical condition, and even age, contribute to prebirth growth and development.

- Health factors, such as preventive care, diseases, illnesses, and accidents in childhood, can affect both the growth and development of the body.

- Environmental factors, such as nutrition, quality of air, and geographic location, affect physical growth and development.

- Age or maturation is a determining factor in the changing body's size and development.

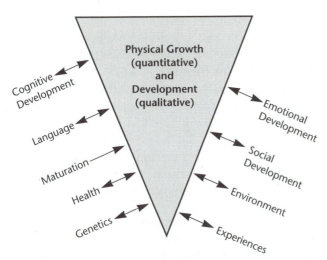

Figure 3.6 Interrelated Factors in Physical Growth and Development

- Social factors, such as opportunities, experiences, and role models, affect development.
- Economic level has an effect on both physical growth and development through nutrition, experiences, and opportunities.

Other areas of development have a two-way influence:

- Cognitive development affects physical development. As the child's thinking changes to higher levels, her movements change. She can do a more complex puzzle, not just because of physical dexterity but ability to visualize pieces of the whole. It is also through physically manipulating materials that the child's cognitive structures build, experiencing soft and hard, hot and cold.
- Language and physical development are interdependent. As the child physically develops, she also learns new vocabulary words for the movements (jump, skip, pirouette). By following verbal directions, processing language, he learns how to perform physical tasks. "Hold the bat up straighter, away from your body."
- Social interactions with other people encourage physical development. By imitating the actions of others, children learn to perform tasks, such as painting, swinging, and riding a bike. As they perform these actions, they interact with other people and their physical development is used to play and work cooperatively.
- Emotional deprivation has been known to stunt physical growth. Emotional development is affected by body growth. Abnormal growth and physical disabilities can affect self-esteem. It influences development because lack of confidence can make someone awkward.

When physical growth or development is adversely affected, whatever the cause, modifications can be made to the environment. This minimizes the social-emotional effects and helps compensate for or improve the skill. This can be accomplished through observation, evaluation, and individualized curriculum planning.

Stages of Physical Development

The common characteristics of development: predictable sequences with individual differences are very evident in physical development.

Predictable Sequence. Development and coordination (voluntary control of the muscles) occur in predictable directions. The infant first gains control of the head, by using neck muscles, then the shoulders and torso. When development reaches the thighs and calves and toes, real crawling and creeping are accomplished. This head-to-toe direction of development is described as **cephalocaudal.** Control of the shoulders and

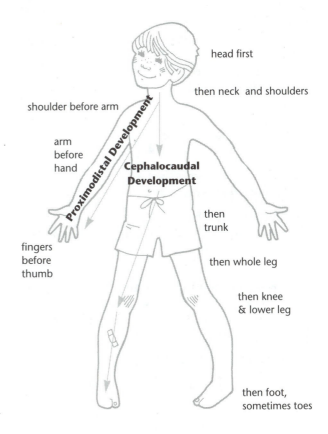

Gaining Control of Muscles in a Downward and Outward Sequence

Figure 3.7 Cephalocaudal and Proximodistal Muscle Development

arms comes before hands, then fingers, from the center of the body outward described as **proximodistal,** or near to far.

Individual Timetable. Some infants purposefully pick up their head and look for the source of a voice or sound by one month. Some do this earlier than others. Some children are walking by 10 months and others not until 16 months. A baby will not walk until she *can*. An adult cannot make a baby walk before the muscles are strong and coordinated enough to accomplish the task.

Readiness. Physical development vividly illustrates the predictable, sequential, individual aspects of development. In other areas of development such as emotional and cognitive development, the stages are not as easily observed. This visual reminder is an important concept to apply to curriculum planning in all areas. The child's body and mind must be ready before they can accomplish the skill. All the other steps have come before it to lead the way, serving as a benchmark of readiness for the next step.

By the age of one and a half, a child has accomplished the basic physical skills of mobility (**large muscle** or gross motor) and manipulation (**small muscle** or fine motor). The next 48 months will see vast increases in coordination and integration of all body structures. By the time children are five, they have acquired body control. The skills of walking, running, climbing, balancing, pushing, pulling, lifting, carrying, throwing, catching, and striking prepare them for life functions and all the sports and recreation skills.

The Role of Observation in Physical Development

Exercise: Watch two people walk across the room. Write a description of how each one walks. What contributed to the differences?

Observation and Recording for Assessment. Watching children move gives the observer information, leading knowledge, and theories about the contributing factors:

height—parents' height, ethnicity

weight—nutrition, metabolism, television habits, parents' physical fitness

movement—age, experiences, inherited capabilities, self-esteem, physical energy level, possible disabilities

Written observations provide documentation for comparisons over time to show progress. From observations, assessments may be made as to the child's growth and development. Further evaluations may be recommended if assessments indicate results fall below the normal range.

Observation for Safety Maintenance. It is the adult's responsibility to prepare a safe environment for children.

Exercise: Using a separate sheet of paper, list five safety features you would plan if you were designing a room for young children.

Accidents occur frequently in the early years because of increased mobility, lack of coordination, inability to anticipate and avoid dangerous actions, or lack of supervision. The newly mobile infant requires crawling surfaces that are sanitary and safe from ingestible objects. Beds and changing tables must have high sides, safety straps, and adult supervision. For the infant and toddler, surrounding equipment must be a stable base as the standing infant pulls himself up. He uses furniture for handles and stabilizers as he begins to walk around. Climbing on objects not meant to be climbed can be dangerous, so the furniture must be secured. Other climbing experiences should be provided, within a manageable range of the child's climbing ability. A soft mat is placed underneath to cushion inevitable falls. All stairways and doorways must be blocked from the little cruiser.

Frost (1992) has devised a Playground Rating System Checklist for Ages 3 to 8 that features criteria on surfaces, equipment, natural aspects, security, storage, safety, and educational usefulness, Figure 3.8.

Exercise: Use the playground Maintenance Checklist to practice Checklist recording and review the criteria for safe environments.

Preschoolers have greater mobility and coordination, increasing the risk of accidents. The independent two-, three-, and four-year-olds have the urge to get things for themselves. Leaving an area, climbing into a cupboard or onto shelves, or attempting tasks beyond their capability and judgment present dangers. Preschoolers need an environment with interesting things to do, opportunities to help themselves in learning centers, and adequate supervision for safety and facilitating play. Then the potential for accidents can be reduced.

Assessing Muscle Development Through the Environment. It is the teacher's role and responsibility to provide a safe environment to meet the developmental needs of the children.

Date Detected	Date Repaired	
		• Hard surfaces under and around equipment in fall zones
		• Resilient surface material pitted or scattered
		• Insufficient space between equipment
		• Equipment not sized for age of children
		• Entrapment areas
		• Excessive or unprotected heights
		• Shearing and crushing mechanisms
		• Cracking, bending, warping, rusting, breaking or missing components
		• Pinching actions, open S hooks, deformed rings, links, etc.
		• Loose or uncapped bolts, nuts, etc.
		• Worn bearings or axles
		• Worn swing hangers (swivels) or chains
		• Metal slides in direct path of sun
		• Slide beds loose, metal edges accessible to fingers
		• Heavy swing seats or seats with protruding elements
		• Exposed or damaged concrete footings
		• Equipment improperly anchored
		• Sharp edges and points
		• Exposed or projecting elements, caps missing
		• Railings of insufficient height
		• Railings invite climbing (horizontal instead of vertical)
		• Exposed metal in tires or swing seats
		• Suspended elements (e.g., ropes, cables) in movement areas
		• Deteriorated (splintered, cracked, rotting) wood
		• Broken or missing railings, steps, swing seats, rungs, deck components, etc.
		• Slippery footing areas on decks, steps, walkways
		• Trash (broken glass, foreign objects, etc.) in area
		• Vandalism (fire damage, broken or missing parts)
		• Obstacles (rocks, roots, trash, badly placed equipment) in movement area
		• Poor drainage (standing water)
		• Accessible electrical apparatus (air conditioners, switch boxes) climbable poles, guy wires, ladders accessing electrical lines
		• Fence not installed or in need of repair, gates not securable (younger children), extra protection for pools
		• Signs illegible and in poor repair
		• Moving parts not lubricated
		• Toxic materials
		• Foreign materials or equipment parts in fall zone

Figure 3.8 Maintenance Checklist. (Courtesy of Frost, J. L., 1992, pp. 348, 349. *Play and Playscapes*. Albany, NY: Delmar Publishers. Reprinted with permission.)

Usually the classroom space is predetermined so the teacher makes decisions of furnishings and room arrangement based on teaching philosophies and priorities for space.

Indoor Play. Lack of space is the reason given by many teachers for not including classroom space for a large muscle area. A climber, space to jump, tumble, and run require open, nonfurnished areas. A clear floor space of 35 square feet per child is the minimum needed for toddlers and preschoolers. Less than 25 square feet of usable space was found to reduce gross motor activity and group play and increase aggression (Smith & Connolly, 1980).

Designer of innovative developmental environmental facilities for children, Ania Rui Olds (1994), bases designs on three essentials:

1. Extensive experiences in the natural world and the inclusion of natural elements indoors
2. Identifiable places for gross motor play inside
3. Use of lofts and varied types of equipment to encourage children's use of their bodies continuously (p. 34)

In the physical environment, the adult assures safety, provides opportunities, and gives support. The developing skill determines the environment, Figure 3.9, that includes all the skill opportunities that have already been attained so they can be refined and practiced. New experiences are added to the old.

Outdoor Play. The outdoor environment should also be considered to maximize development.

Exercise: If you were designing a playground for infants, what kinds of equipment and surfaces would it have?

Crawlers and walkers need materials that are safe and soft for first crawling and walking efforts indoors and out. Carriage and stroller paths past interesting things to look at begin the infant's outdoor experience. Paths later can be used for toddling, walking, and wheeled toys. Gentle inclines provide climbing and rolling down fun. A variety of natural materials such as grass, sand, wood, and smooth rocks provide sensory experiences in texture. Wind chimes, birdfeeders, and portable tape players provide hearing experiences. The area is enriched with a variety of toys for manipulation, pretend play, and construction, Figure 3.10.

Preschoolers need the same type of equipment and surfaces as the younger children but more challenging and separate. They need climbing

SKILL	ENVIRONMENT
Infants	
Rhythmic movement	Rocking chair, music
Crawling	Clean, cushioned surfaces to crawl on, under, through
Pulling up/standing	Stable furniture to hold
Walking, holding on (cruising)	Furnishings placed close together
Walking alone	Smooth, nonslip carpeted surface
Climbing	Low, padded platforms with padded surface beneath
Pushing, pulling, and lifting	Movable materials, tubs, wheeled toys
Toddlers: Above plus	
Climbing	More challenging apparatus, three or four stairs with railing
Scooting	Wheeled toys
Running	Clear, carpeted area for running
Jumping	Sturdy, low platforms
Pushing, pulling, and lifting	Heavier, movable equipment
Throwing	Large, lightweight balls
Preschoolers: Above plus	
Balancing	Climbing and balance apparatus
Pedalling	Tricycles, scooters
Hopping	Floor games and patterns
Throwing and catching	Balls and beanbags, targets
Striking	Bats, rackets, foam balls, wiffle balls suspended from ceiling
Schoolagers: Above plus	
Dribbling and Shooting	Basketballs, baskets, and court
Running races	Team games
Gymnastics	Padded surface, horse, and parallel bars
Dancing	Rhythmic group dancing

Figure 3.9 Developing skills determine the environment.

Figure 3.10 Even the littlest ones need an enriched outdoor environment full of sights, sounds, and a variety of textures.

apparatus and balancing equipment. They need steep hills to climb and roll down and movable construction materials. Riding toys, swings, and sports equipment such as balls, bats, nets, and ropes also facilitate physical development.

Physically challenged children can use the paths for wheelchairs and raised water and sand play areas for accessibility. Children with visual impairments are provided tactile and auditory stimulation materials. A real garden provides gross motor exercise as it is dug, raked, and weeded; it also encourages science, language, and sensory pleasure.

Observation for Curriculum Planning. For infants, body awareness, learning names for the parts of the body, and naming parts as they are washed and moved are the beginnings of large muscle curriculum. Using the developmental assessment Checklist, the adult can see what the child has accomplished and continue to give her practice to refine that skill. If she can roll over, then she is frequently placed on the floor and coaxed, called, lured by a toy, or gently rocked to practice the rolling. She will be sitting up soon, so she can be propped in a sitting position several times a day for short periods to give her a new view. Moving to a beat is an important curriculum goal, so music, rhythm instruments, singing, and dancing are planned daily.

Older infants and toddlers begin the quest to explore beyond their body. Toys and activities to manipulate and move are a necessary part of the curriculum. Activities are planned for interaction with adults and materials chosen to keep interest. The adult models and introduces new ways of playing.

Locomotor movement, such as creeping and crawling, transfers weight from one side of the body to the other. This is a necessary skill for walking because all the more complex skills build on that one. To stimulate creeping and crawling, interesting objects and pictures are placed at floor level, not too far away to be frustrating, but alluring enough to produce forward motion. Crawlers want interesting things to crawl on, such as unbreakable mirrors or pictures under sheets of plexiglass on the floor. A texture maze on the floor and up the first two feet of the wall are stimulating environments planned for infant and toddler motor development. Feeling the steady beat, Weikert (1987) believes, is a primary ability to basic motor skill development so those games of "Patty Cake" and baby rumbas are planned curriculum activities. Reading poetry, repeating fingerplays, and reading stories with repetitive lines provide verbal experiences with rhythm.

For preschoolers, Hall and Esser's useful book of activities for four- to eight-year-olds *Until the Whistle Blows* (1976) suggests large muscle curriculum consists of activities that address the following components of fitness:

- strength—working together to lift and move heavy objects
- coordination—obstacle courses that involve multiple movements such as climbing, crawling, and balance
- flexibility—bending, stretching, and dramatic movement
- stamina—increasing number of repetitive movements
- speed—moving quickly, stopping accurately
- equilibrium—balance beam, walking backward
- power—kicking balls, batting balloons
- cardiovascular recovery—cool down to normal heartbeat through relaxation techniques (p. 10)

Planned activities can be documented using different methods to indicate the child's reaction to the experiences and development of skills. Over time, this record becomes valuable evidence of the efforts and celebrations of accomplishments. The developmental Checklists show skills for practicing to improve and the next skill that is to be introduced and encouraged. Vygotsky (1978) calls this the zone of proximal development, the "distance between the actual developmental level... and the level of potential development... under adult guidance or in collaboration with more capable peers" (p. 86). With the help of an adult or another child, the developing child can approximate the skill before he really can accomplish it on his own. This brings the promise, the feeling of success, and builds rapport with those who support the attempt.

The curriculum is individualized by referring to assessments to determine the level of motor development each child has attained. Daily plans for the whole group would include a variety of large muscle activities. They address the key experiences previously discussed. Individual children benefit from specifically focused activities to help them achieve the next level of development. They must, however, have many opportunities for success at their present level without feeling pressured or required to try something they are not sure they will attain. The skillful teacher uses a blend of addressing needs by combining it with interests like the song line "a little bit of sugar makes the medicine go down."

Planning for exceptional children will build on the abilities they do have. The curriculum is adapted so they have the closest match to what the rest of the class is doing. This is what is known as the **least restrictive environment.** If the class is marching, the child in the wheelchair can push along in the parade or beat the drum. The child with a hearing impairment can watch the beat being tapped out and feel the vibration of the drum. The child who does not speak can lead the band. The child who is visually impaired can play an instrument in one location. The child who speaks no English can move and play with everyone else.

Share Observations with Children and Parents. Relating observations to parents not only informs them of the child's activity that day but is an opportunity to teach child development principles and raise the child's self esteem.

Exercise: How do you think a child would feel about the following comments?

"Now you can stand up all by yourself!"

"Look at that big girl sitting up! You're so strong."

"You worked so hard at that balance beam today."

"You climbed to the top of the climber today. How did it feel up there?"

Accomplishments, as well as attempts, should be relayed to the child and the parents. Telling parents good news in front of the child is a self-esteem booster for both of them. When the formal observation documentation such as Checklists or Anecdotal Records are shown or given to parents, they see the progress and become involved in setting goals and strategies for the next skill or level. If the assessment indicates a significant developmental lag or regression, the parent is consulted in private.

This is to determine if this coincides with what they have observed. Then a follow-up action can be decided. It may be just to wait a while for the skill to develop or to seek further advice depending on the situation and parental decision.

Differences Between Girls and Boys

Exercise: How are boys and girls different besides anatomy?

Physiologically, men are stronger than women but women have greater endurance. There are other differences seen very early in life. Male one-year-olds already spend more time in gross motor activities while girls of that age spend more time in fine motor activities.

The social treatment of girls and boys, regarding toys and movement, begins very early. It is virtually impossible to control for that factor. This makes it difficult to determine what indeed is genetic and what is learned. Many studies have shown gender differences in toy selection, adult interactions with girls and boys, fantasy play themes and types of play. Boys were found to be more aggressive, Figure 3.11, and girls more domestic, boys more physical and girls more verbal. The exact cause of those differences is still under debate.

Figure 3.11 Boys engage in more rough-and-tumble play.

Exercise: How does this picture make you feel? What would you do if you were the adult in charge?

Because early childhood care and education is a field with predominately female personnel, their own genetic and social predispositions guide play expectations for girls and boys. That subtle bias can be seen in the low priority for large muscle equipment and curriculum in early childhood programs. Often female personnel give quick responses and attempt to discourage rough-and-tumble play in the classroom. The biases are not so subtle in comments such as "Boys don't cry," or "Young ladies don't do that."

Pellegrini and Perlmutter (1988) have done longitudinal studies of rough-and-tumble play, defined as active physical running and wrestling accompanied by laughter rather than frowning and hitting. Rough-and-tumble play is not about territories or possessions with participants taking turns as victim and victimizer. Their studies found that rough-and-tumble play was engaged in typically by boys who had high social skills. They contend observation of rough-and-tumble play can be a social competence indicator. It leads to games with rules, role taking, and problem solving. Its use with established guidelines is promoted by Porter (1994). He claims it is a safe, fun activity to be encouraged as "a natural expression of children's exuberance, joy, and affection for each other" (p. 45). The implications give early childhood educators issues to consider.

- Does the environment meet the large muscle needs of all the children in the class?
- What is the response of adults when children are spontaneously using large muscles to run, wrestle, or pretend to box in the classroom?
- Is the dramatic play area designed to attract domestic players and not active players, thereby reinforcing the sex stereotypic play?
- Do children wear casual clothing for physical, indoor, and outdoor activities?
- Do adults wear casual clothing for physical, indoor, and outdoor activities?

Why Physical Development Is Important

Early physical development and fitness affects lifelong health in areas such as posture, balance, muscular strength, cardiovascular endurance, and body leanness. Declining fitness and increasing obesity are national concerns. The American Academy of Pediatrics gives today's children a poor fitness report card.

- Children today are less fit than they were 20 years ago.
- Up to 50 percent of American children are not getting enough exercise to develop healthy hearts and lungs.
- Forty percent of five- to eight-year-old children show at least one risk factor for heart disease—

elevated blood pressure, high cholesterol, or physical inactivity (as cited in Javernick, 1988).

There are many theories about the factors leading to this physical decline. Television, and now video watching and game playing, and computers have been attributed as a major contribution to obesity. Because of children's inactivity and advertisements for high-calorie, fat-laden foods, television is blamed. Changes in family structures with both parents working outside the home turning child-rearing over to others, or to the children themselves, have been blamed for children not playing actively. Violence in the neighborhood has kept some children from playgrounds or playing outside in the street or yard. Schools have been reducing the emphasis on physical education as mandates for academic areas and budgetary woes increase.

Many blame the teacher. Institutions of higher education in teacher preparation were indicted by Gallahue (1982) when he says

> The vast majority of educators are: (1) poorly informed as to why motor development is important, (2) poorly informed as to what forms of physical activity to include in their programs, and (3) inadequately prepared as to how to go about such a task." (p. 366)

Phyllis Weikart (1987) of High/Scope Foundation agrees. A questionnaire she administered to workshop participants with baccalaureate degrees found "fewer than 38 percent, however, had received any type of formal training in movement, and fewer than one-third had attended early childhood movement workshops, or read any books about movement, or had access to a movement consultant" (p. 6).

The teacher's role during playground duty is understood to be supervisory rather than supportive or enriching. Javernick's (1988) study of childhood obesity found that few teachers make an effort to include all children in physical activities or observe carefully to see that especially overweight children participate. She says "merely monitoring children on the playground does not encourage overweight children to be physically active" (p. 19). Too many programs rely on outside free play or a period of free play or time in a gym for motor development.

Scofield (1987) in *School Age NOTES* points out the uses and abuses of free play, Figure 3.12.

Free play in a well-equipped area is important. Programs should also provide an appropriate movement curriculum to develop physical fitness and perceptual motor activities (Poest, et al., 1990). Even for children with severe disabilities,

---

USES OF FREE PLAY

- Free play increases creativity.

- Children learn to set own limits, accept responsibility for operating within those limits, and develop a sense of independence and competency.

- It provides time for one-to-one relationship building of staff to children.

- It provides time for observation of particular children or groups of children and their interests and interactions.

ABUSES OF FREE PLAY

- Not enough activities or raw materials are provided

- Caregivers begin to see it as a "break" for themselves, then become resentful when children want their attention while they are gossiping or reading the paper.

Figure 3.12 Uses of Free Play. (Courtesy of Scofield, R. T. *School-Age NOTES,* 1987. Nashville, TN. Reprinted with permission.)

---

formal psychomotor programs were not as effective as training specific to diagnosis of individual needs. These were most effective when planned individually for children, conducted by the child's teacher and in close communication with parents (Frost, 1992). That is exactly a description of observation, assessment, and individualized curriculum planning with parent involvement. That is appropriate and effective for all children.

Weikart (1987) says early movement experiences have the potential to enhance self-image, and successful movement experiences encourage children to try new experiences. This ultimately affects their academic potential. She has designed movement curriculum around eight experiences as key not only for motor development but visual and aural comprehension. They bring an awareness of rhythm and development of a positive self-concept:

- following simple directions to visual, aural, tactile cues
- describing movements
- moving the body without transferring weight
- weight transfer, such as walking and jumping
- moving with objects—carrying beanbags or scarves
- expressing creativity in movement—fly like a bird

- feeling and expressing a beat—parachute or lumi sticks
- moving with others to a common beat—rhythm band; simple folk music steps (pp. 11, 12)

Researchers say the social and emotional effects of large muscle skills are children's views of themselves and their perceptions of how others feel about them (Gallahue, 1987; Purkey, 1970; Coakley, 1990). Success-oriented physical education not only meets the child's need for motor skill development but the social-emotional development qualities of competence, belonging, and self-worth (Weiller & Richardson, 1993).

Small Muscle Development

The coordinated functions of arm, hand, and fingers are taken for granted.

Exercise: Pick up each of the following items: chair, book, dime, hair. Perform each of the following tasks: zip a zipper; tie a shoe; write your name. Now perform the above tasks with your nondominant hand. Notice the different movements and functions of your small muscles.

For the first few months of life, the small muscles of hands and feet are moved by **reflexes,** rather than purposeful movements controlled by thought. Apply pressure to the palms of the infant and her mouth opens and her head flexes forward (Babkin reflex). Stroke her palm and her hand closes into a grip around the object so strong it can hold her weight. Stroke the sole of her foot and her toes extend. Over the course of the first year, the infant develops control over these small muscles, first by reaching, corralling, and grasping with the entire hand. By one-year-old, the infant can use the thumb and forefinger in a pincer grasp. Letting go, or releasing, comes later than grasping. This explains why an infant holding onto an earring or a lock of hair has a hard time letting go of it.

These small muscle skills are connected to eye and hand coordination, the cephalocaudal and proximal distal development of the whole body, and thought processes. They will continue to develop in the more specific motions needed to twist, squeeze, pinch, button, snap, zip, pour, pick up small objects, insert, and cut. All of these skills are leading to the achievement of readiness to write. Other developmental skills also signal that the child is ready for writing:

Balance without using the hands
Grasp and release objects voluntarily

Handedness predominates with one hand leading and the other following
Eye-hand coordination
Construction experiences—putting things together, parts and whole concept
Increased attention span

The developmental sequence is

Scribbling, holding tool in a hammer hold
Scribbling, with finger hold
Control of tool to close a circle shape
Making straight lines
Drawing with the characteristics of writing
Beginning of alphabet letters
Ability to make a square
Printing name—in upper case letters
Printing name—in upper and lower case
Left-to-right progression of letters and words

Observing Small Muscle Development. The physical environment includes materials and opportunities for the child to practice small muscle skills. The baby touches and grasps any objects within its reach, appropriate or not, grandpa's glasses, a hot coffee cup, or a dust mote floating through the air. The toddler grabs, carries, dumps, fills, manipulates whatever is movable: toilet paper, stones in the driveway, knick knacks on the coffee table, or items on the supermarket shelf. The preschooler practices writing with whatever tools are available, a stick in the dust, Mommy's lipstick, or a paintbrush in tar. The important observer role is to watch what the child is touching, then evaluate its potential for harm. If necessary, the adult intervenes before damage is done to the child, the object, or the environment.

The observer in an educational setting sees the movements as indicators of development and documents what the child can do on this date so that periodically the record is updated to check if progress is being made. Knowledge of the child's abilities at this stage influences the kinds of equipment, materials, and activities the teacher provides. An infant is given items that are easy to grasp and gives some immediate signal such as a rattle, toy with a bell or squeak. The toddler is given items to stack, fill and dump, pound, squeeze, and manipulate such as Play Doh and puzzles with simple, large pieces. The preschooler is provided with smaller manipulatives, such as building bricks, smaller piece puzzles, lacing cards, scissors and a wide array of writing tools and papers.

Documentation of small muscle development can be made with Checklists, Anecdotal Records, and samples of the child's work on paper. The first scribbles, the first alphabet letters, the first name writing, the first "I love you" note are precious and graphic illustrations of the small muscle development as it leads to literacy. These are important evidence to be added to the portfolio and shared with parents to illustrate the child's small muscle development. Stages of small muscle development also are integrally involved in both art and literacy and are discussed again in later chapters.

IT HAPPENED TO ME:
He Sure Can Cut!

We had been working with Andy's small muscle skills, finding ways to interest him in trying some cutting instead of always playing with blocks and on the climber. We found some construction machinery catalogs and invited him to cut and paste to make a book to take home. He worked for several days at it and we saw those cutting skills improve so dramatically we sent home a "Happy Note" about the news. Mom came in a few days later and said, "You know those cutting skills you've been working on with Andy? He's been working on them at home too. He got the scissors and cut up all the chains in my jewelry box into little pieces!" Gulp! Teaching should come with disclaimers, "We cannot be responsible for the application of newly learned skills in a nonsupervised environment."

SPECIAL POPULATIONS AND PHYSICAL DEVELOPMENT

Adapting the environment for children with special needs already has been addressed. Just as any other child, the basis for planning curriculum begins with the assessment of where the child is in that developmental area. More information is usually present about the area of disability, from parental information and the child's file with reports from helping professionals. It is in the areas other than the one affected that the observer needs to attune. It sometimes is the bias or unconscious attitude that other developmental areas are similarly affected. That is not true. Other areas could be right at the age or stage level with other children. They could just as easily be advanced. Objective observation and recording, without bias concerning the disability, is important.

Non-English-speaking children, and children of diverse cultures are usually no different physically than others in the group. It may be in the communication of expectations with both groups that any difficulties may arise. Modeling and acceptance will help all children feel the freedom to try physical activities.

HELPING PROFESSIONALS FOR PHYSICAL DEVELOPMENT CONCERNS

If observation reveals a developmental lag, the parents are consulted, following confirmation by others on the team. They can be referred to their medical helper, such as the pediatrician, for evaluation. Others who may become involved in evaluations of physical developmental lags follow.

occupational therapist—a specialist who evaluates activities of daily living (feeding or dressing themselves) and provides therapy for assisting in the mastery of these activities

neurologist—a physician who specializes in the diagnosis and treatment of disorders of the nervous system, treating symptoms of pain and motor impairments

physical therapist—a specialist who evaluates capabilities for standing, sitting, and ambulation and provides therapy for people who have problems with these functions

Week 3, Assignment A

CHECKLIST ON MOTOR DEVELOPMENT FOR ALL

Copy the age-appropriate Frost-Wortham Developmental Checklist (1992) for each child in the class. The Checklists are included in Appendix D. If these do not fit your group's age or developmental stage, or if your program is already using some other developmental Checklist, substitute the forms in this assignment.

Enter the child's name and age. Assess large and small muscle development this week as the children play and work.

What to Do with It

Enter on the portfolio overview sheet that the Checklist on physical development has been used, the recorder's name (you), and the date. Place the Checklist in each child's portfolio.

Share the child's accomplishments with the parents and the child, if appropriate. For example: "This week we are closely observing the child's muscle development and coordination. I noticed Madeline can skip, walk downstairs using alternating feet, and balance on one leg for several seconds. Those are unusual skills for one not yet four years old," or "Frank, I noticed that you can cut

PHYSICAL DEVELOPMENT		
Documentation	Recorder	Date
CK Lg OK Sm no cutting writing	BAN	9/19
CK Lg-balance? Sm. cut-slash		12/12
CK Lg-fine, skip Sm. cut fine		5/16

Figure 3.13 Portfolio Overview Example

with scissors with either your left hand or your right hand. Do you write better with one hand or the other? Can you show me?"

If a significant lag appears, discuss it with your supervisor to confirm it, then with the parents. Together you can decide on a course of action.

Look at the next level or skill to be developed for each child. Plan activities to encourage that skill, especially inviting this child to participate. Make a note of the child's response. For example, "Monday—put out new building blocks, invite Ben and X, and Y, and Z. Ben worked with blocks for three minutes but had difficulty. I took out the larger blocks, which he worked with for seven minutes."

Date these notes and place them in the child's portfolio.

Week 3, Assignment B

ANECDOTAL RECORDING MUSCLE DEVELOPMENT FOR GROUP B

Select children in group B. On Monday observe the first child in group B, looking for an episode demonstrating physical development. Write an Anecdotal Recording with as many details about how the child moves and uses the body. If the child makes any comments about physical ability, be sure to note it word for word. Comment in the right column on the significance of this event. Was it usual or unusual, above or below expected level for this age? Give some possible contributing factors if you know them. The reader should have the feeling of seeing the episode through your eyes. On Tuesday observe the next child, planning so that by the end of the week, each child in group B has an Anecdotal Recording on muscle development in the portfolio.

What to Do with It

On the child's portfolio overview, note the Anecdotal Record is being included, your name as recorder, and the date. (See the preceding portfolio overview entry.)

Share the recording with the child's parents and the child, if appropriate. For example, "Megan traced her hand and cut it out today. That's quite a difficult task for a three-year-old, but she did it." File the Anecdotal Recordings in each child's portfolio.

If a significant lag is indicated, speak with your supervisor. Discuss with the parent to decide on a course of action.

Plan specific curriculum activities to practice the accomplished skill and next-level skills to give experiences to develop with help.

Week 3, Assignment C

REFLECTIVE JOURNAL

Respond to the following in your Reflective Journal, kept in a private file at home.

Physical activities in my daily routine include…

In thinking about physical development, my own large muscle skills are…

My small muscle skills are…

I think I'm this way because…

It's affected other areas of my life by…

REFERENCES

Allen, K. E. & Marotz, L. (1994). *Developmental profiles: PreBirth through eight.* Albany, NY: Delmar Publishers.

Beaty, J. (1994). *Observing development of the young child, 3rd edition.* New York: Macmillan Publishing Co.

Bentzen, W. R. (1993). *Seeing young children: A guide to observing and recording behavior.* Albany, NY: Delmar Publishers.

Brigance, A. H. (1991). *Brigance diagnostic inventory of early development.* Woburge, MA: Curriculum Associates, Inc.

Coakley, J. J. (1990). *Sport and society: Issues and controversies.* 4th ed. St. Louis: Mosby.

Frankenburg, W. K., Dodds, J. B., & Fandal, A. W. (1990). Denver Developmental Screening II (DDST-II). Denver: Denver Developmental Materials, Inc.

Frost, J. (1992). *Play and playscapes.* Albany, NY: Delmar Publishers.

Gallahue, D. L. (1987). *Developmental physical education for today's elementary school children.* New York: Macmillan.

Hall, N. H & Esser, J. H. (1976). *Until the whistle blows.* Santa Monica, CA: Goodyear Publishing Co.

High/Scope Educational Research Foundation. (1987). Child Observation Record (COR) and Child Assessment Record (CAR). Ypsilanti, MI: High/Scope Educational Research Foundation.

Ireton, H. (1992). *Child Development Inventory (CDI).* Minneapolis, MN: Behavioral Science Systems.

Javernick, E. (1988). Johnny's not jumping: Can we help obese children? *Young Children, 43* (2).

Marotz, L. R., Rush, J. M., & Cross, M. Z. (1989). *Health, Safety & Nutrition for the Young child, 2nd Edition.* Albany, NY: Delmar Publishers.

Meisels, S., Jablon, J. Marsden, D., Dichtmiller, D., & Dorfman, A. (1994). *The work sampling system.* Ann Arbor, MI: Rebus Planning Associates, Inc.

Olds, A. R. (1994). From cartwheels to caterpillars: Children's need to move indoors and out. *Child Care Information Exchange, 96,* May/June 1994.

Pelligrini, A. D. & Perlmutter, J. D. (1988). Rough-and-tumble play on the elementary school playground. *Young Children 43* (2).

Poest, C. A., Williams, J. F, Witt, D. D., & Atwood, M. E. (1990). Challenge me to move: Large muscle development in young children. *Young Children 45* (5).

Porter, R. (1994). Roughhousing as a style of play. *Child Care Information Exchange 96,* May/June 1994.

Purkey, W. W. (1970). *Self-concept and social achievement.* Englewood Cliffs, NJ: Prentice Hall.

Scofield, R. (1987). The uses and abuses of free play. *School Age NOTES,* Nashville, TN: School Age NOTES.

Smith, P. K. & Connolly, K. J. (1980). The ecology of preschool behavior. Cambridge, England: Cambridge University Press cited in J. E. Johnson, J. F. Christie, & T. D. Yawkey, (Eds.) *Play and early childhood development.* 1987. New York: Harper Collins Publishers.

Vygotsky, L. S. (1978). *Mind in society: The development of higher psychological processes.* Cambridge, MA: Harvard University Press.

Weikart, Phyllis S. (1987). *Round the circle.* Ypsilanti, MI: High/Scope Press.

Weiller, K. H. & Richardson, P. A. (1993). A program for kids: Success-oriented physical education. *Childhood Education 69* (3).

RESOURCES

Hall, N. H. & Esser, J. H. (1976). *Until the whistle blows.* Santa Monica, CA: Goodyear Publishing Co.

Weikart, P. S. (1987). *Round the circle.* Ypsilanti, MI: High/Scope Press.

Weiller, K. H. & Richardson, P. A. (1993). A program for kids: Success-oriented physical education. *Childhood education 69* (3), Spring, 1993.

Using Running Records to Look at Social Development

IN THIS CHAPTER

✔ Using Running Records

✔ Topics in Observation: "The Stew"

✔ Looking at Social Development

✔ Special Populations and Social Development

✔ Helping Professionals for Social Development Concerns

USING RUNNING RECORDS

Exercise: Read the Running Record that focuses on Larry, Figure 4.1. Cover the right-hand column with a sheet of paper, make comments or inferences about Larry as indicated from this incident.

From the exercise you see that a **Running Record** uses the same technique as the Anecdotal Recording, Figure 4.1. It is a factual, detailed, written account over a span of time. Actions are described and quotes are recorded as precisely as possible. Commentary or interpretation about the recording is written separately from the actual account. The recorder decides to observe and write for a period of time, focusing on one child or one play area. A nonselective narrative documents a specimen of that child or that area's action.

The Running Record is written as the events are happening, while the Anecdotal Recording usually is written shortly after a significant event. The Anecdotal Recording is a little story with a beginning, the action, and an ending. Running Records are indiscriminate, giving a more objective glimpse into a normal (or what may turn out to be abnor-

mal) segment of time. That is not known, however, before the recorder begins to write. Everything that happens in that time segment is recorded: the mundane, the boring, the unexplained. At the end of a time period, the recording stops. This may not necessarily be at the end of the event. A Running Record is like turning on a video and just letting it run for a certain amount of time, recording whatever occurs. A Running Record is the most useful in giving a naturalistic view of a short time in the life of the child.

When a learning center or area of the classroom is the focus of a Running Record, it can evaluate the usefulness of the area and if the area needs any modifications. Particular learning centers or classroom areas are more suitable for viewing specific skills. A Running Record in the large muscle area obviously gives information on children's climbing, running, or jumping skills but also can yield valuable information on social, emotional, and verbal development. Imaginative play, social interactions, and self-concept are illustrated vividly in the dramatic play area as well as the block area. Small muscle skills, literacy development, and social and verbal skills are observed easily in the art

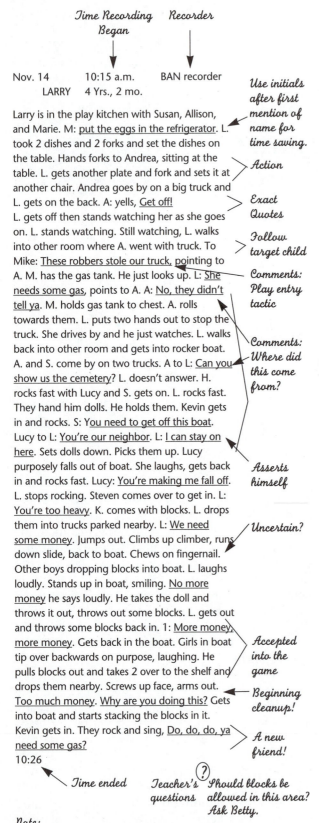

Time Recording Began → *Recorder* →

Nov. 14   10:15 a.m.   BAN recorder
LARRY   4 Yrs., 2 mo.

Use initials after first mention of name for time saving.

Larry is in the play kitchen with Susan, Allison, and Marie. M: <u>put the eggs in the refrigerator</u>. L. took 2 dishes and 2 forks and set the dishes on the table. Hands forks to Andrea, sitting at the table. L. gets another plate and fork and sets it at another chair. Andrea goes by on a big truck and L. gets on the back. A: yells, <u>Get off!</u> L. gets off then stands watching her as she goes on. L. stands watching. Still watching, L. walks into other room where A. went with truck. To Mike: <u>These robbers stole our truck,</u> pointing to A. M. has the gas tank. He just looks up. L: <u>She needs some gas</u>, points to A. A: <u>No, they didn't tell ya</u>. M. holds gas tank to chest. A. rolls towards them. L. puts two hands out to stop the truck. She drives by and he just watches. L. walks back into other room and gets into rocker boat. A. and S. come by on two trucks. A to L: <u>Can you show us the cemetery?</u> L. doesn't answer. H. rocks fast with Lucy and S. gets on. L. rocks fast. They hand him dolls. He holds them. Kevin gets in and rocks. S: <u>You need to get off this boat.</u> Lucy to L: <u>You're our neighbor.</u> L: <u>I can stay on here</u>. Sets dolls down. Picks them up. Lucy purposely falls out of boat. She laughs, gets back in and rocks fast. Lucy: <u>You're making me fall off</u>. L. stops rocking. Steven comes over to get in. L: <u>You're too heavy</u>. K. comes with blocks. L. drops them into trucks parked nearby. L: <u>We need some money</u>. Jumps out. Climbs up climber, runs down slide, back to boat. Chews on fingernail. Other boys dropping blocks into boat. L. laughs loudly. Stands up in boat, smiling. <u>No more money</u> he says loudly. He takes the doll and throws it out, throws out some blocks. L. gets out and throws some blocks back in. 1: <u>More money, more money</u>. Gets back in the boat. Girls in boat tip over backwards on purpose, laughing. He pulls blocks out and takes 2 over to the shelf and drops them nearby. Screws up face, arms out. <u>Too much money. Why are you doing this?</u> Gets into boat and starts stacking the blocks in it. Kevin gets in. They rock and sing, <u>Do, do, do, ya need some gas?</u>

10:26

← *Time ended*

Note:
Bare record could be copied for other children's files if no negative events took place or block other names

Action

Exact Quotes

Follow target child

Comments: Play entry tactic

Comments: Where did this come from?

Asserts himself

Uncertain?

Accepted into the game

Beginning cleanup!

A new friend!

Teacher's questions (?) *Should blocks be allowed in this area? Ask Betty.*

Figure 4.1 Running Record Example

---

area or during play at the sand or water table. Running Records of 10 minutes at any one of these areas can be extremely informative.

The Running Record requires intense concentration and focused attention. Other staff are needed in the room to be sure all children are supervised adequately. Of course, any recording in progress is secondary to a child in need. Anytime recording must be interrupted a line is drawn and the ending and return time is noted. It may be resumed if the situation is now under control.

IT HAPPENED TO ME: Artist's Model?

I was sightseeing on a bus in a foreign country, feeling very special, looking all around at the scenery, when I felt someone watching me. A young man toward the rear of the bus was sketching on a pad. "Oh," I thought, "He's an artist. This country's full of artists. He must be sketching me." So I turned my best side toward him, sat up straighter in the seat, and sat still with a facial expression I wanted captured on his pad. As he was leaving the bus I craned my neck to see the pad. It was a forest scene, apparently from memory, he was working on. Because I thought he was watching me, it changed my behavior.

Exercise: On a separate sheet of paper, describe how you might feel if someone were watching you for 10 minutes and writing notes.

One caution in using the Running Record, or any other recording technique, is the possible effect it may have on the child's behavior, Figure 4.2. It may make them uncomfortable or act in an artificial way. The recorder must be sensitive to that self-consciousness. The writing would then stop and efforts made to be less obvious in the future. In a classroom where observation and recording go on all the time as a natural part of everyday life, children often cease to notice. By showing them the notes, even if they are not yet able to read, they feel more comfortable about the writing. Talking with them about what was observed helps them understand the purpose

Figure 4.2 Observation may change behavior, so the observer attempts to be unobtrusive.

behind the writing. When they hear the teacher talk with their parents about the episodes from the notes, they realize that their actions are important and meaningful. **Warning:** Any negative occurrences or difficulties observed should not be discussed with the parent in the presence of the child.

Uses

The Running Record

- records detailed segments of behavior occurring in a certain time block
- focuses on an individual child to show a naturalistic view of a part of the day
- can be analyzed for evaluation of many developmental areas: physical, social, emotional, language, self-concept, attention span, problem solving, memory, learning style
- documents evaluation of developmental areas for child study
- can focus on a particular learning center or classroom area to see what typically occurs there

Advantages

The Running Record is helpful because it

- details a normal segment of time in the day, giving a more natural view
- reveals many areas of development in one recording
- can evaluate the effectiveness of a Learning Center or area

Disadvantages

The Running Record may

- make the subject feel watched, become uncomfortable, and change behavior, destroying the nature of the recording

- not show in the time segment what normally occurs
- make the adult unavailable to facilitate or observe what is happening in the rest of the room because attention is focused on the recording
- Tire and drain the recorder because of its intensity

Exercise: Practice writing a Running Record. Take a separate sheet of paper right now, fold it in half, select a person to watch, and write down everything that person does and says for 10 minutes.

Rate your Running Record:

- Did you mention the setting so the reader knows where it took place?
- Did you write the date and time you started?
- Did you write your name on it as the recorder?

Look over the words you used to make sure they described actions, not summarized them, or gave reasons. The words should form mental pictures.

- If you used any of the following words, perhaps you fell in the trap of summarizing: *because, wanted to, tried, saw, played, looked (emotion), noticed, pretended.*
- If more than one person was involved, did you write down the conversation word for word?
- Now go back and on the right column write what judgments you would make about this person's physical, cognitive, social, and emotional development. What did this segment of action show about that person? What questions did it raise about why the person acted that way?

Exercise: The following pages contain Running Records on which to practice. Find the recorder's mistakes, then return to this point and check yourself.

In Figure 4.3 the term *plays* is too generic. The recorder should be specific and mention who else is there. "Talks" is not exact quotes. This was an example of good action description. How does the observer know what A thinks? Exact quotes were not written down. This is 15 minutes of action? The recorder exactly documented pronunciation giving the reader more information about the child.

Read Figure 4.4. "Play a lot" is a summary, there is no documentation. It is a good description of placing blocks, but there are no quotes. "As usual" is an unsubstantiated comment. It could be written in the right-hand column. "Convenient" is a

ABC Center   Ann Wade
4 yr. old class   BAN recorder

Sep. 28

9:30   Ann plays with other children at the sand table. She talks

with Q most of the time.

She picks up a shovel and scoops sand into a sifter,

watching it sprinkle and calling it snow.

When Q. picks up the shovel, Ann thinks she should have it

back so she grabs it away. Q. gets another one. As children

come over, Ann gives them attention and asks them questions.

After a while, Ann skips over to another group of children

she wants to play with. She says, "Hey, watcha doin?"

Figure 4.3 Find the recorder's errors: Running Record #1.

ABC Center   Jimmy Fresno
4 yr old class   BAN recorder

Sep. 29

8:20am. Jimmy and T. are in the block area where they play alot together. J.

places four longer blocks in a square on the rug and tells T. to go

get some more. T. obeys as usual and gets on the big truck, making

motor noises. Scoots over to the convenient block shelf. He picks up

blocks with each hand, loads the truck, then drives it slowly to where

J. has started building. J takes 4 blocks & sets them on end. He

decides he doesn't like it so he gives a vicious kick & knocks them

down. T. jumps up screaming at J. because he is so angry. The

teacher tells J. to help build the building up and he does.

Figure 4.4 Find the recorder's errors: Running Record #2.

ABC Center   Nora Camp
4 yr. old class   BAN recorder

Sep. 30

10:35	After circle time the children had free play. N. and her friend J.
	went over to the block area and dumped the blocks on the floor
	and started playing. They play for about 20 minutes. One girl
	stayed by the blocks while N. wanted the teacher to see their
	building. The teacher said she loved it and the two girls smiled.
	After the teacher walked away, the two girls stared at it, then
	they knocked it down and started to build something new. N. got
	bored then and decided to go over to the dramatic play area.
11:00	

Figure 4.5 Find the recorder's errors: Running Record #3.

judgment. Perhaps the writer set up the room? Movement on the trucks and blocks was well described. How does the writer know J. does not like it? "Vicious" is a subjective term with some bias showing. "Because" is a red flag. The open record only describes action. The reasons for the action or reaction can be written in the right-hand column. What exactly did the teacher say? "Go over and apologize and build that back up!" "Look at T.'s face, He is sad. You knocked over his building. Helping him build it back up is a friendly thing to do."

In Figure 4.5, "started playing" is a summary of their actions with no descriptions. Were they just piling them or making the Eiffel Tower? Twenty minutes of playing should contain more details. How did the recorder know what N. wanted? The teacher's words are lost, and it doesn't matter if she loved it. It should be satisfying to the builder unless she commissioned it to be built. "Got bored," what does that *look* like? "Decided" is another red flag word. A recorder only writes what actually happens, not what is decided. That is determined by the actions.

Running and Anecdotal Records are like written movie camera scripts, exactly describing actions, facial expressions, and exact words of the players.

LOOKING AT SOCIAL DEVELOPMENT

Two children are pulling on the same toy, Figure 4.6. "It's mine!" "No I want it!" An adult comes over, takes it away from one and gives it to the other. "You've got to share! Don't be so selfish."

That is not sharing. That is robbery. That is reinforcing the concept that bigger people can take things away from small people. True sharing is the willing relinquishing of one's rightful possession to another person. But how do children learn not to be so selfish?

The Need for a Selfless Society

Moving from selfish to selfless takes more than changing a few alphabet letters. It is a total transformation from self-centered, immediate

Figure 4.6 Attaining social development is not without its struggles.

gratification to other-centered, altruistic, generosity. The goal of maturity in a moral society is to become less concerned with one's own needs and desires by giving priority to others'. A person, group, or society, which only lives for itself, is constantly in conflict. Often more than one person wants the object or their own opinion to prevail and both cannot be satisfied. From that conflict came the rules of the tribe, then laws. Now laws are so numerous and complex that buildings are needed to hold the books that list and interpret them all. People devote their lives to interpreting, enforcing, changing, and even breaking them. There are also some people in a society who cannot fill their own needs so others are needed to generously help if they are to survive. The task of raising the young to be selfless is for the survival of the society. What a responsibility! This is a long struggle that begins with small steps.

Exercise: Think about how the following laws or rules restrict your freedom for the good of society.

- Only licensed physicians can practice medicine.
- Drive on the right side of the road.
- Items in a store must be exchanged for money.
- Use utensils, not hands, for serving items from the salad bar.
- Buckle up your seat belt in the car.

In caring, teaching, or working with young children, the development of the social domain has a high priority. It does not develop separately from physical, cognitive, emotional areas but simultaneously moves forward, influenced by many of the same factors of genetics, environment, culture, and society. Helping a child to learn the rules of the tribe will help him to function in that group. It is a necessary skill for both physical and psychological well-being.

Exercise: List some social rules, not developed naturally, that children must be taught.

The infant is born being only concerned with its own needs, totally dependent on **reflexes** and signals calling for responses to those signals. The hungry baby never considers the mother's dinner getting cold. The baby crying in the middle of the night pays no heed to parents' early work schedules. The crawler pulls the cat's tail, or the toddler takes a truck from another. The needs and wants of the other person are not deliberated, or weighed, or even considered at all. Years and much growing and developing must take place before the child sees the point of view of the other person. It takes even longer before she can place the other person's needs ahead of her own with generosity and empathy. She has much growing up to do before living up to society's expectations and taking on the responsibility for others. Along that path there are stages, developmental milestones, that can be observed, aided in their arrival by interactions with adults.

Theories of Social Development and Their Implications on Early Childhood Professional Practice

Many in the past have pondered the origins of how people relate to one another. Freud (1953) attributes social behavior to the sexual nature of humans hidden in the subconscious. He saw the strong parental role in developing the superego or conscience to balance the id, demanding satisfaction of desires. The parental influences on the child's knowledge and feelings of right and wrong are deeply ingrained and different from one family to another. It is important for the teacher to know and work cooperatively with parents, reducing the dissonance of differing messages and how to cope with them. Freudian theory also reminds teachers that the child also has a sexual nature. Although they are very young, basic sex roles and attitudes are forming through experiences in early childhood.

Erikson's psychosocial developmental theory (1950) looks at not just biology but the changing

TOPICS IN OBSERVATION: "The Stew"

Once upon a time, two shoppers bought the ingredients to make a stew. They presented the different ingredients to a chef who prepared them, and placed them on the stove to cook. After a period of time, the chef took a deep ladle and sampled a bit of each of the ingredients. The chef judged that some were just right, but others needed more time to cook, so the chef turned up the heat and gave the stew more time. The stew was lacking in flavor so some spices were added. It was too salty so a potato was added to take away some saltiness. The chef still was not satisfied with the taste so she called another chef, a stew expert, to give an opinion. The expert gave some advice and the other chefs followed it.

The stew was done so it was served to the first diner. It happened to be the chef's mother who declared the stew "Marvelous!" The hungry man devoured the stew, which satisfied his hunger. The Board of Health inspector closely examined each part, looking for irregularities, without really caring about the whole stew. The vegetarian, repulsed by the meat in the stew, stopped eating, vowing to make comments to the cooks. One diner thought it needed more salt, while another thought it was too salty. The unserved portions of the stew were refrigerated and reheated the next day with flavors mellowed and texture softer. But alas, some of the diners have moved on to other restaurants so they never got the full, aged taste of the stew. Ah, if they could only taste this stew now!

Meaning:

The stew is the child made up of many areas of development. The parents bring the child to the teacher with knowledge, skills, and abilities. The teacher works with those to bring them to a certain expected level. A sample of the child's development is made to determine further action. In some areas, nothing is needed. In other areas, more time will bring the development to the expected level. Added enrichment and individual planning also may help and strategies to decrease undesirable behavior are enacted. Expert advice is sometimes needed so parents and teachers seek the referral and advice of helping professionals.

Hopefully, the parents are pleased with the progress their child is making. Others with no interest in the child or program may not care. The responsibility of some people, such as fire inspectors or the accountant, is to look minutely at some areas while not seeing the whole child. The child's progress may not suit some people who have particular interests or biases. Over time, the child grows, develops, and changes but those other people do not have the opportunity to enjoy the wonderful progress. The parents and teachers see the change and have a record of the change so they will follow that recipe again. The ingredients are always just a little different so no two stews are ever the same. It is sad that not everyone gets the opportunity to appreciate the transformation from raw ingredients to flavorful stew.

mind and emotions and the effects of society in forming behavior patterns. His Eight Stages of Man illustrates the observable, predictable stages through which humans move. They include the positive task of the social role in each stage. Unlike Freud, who looked into the past to find reasons for pathological behavior, Erikson looked to the future, not giving up hope that the past can be overcome. Erikson's theory also stresses the importance of the adults in understanding and meeting children's needs in each stage. This affects how the child feels about himself and interacts with others.

Piaget's work in cognitive theory (Flavell, 1977) has meaning for children's social development.

Children's thinking governs their actions. As the child takes in new information, the child interprets it differently at different stages. Before the infant reaches **object permanence**, the knowledge that objects exist outside their sight, the infant will not "miss" his mother. Once he has cognitively reached that stage, other people's faces are compared to his mental image of hers and that mismatch results in separation anxiety. The young child is described in Piaget's theory as **egocentric**, only able to see things from his own point of view. "I want this ball so I should have it," and takes the ball from another child. When the adult says "How would you like it if he did that to you?" it has no meaning. He cannot mentally place himself with the ball in his hands with another child taking the ball away. This is just too much abstract cognitive processing for his ability at this stage. This is the underlying factor of social actions in the preschool years: the conflict between what one child wants (and thinks he should have) and that of another. Recognizing this, the adults take many actions, such as having enough duplicate toys that the need for possession is met. Once the child becomes verbal, the adult repeats phrases children can use. These help function socially, such as "You could say, `I want to play with that ball when you're done,'" or "Tell her `I don't like it when you take that away from me.'"

Behaviorists' social learning theory (Skinner, 1953; Watson, 1950) describe how learning takes place when it is reinforced either negatively or positively. This behaviorism is the reason that spanking or punishment works (for a while) and praise causes that behavior to occur again. This is external reinforcement of behavior. Parents and teachers want the child to be *intrinsically motivated*, to do the right thing even when no one is there to say, "Good job," or "No, No." When appropriate recognition for *right* and *wrong* deeds is given, the child sees the results from those actions and forms a thinking process for making choices about right and wrong for next time. Hopefully, the adult does not have to be present for reinforcement for the child to make the *right choice*.

Maslow's work (1970) investigating the causes of behavior also was based on met or unmet needs. His "Hierarchy of Needs" chart is familiar to students of psychology. It has the most basic survival needs at the bottom of the triangle, moving up to social needs, and eventually to self-actualization. This is where satisfaction comes, from serving others rather than self. Physical and psychological safety are necessary for children to develop. Schools have learned that a hungry child cannot learn, so national programs provide nutritious breakfasts and lunches. The physical environment influences behavior so homes, schools, restaurants, arcades, and businesses spend millions of dollars on color, furnishings, lighting, and aesthetics to influence human behavior. The classroom environment is an important factor in learning by attending to the physical and psychological needs of the children and adults. The affective needs of acceptance, recognition, affection, belonging, and love are the work of the curriculum of the social development area. From names on the cubbies, to hugs at the end of the day, children thrive socially in the environment that meets their emotional needs.

Hartup (1992) and many others have studied the importance of peer relationships. The critical social purposes of early childhood education are reinforced by his statement:

> Indeed, the single best childhood predictor of adult adaptation is not IQ, not school grades, and not classroom behavior, but rather, the adequacy with which the child gets along with other children. Children who are generally disliked, who are aggressive and disruptive, who are unable to sustain close relationships with other children, and who cannot establish a place for themselves in the peer culture are seriously at risk.

Implications of Social Learning Theory on Early Childhood Practices. Teachers need to

- work cooperatively and closely with parents
- be aware of the sex role formation in young children
- meet children's needs
- consider child's cognitive level for realistic social expectations
- give appropriate recognition for right and wrong deeds, along with resulting consequences
- assist each child toward social competence

Stages of Social Development

The word *development* indicates the changes that take place in the way the child interacts with other people is qualitative. It is not a change that can be measured in numbers but in refinement. It moves from simple to more complex, in a predictable sequence, but at different rates for individual people, Figure 4.7.

Figure 4.7 Stages of Social Development

Self. The newborn infant (neonate) has no social development. Interactions with other people are governed by reflexes:

Rooting reflex—When stroked on the cheek, the neonate turns towards that side. (It is not to see his mother better.)

Babkin reflex—When the palms are stimulated, the neonate's fingers curl around it and grasp it. (It is not to play with daddy's finger.)

Walking and stepping reflex—When held so that feet or toes touch the floor, the neonate makes a walking, stepping motion. (It is not to dance with her sister.)

Moro reflex—When a loud noise, bright light, loss of support is experienced, the neonate startles and flings out his arms. (It is not reaching out to be held because he was scared.)

What is the neonate doing socially? The infant can see very well close up, looking at close faces and registering information about what it sees and hears. The baby's kinesthetic sense (body movement and position) is present so the baby senses she is held, rocked, or touched. Babies usually cry less and are soothed by motion. The baby imitates and matches facial expressions. There is a wonderful example of this in the video *Exploring First Feelings* (1980). An adult is holding a newborn and opens her mouth. The baby gazes intently and matches the movement. Some babies right from the start are more gregarious, responsive to others, open to friendly overtures, Figure 4.8. Others are much more serious, reserved, limiting social contacts to just a few people. This personality type affects social interactions, and may be evident throughout the child's life. All areas of development—physical, cognitive, and emotional—are being affected and are affecting social development.

The implications for social development seem clear. The adult role is to meet the baby's needs, first of all in physical care. The infant who has attention and is prompted to respond to coos and words is being prepared for verbal conversations. The environment stimulates cognitive development. Psychological needs are met by being close, and handling the baby gently and responsively. Interactions are initiated and provide an interesting environment that responds to what the baby indicates she likes. These met needs give the infant a secure base from which to emerge into the social realm with the abilities to function in it.

Self-Gratification. During the first year, the infant is focused on receiving what he needs to survive and be happy, whatever that takes. This is

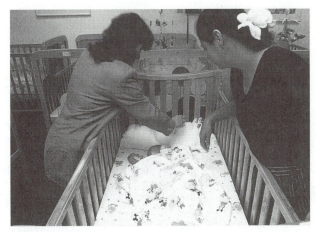

Figure 4.8 Social development begins with the infant's needs being met.

the stage of attachment to his parents and is the beginning of his independence from them. During the first months of life, the baby increases the imitative behavior with smiles and laughs as the adult feeds, dresses, and cares for him. In the second half of the first year, the baby shows separation anxiety, trying to recapture the presence of the ones who meet his needs. He also begins some social exchanges by reaching out his hands and arms to be held, kicking and making noises to gain attention. He is becoming mobile so he now can crawl to mother and pull on her leg. He is beginning to learn that he is no longer allowed to cry, sleep, play, eat, or act by his own desires. He may be put down for a nap when he is not "ready" or be told "No" when he reaches for grandpa's glasses. He cries and uses whatever social skills he has learned to get what he wants. He also is beginning to exert social control by withdrawing, by turning away from the spoon, a plaything, or a smiling auntie, pulling back her social self.

The play that infants engage in during the first year is mainly manipulation. They experience the object in every way possible: touching, squeezing, biting, smelling, shaking to listen, and throwing to see the reaction. A favorite game is Peek-A-Boo, which builds the cognitive structure of what goes away is not gone forever but returns. This game prepares the infant for separation. Another favorite game is throw the toy away and have someone return it. It is a social give and take, action and response. It also reinforces the object permanence, but also that power over other people to do what he wants them to do. It is the precursor for taking turns, sharing, and playing baseball.

This process over the first two years is moving from self to the consideration of others. It is

Phase	Age of Onset in Months	Infant Capabilities	Social Outcome	Function in Individuation Process	Adult Behaviors That Support Individuation
I	0	Sucking, visual tracking; grasping; cuddling	Reflexes	Proximity to mother	Observation of states; prompt basic care
II	1-2	More time quietly alert; sensory learning about people and objects; molding to caregiver's body; continues interesting activities	Mother-infant pair perceived as a unit; beginning social responsiveness; mutual cueing, gazing	Begins differentiation between self and objects; more ways of maintaining proximity	Provide objects; engage in turn taking play; give prompt basic care; respond sensitively to different states
III	4-8	Sits, grasps; creeps; increased interest in objects; sensory learning: mouthing, manipulating, examining, banging, etc.	Recognizes familiar people; shows clear preferences among people; intentionality limited to previously learned actions, playful; social smile, laughter	No self-awareness; beginnings of social expectations; stranger fear; maintains proximity by following, checking back on caregiver after short excursions	Provide a safe environment for floor exploration; establish limit for child; respond predictably
IV	9-12	Walking, climbing, running; joyful exploration; curious, excited; beginning use of language and gesture; person and object permanence becoming clearer; trial-and-error problem solving; intentions conveyed by language, gesture, and action; makes requests	Strong desire for approval, inclined to comply; self-willed; increased self-control; variety of emotions; social play with adults; interest in events	Beginning to recognize that mother is not part of self; maintains proximity by following and calling mother; strong preferences for particular people; protests separation, uses mother as a "base of operations" and moves outward	Protect from hazards (child has mobility without judgment): respond promptly to communicative acts; set and maintain routines and limits; provide opportunity for independence; use language for comfort, explain; leave child with familiar adults; have patience
V	15-24	Increase of all motor tasks; skillful exploration of object, events; rapid increase in language and nonverbal communication skills; likely to carry objects to preferred adults; object permanence achieved at end of phase V	Is likely to cling, then run away; plays "mother chase me!"; self willed: "No" before compliance; considerable amount of self control; self-comforting; may show sudden fear after departure from mother; may cry from relief at her return	Realizes mother's goals are not own goals; may be ambivalent about dependence/independence; can play happily in absence of preferred person; uses "gifts" of toys in seeking proximity, more language	Verbalize about departures, reassure; tolerate rapid changes in approach and withdrawal; use language to discuss events, relationships, objects, etc.; allow child to control some holding on, letting go; make social expectations clear over and over; have patience
VI	24-30	Good understanding of ordinary language; intentionally well developed; mental problem solving; ability to ask for help based on need; goal-directed behavior.	Increasing interest in other children; peer play and communication stronger; mutually regulated social interactions; pretend play	Realistic sense of self and others; uses a wide array of techniques to maintain proximity (helping conversation, play, stories); can cope well with separations	Continue to reassure, support, and provide affection; praise efforts at self-control and independent behavior; provide experience with another toddler

Figure 4.9 The Individuation Process and Appropriate Adult Responses. (Courtesy of Kostelnik, M. J, Stein, L. C., Whiren, A. P., & Soderman, A. K., 1993, p. 34. *Guiding Children's Social Development.* Albany, NY: Delmar Publishers. Reprinted with permission.)

dependent on the infant's capabilities and the supportive adult behaviors. Figure 4.9 graphically portrays the stages, the roles of child and adult, with the desired outcomes (Kostelnik, et al., 1993).

Self-Assertion. In the second year, the child generalizes all other social relationships. She expects that everyone, especially other children, will treat her in the same way as her parents: accepting, acquiescent, providing what she needs and wants. When this does not happen, she cannot understand it.

Language is developing at this time also, so vocabulary and verbal expression come into the social realm. Words and phrases like "No!" "Mine!" and "Gimme" are repeatedly used in social gatherings. "Please" is expected to yield miraculous results with objects or toys being the lure of toddler friendships.

Parten's Stages of Social Play (cited in Rogers & Sawyers, 1988) have long been referred to when classifying the development of social play, Figure 4.10. In **unoccupied play**, the child is not focused on any toy or activity: he follows the adult but does not engage in any sustained way. In **onlooker play**, the child watches other children play but does not get involved. This is used frequently by children in new situations. They can scope out the territory. It is also the style of children who are shy, emotionally depressed, or just not feeling like getting involved. The caregiver attends to both behaviors, assesses possible causes, and decides if action is indicated. The adult may decide to issue an invitation to play. In this way, she can role model how to join in the play. The decision may be to allow the child to have control over joining or not.

Solitary play, playing alone or totally focused on one's own play, is used for manipulation and practice, stress release, or by choice. It is the way of gaining familiarity with a new toy, game, or sports equipment. It is the repetitive motion to make a skill become natural. Many find this relaxing and rewarding.

In **parallel play**, there is minimal social contact. It is not solitary play, but it is not involved either. It involves companionship but not cooperation, affiliation but not association. The young child at this stage is not developmentally able to sustain a higher level of play.

This stage is mainly manipulative, seeing how things work. The developing small muscles are used to twist, insert, pound, shovel, grasp, release, and pinch. The large muscles are used for climbing, pedaling, running, and jumping. The child, at the beginning of this stage, cannot sustain interactive

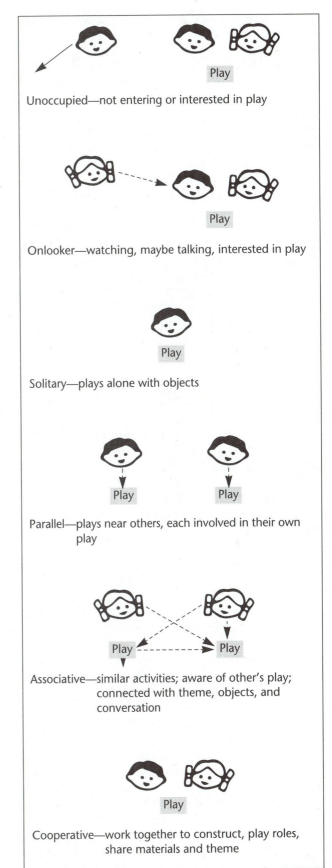

Unoccupied—not entering or interested in play

Onlooker—watching, maybe talking, interested in play

Solitary—plays alone with objects

Parallel—plays near others, each involved in their own play

Associative—similar activities; aware of other's play; connected with theme, objects, and conversation

Cooperative—work together to construct, play roles, share materials and theme

Figure 4.10 The Stages of Social Play

play because of limited language, cognitive, social, and emotional skills. That does not keep the child from seeking out those social contacts. In the second year, walking widens the social world considerably. Now the child can walk over to other children and initiate interactions. Because of social immaturity, however, those overtures to play may be in the form of grabbing a toy, biting, or screaming. The responses may be less than friendly.

By the end of the second year, children have begun to make friends. They recognize other children with whom they have frequent contact. They imitate overtures of affection, such as hugging, kissing, and giving objects to others. Occasionally, they make eye contact, engaging in little conversations. Mostly they are involved in their own play and play objects. Still possessing immature cognitive, social, emotional structures, sharing and turn taking are limited, if present at all. Some very young children have been observed in friendships. Rubin (1980) listed some factors that contributed to these early friendships:

- secure relationships with their mothers
- relationships with older siblings or children
- their mothers were friends
- the children were at similar developmental levels, had similar temperaments, and behavioral styles (pp. 26, 27)

The stages of play are developmental stages that are attained and built upon for the next stage but are revisited again and again through life for various reasons. Regression to an earlier stage is not viewed as peculiar or cause for alarm. The setting, the person's style, and the situation determine how the person will interact.

Besides the stages of play, another dynamic enters play. It is the *how* of play. Four categories of play are seen in the social stages of play, Figure 4.11. In **functional play**, actions are repeated for practice and exploration. A child paints all over the paper, his hands, the legs of the easel. Clay is squeezed, patted, rolled, poked, and cut. Blocks are piled and knocked down, containers filled with them, then dumped. No end product is in mind; it is just manipulation of materials. People do this all the time in sporting goods stores as they take practice swings with golf clubs or baseball bats.

Constructive play produces a product. That manipulation of the paintbrush turns into a recognizable flower. The clay balls are piled on one another and named a "snowman." The blocks are piled, and the builder calls it "The Umpire (sic) State Building."

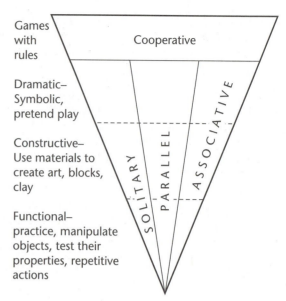

Figure 4.11 Types of Play

Dramatic play takes the player into the world of pretend. The paintbrush becomes a bee buzzing toward the flower, gathering nectar. The snowman is moved along the table, talking to other clay creations and wondering what will happen when the sun comes out. The builder takes a monkey from the jungle set and has King Kong climbing up the building. Participation with or without props, in the world of fantasy, is classified as this type of play.

As children move toward the fifth and sixth years, **games with rules** become part of their play repertoire. This coincides with mathematical reasoning and the social-emotional stage of industry, putting things in order. By this age, children are bringing themselves into control, passing the egocentric stage, so now they can see from another's point of view. This stage also appears at a time when children's language skills are more developed and they are able to play in a more cooperative way.

Self-Initiator. Three-, four-, and five-year-olds are blossoming social beings. They now have the verbal, physical, and cognitive skills to begin to interact more with each other. They engage in **associative play**, doing a similar type of activity, involved in the same play theme or with similar types of toys, but in this stage they still are "doing their own thing." They are not working together toward a common goal, they just happen to be near each other, talking about what each of them is doing.

Cooperative play produces a common product, such as a block building, a road in the sand connecting areas, or dinner in the dramatic area.

All players are working out a common plan. Preschoolers are still in the Preoperational Stage, still egocentric, but they are making advances. The teacher prepares an environment that will enhance social development by providing enough materials so that solitary and parallel play is not thwarted by having to "steal" from others. Cooperation and sharing are planned into the routines and curriculum by such things as helper charts, joint projects, songs, stories, and puppet plays. Competition during this period is not understood, so it is not an appropriate method of group interactions. Games with winners and losers, who can be the best, the fastest, or the neatest reinforce selfish attitudes. Cooperation and concern for others are the major social tasks of this age. Children who have had experiences in rule-making for the classroom and in their enforcement in an acceptable way get along better. They know and understand the reasons for why rules exist. They are careful observers of others who are breaking the rules. This is the beginning of moral development, recognizing right from wrong.

Difficulties between children are best handled not by the teacher as the judge. The teacher's role is facilitator for negotiation, helping those involved to tell each other their point of view. The children decide in a democratic manner.

Excluded children, those who have difficulty being accepted by peers, have some common characteristics. Disliked children often ignore other children's overtures to play, misunderstand peers' emotions, and are aggressive (Kemple, 1992). A strategy to help excluded or disliked children is to pair them with a younger child with whom they can feel more socially confident. Likewise, they may be paired with those who are socially competent as a model. Alternatives to aggressiveness through role plays, books, and puppet plays may give problem-solving ideas to be remembered when conflicts arise.

The Importance of Play to Social Development

Exercise: How do you play?

Play is a part of life, not just for children but for adults as well. Some early childhood programs are criticized for allowing play. "They're not learning anything there. All they ever do is just play." The word *play* is used repeatedly in discussing social development and many other areas as well. An understanding of play and its importance is necessary to child observers because it is a vehicle for learning.

Pugmire-Stoy (1992) captured the value of play in the diagram in Figure 4.12. It illustrates the developmental areas involved in play, kinds of play, its connection with language arts, and the necessary provisions for play. The opposite word from *play* is *work*. The phrase "Play is the child's work," or variations of it, have been the theme or motto for defending play. The constructivist theory (DeVries & Kohlberg 1987) contends it is through play and interaction with the environment that children construct mental images and processes. This is *work* in the sense that it has purpose and a definite goal. When an attempt is made to differentiate play from work, the dividing line becomes blurred. Play has been described and researched by many people. Rubin, Fein, and Vandenberg (1983) formed this description of play:

1. Play is intrinsically motivated.
2. Play is relatively free of externally imposed rules.
3. Play is carried out as if the activity were real.
4. Play focuses on the process rather than any product.
5. Play is dominated by the players.
6. Play requires the active involvement of the players.

It is obvious that play can take place without other people, so solitary play is not just a stage but a type of play. Play with other people involved is democratic, without rules. Each player has some authority over the play. By observing, it is evident that not every player has equal power or as much power as they may want. Conflict in play erupts when the social development of the players is uneven. All the other developmental areas such as cognitive, language, physical, and emotional contribute to play's success.

Observing Play and Social Development

"Kidwatching" (Goodman, 1978) as children interact with each other can be extremely amusing. They reveal so much of themselves and all areas of development as they play. Information on physical, cognitive, language, emotional, and social development can be gathered as children interact with the environment and other people.

Anecdotal and Running Record. Social play observations are caught vividly with Anecdotal and Running Recordings that capture the actions

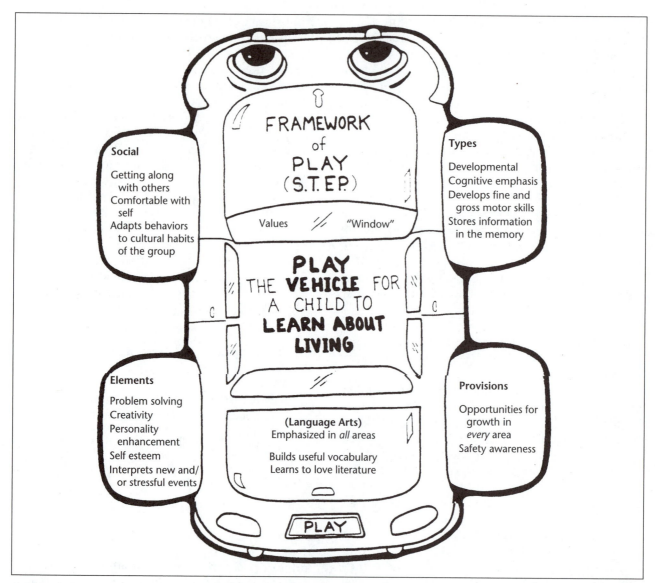

Figure 4.12 Play is the vehicle for learning. (Courtesy of Pugmire-Stoy, M. C., 1992, p. 182. *Spontaneous Play in Early Childhood.* Albany, NY: Delmar Publishers. Reprinted with permission.)

and the words. A narrative gives a lasting memory of an event that can be wrought with meaning to every reader. One of the foremost kidwatchers is Vivian Paley. Her books of Anecdotal Recordings, many about boys and girls in dramatic play, are not only entertaining but full of meaning. In *Boys & Girls: Superheroes in the Doll Corner* (1984), she relates this discussion with the children about where the real work of school is happening in the classroom.

Teacher: The girls think the block area is for play and not for work. Is that what you think?

Jonathan: It *is* for play. But you could be a work person.

Teacher: If you're a work person, then what do you do in the blocks?

Andrew: Build very neatly and don't knock it down and don't play.

Teacher: How can you tell if you're working or playing?

Andrew: No Star Wars or superheroes. None of that stuff.

Paul: No shooting and no robbers.

Jonathan: And no running.

Teacher: What else is work in this room?

Andrew: If you color or put your name on a thing. On a paper.

Paul: It has to be work if you tell us to do something.

Teacher: How about stories? Your own stories. Is that work?

Andrew: No because that could be Star Wars or Superman.

The children are in agreement. Whatever involves fantasy or creates a mess is play. Work is achieved sitting at a table, with a teacher nearby giving orders. (p. 31)[1]

Classifications of Play. Observers of social development should be able to recognize and label social play using Parten's stages (unoccupied, onlooker, solitary, parallel, associative, cooperative) and Smilansky's and Piaget's play categories (functional, constructive, dramatic, games with rules).

Exercise: Using Parten's, Smilansky's and Piaget's terms, classify the following players.

1. Jake and Donald are sitting across from each other, building with separate erector sets. Jake and Donald are in the _____ stage, demonstrating the _____ type of play.
2. Heather, Greg, and Lisa are putting on a puppet play in a cardboard stage. Louise has been watching for several minutes. Louise is in the _____ stage, while Heather, Greg, and Lisa are in the _____ stage, demonstrating_____ type of play.
3. Piku is at the art table making balls of clay and poking them with a pencil. He is in the _____ stage of play, demonstrating _____ type of play.
4. Barry is laying parallel rows of blocks and Birdie is riding a truck back and forth between them. Barry and Birdie are in the _____ stage of play, Barry demonstrating _____ type of play. Birdie is demonstrating_____. She says, "I'm delivering bread to the store." Now her play is _____.

In checking your understanding of the play stages and types, you should have recognized: (1) parallel, constructive, (2) onlooker, cooperative, dramatic; (3) functional, solitary; (4) associative, constructive, functional, dramatic.

Checklists. Most developmental checklists have a section for social play, usually using the stages and types previously mentioned. One that

has been developed to help teachers and parents monitor a child's social behavior is shown in Figure 4.13. It comes with the admonition from the

I. Individual Attributes

The child:
1. Is **usually** in a positive mood
2. Is not **excessively** dependent on the teacher, assistant, or other adults
3. **Usually** comes to the program or setting willingly
4. **Usually** copes with rebuffs and reverses adequately
5. Shows the capacity to empathize
6. Has a positive relationship with one or two peers; shows capacity to really care about them, miss them if absent, etc.
7. Displays the capacity for humor
8. Does not seem to be acutely or chronically lonely

II. Social Skill Attributes

The child **usually**
1. Approaches others positively
2. Expresses wishes and preferences clearly; gives reasons for actions and positions
3. Asserts own rights and needs appropriately
4. Is not easily intimidated by bullies
5. Expresses frustrations and anger effectively and without harming others or property
6. Gains access to ongoing groups at play and work
7. Enters ongoing discussion on the subject; makes relevant contributions to ongoing activities
8. Takes turns fairly easily
9. Shows interest in others; exchanges information with and requests information from others appropriately
10. Negotiates and compromises with others appropriately
11. Does not draw inappropriate attention to self
12. Accepts and enjoys peers and adults of ethnic groups other than his or her own
13. Gains access to ongoing groups at play and work
14. Interacts nonverbally with other children with smiles, waves, nods, etc.

III. Peer Relationship Attributes

The child is
1. **Usually** accepted, versus neglected or rejected, by other children
2. **Sometimes** invited by other children to join them in play, friendship, and work.

Figure 4.13 The Social Attributes Checklist. (Reprinted from McClellan, D. E. & Katz, L. *Young Children's Social Development: A Checklist.* Urbana, IL: ERIC Clearinghouse on Elementary and Early Childhood Education, 1993. EDO-PS-93-6.)

---

1. From Paley, V. G. (1984). *Boys & girls: Superheroes in the doll corner.* Chicago: The University of Chicago Press. Reprinted with permission of author.

authors, McClellan and Katz (1993), that the intent is not to prescribe "correct social behavior." It is to uncover children who may be doing poorly on many items on the list. Those children may have personality and temperament differences that are completely normal for them. Children from diverse cultural and family backgrounds may not *usually* do many of these things. When this checklist shows children are having social difficulties, the teacher assesses the cause and plans for a classroom that is supportive and accepting.

SPECIAL POPULATIONS AND SOCIAL DEVELOPMENT

Social interactions depend heavily on communication. For the child with a hearing loss, this is a barrier. Early involvement with hearing children as social role models and alternative communication techniques are helpful in promoting social development. For the teacher, this also means learning some way to communicate with the child to facilitate social interactions with the child's peers and interpret the classroom environment.

Vision impairment does not necessarily cause social problems but more likely it is society's reaction to the impairment. The more severe the impairment the less negative the reaction, possibly because of the sympathy effect. Children with thick corrective lenses may be rejected as a playmate by other children just from appearances. The teacher can inform children of the nature of the child's vision and how it may affect the child in the classroom, inviting other children's assistance and acceptance. The teacher as a role model provides an environment that is safe but allows all the freedom and challenge as other children receive.

Children with physical limitations are now included in regular classrooms, advertisements, and television shows. Familiarity with prostheses, walkers, and wheelchairs are helping to bring more social peer acceptance in group settings. Children have a desire to be helpful yet the danger exists for them to do too much, reinforcing learned helplessness. It is important for every child to be included in every classroom activity to the fullest of her ability. That will go a long way in facilitating peer acceptance as well.

Children from other cultures may have different social styles, depending on cultural values and practices. The teacher familiarizes himself with the cultures of the children in the group and transfers that awareness to assist the child to feel comfortable socially in the classroom. If a child does not speak English, the teacher, even though he may not speak the child's language, can act as a body language translator and an advocate for the child with the other children. The parents, through an interpreter, can supply the teacher with a list of common words and their meanings.

The social climate of acceptance for all children will be extended to any child with differences. Having a friend is one of the most important motivators in learning and feeling successful and happy. The teacher must do all in his power to make that happen.

HELPING PROFESSIONALS FOR SOCIAL DEVELOPMENT CONCERNS

If all the efforts of the staff and observations documented by Anecdotal and Running Records or social checklists indicate a child is having a problem in this area, some action must be taken. In a talk with the parents, the teacher can discuss his concerns. This is a sensitive area since no parent wants to hear that their child is rejected and friendless. Family dynamics and values are closely woven with social development, so the utmost care should be taken in this approach. The family probably already has clues the child is having difficulty. The child may be reluctant to come to school, with crying and tantrums every morning. The child may be getting into fights, hurting and being hurt. Together some of the possible causes are explored and some plans agreed upon.

If the problem is prolonged or so severe it seems inadvisable to wait, then helping professionals may be consulted. After the medial personnel have ruled out any possible physical cause, then the psychological causes could be examined. Some of those professionals might include a

social worker—counsels individuals and families, serves as advocate or consultant to agencies or schools

family therapist—psychologist specializing in working with families in the treatment of an individual or family group

play therapist—psychologist or psychiatrist using play for diagnosis, dialogue, and treatment of childhood social-emotional disorders

child psychologist—evaluates, diagnoses, and treats children for emotional, social, cognitive, and behavioral disorders

Week 4, Assignment A

RUNNING RECORD OF SOCIAL DEVELOPMENT FOR GROUP C

From group C, assign each of the children to a day this week. Decide on a 10-minute time block to observe each child. Fold lined paper down the middle and write in the left-hand column. When that time comes, whatever that child is doing, begin your recording. Start with the child's name, date, time, and in which area or activity the child is engaged. From that point, write down each action and movement, and any conversation. Be as descriptive as you can without summarizing or giving reasons for the behavior. Record conversations word for word. Later in the day, take the recording and make comments, write questions, or pose theories in the right-hand column. Review the stages of social play. Identify which stage or stages the child demonstrated, and write that in the right column as well.

What to Do with It

Write a few summary words, the date, and your name on the portfolio overview sheet, Figure 4.14.

Share with the parents and the child, if appropriate. For example: "Mrs. Stento, today when I was watching Tony play he was deeply engrossed

SOCIAL DEVELOPMENT		
Documentation	Recorder	Date
CL parallel	MS	9/26
CL assoc	BAN	1/10
CK coop ☺ asserts	BAN	4/30
CK negotiating		5/20

Figure 4.14 Portfolio Overview Example

in pouring sand from one container to another. Another child came to the table and began to play next to Tony. Without missing a beat in pouring, Tony slid one of his containers toward the other child, who took it and also began filling it. Not a word was exchanged but that was a big step for Tony, sharing one of his toys," or "Maxine, I was making some notes as you played today and I wrote down about how you played the big sister going to the doctor with her baby brother. You were very gentle with Robert. That must be the way your sister Irene is gentle with you."

Make a note if further action is indicated and follow through. File the Running Record in each child's portfolio.

Week 4, Assignment B

CLASS LIST LOG OF SOCIAL DEVELOPMENT FOR ALL

Copy a Class List Log from Appendix D and write the names of the children in your class alphabetically. Draw vertical lines to indicate the social play stages: Onlooker, Solitary, Parallel, Associative, and Cooperative. This week during free play time, observe the children as they interact with each other. Place a check mark in the stage next to their name. If you can, you could also indicate what type of play it is: functional (F), constructive (C), dramatic (D), or games with rules (G).

What to Do with It

At the end of the week, take the Class List Log and transfer the stage you observed onto the portfolio overview sheet with your name and date of the observation. (See the example in Assignment A, Figure 4.14.)

Share with the parents and the child, if it is appropriate. For example: "Mr. Nugent, I noticed Max playing for a long time by himself today with the Legos," or "Kathy, I noticed you building together with Laura today in the block area."

File the Class List Log in the class file. Make note if any further action is indicated.

Week 4, Assignment C

REFLECTIVE JOURNAL

Respond to the following in your Reflective Journal kept in a private file at home.

One difference in the way boys and girls played this week was...

I noticed this week that there was no difference in the way boys and girls...

When children have difficulty sharing, I...

When I think about my own social development, I prefer (Onlooker, Solitary, Parallel, Associative, or Cooperative play. I think it's because...

I wish I could...

REFERENCES

DeVries, R. & Kohlberg, L. (1987). *Constructivist early childhood education: Overview and comparison with other programs.* Washington: National Association for the Education of Young Children.

Erikson. E. H. (1950). *Childhood and society.* New York: Norton.

Flavell, J. (1977). *Cognitive development.* Englewood Cliffs, NJ: Prentice Hall.

Freud, S. (1953). *The standard edition of the complete psychological works of Sigmund Freud.* (J. Strachey, Ed. and Trans.). London: Hogarth and the Institute of Psychoanalysis.

Goodman, Y. M. (1978). Kidwatching: An alternative to testing. *National Elementary School Principal, 57* (4), 41–51.

Greenspan, S. (1988). *Exploring first feelings.* (1980) Washington, DC: The Institute for Mental Health Initiatives.

Hartup, W. W. (1992). *Having friends, making friends, and keeping friends: Relationships as educational contexts.* Urbana, IL: ERIC Clearinghouse on Elementary and Early Childhood Education, ED 345 854.

Kemple, K. (1992). *Understanding and facilitating preschool children's peer acceptance.* Urbana, IL: ERIC Clearinghouse on Elementary and Early Childhood Education, EDO-PS-92-5.

Kostelnik, M. J., Stein, L. C., Whiren, A. P., & Soderman, A. K. (1993). *Guiding children's social development.* Albany: Delmar Publishers.

Maslow, A. H. (1970). *Motivation and personality.* New York: Harper & Row.

McClellan, D. & Katz, L. (1993). *Young children's social development: A checklist.* Urbana, IL: ERIC Clearinghouse on Elementary and Early Childhood Education, 1993. EDO-PS-93-6.

Paley, V. G. (1984). *Boys & girls: Superheroes in the doll corner.* Chicago: The University of Chicago Press.

Paley, V. G. (1988). *Bad boys don't have birthdays: Fantasy play at four.* Chicago: University of Chicago Press.

Pugmire-Stoy, M. C. (1992). *Spontaneous play in early childhood.* Albany: Delmar Publishers.

Rogers, C. S. & Sawyers, J. K. (1988). *Play in the lives of children.* Washington: National Association for the Education of Young Children.

Rubin, K., Fein, G. G., & Vandenberg, B. (1983). Play. In E. M. Hetherington (Ed.), P. H. Mussen (Series Ed.), *Handbook of child psychology: Vol 4. Socialization, personality, and social development* (pp. 693–774). New York: Wiley.

Rubin, Z. (1980). *Children's friendships.* Cambridge, MA: Harvard University Press.

Skinner, B. F. (1953). *Science and human behavior.* New York: Macmillan.

Watson, J. B. (1950). *Behaviorism.* New York: Norton.

RESOURCES

Kostelnik, M. J., Stein, L. C., Whiren, A. P. & Soderman, A. K. (1993). *Guiding children's social development.* Albany: Delmar Publishers.

Rogers, C. S. & Sawyers, J. K. (1988). *Play in the lives of children.* Washington: National Association for the Education of Young Children.

Using Frequency Counts to Look at Emotional Development

USING FREQUENCY COUNTS

Exercise: How often did you do each of the following today?

Eat
Go to the bathroom
Talk on the phone
Say your pet phrase ("Oh well," "Basically," or "Whatever")

Much behavior is habitual, done without thinking. Occasionally, those habitual actions become really important. More attention is given to how often and what food is eaten when someone is on a diet. Measuring or counting is a part of decision making. If a person is experiencing an illness, the number of times one goes to the bathroom may be an important symptom. Legislators tally the number of pro and con calls received on an issue. Weight before beginning a diet, the number of phone calls, or an unusual change in body functions is an indicator that provides information for comparison. In behav-

ior modification, a measurement is made, action taken, and then measured again to see the significance of the change.

In the classroom, a **Frequency Count** can measure repeated actions of a child, the whole group, or the teacher. It is sometimes necessary to count behaviors that occur often in one day or session, such as hitting, children running, or the teacher saying, "Don't." Strategies are implemented then to reduce negative actions or behavior, or increase desirable ones.

Exercise: Frequently occurring actions that may occur in a group of preschool children follow. What is your estimate of how many times a day each happens? Which ones would you like to see increased or decreased?

1. Spills
2. Biting
3. Punching
4. "Thank-you"
5. Vomiting
6. Using the book area

7. Sharing
8. "Don't..."
9. "OK, guys"
10. "Teacher, Teacher..."

Candidates for a reduction are numbers 1, 2, 3, 8, 9, and 10. Numbers 4 , 6, and 7 could be increased. Number 5 is an infrequent event and would not be a measurable criterion for a Frequency Count or a reduction plan. It is necessary to note that incident, however, on a health form or a short anecdotal. In an infant room, this may be a more frequent event. Number 2 is more likely to occur in a toddler room, because it is an expected behavior. If it were a frequent behavior in a kindergarten room, with an individual child, or many children, the teacher would begin to search for answers, after she applied first aid, of course. Biting is not expected behavior for kindergarten students.

Frequency Counts are a way of seeing just how often an event happens. The purpose is to try to change undesirable behavior. If the action is negative and excessive for the age or stage expectations, then a plan is implemented to try to reduce it. If an expected behavior is not present or not happening often enough, then a plan is made to try to increase it. After a period of time, another Frequency Count is taken to measure the success. The process is documented by a Frequency Count to "prove" if the remedy or theory works.

This is not recommending a program of behavior modification where positive behavior is rewarded so it will increase, and negative behavior is punished so it will decrease. It is more a measurement of the teacher or learning process, like a pretest and a posttest. It assumes a change will take place. The agents of that change may be time, direct instruction, modeling, planned experiences, and self-regulation. Bandura's social learning theory (1977) recognized that the change, called learning, results from an interaction between thinking, acting, and the environment.

Figure 5.1 is an example of a Frequency Count. Spills seem to be happening many times a day in this classroom and the staff is concerned, besides irritated, at the messes. They complain then talk about some possible reasons. The children may be too young to initiate pouring, or the pitchers available are too heavy with no lids and opaque so the liquid comes out unexpectedly for novice pourers. Perhaps the adults are not sitting at the table with the children but using that time to prepare for the next activity. Each of the possible reasons suggests possible strategies. A decision is reached and the strategy is implemented. A later

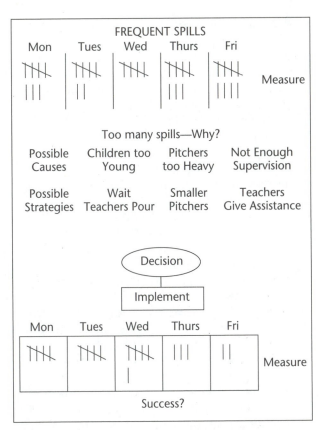

Figure 5.1 Frequency Counts to Measure Reduction of Undesirable Behavior

Frequency Count measures whether the strategy is successful or not.

IT HAPPENED TO ME:
The Spilling Song

In a center I visited recently, a spill occurred. Immediately, a teacher jumped up and turned on a record player with a little song about spilling. She later remarked, "That same child deliberately spills every day." I asked about the song. "Oh, they love it." Do you think the teacher's response to spilling increased or decreased spilling at snack time?

Using the Frequency Count to Document Frequently Occurring Behaviors

Other classroom situations and possible strategies for Frequency Count measurement follow.

- decrease aggressive acts—prosocial or emotional curriculum
- decrease the need for teacher intervention—more self-help shelves for materials and supplies
- decrease inappropriate use of materials—helper chart to encourage responsibility
- document individual child with transition difficulties—individual Frequency Count and implementation of special warning before it is time to change activities
- decrease use of punitive guidance techniques—training in positive guidance
- decrease teacher chatting on the playground—coffee break for chatting before playground duty
- decrease domination of adult voices in the classroom—tape recorder to monitor and make teachers aware of voice level.
- increase cooperative play—buddy time when each child and a friend choose an activity to do together
- increase interactions with parents—weekly happy notes
- increase eye-level talking with children—small chairs in each learning center for teacher to sit on while observing play and talking to children
- increase scanning supervision of whole room—reminder posters for teachers on every wall that display "SCAN"
- increase use of learning area—place an adult there to interact with the children
- increase self-care—equip room with cleaning equipment, low shelves, paint smocks with Velcro, dress up clothes with elastic and Velcro

Using Frequency Counts to Measure Prosocial and Antisocial Behavior

Groups of young children are emotionally and socially immature, resulting in disagreements and a lack of empathy for one another. The goals of adults who work with children are to decrease antisocial behavior and increase prosocial behavior. Frequency Counts can measure the effectiveness of a chosen strategy or intervention, or the progress that children make just from maturation and experience in a group setting.

A Frequency Count tallies each time a frequently occurring behavior occurs. The Frequency Count example in Figure 5.2 shows a group of eleven children on a certain day. Huy made no social contacts. What does that mean? We cannot tell from this recording. That means that it is a closed

method. The recorder observes, in this case looking for certain behavior. When it is observed, a tally mark is made. All the details except for the name of the child involved and the fact that it occurred are lost. The reader does not know the nature of the action, what precipitated it, any conversation from the incident, or the result. The purpose is solely to count.

Exercise: Interpret what the information in Figure 5.2 could mean.

What kind of a player is Carol? Solitary, parallel, cooperative (not the traditional meaning, but play stage meaning)?

What do you think Edward did?

What about Huy? Why do you think he has no tallies?

Probably Carol is in the cooperative stage of play but immature socially. She had a lot of social contacts, but she may not have her emotions under control. After reading the rest of the chapter, particularly the difference between girls and boys, come back and think about Edward here. Huy probably is not making many social contacts because of his language barrier. Isolated children are neither prosocial or antisocial. The common definition of an introverted, withdrawn, quiet person is, "He's antisocial." In this case, it probably is not deliberate or willful, just lack of confidence: "When in doubt, do nothing," syndrome. Prosocial and antisocial Frequency Counts give indicators of the emotional tone of the classroom. Prosocial behavior is the outward manifestation of empathy, caring for another person through an action. In encouraging caring communities, Frequency Counts help the teacher clearly see patterns of individuals who are displaying these behaviors.

Frequency Counts can be used in selected circumstances, not a usual part of the classroom information gathering. Effectively measuring before and after a strategy or a period of time gives important documentation to the significance of the interval.

What to Do with the Information

The information gathered from a Frequency Count is more than food for an inquiring mind, although it may indicate that no change is needed. It is a tool to measure a baseline, the commonplace, not out of the ordinary. It is the basis for

FREQUENCY COUNT Date _March 01 1998_ Recorder _BAN_

Make a tally mark in the column next to the child's name each time you observe a behavior that you would classify as prosocial or antisocial.

CHILD'S NAME	PROSOCIAL Helping, sharing, hugging, calling another child by a kind name	ANTISOCIAL Hurting, hoarding, bad name calling, rejecting another child
Amy	1 1	
Bajic	1 1 1	1 1 1 1
Carol	1̶1̶1̶1̶ 1	1̶1̶1̶1̶ 1
Danielle	1	1 1
Edward		1̶1̶1̶1̶ 11
Fatima	1	
Galina	1 1 1	
Huy		
Irma	1 1	1
Jacob	1 1	1 1
Kara	1 1 1 1	
Totals	24	22

Figure 5.2 Frequency Count example

judgments about the need for change. A strategy is implemented and more Frequency Counts are taken to measure progress and success. The process is a mini-research and experiment in a behavior modification format. Depending on the topic and subject of the research, it can be shared as a victory in progress with parents, other teachers, and the administration. It can be used as a needs assessment for equipment, materials, or teacher training. The postintervention Frequency Count can be used in reporting to funders or the administration the difference the new equipment or the training made. Periodic return to the Frequency Count method will measure how long lasting the effects of the project have been.

Advantages

Frequency Counts are

- a quantitative measurement on which to base strategies for change
- quick to record, with no details just tallies to write
- useful for quantitatively and objectively measuring frequently occurring behaviors

Disadvantages

Frequency Counts can

- lose the raw data, with no details recorded
- only measure one kind of behavior, making the results highly selective
- allow the recorder's bias to enter the recording

Pitfalls

Frequency Counts

- can select behaviors to measure that do not occur often (we hope), such as: accidents requiring stitches, incidents of child abuse, guinea pig escapes
- infer from one sample that this is normal behavior. It may have been an unusual day so results are not indicative of a normal day.
- allow much interpretation from one recorder to another. (For example, "Was that sharing when Aiko handed Katerina the Play Doh because Katerina demanded it?")
- are an intense recording method that requires the adult to be free from child-interaction responsibilities, which is not always possible.

LOOKING AT EMOTIONAL DEVELOPMENT
Stages of Emotional Development

Exercise: What emotions would these events stir in you? How would you express it?

You won the $3 million lottery.

You are asked by your best friend to co-sign a $20,000 loan.

You are told the plane has lost power, prepare for a crash landing.

You have lost an heirloom ring that has been in your family for five generations.

You just got a phone call from the lottery office that they made a mistake. You did not win the money after all.

Emotions are not grown. They change over time from simple to complex. Their development occurs in predictable stages but in very individual ways. Development of emotions is in the expression and control. As the human matures, the capacity for distinguishing between various emotions intensifies, and along with it the ability to recognize those

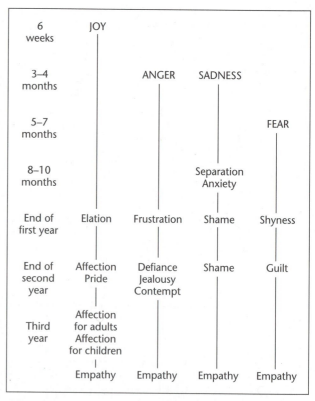

Figure 5.3 Emergence of children's emotions during the first three years of life. (Courtesy of Kostelnik, M. J. Stein, L. C., Whiren, A. P., & Soderman, A. K., 1993, p. 113. *Guiding Children's Social Development*. Albany, NY: Delmar Publishers. Reprinted with permission.)

same emotions in others. A lifelong struggle is fought in the acceptable expression and control of those emotions, and the ability to control the intensity at both ends of the emotional balance.

Studies of emotions have found that there are common emotions to all humans, Figure 5.3. These **core emotions**—fear, rage, and love—were researched by the work of J. B. Watson (1914). These form the basis for all emotions that are just more finite distinctions of fear, rage, and love. Core emotions are, at first, purely responses to stimuli. Within the first year, however, their appearance becomes more deliberate and recognizable, Figure 5.4.

In the infant, these emotions are expressed first by reflexes, varying in intensity. They are usually governed not by the situation but by temperament. One baby expressing joy or contentment may lie passively, while others may move actively about. Babies differ in the intensity of their crying dependent more on their particular style than the range of their discontent. These temperaments are genetic but over time other influences will affect change in responses. Parental influence on temperament

has been studied by many researchers. Thomas and Chess (1977) have done research on long-term effects of mother-child interactions on personality and emotional development. They identified nine temperamental qualities that can be observed not only in the infant but continued throughout life:

1. Activity level—physical motion
2. Rhythmicity—regularity of biological functions
3. Approach or withdrawal—initial reaction to new stimulation
4. Adaptability—flexibility after initial reaction
5. Intensity of reaction—energy level of responses
6. Threshold of responsiveness—intensity of stimulation needed to produce a response
7. Quality of mood—general behavior
8. Distractibility—outside stimulation changing ongoing behavior
9. Attention span and persistence—length of time activities are maintained

Exercise: Think of yourself and one other person you know well and jot down, on a separate sheet of paper, descriptors in the nine categories of temperament.

	Self	Friend
1.		
2.		
3.		
4.		
5.		
6.		
7.		
8.		
9.		

Examine the differences. Why are you different from your friend? Genetics? Family influences? Experiences with peers?

. . . .

IT HAPPENED TO ME: When Are You Going to Control Your Temper?

. . . .

My two sons and I were sitting at the dining room table doing homework when they started arguing over a pencil, the way seven- and nine-year-olds will. The argument got more and more heated until the furious nine-year-old flung the pencil at his brother. The pencil seemed to spin in slow motion as it narrowly missed his brother's eye. I was

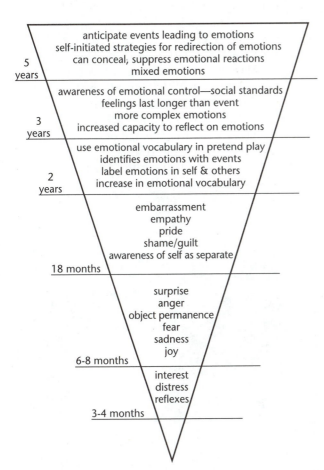

Figure 5.4 Emotional Development

relieved that it missed but outraged that he would do such a dangerous thing. I got right in his face, and yelled, "When are you going to learn to control your temper!?" At that moment I realized I was out of control and he was wise not to say, "When you do, Mother."

. . . .

Socialization of Emotions

As the child develops a more complex thinking process, he can differentiate the range of feelings from pleasant to elated and select expressive behaviors appropriate to the range. Emotional development then is the recognition of the feelings and range of emotions. Most of all, emotional development is learning to control and express emotions in a socially acceptable way. Infants are born with the basic emotional responses that will become more defined in how they are expressed as other areas of development become more mature. As thinking levels develop, the causes of the feelings and more choices of expression are understood. Social factors such as the situation (not to cry so loudly in church as she does in the grocery store) and modeling by those around will affect emotional responses. Kuebli (1994, p. 44) gives four processes by which emotions are socialized:

1. chiding or praising children's immediately prior emotional behaviors
2. giving direct instruction regarding social conventions for expressing emotions ("girls don't brag about their successes")
3. modeling emotional states, expressions, and events—children watch and imitate
4. communicating expectancies, verbally or nonverbally, directly to the child or within his hearing ("When I was your age I was afraid the first time I slept away from home.")

Emotions are socialized or influenced in their recognition and expression by adults in the child's world. Americans display more intense expression of emotions than Chinese and Japanese people. This may cause children from eastern cultures to be ill at ease in a setting where discussion and free expression of emotions are encouraged.

It is difficult to interpret the inner cause for the outward display of emotions. The observer infers the cause based on prior knowledge of development and behavioral cues. Each individual is different, and before language appears, it is impossible to be certain of the emotions of the observed. Between two and three years old, children use the words *mad, scared,* and *happy* to describe their own and other's emotions. Notice the correlation to the core emotions. By five years old they could match and label a broader range of emotions from pictures (Kuebli, 1994).

Joy, Love, and Happiness

Exercise: What does happiness look like? What might be some causes of happiness?

The most recognizable characteristic that suggests joy or happiness is smiling. Those first smiles are reputed to be reflex responses to digestion rather than an emotional state. Smiles in response to human voices are seen at three weeks and to familiar faces by three and one-half months. Laughter, in response to physical stimulation like tickling, then to more social situations, begins at four months. The reciprocal sharing of smiles, coos, and laughter is part of the attachment process needed for the coming separation, cognitively and physically. Emotional development is closely aligned with social interactions and cognitive development. When the infant can differentiate between self and others and realizes the primary caregiver is not with her, anger and fear combine to form separation anxiety. The emotional task of infancy is the formation of trust (Erikson, 1950), the confidence that needs will be met, mother will return, and all is well. That is the foundation for mental health, Figure 5.5.

Joy is manifested after the age of one from situations that have favorable results. To young children, that means it satisfies their own desires. As they work on autonomy, the accomplishment of tasks brings joy in the form of pride. As they near

Figure 5.5 Joy is easy to recognize!

four and five years old, happiness is meeting adult's expectations. They are working toward empathy. They can now find joy for what is happening to others rather than self. That is a goal of social development for the benefit of the whole community.

The Absence of Joy. Factors that influence this emotion begin, as always, with what is inborn. Some infants just have a generally happy behavior. Others are more irritable and harder to find in a state of satisfaction and calm. That inborn temperament may be the beginning point. Interactions with mother, the primary caregivers, and others are extremely important. In cases studied in which infants were deprived of social interactions, physical, mental and emotional disorders were seen contributing to the **failure to thrive**. In situations of neglect, conditions of poverty, or physical illness, emotional damage can be seen as well.

Exercise: Think of someone you know who has had a life of really difficult experiences yet appears to have overcome the obstacles and is emotionally whole. What made the difference for that person?

Exercise: How do you deal with difficult situations?

Some children display behaviors that will allow them to deal with the absence of joy in their life. First, children may be in denial. They may use fantasy or refusal to recognize the difficult situation by acting as if it were not so. Children use this technique to come through abuse, removing themselves emotionally from the situation until it becomes unreal, a sealed off part of their life. Children may regress to an earlier stage of behavior to escape the reality of the difficulty. By recording a child's progress, an observation of regression can be a warning that something may be bothering the child. Withdrawal might be used as protection from facing the absence of joy. By not interacting socially, the pain or risk of pain is thought to make it hurt less. By evaluating children's social behaviors against the typical stages, clues may be noticed that suggest a possible emotional trauma. When children act out, there may be many causes. It may be a realistic behavior for this age or stage, a bid for attention, or a disregard for others because of the emotional pain the child is experiencing. Observing the indicators of defense mechanisms should be noted and studied further.

An interesting phenomenon that puzzles researchers, as well as anyone who wonders about cause and effect, is the coping mechanisms that some children develop. Some children can remain emotionally healthy after experiencing traumatic events. Anthony and Cohler (1987) looked at the common factors in the **invulnerable child**, the one who survives and can rise above expected dire outcomes from difficult, seemingly impossible circumstances. They exhibit empathy, detachment from the dysfunctional behaviors of others, a sense of humor, and personal power. Teachers or caregivers have incredible belief in the capacity for the spirit to overcome difficult situations. This leads them to assist every child learning **coping skills**. The child's competency and empowerment will help bring joy and happiness out of deprivation.

When a child displays a lack of joy, the teacher has some steps to take, Figure 5.6. The first one is to recognize the emotion and not show disapproval or denial even if the emotion is not justified. So often adults say "Don't feel that way," or "You shouldn't feel that way." The emotion is real to the person feeling it and should not be denied by an outsider. Secondly, trying to get the child to forget about the feeling is a short-term solution. Pretending happiness does not help when the child is experiencing loneliness from missing the parent who left him at day care. Acting silly to get the child to smile or involving him in an activity only temporarily relieves the difficulty.

When children learn coping skills, they can generalize to any situation that is unpleasant. In this

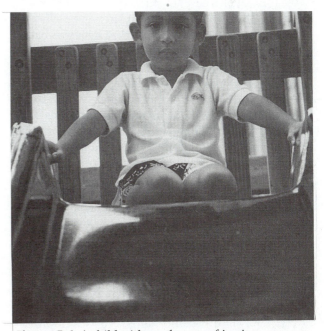

Figure 5.6 A child with an absence of joy is a concern.

way, they can address the difficulty in an emotionally healthy way.

Coping skills are learned in the same ways other skills are learned. The first step is the recognition of the cause of the problem. This will help the child, at her developmental level, understand why she has this feeling. The emotion is named and the normalcy of these feelings will help the child move toward a solution. For example: "You're not happy today because you didn't want to say goodbye to your Dad and see him leave you. Everyone feels sad sometimes when they want to be with someone and they can't. What are some things you could do until he comes back?"

Adults can role model coping mechanisms for children. "I think I'll put on this happy record. It always makes me feel like smiling when I hear this song." Some direct instruction can take place by using discussions following books or puppet scenarios in which characters have similar feelings of sadness or loneliness. Helping children to learn ways to deal with their feelings is a part of the social-emotional curriculum.

Anger and Aggression

Exercise: Using a separate sheet of paper, list 10 things that make you angry. What do you do when you are angry?

Developmental Stages of Anger. Anger grows from the unmet needs of the self. When a baby rolls over and gets stuck next to the bars of the crib, that cry is an angry one. She wants to move, but something is preventing her from carrying out that urge to move. That same feeling will overcome her when she is late for work twenty years later but stuck in traffic. The response is usually different (sometimes not). Anger is energizing. It motivates the child to chase down the one who took his tricycle while he was off picking dandelions. It enables the adult to clean the whole house after an argument with a friend. Some of those actions may address the cause of the anger while others act as a valve to let off steam. This **displacement** of anger's energy has been the subject of much research with varying results. The major objection to it is that it does not solve the problem, just vents the energy.

In the child's second year, she is seeking to be autonomous, to rule herself. She is angry when those attempts are resisted, even if it is for her own safety. Her lack of full language development makes it difficult for her to express her desires or

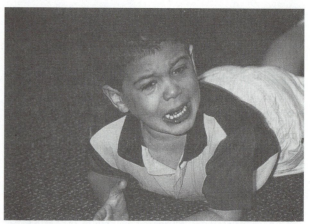

Figure 5.7 Tantrums are common in toddlers, displaying newly developed emotions without the inner controls to manage them.

her feelings about being thwarted or denied, so anger and frustration are increased, Figure 5.7. The egocentricism contributes to angry feelings. The child can only see her own point of view. She cannot understand why she cannot have the tricycle back after leaving it for ten minutes, just because she wants it. She wants it so she believes she should have it. With the struggle for autonomy it is not surprising that defiance, an angry stance against authority, would begin in the second year. The battle of wills is beginning here, and depending on the child's temperament and the parenting style, it may be a long, difficult one or less severe.

Toward the end of the second year a more complicated form of anger—jealousy—appears. It could be caused by adult attention diverted away from the child or a desirable object seen in the hands of someone else. A common reaction to this jealousy is a temper tantrum. These are often seen in the grocery store, or the mall. There is so much visual stimulation. Attractive, desirable objects are all around but so are restrictions the child cannot understand. They are told not to touch when their mother is touching. They are told they cannot have it when it is placed at eye level and within their reach.

The temper tantrum can be seen in the classroom for just the same reasons. With the teacher's time divided among several children, demands for time and attention are many and are divided. Equipment and materials in the toddler room are well thought out to provide many duplicates so that competition for toys is kept to a minimum. Tantrums will still occur, so the caregiver should be prepared to understand their causes and deal with them in an understanding way. He gives attention to the causes and the safety of the child, not the behavior. That prevents it from becoming a battle of wills.

Aggression. **Aggression** is the display of anger that results in physical or emotional damage to people or property. Aggression has been the subject of much research. Gaining an understanding of the causes may result in a reduction of aggression in society (Pepler & Rubin, 1991). Genetic or biological causes are being researched to learn if medications or genetic manipulation could reduce aggressiveness. Family influence on aggressive behavior is being studied to find the cycle over the generations and try to intervene in its recurrence. Society's influence, especially violent television programming, has been a large segment of the aggression research with much of it pointing to high correlations. The predictability and treatment of childhood aggression and the sex differences are other aspects of the studies. All of these underscore the problematic nature of childhood aggression and the complexity of its effects on behavior. These cannot be minimized or trivialized but there are some basic understandings about children and aggression that every teacher should recognize.

Exercise: What does aggression in the classroom look like?

Aggression is developmental. Children are aggressive at various predictable stages (Kostelnik, 1993), Figure 5.8.

Two- and three-year-olds display aggressiveness mainly to attain or maintain possession of items or territories. They will use physical violence, hitting, kicking, and biting to keep or get what they want. "It is important not to assume that such behaviors represent a personality trait," writes Jewett (1992). It is a developmental phase not a prediction of a lifestyle.

Two-year-old aggressiveness is described as instrumental aggression. It works! Hit the person who has the toy and he lets go. Knock the person off the bicycle so now she can get on. As language skills increase, the child can speak rather than act, and eventually negotiate. Preschoolers are beginning to use words to express their desires but may still be resorting to grabbing, stealing, or hiding items to keep them.

Early school-age children use negotiation more often but shift from physical aggression to verbal aggression. Name calling, mean talk, and threatening to withdraw friendships are the ways school-age children are aggressive.

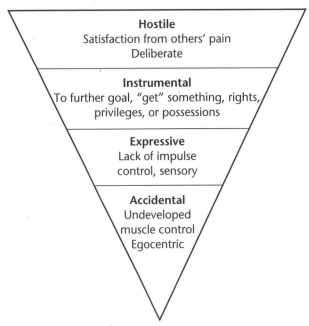

Figure 5.8 Types of Aggression. (Adapted from Kostelnik, M. J, Stein, L. C., Whiren, A. P., & Soderman, A. K. 1993. *Guiding Children's Social Development*. Albany, NY: Delmar Publishers.)

Aggression Can Be Accidental. Young children are physically uncoordinated. Much of the hurtful actions take place because they are inaccurate walkers and touchers, Figure 5.9. Stepping on each others' fingers, exploratory touches that end up hurting, and manipulation of materials and equipment in ways that hurt someone else are common. While digging vigorously in the sand, it flies into someone's eyes. While walking through the block area, she knocks down a pile of blocks. A child slides down the slide and knocks down the person standing at the bottom. All are incidents that can be classified as aggression but were unintentional. However, young children cannot understand intentionality. If they are hurt, they interpret it as aggression, and feel vindicated in hitting back. When the adult says, "She didn't mean it," those words have little meaning for the young child. The observant adult can only reduce this type of aggression by creating a safe environment and constant supervision. Positive guidance techniques such as, "Shovel the sand into the bucket," "Build inside these dividing lines," or "Wait to slide down until that person is out of the way" can help preschool children have a little more control over their behavior.

Aggression Can Be Changed to Assertion. The adult will not always be present to prevent scuffles over toys or disagreements over turns or

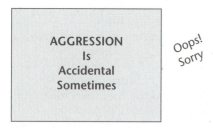

Figure 5.9 Accidental Aggression

Figure 5.11 Day care is not the cause of aggression. Punitive discipline is.

rights. Helping children become more assertive is another of those lessons that has many rewards, Figure 5.10. The child who can express what he wants or needs is more likely to receive it than the child who grabs. The child who can defend himself verbally from aggressors gains self-esteem and prevents himself from becoming a victim. The assertion skills will give the individual the autonomy to make their own needs known. When others must guess, they may do so incorrectly. Assertion too is developmental. It progresses from the two-year-old saying, "Mine," the three-year-old saying "I had that first," and the four-year-old saying, "Maybe we could take turns."

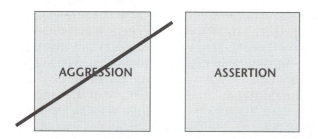

Figure 5.10 Aggression—No! Assertion—Yes!

Aggressiveness Is Not an Outcome of Day Care But of Strict Discipline. Studies have reported that children in day care are more aggressive than those children reared exclusively at home (Haskins, 1985; Thornburg, et al., 1990), Figure 5.11. Another study of preschoolers and aggression (Clarke-Stewart, et al., 1994) found the correlating factor was not the setting but physical control and punishment. The punitive discipline techniques used by either day care workers or parents was the common factor. This is another in the growing body of research that punitive adult behavior increases child aggression. It calls for parents and teachers to develop more appropriate discipline strategies.

Aggression Must Be Reduced. The first reason to reduce aggression is safety, in the classroom or at home, Figure 5.12. This is not just for the present, but for the future. Many studies have shown that aggressiveness in the early elementary grades predicts aggressiveness in early adulthood (Huesmann, et al., 1984). This continuity is disturbing yet holds the promise for early childhood education. The goal of emotional control is a critical one. By lowering aggression before the early elementary age, it can have long-lasting effects. Farrington's study (1991) found high percentages of other causes for aggression. Economic deprivation, family criminality, poor parental child-rearing behavior, and school failure were all measurable at 8 to 10 years of age.

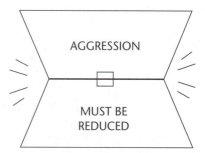

Figure 5.12 Aggression must be reduced!

Aggression Is Different in Boys and Girls. For many years, research has looked at hostile aggression as a greater problem for boys than girls, Figure 5.13. More boys are reported by teachers and parents as aggressive. It has been thought that hormonal differences accounted for this aggressiveness but recent studies are causing scientists to rethink that belief (Seligman, 1995). Tremblay (1991) suggests that girls may be less aggressive in the school years. However, the more aggressive girls tended to show later effects:

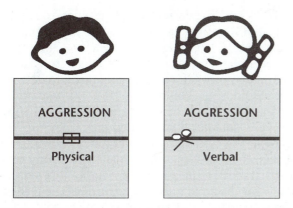

Figure 5.13 Differences in Aggression of Boys and Girls

- More became adolescent mothers.
- More were single parents.
- They experienced higher levels of psychiatric disorders.
- They had children who were more aggressive.

No matter what the cause, aggression is a problem in group settings of children, in the home, and in society as a whole. A task of the early childhood field then is to attempt to reduce the aggression.

Aggression Can Be Reduced. Children can learn to exhibit prosocial behavior through a variety of strategies, Figure 5.14 (Kostelnik, et al., 1993):

Modeling
Reinforcement
Direct instruction, such as teaching prosocial behaviors
Helping children recognize instances of accidental aggression
Helping children deescalate potentially aggressive play

Making it clear aggression is unacceptable
Teaching children alternatives to gunplay
Helping children respond to aggression of others

Other social prevention programs have been found to reduce antisocial behaviors (Burchard & Burchard, 1987). *Early Violence Prevention: Tools for Teachers of Young Children* (Slaby, et al., 1995) offers many suggestions for the physical environment, materials, cooperative activities, guidance techniques, responding, and teaching problem solving and assertiveness skills.

Fear and Shyness

Exercise: What are you afraid of?

Fear and Development. The first fear is of strangers. That only happens after the child has developed an awareness of separateness from others and has formed mental images of those familiar faces that are seen frequently. Sometimes even these may cause terrified screams. This change at around six months old signals a changing cognitive development. The infant is constantly matching new pictures with the old. Any discrepancy, glasses/no glasses, hair up/hair worn down, that does not match the mental image, triggers the fear response, Figure 5.15.

Other fears develop around two-and-a-half once a child's thinking is more advanced. Fears develop from the child's inability to make sense of the world. With limited understanding, everything is magic and anything is possible. There could be a grizzly bear under the bed. The house might blow

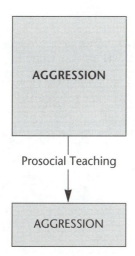

Figure 5.14 Prosocial teaching reduces antisocial behavior, including aggression.

Figure 5.15 Children have many fears.

away. The closet might be full of scary things that come out at night. These fears can be planted by tales the child hears from other people, adults included. Television or a fantasy book, read for fun and imagination, can produce fears. Fears of monsters, and being hurt, and nightmares, persist into the sixth and seventh year, when a firmer understanding of reality and fantasy is formed.

Exercise: What does fear look like?

Fear is exhibited by wide, open eyes; screaming; crying, when some kinds of sounds or language with a shrill tone are heard; rigid body; sometimes uncontrollable trembling; retreat or withdrawal; or seeking adult help. Some of the same strategies to help the child deal with anger can be used with fear. Talking about the fear by naming the emotion, not denying the feeling, and working together to help the child cope with the feeling are approaches that have been successful. The child can be encouraged to draw or act out the fear, write or dictate a story about it, or eventually face up to it little by little.

Shame, a Form of Fear. During the second year, when the child is struggling with autonomy, a stronger sense of guilt or shame is developed. This shows the thinking processes have been categorizing actions as acceptable and not acceptable. This is a necessary step in moral development. When the child does something perceived as nonacceptable, feelings of shame develop. These are extremely strong in children who have strong parental authority without the opportunity to make decisions for themselves.

● ●

IT HAPPENED TO ME:
The Beginning of Conscience

● ●

I was talking with the mother of a two-year-old when the mother looked down. Her little girl had a fist full of little pieces of paper. She admonished her, "Don't throw those pieces on the floor." The little girl looked up at her mom, closed her eyes, and opened her hand. This was a great example of a beginning conscience. She only believed something was wrong if someone is watching. She displayed her egocentric thinking: if she did not see it, neither did her mother.

● ● ● ● ● ● ● ● ● ● ● ● ● ● ● ● ●

Four- and five-year-olds are in what Tom Lickona (1983) calls Stage 1 of Moral Development, "You Should Do What You're Told." Children at this age, he says, believe that "what's right is doing what grown-ups tell you and the reason to do what you're told is you could get in trouble if you don't" (p. 114). Children who develop shame are those who are constantly reminded that they are not doing as they were told. It sometimes leads them to believe there is something inherently wrong with them. It may be the adult's expectations were unrealistic for the child's ability to comply. The feelings of inadequacy and shame are all the child knows in this situation.

Shyness, a Form of Fear. Shyness may be a type of fear that appears at the end of the first year because so many situations and people are new. The child at this age realizes the separateness from parents. The new freedom in mobility and competency is accompanied by feelings of inadequacy. Extra attention causes them discomfort, Figure 5.16. They are often most comfortable observing or withdrawing from the action until they are sure they can function. This should be accepted as a feeling, not to be denied, changed, or negated. The adult helps the child find ways to understand and cope with the feeling. Empty praise is not helpful nor is labeling like, "the shy one." Care should be taken to give opportunities without pushing. The following advice to teachers is adapted from *The Shy Child* (Zimardo & Radl, 1981).

Greet each child individually by name.
Make eye contact at eye level.
Be relaxed; smile; do not be "pushy."
Generate warmth and respect.
Be sensitive to the child's feelings.

Figure 5.16 Children who are labeled "shy" often continue that behavior.

Do not reinforce shyness by giving too much attention.

Give special individual attention, then ease the child into the group. (p. 120)

Children Under Stress. Children may develop stress from fears, both real and imaginary, and experience eating, sleeping, or toileting disturbances. They may not be socially or mentally participating, and may regress in behavior, or act out. They may even become physically or emotionally ill. The family can be the stressors or the stress reliever of young children. Honig (1986, pp. 147–157) lists several stresses in the family:

Poverty
Birth of siblings
Bereavement and loss
    death of a parent
    death of a sibling
    sibling with a handicapping condition
Separation and divorce
Step families
Mental illness in parents
Inept parenting practices, especially parental
    discipline techniques
Child abuse

Families can also be the healing haven for stresses from those very things, depending on how it is addressed. Honig also suggests that close mother and child or parent and child attachment has been shown to decrease stress in situations, such as a parent with mental illness and children in war zone situations. Caring adults can help children be stress-resistant.

Poor quality child care and educational practices can also be stressors. An environment that is psychologically risky, where right answers and unrealistic behavioral and learning expectations are set, can affect the child significantly. It is important for the observer to recognize signs of stress, make notes, and take action to help the child.

· ·

IT HAPPENED TO ME:
A Scary Dream

· ·

A four-year-old girl came into day care one morning, carrying her blanket and looking very serious. (No one spoke to her father as he dropped her off. No one greeted the little girl or noticed her facial or body expressions.) I was there observing a student teacher involved in an activity who also did not notice the girl. She walked over to me, a perfect stranger, and laid her head on my shoulder.

"You look like you're still sleepy," I said.

"No, I had a bad dream last night," she said quietly.

"Do you remember what the dream was about?" I asked.

"It was scary. Dreams are what you think about when you're sleeping."

That was profound, I thought.

"But dreams aren't real," I replied thinking that might help.

"I know, but you still wake up scared." How true. I needed a four-year-old to remind me that even unreal things can make us feel real feelings. We trust that someone will notice, care, give voice to our fears, and help us face them not feeling alone. *Listen to the children.*

· ·

The Emotionally Secure Environment

The role of the family and early childhood environment is to reduce the effects of negative emotions. They can help the child develop healthy attitudes, inner controls, and acceptable expressions. It begins with an atmosphere of mutual trust between the home and the program. The program with predictable room arrangements and routines is reassuring and stress-reducing. The rooms are physically comfortable without too much sensory stimulation. The curriculum is appropriate for the age and stage of the child, reflecting an attitude of acceptance of mistakes and responsiveness to the individual. Learning activities promote internal satisfaction, rather than emphasis on strict obedience or pleasing the adult. The schedule gives freedom to move, make choices, and use creative play outlets. These all contribute to a stress-free environment, control of negative emotions, encouragement of the positive ones of interest, curiosity, and enjoyment. This is accomplished by assessing the children's developmental levels and planning curriculum from topics or themes or projects that come from the children's world.

Exercise: Using a separate sheet of paper, make a list of prosocial (caring and empathetic) actions you would like to see in your classroom.

Now make a list of antisocial actions you probably witnessed but wished you did not. (These are typical behaviors of young children without emotional self-control.)

This is the connection between emotional development and Frequency Counts on prosocial and antisocial actions. They are done occasionally to take the social-emotional temperature of the room. It gives an objective, quantitative measurement of the environment. It may be the temperature is "normal" so nothing else needs to be done. It may reveal there are "hot zones," certain children who are having difficulty controlling aggressive tendencies. They could benefit from some intervention, since aggressive behavior affects social relationships, self-esteem, and ultimately success in school.

The first assessment should be the physical environment and how that affects prosocial development. Holloway and Reichart-Erickson (1988) suggest the criteria in Figure 5.17 for that assessment.

- There is enough usable space indoors and outdoors so that children are not crowded.

- Activity areas are defined by spatial arrangement.

- Space is arranged to accommodate children individually, in small groups, and in large groups.

- A variety of age-appropriate materials and equipment is accessible to children.

- Individual space is provided for each child's belongings.

- Private areas, such as enclosed book corners, lofts, and playhouses, where children can play or work alone or with a friend, are available indoors and outdoors.

- The environment includes many soft elements, such as rugs, cushions, rocking chairs, soft furniture, soft toys, and adults who cuddle children in their laps.

- Sound-absorbing materials, such as ceiling tiles and rugs, are used to cut down on noise.

- The outdoor play area is protected from access to streets or other dangers. A variety of activities can go on outdoors throughout the year.

Figure 5.17 Physical Environment Criteria for Promoting Prosocial Development. (Courtesy of Holloway, S. D., Reichart-Erickson, M. 1988. Early Childhood Observation Instrument, revised. *Early Childhood Research Quarterly, 3,* p. 53. Reprinted with permission from Ablex Publishing Corporation.)

Strategies for adults to help children with emotional development come from many sources. Wittmer and Honig (1994, pp. 4–11) recommend:

- Acknowledge and encourage understanding and expression of children's feelings.
- Facilitate perspective- and role-taking skills and understanding of other's feelings.
- Use victim-centered discipline and reparation: Emphasize consequences.
- Help children become assertive concerning prosocial matters.

Sue Dinwiddie (1994, p. 17) gives many practical suggestions for dealing with aggression, including a social problem-solving method:

1. initiate mediation
2. gather data
3. define the problem
4. generate alternative solutions
5. agree on a solution
6. follow through

Through observation, children's emotional and social situations are examined closely. From that examination, the teacher takes actions to assist the child to move on in the developmental stage. The adult helps the child recognize emotional and social states, gain control of behavior, feel more competent, and move on to the next level of social development. Observation and recording are closely entwined with curriculum to assist this process. This is similar to making a braid, Figure 5.18.

SPECIAL POPULATIONS AND EMOTIONAL DEVELOPMENT

The factors influencing emotional development are observed in all children. For children with developmental delays or disabilities, emotions are affected as well. A growing awareness of differences increases with maturity and experiences outside the home. When children with physical disabilities are included in programs with other children, self-comparisons are made. The other children are also learners with still-developing social skills, understanding, and empathy. Fear, rejection, and curiosity may be the emotions displayed by the classmates causing loneliness, doubt, and low self-esteem in the child with the disability. The teacher prepares the other children in the group, just as the environment is prepared, to receive the child with handicaps. Providing adaptive apparatus, such as wheelchairs, walkers, hearing aid cases, and eye-

TOPICS IN OBSERVATION: The Assessment and Curriculum Braid

Exercise: Try making a French braid in a volunteer's hair. Here are the directions: Section the top and separate into three parts. Place the left strand across the center. Bring the center strand to the left, switching their positions. Place the right strand across the center, bring the center strand to the right, switching their positions. Gather additional hair from behind the left ear, and add it to the strand that is now on the left. Place the strand with the added hair across the center strand. Use the right thumb to gather additional hair from the back of the right ear and add it to the strand that is now on the right. Place the strand with the added hair across the center strand. Keep taking additional hair and combining it with the main strands.

Think of development, assessment, and curriculum as the three main strands. It all begins with the knowledge of child development; the normal expectations of how the child will change over time physically, socially, emotionally, and cognitively. Every group of children brings its own range of development, interests, and today's reality. Children of the 1990s know very little about trains, and may or may not know much about planes. Assessing their knowledge and interest will determine the curriculum vehicle. Reggio Emelia's projects (Edwards, et al., 1993) are based on children's interests and happenings in their town. The projects about the race or the fountains in town demonstrate how the curriculum was real to the children before the activities began. They could then relate it to prior knowledge. Left on their own, children will play the Olympics *after* rather than *before* they happen. The children have then seen it on television and have heard their parents talk about it. It is a part of their real world. When teachers introduce the Olympic theme weeks before it happens, it is a part of the teachers' world but not the child's.

Knowledge of what two-year-olds, or threes or fours are like is one of the main strands in the braid. The specific group is observed and assessed through knowledgeable eyes. They are measured against a range of expectations. They also are observed to poll their interests. This makes assessment another strand of the braid. Documentation is the process of writing down what is seen. It will be remembered and used for a variety of purposes. That also will be a strand that runs through the braid, making a formalized record of what is known, done, and questioned.

Curriculum is the strand that carries the experiences and opportunities for exploration and discovery through the senses. By planning activities that children touch, taste, hear, see, and smell, all the developmental areas are being stimulated. If the experiences are familiar to their world, they make associations or matches. "Oh, I tasted this before. It's a sweet pickle." If the experiences are new ones, they seek to find equilibrium. "This is *called* a pickle but it's *made* out of a cucumber?" The association with the cucumber is unbalanced. What makes a pickle a pickle? A worthy curriculum theme? Science is seeing cause-and-effect changes. Math is following the recipe. Language is learning vocabulary and new, fun songs and rhymes about pickles. Visual perception is the comparison of shades of green in varieties of pickles. They appear in drawings and easel paintings. Social interactions take place in exploring who likes dill and who

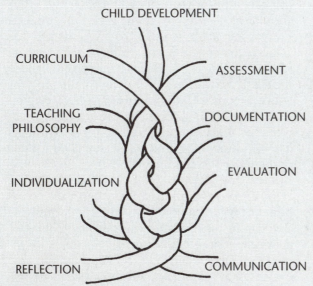

CHILD DEVELOPMENT

CURRICULUM

ASSESSMENT

TEACHING PHILOSOPHY

DOCUMENTATION

EVALUATION

INDIVIDUALIZATION

REFLECTION

COMMUNICATION

Figure 5.18 Development, assessment, and curriculum are three strands of the braid of appropriate programs for young children.

TOPICS IN OBSERVATION: continued

likes sweet pickles. People like different kinds of pickles, and people are different like pickles. Playing "Who's in the Pickle Jar" promotes social and physical development as children run to catch each other. The unstressful, nonacademic theme will produce emotional relaxation through enjoyment and self-esteem. "These are the pickles I made in school today. Bet you can't guess they're made out of cucumbers." Weaving all these activities together is the web, that very fragile but definite unending thread.

Implementation of curriculum is another strand of the braid. The teacher may have the background training in the "plan, do, review" model of High/Scope (Hohmann & Weikart, 1995). The teacher may follow the Creative Curriculum (Trister-Dodge, 1988), which carries the curriculum through the physical environment. The Montessori training may lead the teacher to set up formal lessons with defined procedures for children to follow. If the teacher is like most, the teaching philosophy or professional practice is eclectic. It is a combination of many philosophies that fit into their own learning style, personality, educational background, and also the program goals.

While the curriculum is being carried out, the teacher is the observer. She notes such things as how each child is running in the game, who can count the pickles in the jar, and who has never seen a cucumber before. The teacher writes down the wonderful stories they tell about how the seeds got in there and what will happen if they are swallowed. Every developmental area can be evaluated as children interact with the environment without intrusion or pressure. There will be children on both ends of the range of normal who will need some adaptation of the environment. The child who has not yet reached the levels of most of the other children will need to have some teacher assistance and facilitation to bridge the gap. This is what Vygotsky calls the **zone of proximal development** (Hills, 1992). It allows the child to approximate a level of competency, held up by the teacher's scaffold or mediation. The observer will document (to remember) what the child knows, what he can do, how he behaves, and how he feels about himself. This is all while observing the pickle game.

The teacher evaluates each child against what is expected for this age or developmental stage. Added to that is what the teacher knows about this particular child's circumstances. Because of that knowledge, a decision is made to modify the curriculum for a particular child. A child may need to have a pickle sign placed in his hand as the signal that it is his turn to chase because he cannot hear his name called. Another may need to hear the word in Spanish. The observer may notice that a particular child is easily frustrated when matching the lids to the pickle jars. She notes to take a closer look at possible vision or small muscle problems. The observer may notice that a child was reading all the ingredients to the recipe chart. That child needs a simple reader about pickles to keep him interested and a way to tape record so that others can listen to it. By writing this down (documenting) the teacher will remember to follow through on the plan, or follow up on questions to be answered.

The evaluations are communicated first to the parents. The best way is that face-to-face exchange about specific incidents and their relation to the child's developing knowledge and skill. This is a form of parent education about child development and shows the parents that the teacher is closely watching and recognizing the accomplishments of their child. The child should also hear of their accomplishments. Empty valuative words like "Wonderful" or "Good" are meaningless, compared to specific statements, such as, "When you counted those pickles it was higher than I've ever heard you count before." The communication of evaluations of child development can be used effectively to initiate early intervention. Through careful observation and documentation, developmental concerns are raised that need to be further investigated. After additional observations and consultations with other team members, the validity of the concern is confirmed. The parents and teacher can pursue a course of action to address the concern.

The teacher activates the curriculum and evaluates development. Another strand in the braid reflects on the professional and personal efforts of the process. Attitudes are monitored and decisions reconsidered. Receptiveness to change is measured. The reflective practitioner

TOPICS IN OBSERVATION: continued

returns to the strands of child development and assessment. The process begins again.

As this braid weaves in all these components, it becomes stronger. When any of the strands is weak, broken, or absent, the result is not as effective. In many programs, the documentation of assessment is the weakest strand, leaving individualization and communication to rely on memory and chance. Those are too important to not be supported by data, collected in a natural way through multiple sources. That is how assessment/documentation/evaluation drives curriculum.

What does observing and recording have to do with curriculum? Everything or nothing—it depends on the program and the teacher. All the methods and assignments in this book could be used to compile a vast and impressive portfolio on each child. It would be useless if it only showed where the child was at any given point. It becomes dynamic information when it is used to help guide curriculum. "How is that done?" becomes the question.

How is curriculum formed? Schweinhart (1995) is studying the use of various curriculum models that are being used by early childhood leaders and how extensively they are used. High/Scope, the Creative Curriculum, and the

Bank Street model were the three predominate curriculums being used. Preliminary findings suggest that less than one-third espouse any one model while more than two-thirds use parts of some models, though not extensively. This indicates that curriculum is individualized for program needs and to fit teaching styles of individual teachers.

Schweinhart's study was undertaken to try to measure and compare the outcomes of various models. With this much variation in how they are used, it is impossible to assess the outcomes of any one model using standardized testing. By observing and assessing individual children, however, the curriculum and the teaching methods can be evaluated, not just measured to a standard but to become the basis for change. That is what Rosegrant and Bredekamp (1991) call transformational curriculum—curriculum that helps bring about change. One strand of the braid is assessment of prosocial and emotional control with a Frequency Count. Another is implementation of curriculum. The third is evaluation of individual children's social interactions and emotional nature and controls. These are woven together in the braid to make a strong, efficient, and neat model.

glass frames, the children can experiment how it feels to use these things. Many more books now include children with differing abilities, both in regular storylines and in nonfictional, child-level explanations of disabilities.

Children with emotional disorders in the classroom will affect the emotions of both the staff and other children. Difficult behaviors, aggressiveness, withdrawal, and acting out always are challenges for staff. For the child with chronic emotional disorders, it is an even greater challenge. Acceptance and a knowledge of the disorder and approaches to use will be part of the preparation for this child. Parental information, records from other professionals working with the child and the family, and individual research will provide the teacher with a background and strategies to deal with the child. The other children can be informed and helped to understand the nature of this child's needs so that a caring atmosphere is created for all.

HELPING PROFESSIONALS FOR EMOTIONAL CONCERNS

Helping professionals, such as social workers, psychologists, or psychiatrists may be involved in consultations, assisting in emotional development difficulties. The staff will use each other for resources to seek answers to emotional behavior problems. Discussions with parents in the initial interview and intake process, in open communication opportunities such as open house, parent meetings, and social events give the teacher insight about the child. When all other attempts are not working, a more formalized discussion with the parents may be necessary. The emotional realm is subjective and also personally connected with the parents' and teacher's emotions. This conference should be approached sensitively, seeking a partnership of ways to help the child. Caution is taken not to lay blame, make diagnoses, or criticize. The teacher is prepared to suggest referrals for further evaluation. They may include

medical personnel—pediatrician, neurologist (treatment of brain and central nervous system disorders)

mental health professionals—psychiatrists, psychologists, social workers, therapists

support groups—mentor parents; parent resource centers; cooperative extension agents; school, religious, or community agencies

Week 5, Assignment A

FREQUENCY COUNT—SOCIAL/EMOTIONAL

Make at least two copies of the Frequency Count form in Appendix D. List the children in groups A and B on one form and groups C and D on another. Use the alphabetical name list from the Class List Log. On one day during free choice time, observe for 30 minutes, looking for evidence of prosocial or antisocial behaviors on one sheet. On another day, observe the children on the second sheet. Each time one of these behaviors occurs, make a tally mark next to the name of the child in the appropriate column.

What to Do with It

Analyze and plan. Look at the results. Do you see a few children with very high numbers in the antisocial column? Write a short theory as to why these children have scored in this way. (Do not put this in the child's portfolio. This is for your use.) Use some of the Resources to make a plan for the class or for individual children to foster prosocial/emotional development. You may want to try another Frequency Count at intervals during and following your plan to measure if it has been effective.

Week 5, Assignment B

ANECDOTAL RECORD OF EMOTIONAL DEVELOPMENT FOR GROUP D

Select the children in group D. Divide them among the days of this week and plan to write an Anecdotal Recording on each child about an incident that gives information about emotional development, such as the child displaying joy, happiness, anger, aggression, or fear. Make notes as the incident is happening, or shortly thereafter. By the end of the day, write an Anecdotal Recording about the incident. Include as many details as possible about the incident in the left column of a sheet of paper. In the right column, comment on the significance of the incident, if it was usual or unusual, and possible contributing factors. You may want to comment on:

Knowledge—recognition of emotions, vocabulary of emotions
Skills—what the child can do to control emotions
Dispositions—behaviors related to emotions
Feelings—how the child's self concept is involved with emotions

What to Do with It

In the child's portfolio, jot a few summary words on the overview sheet that the Anecdotal Recording is present, the date, and your name, Figure 5.19.

Share the observation with parents and the child, if appropriate, such as "I was observing Carlos today and saw him go to the bathroom all by himself. He had been afraid to go down the hall alone, but today he did it." File in each child's portfolio.

If a strategy to help the child cope with emotions is indicated, discuss it with the parents or your supervisor to decide on a course of action. Follow through.

EMOTIONAL DEVELOPMENT		
Documentation	Recorder	Date
FC ++	*MS*	10/6
RR "Be my friend"	*MS*	12/27
FC pro soc ++		3/30
FC some ⊖ ? new baby		5/25

Figure 5.19 Portfolio Overview Example

Week 5, Assignment C

REFLECTIVE JOURNAL

Would you describe yourself as shy? If so, think about these suggestions from Zipardo and Radl (1981), *The Shy Child:*

Decide to get over it.

Learn *why*.
Build self-esteem: What are your best qualities?
Pay attention to your personal appearance.
Be your own best friend.
Practice social skills. (pp. 214–227)

Respond to the following in your Reflective Journal kept in a private file at home.

I feel shy when…

I think it's because…

From the above list, maybe I could try…

When I see a child angry, it makes me…

When I looked at the Frequency Count and compared boys to girls, I was surprised to see…

It might make me…

I really would like to help _____ control emotions. I'll try…

REFERENCES

Anthony, J. E. & Cohler, B. J. (Eds.). (1987). *The invulnerable child.* New York: The Guilford Press.

Bandura, A. (1977). *Social learning theory.* Englewood Cliffs, NJ: Prentice Hall.

Bos, B. (1990). *Together We're Better.* Roseville, CA: Turn the Page Press.

Burchard, J. D. & Burchard, S. N. (Eds.) (1987). *Prevention of delinquent behaviors.* Beverly Hills, CA: Sage.

Clarke-Stewart, K. A., Gruber, C. P., & Fitzgerald, L. M. (1994). *Children at home and in day care.* Hillsdale, NJ: Lawrence Erlbaum Associates, Publishers.

Dinwiddie, S. (1994). The saga of Sally, Sammy, and the red pen: Facilitating children's social problem solving. *Young Children, 49,* (5), 14–24.

Edwards, C., Gandini, L., & Forman, G. (Eds.) (1993). *The hundred languages of children: The Reggio Emelia approach to early childhood education.* Norwood, NJ: Ablex.

Erikson, E. H. (1950). *Childhood and society.* New York: Norton.

Farrington, D. P. (1991). Childhood aggression and adult violence: Early precursors and later-life outcomes. In D. J. Furman, (1995, January). Helping children cope with stress and deal with feelings. *Young Children, 50,* (2).

Haskins, R. (1985). Public school aggression among children with varying day-care experience. *Child Development, 56,* 689–703.

Hills, T. W. (1992). Reach potentials through appropriate assessment in Bredekamp, S. & Rosegrant, T. (Eds.) *Reaching Potentials: Appropriate Curriculum and Assessment for Young Children, Volume 1.* Washington: National Association for the Education of Young Children.

Hohmann, M. & Weikart, D. P. (1995). *Educating young children: Active learning practices for preschool and child care programs.* Ypsilanti, MI: High/Scope Press.

Holloway, S. D. & Reichart-Erickson, M. (1988). The relationship of day care quality to children's free play behavior and social problem-solving skills. *Early Childhood Research Quarterly, 3,* p. 53.

Honig, A. (1986). Stress and coping in children, in McCracken, J. B. (Eds.) (1986). *Reducing stress in young children's lives.* Washington, DC: National Association for the Education of Young Children.

Huesmann, L. R., Eron, L. D., Lefkowitz, M. M., & Walder, L. O. (1984). Stability of aggression over time and generations. Developmental *Psychology, 20,* 1120–1134.

Jewett, J. (1992). *Aggression and cooperation: Helping young children develop constructive strategies.* (1992). Urbana, IL: ERIC Clearinghouse on Elementary and Early Childhood Education, EDO-PS-92-10.

Kostelnik, M. J., Stein, L. C., Whiren, A. P., & Soderman, A. K. (1993). *Guiding Young Children's Social Development.* Albany, NY: Delmar Publishers.

Kuebli, J. (1994, March). Young children's understanding of everyday emotions. *Young Children, 49,* (3), 44.

Lickona, T. (1983). *Raising good children.* New York: Bantam Books.

Morrison, G. (1990). *The world of child development: Conception to adolescence.* Albany: Delmar Publishers.

Pepler, D. J. & Rubin, K. H. (Eds.). (1991). *The development and treatment of childhood aggression.* Hillsdale, NJ: Lawrence Erlbaum Associates, Publishers.

Rosegrant, T. & Bredekamp, S. (1991). Reaching individual potentials through transformational curriculum. In S. Bredekamp and T. Rosegrant (Eds.). *Reaching Potentials: Appropriate Curriculum and Assessment for Young Children, Volume 1.* Washington, DC: National Association for the Education of Young Children.

Schweinhart, L. (1995, June). *Early childhood curriculum models: Who needs them?* Research presented at the meeting of the National Institute for Early Childhood Professional Development, San Francisco, CA.

Segal, M. & Adcock, D. (1993). *Play together, grow together: A cooperative curriculum for teachers of young children.* Ft. Lauderdale, FL: Nova University Publications.

Seligman, J. (July 3, 1995). Testosterone wimping out? *Newsweek,* p. 61.

Slaby, R. G., Roedell, W. C., Arezzo, D. & Hendrix, K. (1995). *Early violence prevention: Tools for teachers of young children.* Washington,DC: National Association for the Education of Young Children.

Smith, C. A. (1993). *The peaceful classroom.* Mt. Ranier, MD: Gryphon House.

Thomas, A. & and Chess, S. (1977). *Temperament and development.* New York: Brunner/Mazel.

Thornburg, K. R., Pearl, P., Crompton, D., & Ispa, J. M. (1990). Development of kindergarten children based on child care arrangements. *Early Childhood Research Quarterly, 5,* 27–42.

Tremblay, R. E. (1991). Aggression, prosocial behavior, and gender: Three magic words but no magic wand. In D. J. Pepler & K. H. Rubin (Eds.), *The development and treatment of childhood aggression.* Hillsdale, N. C. Lawrence Erlbaum Associates.

Trister-Dodge, D. (1988). *The creative curriculum for early childhood.* Washington, DC: Creative Associates International, Inc.

Watson, J. B. (1914). *Behavior: An introduction to comparative psychology.* New York: Holt, Rinehart, & Winston.

Wittmer, D. & Honig, A. (1994). Encouraging positive social development in young children. *Young Children, 49,* (5), 4–11.

Zimbardo, P. & Radl, S. (1981). *The shy child: A parent's guide to preventing and overcoming shyness from infancy to adulthood.* New York: McGraw-Hill.

RESOURCES

Bos, B. (1990). *Together we're better.* Roseville, CA: Turn the Page Press.

Segal, M. & Adcock, D. (1993). *Play together, grow together: A cooperative curriculum for young children.* Ft. Lauderdale, FL: Nova University Publications.

Slaby, R. G., Roedell, W. C., Arezzo, D. & Hendrix, K. (1995). *Early violence prevention: Tools for teachers of young children.* Washington, DC: National Association for the Education of Young Children.

Smith, C. A. (1993). *The peaceful classroom: 162 easy activities to teach preschoolers compassion and cooperation.* Mt. Rainer, MD: Gryphon House.

Using Interviews to Look at Language and Speech

IN THIS CHAPTER

✔ Using Interviews As an Observation Method

✔ Looking at Language and Speech

✔ Special Populations and Language Development

✔ Topics in Observation: Diversity

✔ Helping Professionals for Speech and Language Concerns

USING INTERVIEWS AS AN OBSERVATION METHOD

Exercise: What might the following sentences tell you about the person speaking?

"Howdy, ya'll."

"I've just had a dialogue with my stock broker..."

"When I was in France..."

"I'm so stupid..."

"Thith ith fun!"

"I ain't got no job."

"Dey gonna come get you bein' bad."

"Wa wa."

"You raise sheep? How do e-w-e do it?" (spells out ewe)

"Na na, na na, na."

"You sister him?"

Observing by listening is done naturally all the time. The message received by the listener is not just the words and their meaning. Inferences are made about where the speaker is from, their self-esteem, educational background, social situation, ethnic group, and even mental age. Subtle, and

sometimes not so subtle, clues are given about their interests, economics, and experiences. The listener notices teeth formation, facial expression, body language, eye contact, sense of humor, and vocabulary choice. All of these may give more information about the speaker than the actual words spoken.

Exercise: When you want to know something about the following subjects, whom do you ask?

What postage is due on this package I'm mailing?

How many automobiles were shipped into the United States last year?

How long do I cook a five-pound roast?

What medicine can I take for this cold?

Do I need a haircut?

Where does it hurt?

To receive a reliable answer to a question, it must be addressed to the person who most likely knows the answer. Scramble the answers to the questions in the preceding exercise to see how foolish it is to ask the wrong person, or even guess the answer. It only makes sense, then, to gather information *about* the child *from* the child. Harste and colleagues (1984) use the phrase, "the child as the informant." By listening to the child, both what is said and how it is said, information is transferred upon which evaluations are made.

Exercise: Using a tape recorder, talk to five children of different ages. Try to find a child of one, two, three, four, and five. This tape will be used repeatedly in this chapter to illustrate speech and language development.

Carry on a little conversation beginning with a greeting, "My name is _____. What's your name? How old are you? What are you doing? Where did you get that? What are you going to do with it?"

What differences did you hear in the way children of various ages answered the questions?

Interviewing, or asking children questions to find out what they know or what they are thinking about, is an age-old technique. The early childhood field has a prestigious role model for interviewing children in Piaget (Evans, 1973), who used the "clinical" interview, writing meticulous notes on the questions and answers. He began with his own children but extended his interviews to others to delve deeper into their thinking and understand their wrong answers to questions.

Talking with young children can be interesting and rewarding, Figure 6.1. It also can be frustrating because of their short attention span and egocentricism (only understanding from their point of view). Sometimes they do not speak clearly enough to be understood. Questioning children brings surprising results: Ask a child, "What color is a banana?" The child may say white or may say yellow. The part we eat is white. Ask a child, "What color is an apple?" The answer may be white. Is that a wrong answer? It probably would be considered wrong on a standardized test, although it is correct technically.

There are many formal tests of speech and language that use picture recognition, imitating letter sounds, comprehension, and sentence completion. These are used primarily by speech and language pathologists in determining a child's level of speech and language ability. The parent, teacher, or caregiver is most concerned, however, in communicating with the child. Formal evaluation measures are used only when that communication seems to be hampered by speech or language delays or difficulties.

Social discourse or discussions and questioning methods were first called **action research** by Kurt Lewin in 1958. It is a way for teachers to find out what they want to know and to seek answers about their own classroom. Interviewing children and their self reporting are accepted fact-finding methods (Moxley, et al., 1990). Interviews take several forms, depending on the age of the child, situation, and information to be gathered. **Informal interviews** happen all the time in the normal functioning of the child in the environment. As the adult talks with the child about her actions, he asks, "Wow! How did you get that to stand up on that little end like that?" or "Can you think of another way to use these old pieces of plastic someone gave us?" Snack, mealtimes, and discussions after stories are excellent times for information discussions or interviews. This style allows the conversation to flow in a natural way and to gather spontaneous samples of what the child is doing and thinking. Besides listening to the message, the hearer can also examine how the child is using language and the quality of the speech production. It then becomes an informal **diagnostic interview** as well. Interviewing can be a process to confirm a problem that may need remediation. Both casual conversations and structured interviews can be diagnostic.

A more **structured interview** gathers specific information about the child's understanding of certain concepts. The adult sets up items for the child to choose big/little; short/long; over/under; red/blue; things that go together or things that do not belong. Selected pictures or books often are used to elicit conversation. During the interview, speech and language skills are assessed also (Wortham, 1995). An Interest Questionnaire (Almy & Genishi, 1979) can give older children an opportunity to express their likes and dislikes and give insight into a child's happiness or self-esteem, with

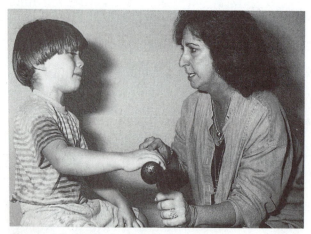

Figure 6.1 Talking with a child can be interesting and a source of developmental assessment.

questions like: "What would you like to know more about?" or "The most interesting thing I have done at our school during the past week is?" or "What is your favorite thing to do at school?"

Responses may be written in a log by older children or dictated to the teacher, Figure 6.2. Dictation gives the child a role model for literacy, seeing spoken words translated into permanent print. It also gives the child an opportunity to think and reflect on the past. Through dictation, the child expresses feelings by elaborating on thoughts and feelings. Opinions are stated or interpretations or reasons for an event can be explored. The interview is a little conversation with a purpose. Newman (1993, p. 258) suggests this mini-outline:

A greeting of some kind—"Hello, Anita."
Expression of interest—"I have some new markers. Would you like to try them and draw some things that you like to do at school?"
Taking turns at speaking—As Anita draws, she says, "This is the easel." The teacher says, "Yes, you like to paint just about every day. What else is in this drawing of favorite things?" Anita says, "I like to get in the TV and sing like I'm on a show." The teacher reponds, "That big old TV cabinet holds you and your friend."
Some pausing—Gives child time to draw and think. "And here we are!"
Leave-taking, or way to end the conversation—"I enjoyed our little talk and hearing about your favorite things. Let's go into the office and make a copy so we can put one into your portfolio and you can take this one home. I hope the purple and orange markers you used copy all right."

Efficient questioning techniques and skills make the most of the interviewing method. There is a hierarchy of questions (Bryen & Gallaher, 1983) that yield progressively more information while requiring more complex levels of comprehension.

Yes/no questions—"Do you want a drink?"
What (object)—"What's this?"
What (action)—"What are you doing?"
Where (location)—"Where's the dolly?"

Figure 6.2 Children's dictations and drawings give insight into their thinking.

What (attributes)—"What color is this?"

Who (persons)—"Who is picking you up today?"

Whose (possession)— "Whose boots are these?"

Which (selection)—"Which cookie cutter do you want?"

When (time)—"When are you going to paint today?"

How (manner)—"How did you make those dots?"

Why (cause-effect)—"Why did that paper rip?" (p. 103)

Each type of question requires more thought; understanding of the *Wh*-questions, and longer, more revealing answers. **Closed questions** are those for which the asker already knows the answer and is testing the receiver. All but the last two of the preceding list are closed questions. They may give information about a child's specific knowledge but not about thinking processes or creativity. **Open questions** such as, "What's another way…" or "Can you tell me how…?" give more insight and are more natural conversation models.

Asking children open-ended questions (those for which the person asking does not know the precise answer) is a technique to help the child think, imagine, and solve problems.

Exercise: Here are some typical questions. Put a checkmark by the open-ended questions.

❑   Observing—"What do you notice here?"
❑   Recall—"What did you see at the zoo?"
❑   Differences—"How are they different?"
❑   Similarities—How are these the same?"
❑   Ordering—"Can you order these colors from lightest to darkest?"
❑   Grouping—"Which of these go together?"
❑   Labeling—"What is the name of that group?"
❑   Classifying—"Which cubes here are red?"
❑   Concept Testing—"This cube is blue but does it belong?"
❑   Causes—"Why do you think that happened?"
        "f…?"
            she feels?"
                  happens to

            ask her?"
            hink will hap-

        e would you

    ning Model in

All but naming, labeling, classifying and concept testing are open-ended questions.

Selecting an interview type depends on what the adult wants to know about the child, the cognitive level, and the emotional state of the child.

The style of the questioner is also a factor in interviewing. Some people are more comfortable engaging in a conversation that is spontaneous and flows from the exchange between child and adult. Others may prefer a more structured format for uniformity and comparison as well as comfort with the method. Questions for discussion or interviews with preschool children will be provided for the interview assignments, but the observer or recorder is free to record more natural conversations if that is more comfortable.

How to Record Conversations and Interviews

In the context of this book, **record** is a word used for writing down information. Using interviews it can have the more traditional meaning referring to electronic recording such as audio tape recording. This is an effective method for preserving the conversation for later transcription into words and for a more careful analysis of the child's speech and language. It depends, however, on the comfort zone of both the adult and the child. Tape recording can be intimidating and intrusive. If it is, it modifies the results. Frequent use of the tape recorder for children to record themselves and each other reduces the intimidation and familiarizes them with the tape recorder.

A tape for each child with a collection of recordings made throughout the year is an appropriate addition to the portfolio. Most children enjoy taping and listening to themselves. The teacher also makes written summaries or notes of the tape recordings. This method is recommended for the beginning interviewer so that concentration is focused on the conversation rather than note taking.

Advantages of Interviews

Interviews can

*   yield multitudes of information both in content and in language production from natural situations
*   be analyzed later
*   show progress of speech and language over time
*   raise child's self-esteem as the focus of a one-on-one conversation, with a closely attentive listener

Disadvantage of Interviews

Interviews are

- time-intensive when focusing on one child
- intimidating so the child may be reluctant to speak under certain circumstances
- confidential and may be intrusive to child or family

Pitfalls to Avoid

Children may be uncomfortable with interviews. It is important to emphasize the special conversations will be held with *each* child and *everyone* will have a turn. If a child appears anxious during the interview and is reluctant to speak, the interviewer should stop and observe the child in a more natural setting.

A busy classroom may interfere with the interview, but isolation in another room is not recommended. Find a quiet spot, as free from distractions as possible, within the classroom.

Any information revealed by the child of a personal nature should not be recorded unless it is a child abuse disclosure. (See Chapter 12 for a full discussion of this subject.)

What to Do with It

The Structured Interview questions and answers are filed in the child's portfolio. Anecdotal notes or jottings from an Informal Interview are also filed in the portfolio. Significant parts can be highlighted with a marker to draw attention. The information yielded can be noted in respective categories on the overview sheet, such as cognitive, social, self-identity, or emotional.

Tape recordings are also filed in the portfolio. A sheet is attached to the tape, listing the dates and subject (and counter number, if possible) of each recording. Full transcriptions are not necessary unless there is some reason to amplify documentation of a developmental area, or provide the raw data, exact wording, for a referral.

The tape recorded conversations or interviews make excellent resources for listening closely to a child's speech and language. The next section on speech and language development gives guidelines for listening and evaluating, both from live and tape recorded conversations.

LOOKING AT LANGUAGE AND SPEECH

"Listen before you speak" is not just wise advice but actually the progression of language develop-

ment. Listening is also described as **receptive language**.

Receptive and Expressive Language

An important principle of language development is that the receptive language always is greater than the **expressive language**, Figure 6.3. The one-year-old is told "Go give grandma a kiss." The infant crawls, or walks, to grandma and gives her a kiss. He cannot say anything close to, "I want to kiss my grandma," but from his actions that is interpreted. He can understand the words of the request, act on them, but not say or express the words himself. When people are learning a second language, they always can understand far more than they are able to actually say themselves. This principle is also displayed when a person has a thought or idea but has difficulty explaining it to someone else. They say, "I know what I mean, but I just can't explain it." Receptive language, understanding verbal communication, is always greater than the ability to express thoughts verbally.

This has some direct implications for anyone around young children. The phrase, "Little pitchers have big ears" comes from this principle. Although children are physically small, unsophisticated, and unable to speak themselves, they are "taking in" what they hear. It will eventually be expressed. Not only is this a warning for adults to monitor their conversations in the presence of young children, but it is a reminder that this is a fertile learning time. All that is said, read, and sung is received. It emphasizes the importance of adults talking to babies who cannot yet communicate back. The foundations for vocabulary and language not yet present are laid in these early months and years.

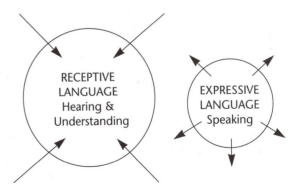

Figure 6.3 Receptive language is always greater than expressive language.

Language Acquisition

Exactly how language is acquired has been the focus of much study and controversy. B. F. Skinner's behaviorist theory (1957) attributes language development to reinforcement and imitation. In Chomsky's (1965) Language Acquisition Device (LAD) theory, the capacity to acquire language is present in all humans, but not animals. Proof of this are the choices in grammar that children make automatically. No one teaches a child to say "goed." It comes from the internalization of language. The process converts to a past tense using an untaught rule. It also causes the switch from "goed" to "went" a little later. Other language theorists include heredity and environmental influences to explain language development. Imitation of sounds is unquestionably a part of language acquisition. The repetition of words they hear is how children learn vocabulary. They associate objects with words, and eventually feelings with words that describe them. Imitation is not the whole answer either, for children form sentences they have never heard. Piaget (1955) emphasizes the initial cognitive development before language is present, whereas Vygotsky (1962) disagrees and believes children are speaking internally to solve difficult problems.

The adult role in language acquisition cannot be denied. When children are provided an environment where people are talking to them, they talk sooner. When adults respond to babies' early sounds, those sounds occur more frequently. Reinforcement, encouragement, expectation, and rewards for language stimulate development. Probably, it is a combination of all of these factors working together. The important principle for parents and teachers of young children is the recognition and response to each child's attempts to communicate.

Speech Development

Exercise: Read the following sentence out loud:

"Eres el/la heredero de una herencia. Ve inmediatemente a Madrid y pregunta por el alcalde. El te va a indicar lo que debes hacer."

You have just spoken Spanish. You have the speech. You have the sounds, but you do not have the language unless you know the meaning. Have you communicated in Spanish? Only if the hearer or receiver knows the language. (The sentence means: "You are the heir of a fortune. Go at once to Madrid and ask for the mayor. He will direct you.") It would be important to be able to receive that message!

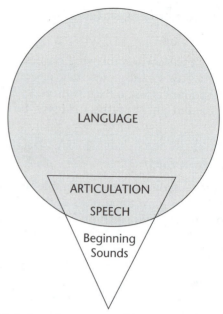

Figure 6.4 Speech as a part of language development

As explained in Chapter 1, the words *growth* and *development* often are used interchangeably. However, they have different meanings. The words *speech* and *language* are so often used together that most people think they are the same also, Figure 6.4. Not so! **Speech** is the sound produced to make the words. **Language** is the term for words and phrases that convey meaning. There can be speech without language (just making random sounds). There can be no audible language without speech. Nonverbal communication is body language or gestures, the way of conveying messages without speaking.

The smallest units making the sounds of the words are the **phonemes,** the sounds of speech. These are phonemes /u/, /o/, /a/, /m/, /p/, /b/, /t/, /n/, /k/, /ng/, /y/, /g/, /f/, /v/, /sh/, /zh/, /l/, /rth/, /ch/. These are in the order in which they appear developmentally. Along with vowels to link them, words are formed. These are called **morphemes**, small units of sound that have meaning. It is interesting that /m/ is the first sound an infant can make, and in most languages of the world, the word for the person who bore them begins with the /m/ sound: *mother, mama, mamone* (Ouseg, 1962).

The infant begins to make sounds at birth, crying, not purposefully but by reflex, just like reflex actions in other developmental areas. Within the first month, the crying becomes more differentiated so the caregiver can begin to tell the difference between the hungry cry and the painful cry. During that first month, preverbal infants can even differentiate between the sounds of /ba/ and /pa/ (deVillers & deVillers, 1979).

During the second month, more purposeful and pleasant sounds emerge: cooing and squealing. Those can be written down because the sounds are phonemes that are recognizable as vowels. As the infant gains muscular control of the lips and tongue, the consonants appear in babbling and later imitation of adult talking. "Ba ba, ma ma, da da, pa pa," understandable approximations of longer words, are usually frequent by the end of the first year.

Another interesting fact about infants' phoneme production put forth by deVillers (1979) is that the range of sounds infants make is found in every language. The click sound in Southern African languages, or the blowing through his lips like a cross between a /p/ and an /f/ in the Japanese language, are made but later lost by English-speaking children. These sounds are heard in babbles of all babies around the world but disappear or are added around one year, depending on the language they are learning. This accounts for the difficulty adult learners have with certain sounds of the second language they are learning. The ability to make those sounds has disappeared from their repertoire. It also makes the case for exposing infants and toddlers to other languages to help preserve those sounds.

The precise articulation or production of phonemes, the sounds of language, is a long developmental period. Some of the more difficult combinations of sounds may not be present until six or seven years old.

Exercise: Listen to the tape you made in the exercise again, listening closely and looking at the following articulation chart. This outlines the usual progression and expectation of acquiring certain sounds. Did the children you listened to produce these sounds clearly?

p, w, h, m, n (usually by three years)
b, k, g, d, y (usually by four years)
f, ng, t, r, l (usually by six years)
ch, sh, j, s, z, v, th, zh, br, tr (clear by seven to eight years)

By the time children are four years old, they have usually developed the vocabulary, language structure, and grammatical rules needed to communicate about their world. Because young children are learners, their speech and language will be imperfect. They still may have **articulation** (sound) errors, which will continue to develop into the seventh year, especially those combinations like *wh* (whether), *rth, ch, sz*. Those imperfections

can be categorized but are not necessarily cause for alarm. Some of the common mispronunciations in the preschool years are:

Substitutions—"wabbit" for "rabbit"
Omissions—"tar" for "star"
Distortions—"caaa" for "car"
Additions—"pisghetti" for "speghetti"
Lisps—"thith" for "this"

Speech and language screening in the preschool years is recommended and especially indicated if the child is very difficult to understand. The role of the early childhood educator is one of facilitator, interpreter, and responder rather than remediator. Content and meaning are the most important aspects when talking with young children.

Stuttering. Dysfluent, repetitive speech, or stuttering, "I, I, I, I want it," occurs frequently in the four-and five-year-old. The adult listener should listen patiently without telling the child, "Now, just slow down," or "Don't talk so fast," or "Your ideas just get ahead of your tongue" (Gottwald, et al., 1985). Statements like these draw the child's attention to the stuttering and add to the stress. Avoid placing the child in the spotlight to speak or feeling the pressure of the whole group waiting. If this does not pass in a few weeks, further investigation may be needed to look for stressors or other factors. A private conversation with the parents should begin the investigation, along with notes on when the stuttering began and the child's reaction to it.

The Development of Language

From the first birthday, vocabulary grows (because it can be measured in numbers) at a fantastic rate, Figure 6.5. Listen again to the taped conversations: Count the number of different words each child said. Did it increase with age? Look at the vocabulary explosion, Figure 6.6.

Exercise: Here is a mathematical problem for you. Using Figure 6.6, what is the percentage rate of vocabulary growth between one year (use 15 words) and six years?

Beginning Communication

Exercise: "Mama" is one of the first words a baby says. How many meanings can be interpreted by the way you say it?

The beginning talker starts with one word. It quickly is joined by others, all names for people or objects. They are spoken with various inflections

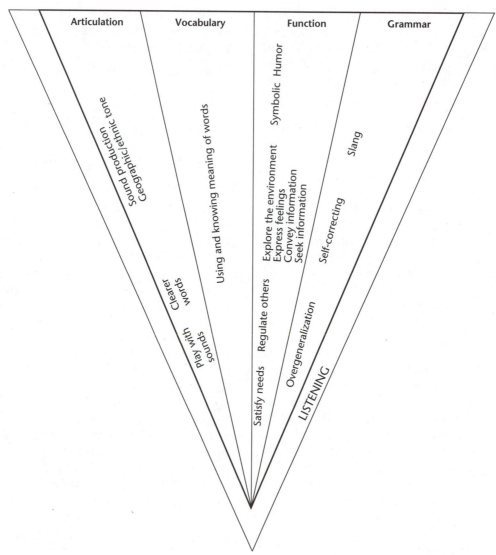

Figure 6.5 Speech and Language Development

and sometimes accompanied by gestures, such as pointing or arm movements that convey a more sophisticated message than labeling. Single words between 12 and 18 months become requests or questions. These one-word utterances that have meaning are **holographic** phrases, which are soon followed by short two-word sentences called **telegraphic** phrases. Examples of the telegraphic phrases are "Doggie gone," and "Look baby." When telegraphic phrases occur, the child has acquired language. She is expressing herself using the sounds of speech.

Exercise: Listen to the children on the tape. Did any of them use just one word to convey a whole thought?

Language is developing, changing from simple to complex in a predictable pattern but at individual rates. The child is developing a sense of **syntax**, the order of words in a sentence that make it understandable to others: "Mama go," "Baby ba ba." Their language is the combination of heredity, social interactions, and emotional environment. Cognitive or learning ability and physical development all combine to make this happen. The interdependence and simultaneous development of many areas are vividly illustrated in language development.

Exercise: Describe how speech or language might be affected by:

Hearing:

Muscle development:

Geography:

Abuse:

Siblings:

Heredity:

Ethnicity:

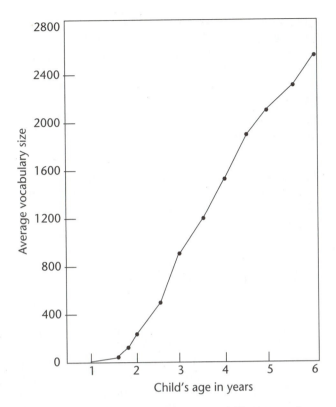

Figure 6.6 The Vocabulary Explosion! (Courtesy of Machado, J. M. 1990. *Early Childhood Experiences in Language Arts.* Albany NY: Delmar Publishers, p. 55. Reprinted with permission of author.)

Exercise: From the children you listened to, could you gather any of the preceding information?

It takes many years for the grammatical construction to move from one-word holographic sentences to the telegraphic but meaningful few-word sentences to complex sentences with prepositional phrases and correct tenses and plurals. Children seem to have an inner sense of picking up plurals and past tense from hearing adults speak. At first they say "mouses," instead of "mice," because they have heard "houses" meaning more than one house. They will say, "I *goed* to the store," though they have never heard anyone say that. They have heard others say, "I *washed* the dishes." This application of simple grammatical rules to all plurals and past tense words is **overgeneralization**. Children internalize the grammatical rule and apply it to all words in that category. Over time, this self-corrects, usually by five years of age.

The development of grammatical construction (Bryen & Gallagher, 1983) follows this progression:

Uses correct word order (by two and one-half)
Uses pronouns (by two and one-half)

Gives name (by three)
Uses plurals and some prepositions (by three)
Tells day's schedule in sequence (by four)
Can tell an imaginative story about a picture (by four)
Speaks in adult-like sentences (by four)

Exercise: How complex were the sentences in the tape recording of conversations? Were there any examples of overgeneralization?

Functions of Language. Children develop in the more complex use of language. Their first single words convey recognition and description, "Ma ma," "Ba ba." Very quickly they learn that their language can be used to influence others. Those same words can now call others to communicate a need. "Ma ma, "Ba ba." As they gain vocabulary and willfulness, the communication takes the form of commands like "Go," "No bath."

With mobility and experience in a wider environment, their language expands not only in vocabulary but in using it to describe what they see, "Red ball." They convey information, "Ball all gone," as they watch the ball going down the toilet. They seek information in the third and fourth years with the constant, "Why?" questions, and begin to express feelings, "So sad." After a scolding, the "So sorry," may soften a grandma's heart. Cognitive development is moving toward the symbolic stage when reading and writing develop. The symbolic stage appears in language too, "I have an idea." Humor may emerge in double meanings of words and puns. The concept of rhyming may be understood.

Social and Nonverbal Language. Acredolo and Goodwyn (1985) found that nonverbal gestures as signs or signals come before words. A baby with arms outstretched is making an understandable but silent plea. Asking a one- to two-year-old, "Where's your nose?" elicits a knowledgeable response months before the child can say the word *nose*. By observing gestures and also listening for words, the caregiver can learn about the child's needs, what he knows, and even what he is thinking.

Children show social and cognitive skills in their language as well. Think about each of the children on your tape as they talked with you.

Did they demonstrate a "turn-taking" kind of conversation where they knew they were to speak then you would have a turn, or was it more of a monologue?
Did they make eye contact?
What was the facial expression as they spoke?

What gestures did they use, if any?

What could you tell from the tone of voice that just writing down the words would not convey?

IT HAPPENED TO ME:
He Shared His Expertise

Jason was a very quiet four-year-old when he started preschool. Several weeks went by while he just watched other children, without interacting or speaking in the classroom. Some children just need more time to adjust to a situation. We spoke to him about the day, what he was doing, greeted him at the door without pressuring him to speak or commenting on his silence. In private talks with his mother, she said that was his way of coping with new situations. She assured us he was very verbal at home. This continued for weeks and into months with his mother assuring us this was his little game. He did begin to play with objects in the classroom, first the sand and blocks. He eventually began to interact with other children but still without speaking. We still tried not to draw attention to it but spoke to him as we did all the other children in conversation as they played.

One day in February, when dinosaurs were the project theme, he brought in a book from home. At the door he held it open to me and said, "This is a stegosaurus." I was shocked and the children even commented saying, "He talked!" I said, "Jason, that's the first thing you've ever said to me. I wonder why you chose today to talk." He said matter of factly, "I wanted to share my expertise about dinosaurs with you." (Exact words, I swear.) From that day on, he talked occasionally with peers and teachers as he played. I often marvel at the strength of will he had all those weeks. His willpower held us all hostage to his little game.

Exercise: Practice your ability to place bits of language in chronological order of their normal development. Number the following from the earliest to the latest in the progression of development:

☐ "Want milk"
☐ "Waader"
☐ "When I grow up, I'm gonna be a ballerina."
☐ "No"
☐ "mum mum mum mum mum"
☐ "I goed to the store."
☐ "Wha's dat?"
☐ "Eeeeeeeeeeeeeeeeeee"

The sequence is vowels, consonants and vowels, approximations of words, telegraphic speech, questions, refusals (this can come anytime after item number 2), imperfect grammar, and adult-like but self-centered.

Answers are: 6, 3, 8, 5, 2, 7, 4, 1.

Language Role Models. Adults are language role models for children, Figure 6.7.

Exercise: Set up a tape recorder in the classroom or wear a small portable one in your pocket. Tape a 30- to 60-minute sample of yourself "for your ears only." Analyze it for your common language habits, and see if any changes need to be made in the language role model you are presenting to children.

Teachers of young children fall into some habits that are not helpful to children. Some are reviewed here to alert the reader to consider the impact on the child.

Figure 6.7 Language Role Models?

The Tester. Many teachers of young children know the way to find out what children know is to ask questions. Unfortunately, they translate this into a series of test questions: "What color is the coat you are wearing today?" "Is it sunny or rainy?" "How many colors in your picture?" "What month is it?" The child might answer sarcastically, "You're supposed to be the teacher and you don't know so you're asking a little kid?" As language role models and empathetic humans, adults should speak to children in the same manner they speak to peers. An adult would not ask a bystander "What color is your shirt?" or a friend "How many bracelets are you wearing today?" Questions asked of children should be motivated by natural interest and desire to explore the child's thinking, rather than checking if the child knows.

The Helper. Adults fall into the trap of speaking of themselves by name in sentences spoken to young children, like the much criticized "we" of the health profession. Often teachers say, "Let Mrs. M. help you with your boots," or "Do you want Miss Barbara to push you on the swing?" If a child said of herself, "Mary can do it" it would be considered an irregular language pattern, not using pronouns. As language models, teachers can and should use pronouns when speaking of themselves in sentences. A neighbor would think it odd if a person spoke of themselves when saying, "Mrs. Smith (the speaker) heard your dog barking all night."

"Use Your Words." The underlying reason for this phrase is to encourage children to verbalize their feelings. These words do not help the child do that. Neither does its accompanying, "Tell him you don't like it when he..." It tells the child what she should do but does not give assistance in how to do it. If she knew how to use her words to tell him, she would have said it already. A more appropriate and helpful phrase might be, "Tell him, 'I don't like it when you...'" It reminds the child that words are preferred to hurtful actions. The child is given the exact words to say. She also does not have to make the shift from "you" to "I" when using the sentence. Imagine a car stopped at the red light, and the driver behind it sounds his horn. The first driver leans out and says sweetly, "Use your words."

How Would You Like It if She Did That to You?" One of the major characteristics of the egocentric, preoperational child is the inability to see from another's perspective, the inability to put oneself on the receiving end of the action or word. This phrase then becomes meaningless and useless to the child under five or six. A more understandable phrase might be, "Remember when you got sand in your eyes from someone flipping the shovel? That's what you just did to Lois. It hurt your eyes and now her eyes are hurting in the same way. Can you find another way to use the shovel?"

Incorrect Grammar, Slang, and Lazy Articulation. The disagreement of noun and verb plurals is a common grammatical habit. Saying, "We was" rather than "We were" gives children a poor example of grammar. Calling all the children "Kids," or "Guys" rather than by their names is disrespectful. Dropping the /g/ at the end of those -*ing* words is a habit adopted by language learners. By listening to a tape of themselves, teachers can become aware of those habits and try to correct 'em (them). Teachers become better language role models for young children with an awareness of the potential for misunderstanding or imitation.

What Can You Tell About a Child from Listening?

Exercise: In the following categories, list on a separate sheet of paper what you might learn about a child by listening to speech and language as well as content.

Family:
Culture:
Physical development:
Health:
Age or stage of development:
Socioeconomic level:
Cognitive development:
Self-concept:
Needs:
Temperament:
Activity level:
Humor:
Television viewing habits:
Imagination:
Problem-solving abilities:
Social development:

In each category, there are the obvious bits of knowledge that can be acquired by listening or asking the child questions.

Family—manners, attitudes, besides finding out inside information like a new baby is on the way

Culture—customs, holiday celebrations, common activities

Physical development—abilities like ride a bike with no training wheels, interests such as dancing or karate, missing teeth, muscles or structure of the mouth and jaw

Health—nasal congestion, "I threw up before I came to school," "My arm hurts."

Age or stage of development—grammatical construction, "Me do it."

Socioeconomic level—"We're flying to Disney World," or "We slept in the car last night."

Cognitive—"If I want more cookie I can just break this one up and have lots," "Eight, nine, ten, eleventeen, twelveteen."

Self-concept—"Nobody likes me."

Needs—Help me, I can't do it."

Temperament—"I CAN'T DO IT!"

Activity level—"I'm gonna swing on a swing then I'm gonna ride a bike, then I'm gonna dig in the sand, then I'm gonna..."

Humor—"Where does a sheep get a haircut? In the baabaa shop."

Television viewing habits—"I'm gonna be a Power Ranger."

Imagination—"I have this refrigerator and it follows me wherever I go so I can have a cold drink whenever I want it."

Problem-solving abilities—"I tried it this way but it didn't work so I tried this and it worked!"

Social development—"If you don't give me a turn I won't invite you to my birthday party."

Listen to children talk, sometimes prompted by a few open-ended questions like

"Do you want to tell me about...?"

"How'd you do that?"

"Then what happened?"

"What do you think will happen next?"

"Hmmmmm"

Confidentiality Issue

Just a reminder to teachers that the child is the client. In that special relationship, what a child tells a teacher is privileged information, just like a doctor or a lawyer. It is important not to use this information for a general topic of conversation, only to help the child. In a later chapter, the child's disclosures of possible abuse are discussed.

SPECIAL POPULATIONS AND LANGUAGE DEVELOPMENT

Society is increasingly more culturally and linguistically diverse as well as aware of differing abilities. It is advisable for teachers to be bilingual, whether in a second cultural language or sign language.

Figure 6.8 Teachers must be ready to receive families of diverse cultures.

Accepting Other Languages and Dialects

Schools and caregivers must be ready to receive a child speaking languages other than English, Figure 6.8. Some statistics by Imhoff in *Learning in Two Languages* (1990) enforce that fact:

- The language-minority population is growing faster than the rest of the population, not limited to urban areas but now in suburban and rural areas.
- Of the limited English students in schools, 65 percent are Spanish speaking with 145 other language groups making up the remainder.
- By the turn of the century, 20 percent of the school population will be speaking Asian languages. (p. 22)

Bilingualism is a great advantage for teachers. There are so different languages spoken in many classrooms, however, it would be impossible to have teachers fluent in all of them. Therefore, it calls for a sensitivity to the child's needs who does not speak the language of the classroom or the teacher. It may be the child speaks a nonstandard dialect such as Black English **Ebonics** (Hendrick, 1992) in which the hearer recognizes the words and phrases but not the meaning. Many group settings include children who speak English as a second language with another as their first or come into the group knowing no English at all. Many schools have labeled these children limited English Proficient (LEP), seeing their lack of English as a deficit rather than recognizing their proficiency in the language they have already learned. In the past, assessments given in English indicated major delays and mistakenly prescribed remediation for many of these children.

More tolerant approaches have developed to help the child become bilingual, not pushing to be monolingual, nor attempting to extinguish the first language. The approach is described as additive, supporting the native language, while adding a second. This can be accomplished by

- providing time to explore
- listening to the child for meaning regardless of language
- giving ample social opportunities
- offering diverse linguistic opportunities
- valuing home cultures
- using informal observations
- providing an accepting classroom climate (Soto, 1991).

A basic early childhood principle is the acceptance of each child. It provides an environment, experiences, and support to help the child progress to the next level. Children learning a second language will progress through the same language development stages as an infant and toddler, beginning with single important words, then to telegraphic stages. They proceed through them with the same stage predictability of any other child learning language. The same techniques of teaching and observation are used regardless of the language the child speaks. See more about assessment and culture in this chapter's Topics in Observation.

Children with Differing Abilities in Regular Classrooms

Children with differing abilities of speech, language, or hearing may be placed in regular classrooms. Other children become their role models and communication skills become more functional in the responsive environment. The same strategies that are recommended for effective therapy carried on in the classroom are applicable to any early childhood teacher. Cook and Colleagues (1992) make the suggestions to

- listen attentively
- not ask quiz-like questions—"What color is your shoe?"
- talk about the here and now
- speak in a calm, normal tone of voice
- expand sentence length as the child's understanding expands (pp. 335, 336)

Sign language, or manual communication, and speech reading (commonly called lip reading) are debated between experts and families of the hearing impaired. The family makes the decision about their child. The early childhood program responds to that decision just as it would to any other family decisions, with sensitivity, and willingness to adapt to meet the needs of the child.

TOPICS IN OBSERVATION: Diversity

Exercise: In a crowded place—the supermarket, at the fair, on a bus—just take a look around. Do you see any two people the same? Look at noses. Just noses. Are any exactly the same shape or size? People-watching is a fascinating pastime.

Every person is different and yet the same. All have two ears and a nose that are parts of the whole. Because all people are members of the same species, there are expectations of how the parts work and how they change over time. Genetics, age, environment, or trauma cause the variations in the basic mold of a human.

Generalities help to make sense of the whole. Averages have been calculated based on large numbers of people but even then some will not fit within the range of average. Assessments and professional practice are based on averages that may not be a valid measurement.

How can a teacher measure vocabulary when the teacher does not speak the same language? How can a teacher write down how long the child can stand on one leg when the child is in a wheelchair? How can a teacher comment on the child's separation and adjustment to the classroom when the child has been in eight foster homes in three years? The dilemma is real!

Diversity is a fact of life, but thinking and attitudes sometimes are so narrow that the truth is overlooked. Adults are supposed to be past the egocentric stage, so they should understand statements such as, "How would you like it if

no one learned how to pronounce your name?"

there never were any pictures of people who looked like you around in your classroom?"

TOPICS IN OBSERVATION: continued

the food never had familiar flavors and spices?"

no one would hold your hand in a circle?"

the teacher planned activities that were always too difficult for you to do?"

you had to have money for school tomorrow for a field trip and your family didn't have it?"

letters always went home addressed to parents and you didn't have two parents (or any)?

everyone else was thin and you were fat?"

Different notes in a song, colors in a rainbow, or flowers in a field are valued. Why not individual differences? They are often rebuffed, ignored, and rejected, causing disharmony, and hurt feelings. While working with children, observing, and evaluating their development, comparisons to norms must be done very cautiously. The environment should represent and reflect everyone's individuality, and an attitude of acceptance of all must prevail. Here are some practical ways of accomplishing this.

Individual Differences. While norms give a range of expected growth and development, there will always be some children at both ends of the range that demand attention and decision-making about that difference. No child will be at the same developmental level as another. Even within each child, the level of development may be different in different areas. The child may be more advanced in language, less advanced in large muscle development, in the mid-range of emotional development, and off the map in cognitive development. Those differences deserve to be observed, evaluated, and acted upon if needed, but not seen as unusual or strange.

Special Needs. Some children have not developed within the normal range of expected levels. A strengths model looks at the abilities of the child as decision points for the placement. The role of the program is to keep the areas of special need from interfering with other normally developing skills. This opposes the deficit model focusing on the need. Instead, the child should be placed where the child can function to capacity where able, and assisted in areas of lesser ability. Authentic assessment, for every child, then looks at the individual areas of development to note the highest level of achievement rather than what the child cannot yet do.

Cultural/Ethnic Diversity. Caution is advised when broadly accepting any standard of evaluation or professional practice. It might be in conflict with the values or style differences in culture or ethnicity. Developmental and behavioral norms and professional practice are based on the majority culture and may be diametrically opposed to those of a minority culture. Familiarity and sensitivity to the cultural and ethnic differences of the population of the classroom is the only way to meet each child's needs. For example, the separation and independence and move toward autonomy in Chapter 1 may not fit the interdependence highly valued in Middle Eastern families.

Toilet training in Chapter 2 is a topic with great cultural variation and should be approached with the family's preferences in mind. Communication differs in some cultures using more through body language and implicit cues. Other cultures respond more to precise, direct language. Cultural differences must be considered when talking to parents about their child. Family decision makers vary between cultures, as do expectations for girls and boys. Acting honestly with a heightened awareness of the differences will help the child. By displaying a willingness to learn and a desire not to offend, families and teachers will build a partnership for the child.

What's in a Name? Throughout this book you will notice children's names, when used as examples, are from a variety of nationalities. A deliberate effort sought out the most popular names in many different cultures from a baby name book. It is extremely important to learn the correct pronunciation of the first and last names of all the families in the class, not giving them American nicknames unless the parents especially request it. It is a learning experience for the teacher and the other children to learn to pronounce ethnic names and can be a point of teaching tolerance, understanding, and cultural awareness. It must begin with the teacher's attitude.

HELPING PROFESSIONALS FOR SPEECH AND LANGUAGE CONCERNS

Speech and language disorders are often diagnosed first in early childhood programs. As children develop, parents expect their verbal skills to be emerging but often are not aware, or choose to ignore, what may be a problem in this area. It is not life-threatening; it often is compensated by the parent and other children in the family; and it can be cute and entertaining.

A speech and language screening is routinely administered to preschool children to detect possible difficulties. Informal interviews may act as that screening.

When to Seek Help in Speech and Language

Parents are consulted if the child is nearing three years old without much language. Documented observations over a time showing little progress when compared to a chart of norms can help explain the concern. The teacher presents options for referrals to professionals who will conduct screening or full evaluations. That referral should begin with medical personnel or the pediatrician. Chronic ear infections often go unnoticed and can cause hearing loss that may affect language development. There are many other possible causes. Early detection for diagnosis and possible intervention is recommended. This dialogue takes place with empathy for the parent's feeling and also a knowledge of community resources. If potential problems are indicated, a full evaluation usually is recommended either by the child's pediatrician or the program team. Teachers and early childhood programs should have referral lists from which the parents can choose an agency or professional to perform this evaluation. Some of the helping professionals that may be involved are

audiologist—conducts screenings and evaluations and diagnoses hearing problems. Assesses hearing aids and teaches clients to conserve hearing and to use residual hearing

speech and language pathologist—conducts screenings, evaluation, diagnosis, and treatment of children with communication disorders

otolaryngologist—physician who specializes in diagnosis and treatment of earn, nose, and throat disorders; sometimes known as ENT (ear, nose, and throat) physician

American Sign Language interpreters—translate spoken language into sign language and vice versa for people with hearing impairments.

Week 6, Assignment A

INTERVIEWS OF SPEECH AND LANGUAGE FOR GROUP A

Select each child in group A to interview each day this week. If possible, tape record the interview Informal or Structured (see the following suggestions) as well as make written notes (literacy role model) as you speak with each child.

Informal Interview

If you wish, record a conversation you have with the child about the child's play, an event, or an explanation of a piece of art or construction. Afterward, analyze the interview for what it reveals about the child's knowledge, emotional state, social development, and about the child's speech and language using the following checklist.

Structured Interview

Two- and three-year-olds:

"What's your name?"
"How old are you?"
"Go get the book." (receptive)
Say, "I want the ball."
"What's this?"
"What's this sound?" (Ring a bell without child seeing it.)
Show a mirror. "Who is that? "What's his/her name?"

Four- and five-year-olds:

"What's your name? Last name?"
"Look around the room and tell me what you see."
"What makes you happy (sad or mad)?"
"What do you like to do best at school?"

"Can you tell me about a dream you've had?"
"Do you know any jokes?"

What to Do with It

Copy the Speech and Language Checklist found in Appendix D for each child interviewed.

Analyze the interview for what it reveals about the child's knowledge, emotional state, social development, and the child's speech and language development. Enter a summary, recorder, and date on the portfolio overview sheet, like the example in Figure 6.9.

If a significant lag appears, discuss it with your supervisor to confirm it; then discuss it with the parents. Have a list of resources available for the parents to locate agencies for a speech and language evaluation.

Share with the parents and the child, if appropriate, something of interest that came from the interview. For example, "Mrs. Santiago, I was talking with Manuel and he told me about the trip you have planned to visit his grandparents. He is very excited about it. When he gets back

we'll be sure to invite him to tell the class about it if he would like to," or "When we had that little talk the other day, Sarah, it really was interesting the way you described your painting. I liked listening to the words you used about the shapes and colors. Anytime you want to listen to the tape, let me know."

Is any followup needed from the Speech and Language Checklist? Make a note of it, and seek answers or take action.

SPEECH/LANGUAGE		
Documentation	Recorder	Date
I. taped ck - lisp?	BAN	10/11
CK clearer sp.	BAN	1/6
I taped - Valentines	MS	2/15
I taped - going to K	BAN	6/19

Figure 6.9 Portfolio Overview Example

Week 6, Assignment B

CLASS LIST LOG OF SPEECH AND LANGUAGE FOR ALL

Use one of the Class List Log forms found in Appendix D, listing children by first names, alphabetically. Jot notes about each child concerning clarity of speech (understandable?), use of language for communication, irregularities, or concerns.

Note an observation on each child's portfolio overview sheet.

What to Do with It

This is a screening for your own use to listen closely to every child's speech and language development this week. In the next month, you will be individually interviewing and audio-taping each child to listen more closely. Discuss any concerns with the other staff or your supervisor, then the parents.

Note an observation on each child's portfolio overview sheet.

File the Class List Log in the class file.

Week 6, Assignment C

REFLECTIVE JOURNAL

Respond to the following in your Reflective Journal, kept in a private file at home.

I like to talk with children about…

I feel much more apprehensive when talking about…

I think it is because…

The language habit I need to work on most is…

My thoughts about diversity are…

REFERENCES

Acredolo, L. P. & Goodwyn, S. W. (1986). Symbolic gesturing in language development. *Human Development* No. 28, 53–58.

Almy, M., Genishi, C. (1979). *Ways of studying children.* New York: Teacher's College Press.

Bryen, D. N & Gallaher, D. (1983). Assessment of Language and Communication in K. D. Paget, & B. A. Bracken (Eds.) *The psychoeducational assessment of the Preschool Child.* New York: Grune & Stratton.

Chomsky, N. (1965). *Aspects of the theory of syntax.* Cambridge, MA: MIT Press.

Cook, R. E., Tessier, A., & Klein, M. D. (1992). *Adapting early childhood curricula for children with special needs.* New York: Merrill. (An imprint of Macmillan Publishing Company.)

deVilliers, P. A. & deVilliers, J. G. (1979). *Early language.* (1979). Cambridge, MA: Harvard University Press.

Evans, R. I. (1973). *Jean Piaget: The man and his ideas.* New York: E. P. Dutton.

Gottwald, S. R., Goldback, P., & Isack, A. H. (1985). Stuttering: Prevention and detection. *Young Children 41,* (1) 9–14.

Harste, J., Woodward, V., & Burke, C. (1984). *Language stories & literacy lessons.* Portsmouth, NH: Heinemann.

Hendrick, J. (1992). *The whole child.* New York: Merrill. (An imprint of Macmillan Publishing Co.)

Hildebrand, V., Phenice, L. A., Gray, M. M. & Hines, R. P. (1996). *Knowing and serving diverse families.* Englewood Cliffs, NJ: Prentice Hall.

Imhoff, G. (1990). *Learning in two languages: From conflict to consensus in the reorganization of schools.* New Brunswick: Transaction Press.

Lynch, E. W. & Hanson, M. J. (1994). *Developing cross-cultural competence: A guide for working with young children and their families.* Baltimore: Paul H. Brookes Publishing Co.

Machado, J. M. (1990). *Early childhood experiences in language arts.* Albany: Delmar Publishers.

Moxley, R. A., Kenny, K. A. & Hunt, M. K. (1990). Improving the instruction of young children with self-recording and discussion. In *Early Childhood Research Quarterly,* 5, 233–249.

Newman, S. B., & Roskos, K. A. (1993). *Language and literacy learning in the early years.* Fort Worth, TX: Harcourt, Brace Jovanovich.

Ouseg, H. L. (Ed.). (1962). *International dictionary in twenty-one languages.* New York: Philosophical Library.

Pelligrini, A. D. (1991). *Applied child study: A developmental approach.* Hillsdale, NJ: Lawrence Erlbaum.

Piaget, J. (1955). *The language and thought of the child.* New York: Noonday.

Skinner, B. F. (1957). *Verbal behavior.* New York: Appleton-Century-Crofts.

Soto, L. D. (1991). Understanding bilingual/bicultural young children. *Young Children 46,* (2) 30–36.

Vygotsky, L. S. (1962). *Thought and language.* New York: John Wiley.

Wortham, S. C. (1995). *Measurement and evaluation in early childhood education.* Englewood Cliffs, NJ: Prentice Hall.

RESOURCES

Derman-Sparks, L. (1988). *Anti-bias curriculum: Tools for empowering young children.* Washington, DC: National Association for the Education of Young Children.

Hildebrand, V., Phenice, L. A., Gray, M. M., & Hines, R. P. (1996). *Knowing and serving diverse families.* Englewood Cliffs, NJ: Prentice Hall.

King, E. W., Chipman, M., & Cruz-Janzen, M. (1994). *Educating young children in a diverse society.* Boston: Allyn and Bacon.

Lynch, E. W. & Hanson, M. J. (1994). *Developing cross-cultural competence.* Baltimore: Paul H. Brookes Publishing Co.

Using Time Samples to Look at Attention Span

USING TIME SAMPLES

Exercise: How much time did you spend in the last week sewing? reading? golfing? shopping? When is your attention span the longest?

Think about the choices you make. When there is a choice of activities, it is governed by some assumptions:

- You are more likely to do what you *like* to do rather than what you *have* to do.
- You do what you have the opportunity to do. Your sewing machine may be broken. You have no new novel to read. You have no money for golfing or shopping. You would if you could.
- If your first choice, your favorite pastime, is not available, you may choose a related activity. Your sewing machine is broken so maybe you do some hand sewing. You have no new book to read so you reread an old one. Instead of golfing or shopping, you read about it in magazines or the newspaper.

- If you have finished all the sewing projects, read all the books, played that course, or shopped that mall already, you may be bored with those choices.
- If you have a new pattern you want to try, a best-seller waiting, a new golf course or mall just opened, you cannot wait to try it and will avoid all other choices, people, or tasks.
- You are more likely to do it if you feel you will be successful or challenged, but not frustrated. You know you can sew a dress so perhaps you decide to try a jacket. You will work on it until you get to a difficult part. Depending on your personality, you may work at it, rip it out and start over, or abandon the project. If you are a slow, deliberate reader then probably reading is not a favorite pastime. If you feel awkward at physical things, then golfing may not be your forté. A person planning to lose weight before the next season might be frustrated with shopping and leave the store after trying on only one bathing suit.
- You may choose your activity because your friends are doing it too. They call and say, "Let's go golfing or shopping." You had not

planned to, but you want to be with them so you join them.

- While you are at a task of your choosing, time passes quickly. You look up at the clock and cannot believe you have spent four hours working on that garment, reading that book, playing that golf game, or shopping at that mall. The total absorption in the activity also resents intrusions and attempts to draw you away. The phone rings, you let the answering machine get it. It is time for lunch, so you grab a sandwich and eat it while you are reading. You hurry home from the golf course or shopping and pick up a pizza for dinner. If someone comes and tells you it is time to stop doing that and to come do something else, it makes you angry. You may ignore the first call, the second, and the third.

Factors Influencing Children's Attention Span

What does this have to do with observing young children? When they have their choice, where, what, and with whom do they choose to spend their time? By observing children's choices of activities, a spectrum of information is gathered. The same principles lead children's activity choices.

The child's choices reveal interests. Avoidance or cursory completion of assigned or chosen tasks may suggest lack of competence. Bessie just loves painting at the easel so she rushes to get there first, puts on her smock, and gets ready. Miss Jones says, "Bessie, before you start painting I want you to come and paint this hand plaque for your mother." Bessie reluctantly goes to the table, quickly paints the plaque, and returns to the easel where she paints for the next 15 minutes. Miss Jones wonders to herself, and maybe even writes on her Class List Log, "Short attention span, painted part of plaque and left." Was Bessie interested in painting and does she have a long or short attention span? What made the difference?

The child may select related activities when their first choice is not available. William headed straight for the water table after he hung up his jacket. It was closed. He moved to the climber, but it was taken down, replaced by a writing center. He went into the bathroom, ran water in the sink and wadded up paper towels and blew them around in the water. Someone had to use the bathroom so he came out. He climbed up on the shelf and jumped off, three times, before the teacher came over and tried to get him to come to the new writing center. He refused. She wondered, "Why is he doing these things

Figure 7.1 New activities attract attention.

today?" Children will find a way to do what they want and need to do. William found water play soothing and climbing helped him work off extra energy. Those were two activities his body, temperament, and development needed but were denied by the environment so he manufactured them himself.

Novel, new activities attract children's interest, Figure 7.1. The next day when William came to the classroom, he saw that there was a computer in the writing center. He ran right over and started touching the keys. Marvella showed him how to turn it on and asked him if he wanted to use the dinosaur program to write a story with her. "Sure." Miss Jones wondered, "I couldn't get William over here yesterday. I wonder what made the difference?"

Children will choose and give attention to activities where they find success. Bessie may have rejected the teacher's painting project, preferring her own. Maybe she never painted a plaque before and was afraid to try. She had trouble controlling the small brushes the teacher provided but she knew how to use the big brushes and many colors at the easel. Easel painting she knew would be successful. William was not lured by the teacher's invitation to the writing center. He had tried to write his name when his mother made him practice, and he could not do it to please her. If he went to the writing center he probably would have to write, "No way! Stay away! I'll just stick with water play and climbing and jumping. I know I'm good at those."

Children are influenced by their friends' choices of activities. Bessie looked over at the art table. "Oh, my friends are all at the art table with shells and twigs and leaves and stones and bottles of glue. They're calling me over. I've never used glue before. My mom says it's too messy." She joins them and watches for a few minutes. "Now I know how to do it," and works as long as they are there. When they leave she may decide to finish her collage or leave it and follow them to the next activity they choose. She may choose an activity because that is where the adult is. She likes to be near Mr. Jim. If he had invited her to do the plaque she would have stayed there longer.

Children involved in an activity may be reluctant to bring it to a close. Timmy's block building is growing taller and wider. He gets more blocks and makes a road up to the building's door. He gets out the little animals and builds a pen for them. Then he gets a tub of cars and drives it up the road to deliver new animals. The teacher says, "Time for everyone to come to circle time." He keeps building. She says, "Timmy, put the blocks away and come to circle time. You have played there a whole hour." There are too many blocks and animals and cars to put away and the building does not yet have a roof or a barn for the animals. It is not finished and he realizes he did not even have time to play in the water table yet and he always plays in the water before circle time. He has been in the block area the whole free choice time.

Measuring Attention Span with Time Samples

One of the characteristics commonly used to describe young children is "short attention span." Parents will often report that children who cannot sit still one minute at the dinner table will sit for two hours watching a video and never move. (Is it any wonder that parents do not fully cooperate with "Television Turn-Off Day?") From the preceding adult and children's examples, there are many variables that determine the length of attention span. By watching children as they choose and participate in the activities, a wide spectrum of development and behavior can be assessed and evaluated.

The **Time Sample** is an efficient recording method that tracks children's choices, their playmates, and the time they spend in one area. It is a method suitable for children three years old and older in group settings. It may be a mixed age group or homogeneous age group. Obviously, if it is recording the children's choices, it is only used in a program and at a time when children have choices. That assumption is based on developmentally appropriate practice for young children three through eight years old (Bredekamp, 1987):

> Three-year-olds—Adults provide large amounts of uninterrupted time for children to persist at self-chosen tasks and activities... (p. 48)

> Four- and five-year-olds—Children select many of their own activities from among a variety of learning areas... (p. 54.)

> The primary grades—Many learning centers are available for children to choose from. (p. 68)

Here is an example of a Time Sample, Figure 7.2. A segment of the free choice time is selected. One-half hour works well, begun after the children have all arrived and are actively engaged. The learning centers or choices are listed down the left margin. Five-minute intervals are filled in across the top from when the recording is begun. The recorder looks at each area and writes down the names of the children who are in that area at that moment. After a quick glance, a circle can be drawn around the names of the children who are playing cooperatively. That does not refer to the absence of arguments but to the social stage of working together for a common goal, as described in Chapter 4. The recorder notes also if an adult is in that area, then looks on to the next area to be observed. The areas are all scanned, and names of players are written down. A category at the bottom designates the names of children not in any area at the time, perhaps in transition, perhaps wandering around not involved in play.

When the next five-minute period begins, the process is repeated. If the recorder knows a child remained in the area from the last five minutes, a straight line is drawn, saving a few seconds. If the child left and returned, the name is rewritten. Children do move quickly. Every five minutes the process is repeated.

Exercise: From the Time Sample example, choose one child and follow the child for a one-half hour segment. Draw some conclusions about:

- the child's interests
- where the child feels competent (probably is most developed)
- where the child may not feel competent (may be the least developed area)
- the stage of play
- the length of attention span
- if the child is teacher-dependent or avoids the adults
- what questions it still leaves in your mind about this child.

Of course, a total evaluation of a child's development is not drawn from one recording, any more than it should be drawn from one test score. Time samples should be done periodically to see trends and to amplify other documentation methods.

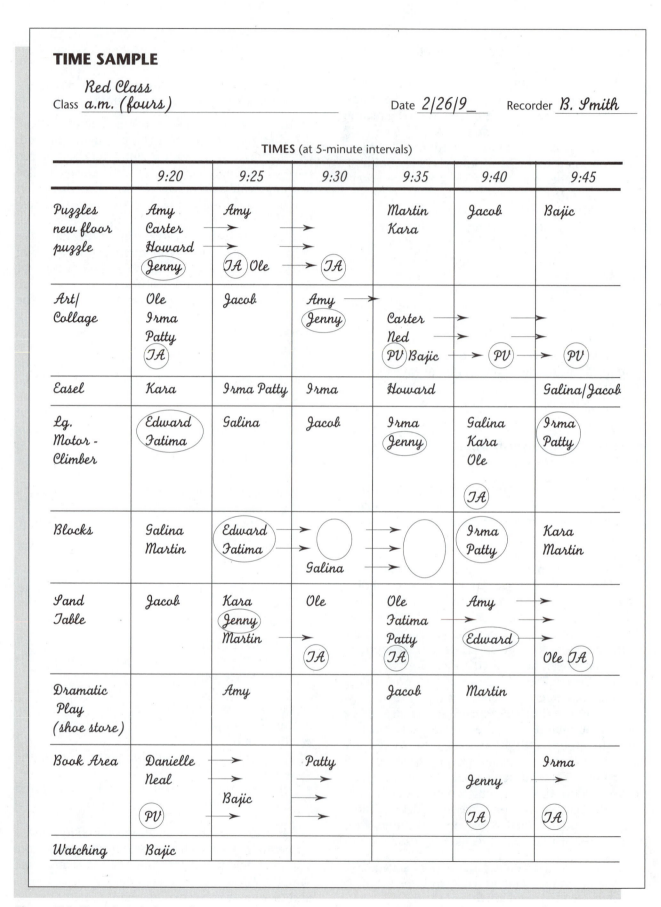

TIME SAMPLE

Class _Red Class_
a.m. (fours)   Date _2/26/9_   Recorder _B. Smith_

TIMES (at 5-minute intervals)

	9:20	9:25	9:30	9:35	9:40	9:45
Puzzles new floor puzzle	Amy Carter → Howard → (Jenny)	Amy → → (TA) Ole →	→ (TA)	Martin Kara	Jacob	Bajic
Art/ Collage	Ole Irma Patty (TA)	Jacob	Amy → (Jenny)	Carter → Ned → (PV) Bajic →	→ (PV) →	→ (PV)
Easel	Kara	Irma Patty	Irma	Howard		Galina/Jacob
Lg. Motor - Climber	(Edward Fatima)	Galina	Jacob	Irma (Jenny)	Galina Kara Ole (TA)	(Irma Patty)
Blocks	Galina Martin	(Edward Fatima) → → Galina →	○ → ○ →	○	(Irma Patty)	Kara Martin
Sand Table	Jacob	Kara (Jenny) Martin →	Ole (TA)	Ole Fatima Patty (TA)	Amy → → (Edward) →	→ → Ole (TA)
Dramatic Play (shoe store)		Amy		Jacob	Martin	
Book Area	Danielle → Neal → (PV) →	→ Bajic →	Patty → →		Jenny (TA)	Irma → (TA)
Watching	Bajic					

Figure 7.2 Time Sample Example

Analysis of the Time Sample Example

Who do you think is the oldest child in the class? Probably Edward. He appears to have the longest attention span and is a cooperative player.

Who is probably the youngest? It might be Bajic, or possibly he is just new to the class.

Whose parent was probably the volunteer (see PV for parent volunteer)? The PV was probably related to Ned, or else he is the most dependent.

Who likes to be with the teacher assistant (TA)?

What are the most popular areas of the classroom? Large motor and sand.

What is the least popular area? Dramatic play. What might be a remedy?

What strategy did the TA use? The TA went to where the most children were.

Where was the teacher (T)? The teacher possibly was recording the Time Sample.

What child is missing half-way through the Time Sample? Danielle. She might have gone home sick or gone to a pull-out program such as speech. It is possible she was in transit between areas or just missed. Mistakes do happen.

Who is the child who needed the teacher's attention? Lenny. What finally worked? The book area.

What well-used area did not sustain long periods of play? Large motor. What might be the reason?

How long would you expect four-year-olds to stay at a task? A rule of thumb is a minute for a year of age *unless* one of the preceding variables affects it.

A Time Sample is a closed method because the recorder writes down where children are at that moment (raw data) but does not include details of what they are doing, how they are doing it or what they are saying. The symbols indicate inferences the observer makes as notes are recorded such as: circles for cooperative play, arrows for uninterrupted play, and a jagged circle for aggressive play. A Time Sample is a very revealing method of gathering and recording information that can be interpreted for many purposes. It even reveals where the adults spend their time and the most and least used areas of the room. Evaluation of children, adults, and curriculum choices all can be made from the Time Sample.

Advantages of the Time Sample Method

The Time Sample is helpful because it

* gathers information on all the children in the class at one time
* gives quantitative (numerical) information about attention span (Cindy spent _____ minutes at the easel.)
* indicates child's play and interest preferences
* gives clues as to children's strongest areas, inferred by choices
* gives clues about child's less developed areas, inferred by avoidance
* can indicate the stage of play the child is in
* can show preferred playmates
* can track adult positions in the room
* shows which areas of the classroom are most used
* shows which areas of the classroom are under utilized

The recorder can develop abbreviations and adapt the form and method to meet the individual program.

Disadvantages of the Time Sample Method

The Time Sample

* records no details about the nature of the play
* may not capture children moving while recorder is writing
* makes inferences that may not be accurate
* is time-intensive for the recorder
* is effective only where a long period of free choice play is offered
* is not as effective for toddlers because most play is solitary or parallel, and movement from area to area is more frequent due to the children's shorter attention spans
* must be done periodically, or it is too judgmental

Pitfalls to Avoid

Time Samples should be repeated every few weeks so that too much credence is not placed on one isolated Time Sample (as in the exercise interpreting this Time Sample).

The Time Sample is very time-consuming but is a method that a parent or a volunteer, a nonparticipant observer, could be assigned.

Children must have free choice of activity areas for the Time Sample to be effective. If there is a teacher-led activity during that free choice time, it can be indicated.

LOOKING AT COGNITIVE DEVELOPMENT

Exercise: Try this exercise to determine your learning style.

HOW DO YOU LEARN?

For each item below, check the response that most clearly describes your typical behavior.

1. In a meeting, I
   - ❏ A. Take lots of notes, often with lots of doodles
   - ❏ B. Sit near the action so I can hear and participate in discussions
   - ❏ C. Tend to get restless quickly, have the urge to move around

2. I get the most out of workshops where the presenter
   - ❏ A. Uses lots of audio-visual aids and handouts
   - ❏ B. Is a good speaker
   - ❏ C. Involves participants in exercises and hands-on experiences

3. When someone asks me to critique something they wrote, I prefer to
   - ❏ A. Read it quietly to myself
   - ❏ B. Have it read to me
   - ❏ C. Read it aloud while pacing about

4. When I need to make a big decision, I prefer to
   - ❏ A. Analyze my options on paper
   - ❏ B. Sit in a comfortable place and listen to music
   - ❏ C. Do something active like jogging, walking, or working in the yard

5. When I studied a foreign language, I learned best when
   - ❏ A. Reading and writing the language
   - ❏ B. Speaking the language in the classroom
   - ❏ C. Trying the language out in real life situations

6. Prior to purchasing a major appliance, vehicle, or piece of equipment, I evaluate my choices by
   - ❏ A. Reading about them
   - ❏ B. Talking to friends and associates for their advice
   - ❏ C. Trying the item out or seeing it in person

7. When learning how to use a new appliance, I
   - ❏ A. Read all the directions before trying it out
   - ❏ B. Like to have someone tell me how to get started
   - ❏ C. Like to set it up and try it out first

8. When I get angry, I
   - ❏ A. Clam up and keep it to myself
   - ❏ B. Quickly let others know I am angry
   - ❏ C. Clench my fists, pound the table, storm off

9. In my spare time, I prefer to
   - ❏ A. Watch TV, go to movies, attend a play, or read
   - ❏ B. Listen to the radio, play records, or attend a concert
   - ❏ C. Engage in a physical activity

Interpreting your answers: Total how many times you selected the A, B, and C responses. If most of your answers were A's, this would tend to indicate that you are primarily a visual learner; if most are B's, an auditory learner; and if most are C's, a kinesthetic learner.

This evaluation form was adapted from questions field tested by Patricia Scallan for Child Care Information Exchange as well as from the research of Walter B. Barbe and Michael N. Milone, Jr.

Figure 7.3 How Do You Learn? (October, 1988, p. 11. Reprinted with permission from *Child Care Information Exchange,* PO Box 2890, Redmond, WA 98073, 1-800-221-2864.)

Learning is not just a matter of memorizing information. It is highly complex and individually different. Some people learn best by hearing, reading, and memorizing, whereas others learn best by touching, moving, and interacting either with materials or people. The art of teaching does not begin with knowing the pupil, but with knowing oneself. Recognizing that others learn in ways different from ourselves profoundly affects understanding and teaching. Teaching then becomes the orchestration of experiences for all modalities or ways of learning. Traditional recite, memorize, and test have been unsuccessful for many people. The development of cognition, thinking processes, is observable and an area for teachers to consider in environment and schedule planning as well as daily lesson planning.

The development of cognition entwines all other areas already discussed—attachment and separation, physical development, language, and social and emotional development. In the next few chapters, it will be the focus of a closer look. Observers need knowledge and clues to examine closely the changes that take place in children's mental processes. Whether the process is called knowledge, imagination, creativity, reasoning, problem solving, classification, logic, symbolizing, or logical-mathematic reasoning, it all is relevant to cognitive development. The chapter and section divisions are for ease of categorization and description, not separate from one another as the divisions infer.

Piaget and Cognitive Development

No discussion of cognition can be complete without a review of the work of Jean Piaget (1896–1980) and his interpreters (Flavell, 1987; Furth, 1969, Ginsburg & Opper, 1969). He described the kinds of knowledge and the stages of children's cognitive development.

Jean Piaget, born in 1896, was a Swiss scientist, psychologist, and epistemologist (a person who studies the methods and grounds of knowledge). His early work studied the adaptation of mollusks (related to the clam) to different types of water; he was trained in exacting observation skills. He had to look closely to see changes in a mollusk. His life changed dramatically, as most do, when he became a parent. He then transferred those observation skills to a more fascinating subject, his own children, looking and theorizing the source and meaning of each movement and new skill. Out of those close observations and sixty years of study (talk about long attention span!) came the founda-

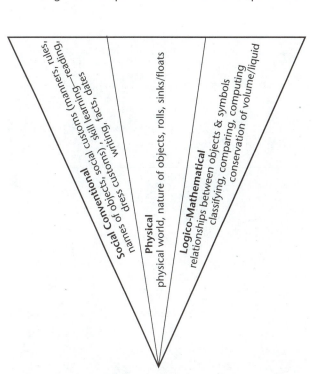

Figure 7.4 Kinds of Knowledge. (Adapted from Peterson, R., Felton-Collins, V. 1986. *The Piaget Handbook for Teachers and Parents*. New York: Teachers College Press.)

tion for most of what is known about infant and young child maturation cognitive processes.

Kinds of Knowledge. Piaget categorized not only the stages of cognitive development but the types of knowledge developed, Figure 7.4.

Social Conventional Knowledge. **Social conventional knowledge** is described as "the rules of the tribe." It is the type of knowledge that parents teach by instruction and example. These are the accepted social and cultural norms for dress, behavior in different settings, greetings, and ways of addressing others. Some might call this category manners or customs. Language development is another major cognitive category in conventional knowledge. The interactions with other people affect language directly, but certain cognitive processing must be possible before language can appear.

Physical Knowledge. **Physical knowledge** is the accumulation of facts about how the world works. As the child rolls, scoots, crawls, stands, cruises and climbs, she is inspecting her environment, Figure 7.5. She finds that pushing a ball makes it roll, but pushing a block does not have the same effect. She soon adapts her hand movements and expectations of results when she pushes round objects and grasps square ones. During

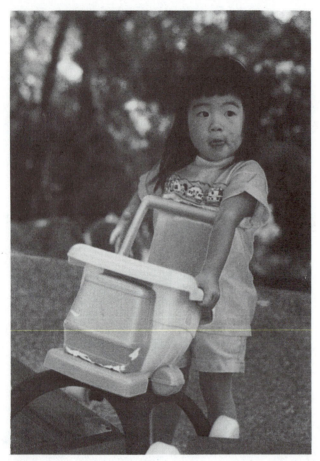

Figure 7.5 Physical knowledge is acquired through experiences with real objects.

the sensorimotor stage, the child is gathering data about the properties of all that is around her by manipulating it and watching the results.

- -

IT HAPPENED TO ME: Beginning Geometry

- -

A group of parents and toddlers were gathered to share stories, frustrations, and advice. A less-than-two-year-old toddled over to a swinging door with an automatic closer. When he leaned against it, it opened a little way, then closed with a hissing sound. He seriously looked at the door and tried it again. Push, close, hiss. Push, close, hiss. All this time he was looking up at the top of the door jamb. Mom came running over, "Come away from there." She was probably concerned about pinched fingers and what would happen if he pushed too

hard and went on through the doorway. I was fascinated that he was not tempted to do that. He was mesmerized by the action and reaction of the door.

As we took his point of view and looked up as he was, we saw the ceiling produced a bright changing triangle as the door closed. He formed a mental image (schema) of triangles and their changing shapes that day that will be the foundation of later geometry equations. Someday he will measure the degrees of the angles in a triangle. I like to think about the connection between that task and the day he pushed the door open and watched it close.

- -

Logico-Mathematical Knowledge. **Logico-mathematical knowledge** is the primary area usually associated with cognitive development, the processing of information to draw conclusions, either verbal or mathematical. Seeking relationships is the main task of this type of processing. It is all about the observation of similarities, differences, and commonalities. Variables are manipulated and the results measured. These abstract concepts are clarified when we watch as a child plays with blocks:

- Similarities and **matching**—He places the same size blocks on top of each other.
- Commonalities and **classification**—He places all the blocks together and all the toy animals together.
- Cause and effect—He tries to stand the toy horse on the small block too small for all four feet. Then he tries to stand it up on the large block, which succeeds.
- Measuring and **seriation**—He places the animals in a line according to size.
- **Rote counting**—He orally counts, perhaps inaccurately, or out of order, "1, 2, 3, 6, 8."
- **One-to-one correspondence**—He points to each animal as he accurately counts, "1, 2, 3, 4."
- **Object permanence**—He knows that if one of the animals falls off the table, out of his sight, it still exists. If he looks for it, he can find it.
- **Conservation**—He knows if he sawed one of the two blocks in half, the two halves would weigh the same as the whole block.

These three areas of cognitive development—social conventional knowledge, physical knowledge, and logico-mathematical knowledge—change in a predictable pattern from simple to complex, over a period of time, at individual rates. They have implications for curriculum planning and assessment.

Piaget's Stages of Cognitive Development

Infancy—Sensorimotor Stage (Birth to 24 Months). Piaget's label of the **Sensorimotor Stage,** birth through 24 months old, gives clues of how the infant is processing information through the senses and acting on information with developing large and small muscles. Vision in a newborn is at the legally blind level (Flavell, 1987) because of the inability to focus or fixate. However, the newborn is able to distinguish between high and dark contrast about 7 to 8 inches away, figure-ground, shape, and contours. That is just what is needed to look at a human face at close distance. Visual acuity increases rapidly, and by six months it is at the adult level. Hearing is at a near-adult level at birth. Some research suggests an infant can discriminate the mother's voice from others, if it was in "motherese," an up and down quality that adults naturally use with babies. The infant has been found able to discriminate between "pa" and "ba" sounds at an early age as well. Touch is well developed, especially the sensors for receptive touch that have caused an interest in baby massage. Those perceptions, along

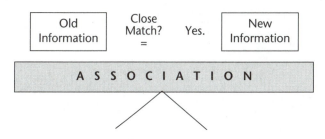

Figure 7.7 Association

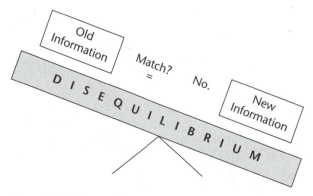

Figure 7.8 Disequilibrium

with taste and smell, are present at birth, though at rudimentary levels. Their rapid development necessitates parents and caregivers to provide a sensory-rich environment and experiences for even the youngest infant. In this way, they have a healthy start on the road to cognitive development.

Piaget described intricate substages in which information and physical abilities take a circular path. Each new piece of information goes through this chain, trying to make a match. Piaget called this constructing knowledge. This basic principle is the foundation for professional practice. The child is involved actively in exploration and experimentation to form his own knowledge. Knowledge is not the transfer of abstract information but the formation of associations based on information from the senses.

For the readers who are familiar with this theo-, the diagram in Figure 7.7 is **association.** You take in" the information from the diagram and make a close match with what you already know.

If it is new information for you, you are in **disequilibrium** (mental confusion or imbalance) until you make a match, Figure 7.8. Once you take in the information and form a bridge or relationship to what you already know, it is **assimilation.** You have added another building block, or schema, to existing information or deepened your understanding.

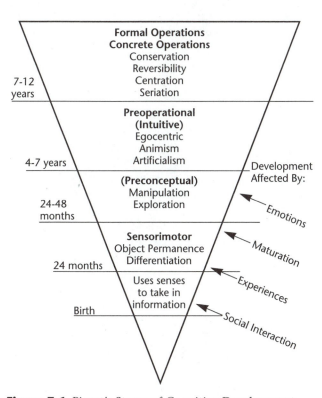

Figure 7.6 Piaget's Stages of Cognitive Development

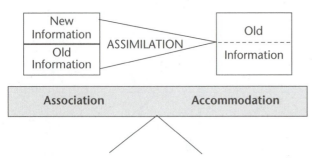

Figure 7.9 Assimilation

When the new information is associated, assimilated, and added to the old information, you have achieved **accommodation**. You have somewhat changed the structure of what you previously knew and formed new ideas or blocks of knowledge. That is the process of assimilation. Now all of that becomes old information to begin the process all over again the next time a new piece of information is received. You will try to associate it, assimilate it, go into disequilibrium and then accommodate it, Figure 7.9.

Here is an example: An infant suckles her mother's breast and receives milk. She builds an association between sucking and milk. As she is rolling around in her crib a few months later, the blanket brushes her lips. The reflex motion causes her to suck. "Ugh! I'm not getting milk!" She could not make a match between the previous milk she received and this new substance. She has tried to associate the substance to what she already knew, but it was lint instead of milk. She was in disequilibrium. She spit the blanket out and has now another action or reaction to sucking. She can continue or she can spit it out. She can now assimilate, or make a judgment, and decide on a new course of action, accommodation. She may decide that it is a second-best alternative and continue to chew on it when the nipple is not available.

This process occurs thousands of times a day in nanoseconds (one billionth of a second) without any awareness or conscious decision of the thinker.

The cognitive tasks of the Sensorimotor Stage are self-differentiation and object permanence. Around six months of age, the infant forms the concept that he is a separate entity from the crib, from the car seat, but most of all from the humans around him. This has implications when adults leave the room and the infant wants them back. Remember the discussion on separation in the first chapter?

Very closely allied is the knowledge that items and people still exist even when out of sight. If they drop a spoon over the side of the high chair tray, they will look for it. When their parent leaves the room, they may whine or cry until he comes back. By the end of the second year, infants have both mental representations that are leading them into the development of language and on into the Preoperational Stage.

The Preoperational Stage (Two to Seven Years). The Preoperational Stage consists of the Preconceptual Period (two to four years old) and the Intuitive Period (four to seven years old).

According to Piaget (Peterson & Fenton-Collins, 1986) there are four factors that guide development from one substage to the next:

1. emotions that create feelings and motivate learning
2. maturation of physical growth, including the nervous system
3. experiences (own learning and self-discovery)
4. social interaction and influence of parents, teachers, and peers (p. 4)

Having an understanding of these factors assists the early childhood educator to assess and plan for an environment and curriculum that meets the cognitive needs of this stage.

In the Preconceptual Period, the child is an active participant in learning, intentionally acting on the environment and finding how things work. Problems are attacked mostly by trial and error and manipulation of materials. Instead of just using a spoon to feed herself, she will use it to feed her dolly. This moves her from the function performed on herself, to acting on another. She may even move to the symbolic or dramatic use of the play when she uses the spoon as a microphone like she saw the singer on television last night. Throughout this substage, the major task is classification, making connections by physically and mentally placing items in pairs and groups. The vocabulary is rapidly building and grammar is expanding. Now sentences convey messages and control the environment and other people.

In the Intuitive Period, as described by Piaget, for the early childhood years four to seven years old, the reasons the child gives for phenomena are based on appearances or intuition rather than understanding. There are many mental processes the child cannot do until the next stage, the Concrete Operations stage. Flavell (1987) and others have looked at this stage in a more positive light, finding that children in this stage have built large knowledge structures. Although they are present, the child may not yet represent them either in language or art. The receptive processes are greater than the expressive. The child understands much more than he can convey either in words, drawings, or writing.

Some classic terminology and experiments demonstrate what a Preoperational child will attain in the next stage:

egocentrism—The child believes that everyone thinks and feels as he does. (A small screen separates the child and a toy from the examiner who asks, "Can I see the toy?" If the child can see it, she will answer, "Yes," even if a screen blocks the examiner's view.)

conservation—The child does not understand the variables that can make quantity look different although the volume is unchanged. (There are two glasses of water with the same level of liquid.) The examiner asks, "Are they the same?" Then liquid is poured from one glass into a tall, thin beaker. The examiner asks, "Are they the same now?" The Preoperational child, without the understanding of the properties of volume, will say, "No. This one has more." The child will answer by appearance.

reversibility—The child is not yet able to mentally reverse an operation. (The examiner asks, "What will happen if I pour this back? Then will it be the same?"

centration—The Preoperational child is only able to focus on one attribute at a time. (If the child is sorting by color but the blocks also have different shapes, he will have difficulty centering (concentrating) on sorting by color, ignoring the shape.

seriation—The Preoperational child is not able to place items in a series according to a rule such as height or weight. (They can probably pick out largest and smallest but have difficulty with those in between.)

The Preoperational child makes cognitive errors based on appearance, not reasoning, such as:

animism—The child believes that all objects have properties of being alive ("My book will be lonely if I leave it home.")

artificialism—The child believes that natural phenomena are man-caused. ("Daddy, make it stop raining so we can go on our picnic.")

Concrete Operational Stage (Seven to Eleven Years). All the processes that the Preoperational child is developing come to bloom in the **Concrete Operational Stage**. Children now can use logical and rational thinking to understand and explain the properties of volume and number, classifying, seriating, centering, and reversing. It does not occur as they celebrate their seventh birthday; it happens in small, incremental steps. Sheldon White (1965, 1975) called this "the five to seven shift," when major neurological changes take place. Around seven years old, the ways of thinking have changed. The child is now ready physically, socially, emotionally, and cognitively to apply the experiences of the past seven years to the serious business of learning.

The tasks of sorting and classifying, recognizing similarities and differences, is *the* recurring curriculum theme. This is not to be interpreted that ways of learning change from those experiential, hands-on explorations. Piaget's theory is complex and full of terminology but it has practical application for methods, materials, environment, and curriculum in any early childhood program. The environment and curriculum allow each child to construct knowledge by exploration, manipulation, and sensory experiences the adults provide. The role of the adult is still to prepare the environment, facilitate the exploration, support and scaffold approximations of development, and record the progress. If the first roles are fulfilled, there will be progress to record.

Memory

During the Sensorimotor and Preoperational stages, the child interacts with real objects and building memory of the properties of these objects and how they react. This assimilation and accommodation is stored in the memory. John Flavell, whose whole career has been devoted to studying cognitive development, reinforces the importance of providing young children with experiences that will increase their knowledge of the world in which they live. He says, "What the head knows has an enormous effect on what the head learns and remembers" (Flavell, 1987, p. 213). Memory is the construction material of cognitive development.

Exercise: Respond to the following statements about yourself:
I have a (bad/good) memory.
It helps me to remember if I…

There are many different aspects of memory. Recognition is the most basic. Piaget's term for it was *association*. It is that matching to a past piece of information. Studies of infants and young children show this basic ability is very high early in life. A 1993 article in *Life* magazine entitled, "Babies Are SMARTER Than You Think," reviewed amazing research experiments. Six-week-old infants remembered lab experiments up to two years later when the same retrieval cues were given (Bernstein & Hollister, 1993).

Visual recognition has very high rates of memory. "Ah, yes, I've met you before but I don't remember your name." Recall, the next phase after recognition is more difficult, placing the name with the face recognized. The strategy used to help in that recall or retrieval of information is mnemonics. Figure 7.10 illustrates six keys that might be used to "unlock" memory:

- Wait time—One of the most natural keys, used by all ages, involves waiting for a period of time and letting the mind work.
- Rehearsal—Repeating, either aloud or silently, is a technique that experimenters have taught young children to use (Kail, 1979). However, it is not long-lasting nor does it become spontaneous.
- Categories or word associations—Older children and adults use this technique to put words into categories to aid in retrieval.
- Sensory cues—Kail (1979) found that young children use visual and sensory retrieval cues. This reinforces the emphasis on an active, real approach for teaching young children, using multisensory experiences. For example, reading a story about an apple, accompanied by eating one, will help children remember the story about the apple.
- Chunking—Memory is aided by breaking strings of information down into smaller parts, such as Social Security numbers, telephone numbers, or song lyrics. (For example, two, forty-eight, eleven, seventy-nine, seventy-six, or 1-800-FORKIDS.) Teachers who use rebus charts to teach children song lyrics use visual cues and teach small portions of the song at a time.
- Writing—Writing words down helps implant them in the memory and aids in recall. That is the major reason for *written* observations.

The awareness of the need to remember begins in the Preoperational period. Preschoolers were found to be inaccurate predictors of what they could remember, and ill-equipped to develop or act on strategies. By the time they were seven, however, they could group material into similarities or categories to help them remember. They used common aids like making lists or placing items to remember by their coat (Kail, 1979).

The strategies that different people use to learn and remember have been explored from a number of theories. Multiple intelligences and learning styles are ones that have caught the interest of researchers. Educators also see the profound differences between children, bringing that recognition to the next step, which is adopting an individualized curriculum and expectations based on each child's learning style and strength.

Multiple Intelligences and Hemisphericity

Howard Gardner (1983) has looked beyond learning styles and identified seven types of intelligence he calls Frames of Mind. He criticizes schools that only measure and value some while ignoring others. The **multiple intelligences** are:

1. Linguistic intelligence—remembering what one hears and reads
2. Logical-mathematical intelligence—figuring things out logically using reasoning and problem solving
3. Spatial intelligence—recreating what one sees, imagines, visualizes, or creates
4. Bodily-kinesthetic intelligence—using one's body to learn, interact, and express oneself
5. Musical intelligence—innate musical talent
6. Interpersonal intelligence—understanding, cooperative, and communicative with others

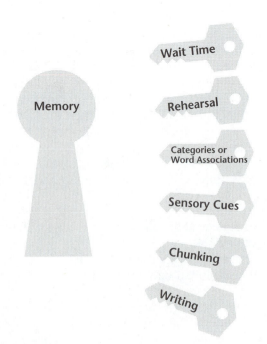

Figure 7.10 Keys to Unlock Memory

7. Intrapersonal intelligence—comfortable with self, works best alone, and pursues one's own interests

Faggella and Horowitz (1990) thought about the seven intelligences displayed in the classroom by choices and strengths and suggest using these categories as ways to individualize the curriculum to promote each child's type of intelligence.

Exercise: Think of people you know who fit into each of the multiple intelligences. Where are your strengths or gifts?

By observing and recognizing each child's cognitive style, the teacher can better understand and individualize the curriculum. An environment providing for all modalities sounds very much like a developmentally appropriate early childhood classroom:

- language-based, print-rich materials
- real objects to explore, manipulate, and experiment with
- art and construction materials to create without models
- music, rhythm, and songs for transitions
- large muscle equipment and opportunities, creative movement

- cooperative activities and a social atmosphere
- alone spaces and individual activities

Another related theory is brain hemisphericity. The two hemispheres, or sides, of the brain deal with information and behavioral functions in different ways (Brooks & Obrzut, 1981). The study of brain lateralization has led Cherry and colleagues (1989) to point to the overemphasis in formal education of the left side of the brain where the literacy, logical mathematical functions reside. In *Is the Left Brain Always Right?* Cherry, noted early childhood educator, explains:

Left—analytical, logical, sequential, orderly, verbal, computational, linear, concrete

Right—Intuitive, spontaneous, random, casual and informal, holistic, uses body language, sensory, visual, metaphoric. (p. 13)

Cherry, Gardner, and others feel traditional educational teaching and testing methods ignore sensory, visual, and intuition functions of the brain. The labeling of right-brained learners as learning disabled is an injustice that lateralization and learning styles theorists seek to eliminate (Armstrong, 1987).

TOPICS IN OBSERVATION: Measuring Cognitive Development—Why Not Test?

Exercise: Imagine that you took a test and found out you failed. Jot down how each of the possible reasons that follows might have been the cause of your failure.

The room
The person giving the test
The subject matter of the test
The importance of the test to you
The new format of the test
The way the test was scored
Your health
You are physically challenged
You are in big trouble that has nothing to do with the test
Your native language is Russian. The test is in English.
Your friend left you here in this strange building to take the test, but you do not know how you will find her later

These same influences affect the outcomes of a young child taking a test, only more so because they are not able to understand, rationalize, or adjust. This section is a policy statement to defend and uphold authentic assessment methods over standardized or achievement tests. There are three major issues in testing young children: the test itself, the child, and the use of the test.

A **standardized test** is an evaluation instrument written for a definite purpose and application. When it indeed does measure what it proposes to measure it is described as **valid**. Early forms of the test are tried out on a segment of the population that will be taking the test eventually. This early test group is the **norm** group against which the rest of the scores are measured. If the norm group is significantly different from the subjects taking the

TOPICS IN OBSERVATION: continued

test then the scores will be inaccurate. For example, suppose the norm group in the tryout of a new test is 10 children. There are eight boys and two girls, ranging in age from five to eight years old, living in south Florida, all attending the same school. Two children are black, three are Puerto Rican, and one has been sexually abused. Their scores on the test will set the standard against which children in Idaho, Connecticut, and Minnesota will be measured. This is an extreme example to demonstrate the point, but unfortunately is not far from reality. It is difficult to select a norm group that represents all the variables in exact proportions to the subjects taking the test. Standardized tests have a high risk of being discriminatory because of the scoring against the norm group. The results may be skewed by factors such as geographic region, urban, suburban or rural, different socialization experiences due to culture, economic situation, family dynamics, and native language.

The second major concern of using standardized tests on young children is the nature of the child. Because young children are just that—young—taking tests may be a new experience for them. The way that children confront new experiences varies from child to child. Some just observe, watch, and wait, paralyzed by the novelty. Others will manipulate it and play with it, not recognizing the purpose. They may not understand or follow directions but explore and adapt it to their own style. If the child takes another form of the same test again in a short time, the score may be drastically different. Now they have experience, or have thought of other ways to try it out.

The expectation of standardized tests is that the same subject taking the same type of test in a reasonable period will obtain a similar score. This is test **reliability**. Many standardized tests for young children are not reliable. They are easily influenced by the new place. The examiner may be a stranger to them. They are separated from their parent and may not know how to take a test. They lack the ability to screen out noises, hunger, or fear that may divert their attention.

The original intelligence test developed in France by Binet was for a noble purpose, to pro-

vide adequate education for children who were mentally retarded. Many tests administered to children today are for a similar purpose, to identify handicapping conditions for which early intervention would be provided.

Many federal and state laws mandate such testing. P. L. 94–142 (1975) provides a free and appropriate public education for children with disabilities between the ages of 3 and 21. P. L. 99–457 (1986) includes infants and toddlers and their families in comprehensive early intervention services. To implement these mandates, it was necessary to identify children who needed services. This was accomplished through a **screening**, an initial step in identifying those children who had a high probability of developmental delay. Once a screening indicated there might be a delay or problem, a full evaluation or follow-up provides the diagnosis. The diagnosis will determine the type of intervention needed to provide services for the child in the least-restrictive environment. These laws have been effective in helping many children and families receive the services they need.

The problem arises when the screenings and tests developed for one purpose are used for others, possibly less helpful ones. Meisels (1987) has criticized the Gesell Preschool Readiness Test as an invalid predictor of success in kindergarten. Many schools use this as a developmental screening tool. Based on its results, a recommendation may be made to delay school entrance or a year in a transitional grade between kindergarten and first grade. Meisels contends this is a misuse of a test that lacks reliability and validity. Tests are misused when they are the sole factor in decisions to place a child in special education, or label them as an individual with a handicapping condition. The *NAEYC Position Statement on Standardized Testing of Young Children 3 through 8 Years of Age* (1988) addresses the necessity for reliable, valid standards. "Decisions that have a major impact on children, such as enrollment, retention, or assignment to remedial or special classes, should be based on multiple scores of information and should never be based on a single test score" (p. 44).

The NAEYC Position and constructivist writings, such as Kamii & Kamii (1990) in

TOPICS IN OBSERVATION: continued

Achievement Testing in the Early Grades: The Games Grown-ups Play, enumerate the abuses of testing:

- Results of standardized tests might be inappropriately used as readiness screening tests for placement decisions.
- Standardized testing increases the academic emphasis of the curriculum, which should be localized not centralized.
- Achievement tests frequently do not reflect current theory or research about how children learn.
- Many schools "teach to the test" to raise school scores.
- Standardized tests cannot predict how well students will do in the future.
- Below third grade, development is uneven and still emergent.
- Racial, cultural, and social biases are evident.
- Numerical results are not useful in curriculum planning for individual students.

How can the effectiveness of teachers and schools be measured if children are not tested? How can a teacher know if the child is learning? How could school boards and voters know their education tax dollars were well-spent but still be sensitive to the population it was examining?

Authentic assessment assumes that children in a supportive setting will initiate and direct their own learning, constructing knowledge at their own rate physically, emotionally, socially, and intellectually. It also assumes that learning proceeds from concrete to abstract. Children learn by interacting with the enriched environment that recognizes and values different intelligences and is facilitated by an adult who has specialized training and skills. Teaching is individualized and in small groups. Individual learning needs are acknowledged based on objective evaluation of each child's strengths, moving the child forward in the continuum of learning through relevant curriculum. Assessment is rooted in principles of child growth and development and involves a collaboration of child, teacher, parents, and other professionals as needed (Puckett & Black, 1994).

The form of that assessment is in question. Teachers ask, "How can a test manufactured in New Jersey measure what the children have learned about magnets in my class in Nevada? How can the test maker in New Jersey even know if my class in Nevada has worked with magnets?" The test can only measure it if the teachers know what is on the test and make sure that it is taught in the classroom. In this way, it is the test determining the curriculum, instead of measuring achievement. Methods of authentic assessment, then, must be locally based to measure progress of a distinct group of children. This is done by "keeping track" (Kamii & Kamii, pp. 120, 121) of their work on three levels:

1. Descriptive data about each child that can be analyzed by the teacher as well as outside evaluators.
2. Summaries and interpretations of that data by the teacher to evaluate the effectiveness of teaching methods and the individual progress of the child.
3. Quantitative information that gives statistical analysis of the whole group, against which individual children may be compared to adjust the curriculum.

These principles of performance assessment are consistent with the knowledge of child growth and development, and developmentally appropriate practice. Assessment by observation and recording using a multiple of techniques is repeated in a systematic way. The portfolio documents the child's progress and is shared with the parents and the child. That describes what can be achieved by *Week by Week* assessment planning.

SPECIAL POPULATIONS AND ATTENTION SPAN

Cognitive development, with respect to memory and attention span, are affected by physical, emotional, and cultural influences.

Mental Processing Difficulties

Different causes such as birth defects, maternal drug use, and poor nutrition may result in difficulties in the basic cognitive processes.

Attention. Attention is defined as the ability to focus on a specific aspect of the environment and ignore the other stimuli. Some children with extremely short attention spans, difficulty concentrating, and high distractibility have been diagnosed with Attention-Deficit Hyperactivity Disorder (**ADHD**) or Attention Deficit Disorders (**ADD**) without hyperactivity. Children with these disorders have been mislabeled sometimes as emotionally disturbed, mentally retarded, or autistic. It is the nature of young children to be impulsive and easily distracted, especially when the classroom does not provide outlets for their energy or appropriate curriculum. This makes the disorder difficult to diagnose. Is it the environment, the curriculum, or the child? Diagnosis begins with gathering information of physical, mental, and social-emotional development from parents, medical professionals, and teachers. Federal laws, such as the Individuals with Disabilities Education Act (IDEA) and Section 504 of the Rehabilitation Act of 1973 provide coverage for children with ADD (Council, 1992).

The Time Samples of the group will give a quantitative recording of the attention behavior. It also will compare the child in question to his peers. (The word *his* is selected purposefully here because more boys than girls are diagnosed with ADHD.)

Running Records focusing on the child will also aid helping professionals in the diagnosis. Even though a child has a short attention span, high distractibility, high activity, and impulsivity, he may not have ADHD.

It is important for the parent or program staff not to impose a label or a diagnosis, leaving that to the professionals. There are brain functioning tests and a breakthrough link to identify the specific gene, recently discovered at the University of Chicago. (*Advance*, 1995, p. 2). Most children with this disorder respond favorably to a stimulant that paradoxically increases attention and decreases impulsivity and activity, along with child and family counseling. There is a national information support group: Children with Attention Deficit Disorders (CH.A.D.D.), (305) 587–3700.

Perception. Perception is the ability to interpret the objects and events stimulating the senses. For children with a limited ability in hearing, sight, taste, smell, or touch, the intake of information limits their cognitive processing. The other modalities may compensate for the limited ones but only as much as the cognitive capacity is able to accommodate. Young children especially depend on sight to cue all kinds of behavior with less attention to verbal language. They carefully watch and imitate rather than listen and do.

Perception depends on the ability to discriminate between appearances, sounds, and textures. With impairments of the receptors or the cognitive structures to process the information, these sensory cues go unrecognized and ignored. The teacher of children with such impaired sensory abilities makes adaptations for the other senses to receive a similar message, such as tapping a rhythm that cannot be heard or associating textures with the words *cool, warm, rough,* and *soft.*

Memory is the third basic cognitive process, received through attention and perception. It is stored in the central nervous system in the various categories of short-term, long-term, visual, rote, recognition, and recall: Children with nervous system difficulties, such as muscular dystrophy or multiple sclerosis, as well as limited cognitive ability, may experience memory difficulties.

As with all cognitive, physical, or emotional disorders, parents, teachers, and Committees on the Handicapped seek to place the child in the least restricted environment, that in which the child can maximize the abilities that are present and make modifications and allowances for the areas of lower functioning.

Cultural Differences in Memory and Attention Span

Research on various cultures has had mixed results. People from a culture with little or no formal schooling or technological tools to aid problem solving, such as alphabets, calculators, or computers, seem to be more concrete thinkers (Luria, 1976; Dasen, 1977). The assessment of cognitive development must consider the cultural context. When memory tasks used for assessment are unrelated to the child's world they do poorly (Rogoff, 1990), but when tests were culturally relevant few differences in memory are found (Mandler, et al., 1980). This is consistent with the principles of fair testing: The test should be culturally relevant to be a valid measurement of ability.

HELPING PROFESSIONALS FOR ATTENTION CONCERNS

If a difficulty with memory, attention span, or cognitive processing is observed, those concerns are addressed by the teaching team, program supervisor, and then brought to the attention of the parents of the child with tact and sensitivity. They are nebulous and often extremely difficult to diagnose and even more difficult to treat and strategize. People who may be able to help are described here.

pediatrician—physician specifically trained to treat children

psychologist or psychiatrist—professionals trained in areas of emotional disorders

neurologist—physician specifically trained in sensory or motor responses due to nervous system impairments

special educators—specialists with knowledge or normal and atypical children's development and appropriate education strategies

Week 7, Assignment A

TIME SAMPLE OF ATTENTION SPAN FOR ALL

Select a day this week during a normal free play time. Prepare a Time Sample form by copying the Time Sample Form from Appendix D and adapt it to reflect areas in your classroom. List the learning center areas down the left margin. Begin by noting the time in the top column and proceed to write down each child's name as you scan each learning area. If you have time, circle those children's names who are playing cooperatively, a jagged circle around any who are aggressive. Note where the adults are and if any child is just standing and watching. Five minutes from the beginning time, scan the areas once again. If the child has not left the area, draw an arrow to the next time block and move on. Every five minutes, repeat the scanning and recording.

What to Do with It

Later that day, draw conclusions and write notes on each child's portfolio overview about the child's attention span, play preferences, or social interactions as recorded on the Time Sample, Figure 7.11.

File the Time Sample in the class file. If this Time Sample showed an unusual pattern or you have an explanation for why a certain thing happened, write that down as well. Your incidental

MEMORY AND ATTENTION SPAN		
Documentation	Recorder	Date
TS +Dram Play no book	MS	10/18
TS absent		1/5
TS Dr. Play 10 min Book	MS	3/1
TS +Blocks Art 20 min	BAN	6/26

Figure 7.11 Portfolio Overview Example

observations are important too. For example, note if you observe that there were a lot of children around the water table today because it is new.

Discuss your observations with parents or the child, if appropriate. For example: "Mrs. Johnson, while I was observing in class today I noticed that Shawnalee spent 12 minutes at the easel painting. That was a lot of concentration for a three-year-old." or "Anthony, I noticed today you never played at the new water table. Did you want a turn? There were times when you weren't busy other places. It'll be out again tomorrow so you'll have another chance if you want to play there."

If you notice a learning center is avoided by all children, you may want to consider the reasons for it and work to make it more interesting or change it to some other emphasis.

Week 7, Assignment B

INTERVIEWS IN SPEECH AND LANGUAGE FOR GROUP B

Continue with Interviews begun last week, selecting children from group B to Interview each day this week. If possible, tape record the Interview as well as make written notes as you speak with each child. Do an informal or structured Interview as described in Week 6, Assignment A.

What to Do with It

Analyze each interview for what it reveals about the child's knowledge, emotional state, social development, and the child's speech and language. (Use the Speech and Language Checklist found in Appendix D.)

Enter the summary. Note your name and the date on the portfolio overview sheet. If a significant lag appears, discuss it with your supervisor to confirm it. Then approach the parent. Have a list of sites where a speech and language evaluation may be obtained to give to the parent.

Week 7, Assignment C

REFLECTIVE JOURNAL

Respond to the following in your Reflective Journal, kept in a private file at home.

I think I am a _____ learner because...

When I look at children's learning, I'm interested especially in...

I found doing the time sample...

It really showed me...

I wonder if...

REFERENCES

Advance for Speech Pathologists, (5), 16. Researchers Identify Specific Gene for ADHD. April 24, 1995.

Armstrong, T. (1987). *In their own way*. New York: G. P. Putnam's Sons.

Bernstein, S. & Hollister, A. (1993). Babies are SMARTER than you think. *Life*, July, 1993, 46–60.

Bredekamp, S. (Ed.). (1987). *Developmentally appropriate practice in early childhood programs serving children from birth through age 8: Expanded edition*. Washington, DC: National Association for the Education of Young Children.

Brooks, R. L. & Obrzut, J. T. (1981). Brain lateralization: Implications for infant stimulation and development. *Young Children, 36* (3), 9—16.

Charlesworth, R. (1996). *Understanding child development: For adults who work with young children, third edition*. Albany: Delmar Publishers.

Cherry, C., Godwin, D., & Staples, J. (1989). *Is the left brain always right: A guide to whole child development*. Belmont, CA: Fearon Teacher Aids.

Council for Exceptional Children. (1992). *Providing an appropriate education to children with attention deficit disorder*. ERIC Digest ED352747-92.

Dasen, P. R. (Ed.). (1977). Piagetian psychology: Cross-cultural contributions. New York: Gardner.

Faggella, K. & Horowitz, J. (1990). *Different Child, Different Style: Seven Ways to Reach and Teach All Children*. Instructor. Sept. 49–54.

Flavell, J. H. (1987). *Cognitive development*, second edition. Englewood Cliffs, NJ: Prentice Hall.

Furth, H. G. (1969). *Piaget and knowledge*. Englewood Cliffs, NJ: Prentice Hall.

Gardner, H. (1983). *Frames of mind: Theory of multiple intelligences*. New York: Basic Books.

Ginsburg, H. & Opper, S. (1969). *Piaget's theory of intellectual development*. Englewood Cliffs, NJ: Prentice Hall.

Kail, R. (1979). *The development of memory in children*. San Francisco: W. H. Freeman & Co.

Kamii, C. & Kamii, M., (1990). Why achievement testing should stop in C. Kamii, (Ed.) *Achievement Testing in the Early Grades: The games grown-ups play*. Washington, DC: National Association for the Education of Young Children.

Luria. A. R. (1976). *Cognitive development: Its cultural and social foundations*. Cambridge, MA: Harvard University Press.

Mandler, J. M., Scribner, S., Cole, M., & DeForest, M. (1980). Cross-cultural invariance in story recall. *Child Development, 51*, 19–26.

Meisels, S. (1987). Uses and abuses of developmental screening and school readiness testing. *Young Children, 42* (2), 4.

NAEYC position statement on standardized testing of young children 3 through 8 years of age. (1988). *Young Children, 43*, (3), 42–47.

Owens, K. (1993). *The world of the child*. New York: Macmillan Publishing Company.

Peterson, R., & Felton-Collins, V. (1986). *The Piaget handbook for teachers and parents; Children in the age of discovery, preschool-third grade*. New York: Teachers College Press.

Puckett, M. B. & Black, J. K. (1994). *Authentic assessment of the young child: Celebrating development and learning*. New York: Merrill. (An imprint of Macmillan College Publishing Company.)

Rogoff, B. (1990). *Apprenticeship in thinking: Cognitive development in social context*. New York: Oxford University Press.

White, S. (1965). Evidence for a hierarchical arrangement of learning processes. In L. P. Lipsitt & C. C. Spiker (Eds.), *Advances in child development and behavior*. New York: Academic Press.

White S. (1975). *Speculations on the future fate of early childhood education*. Paper presented at the American Education Research Association, Washington, DC.

RESOURCES

Cherry, C., Godwin, D., & Staples, J. (1989). *Is the left brain always right: A guide to whole child development*. Belmont, CA: Fearon Teacher Aids.

Kamii, C. & Kamii, M. (1990). Why achievement testing should stop in C. Kamii, (Ed.) *Achievement Testing in the Early Grades: The Games Grown-ups Play*. Washington, DC: National Association for the Education of Young Children.

Peterson, R. & Felton-Collins, V. (1987). *The Piaget handbook for teachers and parents: Children in the age of discovery, preschool–third grade*. New York: Teachers College Press.

Using Cognitive Task Experiments to Look at Cognitive Development

IN THIS CHAPTER

✔ Using Cognitive Task Experiments and Assessments

✔ Looking at Cognitive Development: Math and Science

✔ Topics in Observation: "Real" Curriculum

✔ Special Populations and Cognitive Development

✔ Helping Professionals for Cognitive Concerns

USING COGNITIVE TASK EXPERIMENTS AND ASSESSMENTS

Experiments are attempts to discover the unknown or to test a theory. While observing young children as they play and work, their cognitive development in the area of logico-mathematical principles and physical knowledge can be assessed using the scientific processes of information gathering:

- Observing—watching natural phenomena, watching children as they play and work
- Identifying—recognizing, naming (He is using a math skill by setting cups on the table.)
- Describing—isolating characteristics, one-to-one correspondence, using appropriate terminology
- Classifying—compare/contrast, (She is placing them in rows. He is placing one at each chair.)
- Designing investigations—asking questions (How are you deciding how many cups to put out?)
- Following procedures—I will make notes on who places cups in rows and who places them at each chair.

- Collecting data—taking notes, measuring, Anecdotal Recording of answers, Class List Log of cup placement
- Interpreting data—theories of cause and effect (I'll look at their birthdates to see if there is a correlation.)
- Communicating the results—summarizing, describing (I'll show the other staff my study and the results.)
- Formulating conclusions—evaluating, generalizing, analyzing (If age is a factor then at this age a change should take place in these "cup in a row" people.)

Presenting children with concrete materials and asking them formalized questions about them also can give insight into what they know, Figure 8.1. Piaget was intrigued by children's "wrong" answers to his probing questions. This is one of the methods he used to form his theories. Using task experiments helps to understand theories better. After a few of these task **experiments**, cognitive developmental theory will be clear. *These will not be done with every child.* These should be done at selected times on selected children of various ages.

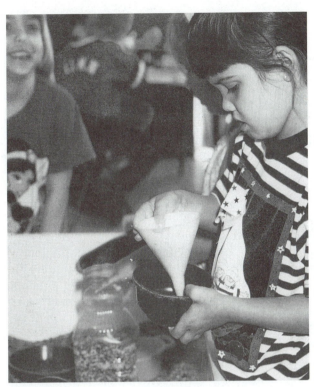

Figure 8.1 Math concepts are learned best with real objects.

"Yes"

"What's the same about them?"

"They're red."

"Yes, that's right. Both of them are the same color. They're red. Is there any other way they are the same?"

"Yes. Size."

"Oh, they're the same size, the same length?"

"Yes"

You move the top one to the right about 3 inches. "Now are they the same size or length?"

"No. This one is longer. (Jolene points to the top ribbon.)

"This one's longer than this one? Show me how you know that."

"See." She points to the end of the top ribbon, and the end of the bottom ribbon.

You move the bottom ribbon 3 inches to the right, under the top ribbon.

"Now are they the same or is one longer?"

"Nope. They're the same."

1. How would you interpret the data?
2. What theory does this illustrate?
3. What terminology is used to describe this concept?
4. How would you communicate the results?
5. What conclusions would you draw? What decisions would you make about the environment
6. When would you try this experiment again, expecting to see change?

They will help the observer fully understand the theory of cognitive development and give fuel to reflective thinking about teaching practices. An awareness of the theories will help the observer see the principles in the child's natural environment, rather than in structured situations.

These experiments are not tests of children's intelligence because the outcome is not a quantitative score. They are illustrations of the stages of thinking. By repeating them in a few months, the effect of maturation and experience is seen. On children of various ages, the theory is replicated. Behavior is not manipulated nor is the experiment seeking to change the child or teach a concept. It is a process of presenting tasks and observing how the child performs them. Conclusions are drawn about their development to make curriculum decisions. Additions to the environment for the group or individual child are based on inferences from the observation. The effects of maturity and experience are seen when the experiment is repeated.

Exercise: You have two pieces of ribbon 12 inches long. You are working with Jolene, who is three years, six months old. Read the following dialogue and, using a separate piece of paper, answer the questions that follow:

"Are these the same?"

This scenario illustrates the concept of conservation, usually attributed to the Concrete Operational Stage. The Preoperational child will have difficulty with it because the child decenters, using intuition rather than logic. She looks at the ends of the ribbons at the left or right to make her decision without taking the position of the opposite ends into consideration. She considers only one part of the situation. This is not a skill that is taught. It will develop as the child's cognitive processes mature and she has opportunities to manipulate objects. The learning environment should contain open-ended materials, such as string, ribbons, scarves, beads to string, and all kinds of materials to add to and take away from. By the time Jolene is between five and six, this simple experiment will no longer stump her.

Several logico-mathematical task experiments to use individually with children ages three through seven years follow. For more tasks in each cognitive level, see Charlesworth and Lind (1995),

Math and Science for Young Children, Delmar Publishers, pages 499–526. Evaluating children's knowledge of math and science as they interact with the environment will be discussed in the next section.

Numbers and Counting. Ask the child to count aloud to 10 (rote counting). Present 10 objects (all the same) and ask the child to count them (one-to-one correspondence).

Conservation. Line up objects in two rows of five, evenly spaced. Are they the same? Now spread one row out. Now are they the same?

Classifying. Provide an assortment of toys with duplicates: two crayons the same color, two blocks the same color but different shapes, two blocks the same color but different sizes, a related pair such as a hammer and a nail. "Put together the things that are a family. Which ones belong together?"

Seriation. Cut paper towel rolls into lengths 2, 4, 6, and 8 inches long. Ask the child to stand them up and put them in a row. "Will you place these in a row by size?"

Visual Spatial. Trace three blocks of different sizes on a piece of paper. Point to one of the blocks. Ask the child, "Just by looking, which block on the paper is the same as this one?"

Problem Solving. Show the child a ball of clay. "Two people want to play with it. What can they do?" "Now someone else comes and wants some. What can they do?"

Advantages

Task experiments

- give evidence of the cognitive development theory to the observer
- allow an opportunity for one-on-one time with each child
- illustrate the concepts of cognitive theory in a concrete way for the observer
- provide hard data and documentation against which to compare later. They illustrate the principle of development, the progressive change over time that comes about through maturation and experience.

Disadvantages

Cognitive task experiments may be difficult because they are

- time-consuming

- dependent on the child's cooperation
- teacher-directed rather than child-led
- possibly misleading to think that the concepts need to be "taught"

Pitfalls to Avoid

Advice for the use of task experiments follows.

- The uncooperative child—Begin with a child you know will be eager to participate in the experiment. If a child appears reluctant, stop and try to observe the same principles in a more natural way.
- The bored child—Try to make it a game by only doing a few concepts at a time. In this way, it does not become test-invoking anxiety or forced attention.
- Delay while you gather materials—Be prepared with materials. Be familiar with the script of the questions and have a data sheet on which to quickly record responses.
- The rest of the room is unsupervised while you are occupied—Choose a location where you are not isolated and can scan the room. This will also help children want to cooperate but may make for some distractions. Be prepared to interrupt observation if intervention is needed somewhere else in the room.

LOOKING AT COGNITIVE DEVELOPMENT: MATH AND SCIENCE

Exercise: How do you feel when you read these words?

Mathematics
Physics
Geometry
Hypothesis

In looking further at **cognitive** development, observing and assessing intellectual development, it is important to consider not just the knowledge of the subject matter but the other dimensions of development. Lillian Katz (1988), a great thinking stimulator of the early childhood field, reminds educators that learning is not just knowledge as an accumulation of facts, skills, or the ability to function in a certain way. Knowledge also involves dispositions, habits of the mind. Those are the ways that each individual responds to experiences. Some people have the disposition to quit after a defeat or embarrassment. The same situation may cause someone else with a different disposition to try harder, while another casts blame or another reflects and seeks advice.

The dispositions, feelings, or emotional responses to the fields of mathematics and science affect many early childhood educators. Perhaps it is the nonacademic track through which some have entered the field. Perhaps it is the manifestation of learning style theory that people with strong logical thinking skills become engineers, while those with interpersonal learning styles and skills become educators. Whatever the cause, the math and science aversion has kept many early childhood classrooms from having interesting and challenging math and science learning areas. Consequently, the foundations have not been adequately laid on which children can build knowledge.

Rivkin (1992), an early childhood teacher educator, addresses the emotions of science and urges a joy in the beauty of nature and a childlike curiosity and quest to make sense of things. She urges teachers to examine sexist messages that science is a man's field and questions the perpetuation of that idea. She heralds Bess-Gene Holt's (1977) "science is a way of life" philosophy in suggesting these essentials for teachers of science:

1. Providing time—to play with things, ask questions, not feel rushed to cover a set amount of information.
2. Knowing something—get some guide books and read about trees, birds, or rocks; share that interest and new knowledge with children.
3. Being open to one's own ignorance—admit to not knowing then consult more knowledgeable people or find out some other way.
4. Valuing one's own interests and interpretations. Science is not something you have to learn. It is in the quest for knowledge that value is found.
5. Valuing the symbolizing of experience and knowledge. By writing down and drawing what we see and helping children to do the same, we remember.
6. Providing the supplies of science for exploration, even if it means snakes, rodents, slime, slush, and softness (p. 16).

If teachers have feelings of inadequacy and avoidance of math and science, there will be little to observe. The teacher must become conscious of these emotions. The concepts that follow can be used to heighten awareness of what children are doing as they manipulate their environment. They are actively engaging in math and science,

even though it may not be on the daily curriculum plan. This will serve also as a curriculum guide of the concepts that can be incorporated into the early childhood program, enriching children's experiences in math and science. Reflective thinking and concept-building encourage the teacher's explorations.

Observing Developing Mathematical Concepts

Exercise: Which of the following children are learning math?

❑ The class is looking at the teacher holding the calendar and counting up to today's date, the 23rd.
❑ Two children are setting the table for lunch.
❑ Two children are shoving each other at the door to go outside.
❑ A child is eating orange sections.
❑ Two children are playing with clay.
❑ Three children and the teacher are making instant pudding.
❑ A child is painting at the easel.
❑ The group is sitting on a rug singing, "This Old Man."
❑ Four children are picking up the blocks and placing them on the shelves.
❑ A child in the housekeeping area is squeezed into a doll high chair.
❑ A child is passing out birthday party invitations and has one left over.
❑ A child is lining up all the shoes in the dressup corner.

If you checked all of the items except the first one, you are correct.

Rote counting with nothing to touch or manipulate has little relevance to the child's life. (Why should the child care if it is the 23rd or the 89th?) This is not how children learn mathematical concepts. More effective ways of using the calendar to support children's concepts of time are with shared experiences (Van Scoy & Fairchild, 1993). Calendars record an event that has happened, like a birthday, with an artifact from that event. Children could record individual experiences, much the same as Show and Tell, but drawn, dictated, or written on a calendar by the child. The calendar can be used to plan for anticipated events, how many days until the picnic, and what must be done each day in preparation for it. In this way, calendars are relevant and perform concrete purposes rather than the recital of numbers and words that have little meaning.

It is through direct interaction with real objects that children construct meaning and make those associations that lead to cognitive development, Figure 8.2. Kamii (1982) has studied Piagetian principles and applied them to mathematics in the early years. She says, "It is good for children to learn to count and to read and write numerals, but a more important objective is for the child to construct the mental structure of number" (p. 25). She advocates teaching number through indirect ways in the environment. "Indirect teaching can vary from encouraging the child to put all kinds of things into all kinds of relationships, to ask him to get just enough plates for everybody at his table" (p. 27). While they are working, the observer records and assesses the child's mathematical and physical knowledge. The activities that follow illustrate children learning math concepts in indirect ways from the environment.

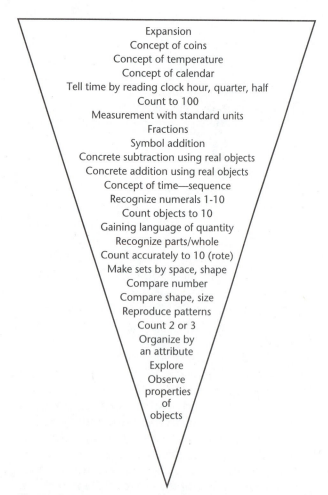

Figure 8.2 Developing Math Concepts

One-to-one Correspondence. When children are setting the table, placing one cup or one napkin at each place, they are demonstrating the concept of oneness, the most basic concept of number. This is practiced and can be observed in any number of ways. A child puts on a boot and knows she has two feet so there must be another boot somewhere. She does not try to put the second boot on the same foot. Materials in the classroom with pieces that fit, match, or can be counted if the child is at that level all add to the acquisition of one-to-one correspondence.

Ordinal Numbers. The idea of **ordinal numbers** (first/second) is learned quickly by children in group settings or in families with siblings. The two-year-old wants his "first." The boys at the door want to be the "first" out. Not that it makes any difference once they get out but it is the competitive drive for first and the disappointment of "last." Would they then tussle to be the "first" in or the "last" in? That would be an indication of their understanding of the terminology of ordinal numbers. In the classroom, the familiarity with the schedule becomes rigidly defined in the lives of two-year-olds. Song time *must* come before the story, and then outside time. If the teacher decides that it looks like rain so today they must go outside "first," many will protest. Having older preschoolers decide which activity to do first, or who will have a first turn, and why, is an excellent way to observe children's understanding of ordinal numbers.

Whole/Part Terminology. As children interact with the environment, the role of the adult is to observe and provide descriptions for their actions like, "You've eaten half your orange." By inquiring, the adult can encourage further exploration, "How many sections were in the orange?" "Did each section have a seed or only some of them?" This type of description can go on incidentally throughout the day. It shows children individual attention by describing ordinary actions. It adds to their vocabulary, raises self-esteem, and promotes thinking.

Conservation. Clay manipulated into balls and snakes and scrutinized for more and less is an excellent math medium, Figure 8.3. The conservation of volume is the Piagetian concept that the Preoperational child (two to six years old) has not yet attained. The child uses intuition or appearances by centering attention on one attribute and judging volume by that. Two children have equal size balls. One breaks the ball into several little

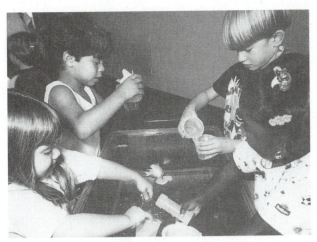

Figure 8.3 The amount never changes even if the shape does—that's Piaget's conservation.

ones and declares, "I have more." The other one shouts, "Not fair." There have been efforts to teach conservation with limited results but the viewpoint now is that it should develop naturally and *not* be taught. However, clay and the water experiments with tall containers and a short squatty one are excellent ways to question children's reasoning to test this hypothesis.

Measurement. Cooking is an excellent way to apply mathematical principles of measurement, sequence, cause, and effect. In following a recipe, quantities are specified, then measured by different-sized cups and spoons. Johnson and Plemons, in *Cup Cooking* (1993), suggest using multiple measuring utensils, such as three individual teaspoon measuring spoons rather than filling the teaspoon measurer three times. In this way, the child sees the quantity "three" physically present before adding them to the recipe. Recipes are practices in sequencing. The observation of before and after cooking or baking demonstrates cause and effect of heat and prompts description of attributes like hard and soft, liquid and solid.

Geometry of Shape. The recognition of circle, square, and triangle begins in infancy when the baby reaches out for a ball or a box or a sharp triangular shape. The infant uses all the senses, touching, chewing, seeing, and hearing. Someone says "Ball," "Box." The words are stored and each experience associates with the prior one. "Is this shape like that one? Yes? Then it must be a ball too." The baby is handed an orange. She says "Ball." She is overgeneralizing in calling all round objects balls. As she absorbs more information,

those shapes will be differentiated from one another. They will take on more and more meaning by their various differences. They eventually will be the symbols that are represented in drawing and later writing. Attention to the details and differences are really training for writing skills.

Geometry of Pattern. Pattern can be the visual image of the regular bars of the crib and the figures printed in a row on the sheets. The repetition of sounds in language and singing also form a pattern. Patterns are expressed in lines painted on the paper at the easel, and the rhythmic clapping of name syllables as they go to wash for lunch. Formal pattern materials are supplied with the card to guide the sequence of shapes, colors, or beads. They begin with two element patterns and gradually increase in complexity. Scientific observation skills are built as the child notices similarities and differences. The teacher watches and notes how the child uses blocks, buttons, and sound to make patterns.

Classifying. Sorting is such an important skill to cognitive development that it is taken for granted or overlooked as a cognitive activity. The toddler fills and dumps, then puts some in this bucket and some in that one. Finally, by some criteria, he purposefully sorts and selects which ones will go into each bucket. He is on the road to classification skills, which are the basis for scientific discovery. In the block area, the shelves are labeled with the shape of the block that belongs there. All the manipulatives have boxes or trays with picture and word labels. Replacing them is more than keeping the room tidy, it is a cognitive exercise. In the dramatic play area, tools are outlined above the woodworking bench for their replacement. In the art area, supplies are on labeled shelves. Spontaneous classifying occurs at snack time by eating the round pretzels before the straight ones, or separating the peas from the carrots. These all are building cognitive schema against which future associations will be made. Children will sort in ways that are not always predictable. This ability to sort as well as the "wrong" way can be observed, noted, and questioned to investigate the child's thinking.

Visual Spatial Skills. The estimate of how much space an object will fill sometimes is overcome by strong desire. Fitting into small spaces is a challenge to young children who are still learning the fine art of spacial awareness. They are prone to put fingers into tiny holes, heads through spaces, and bodies into containers. Withdrawing from those spaces sometimes is difficult.

This spatial awareness is seen on the playground when a child playing "Duck, Duck, Goose" has difficulty finding the spot to join the circle. It can be observed when a child is doing a puzzle, trying to pound the piece in by force rather than turn it to get it to fit. The sand player fills the container, yet continues to shovel and shovel and shovel. The container overflows with each scoop. Still the child does not indicate a recognition that the space is full and can hold no more. Then comes the day when he lines the containers up and fills each one to the top. Ah ha! A new phase of cognitive development appears.

Problem Solving. It is James's turn to pass out napkins. Maxine had counted them out because she knows how many children are in the class. "Why do you have one left?" This question invites the child to apply the math skills of how many he started with, how many are in the class, how many children are absent, and then the observation and memory task of deciding who did not receive one. Offering opportunities for problem solving, which uses mathematics, can show children the usefulness of their newfound knowledge. "There are eight crackers left and four children at the table. How can we decide who can have more? How many can they have?" At the computer there are two chairs and the rule is two workers, but three people want to use it. Problem solving does not have to have a mathematical solution to be helpful in cognitive development. It is also the logical process of mentally creating the situation, the dilemma, generating possible solutions, and deciding on one by some criteria. Problem-solving strategies are universal.

Seriation. Placing objects in order according to some rule, such as size, texture, or color, helps the child to look for similarities but also to distinguish differences. The vocabulary of seriation begins with comparisons (big/little, short/long, heavy/light, empty/full) and expands to middle points and closer variations. This shows the ability to center attention on the one critical variable by which the items are being placed in a series. It is a complex skill that can be observed in its progression. Stories like "Goldilocks and the Three Bears" can lead to concrete activities for manipulating props from the hand to the mind. Concepts of small, medium, and large; first and last; and in and out are introduced. Observing what strategies the child uses to come to conclusions about an item's placement also gives clues about the child's thinking processes.

Observing Developing Scientific Concepts

Exercise: Check the following science activities that would be appropriate for young children.

☐ Let's learn all about cacti.
☐ Men are stronger than women.
☐ There can be an eclipse.
☐ Thunder is a bowling game in the sky.
☐ Monsters are real.
☐ Pollution is a major problem today.
☐ Materials sink and float.
☐ The rotation of the earth causes day and night.
☐ Some colors make us feel happy.
☐ Milk comes from cartons in the store.

(Excerpts adapted from *Science Everywhere: Opportunities for Very Young Children* by Barbara J. Taylor (1993), Holt, Rinehart, and Winston, Inc. Reprinted by permission of the publisher.)

Learning activities are appropriate if they are relevant or real to the group of children and the concept can be tested through investigation. Learning about cacti would be relevant for a school in New Mexico but probably not one in New York, that is, unless the class was invited to visit a greenhouse specializing in cacti.

It would be interesting to plan a way to investigate whether men are stronger than women. Older children would really be interested, and it might be relevant to them.

Eclipse is a natural phenomenon that would be appropriate if it were going to be visible while the children were at school. This is a difficult topic to make relevant or understandable for young children, due to their egocentrism.

The thunder idea should be put in the scrap heap and replaced with a more relevant topic from the children's daily life. Thunder and lightning are interesting and frightening so an innovative teacher may find a way to help older children explore it but it might be difficult.

Monsters is a topic children are interested in but approaching it would be difficult. From the philosophy that the only way to overcome a fear is to confront it, going through the discovery process about monsters may be appropriate.

The preservation of our environment should be incorporated into every day's activity by responsible use of materials. Pollution of the world is a vast topic that would be difficult to approach unless there had just been a catastrophe like the Valdez oil spill that was in the news and on television. Three years later, however, it would not be relevant to young children, though it may be to adults.

Sinking and floating is fun experimentation but just putting objects into the water table and calling that the day's science activity is not enough. Follow-through in the scientific process is mandated.

Do you understand the rotation of the earth and how it makes night and day? It is difficult to present concepts that we do not understand ourselves. Day and night and the differences would be a more appropriate topic.

Colors and their affective attributes would be a difficult concept for children who are still differentiating the levels of emotional responses to events and people. To complicate it with color's effects is beyond their level. Exploration of colors and exploration of feelings are worthwhile topics to integrate into curriculum when children have an interest or need.

The concept of where milk comes from might be an interesting hypothesis to investigate. It may evolve from children's observation of their real world and calls for further investigation. Perhaps the class would take a field trip to the back room and loading dock at the store, then follow the truck back to the milk processing plant, back to the bulk tanker, back to the farm, back to the cow, back to the corn, and eventually back to the seed. That sequence with its implications and connected language, reading, writing, and social studies curriculum would be appropriate discovery learning.

The same cognitive processes the child uses for math are also used for science, Figure 8.4. Scientific discovery and mathematic awareness come from exploring the physical properties of objects through all the senses and identifying the similarities and differences between objects and events. Meaning is attached to the symbols of the environment, such as day and night, summer and winter. The ability to focus on selected pieces of information while ignoring the irrelevant is developed. Vocabulary is expanded to express the concepts of knowledge in various subject areas (Kostelnik, et al., 1993). These processes have been pointed out as necessary for literacy as well, such as perceptual skills, matching, discrimination, sequencing, describing, and classifying. Science, math, literacy are all connected to cognitive development. The world of science for the young child contains all of these elements. Their learning is enriched by reading and listening to stories about the natural world, discussing, and hypothesizing.

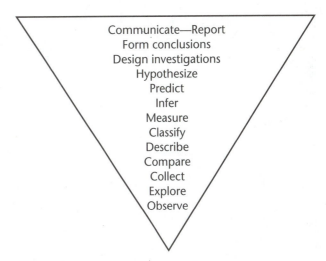

Figure 8.4 Developing Science Concepts

They wonder about how the guinea pig had babies in the night and what happened to the snowman. Small muscles are used in carefully picking up a worm, and large ones are used when they run with paper streamers in the wind. They listen and count the heart beats of Stephanie's unborn sibling with a stethoscope on her mother's abdomen. Let's get ourselves, then children, excited about science!

What are the building blocks of science in the early years? They are the same ones used in chemistry laboratories in real life. The problem-solving skills in science (Charlesworth & Lind, 1995) are explored every day by young children, constructing their own knowledge.

Exercise: Look at the skills and tasks in the chart in Figure 8.5. Think of activities to provide these kinds of experiences from the child's interests and familiar world.

**IT HAPPENED TO ME:
Tornados**

I was observing a student teacher leading a "science" activity. She had joined two soda bottles at the neck and gave each child in the circle a turn at tipping them over. They watched the vortex of swirling water as it drained from the upper bottle to the lower one. Some waited patiently, others impatiently, as they waited for a turn to make a "tornado." When it finally completed the circle, she asked the question, "And

SKILL	TASK	ACTIVITIES
OBSERVING	Discriminating alike, different	
IDENTIFYING	Recognizing, naming	
DESCRIBING	Isolating characteristics Using appropriate terms Building vocabulary	
CLASSIFYING	Comparing/Contrasting Arranging/Matching Categorizing	
DESIGNING INVESTIGATIONS	Asking questions Looking for relationships Following procedures	
COLLECTING DATA	Taking notes Measuring	
INTERPRETING	Theories of cause and effect Organizing facts	
COMMUNICATING RESULTS	Summarizing Sequencing Describing	
FORMULATING CONCLUSIONS	Evaluating Generalizing Analyzing critically Applying to other situations	

Figure 8.5 Problem-Solving Skills in Science

what did we learn about today?" Many were blank and silent but one dare-to-risk child said "Tomatoes!" There was surprise on the student teacher's face with a where'd-he-get-that? look.

Afterward we talked about a child's need to manipulate, a child's inability to wait, and the importance of relevancy. We discussed why the child said "Tomatoes." She had no idea other than it sounded like tornados. For children living in Kansas who had seen funnel clouds and knew the word *tornado*, this lesson might have been more effective. Four-year-olds in New York could make no connection between a tornado and the water in the bottle. Should she not have done it? Possibly. Perhaps with other kinds of preparations about wind, funnels, pipes, it would have had meaning. This activity did little to promote cognitive development, or any other kind.

. . . .

Science for Young Children. Appropriate science content that would have meaning to the young child is suggested in Charlesworth and Lind's useful guide *Math and Science for Young Children* (1995), Figure 8.6.

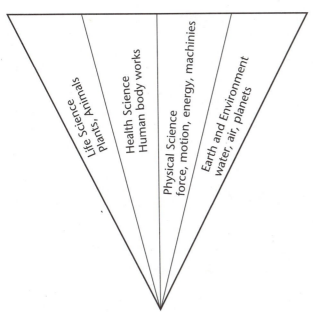

Figure 8.6 Young Children"s Science Curriculum Topics

Life Science. Life science is the study of plants, animals, and ecology. Appropriate to every early childhood classroom are growing, living things. Plants on a window sill, guinea pigs in a cage, fish in a tank, or a recycling bin next to the garbage can are all informal ways of incorporating life science into the curriculum. These can become more formalized with specific activities to observe, identify, describe, classify, and so on.

Health Science. The most relevant lesson to all is health science, the human body, its workings, and healthy practices. This is a vital area for foundation building, illness prevention, and promotion of lifelong wellness. Everyday practices, such as handwashing, are probably the most important health lessons that early childhood programs teach. Children are curious about their bodies, the appearance, and function internally and externally. Measuring, weighing; and charting hair color, eye color, or number of teeth are relevant math and science activities for young children. Having a class baby is a very beneficial activity. At the beginning of the year the class "adopts" a mom having a baby in a month or two. She visits the class and they ask questions and learn about the baby growing inside her. After its birth (which is a class celebration!) the mother visits the class regularly for the children to observe, measure, and investigate the baby's growth. By the end of the school year, the baby is sitting up, crawling, getting teeth, and becoming social. The children have learned many

concepts in math, science, social studies, language, and physical development.

Physical Science. Physical science is the study of force, motion, energy, and machines. Children themselves are force, motion, and energy in one machine. Their fascination with carrying each other around, moving objects and what makes things run can be capitalized in the classroom. Heavy objects to be moved can be moved easily (once they all get moving in the same direction) by a group of 8 or 10 preschoolers. Even the teacher sitting on a table can be carried from place to place. Magnets have always been a part of the classroom without deep explanation of poles of attraction. Manipulation, exploration, and observation can be augmented with charting what the magnet will pick up or attach to and what it will not. Blocks, a staple area of the classroom, can be augmented with ramps, cardboard tubes, and a facilitator who asks what-if questions to expose children to principles of gravity and give experiences in making predictions. "From which tube will the ball come out first if we start them both at the same time—the long one or the short one? Does it make any difference if it is a big ball or a small ball? Does it make a difference if we tip the short tube up higher? Why?" These concepts cannot be fully understood at this age. Most adults use electricity and television without understanding the principles behind them. The exploration of the effects of the forces of air, water, and machines are suitable activities for the early childhood classroom to explore and pose questions. The physical science area is important as these children grow up in the technological age where these skills affect their daily life.

Earth and Environmental Science. All children are in daily contact with weather, water, air, dirt, rocks, sun, moon, and stars. Charting and measuring temperature and rainfall are concrete activities that can be carried on in an early childhood classroom. Experiments with water are carried on naturally as they stick their finger in the faucet to see what happens, or as they plunge a container into the water table and hold it up high to watch the water spill out. The magic of air's invisibility yet power can spark some interesting investigations for young children, laying foundations for the study of aerodynamics or hot air ballooning. Collecting rocks has been done naturally since the child was a toddler, picking up gravel stones from the driveway. Size, color, weight, geography, and effects of the environment all can be concepts to explore in this area. The sky and its lights have fascinated children and poets. Exploring these from all kinds of curriculum areas begins with familiar stories, such as "Good Night, Moon," and singing "Twinkle, Twinkle, Little Star."

Will children understand all the math and science concepts? Probably not. Most adults do not understand how turning a switch will light a lamp, but it is used. Giving children experiences that provide exploration expands their knowledge and logical thinking processes, and poses greater questions that will continue to be explored as they grow older.

Math and science curriculum topics begin with ideas from children's interest, current events, and the natural world around them. Projects and curriculum themes can be webbed or integrated into all of the curriculum areas. These are opportunities to make associations, broaden the experiences, and meet the needs of different learning styles. Here is an example of a curriculum web exploring topics relating to dirt, Figure 8.7.

Exercise: Select one of the topics mentioned in this chapter and make a web to explore possible

activities in each of the learning centers of your classroom or curriculum areas. Use the blank curriculum web in Figure 8.8.

Mathematics and science are interwoven into daily life so math and science concepts are interwoven into the curriculum in much the same way. They are not discrete subjects but useful ways to

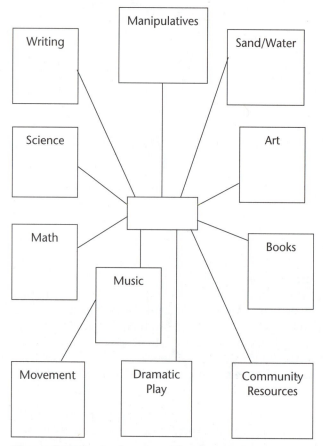

Figure 8.8 Curriculum Area Planning Web

make connections and meaning. Every individual is affected. Everyone uses mathematics and science in their daily lives.

Assessing Other Developmental Areas While Observing Math and Science Activities

As children interact with math and science experiences in the classroom in integrated curriculum, developmental areas other than cognitive development can be observed simultaneously. The interdependence of development both contributes to and is an outcome of math and science activities.

Figure 8.7 Science Curriculum Theme Web

Self-Care Skills. The autonomy of doing things for oneself comes as children feel more competent in their environment. When children can count how many napkins they need to set the table for the group, or a child sees her name on the chart as the floor sweeper around the table where marigolds were being planted today, the skills interact.

Large Muscle Development. The coordination of the body is observed as the child is running under the parachute to experience the wind or as she follows the game rules to take six steps backward. Both counting to six and walking backward are observed.

Small Muscle Development. The child places one shell in each compartment of the egg carton in one-to-one correspondence. He gently picks up the baby chick that has just been hatched. Observation of small muscle skills and math and science come together, Figure 8.9.

Other Areas of Development. Visual perception and knowledge of size comparison vocabulary

can be noted when the child picks up the bowling ball and calls it the "heaviest."

Language can be assessed by listening as the child speaks about solving the dilemma of three friends who want to sit by her at lunch. There are only two chairs left. Where will the third child sit? The logical resolution considering number of chairs as well as social interactions are observed while listening for clear speech and complexity of sentence structure.

Sharing Play Doh, dividing cookies, and taking turns on two bicycles are opportunities to observe both mathematical concepts and social development. Cooperation in working together to move a heavy object displays not only scientific principles but an understanding of community.

As children discover math and science concepts in a free environment without fear of "wrong" answers, they do not have to memorize or parrot back "right" answers in reply to closed questions. They can take risks to experiment. That is the basis for all inquiry: the elimination of wrong answers until the right one is arrived at through understanding. Children in the classroom environment dedicated to developmental learning can build and demonstrate that kind of self-concept.

Figure 8.9 Other areas of development may be assessed during math and science activities.

• •

IT HAPPENED TO ME:
Toads

• •

I was observing in a first-grade classroom where the teacher told the children to turn to page 45 in their workbook. She asked, "What is that animal?" One of the children said, "Frog." "No, it's not a frog. It's a toad, /t/, /t/, /t/. The letter of the day is *T* so this has to be a toad. Now copy the word *toad* at the bottom of the page and you can color it in."

It looked like a frog to me. What is the difference? More importantly, what a learning opportunity was missed for the children and me to learn the difference. Instead, a negative message was sent to the one who answered the question. Do any of those children now know about toads because they wrote the letter or colored it? What if the class had gone out and gathered toads from the window well, watched them squirm down into the dirt, felt them wiggle, and measured their jumps? What if they compared them to a frog someone had captured in a pond and to tadpoles (another *T*

TOPICS IN OBSERVATION: "Real" Curriculum

Educational advertisements fill teachers' mailboxes, promising easy, fun, ready-to-do activities for every curriculum area, especially math and science. They come with attractive containers, dividers for organization, and free sample plans. Most of these and many idea books for math and science curriculum are adaptations of the workbook format. Directions are given such as, "Draw a line to the one that is the same." "Count the red balloons and select the numeral." "Circle the bead that completes the pattern." The purpose of these activities is to teach and assess cognitive concepts. Visual discrimination and classification, count-ing and reading numbers, and patterning are appropriate learning objectives for activity plans. Using paper and pencil tasks, or even teacher-made paper games is not showing the teacher's knowledge of child development.

We know the attributes of the young, devel-oping child. By knowing child development principles and observing and assessing the individual child's physical, social, emotional, and cognitive development, we can develop curriculum and teaching practices, Figure 8.10. It is not necessary nor effective to use work-book pages or folder activities to teach or test concepts. Just watch the child.

BECAUSE WE KNOW . . .	WE DO
Children learn through their senses.	We do provide real, three-dimensional objects for them to manipulate.
Children are making associations with previous knowledge.	We do provide materials that are familiar.
Children need time to organize their thoughts.	We do provide long periods of uninterrupted time for them to explore.
Children cannot share.	We do provide duplicates of popular materials.
Children cannot wait.	We do not require them to all do the same thing at the same time.
Children have different attention spans.	We do provide a flexible schedule so children can move at their own pace.
Children are egocentric, only seeing things from their own point of view.	We do not force them to internalize someone else's point of view.
Children learn what they want to know.	We do listen to them and provide ways for them to learn it.
Children learn from making mistakes.	We do allow the mistakes to happen.
Children are frustrated easily.	We do provide an enviornment and materials that are accessible and easy to manage themselves.
Children learn from accomplishing hard tasks.	We do let them try without rushing in with solutions.
Children construct their own knowledge.	We do provide a way for them to "teach" themselves.

Figure 8.10 Because We Know, We Do

word to add to their vocabulary)? Then they could have written, drawn, and dictated a story about a toad and a frog. The teacher would have really met her objective to familiarize them with toads and the letter *T* in a way that they would be more likely to remember. Authentic assessment is a real, not contrived, measurement of a real, not contrived curriculum.

● ●

SPECIAL POPULATIONS AND COGNITIVE DEVELOPMENT

Cognitive development is different for each person, affected by learning styles, strong areas of intelligence, physical, and experiential factors. Early childhood teachers are faced with the challenge of meeting the learning needs of each child. There are some special populations whose cognitive development presents even more challenges.

Minority and Poverty Effects on School Achievement

Equality of educational opportunity has been the theme of Head Start for over thirty years. The Children's Defense Fund monitors poverty's effect on school achievement and has found that "each year spent in poverty by a child increases by two percentage points the chances that he or she will fall behind in school and reduces by two percentage points the likelihood that the child will finish high school by age 19" (1995, p. 92). Minority children have higher rates of illiteracy and lower reading levels.

In Oakes and colleagues' (1990) study of the effects of minority status and socioeconomic levels, she found that minority classes were "seven times more likely to be identified as low-ability than as high-ability" (p. 23), with teachers relying more on tests than hands-on learning. There are many factors contributing to these depressing statistics. It is even more depressing to know that teaching and assessment methods exacerbated rather than helped minority children and children in poverty to learn. The well-known Rosenthal effect (Rosenthal & Jacobson, 1968) may affect these populations. Teachers' expectations, using IQ scores or labels to categorize people, may contribute to the inequities. Jonathan Kozol's *Savage Inequalities: Children in America's Schools* (1991) captured in several vignettes the differences in schools for the haves and the have nots. Teachers

who gave their all to their students under extremely harsh conditions were portrayed along with teachers who did much harm. The book is a call to self-reflection about attitudes and actions by everyone who works with children.

Children Who Are Mentally Retarded

A whole group of cognitive impairments is categorized as mental retardation, subaverage intellectual function, and adaptive behavior, Figure 8.11. There are many causes, some of which are genetic disorders such as Down syndrome, prenatal influences (maternal illness, drug abuse, fetal alcohol syndrome [FAS]), birth complications such as anoxia (oxygen deprivation during the birth process), postnatal causes, such as illnesses with high fevers, head injury, lead poisoning, and environmental causes such as parental abuse and neglect. The identification and labeling of mild cognitive impairments is difficult in young children because of inaccurate diagnostic methods

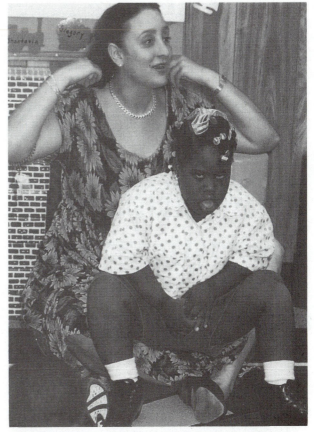

Figure 8.11 Cognitive development can be affected by many factors, but inclusive programs accept and adapt.

such as IQ tests and wide cultural definitions of "normal" intelligence. Some symptoms or clues are:

- extremely short attention span
- language delays of more than one year
- social and emotional difficulties

Children with undiagnosed cognitive impairments often are detected first by preschool teachers. Approaching families with suspicions or concerns is a very sensitive task, done with concrete data, surrounded with care, understanding, and tact. The teacher may refer the family first to the pediatrician or a clinic specializing in full developmental evaluations.

After diagnosis, a placement decision is made for the child in the least restricted environment. It may be the child can function in a regular classroom. Cook and colleagues (1992, p. 381) give these recommendations for children who need extra time and spaced practice:

1. Provide concrete, multisensory tasks.
2. Find the child's most efficient mode of learning.
3. Monitor pacing; provide shorter work periods with less information.
4. Provide repetition.
5. Plan for modeling and imitation.
6. Task analyze; use short, simple steps in sequence.
7. Give explicit directions.

Children Who Are Talented and Gifted

This beyond-the-range-of-normal category is one of the most neglected in working with children with exceptional needs. While high cognitive abilities characterized by advanced linguistic, reasoning ability, curiosity, and superior memory are the most obvious indicators of cognitive giftedness, other areas also are considered in this category. Children with advanced social skills, physical prowess, and musical ability also are included. The same hindrances to early identification of mental impairments also apply to giftedness. Developmental assessments can indicate advanced attainment of milestones and document behavior that alerts teachers and parents of the child's exceptional abilities. The teacher then individualizes the curriculum to provide enrichment opportunities to support the child's area of strength as well as the areas of normal development.

HELPING PROFESSIONALS FOR COGNITIVE CONCERNS

Families with a child with exceptional cognitive development at either end of the range of normal can first seek help from the following medical personnel.

pediatrician—physician specializing in the health and development of children

neurologist—physician specializing in the nervous system and in brain functioning

Within the educational system, specially trained professionals help the classroom teacher and the family meet the needs of the child whether cognitively impaired or gifted.

itinerant teacher—visits classroom or home regularly to see that appropriate methods, materials, and services are provided

resource teacher—assesses placement and provides instructional time outside of the regular classroom

Week 8, Assignment A

COGNITIVE DEVELOPMENT TASK EXPERIMENT FOR CHOICE

Try some of the following task experiments on children three through eight years old. Try to observe these tasks while children are at play in activities of their own choosing, or make a game of the activities. Make notes of their responses.

Numbers and Counting. Ask the child to count aloud to 10 (rote counting). Present 10 objects (all the same) and ask the child to count them (one-to-one correspondence).

Conservation. Line up objects in two rows of five, evenly spaced. Are they the same? Now spread one row out. Now are they the same?

Classifying. Provide an assortment of toys with duplicates: two crayons the same color, two blocks the same color but different shapes, two blocks the same color but different sizes, a related pair such as a hammer and a nail. "Put together the things that are a family. Which ones belong together?"

Seriation. Cut paper towel rolls into lengths 2, 4, 6, and eight inches long. Ask the child to stand them up and put them in a row. "Will you place these in a row by size?"

Visual Spatial. Trace three blocks of different sizes on a piece of paper. Point to one of the blocks. Ask the child, "Just by looking, which block on the paper is the same as this one?

Problem Solving. "Here is a ball of clay. Two people want to play with it. What can they do?" "Now someone else comes and wants some. What can they do?"

For more tasks in each cognitive level, see Charlesworth & Lind (1995), *Math and Science for Young Children*, Delmar Publishers, pages 499–526.

What to Do with It

Share findings with coworkers and file documentation in the class file. Try the same activities with the same children in six months to see changes. Remember these are not tests but are activities to test theories, one of the purposes of observation and recording. The achievement of each concept signifies developmental milestones for which adults provide the environment, experiences, and support but do not formally *teach*.

Week 8, Assignment B

MATH AND SCIENCE ASSESSMENT FOR ALL

Copy the Math and Science Checklist in Appendix D for each child, or use the cognitive portion of the developmental checklist used by your program. During this week, observe and mark as many of the criterion as you can from natural activities.

What to Do with It

Note the assessment on the portfolio overview sheet with the date completed and your name, Figure 8.12.

Share your observations with the parents or the child, if appropriate. For example: "Mrs. DeRienzo, when I was observing Gino counting today I noticed that besides being able to say the numbers to 10, he can count up to five objects. The count-ing comes first then the understanding of number," or "Carmine, here on this paper I'm writing all the numbers and colors and shapes you know. After the holiday, I'll take this paper out again and see how much more you've learned."

File the checklist in each child's portfolio.

COGNITIVE DEVELOPMENT		
Documentation	Recorder	Date
Cog Task AR	Ban	10/20
CK ++Math	MS	1/10
CK OK	Ban	4/11
CK OK		6/27

Figure 8.12 Portfolio Overview Example

Week 8, Assignment C

INTERVIEWS USING SPEECH AND LANGUAGE CHECKLIST FOR GROUP C

Continue with the Interviews begun in week 6, selecting children from group C to interview each day this week. If possible, tape record the Interview as well as make written notes as you speak with each child. Do an informal or structured Interview as described in Week 6, Assignment A.

What to Do with It

Analyze each interview for what it reveals about the child's knowledge, emotional state, social development, and the child's speech and language. (Use the Speech and Language Checklist found in Appendix D.)

Enter the summary. Note your name and the date on the portfolio overview sheet. If a significant lag appears, discuss it with your supervisor to confirm it. Then discuss it with the parents. Have available a list of sites where a speech and language evaluation may be obtained to give to the parents.

Week 8, Assignment D

REFLECTIVE JOURNAL

Respond to the following in your Reflective Journal, kept in a private file at home.

Reading about the emotions and the subjects of math and science made me think that...

I wish I knew more about...

I remember math and science in school as ...

I think I'll try...

REFERENCES

Charlesworth, R. & Lind, K. (1995). *Math and science for young children*. Albany: Delmar Publishers.

Children's Defense Fund. (1995). *The state of America's children yearbook, 1995*. Washington, DC: Author.

Cook, R. E., Tessier, A., & Klein, M. D. (1992). *Adapting early childhood curricula for children with special needs, third edition*. New York: Merrill, (An imprint of Macmillan Publishing Company.)

Holt., B. (1977). *Science with young children*. Washington, DC: National Association for the Education of Young Children.

Johnson, B. & Plemons, B. (1993). *Cup cooking: Individual child-portion picture recipes*. Ithaca, NY: Early Educators Press.

Kamii, C. (1982). *Number in preschool and kindergarten: Educational implications of Piaget's theory*. Washington, DC: National Association for the Education of Young Children.

Katz, L. G. (1988). *Early childhood education: What research tells us*. Bloomington IN: Phi Delta Kappa.

Katz, L. G. & Chard, S. C. (1994) *Engaging children's minds: The project approach*. Norwood, NJ: Ablex Publishing Corp.

Kostelnik, M., Soderman, A., & Whiren, A. (1993). *Developmentally appropriate programs in early childhood education*. New York. (An imprint of Macmillan Publishing Company.)

Kozol, J. (1991). *Savage inequalities: Children in America's schools*. New York: Harper Perennial.

Oakes, J., Ormseth, T., Bell, R., & Camp, P. (1990). *Multiplying inequalities: The effects of race, social class, and tracking on opportunities to learn mathematics and science*. Santa Monica, CA: Rand Corporation.

Rivkin, M. (1992). Science is a way of life. *Young Children, 47* (4), May 1992.

Rosenthal, R. & Jacobson, L. (1968). *Pygmalion in the classroom: Teacher expectation and pupils intellectual development*. New York: Holt, Rinehart, and Winston.

Taylor, B. A. (1993). *Science everywhere: Opportunities for very young children*. Fort Worth: Harcourt Brace Jovanovich.

VanScoy, I. J. & Fairchild, S. H. (1993). It's about time! Helping preschool and primary children understand time concepts. *Young Children, 48*, 2, 21–24.

RESOURCES

Charlesworth, R. & Lind, K. (1995). *Math and science for young children*. Albany: Delmar Publishers.

Holt, B. (1977). *Science with young children, Revised*. Washington, DC: National Association for the Education of Young Children.

Kamii, C. (1982). *Number in preschool and kindergarten: Educational implications of Piaget's theory*. Washington, DC: National Association for the Education of Young Children.

Peterson, R. & Felton-Collins, V. (1986). *The Piaget handbook for teachers and parents: Children in the age of discovery, preschool-third grade*. New York: Teachers College Press.

Using Rating Scales to Look at Literacy

IN THIS CHAPTER ....

✔ Using the Rating Scale

✔ Looking at Literacy

✔ Topics in Observation: Books in the Sandbox

✔ Special Populations and Literacy

✔ Helping Professionals for Literacy Concerns

USING THE RATING SCALE

Exercise: How hungry are you?
    Starved?   A little hungry?   Fully satisfied?
How is the temperature?
    Too cold?   Just right? · Too Hot?
How well do you sing?
    Off key? Comfortably with a group? Soloist?

A **rating scale** gives a range of criteria from which to choose rather than just the decision of present or absent, yes or no. Rating scales are used to measure specific skills or criteria. They are the most reliable when the criterion is clearly defined and easily identified by observation. More than two choices are offered but the choices are not limitless. A rating scale of 25 choices for a criterion would be unwieldy. The rater is familiar with the child or spends a reasonable time observing to make a fair judgment in selecting a rating of the criterion. Once familiar with the instrument, it could be used by the teacher, parent, volunteer, or outside observer.

When more than one rater uses the same instrument on the same child, the validity increases, reducing rater bias. This is called **inter-rater reliability.** The scores are compared and, depending on the number of raters, the highest and lowest scores are cast out and the remaining scores are averaged. This technique is used in research and in Olympic sporting events.

The **quality point** choices of rating are arranged from least developed, or the lowest, on the left to the most developed, or highest, on the right. There can be any number of quality points between. It contains the same information of a developmental checklist (one that has a list of skills in order of their appearance) but it is arranged horizontally rather than vertically. It is visually arranged to show forward movement along a continuum rather than going downward like a checklist.

Checklist Example

❑ Recognizes logos and signs
❑ Recognizes name
❑ Recognizes some alphabet letters
❑ Demonstrates purpose of a book
❑ Can tell the story from pictures after hearing it once

❑ Catches the reader if words are changed
❑ Can read some words out of context

Rating Scale Example

These same criterion are displayed in a rating scale format horizontally, Figure 9.1.

The quality points take several forms, depending on the design of the rating scale. The scale in Figure 9.1 describes the criteria from which the rater selects the most accurate choice based on observation and the rater's knowledge of the child. Many rating scales translate the verbal criteria into a number rating that can be added with others to obtain a quantitative score. The Harms and Clifford *Environmental Rating Scales (ECERS)* are constructed like this, Figure 9.2. Observations are compared to carefully explained criterion points and given a numerical rating.

There are 37 criteria rating the environment in categories of personal care, furnishings and display, language and reasoning, fine and gross motor, creative activities, social devlopment, and adults. These are then arranged on the summary sheet for a quantitative score and a graphic report of areas of strength and areas that need attention, Figure 9.3.

Other rating scales, such as *The Work Sampling System* (Meisel, et al., 1994), use quality points of "Seldom, Usually, Always," or "Not Yet, In Process, Proficient."

Rating scales can be used to measure criteria of the environment, the program, or the teacher's abilities. Tools, such as the National Association for the Education of Young Children (NAEYC) Accreditation Self Study, are rating scales with the criteria rated as "Unmet, Partially Met, or Fully Met." Since the rating is more than a yes or no decision like the checklist, it is a rating scale. Figure 9.4 illustrates one of the criterion that rates language and literacy in the curriculum.

Rating scales, like checklists, are used to track a child's development. They can be self-made or purchased developmental age and stage rating scales. It is helpful to see what the child has attained in that specific area and what skill to plan for next. This gives the teacher that zone of proximal development (Berk, 1995), the not-yet-attained skill that can be scaffolded and helped along with support. For example, a child who can print the first letter of his name is encouraged to do so at every opportunity with the teacher finishing it. Eventually, the child will write more of the letters himself.

Because the rater is looking for signs of the specific criteria, a rating scale is a highly **selective method.** Other observations are irrelevant and not recorded while looking for the specific criteria, Figure 9.5. A Rating Scale is considered a closed method since no raw data, or details, are recorded. Exact details about how the child fulfills the criterion are lost. In the preceding example from the *NAEYC Accreditation Criteria and Procedures,* exactly what the teacher does to encourage literacy is not recorded. The *ECERS* does have a small space for rater's notes that could preserve a few words. It is still a closed method since the outside reader does not have enough data on which to draw her own conclusions, unlike the Anecdotal or Running Record.

A Literacy Rating Scale has been developed for this area to assess the interest, skill, and knowledge of young children's reading and writing. (See Appendix D for a blank reproducible Literacy Rating Scale.)

A form should be duplicated for each child's portfolio and should be reviewed periodically. Each criterion is rated from observation of the child and dated at its highest level of attainment. When progress is not observed, individualized curriculum or activities are planned for that child to encourage this area of development. It may be that the environment is not conducive for this child's learning style to spawn interest in reading or writing, or the materials are not accessible or meaningful. The tool is a way to accomplish the end result, to stimulate and encourage literacy development.

Figure 9.6 is an example of a completed Literacy Rating Scale.

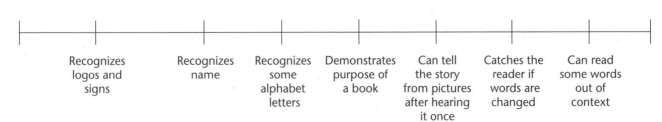

| Recognizes logos and signs | Recognizes name | Recognizes some alphabet letters | Demonstrates purpose of a book | Can tell the story from pictures after hearing it once | Catches the reader if words are changed | Can read some words out of context |

Figure 9.1 Literacy Rating Scale

Item	Inadequate 1 2	Minimal 3	Good 4 5	Excellent 6 7	SAMPLE SCORING STRIP
◆10. Child related display (Infants/toddlers)	No materials displayed.	Inappropriate materials for age group displayed (Ex. materials designed for school-aged children or church materials).	Colorful, simple photographs and pictures displayed on child's eye level (Ex. in feeding area, near cribs and crawling areas or where children can be held up to see them). Mobiles and other colorful objects for children to look at.	Everything in 5 plus staff point out pictures and talk to infants about them. Ample use of photographs of children in group. Early scribble pictures done by infants/toddlers are displayed.	Total Furnishings/display (Items 6-10)
Language-Reasoning Experiences					
11. Understanding of language (receptive language) Materials: Books, records, picture lotto and other picture card games, flannel board materials, etc.	Few materials present and little use of materials to help children understand language (Ex. no scheduled story time daily).	Some materials present, but either not available on regular basis (closed cabinets) or not regularly used for language development.	Many materials present for free choice and supervised use. At least one planned activity daily (Ex. reading books to children, story telling, flannel board stories, finger plays, etc.)	Everything in 5 plus teacher provides good language model throughout day (Ex. gives clear directions, uses words exactly in descriptions). Plans additional activities for children with special needs.	11. Understanding language 1 2 3 4 5 6 7
12. Using language (expressive language) Activities: Puppets, finger plays, singing, rhymes, answering questions, talking about experiences, interpreting pictures, child dictated stories, dramatic play.	No scheduled activities for using language (Ex. no children's planning time, talking about drawings, dictating stories, show 'n tell, etc.).	Some scheduled activities for using language (Ex. show 'n tell) , but child language not encouraged throughout the day.	Many scheduled activities for using language available during free play and group times, but not planned specifically for expressive language development.	Daily plans provide a wide variety of activities for using language during free play and group times. Opportunities to develop skills in expressing thoughts are part of a language development plan based on individual needs. Teachers encourage expressive language throughout the day.	12. Using language 1 2 3 4 5 6 7
13. Using learning concepts (reasoning) Materials Infants: shape sorting boxes, beads. Preschool: sequence cards, same-different games, size and shape toys, sorting games.	No games, materials, or activities to extend and encourage reasoning (Ex. no matching, sequencing, categorizing, etc.).	Some games, materials, or activities present, but not used with teacher guidance or not readily available.	Sufficient games, materials, and activities available on a regular basis. Children use by choice with teacher available to assist in developing concepts by talking to a child and asking questions to stimulate child's reasoning.	Everything in 5 plus a plan for introducing concepts as children are ready, either individually or in groups. Teacher encourages children to reason throughout the day, using actual events and experiences as a basis for concept development (Ex. children learn sequence by talking about their experiences in the daily routine, or recalling the sequence of a cooking project).	13. Reasoning 1 2 3 4 5 6 7

Figure 9.2 Language and Literacy Rating Scale from *ECERS*. (Courtesy of Harms, T. & Clifford, R. M. 1980. *Early Childhood Environment Rating Scale*. New York: Teachers College Press. Reprinted with permission of author.)

Item	Inadequate 1	2	Minimal 3	4	Good 5	6	Excellent 7	SAMPLE SCORING STRIP
14. Informal use of language	Language outside of group times primarily used by staff to control children's behavior and manage routines.		Staff sometimes talks with children in conversation, but children are asked primarily "yes/no" or short answer questions. Children's talk not encouraged.		Staff-child conversations are frequent. Language is primarily used by staff to exchange information with children and for social interaction. Children are asked "why, how, what it" questions, requiring longer and more complex answers.		Staff makes conscious effort to have an informal conversation with each child every day. Staff verbally expands on ideas presented by children (Ex. adds information, asks questions to encourage child to talk more).	14. or ◆14. Informal language 1 2 3 4 5 6 7

OR

Item	Inadequate 1	2	Minimal 3	4	Good 5	6	Excellent 7	
◆14. Informal use of language (Infants/toddlers)	Little or no talking to infants and toddlers.		Language used primarily to control child's behavior (Ex. No, no!).		Caregiver responds to sounds infants make, engages in verbal play (Ex. sings to child, imitates child's sounds). Staff repeats what toddlers say, expanding and elaborating when appropriate.		Everything in 5 plus staff talks to child during routines describing activity child is engaged in. Encourages toddlers to use words. Maintains eye contact while talking to child.	Total Language/reasoning (Items 11-14) _____

Notes for Clarification

11, 12, 13
For infants, it is very difficult to clearly divide language-reasoning experience into these three categories. However, since language stimulation experiences should start in the first months of life, we suggest these items be scored for infant/toddler rooms with the modifications noted below. For all ages of children, look for evidence of planned times for use of materials as well as availability of materials.

11. Activities for infants: action rhymes such as pat-a-cake, singing, adult commentary accompanying children's activity, simple picture books and pictures on walls where infants can see them used to introduce words.

12. Activities for infants: encourage imitation by repeating gestures and words for Hi, Bye Bye, and pat-a-cake; show pleasure in child's beginning sounds and early imitations of words and gestures. For a 7, the language development plan should contain formal experiences, such as stories and games, as well as informal experiences, such as teacher-child conversations and "talking times."

13. Remember, activities should be age appropriate. For infants, games such as hiding an object under a blanket and asking where it went, help to develop reasoning. For toddlers, some free choice of materials is important.

14 or ◆14
In case two raters are rating a room, they must decide which of these two items is most appropriate for the age group in the room.

◆14. Evidence of much elaboration and expansion of what toddlers are saying is needed for a rating of 5.

Figure 9.2 (Continued.)

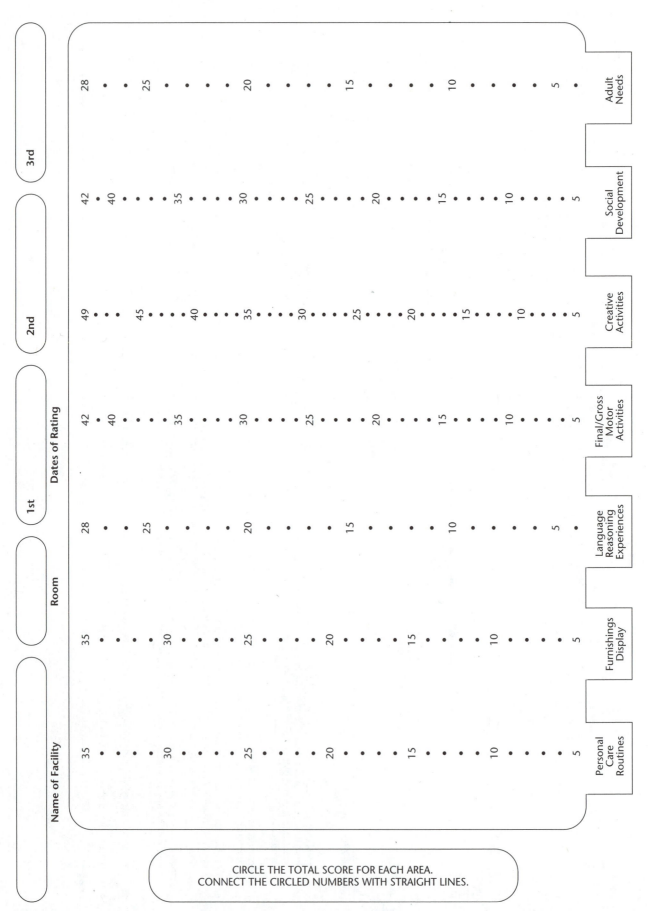

Figure 9.3 Summary Sheet from *ECERS*. (Courtesy of Harms, T. & Clifford, R. M. 1980. *Early Childhood Environment Rating Scale*. New York: Teachers College Press. Reprinted with permission of author.)

Advantages

The Rating Scale is

- quick and easy (The rater reads, decides, circles, or checks.)
- efficient for measuring a large number of criteria quickly

RATING

Not met   Partially Met   Fully met

| 1 | | 2 | | 3 |

For example,
Infants/younger toddlers
Engage in many one-to-one, face-to-face interactions with infants.
Look at simple books and pictures.
Talk in a pleasant, clam voice, using simple language and frequent eye contact while being responsive to the infant's cues.
Verbally label objects and events within the infant's experience.
Respond to sounds infant makes, occasionally imitating infant's vocalization.
Describe children's and adult's actions and the events that occur in the child's environment.
Respond to toddlers' attempts at language in supportive ways, such as expanding their utterances and answering their questions, engaging in meaningful conversation about everyday experiences.

Older toddlers/ preschoolers
Read books and poems, tell stories about experiences, talk about pictures, write down experience stories children dictate.
Provide time for conversation, ask child questions that require more than a one-word answer.
Answer children's questions.
Add more information to what a child says.
Label things in room, use written words with pictures and spoken language, provide a print-rich environment.
Use flannel board, puppets, songs, finger plays.
Encourage children's emerging interest in writing (scribbling, drawing, copying, and inventing own spelling).

School-agers
Provide opportunities to read books.
Write and produce plays, publish newspapers, write stories.
Share experiences with friends or adults.
Use audio-visual equipment such as tape recorders.
Make own filmstrips.

COMMENTS

_____

_____

_____

_____

Figure 9.4 NAEYC Accreditation Self-Study Criteria. (Permission to reprint granted by National Academy of Early Childhood Programs, 1991. *Accreditation Criteria and Procedures.* Washington, DC: National Association for the Education of Young Children.)

- informative of what "should be" expected
- useful for tracking progress or warning of developmental lags
- an assessment measurement against the ideal and used as a plan for improvement (accreditation)
- revisited to see progress over time

Disadvantages

The Rating Scale is not

- backed up with raw data
- objective (Judgments are made as observation is taking place with little time for considering the criteria and no place for explanation of circumstances.)
- free of rater bias, with no way for the reader to know that
- useful as a method to record spontaneous actions or conversations
- sensitive to a wide range of individual differences

Figure 9.5 Literacy components of the environment and individual children can be documented during the regular classroom routines.

LITERACY RATING SCALE

Child's Name *Jeremiah Jones*

INTEREST IN BOOKS

No interest, avoids	Only if adult-initiated	Brings books to adult to read	Looks at books as self-initiated activity
9/10	*10/17*		

LISTENING TO BOOKS

Wiggly, no attention	Intermittent attention	Listens in one-on-one situation	Listens as part of a group, tuning out distractions
9/21 10/6	*11/17 can't last thru whole story*		

INVOLVEMENT WITH BOOKS BEING READ

Little or no response	Emotional response, laugh, frown	Comments, asks questions	Joins in during reading
11/11			

HANDLING BOOKS

No voluntary touching	Rough handling	Exploratory manipulation	Books as favorite toys
	9/30	*10/29 Stacking up in piles by color!*	

CONCEPT OF BOOK FORMAT

No idea of front/back, up/down	Holds book right side up but skips pages	Demonstrated front/back concept	Looks at pages left to right
0	*0*	*10/29*	*2/7 He sat & looked at every page of dinosaur book*

CONCEPT OF STORY BOOK

didn't realize he was listening even though he wasn't sitting

Labels pictures	Retells story in sequence from pictures	Accurately repeats some story lines	Points to print while accurately re-telling from pictures
11/21	*1/16*		

PRINT IN THE ENVIRONMENT

no obs. in this area

Notices signs, labels	Asks, "What's that say?"	Reads signs, labels out of context	"Writes" signs to label constructions
0 *0*	*0*	*0*	*0*

BEGINNING READING

a start. "J"

Recognizes own name	Recognizes letters in name in other words	Reads simple words	Sounds out letters in unfamiliar words
11/15 *0*	*3/17*		

CONTINUED

Figure 9.6 Literacy Rating Scale Example

LITERACY RATING SCALE (continued)

MANIPULATION OF WRITING TOOLS

Fist hold	High hold on pencil	Adult grip, little control	Adult grip, good control
9/30	*11/6*	*4/17* *Work on this!*	

COMMUNICATION THROUGH WRITING

no interest

Communicates ideas through drawing	Will dictate on request	Initiates dictation	Draws and writes words
2/16 0	*4/20 0 0*		

BEGINNING WRITING

Scribbles, no reference to writing	Named scribbles "Says my name"	Single letters, random	Writes name

WRITING IN PLAY

No reference to writing	Asks for signs, words to be written	Asks for adult to spell words	Sounds out words and writes on own

Figure 9.6 (Continued)

Pitfalls to Avoid

The Rating Scale recorder should

- make sure the Rating Scale criteria matches the goals and objectives of the program and developmental range of the children
- have more than one person use the same rating scale and compare ratings for inter-rater reliability to limit observer bias
- become familiar with rating scale criteria before using it and be sure that each criterion is observable rather than judgmental: Scribbles/ Forms alphabet letters/Writes cursive *not* Still scribbling/Poor spelling/Good writing
- be sure the quality points describe behaviors rather than attitudes: Leaves when story reading begins/Stays, plays with toys during story reading/Sits, watching pages displayed during story reading *not* Not interested /Some interest/ Very interested

LOOKING AT LITERACY

Exercise: What did you read today? What did you write today?

Reading and writing is so natural that it is done automatically. When reading the preceding exercise, thoughts might have gone to formally picking up a book or writing a letter. Do not forget about:

The numbers on the clock
The name of the toothpaste you used this
   morning
The on/off light switch
Signing a check
Jotting down a phone number
Reading and writing this exercise

Literacy, the ability to read and write, is a natural part of modern life, but how is it learned? For some people, it is difficult. For most people, though, once it is learned it is there forever, and *very* useful. Becoming literate is like the childhood game of "Mother, May I." It comes in baby steps, tiny little forward motions, then giant steps, leaps that propel it forward. Literacy is not an isolated skill from other development for it involves motor skills, visual perception, hearing, small muscle development, cognitive development, social interactions, and emotional control. It is simultaneously developing along with language.

Receptive language skills are greater and earlier than expressive skills. This is true in literacy as well. Hearing and understanding words precedes speaking them. Reading words usually occurs before writing them. Reading and comprehension ability will always be greater than the ability to write as an expressive form (though some writing seems to be done without thinking).

Holdaway's classic, *The Foundations of Literacy* (1979), chronicled the history of schools' reading instruction by reviewing the alphabetic versus phonetic, versus whole-word approaches. Then came the whole-word versus sentence, then book approaches versus language experiences, and many variations of each. The basal readers were stories consisting of the most common English words, most of them boring. Writing and reading were taught as separate subjects. The whole language movement of the eighties brought back the integrated method with the decoding process still in debate (Ollila & Mayfield, 1992). Holdaway (1979) and many others since have emphasized that children learn to read and write like they learn to speak, in a natural progression of meaningful experiences. It all begins with receiving information about print.

Literacy Development

The formal instruction of reading and writing was thought to began in the first grade. As the field of **emergent literacy** expands, it is believed that literacy begins much earlier, Figure 9.7. Children come to school knowing much about reading and writing already.

Exercise: Look around you right now. List all the reading and writing materials in view.

Probably your list is very long. It may contain: labels on the television set, phone books, recipe cards, magazines and every other form of print, pens, pencils, markers, paper, computers, and brand labels on manufactured items.

Becoming a reader and writer begins by immersion in a world of print. Young children's environments are filled with the alphabet on everything from blocks, sheets, and cereal boxes. Colorful logos like McDonalds and Sesame Street are recog-

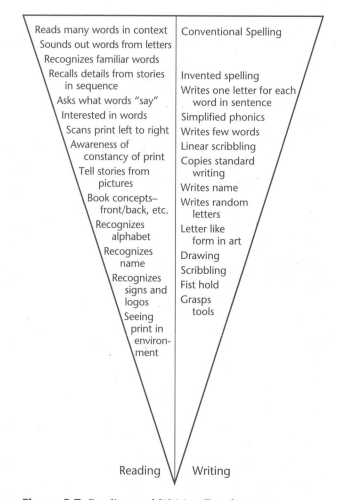

Figure 9.7 Reading and Writing Development

nized long before the actual individual letters and their sounds are known. This is **contextualized literacy,** words and phrases that can be read because they are defined by their context, shape, color, and position. Besides an environment full of print, children look to role models. They see parents reading the newspaper, the advertising on television, or directions on how to put together the tricycle. They often imitate those actions by picking up papers and babbling or pretending to read. Almost every child has picked up a pencil, pen, lipstick, or permanent marker and made some scribbles in a place not meant for writing.

IT HAPPENED TO ME: Permanent Name Writing

A mother came to school one morning and said, "I'm really glad you've been working with name writing and journal writing but last night Jason wrote his name on the side of the car with permanent marker!" Oops, no guarantees.

• •

Babies and Books. An important step toward becoming literate is the shared experience of reading a book with bright pictures and simple words about the child's world.

Exercise: Picture this in your mind: An adult and a young toddler are curled up in a big armchair looking at a picture book together. The smiling adult has a hand lightly resting on the child's head and the other pointing out something in the book. The child is looking at the book with sparkling, wide eyes, mouth agape, and hands holding onto the book.

How does this picture make you feel?
What do you think the adult is feeling?
What do you think the child is feeling?

Young babies are at the sensorimotor stage, so their books have to be touchable. The small, cardboard books, ones with texture, cloth, or plastic ones they can pull on and chew, provide those first experiences. Because infants' language development is at a simple stage, one-word books with repeating sounds soon become their favorites. Even if the reading material is the *New York Times*, building blocks of literacy are being cemented together. The bodies are close. There is a difference in the reading voice from the speaking voice. Awareness is growing that those little marks on the page mean something.

As the child moves into the second year, the memory is lengthening. The child is becoming familiar with books and pointing, laughing, and saying words of identification, like "Choo choo," and "Wha's dat?" They become participants by pretending to read. Words and familiar phrases from favorite books are added to their vocabulary. They ask for their favorites to be read over, and over, and over. When the adult changes a word in a familiar book, the child notices and protests. This shows that they know print and speech are related. By the end of the third year, the child can accurately tell the story from the pictures in familiar books. They will begin to move eyes and fingers along the row of print while saying the words. This is an indication of the child's awareness that those lines and circles are a code to be deciphered.

Reading and Preschoolers. Children learn to listen and speak effortlessly without direct instruction. Traditionally, reading and writing have been taught in formal education. In separate, isolated exercises, the vision and mind for reading and small muscles were trained with "readiness" worksheets or activities. The term *emergent literacy* is a broader term, differing from isolated skills, coming out of the whole-language movement (Clay, 1975). It fits very well into the paradigm of developmentally appropriate practice, child-centered, developmentally based, using curriculum of themes and projects.

Preschoolers who have a knowledge of literacy at age five have been shown to have a high success rate in later school achievement (Wells, 1986). The common characteristics of these children have most to do with their home environment.

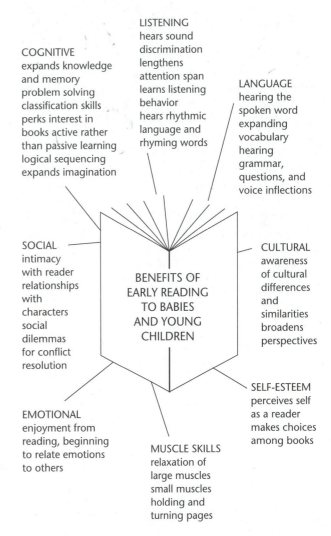

Figure 9.8 Benefits of Early Reading to Babies and Young Children

They

- were read to on a regular basis
- had a wide variety of print available in the home, such as books, magazines, and newspapers
- had paper and pencil available to scribble and draw and copy objects and letters
- people in the home stimulated the child's interest by supporting reading and writing as a worthwhile activity (Trelease, 1985)

This is not an endorsement for the "superbaby syndrome." Early reading to babies and young children brings many benefits, Figure 9.8. Forced acceleration of reading training has been shown to have no positive effect on school performance by the third grade. While those two concepts seem against each other, the difference is in the approach. Young children (as early as two years old) have been taught to read and do mathematics through drill and practice. David Elkind, noted child psychologist, has sent out the warning against the "superkid" practices in his book *Miseducation: Preschoolers at Risk* (1987). These techniques are based on behaviorist philosophies rather than on the developmentalists such as Piaget and Erikson, on which most early childhood principles and practices are founded.

So how then should young children interact with literacy? (See Figure 9.9.)

Literacy begins with communication, verbally and nonverbally. Even the unborn child hears the muffled mother's voice and the rhythm of her heartbeat. Early in the child's life, long before the child can speak to convey thoughts or express feelings, music and visual arts and crafts can be the symbols of thought. The Carnegie Foundation report *Ready to Learn* (1991) reported that only

about one-third of America's parents regularly engage in music or arts with their children.

Between two and three years, children begin to recognize the letter names and the sounds of the letters. They know which side is up in a book and the concept of front to back. In the third year, many recognize familiar logos and signs, their own name, and some short words. They begin to take an interest in the words in books and in the environment, and ask what specific words say. They understand the purpose of a book and begin to turn pages from front to back and scan the pictures from left to right pages. The story sequence of beginning, middle, and end is recognized and can be retold from the pictures. An awareness of rhyming words appears and an association of letters and sounds.

Four- and five-year-old children recognize books as sources of information and entertainment and recognize the difference between story books and pictionary or dictionary format. They can fill in story lines from rebus picture books and sometimes read simple stories word by word. They can retell the story from memory. The story is reconstructed from the pictures. Predictions are made about what might happen next or why a certain event happened, relating the cause and effect concept. Many words are recognized by sight and they are sounding out other words by alphabet letters. They are beginning to notice the space between words and the punctuation marks at the end of the sentence and change their inflection depending on the mark. They act out story characters in their play. Their conversations relate to situations and dilemmas the characters faced and how they solved them. They take an interest in creating and illustrating their own books, either in pretend writing, phonetic spelling, or dictation. Some of them have become readers, either by parents' direct instruction, or by natural association of letters and sounds.

· ·

IT HAPPENED TO ME: Office

· ·

Walking down the hall, a child in my preschool class asked, "Where's the ice?"

"What do you mean? Where's the ice?" I asked incredulously.

He pointed to a door with the sign OFFICE. "It says, 'off ice.' I wonder where the ice is?"

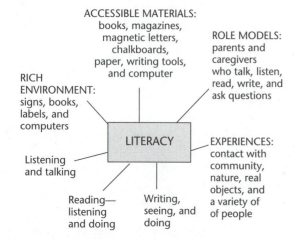

Figure 9.9 Interacting with Literacy

He had learned one aspect of print, the decoding of letters into meaningful words, but had not yet mastered the importance of spacing.

●●●●●●●●●●●●●●●●●●●●●●●●●●●●●●●●●●

Children enjoy and learn different things from different types of books. They should be exposed to many types. Machado (1990) lists the types, the learning possibilities, and why children like them, Figure 9.10.

Young Children Write

Young children's writing emerges along with language and reading, as well as art. The myth that oral language must be mastered before written language can develop is attacked by Schickedanz. Her book *More Than the ABCs: The Early Stages of Reading and Writing* (1986) is a helpful resource for the early childhood educator and parents. The first step in writing begins with the small muscle control of the writing tool, pencil, marker, or crayon. This is influenced greatly by the environment that makes these accessible. The adult is a role model for writing lists to remember. Labels are written on items to signify possession. Writing is demonstrated by the adult who says, "This is how you write your name."

Writing is more than mastery of the tools, or symbols of reading. In fact, researchers have found that many children actually write before they read, driven by the urge to communicate although they are limited in the knowledge of writing conventions (Clark, 1976; Durkin, 1966; Wells, 1986). Wells calls this Writing to Read with this powerful statement: "When one has something important to say, and other people are interested in hearing it, it is then that language and thinking most fully interpenetrate in the struggle to make meaning that captures what one has observed and understood and communicate it to others" (p. 107).

●●●●●●●●●●●●●●●●●●●●●●●●●●●●●●●●●●

IT HAPPENED TO ME:
B L D Z R

●●●●●●●●●●●●●●●●●●●●●●●●●●●●●●●●●●

This was demonstrated to me by a group of five-year-old boys who predominated a class I had. As we approached the holiday season, they were interested in making their gift wish lists. Having just been inspired by Schickedanz's book

(1986), instead of dictating their lists to me, I urged them to write or draw their own. To my amazement they worked hard at it for many minutes (which was amazing in itself). Even more amazing was that I could really read what they wrote:

B L D Z R (bulldozer)
G N (gun)
2 W E L R (two-wheeler)

They were struggling to communicate meaning, and they had done so!

●●●●●●●●●●●●●●●●●●●●●●●●●●●●●●●●●●

Stages of Writing. Writing develops in predictable stages. They are:

Scribbling. The child makes marks as soon as she can hold a writing tool. She begins by stabbing at the paper, the dragging action making lines. She progresses to unclosed circular motions, then to closed circles, vertical and horizontal lines, and eventually boxlike or square shapes. This phase is the preparation for both drawing and writing. Many children extend scribbling into wavy lines that they call writing after observing adults writing cursive, Figure 9.11.

Drawing. Written communication in the form of pictures has its historical roots in the Egyptian pictorials inside the pyramids. Children (and societies) without writing convey meaningful messages by drawing. Young children are hindered by their lack of small muscle coordination and the ability to represent on paper the ideas they have in their head, Figure 9.12. They have a mental image of horse but what they draw may not be recognizable as a horse to the viewer. Again, the receptive is greater than the expressive.

Making Letters. Between the ages of three and four, children come to realize there is a difference between drawing and writing although it may not be evident to the viewer. The first letter they write is usually the first letter of their name. As their knowledge of the sounds and shapes of more letters expands, they will begin to write sentences, Figure 9.13. The first letter of each word is sounded out and written down, expecting the reader to be able to decipher the message. It is an approximation that is bringing them closer to the symbols that combine to make words in a sentence. They will often ask for words to be written so they can copy them. They try their hand at **invented spelling,** as the boys did on their gift

Types	Features Teachers Like	Features Children Like
Story books (picture books) •Family and home •Folktales and fables • Fanciful stories • Fairy tales • Animal stories • Others	Shared moments children enthusiastic and attentive Making characters' voices Introducing human truths and imaginative adventures Sharing favorites Easy for child to identify with small creatures	Imagination and fantasy Identification with characters' humanness Wish and need fulfillment Adventure, Excitement, Action, Self-realization, Visual variety, Word pleasure
Nonfiction books (informational)	Expanding individual and group interests Developing "reading-to-know" attitudes Finding out together	Facts, discovery of information and ideas Understanding of reality and how things work and function Answers to "why" and "how" New words and new meanings
Wordless books	Promote child speech, creativity, and imagi- nation	Supplying their own words to tell story Discovery of meanings Color, action, and visual variety
Interaction books (books which have active child participation built-in)	Keeping children involved and attentive Builds listening for directions skills	Movement and group feeling Individual creativity and expression Appeal to senses Manipulative features
Concept books (books with central concepts or themes that include specific and reinforcing examples)	Promotes categorization Presents opportunities to know about and develop concepts Many examples	Adds to knowledge Visually presents abstractions
Predictable books (books with repetitions and reinforcement)	Permits successful guessing Build's child's confidence Promotes ideas that books make sense	Opportunity to read along Repetitiveness Builds feelings of competence
Reference books (picture dictionaries, encyclopedias, special subject books)	Opportunity to look up questions with the child Individualized learning	Getting answers Being with teacher Finding a resource that answers their questions
Alphabet and word books (word books have name of object printed near or on top of object)	Supplies letters and word models Paired words and objects Useful for child with avid interest in alphabet letters and words	Discovery of meanings and names of alphabet letters and words
Novelty books (pop-ups, fold-outs, stamp and pasting books, activity books, puzzle books, scratch and sniff books, hidden objects in illustrations, talking books	Adds sense-exploring variety Stimulates creativity Comes in many different sizes and shapes Motor involvement for child	Exploring, touching, moving, feeling, smelling, licking, painting, drawing, coloring, cutting, gluing, acting upon, listening to a mechanical voice, and getting instant feedback
Paperback books and magazines (Golden Books, *Humpty Dumpty Magazine*)	Inexpensive Wide variety Many classics available	Children can save own money and choose for themselves
Teacher- and child-made books	Reinforces class learnings Builds understanding of authorship Allows creative expression Records individual, group projects, field trips, parties Promotes child expression of concerns and ideas Builds child's self-esteem	Child sees own name in print Shares ideas with others Self-rewarding
Therapeutic books (books helping children cope with and understand things such as divorce, death, jealousy)	Presents life realistically Offers positive solutions and insights Presents diverse family groups Deals with life's hard-to-deal-with subjects	Helps children discuss real feelings
Seasonal and holiday books	Accompanies child interest May help child understand underlying reasons for celebration	Builds pleasant expectations Adds detail
Books and audiovisual combinations (read- alongs)	Adds variety Offers group and individual experiencing opportunities Stimulates interest in books	Projects large illustrations Can be enjoyed individually
Toddler books (durable pages)	Resists wear and tear	Ease in page-turning
Multicultural and cross-cultural books	Increases positive attitudes concerning diver- sity and similarity Emphasizes the realities in our society	Meeting a variety of people

Figure 9.10 Types of Books for Young Children. (Courtesy of Machado, J. M. 1995. *Early Childhood Experiences in Language Arts, 4th edition*. Albany, NY: Delmar Publishers. Reprinted with permission.)

Figure 9.11 Linear scribbles approximate writing.

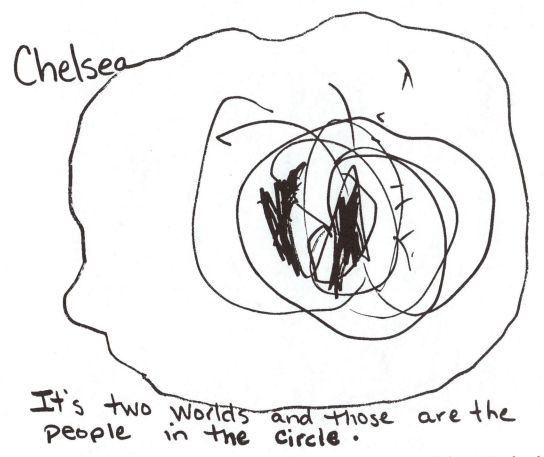

Figure 9.12 Children's drawings often are the expression of inner thoughts and words before writing has developed.

list, by sounding it out and writing the letter sounds that they hear.

Organizing Print. Writing is more than knowledge of letters and their sounds; it is the proper sequence, organization on the page, and spaces between that form written language. Random letters will appear in children's paintings and art work whether they have meaning or are just practicing the style.

Backward letters. Preschoolers in their experimentation with letters, and perhaps due to their still-developing visual perception, often reverse letters to their parents' alarm. Sulzby, who has studied children's writing for over 15 years, says it is common for preschoolers to write backward and switch from backward to forward (Sulzby, 1993), Figure 9.14.

Incorporate Writing into Play. By ages five and six, children realize that writing serves the function of conveying information. They will make signs to designate territory or "Do not disturb," print their name on their art work so they can take it home, and use writing to tell stories or write letters. In the dramatic play area, writing materials are provided as they would appear in context. In housekeeping, put a note pad by the phone, include grocery advertisements, list paper, and a pencil nearby. A shoe store would include sales slip books. A restaurant would need menus with pictures and words, server pads, and checkbooks. A grocery store would need flyers, open and closed signs, help-wanted signs, and worker sign-in sheets.

Journal writing. Many early childhood classrooms have begun daily journal writing for children to make an entry about the day. It may begin as pictures but move to include or become exclusively print. If the child dictates as in Figure 9.15, or the teachers read and interpret the pictures and print, it is a form of personal communication, but also provides a way of ongoing assessment (Williams & Davis, 1994).

∙∙∙

IT HAPPENED TO ME:
Make Love

∙∙∙

Another writing incident is an anecdote I will always remember. A dear, sweet little four-year-old girl came over to me in class one day and said, "Mrs. Nilsen, I know how to make love. Want me to show you?" Gulp! "Sure." She got a sheet of paper and proudly wrote L U V. We rejoiced together!

∙∙∙

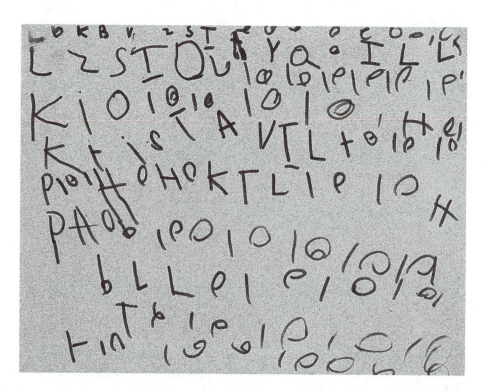

Figure 9.13 Invented spelling, sounding out words, is the beginning of writing for meaning and purpose.

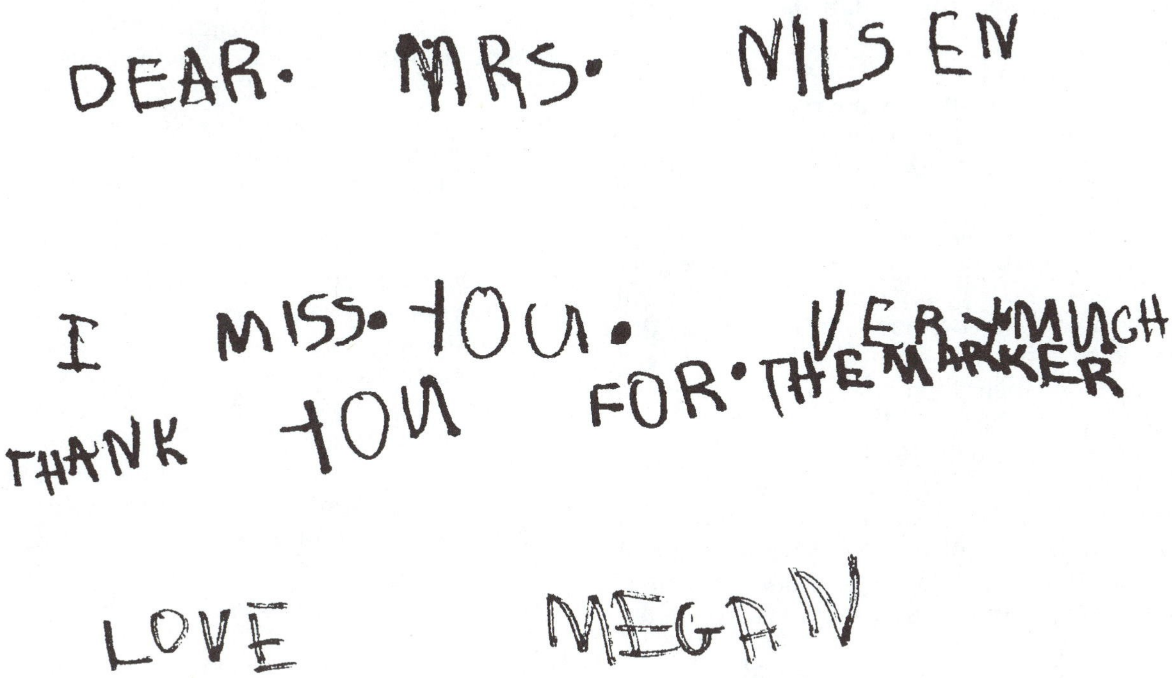

DEAR. MRS. NILSEN

I MISS. YOU. VERY MUCH
THANK YOU FOR THE MARKER

LOVE MEGAN

Figure 9.14 Early writing ignores many rules but is precious for its effort and meaning.

This is a letter to my Gramda. She is getting sick and she is getting better. You better mail it out.

Put it in a basket and mail it up the hill with the grandchildren

Krista
5-6-92

Figure 9.15 Children dictate important messages they want to communicate. This one also demonstrates her egocentricity.

Literacy and Computers

Exercise: How computer literate are you?

Now more than one-third of American homes have computers and many schools and early childhood programs have them as well. Young children have a great interest in using them to imitate adults, Figure 9.16. With the myriad of software available, they are actively involved in the manipulation of symbols, pictures, and letters. The explosion of software for young children has addressed this market but not without controversy. In this age of technology, all advances must be carefully considered for their appropriateness and value to the development of the child.

Computers can serve the same purposes as any other learning area. They can be explored by manipulation, a vehicle of social interaction with peers, and provide a time of interaction with an adult. These all add to the child's general development as well as literacy competency. With the computer,

Figure 9.16 All writing tools begin with manipulation, mastery, then meaning.

children produce their own pictures, text, and even their own books. Holdaway (1979) prophetically stated, "The difficulty of handwriting and spelling tend to delay any genuine desire to produce written language for a purpose" (p. 36). The computer removes that obstacle with software that accepts phonetic spelling, spell checks as words are written, and provides picture and word combinations.

The integration of computers into the learning environment is their most effective use. This does not mean a computer lab down the hall where children spend a period of time. True integration of a computer in the classroom uses it as a tool to explore. The computer can enhance language, mathematics, and science and also social interactions (Davis & Shade, 1994).

Children with learning disabilities and different learning styles have been found to use the computer as a way of finding success in learning. Assistive technology devices were included in the Education of the Handicapped Act Amendments of 1986 (P. L. 99-457) and the Individuals with Disabilities Act (IDEA: P. L. 101-476). Computers promise new ways for the disabled to access not only learning and knowledge but focused behaviors. Behrmann and Lahm (1994) also emphasize the use of computers as a play form in special education that allows children choice, independence, and a mode of expression.

Beaty (1992) suggests that watching the child using the computer will tell the observer about the child's

- thinking—trial and error, problem solving, matching
- language—giving and receiving directions and questions
- creativity—drawing and writing software programs
- attention span—duration of concentration
- letter and word recognition—software selections
- small motor skills—keyboard manipulation
- self-esteem—power over an adult machine, special knowledge
- social development—isolation or sharing and turn taking

An issue of concern is the inequity of access. White families are three times as likely as African Americans or Hispanics to have computers at home. Schools with poorer children have fewer computers (Fineman, 1995). Girls have been found to use the computers less than boys, widening the gap in perceived abilities in the math and science areas. These are valid concerns observant teachers need to keep in mind. Technology offers opportunities beyond imagination but many teachers are still "techno-phobic." Fears of the "teaching machine" are dis-counted by Davis and Shade (1994): "Potentially powerful and stimulating, the computer is only an inert object that can never be a substitute for the personal touch of the classroom teacher."

Ways to Document Reading and Writing Progress

Literacy involvement can be observed across all learning areas. A multitude of methods, then, are used to observe the various forms that literacy takes.

Class List Logs can survey the group for a read-ing and writing interest, behavior, skill, or partici-pation. Taped on the wall in the book area, it is used to record each time a child selects a book as a choice activity, acting as a Frequency Count. A Class List Log could be used to record a child's lis-tening behavior during story reading time. Time Samples indicate how long a child chooses to spend in the book area or writing center. Interviews or asking questions about a story can document the child's understanding of what was read. Anecdotal and Running Records might contain information about the child's use of literacy in structured and unstructured situations. Photographs and videos capture children's reading and writing graphically while their computer-generated stories provide technological evidence. Tape recordings of a child reading or pretending to read give clues not only of reading ability but speech production.

More formalized assessments like checklists of specific reading and writing skills can be purchased or self-made. Samples of the child's writing, dicta-tion, and bookmaking provide information about the level the child has attained. Reading records, sometimes called Running Records, are notations made on scripts of book texts during oral reading (Chittenden & Courtney, 1989). This system requires the individual, concentrated attention of the teacher.

Whatever method is selected, a systematic gathering of documentation shows the progress of literacy.

SPECIAL POPULATIONS AND LITERACY

Language, whether spoken or written, occurs in the context of children's lives. When physical or mental limitations are present, literacy develop-ment may be affected. Children who are Limited English Proficient (LEM) may or may not be literacy limited. It depends on the culture and the family circumstances. All children should be assessed to find the level of development approached as a strength or level of achievement, then individual-ized plans should be made to help the child attain the next level. When literacy materials are placed throughout the classroom environment, this indi-vidualization for special populations is also possible.

Physical Disabilities and Literacy

Visual impairments will slow or prevent the progression of reading and writing. By providing high-contrast documents and writing tools, along with tactile materials such as sandpaper, plastic magnetic, or raised alphabet letters, children with limited vision can be included in the world of lit-eracy. Reading to them is also an important part of their literacy world. Children with hearing impair-ments may have affected language development, which also affects literacy. Using visual cues for communication may be even more important. It is a critical component of both receptive and expres-sive language. Working with children with hearing deficits in the area of reading and writing is an important facet of the teacher's role.

Learning Disabilities and Literacy

Literacy, the ability to read and write, is the area in which learning disabilities are the most evident. One of the early labels of reading difficulties was **dyslexia,** often characterized by writing alphabet letters backwards or confusing similarly shaped letters like *b* and *p*. This is just one symptom of a larger range of difficulties. The term **learning dis-abilities** describes people within the range of nor-mal intelligence, without significant behavioral disorders, but with low academic achievement because of the inability to read and write.

The actual causes for learning disabilities are still under study. Neurological causes, a brain dys-function, is one explanation. Vision and percep-tual processing difficulties is another theory that has spurred some to seek vision training as a rem-edy with mixed results. Psychological and emo-tional causes have been investigated, but academic difficulties affect a child's psychological and emotional well-being so it has been difficult to determine if this is a cause or an effect. Envi-ronmental causes, such as extreme poverty and a lack of cognitive stimulation, have been recog-nized as connected to learning disabilities, how-ever, there many middle-class children with learning disabilities, so environmental causes can-not be the total answer either.

A recognized definition, diagnosis, and label were needed to secure needed services for children with academic underachievement. The Association for Children with Learning Disabilities has defined the term *specific learning disability* as "a chronic condition of presumed neurological origin that selectively interferes with the development, integration, and/or demonstration of verbal

. . . .

TOPICS IN OBSERVATION: Books in the Sandbox

. . . .

Exercise: List the literacy materials (reading or writing) in each of the rooms in your home.

Kitchen
Living room
Bedroom
Bathroom

Most homes have some kinds of literacy materials in every room. From cookbooks to magazines, every room has literacy materials. Why then does the early childhood classroom restrict books to the book area and writing materials to the writing center or art area? It probably is for the protection of the books or the walls from indiscriminate writers. What it does, however, is artificially restrict literacy to certain areas, unlike real life. If the classroom is to be a microcosm of the world outside, then perhaps these restrictions need to be reconsidered. Use the placement and proliferation of books and writing materials throughout the environment as an assessment tool of the literacy-rich environment and the teacher's own literacy priority.

How about books about the beach or archaeology in or near the sandbox? In the art area, books about colors, even art books with prints of the masters, could stimulate interest in color, form, texture, and art expression. Books about buildings and skyscrapers, and pencils and paper to trace blocks or sketch buildings will add a literacy component to the block area. Books or magazines on the back of the toilet might capture the interest of a child not ordinarily sitting in one place very long.

In the dramatic play area, books or magazines and writing materials can connect literacy to whatever dramatic play theme is set up there. A medical office would have an appointment calendar, magazines in the waiting room, and books of anatomy or stories about the hospital. The car repair shop would have auto repair manuals, car magazines, order forms for repairs, and invoices.

Another artificial classroom literacy behavior is reading to the whole group of children at one time. In the outside world, reading and writing are usually individual activities. Individualized reading is enhanced when books and reading materials are integrated throughout the classroom environment. Then the adult can read to every child connected with the context of their play or suggest writing as a mode of communication that facilitates the play. Reading and writing are then associated with their play theme, and assimilated and accommodated into their knowledge base. It is connected with real objects and real purposes, not just another isolated routine on the daily schedule.

By desegregating literacy from the library or writing centers, children see the practical use of reading and writing. The adult role is to help fill the span between their actual ability to read and write and a higher level, to provide that scaffold, by suggesting researching books for answers to questions, or writing as a way to communicate ideas or preserve details.

Care of the books and writing materials is a valid concern, but some principles can reduce the worries:

* Once the decision is made that literacy materials will be accessible throughout the environment, preparations are made for book pockets or racks near the sandbox, easels, and other play areas. A section of the block shelf can just as easily hold books and literacy materials along with wheeled vehicles and block accessories.
* When materials are useful and important to children, they will treat them carefully.
* Adult role models of caring for books and using writing materials in a constructive way will be attended to by the children.

Think about how the opportunities to observe children's literacy skills will be expanded if the materials are included in every area.

or nonverbal activities" (in Hallahan and Kaufman, 1986). Young children with learning disabilities are extremely difficult to diagnose because they are in the prereading stage. The two primary behaviors characteristic of learning disabilities are impulsiveness and indiscrimination (the inability to tune out distractions or concentrate on a task in an orderly fashion), as defined by Samuel Kirk, who coined the term *learning disabled* (as cited in Hallahan & Kaufman, 1986). These two characteristics are common in all young children. When they are prolonged or exaggerated, learning disabilities may be suspected. They are also characteristics of hyperactivity and ADDH.

The role of the early childhood observer is to closely monitor the literacy progress, along with other areas of development and behavior, aware of indications of difficulties and referral agents from whom help may be secured.

Literacy and Children Whose First Language Is Not English

Children who are native speakers in a language other than English probably will come into the early childhood setting with literacy exposure as well. They have observed adults writing and seen a written form of their own language, such as books, newspapers, and letters. They may have story books printed in that language. Early writing follows the same stages: scribbling, drawing, and forming letters. The writing may appear in another form if the symbols are not alphabetic, with scribbles appearing vertically rather than horizontally for Asian children, for example. They continue to acquire native language literacy from home and an expanded language and literacy in English from the early childhood setting. Children who have little or no early experiences with print come to school at a disadvantage. Newman and Roskos (1993) says, "Bilingualism often has a negative effect, leading to low levels of ability in both languages" (p. 80).

For all children, and especially those with Limited English proficiency, (LEP) picture books are excellent ways to communicate universal messages and have a shared experience not based on spoken language. Looking at picture books enhances vocabulary growth. Literacy success in the second language depends on the same factors as oral language for all children, an environment filled with materials and activities. Individual interactions enhance both language and literacy. The environment and curriculum includes real opportunities to use literacy, such as name lists, drawing and writing materials, story books to look at, and adults reading and pointing to pictures and words. Children will write if they have reason to do so, even if they are not able to speak the language (Urzua, 1987). All children need an accepting social atmosphere of language attempts. Adults who allow and encourage native language speaking and writing demonstrate an overall acceptance of the child and the family. Pictorial and word labels in the classroom will help all children associate the object with the written word. Meaningful opportunities to write give older children with limited English a way to communicate. Young children with limited English proficiency can learn vocabulary, customs, and find enjoyment through books and literacy materials. As mentioned previously, the home may already be literacy-rich with books and writing in the parents' language. Stories recorded on tapes, dictionaries that have familiar items in both languages, and books in the first language of every child are helpful toward literacy development. Literacy materials can be sent home for reinforcement and enjoyment by the whole family.

- -

IT HAPPENED TO ME: Working to Communicate

- -

One of my college students was in a practicum placement in a program in which there was a child from Vietnam who spoke no English. She struggled to communicate. Finally, on her own initiative, she made a book of common items in the classroom from a mail order catalog. She found a translator to write the words for the items in the child's language, as well as phonetic spelling in English so she could pronounce it. That book went back and forth from home to school, aiding both in communicating. Everyone benefited. She received an A.

- -

Cultural differences other than native language also affect the child's literacy development. Heath's (1983) ethnographic research on families in two communities in Appalachia found cultural differences in how families encourage and listen to children's language. Cultural differences also have been found in the amount and type of early vocalization with infants and young children. Middleclass families and teachers are more verbally responsive and referential, giving names to items and repeating them, such as "Doggie. Doggie." Nonmainstream cultures relied more on body language, teasing, and traditional stories using dialects and nonstandard English. Many cultures do not consider literacy an important component of the young child's world but hold it as a rite of passage into the adult world. This cultural difference will pose challenges to the early childhood program in helping these children reach the level of familiarity with not only the spoken language but the written language as well.

HELPING PROFESSIONALS FOR LITERACY CONCERNS

Children who need further help in the area of literacy development, reading, or writing should begin first with a physical examination. Vision,

hearing, or neurological problems may interfere with literacy development. Speech and language difficulties could be contributing factors, so evaluations in these areas may be considered. Helping professionals in the area of literacy are

reading specialists—teachers with specialized training in the teaching of reading, and diagnosis and remediation of reading and writing difficulties

special education teachers—teachers with knowledge of literacy disorders and strategies for overcoming learning disabilities

bilingual teachers or interpreters—people who can translate writing materials and communication in the family's first language

Week 9, Assignment A

RATING SCALES IN LITERACY FOR ALL

For each child, copy the Literacy Rating Scale found in Appendix D, or use the literacy assessment tool chosen by your program. Sometime this week, watch how each child uses books, listens to story books being read, and uses writing. Mark the Rating Scale with the date on each attained level. Return to this later in the year to evaluate progress.

What to Do with It

Make a summary note on the portfolio overview sheet, and file the Rating Scale in the child's portfolio, Figure 9.17.

If lower levels of literacy than expected are observed, make notes in your daily plans to give the child some attention or planned activities in that area.

Share your findings with the parents or the child, if appropriate. For example: "Mrs. Chen,

LITERACY DEVELOPMENT		
Documentation	Recorder	Date
RS +name 0 books	*BAN*	11/3
RS reads name, written name see pg. sample		1/18
RS Reads short words		4/17
AR Reading to others		4/29

Figure 9.17 Portfolio Overview Example

while I was noting each child's interaction with books, I saw how Mashiko listened so closely to the story and was able to tell it back word for word. That's the first step in learning to read," or "Today when you were playing in the grocery store I saw how you made that sign that said "Coke." I didn't know you knew how to write!"

Week 9, Assignment B

INTERVIEWS IN SPEECH AND LANGUAGE FOR GROUP D

Continue with the Interviews begun in week 6, selecting children from group D to interview each day this week. If possible, tape record the Interview as well as make written notes as you speak with

each child. Do an informal or structured interview as described in Week 6, Assignment A.

What to Do with It

Analyze each interview for what it reveals about the child's knowledge, emotional state, social development, and speech and language development. (Use the Speech and Language Checklist found in Appendix D.)

Enter the summary. Note your name and the date on the portfolio overview sheet. If a significant lag appears, discuss it with your supervisor to confirm it. Then discuss it with the parents. Have a list of sites where a speech and language evaluation may be obtained to give to the parents.

Week 9, Assignment C

REFLECTIVE JOURNAL

Respond to the following by copying this page, making notations and filing it with your Reflective Journal, kept in a private file at home.

My own literacy rating scale:

I am a reluctant reader, for necessity only	I read the daily newspaper and that's about it	I read on vacation or to kill time	I love to read and always have a book going

I think I developed into that kind of reader because...

My favorite type of reading is_____

section of the daily newspaper, magazines such as _____

_____, religious reading such as _____,

novels about _____, nonfiction about _____

I write for:

necessity	to help me remember	to communicate with distant friends/relatives	to clarify or express my thoughts and feelings

This Reflective Journal...

REFERENCES

Beaty, J. (1992). *Preschool appropriate practices.* Fort Worth: Harcourt Brace Jovanovich College Publishers.

Behrmann, M. M. & Lahm, E. A. (1994). Computer applications in early childhood special education. In Wright, J. L. & Shade, D. D. (Eds.). *Young children: Active learners in a technological age.* Washington, DC: National Association for the Education of Young Children.

Berk, L. E. & Winsler, A. (1995). *Scaffolding children's learning: Vygotsky and early childhood education.* Washington, DC: National Association for the Education of Young Children.

Boyer, E. L. (1991). *Ready to learn: A mandate for the nation.* Princeton, NJ: Carnegie Foundation for the Advancement of Teaching.

Chittenden, E. & Courtney, R. (1989). Assessment of young children's reading: Documentation as an alternative to testing. In Strickland, D. S. & Morrow, L. (Eds.) *Emerging literacy: Young children learn to read and write.* Newark, DE: International Reading Association.

Clark, M. M. (1976). *Young fluent readers.* London: Heinemann Educational Books.

Clay, M. (1975). *What did I write?* Auckland, New Zealand: Heinemann Educational Books.

Davis, B. C. & Shade, D. D. (1994). Integrate, don't isolate!: Computers in the early childhood curriculum. *ERIC Digest.* Urbana, IL: Clearinghouse on Elementary and Early Childhood Education. EDO-PS-94-17.

Durkin, D. (1966). *Children who read early.* New York: Teacher's College Press.

Elkind, D. (1987). *Miseducation: Preschoolers at risk.* New York: Alfred A. Knopf.

Fineman, H. (1995, February 27). The brave new world of cybertribes. *Newsweek, 9,* 30–32.

Hallahan, D. P. & Kaufman, J. M. (1986). *Exceptional Children.* Englewood Cliffs, NJ: Prentice Hall.

Harms, T. & Clifford, R, (1980). *Early childhood environment rating scale (ECERS).* New York: Teachers College Press.

Heath, S. B. (1983). *Ways with words: Language, life and work in communities and classrooms.* Cambridge, England: Cambridge University Press.

Holdaway, D. (1979). *The foundations of literacy.* Sydney, Australia: Ashton Scholastic.

Kirk, S. A., Kliebhan, J. M., & Lerner, J. W. (1978). *Teaching reading to slow and disabled learners.* Boston: Houghton Mifflin.

Machado, J. M. (1995). *Early childhood experiences in language arts, fourth edition.* Albany, NY: Delmar Publishers.

Meisels, S. J., Jablon, J. R., Mardsen, D. B., Dichtelmiller, M. L., & Dorfman, A. B. (1994). *The work sampling system.* Ann Arbor, MI: Rebus Planning Associates.

National Academy of Early Childhood Programs. (1991). *NAEYC Accreditation criteria and procedures.* Washington, DC: Author.

Newman, S. B. Roskos, K. A. (1993). *Language and literacy learning in the early years: An integrated approach.* New York: Harcourt Brace Jovanovich.

Ollila, L. O. & Mayfield, M. I. (1992). *Emerging literacy: Preschool, kindergarten and primary grades.* Boston: Allyn and Bacon.

Schickedanz, J. (1986). *More than the ABCs: The early stages of reading and writing.* Washington, DC: National Association for the Education of Young Children.

Sulzby, E. (1993). Encouraging emergent writers. *Scholastic Pre-K Today, 7* (4) 30.

Trelease, J. (1985). *The read-aloud handbook.* New York: Penguin Books.

Urzua, C. (1987). "You stopped too soon": Second language children composing and revising. *TESOL Quarterly, 21,* (3), 279–305.

Wells, G. (1986). *The meaning makers: Children learning language and using language to learn.* Portsmouth, NH: Heinemann.

Williams. R. P. & Davis, J. K. (1994). Lead sprightly into literacy. *Young Children, 49,* (4) 37–41.

RESOURCES

Machado, J. M. (1995). *Early childhood experiences in language arts, fourth edition.* Albany: Delmar Publishers.

Schickedanz, J. (1986). *More than the ABCs: The early stages of reading and writing.* Washington, DC: National Association for the Education of Young Children.

Strickland, D. S. & Morrow, L. (Eds.) (1989). *Emerging literacy: Young children learn to read and write.* Newark, DE: International Reading Association.

CHAPTER 10

Using Work Samples to Look at Creativity

IN THIS CHAPTER ....

✔ Using Work Samples to Observe a Child's Development

✔ Looking at Children's Creative Development

✔ Topics in Observation: Responding to Children's Creative Work

✔ Special Populations and Creativity

✔ Helping Professionals for Creative Arts

USING WORK SAMPLES TO OBSERVE A CHILD'S DEVELOPMENT

Exercise: What can you tell about the child who created the drawing in Figure 10.1?

You could probably tell this child has observed a dog closely. The drawing is accurately proportioned and detailed, so the age of the artist could be estimated, by one who knew the usual progressive stages of children's drawing, to be about six

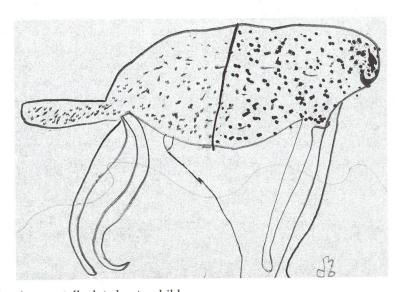

Figure 10.1 A drawing can tell a lot about a child.

years old. Actually, this drawing was done by an active four-year-old with an avid interest in art. Compared to the stages of creative development, it is advanced for the chronological age of the artist.

IT HAPPENED TO ME: The Story of the Dog Drawing

The child who made me the drawing in Figure 10.1 was an imp of a boy with freckles and a sense of humor. He gave me the drawing as a surprise gift. It was preceded by a promise that I would display it on my refrigerator door. It has been displayed to a far wider audience as a prime example of a child's creative work going beyond expected stages. The drawing reveals so much about him and his development. His sense of humor is seen in the face of the dog.

Creativity comes from within and reveals the self, whether it is a three-year-old with a crayon drawing on the wall, or a great master with oils and canvas. The child's creative products can be used as effective revelations of developmental progress. Almost every developmental area can be assessed from observing a child manipulate creative **media.**

The old saying, "A picture is worth a thousand words," is true also of children's creative products. Children's work, done in the natural home or classroom setting, provides information that would take paragraphs to convey. Individual children and groups produce work that can serve as raw data for assessment. They can be collected over time, showing changes in development (McAfee & Leong, 1994). Many areas of development are revealed in children's work samples, Figure 10.2.

Materials can be contributed to the portfolio from various sources—the parents, the teacher, or the child—depending on its purpose. In the *Week by Week* portfolio, information and documents are gathered from all three, with equal access as well. The child's access, of course, depends on the age, but even very young children can understand the portfolio is about them. They often want to see it, just as they love to look at photographs of themselves as babies. By including samples of their work, whether drawing, writing, or photographs, they realize its purpose as a chronicle of their development.

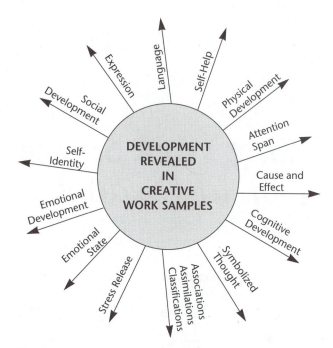

Figure 10.2 Development Revealed in Creative Work

Children should be aware of the portfolio and its purpose as a receptacle for information about them. They are invited to add to the portfolio when they have work they feel is important to them (Meisels & Steele, 1991). If the portfolio is a file folder, the child can decorate the four panels of the file folder, periodically over the quarters of the school year. This personalizes it, but also makes it an episodic documentation of the child's work. The children can comment on their own work as a way of exploring their thinking. The observer listens to the child describe the memory of the work and comments on the progress from the child's viewpoint.

Children are very possessive of their work (as they should be) but usually are generous in allowing copies to be made on a copier. The color is lost but the line and form are preserved. Actually having a notebook for each child to draw in over the course of a year is another way of collecting drawings. It is more structured, drawing at the adult's request, and yields less spontaneous and natural art products. It also limits the types of media that can be used.

Three-dimensional creations such as sculpture, collages, mobiles, woodworking, sewing, and even movement can be preserved with photographs, documented, and added to the portfolio, Figure 10.3. Work can be explained with notes attached to the back. The background of the work, how it came to be done, and any dictation or child's

Figure 10.3 Work samples can be three-dimensional.

words about the work can be written there. The teacher can make notations concerning the child's development that this work especially illustrates.

Portfolios contain samples of the child's work to document progress and illustrate the child's thinking. Because development is seen in children's graphic art products, they are a concrete way to document development. Children's drawings, paintings, scribbles, and block structure photographs or sketches are collected periodically to add to the portfolio. Genishi (1993) recommends reviewing children's art work portfolios when it is time to write progress reports or hold parent conferences. "When you review, look to see how well each child's portfolio captures his or her story of development… For example, include a series of paintings that shows a child's changing use of patterns. Use these stories to inform and enrich your written reports and your conversations with parents" (p. 67).

Other Work Samples for the Portfolio. Figure 10.4 is a list of various types of work samples.

The areas of development and other information the teacher gathers about the child can be observed from a child's creative work. Figure 10.5 is the Work Samples Checklist, which includes areas covered in *Week by Week* and some assessment criteria in the creative realm.

Advantages of Collecting Work Samples

Collecting work samples is an effective recording technique because it is done

- in a natural classroom setting, with the child selecting materials and working at her own pace and direction, illustrating many areas of development

activity choices	manipulative maps
audio tapes	math games
baking projects	models
block constructions	murals
photos	pantomime
sketches	photographs of work
book illustrations	photography by child
book lists	plans and projects
book making	plays
charts and graphs	posters
child-authored books	projects
clay and Play Doh	puppets
manipulations	puzzles
collages	raps
collections	rebus stories
computer constructions	replicas
crafter's handiwork	rhymes
creative movement	rhythms
demonstrations	role play
dictations	rules
dramatic play scenarios	sculptures
exhibits	signs
flannel board depictions	silly sayings
group projects	skits
humor	sociodramatic songs
illustrations	sticker designs
innovations	story themes
jokes and riddles	typing
jump rope rhymes	videotapes
lists	woodworking

Figure 10.4 Work Samples. (Adapted from Puckett, M. & Black, J., 1994, p. 196. *Authentic Assessment of the Young Child: Celebrating Development and Learning.* Reprinted with permission of Prentice Hall, Upper Saddle River, NJ.)

- over a period of time, showing progress of development
- as an expression of the child's thoughts and feelings more accurately and powerfully than an observer can describe them

Disadvantages

Work samples might

- make the child overly conscious of manipulation or practice, not meant to be a statement
- lead the observer to draw erroneous conclusions from creative work

WORK SAMPLES CHECKLIST

Child's Name_____ Dates _____

COMMENTS

Separation
❏ Separates from adult to do creative work alone
❏ Works independently without requiring adult presence or direction

Self-Care
❏ Independently selects materials
❏ Makes preparations to work (Example: Puts on a smock)
❏ Uses materials independently
❏ Cleans up spills, messes
❏ Writes name on work
❏ Places finished product in proper place
❏ Washes and dries hands if necessary
❏ Replaces materials to storage place

Physical Development
❏ Controls whole body movement during work
❏ Controls small muscles to hold tool
❏ Controls tool to form desired product
❏ Draws, prints, paints, pastes
❏ Squeezes glue bottle
❏ Picks up collage materials
❏ Manipulates clay or Play Doh
❏ Cuts with scissors
❏ Controls body to stay within the space (on the paper, building on a rug, clay on table)

Social Skills
❏ Represents important people in his life in his work
❏ Desires and can work near other children
❏ Shares materials and supplies
❏ Engages in positive commentary on other children's work
❏ Works cooperatively on a joint project

Emotional Development
❏ Uses art work to express emotions of happiness, anger, fear
❏ Verbalizes feelings about work
❏ Enjoys manipulation and creation
❏ Controls emotions of frustration when work meets difficulties
❏ Uses the media as a stress release, pounding clay, tearing paper, painting

Speech and Language Development
❏ Names scribbles, buildings, creations
❏ Talks about work using vocabulary connected with art materials and design
❏ Uses language to describe process, intent, and satisfaction with product
❏ Vocabulary reflects knowledge of shapes (circle, square, triangle, rectangle, lines)

CONTINUED

Figure 10.5 Work Samples Checklist Example

WORK SAMPLES CHECKLIST (continued)

COMMENTS

Memory and Attention Span
❑ Includes details in art from memories of experiences
❑ Focuses attention on project to produce a finished work
❑ Tunes out distractions of simultaneous play, talk, and work
❑ Gives attention and makes connections between designs, colors, patterns in environment, and own work

Math and Science
❑ Includes numerals and quantity in work
❑ Shows one-to-one correspondence in work designs
❑ Shows perceptual awareness of color, space, form
❑ Explores cause and effect and experimentation with variables in art media
    (Example: sees differences in paint when water and sand are added)
❑ Observes similarities and differences, forming theories, and testing them out by manipulating the medium
❑ Working with clay or liquid—displays knowledge of the concept of conservation
    (volume stays the same even though form changes—ball flattened is the same amount)

Literacy
❑ Includes alphabet letters in art work
❑ Recognizes the difference between drawing and writing
❑ Uses creative products as symbols of ideas
❑ Work illustrates or connects with stories
❑ Gives attention to art in story books and knows the difference between text and illustrations

Creativity
❑ Uses materials in a novel way, displaying flexibility in seeing new possibilities in materials
❑ Explores all facets of the medium
❑ Draws from experiences to create representations
❑ Incorporates creativity into other areas of play, constructing with blocks, drawing and constructing in
    dramatic play, forming designs in sand and other media
❑ Demonstrates creativity in sensory awareness (seeing, hearing, touching, smelling, tasting)

Self-Identity
❑ Displays risk-free attitude in work
❑ Reveals self in content of work
❑ Work shows a sense of identity and individuality
❑ Expresses satisfaction in art work, confident self-esteem
❑ Portrays self, family, world in creative work
❑ Work demonstrates child's sex-role identification
❑ Work shows child moving from egocentric view of self to an awareness of self as part of larger society
❑ Indicates favorite art medium (singular), media (plural)

Group Time Behaviors
❑ Participates in cooperative and collaborative work

Interaction with Adults
❑ Involves adults in art work as (facilitator, participator, director)

Figure 10.5 Work Samples Checklist Example

- reflect the inferences of the selector (The teacher may only gather scribbling or experimental pieces when actually the child does much more advanced work.)

Pitfalls to Avoid

For work samples to be part of an authentic assessment plan, they should be:

- dated (The changeable date stamp comes in handy here. Children can learn to date their work themselves.)
- gathered periodically by joint decision of the recorder and the child
- accompanied by commentary or narrative concerning the work
- kept in a separate folder from the portfolio if they become overwhelmingly large if children want to submit many pieces

Observing Creativity with Other Recording Methods

Observing a child during the creative process and preserving the finished product as documentation provides valuable developmental information. The products are not only the outcomes of the child's development but are affected by it as well. Creativity is affected by development, yet by observing creativity, development can be observed and assessed, Figure 10.6.

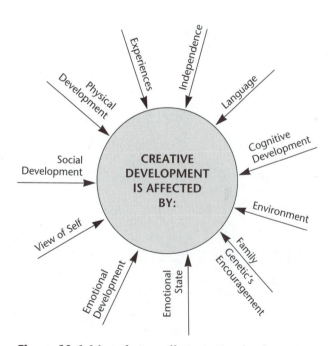

Figure 10.6 Many factors affect creative development.

Developmental checklists with a section on creative development can be used to gather quickly general observed behaviors for the portfolio. The actual work or replicas of it serve as the documentation or evidence for the decisions made on the Checklist or Rating Scale.

Anecdotal Recordings, detailed narratives of the action, and exact words the child uses during and after the creation phase are like the caption to the illustration. The dictated words or quotations give the background or setting of the work. The action of the work is documented along with the exact quotes of the artist. It can inform the viewer and reader of the special circumstances that affected the child and the work.

Interviews while a child is working on a project are another way of gathering information. They reveal the child's understanding of concepts and increase the observer's understanding of the child's work. The child conveys the process and intent. Then it is not misconstrued by the observer. The child can narrate his thinking during the process. Isenberg and Jalongo (1993, p. 303) suggest questions to ask of the artist:

A Process Interview for the Visual Arts:

1. Why do people (paint, draw, sculpt, weave, etc.) pictures?
2. How do you get ready to make a picture?
3. How do you decide what to make?
4. Do you ever do art work at home? If yes, how is art at home different from the art you do at school?
5. If you had to explain to a little child how a person makes a picture, what would you tell him or her to do?
6. Show me or tell me about your best art project. Why do you think this is your best work?

LOOKING AT CHILDREN'S CREATIVE DEVELOPMENT

Analyzing children's creative work is a visual demonstration of developmental principles. All children, all over the world, in whatever age they have lived, progress through the same basic stages in art or graphic representation. Historians who have studied pictorials on caves and rocks and alphabetic systems see the same designs that are seen painted by a child in day care in Chicago. Those combinations of circles, squares, straight lines, and curved lines had meaning for those people long ago, just as they do for today's child. Sylvia Fein, in her fascinating book *First Drawings:*

Genesis of Visual Thinking (1993), compares artifacts from all over the world with children's first attempts at art. From handprints to scribbles, circles, and beginning human figures, early artists in every age follow the same orderly progression of growing complexity, Figures 10.7 through 10.10.

Children's creative work is recognized as a window into their mind. Before a child symbolizes in writing, and sometimes even verbally, they use drawing as an expressive outlet. Many intelligence and psychological tests analyze a child's art to gain insight on the child's thinking and feeling. Careful study and classification of children's drawings have found predictable stages common to children worldwide, with curiously little variation (Kellogg, 1970; Lowenfeld & Brittain, 1975). This reinforces developmental theory that drawing is the representation of inner thought and connected with stages of development. The same factors that affect all other areas of development also affect the creative: genetic, environmental, and cultural. To accurately observe and assess a child's development from creative expression then, knowledge of the stages of creative development is vital.

Figure 10.7 Bronze hands fashioned c2500bp were embossed with triangular spirals and nailed to a wooden container for the ashes of the deceased in a burial site near Kleinklein, Styria, Austria. (Courtesy of Fein, S. 1993. *First Drawings: Genesis of Visual Thinking,* p. 3. Pleasant Hill, CA: Exelrod Press. Reprinted with permission of author.)

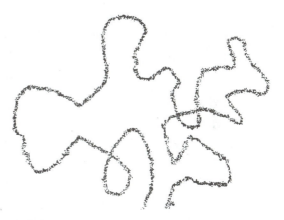

Figure 10.8 An ancestor c2500bp pecked this wandering line into a rock at Dreikopseiland, South Africa. (Courtesy of Fein, S., 1993. *First Drawings: Genesis of Visual Thinking,* p. 17. Pleasant Hill, CA: Exelrod Press. Reprinted with permission of author.)

Figure 10.9 Concentric circles every four-year-old makes are similar to these ancient "runic stones" in Norway. (Courtesy of B. Nilsen.)

Figure 10.10 Caribs on the island of St. Kitts in 2500 drew people in the rocks that resemble preschoolers' early self-portraits. (Courtesy of B. Nilsen.)

Stages of Children's Art

Figure 10.11 illustrates the four stages of creative development.

Stage I. Mark-Making Stage (Birth to Two Years). The marks are random, done for pleasure and exploration, involving visual and physical movement. The child uses large muscles and whole-arm movement. Over time, the marks become more organized and are repeated. The tool is held in a tight fist grip, with a rigid wrist.

Stage II. Scribbling Stage (Two to Four Years). Kellogg (1970) analyzed the scribbles of thousands of young children and cataloged them into separate substages. **Scribbling** becomes more controlled with the development of the small muscles, eye-hand coordination, and cognitive abilities. The child uses a finger grip, with small, more-controlled movements. The marks usually

are controlled to the confines of the paper. During this stage, the child is still experimenting with line and practicing muscle control. The child intently works and develops designs in variations of the circle. Once language is developed, the child attaches names to the scribbles. She may have a mental image when she draws but the mind and muscles are not coordinated enough so the drawings are usually not recognizable to others. She might identify drawings, and as the stage progresses they become more representative of her mental image, to the point that the viewer recognizes the object. The first representation of humans begins to appear in this stage.

A definite progression of geometric shapes and representations occurs in this order:

A. Circles. As small muscle coordination develops, the circle becomes rounded. Finally, the line connects to close the circle completely.

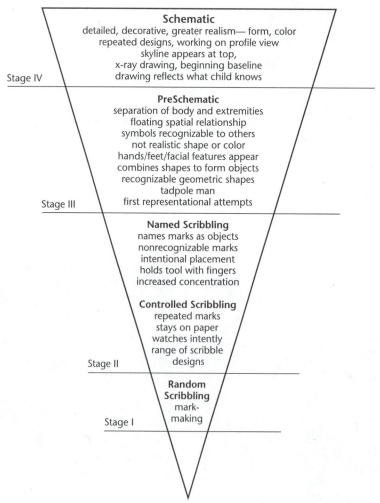

Figure 10.11 The Four Stages of Creative Development. (Adapted from Kellogg, 1970; Lowenfeld & Brittain, 1975; Schirrmacher, 1993)

B. Vertical and horizontal lines. These become more deliberate and crosses and Xs become part of the experimentation with the art medium.

C. Mandalas. A **mandala** (Figure 10.12) is a combination of a cross inside a circle. The word means *circle* in Sanskrit. In Oriental religion, it is regarded as the symbol of the cosmos. In Jungian psychology, the mandala is representative of the psyche with the collective unconscious (Kellogg, 1970, p. 68). These extended meanings raise the mandala's significance. All children universally pass through this stage.

D. Suns. The circle with radiating lines (Figure 10.12) becomes one of the first symbols children draw.

E. Radials. Straight lines radiate from a central point to form a circlelike shape (Figure 10.12). Radials also occur in the controlled scribbling stage.

F. Tadpole man. During the third and fourth years, children begin to represent humans in a curious symbol that resembles a **tadpole man** (Figure 10.12). They combine the circles and lines into a head with features. This is understandable when the earliest images are considered. For months, the infant concentrates closely on the human face. The arms and legs are added later just as their awareness of them came later. The circle represents the whole body as they know it, so a circle with dots for eyes and a line for a mouth is the early person drawing. Arms, then legs, then fingers and toes, and more features appear in an orderly progression. This should remind the student of child development of the principle of cephalocaudal and proximaldistal development.

Stage III. Preschematic (Four to Seven Years). Lowenfeld and Brittain (1987, p. 258) call the symbol a child draws for familiar objects a **schema.** The child experiments with drawing through the scribbling and the **preschematic** stages to develop these symbols. They are unique to each child yet similar because they follow the physical and mental developmental stages through which each child moves. Schirrmacher (1993) calls this stage Attempts at Public Representation. These attempts are **nonrepresentational.** It is difficult, if not impossible, for children in this stage to "Think of your favorite... and draw it." They are able to think of it but lack the fine muscle skills and cognitive ability to physically represent their thoughts. They are more likely to draw what they can, even a scribble, and say, "This is a butterfly." To the viewer, as well as the artist, it is a blob.

Older preschoolers are trying to represent their mental images to others and yet much of what they create is still nonrepresentational and without realism to the viewer. They draw what they *know,* not what they *see.* They surely see more than they are able to draw. They experiment with the medium and often play with the tools. No message or intent for representation may be present.

At the beginning of this stage, there is little regard for realism in color, size proportion, or exact details. These aspects continue to be more evident as the stage progresses. By the end of this stage, the child can copy a square by bringing a single line back to the beginning with defined corners.

Details on the human figure increase, with the body becoming more like a snowman. The neck separates the head and body circle, and ovals appear, representing the arms and legs. Hands move from single lines, to more lines, then accurately drawn five digits, and eventually more of a glovelike hand. Anatomical representations appear as the child is striving for realism and gaining knowledge of gender differences.

By the end of this period, the child draws an accurate triangle and often uses a repeated pattern

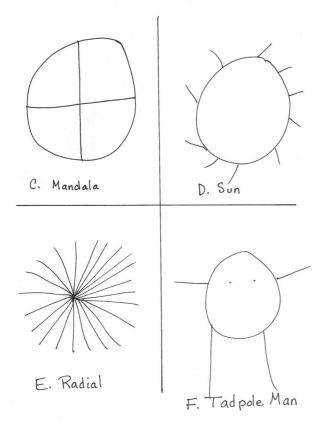

C. Mandala   D. Sun

E. Radial   F. Tadpole Man

Figure 10.12 Early Stages of Drawing

or design of symbols. The child begins to use drawings to express feelings, as well as visual images.

Stage IV. Schematic (Seven to Nine Years). In the **schematic** stage the child now has a well-developed schema repeated in all drawings to represent humans, homes, trees, clouds, all the relevant, important objects in the child's life. The child's drawing still represents concept rather than perception (what he knows versus what he sees). This is observed in a perspective problem: what to do with the hidden leg of a horse rider or the eyes in a profile view? The child draws these like x-ray vision or with both eyes, signifying he knows there are two legs or eyes. Drawing only one is not acceptable mentally to him. The baseline and skyline appear with a partial sun in the corner. Chimneys on roofs are at right angles to the roof line, making them askew to the baseline. As the child's

cognitive development improves, the chimney becomes erect. Attempts at three-dimensional representation are beginning by drawing three sides of a building.

Exercise: Based on the developmental stages discussed, number Figures 10.13 through 10.18 one to six, in order of creative development.

Figure 10.13 is an example of a tadpole man with the beginning of some features. The circles and firm, straight lines show small muscle control. The artist is four years, one month old.

Figure 10.14 is definitely a scribble but a controlled scribble. The child left a margin around the

Figure 10.13

Figure 10.14

Figure 10.15

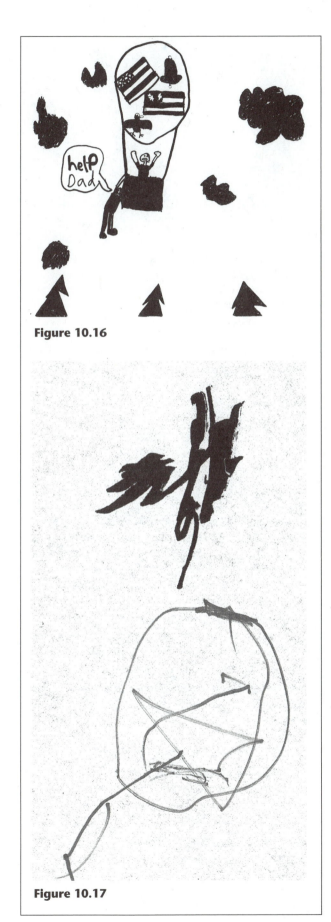

Figure 10.16

Figure 10.17

page and confined marks to a located area. The artist is three years, two months old.

Figure 10.15 shows the glovelike hands, separated body parts, and details. There is a baseline with the stylized flowers, but the person is floating. The sun is only partly seen. There are many signs this child is moving beyond the preschematic stage. The artist is five years, eleven months.

Figure 10.16 is very realistic. Of course, this was by the oldest artist in the group. The baseline is actually above the trees. Only the tops are seen. The other features are in perspective. There are many details and a message from the work. The artist is eight years, five months.

Figure 10.17 was done by the youngest artist at two years, eleven months. There is a closed circle but the other lines show that muscle control is still developing. The marks go off the paper.

Figure 10.18 is the artist's practice, drawing the same form over and over, changing it slightly by the features. Alphabet letters are mixed in with the drawings. The artist is four years, five months.

Your sequence of stages should have been 1—Figure 10.17; 2—Figure 10.14; 3—Figure 10.13; 4—Figure 10.18; 5—Figure 10.15; 6—Figure 10.16. Comparing creative work from different children into developmental stages is not dependable but these are representative of the stages and their ages happened to correspond. It is not always so. The principles of development prevail. The stages are sequential, but children do not pass through them at the same age. Collecting and comparing the drawings of each child to ones drawn previously is dependable documentation of progress.

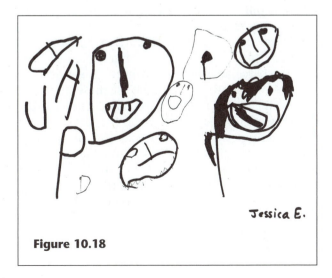

Figure 10.18

Blocks As a Creative Medium

Construction materials are open-ended, used in very different ways by each child. This type of material, like any creative medium, gives the observer knowledge about many developmental areas. Blocks are varied in type but provide this kind of experience. They can be

Plastic interlocking blocks, such as Legos or Duplos

Unit blocks—standard units are multiples of each other

Hollow blocks—standard units of each other but are large; constructed of many pieces nailed and glued together

Cardboard blocks—lightweight, often home-made from milk cartons

Foam blocks—geometric shapes and units; lightweight

Special building sets—Lincoln Logs, Erector sets, Tinkertoys, A-B-C blocks, PVC pipes

Cube blocks—one unit blocks either of wood or plastic, sometimes with locking features

The placement of shaped blocks on shelves, labeled with exact tracings of the block, builds one-to-one correspondence skills. The association of the shapes—square, rectangle, triangle, cylinder— is made not only with the shape but the word, making the literacy connection. Much of what goes on in the block building area is more than construction. It involves dramatic play, social skills, and language practice. The towers with resultant crashes bring excitement and danger themes to the block area. Accompanying props, such as farm and zoo animals, transportation vehicles, and miniature people, expand the play from functional to symbolic. By including textures, such as rug and fabric pieces, small pieces of turflike carpeting, and soft pillows, the area becomes a stress reducer as well, Figure 10.19.

There are often physical barriers between the dramatic play area (housekeeping or family area) and the block area. This contributes to gender segregation, which is so common in these areas. By physically removing the barrier and encouraging the crossover of materials, it can help break down the stereotypes of play materials that are already present in preschoolers. Blocks can be taken to the oven to bake as bread. Block structures become homes where dishes and dolls can be added. By carefully planning the environment, the block area becomes another microcosm of development, affording the observer an excellent view of all areas of development.

Figure 10.19 Block areas with accessories, literacy materials, and cross-over play from the dramatic area promote creativity.

Stages in Block Play. There are progressive stages in the way children interact with blocks, dependent on cognitive, social, emotional, and physical development, Figure 10.20 (adapted from Hirsch, 1974, & Day, 1994).

Stage I. Carrying, Filling, and Dumping (Under Two Years). Children are in the sensori-motor stage, so they are exploring the attributes of blocks by feeling, lifting, and moving them from place to place.

Stage II. Beginning Block Building (Two to Three Years). Children make horizontal rows, laying blocks end to end or stacking. They repeat stacking and knocking down. They are beginning to observe the unstable effect of a small base with large blocks piled on.

Stage III. Bridging (Three Years). Two blocks are placed vertically as pillars with a third block placed across the top. This takes visual acuity, small muscle coordination, and balance.

Stage IV. Enclosures (Three and Four Years). Four blocks are placed at right angles to enclose a space. This corresponds to the child's ability to draw a square, recognizing the connectedness of the angles and associating inside and outside concepts.

Stage V. Patterns (Four Years). Bridges and enclosures are repeated to form a horizontal or vertical pattern. Symmetry, a sense of balance and equal, is demonstrated.

Stage VI. Naming Structures (Four to Six Years). Names and functions of buildings are assigned to the structures. Additional pieces like cars, animals, and play people add to the play. The play becomes more symbolic.

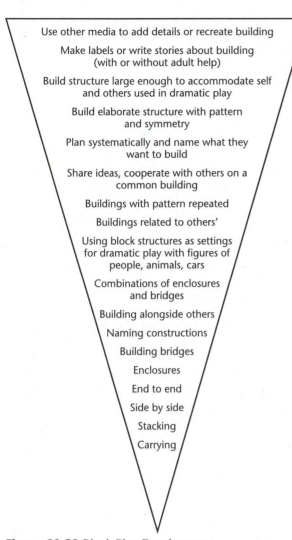

Use other media to add details or recreate building

Make labels or write stories about building (with or without adult help)

Build structure large enough to accommodate self and others used in dramatic play

Build elaborate structure with pattern and symmetry

Plan systematically and name what they want to build

Share ideas, cooperate with others on a common building

Buildings with pattern repeated

Buildings related to others'

Using block structures as settings for dramatic play with figures of people, animals, cars

Combinations of enclosures and bridges

Building alongside others

Naming constructions

Building bridges

Enclosures

End to end

Side by side

Stacking

Carrying

Figure 10.20 Block Play Development

Stage VII. Reproduce True Life Structures (Five Years and Up). This stage is an expansion of Stage VI by trying to build more realistically and to incorporate dramatic play into the structures by moving play people and animals according to a script. These block-building stages parallel the drawing stages: manipulation, simple experimentation, patterns, naming, and realistic reproduction.

Trister-Dodge and Colker (1992, pp. 75–76) outlined the goals and objectives of block play that serve as key points in observing block play, Figure 10.21.

Other Creative Media

Other materials or media such as clay, woodworking, or collage illustrate the child's development through stages similar to drawing. Small muscles interact with creativity to produce three-dimensional products. These often are not preserved but are materials returned to be manipulated in another way. The stages correspond to drawing, Figure 10.22.

Interaction with a tangible, movable medium is sensory, involving seeing, feeling, and often

---

Objectives for Socioemotional Development

- Work independently and in a group (deciding when, how, and with whom to play).
- Express needs, concerns, and fears in socially acceptable ways (creating a hospital or cave with monsters and playing make-believe).
- Share and cooperate with others (trading materials and props, and planning joint building projects).
- Demonstrate pride in accomplishments and a positive self-concept (sharing their buildings by talking about what they have created).

Objectives for Cognitive Development

- Develop an understanding of concepts of length, height, weight, and area (carrying blocks and using them in constructions).
- Classify and sort objects by size, shape, and function (placing blocks of the same size together).
- Make use of physical principles (weight, stability, equilibrium, balance, and leverage).
- Predict cause-and-effect relationships (seeing how high they can build before the blocks fall).
- Solve problems related to construction (bridging a bridge or making steps to a house).
- Organize in a sequence (laying out blocks from short to tall and counting in correct order).
- Use addition, subtraction, and fractions (judging how many blocks are needed to fill a space).
- Utilize emergent reading and writing skills (making signs for buildings).

Objectives for Physical Development

- Use large and small muscle skills (grasping, lifting, placing, and balancing blocks).
- Develop eye-hand coordination (placing blocks in desired patterns).
- Control the placement of objects (under, over, above, below, on top of, and next to when constructing with blocks).

Figure 10.21 Blocks Are Important: Objectives for Children's Learning. (Reprinted with permission from Diane Trister Dodge and Laura J. Colker, *The Creative Curriculum® for Early Childhood, 3rd edition.* ©1992 by Teaching Strategies, Inc. PO Box 42242, Washington, DC 20015, pp. 75–76.)

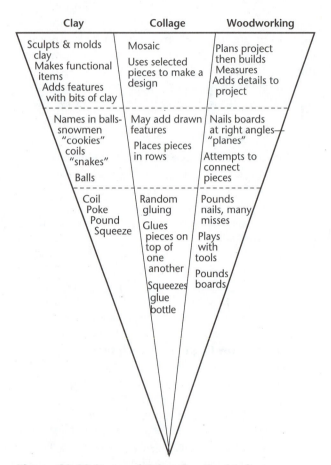

Figure 10.22 Stages of Other Creative Media

smelling. It helps the development of logico-mathematical thinking through manipulation. Physical properties of volume, weight, and length are transformed through play.

Creativity and Cognitive Development

Thinking and all the processes that link thinking and learning are integral to creativity. It should not be surprising. There are parallels between the stages of Piaget's cognitive theory (Flavell, 1963), art stages of Kellogg (1970) and Lowenfeld and Brittain (1987), and the social-emotional stages of Erikson (1950). They correspond to stages of development of language, reading, and writing. The ages of these stages are merely guideposts, not firm changepoints, Figure 10.23.

Creativity is dependent on symbolic thought. It is necessary to have existing structures and beliefs in reality against which to measure new data. It is dependent on cognitive ability, past experiences, and the present environment. Observing children's creative efforts can indicate:

1. Long attention span—When the activity captures their interest, they attend longer.
2. Capacity for organization—The organization of their creative work indicates their classification skills.

Piaget's Stages of Cognitive Development	Stages of Art Kellogg, Lowenfeld and Brittain, Schirrmacher	Language Development	Writing/Reading	Erikson's Psycho-Social Stages
Sensorimotor (b–24 months) Moving from reflexes to object permanence	Scribbling and Mark-making (birth to two) Random exploration Nonintentional	Pre/Language (b-2 years) Sounds, telegraphic sentences	Book Handling Skills (b–2 years) Right side up, front/back, turn pages	Basic Trust vs. Mistrust (birth–2 years) Consistent experiences
Preoperational 2–7 years Egocentric Representation of objects and events by appearances	Personal Symbol and Design (two to four) Controlled scribbling, named scribbling	Beginning Language (2-4 years) Acquiring vocabulary, grammar, social speech	Function of print (2–4 years) Reads symbols in context Read pictures Beginning writing	Autonomy vs. Shame/Doubt (2–4 years) Independence, sensory exploration
	Preschematic (4–7 years) Generalized symbols recognizable to others Nonrepresentational	Language (4-7 years) Symbolic language Humor	Readers and Writers (5–8 years) Decode print Invented spelling Word identity	Initiative vs. Guilt (4–7 years) Constructive activities, own decisions
Concrete Operational (7–11 years) Logical, concrete thinkers. Can conserve, classify, seriate	Schematic/Realism (7–9 years) Representation of what he knows, not necessarily what he sees.			Industry vs. Inferiority (7 years to puberty) Sense of duty, academic social competence

Figure 10.23 Stage Comparison of Cognitive and Creative Theorists

3. Seeing things in a different perspective—This does not go against the egocentric idea but refers to the child's ability to see things without preconceived notions.

4. Exploring before formal instruction—They have the need to manipulate first, and later organize into more conventional uses of tools and materials.

5. Using silence and time—Every parent knows that a quiet child is one that needs to be investigated for there probably is some trouble brewing. Children get into trouble because they try things they do not know are dangerous or forbidden. This is an aspect of creativity like drawing on the sheets with lipstick or painting on the recreation room wall with tar.

6. Taking a "closer look" at things—Creative thinking involves manipulation and being close. It could be apples in a plastic bag at the supermarket or a climb to the top cupboard in the kitchen to investigate.

7. Using fantasy to solve developmental problems—Normal aspects of children's thinking are considered frivolous and even deceitful by adults. Children use creative ideas to explain, defend and problem solve, such as, "The dog must have ridden my bike to the corner and left it there."

8. Storytelling and song making—Playing with words and music combines mental and creative abilities. Children need opportunities and encouragement to express themselves in the arts.

The child's creativity gives information about their cognitive development. The child does not go to bed one night in one stage and wake up in another. It is a spiral moving slightly upward that keeps returning to previous stages to find reassurance, success, and comfort when new stages become too stressful. Constance Kamii (1982) tells the story of the boy setting the table, who moved from one-to-one correspondence to counting out the tableware. When guests were expected, he was not able to mentally add the number of guests to the number in the family. He had to go back to one-to-one correspondence again.

Disequilibrium sometimes invokes a return to a previous stage or strategy. It is seen in the child who has had a traumatic event in her life return to thumbsucking, which brought so much comfort in a previous stage. In creative work, there is the return to the manipulation stage with the introduction of each new medium. The child uses sensory exploration of the materials, play without any purpose other than to get in touch with reality without pressure, before going on to actually represent thought.

Giftedness: Creative and Cognitive Development Beyond Expected Levels. Many parents believe their child is gifted. The definition traditionally referred to an exceptionally high score on an intelligence test but has been broadened to include exceptional ability in other areas as well. In 1969, P. L. 91-230 contained a model program provision for gifted and talented children. Because of the limitations of standardized tests (see Chapter 7), many children were not identified as gifted because of cultural bias of the tests, resulting in low numbers of minorities in gifted programs. Little federal funding has been allocated for gifted programs but much research has been done in trying to define and identify giftedness. Some have to do with **precocity,** early development in areas such as language, music, or mathematical ability. The Renzulli-Hartman scales (in Torrance, 1983, p. 514) are commonly used for assessing creativity in preschool children:

1. The child has unusually advanced vocabulary for age level.
2. The child possesses a large storehouse of information about a variety of topics.
3. The child has rapid insight into cause-effect relationships.
4. The child is a keen and alert observer; usually "sees more" or "gets more" out of a story, picture, film, sightseeing trip, and so on.
5. The child becomes absorbed and truly involved in certain topics or problems.
6. The child strives toward perfection or excellence and is self-critical.
7. The child is interested in many "adult" problems such as religion, politics, sex, race, and so on.
8. The child likes to organize and bring structure to things, people, and situations.
9. The child displays a great deal of curiosity about many things and an intense curiosity about something.
10. The child displays a keen sense of humor and sees humor in situations that may not appear humorous to others.

Divergent thinking is the ability to think of a wide range of possibilities. It is associated with giftedness, rather than **convergent thinking,** the ability to arrive at a single answer. Its identification and measurement at an early age is complicated and inaccurate but close observers of children may see signs of giftedness. Assessment of every child's learning level helps meet the child's needs through curriculum planning. This same reason applies to giftedness.

Using Self-Portraits to Know the Child

Exercise: Look at the self-portraits by children four to five years old, Figures 10.24 through 10.27. Describe how very different they are in control, detail, and the mood they present.

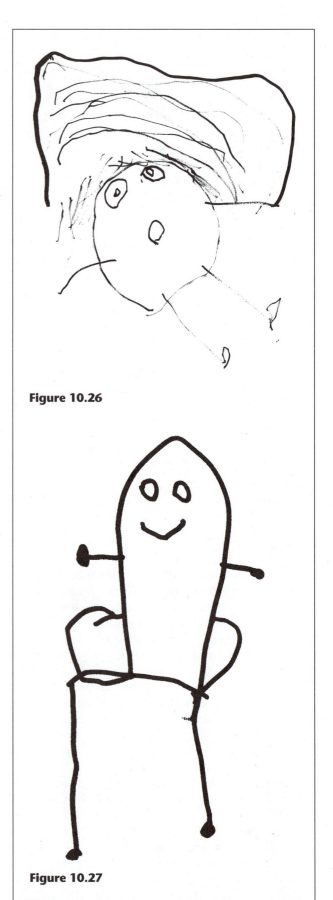

Figure 10.26

Figure 10.24

Figure 10.25

Figure 10.27

The child's drawings of humans evolve from the beginning circle with dots for eyes. The child is drawing what is known. The human face, with eyes as predominant feature, represents family and self, drawn by hands still developing control. Arms and legs later protrude from this head and eventually more and more details appear as more "humanoid" drawings in the fourth year. As the child is closer to five, the neck separates the head and body, and limbs begin to take on more substance than just a line. Between five and six, the child usually can outline a drawing of the whole body in one stroke and begin to proportion the height of adults and children more accurately. This is in a predictable sequence (Kellogg, 1970). Three-dimensional work follows a similar sequence. In knowing that sequence, just like in knowing all developmental stage milestones, it helps the observer to recognize change and to anticipate and recognize the next stage when it appears.

The Goodenough-Harris Drawing Test (1963), also called the Draw-A-Man Test, has been used widely as a measurement of intelligence. It is non-verbal and easy to administer, but there are questions concerning its validity (measures what it intends to measure) and its cultural bias. The self-portraits in Figures 10.24 through 10.27 were drawn by four-year-old boys. It would be presumptuous to interpret levels of development from one drawing. However, when the observer periodically collects children's self-portraits, along with the child's commentary about the work, the result is a more valid indication of cognitive and creative development.

IT HAPPENED TO ME:
Instinct Over Knowledge

I had just discussed the responses to children's art with my college class. The next week, a mother with a newborn came to class to demonstrate the reflexes that were still present. She also brought her preschooler with paper and markers to occupy her while we watched her baby brother. As the demonstration drew to a close, I went over to the big sister and looked at her drawing. Out of my mouth came, "What is it?" The whole class gasped then laughed at my embarrassment at doing what I said not to do. It showed how ingrained those old habits are and how easily the instinctive comments slips out from among the learned behaviors. It takes practice and a concentrated effort!

Reggio Emilia and Children's Art

A discussion of children's creative development would not be complete without mentioning the child care centers and preschools in Reggio Emilia, Italy. They are the model of community and parent collaboration and the integrated project approach to curriculum, but most of all, the incredible creativity of the children. Thousands of visitors from all over the world have been enthralled with the visually sensual learning environment that stimulates children to use a vast array of art materials. The adult follows the children's interests and explores it to its greatest potential. It is rewarded by the children's application of energies and creativity to tasks considered far beyond developmental expectations.

The Hundred Languages of Children (Edwards, et al., 1993) brings Reggio children's projects to the world both in book and in exhibit form. The beauty and richness of the colors, the complete absorption of the children in the work of art, and the planning of each project piques the curiosity of the viewer. New (1990) points out key aspects that could be incorporated into early childhood settings in the United States. Strong parent involvement, the social and cultural climate of the environment of the classroom, emphasis on the arts and aesthetic sensibilities, meaningful work for children through curriculum, and projects that relate to their everyday world are possible. After visiting Reggio Emilia, Carol Seefeldt (1995) describes the philosophy of considering creativity a serious work by teachers who

- understand cognitive theories of art
- motivate children to produce art
- carefully select teaching strategies (p. 39).

Assessing Creative Program Goals

An assessment of the child's creativity is linked with an assessment of the creative environment and reflects this philosophy in the curriculum. *NAEYC Guidelines for Developmentally Appropriate Practice* (Bredekamp, 1987) recommend:

- interactive environment

●●●

TOPICS IN OBSERVATION: Responding to Children's Creative Work

●●●

While observing children working, whether it is just enjoyably watching, or observing for a purpose, the adult is often called upon to comment on a child's work. The child may ask, "How is it?" or "Do you like it?" A ready answer is necessary, one that agrees with personal style, program goals, and theoretical philosophy. The following are presented for consideration and practice so that the teacher's repertoire of comments is consistent with beliefs. Different common responses are listed here, along with commentary and suggestions for improvement.

Complimentary

The child may ask or expect a reaction from the adult. A natural response is generalized, polite praise such as "Oh, lovely," "Very nice," "Beautiful." The problem with this approach is that they are empty words with no specific reaction. The child's purpose may not have been for it to be "nice" or "lovely." It may be a frightening spider or a bad dream. The adult's comment is a casual remark lacking sincerity. It becomes a denial of the purpose of the artist. It may have been for exploration and practice, not beauty.

Instead: "You worked a really long time at that."

Judgmental

"Great!" "That's wonderful." Again, these are empty words that may not be truthful or reflect what the child is trying to portray. It is valuative from the viewer's opinion. When we consider that young children are egocentric, they only imagine that the viewer will see it just as they do. It is more important for the viewer to determine the child's opinion of the work.

Instead: "What do you like about it?" or "Can you tell me how you did it? What part did you do first?"

Valuing

The adult expresses her personal opinion, "I love it." The goal is to help the child find self-satisfaction as the measuring stick of creative work. An outsider's evaluation is not necessary nor advisable. What the *adult* sees or thinks is not important. How the *child* feels or thinks about it is the important point.

Instead: "What do you like about it?"

Questioning

When the adult asks, "What is it?" or "What's this supposed to be?" a loud message is conveyed, "You were supposed to make something I could recognize. I can't see it so you are not doing it right." The adult should know that young children up to age six and seven are nonrepresentational in their art. They may have a mental image of what they want to draw but their physical abilities for control of the medium and cognitive development concerning perception and reality are still in the formative stages.

Instead: "Would you like to tell me about it?" The child still has the option of saying, "No," rather than answering the command, "Tell me about it."

Probing

When the questioning approach asks the significance of every piece of work, it may be overused and it is probing. From what is known about children's art, much of it is for exploration of the medium. The child is getting the feel of the fingerpaint, or practicing rolling snakes and balls of clay, or watching the glue flow out as the bottle is squeezed.

Instead: Just observe. Watch for indications of what the child is getting from the experience. A simple "Hmmmm" suggests interest, invites the child to comment if she chooses.

Correcting

Of course, early childhood educators should know that children's drawings are unrealistic, so telling a child, "Grass isn't orange. Here's a green crayon for grass" is inappropriate.

Instead: Allow the child to use materials in any way they wish as long as it is safe for them-

TOPICS IN OBSERVATION: continued

selves and the environment. Give redirection reminders, such as, "We paint on the paper, not on the wall," or "When you walk around with the brush, you are dripping paint all over. If you want to look at Lizzy's side of the easel, place the brush in the container first."

Psychoanalyzing

Much study has been done on the emotional and psychological meaning of children's creative work. It makes fascinating reading, but it is not for amateurs. Deep psychological significance should not be placed on children's art. It is inappropriate for people without training to make diagnoses about the child's emotional state. Some have said, "She uses black all over the page. She must be depressed." The content of children's creative work and their choice of color is not realistic. The teacher mistakenly commented on the red paint the child used and thought, "He told me this was all the blood from the baby. He must wish his new baby brother was dead. Maybe he's planning to stab him." Forming conclusions about the child's inner mind from one drawing is just as unfair and dangerous as evaluating the whole child from one test.

Instead: Note curious, strange, bizarre creations or comments from the child on a notepad for your own use. If they are repeated or accompanied by behavioral indicators, follow it up. If you are alarmed, talk to your supervisor, then possibly the parents, to search for further clarification or evaluation. Sometimes children's art *can be* their way of expressing fears or traumatic incidents that cannot be verbalized.

Modeling

This is an acceptable teaching technique in every other area of early childhood practice *except* art. Modeling in the sense of making a pattern for a child to follow is not good professional practice. Planned art "projects" sometimes present materials for the child to construct the adult's idea of a caterpillar, clown face, or dinosaur. These thwart the whole purpose and theory of children's creative develop-

ment and its benefits. Many teachers say, "Well, I'm just providing the materials for the clown face, they can do it any way they want." The child knows the adult's expectation but may not have the experience with a clown's face or the desire to make one.

Instead: Provide the child with rich experiences in the world around him. Provide creative materials that the child can use himself and allow the child to create whatever he chooses from those experiences.

Model an accepting attitude to children's explorations.

Model an interest in texture, design, color, and use vocabulary words about them, such as rough, smooth, ridges, pattern, balance, horizontal and vertical, swirls, border, and color names like mauve, lavender, chartreuse. This makes association between the visual image and the word. Young children love big words.

Model processes of using materials by sitting at the clay table and throwing clay to soften it, rolling balls and snakes and pinching pots. This is not direct instruction but scaffolding manipulation techniques that children will adopt when they are ready.

Describing

This is the best *Instead* of the preceding approaches. Every area of development that is seen through creative work can be described (not all at once): physical movement, control of the tools, utilization of the space, self-help skills in working on the project, social interactions in the art or in the process, control or expression of emotions, vocabulary to describe the product, writing associated with the creations, math and science concepts, self-identity revealed through the art, and interactions with the group and adults through the process.

"You used a lot of red today." (Making the association between the visual color and the word *red*.)

"You covered the whole page with paint. That took a lot of concentration." (Commenting on space and attention span)

"You made a lot of blue vertical lines and yellow horizontal lines. It made a design that's sometimes called plaid. Look at this. There's the

TOPICS IN OBSERVATION: continued

color green where they come together. I don't see any green paint out today. I wonder how that happened?" (Using vocabulary of design, pointing out colors, helping child observe cause and effect and wonder. If he does not understand it this time, he might the next time. The association has been made and the disequilibrium has been pointed out. The child will accommodate this new knowledge into color concepts.)

Exercise: Go back to Figures 10.13 through 10.18, which were the drawings in the exercise on the stages of art, and practice your comments to the artist who asks, "How do you like it?"

- prepared environment
- concrete, real materials
- learning materials and activities relevant to the lives of young children
- provisions for a wide range of developmental interests and abilities
- adults who meet the needs of those outside the range of normal
- daily opportunities for aesthetic expression and appreciation
- a variety of media available (pp. 4, 56)

The *NAEYC Accreditation Criteria and Procedures* (1991) self-study asks programs to rate their opportunities for creative expression and appreciation for the arts.

Koster in *Growing Artists* (in print) gives practical suggestions in preparing the environment so that concern over messes does not inhibit the creative process:

1. Allow plenty of space for each child to work. The younger the child, the more space is required.
2. Protect any surface or clothing that might be damaged by the material in use. Make sure the protective covering clearly is different from any supplies being used. It is not necessary to cover surfaces that are easily washed up.
3. Provide a sufficient amount of supplies so that no more than two children have to share the same resource at a time. Certain supplies, such as scissors, should not be shared as they can be dangerous when passed from child to child.
4. Have plenty of easy-to-use cleanup supplies on hand for the children and you to use.
5. Locate activities that make the hands messy very close to a water supply.
6. Define areas in which certain materials must be kept.

Exercise: Rate your classroom creative environment according to the preceding criteria.

Unmet   Partially Met   Fully met

On a separate sheet of paper, write an action plan to improve aspects of the environment to allow for more creative expression.

SPECIAL POPULATIONS AND CREATIVITY

Creative work is both expressive and receptive. It requires no spoken language to create or enjoy someone else's creation. Even with limitations of language barriers, physical, cognitive, or psychological impairments, creative arts can be a form of two-way communication.

Cultural Diversity

Art is a universal language. The child may not speak a common language with the rest of the people in the group or share a common culture. Creative work can be a vehicle for becoming absorbed in activity without pressure to speak or conform. Giving children creative materials with a minimum of direction is appropriate for this population and can be a comforting and successful activity in which to engage these children. It also gives them a way to express feelings and ideas nonverbally.

Ability Diversity

Art plans that are open-ended, designed to explore the medium, can be adapted to meet the needs of special abilities populations. Children with sight or hearing impairments can find great success in manipulating creative materials. Adaptive devices, such as bicycle grips on paintbrush handles, textured finger paint, and Play Doh with scent from powdered, nonsweetened drink mixes, add multisensory aspects to art medium. The manipulation of art materials is also soothing and sustaining for children with attention disorders.

Whatever the cognitive or physical functioning level of the child, open-ended art plans can be implemented and adapted to the child's capability. Frustration and lack of creativity are the outcomes of project-type art (really crafts) that demands a model and closely followed directions. The ability to succeed with these projects is very narrow, leaving most of the group either bored or disappointed.

Creative media are essential parts of every early childhood program. Art involves every developmental area and easily meets the needs of every child, despite their situation. It is a natural place to focus assessment in a nonintrusive way.

HELPING PROFESSIONALS FOR CREATIVE ARTS

Programs or individual teachers who want to enrich the creative environment can enlist the assistance of

art educators—teachers who specialize in the incorporation of the arts into the curriculum

Individual children may be assisted in resolving emotional conflicts or behavior disorders by specialists who use the arts as therapy, such as

art therapist—credentialed professional who helps increase self-understanding and emotional release through art media

music therapist—certified professional who uses music in treatment goals for people with handicaps for physical and mental health

---

Week 10, Assignment A

CREATIVE WORK SAMPLE FOR ALL

This week collect a sample of creative work from every child. Use the Work Samples Checklist (See Appendix D) or the creative portion of your program's checklist. (You could have them draw on the second panel of the portfolio file folder.)

What to Do with It

File the Work Samples and Checklist in the child's portfolio. Note the presence of the work on the portfolio overview sheet, Figure 10.28.

Share with the parents and child, if appropriate. For example: "Mr. Tower, I made a copy of this drawing Mackenzie did today for her portfolio. She's still in the scribbling stage but she is now staying on the paper. She said this was a bee. I think she was watching the fly we had pestering us in the classroom go round and round. I saw her eyes following it while she was working at the table with crayons. In the next stage we will begin to see more recognizable shapes like a circle. She's just practicing so we provide her with lots of

CREATIVE – ART AND BLOCKS		
Documentation	Recorder	Date
Painting - self		9/10
AR about drawing	MS	10/22
self-portrait		11/7
Family		1/23
"Designs"		4/17
My school		5/30

Figure 10.28 Portfolio Overview Example

paper, time, and encouragement," or "Caroline, this is the file folder where I keep all the notes I write about you. Would you like to draw a picture to decorate the cover? You could make a design or draw whatever you wish with the markers on this side, then I'll put it in the drawer with the rest of the papers."

Week 10, Assignment B

ANECDOTAL RECORDING IN CREATIVITY FOR GROUP A

Select all the children from group A and each day write an Anecdotal Recording about how each child used creative materials. Include all the details and exact quotes written on the left column of the paper. In the right column, comment on each child's development, any special circumstances, and whether this was a usual or an unusual occurrence.

What to Do with It

Note the recording on the portfolio overview sheet with the date and your name. (See Figure 10.28.)

Share the Anecdotal Recording with the child's parents or the child, if appropriate. For example: "Mr. Gonzales, this is Arturo's first painting at school. He's spent a long time watching other children. Today we piled leaves and jumped in them and brought a pile inside and glued them to the bulletin board. He went to the easel and I made notes while he painted. It was fascinating! He just used dabbing strokes with all the fall colors until the whole sheet was full. It really shows his interest in those colored leaves made permanent in paint. I took a photograph of it to put into his portfolio. I'm sure he wants to take the painting home when it's dry," or "Mimi, here's your clay ball you wanted to take home. I wrote about how you made it today and how you took the pencil and made all those little holes all over it. You kept saying, 'Let the air out. Let the air out.' 'Yep'." Sometimes you never know what they were thinking.

File the Anecdotal Recording in the child's portfolio.

Week 10, Assignment C

REFLECTIVE JOURNAL

Respond to the following in your Reflective Journal, kept in a private file at home.

When I think about creativity, I...

My own background in art has been...

It has caused me to...

My favorite kind of creative expression is...

I (regularly, sometimes, or never) go to art galleries or museums because...

REFERENCES

Accreditation Criteria and Procedures (1991). Washington, DC: National Association for the Education of Young Children.

Bredekamp, S. (Ed.). (1987). *Developmentally appropriate practice in early childhood programs, serving children from birth through age 8, expanded edition.* Washington, DC: National Association for the Education of Young Children.

Day, B. (1994). *Early childhood education: Developmental/experiential teaching and learning, fourth edition.* New York: Merrill, an imprint of Macmillan College Publishing Company.

Edwards, C., Gandini, L., & Forman, G. (Eds.) (1993). *The hundred languages of children: The Reggio Emilia approach to early childhood education.* Norwood, NJ: Ablex.

Erikson, E. H. (1950. *Childhood and Society.* New York: Norton.

Fein, S. (1993). *First drawings: Genesis of visual thinking.* Pleasant Hill, CA: Exelrod Press.

Flavell, J. H. (1963). *The Developmental Psychology of Jean Piaget.* New York: Van Nostrand.

Genishi, C. (1993). Art, portfolios, and assessment in *Early Childhood Today, 8* (2), 67.

Hirsch, E. S. (1974). *The block book.* Washington, DC: National Association for the Education of Young Children.

Isenberg, J. & Jalongo, M. (1993). *Creative expression and play in the early childhood curriculum.* New York: Merrill, an imprint of Macmillan Publishing Company.

Kamii, C. (1982). *Number in preschool and kindergarten.* Washington: National Association for the Education of Young Children.

Kellogg, R. (1970). *Analyzing children's art.* Palo Alto, CA: National Press Books.

Koster, J. (1997). *Growing artists.* Albany, NY: Delmar Publishers.

Lowenfeld, V. & Brittain, W. L. (1987). *Creative and mental growth, 8th edition.* New York: Macmillan Publishing Co., Inc.

McAfee, O. & Leong, D. (1994). *Assessing and guiding young children's development and learning.* Boston: Allyn and Bacon.

Meisels, S. E. Steele. (1991). The Early Childhood Portfolio Collection: Process Center for Human Growth and Development. Ann Arbor, MI: University of Michigan.

New, R. (1990). Excellent early education: A city in Italy has it. *Young Children, 45* (6), 4.

Puckett, M., & Black, J. (1994). *Authentic assessment of the young child: Celebrating development and learning.* New York: Merrill, an imprint of Macmillan.

Schirrmacher, R. (1993). *Art and creative development for young children.* Albany: Delmar Publishers.

Seefeldt, C. (1995). Art: A serious work. *Young Children, 50* (3), 39.

Torrance, E. P. (1983). Preschool creativity. In Paget, K. & Bracken, B. (Eds.), *The psychosocial assessment of preschool children.* Philadelphia: Grune & Stratton, a subsidiary of Harcourt, Brace.

Trister-Dodge, D. & Colker, L. J. (1992). *The creative curriculum for early childhood, 3rd Edition.* Washington, DC: Teaching Strategies, Inc.

RESOURCES

Church, E. B & Miller, K. (1990). *Learning through play: Blocks, a practical guide for teaching young children.* New York: Scholastic, Inc.

Edwards, C., Gandini, L., & Forman, G. (Eds.) (1993). *The hundred languages of children: The Reggio Emilia approach to early childhood education.* Norwood, NJ: Ablex.

Kellogg, R. (1970). *Analyzing children's art.* Palo Alto, CA: National Press Books.

Koster, J. (1997). *Growing artists.* Albany, NY: Delmar Publishers.

Lowenfeld, V. & Brittain, W. L. (1975). *Creative and mental growth.* New York: Macmillan Publishing Co., Inc.

Using Media to Look at Sociodramatic Play

USING MEDIA AS DOCUMENTATION

Imagine the end of the day. A parent comes to pick up her child at the child care center. She sits for a few minutes with a cup of coffee and puts on virtual reality glasses. Through them, she views her child in selected videotaped segments of the day's activities. The parent sitting next to her is doing the same, watching his own child in a virtual reality recording. Each child has been videotaped simultaneously, cued to their movements by the "school button" they put on each day as they arrive. The teacher has ended the day's taped segment with a reminder for an e-mail response to the parent survey. Other parents have watched portions of the day from home or their workplace through a classroom video connected via the Internet. Parenting workshop choices are reviewed for reception on their television monitors in the next month. They are also reminded to pay the balance of their tuition bill by electronic bank transfer.

Far out? All of this technology exists. Can we afford it? Do we agree with it? Do we want it? These are questions many teachers and directors will be answering soon.

Using technical or electronic medium is not an innovation in classrooms. Tape recorders, cameras, and overhead slide and filmstrip projectors have been used for years. However, electronic and digital technologies have increased the range and quality of products, and ease of equipment use. Lower costs have made electronic media a viable option for documentation in the classroom. Electronic media can capture details that not even the most fluent writer can convey. Tone of voice, little nuances of movement, and a visual image all make an incident as alive for the viewer as it was for the original observer. There are considerations of legal and ethical natures that are discussed in the Topics in Observation section of this chapter. A sample release is included in the Assignment section.

This recording method section presents the possibilities that are available but many are out of the question for most programs today. In just the right situation, in the future, however, they may be realistic options. A few years ago, who would have dreamed that computers would replace typewriters. Who knows what the future holds?

Negroponte opens his book *Being Digital* (1995), saying, "Computing is not about computers any more. It is about living."

Types of Media for Observing and Recording

There are many electronic recording devices. With the arrival of computerization, the options and adaptations are wide. Each has its usefulness along with disadvantages. The early childhood practitioner's knowledge, skills, experience, and creativity may extend far beyond direct interactions with children, into the world of multimedia.

Audio Tape Recording. Recording voices is especially useful for conversations to gather speech and language samples (see Chapter 6) and cognitive task questions (see Chapters 7 and 8). Inexpensive tape recorders are available at any electronics supply store. Children's tape recorders make lower-quality recordings but allow the children to record themselves or each other. These can be used as dramatic play props or on project work. Children can record and play back sounds, voices, and music.

Voice-activated **audio recorders** are available. These can be placed in a selected location where conversations from sociodramatic play, for example, are taking place. The nonintrusive quality is the advantage of this feature, since it does not need the teacher to walk over and turn it on. Natural, clear recordings are preserved and may be transcribed and analyzed to assess and evaluate social play level. Problem-solving techniques, learning styles, dramatic play roles, and how the child sustains the role over time can be evaluated.

Parabolic or shotgun microphones (the type sports broadcasts use to catch the coach's instructions and the players' grunts) can be aimed to pick up sound across the room. They can focus on a small, low conversation and screen out all the background noise that is usually going on in an early childhood classroom. They are effective for catching a conversation at the Play Doh table about who has more Play Doh, who made the long snake, or who made all the little balls. Recordings at the sand table might document Caroline's explanation of how she knows which sand is hers and which belongs to Debbie. The self-talk Nicholas uses as he sets the table for snack is captured. His math skills are assessed as he puts out all of the napkins, saying, "Here's one for this chair, one for this chair, one for this chair. Hey, where's the chair for this napkin?"

The advantage of unobtrusiveness is also a disadvantage. Some regard recording without the subject's approval or knowledge as an invasion of privacy. (See Topics in Observation in this chapter.) Another disadvantage is the cost: approximately $200 to $1,000 and up. It also takes some training to become proficient in its operation. This method would be ideal for the classroom with a separate observation booth. Often the sound quality in a teaching lab observation booth is so poor that the value of the audible observation is lost. Remote control of the microphone would help overcome this problem.

What to Do with It. Audio tapes of an individual child are kept in the child's portfolio. They can be analyzed for speech and language development. Dictated stories or reading abilities, or informal or structured interviews, can be filed there. These preserve an audible record of the child's personality revealed through language.

Video. Many people have **video recorders** today and many children are accustomed to being photographed in this way. Cameras are becoming more affordable, and they are smaller, easier to use, and efficient in almost any kind of light and setting. Zoom capabilities allow recording from a distance. Combined with a parabolic microphone, the video and audio can be remotely controlled from across the room. Mounting a camera on the wall, or in a central location in the room, can record all the events happening in one area. The block area could be recorded on one day and the dramatic play area on another. By mounting the camera and letting it run, children act more natural than if a person is manually pointing the camera at them. If a videographer is used, it is important for the children to become familiar with the process and the person taking pictures. With familiarity, their self-consciousness decreases. A camera could be present, or have a camera person taking blank pictures, days before the actual "shoot" to allow the children to become accustomed to being videotaped. Cameras ranging in price from $900 to $1,500 have point-and-shoot controls, optional date and time, freeze and fast frames, and a bookmark to find the end. The tape can be viewed immediately on a television monitor through the camera. They have a taping capability of 30 minutes to 4 hours (Holzberg, 1993).

Lavalieres (electronic signal devices) can be worn that automatically turn the camera to aim at the subject. These are used in distance learning studios by professors who wander around the room. Extremely small cameras, the size of a pencil, can diminish the awareness of being taped. A teacher could wear one behind his ear or in a pocket. Then he can walk around the room or sit "watching" the children play while he is actually videotaping. Videotaping selected areas could also be done by remote from a control or observation room.

Hours and hours of tape are unmanageable. There may be segments that are profound, while much of the taping yielded nothing usable for the purpose. Editing the tape can be done by retaping segments from one recorder to another. This is time-consuming and the tape is then second-generation quality. Many public or technical schools have editing machines that may be available to perform this function. The digitizing of video reduces images to mathematical symbols that computers can read. Editing video on a computer with CD-ROM is simple, much the same way paragraphs of text are moved with a computer. They also can be manipulated visually and enhanced, and parts can be erased. Captions and background music can be added to make a very professional production with a minimum of technical training. Nonlinear editing allows changes in sequence of segments or individual images. Large amounts of tape can be stored on one disk, useful when cataloging large amounts of information in the computer's memory for sorting, filing, and rearranging. This sophisticated and expensive equipment may be available through the program's affiliations in the community. Parents are frequently resources for technical work.

IT HAPPENED TO ME: Videotaping Lesson

A college video team spent two whole days in my preschool classroom, complete with cameras on tripods, spotlights, and cords (before the sophisticated equipment we have today). We were trying to tape portions of children's play to use for practice observations. After viewing about 12 hours of video, we got very little usable footage. The children were self-conscious, the interactions between teachers and children were unnatural, and the background noise made conversations almost inaudible. It was not as easy as it seemed. Equipment has changed a lot since then. With that and some practice, the results can be much better.

That videotaping experience in my classroom taught me many lessons. An impor-

tant one is to view the tape through the lens of the parents. In that tape one child walked around the whole time holding his genitals. This was such a common stance I did not notice it. When the tape was shown to parents at a dinner, his mother was mortified and asked that those segments be edited out. That just about meant he was never on the tape.

What to Do with It. A videotape is a replay of live action. The episode can be relived repeatedly, hearing and seeing what took place. Segments can be closely examined for relevance to developmental assessment. A commentary can be added for parents, or other teachers, or referral agents by voice overlays. The accompanying narrative can point out important details, such as, "Watch the way he is picking up that napkin. Watch the movement of the thumb. Let's go back and slow it down. We can stop it right here."

Other valuable uses of video recorders in the classroom follow.

- Historic record. A videotape can be a memento of a special occasion for the whole class. Later viewing of important events, such as the first day, a special visitor, a field trip, or just a normal day, serve as enjoyable memories. Events can take on added importance in the future. Looking at the tape, children can see how much they have grown.

- Replay for discussion with the children. A play segment could be taped, shown to the children involved, and discussed, such as, "What happened here? When Audrey did this, see what happened? What could she have done instead?" The tape is then used for problem solving and instruction, more real than any puppet play or discussion with no visual connection.

- Video field trip. A teacher was going on a trip so she taped it from the child's viewpoint, as if the child were along with her. She pointed out, "Watch out for that," and "Look over there, see that." It was very effective when accompanied by her artifacts and books. Video can be a teaching tool.

- Teacher observation practice. Teachers can watch a selected segment and practice recording methods such as Anecdotal and Running Recordings, Frequency Counts, Checklists, and Rating Scales. Then the teachers can compare ratings (inter-rater reliability) to see if they are interpreting the behavior in relatively the same way. This helps them see deficiencies in the system of recording or finding biases that were not realized before. This would make an excellent staff training for improving teachers' professional practice and reviewing child development principles.

- Reevaluation and referral. A video recording, authorized with a written release by the parents, can be shown to helping professionals for their interpretation or a resource person for an evaluation. It shows the child in a natural setting, capturing usual behavior.

- Research. Analyzing videotape can compare small bits of data for research. Ethical principles of voluntary, informed consent are necessary. Parental signatures are required after they have been informed of the nature of the research and the techniques to be used. This must be in language they can understand. It is the investigator's responsibility to carefully evaluate the ethical acceptability of the study regarding the "subject at risk" (*American Psychology Association,* 1990, pp. 390–394).

- Teacher self-evaluation and reflection. The tape can be used by the teacher to monitor and receive reactions to teaching practices or for personal reflection. The teacher may be unaware of habits revealed on videotapes. The tape may be used to self-evaluate intervention strategies, play involvement, or language usage (Wood, et al., 1980).

Exercise: Record a segment of your classroom if you work with children, or normal routines of your day. Listen and analyze what the recording reveals about yourself.

- Live Internet connections. Many parents cannot physically spend time in the classroom, observing normal activities or even arrange to be present for special events. Another new technology that now exists is live video through a camera and microphone called QuickCam from Connectix Corporation, available through many computer mail-order houses. The software needed is CU-See Me, a free videoconferencing program developed by Cornell University that can be downloaded from their web site:

http://cu-seeme.cornell.edu

This is being used by Florence Poor (1995) in her fourth grade classroom in Lexington, Massachusetts. She says, "Although there is quite an open policy of visitation we still do not reach more than one-eighth of our parents. The camera would invite many parents a peek into their child's life in school that could prove more relevant than physically dropping in. Classrooms need to be opened up more than they are presently. This does not imply that a teacher would have to be constantly watched, but for special events parents could be included and increase the camaraderie that we in the classroom often feel. Those teachable moments wouldn't go unappreciated."

IT HAPPENED TO ME: The Gloved Hand

During the days of the taping our hatched chickens were getting bigger so they were allowed some freedom within a circle of children. It made wonderful footage but one got out. Not being an animal person, I had to put on work gloves to pick up the chickens. (I told the children I was allergic.) In one short clip of the tape a black gloved hand appears to scoop up a wandering chicken. Only I know (and now you) the story behind the glove.

Photography. Ah, at last something more familiar. Point and shoot. Quality photographs have become much easier to take with automatic focusing, built-in flash, and zoom capabilities. The quality of pictures is *almost* foolproof. Most children are accustomed to being photographed so that photos become a natural documentation of play. That is only true if it is done often throughout the year. This can be expensive but there are ways to reduce the cost. Buying film in bulk makes it the least expensive part of the operation. Developing has become much less expensive with many places offering discounts for nonprofit organizations. Check with the developer for what is known as contact sheets. These are small, postage-sized prints, all on one page. When looking for "just the right shot" this allows many, many pictures to be taken and only the selected ones to be developed.

The computer age has arrived in photographs as well. Instead of prints, film can be placed on a compact disk (CD) to be viewed on the computer monitor. Some video and still cameras can also record on a CD. No processing is necessary. One disk holds 43,500 still images. It can then be printed out on the printer, copied, and distributed. These can be arranged into a desired order, perhaps to show step by step in a project. It can be used to make a book for the children to revive the memory. These images can be incorporated into the curriculum for a sequencing activity. Printing it out on paper is much less expensive than photo prints, and the size is almost limitless.

What to Do with It. Many teachers use a photo album in the classroom as a prereading experience, inspiring children to recall details of past events. It helps children get better acquainted with class members. The teacher sends home a school album with a different child each week. In this way, the family can see the other children in the class and some events that have taken place. Conversations about school now have a focus and the family feels more of a connection to the school. A Polaroid educational program, "Presenting Bright Ideas for Child Development" (Herr, J. & Libby Y., 1995) gives many other activity ideas for using photographs in the classroom.

Photographs can be added to the portfolio to illustrate comments about areas of development. They add visual information to Anecdotal Records or can be used themselves as the main observation method with notes explaining the photograph. For example, what area of development might the photograph in Figure 11.1 document?

Photographs can be used during the year as vehicles to help the child remember and talk about specific incidents. The visual image is a springboard for a description of the event and the feelings surrounding it. The child's narrative could also be taped or dictated, adding a literacy dimension to the experience.

Photographs of each child taken the first week of school (double prints) can be used in an activity for matching or a concentration game. This is a personal and unique way for children to get to know each other. Children can dictate captions for photographs taken in the classroom or during special events, adding them to the class album or making a book of their own. Photographs are self-esteem boosters.

Photographs taken throughout the school year are excellent mementoes to give the children at the end of the year. They are a lasting reminder of that school year. Photographs taken of the children could be used in an album, a bulletin board, or placed in the portfolio. At the end of the year, they should be distributed to the children. If the teacher or school is retaining any photographs, a special release form should be signed so the parent is aware of that fact and acknowledges consent.

IT HAPPENED TO ME: Do You Want to Be Pink?

One of the highlights of my days in the classroom was an intergenerational project in which one class of four-year-olds made weekly visits to a nearby nursing home. There are a million stories connected with that but my favorite is about Ethel. She was blind and had David for a little friend. He showed empathy that is supposed to be beyond his Preoperational stage.

One spring day we were making drip dot paintings, so he helped her by placing the paintbrush in her hand and shaking it to make the drips. She got paint on her hand so he asked me for a tissue to wipe it off. As he was wiping, she asked, "What color is it, David?" He answered, "Blue, the color of robin's eggs." (Perceptive, eh?) She sighed, "Oh!" He looked at her and at me and said, "Do you want to be pink?" "I'd love to be pink," she replied. He painted each finger a pastel color and I snapped the most rapturous photograph of her face glowing, with hand outstretched with pastel fingers. The significance of the incident and photograph was even more poignant when I learned later from the activities director that Ethel's love of her life was painting. That photo is precious but, alas, I have no permission to print it, so it will have to glow in your own imagination.

Figure 11.1 What do you see in this photograph?

Media As Documentation for Other Areas of Development

Audio or videotaping or photography can be used to record and document any area of development. Arrivals and separations can give poignant images of hellos and good-byes. Self-care photos can illustrate the accomplishment of milestone tasks, such as dressing for outside or tying a shoe. A video of outside play could be a delightful reminder of the physical, emotional, language, and social actions of the child. It could picture children run-ning down a hill, climbing a slide, or wading in a creek. Social interactions can be preserved with photographs or taped conversations. Emotionally troubled moments are usually best kept private, but there may be circumstances when these might need to be preserved visually or audibly. Language segments on audio or videotape preserves not only the words, but facial and body expressions to make them even more illuminating. Visual and auditory reminders of past events help expand memory and attention span. They are good teaching tools and document important events. Creative moments,

---

TOPICS IN OBSERVATION: Protecting the Rights of the Child

It is essential to receive the permission of each child's parent to permanently record their child using audio, video, or photographic recording methods, Figure 11.2. There are instances when this permission may be denied:

- Some religious groups do not allow pho-tographs.
- The child is under protective services in a protected, confidential placement. An inno-cent newspaper photograph of an activity that included the child may jeopardize the child's safety.
- There may be personal reasons the parent may deny permission.

It is important for all staff members to be aware of the prohibition. Just as a life-threaten-ing allergy must be made known to all staff, this is important information to be conveyed. The staff should find alternatives to audio taping the child's language sample. If video or still photography is used, either for formal or infor-mal uses, the staff is responsible for making the photographer aware of the prohibition. Sensi-tivity to the child's feelings is a high priority. The age of the child and reason for prohibition will govern how this exclusion is made. The exclusion from photography or taping should not be obvious to the other children or their parents, or even the child, unless it is by the child's request. Techniques of photography could be used to take group casual pictures from the back of the child. All diligence should be given to this serious ethical and legal issue.

Occasionally, photo contests or commercial purposes may occur. If the recordings are used for other than educational or publicity use, the individual child's parents should be consulted. A special release form for that use should be obtained. It is better to be cautious and guard against any possible recriminations.

Any child who does not want to be taped, video recorded, or photographed has the right to refuse. The program staff has the responsibility to respect the child's wishes, even if the parent has given per-mission. No child should be forced to participate in this kind of an activity. This should be a pol-icy in the program, staff, and parent handbook.

AUDIO/VIDEO/PHOTO RELEASE

I give permission for my child to be tape recorded, video recorded, or photographed for educational or publicity purposes while participating in the regular activities of this program.

Date _____

❏ YES   ❏ NO

Signature _____

Figure 11.2 Sample Release

The media portion was written with the help of Katharyn Nannaman.

whether art media manipulation or sociodramatic play, are meaningfully captured on film or audio tape. Incidents illustrating self-identity, group interactions, or relationships with adults in the classroom are vividly documented more with pictures or audio tape. Any observation can be augmented or recorded using these methods. Further commentary will enhance or add the observer's conclusions to the photograph or tape.

Advantages of Using Media As an Observation Technique

Photographs, video and audio taping are effective observational recording tools because

- they capture visual or real sound images of the episode
- they are less subject to the recorder's bias or inferences
- they allow the viewer to form judgments independent from the recorder's
- they can be analyzed in a number of ways, for different purposes, at different times
- they are less time-consuming if automatic systems are used

Disadvantages of Using Media As an Observation Technique

Photographs, video, or audio taping can be

- expensive
- complicated and time-consuming
- intrusive to children and teachers
- a factor causing unnatural behavior
- against parents' values

LOOKING AT DRAMATIC PLAY

During dramatic play, observers see many interesting scenarios unfold. A child puts on a hat, picks up a briefcase, and says, "See ya, honey, I'm goin' to work now." And off she goes. A toddler holds his sweater coiled up in a ball and strokes it saying, "Nice kitty." A four-year-old at the art bench says to himself, "I need a big piece of paper 'cause I'm gonna' make a big truck with a trailer. No I'll use another piece of paper for the trailer and hitch 'em togedder with a piece of tape." Each of these children is displaying imaginative play through their thoughts and actions. They are cute to the untrained observer but meaningful to those who know what each incident reveals about the child's development.

While *play* is the word used for not performing any worthwhile function, for young children (and for us all), it has many benefits. Research on dramatic play, solitary imaginative play with or without props, and **sociodramatic play,** a fantasy episode interacting with other children, has important implications for teachers of young children. Studies have found that children who regularly engage in sociodramatic or imaginative play are more friendly, popular, cooperative, verbal, and creative. They are usually less impulsive and aggressive and more likely to take the perspective of others (Fein & Kinney, 1994). These are logical outcomes of sustained interactions with peers. Other benefits are documented as well. Children between two and a half and five years old who participate in make-believe play are more advanced in general intellectual ability, have better memory, and display higher reasoning ability (Berk, 1994). Nonparticipants, however, had lower school achievement later and exhibited less self-control in social situations and higher rates of delinquency (Singer & Singer, 1990). With these benefits, can early childhood programs and elementary schools ignore the importance of providing and encouraging this kind of play?

Stages of Dramatic Play

Children play in different ways at different ages and stages, Figure 11.3. Piaget equated that difference in the way they played with the difference in their thinking (Peterson & Felton-Collins, 1986). The changes in imaginative play are easily observed and do correspond with stages of development by several theorists, including Piaget, Erikson, Smilansky, and Vygotsky.

Infancy. The infant and adult are gazing at each other intently. As the adult opens and closes his mouth and slowly sticks out his tongue, the infant imitates the action. Imaginative play has begun. This has been documented to occur in the early days of the infant's life, setting the stage for responding to another human and turn taking. The game of Peek-a-Boo is really the pretend theme of "I'm going away and now I'm back." The repetition of these adult-child interactions is building the foundation for the later plots of sociodramatic play with peers.

Young Toddlers. Between six and eighteen months, the child is exploring the physical world by playing with objects. Close scrutiny of this play illustrates various patterns.

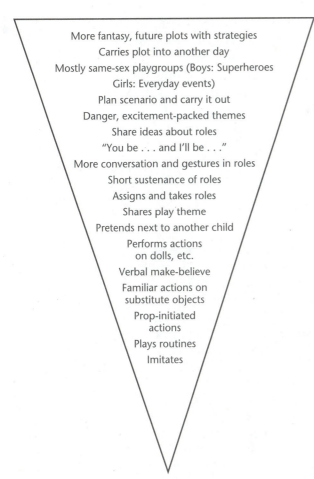

More fantasy, future plots with strategies
Carries plot into another day
Mostly same-sex playgroups (Boys: Superheroes
Girls: Everyday events)
Plan scenario and carry it out
Danger, excitement-packed themes
Share ideas about roles
"You be . . . and I'll be . . ."
More conversation and gestures in roles
Short sustenance of roles
Assigns and takes roles
Shares play theme
Pretends next to another child
Performs actions
on dolls, etc.
Verbal make-believe
Familiar actions on
substitute objects
Prop-initiated
actions
Plays routines
Imitates

Figure 11.3 Dramatic Play Development

Repetition with Objects. Manipulations are repeated with the objects in every conceivable way. The young toddler takes her bottle and shakes it, throws it, chews on it, sucks on all parts of it, listens to it, and minutely examines it.

Repetition Without Objects. The functions she has learned are played out in her imagination without the object. This is the beginning of imaginary play. She puts her fist to her mouth and makes sucking movements and sounds, pretending to suck the bottle.

Substitution. Other objects become stand-ins for the imaginary one. She picks up anything she can handle and puts it to her mouth and pretends, or really, sucks it like a bottle. She is mentally substituting this object for the bottle.

Older Toddlers. Vygotsky's theory (Berk & Winsler, 1995) is that this happens just at the time when social rules are being enforced by adults. These rules restrict behavior, such as avoid dangerous situations and do not tear up books or take toys from others. The child then substitutes imag-

inary situations in which she is in control of the rules and can work them through as she delays immediate gratification. Her parents may be offering her milk from a cup, so she plays the pretend bottle routines as a symbolic way to cope. She now separates thought from action and renounces impulsive action in favor of this situation. She makes the rules.

The child is the center of imaginative play with rituals such as eating and sleeping. The actions become more decentered. Now she is feeding the teddy bear rather than being fed herself. She now can use more language and muscle skills to participate in shared-meaning play with others, but self-control is a problem. Each player must do the acting with the same objects, and none is willing to forego her own desire to possess the toy.

Preschoolers. The three-year-old has an expanded sense of fantasy using semirealistic props for adult roles. Each player has his own role related to the theme but acts independently. The players are trying to represent themselves in roles with which they are familiar. This helps them understand and feel powerful. To be the parent giving the commands, the superhero with super power, or the firefighter as a rescuer, the child takes on the characteristics of another person. They are only able to do this because of expanded vocabulary, experiences with models, and objects that they can mentally transform into props.

Toward the end of the preschool age, the ability to have empathetic thoughts and to want social companionship expands the dramatic play into the sociodramatic stage. Most children are becoming less egocentric and more empathetic. They understand others' points of view and feelings. They are in the Initiative Stage, taking control and leadership of their own play, not dependent on specific props or adult leadership. They are likely to play roles such as family, stereotyped television characters, powerful helpers from the community (firefighter or police), cowboys, pirates, or space creatures. However, now roles are assigned and imaginary experiences are shared through explanations outside the role. Children are frequently heard saying things like, "You be the guy on fire and I'll come with the hose and put the fire out." This often meets with a counter-proposal from the victim, "No, *you* be the guy on fire and *I'll* come with the hose." Resolution of the dilemma may indicate language development for negotiation, problem-solving ability, and social status in the group.

Young School-Agers. Sociodramatic play declines in the early school years. The child has a growing contact with reality, feelings of industry, and pride in their motor and intellectual skills. Games with rules are the outlets for these skills and attitudes. Interactions with other children are growing more competitive. Katz and Chard (1989) call this the age of investigations. They are concrete-operational thinkers, ready for group play. Their investigations may be focused on collections of whatever the fad is this week, though Barbie's and sports cards have sustained their favor. Games with rules become the play pattern of this age child now that they can accurately keep score, easily take turns, and strategically plan. The sociodramatic play of the earlier stages has prepared the child for these activities.

Using Play Stages to Assess Dramatic Play

The social play stages can be used again when assessing and describing dramatic play (see Chapter 4). A variety of methods can record the play, such as Class List Log, Checklist, Anecdotal or Running Record, Rating Scales, or electronically for later analysis.

Onlooker Stage. The child watches the dramatic play of others. The child may lack the entry skills and self-confidence to join the organized play of other children. It may be the child's learning style to watch others before he attempts the play, or it may be the shy personality of the child. The adult can give assistance in play entry techniques if it is warranted.

Solitary Dramatic Play. Any age child may choose to play out individual dramatic or fantasy play alone. The child selects the props for play and may internally or audibly carry on a dialogue. The observer, just as in the Onlooker Stage, can assess the play and decide if intervention is needed to help the child move to social interaction in the play. The scaffolding of an adult as a parallel player may help the child move to the next stage.

Parallel Dramatic Play. Two-, three-, and four-year-olds are social beings and often play out their dramatic roles alongside other children without interactions. The observer, like in the Solitary Stage, assesses the child's social level and choice of parallel play partners. If it is indicated, she can act as an intermediary. Statements such as, "Suzie, you are a Mommy and Joe is a cook. Maybe you could go to his restaurant and order a Kids Meal."

Howe's Peer Play Scale (in Johnson, et al., 1987) classifies sociodramatic play in levels.

Level 1—Simple Parallel Play. Children are in close proximity with similar activities, but there is no eye contact or social behavior.

Level 2—Parallel Play with Mutual Regard. Children are involved in similar activities, making eye contact and often imitating each other's play.

Associative Dramatic Play. In the associative stage, children are still each playing parallel but share play theme and conversation. This is Howe's:

Level 3—Simple Social Play. Children are talking, smiling, offering objects, and corresponding to associative play. It is the stage of social play in which children are playing near each other, in the same play theme, but not together. They do not share props or final results.

Cooperative Dramatic Play. In the cooperative stage, children are working together toward a common goal, contributing parts to the whole. These are Howe's:

Level 4—Complementary/Reciprocal Play with Mutual Awareness. Children offer objects to build a mutual structure, taking turns, but there is no other social exchange. It is a higher level of associative play.

Level 5—Complementary/Reciprocal Social Play. Children engage in social exchanges. They plan and act out make-believe stories.

Smilansky (in Johnson, et al., 1987, p. 160) further defines this level of sociodramatic play as:

- Role playing—adopting roles
- Make-believe transformations—symbols stand for objects, actions, and situations
- Social interactions—directly relating to each other in roles
- Verbal communications—(1) statements to organize the play designating the situation, assigning roles, planning story lines and rebuking players who act in an inappropriate way and (2) pretend communication within the role. (p. 158)

By using these finer distinctions in describing dramatic play, the observer can make decisions about the need or desirability of intervening in the play. The adult can help dramatic play by role modeling, making suggestions, asking open-ended questions, or giving direct instruction in carrying out the role. Each of these may help the child extend the play and become a more acceptable play partner.

Exercise: Look at photographs of children in the dramatic play area. Using the preceding stages of Howe and Smilansky, determine each child's level or role.

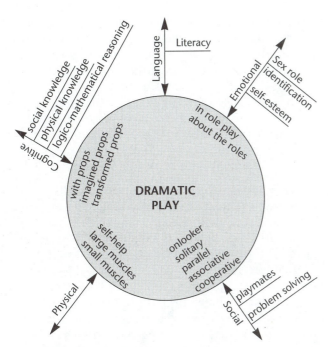

Figure 11.4 Developmental Skills Used and Revealed in Dramatic Play

Observing Dramatic Play for Assessing Other Developmental Areas

While children are engaging in dramatic play, they are using other skills and behaviors that can be observed and assessed simultaneously, Figure 11.4.

Cognitive. Sociodramatic play is a progressive step toward abstract thinking. The movement from the real toy to the symbolic leads the preschooler to abstract thinking. This is the link with the Concrete Operations stage of Piaget. Correlations have been made between IQ scores and sociodramatic play. Children who enjoy pretending score higher on imagination and creativity (Berk & Winsler, 1995). During dramatic play, children shift away from self and take the role of another that helps them see situations from a different viewpoint, moving them out of egocentrism. The reversibility of the role, knowing they can leave it any time, helps develop the cognitive structures for understanding the reversibility of operations such as the clay balls and equal amounts of water in different-sized containers (Johnson, et al., 1987). The planning and carrying out of a thematic role through story and fantasy play have been shown to help children's memory for story lines and serve as a foundation for later memory strategies (Berk & Winsler, 1995).

Language. Sociodramatic play gives children practice in turn taking and using language to plan as well as carry out roles, sometimes with great expression. This shows the child's ability to move out of egocentrism into the role of another, even using different voices, vocabularies, and gestures for the role. The inner speech, or private speech as Vygotsky (in Berk & Winsler, 1995) calls it, often is audible as children work through a dramatic play episode whether alone or with other children. It reveals the child's inner thoughts. It is as if they were being transmitted directly out of the brain, such as, "Now this is my baby and she has to go to the doctor. Oops, her arm just fell off. I think James did that." Accompanying sound effects and directions to inanimate objects, such as, "Get outta here chair," are often heard in fantasy play.

Literacy. Sociodramatic play is a natural way to integrate literacy into the child's environment, to become a natural and important part of the play theme. The use of literacy materials in areas can be observed, such as sign-making in the block area, letter writing, and list making in the dramatic play area. Often children will spontaneously, or the teacher may gently suggest, that a sign or a list could fill a need in the play. It may direct players like an "Open" or "Closed" sign for a grocery store or labels for buildings with the name of the builder or request to preserve it. Watching the use of literacy materials, including books during play, can give the observer clues about the child's understanding of the usefulness of print.

Social. Dramatic play is encouraged by parents who engage in fantasy with their child, provide props, and comment on the play as real. These children tend to be more securely attached and more imaginative. Children's involvement and success with dramatic play depends also on their level of social development (see Chapter 4). When the child is in the parallel play stage, she wants to be near other children playing, but does not have the language, emotional, or cognitive development to engage in interactive play. The adult can recognize the level of social development, help the child find a role that she is capable of, and support her success in that role. Experience in groups greatly affects the child's ability to participate in sociodramatic play. Solving problems in play situations helps children learn the art of negotiation while they divide roles, take turns, and share props. Interacting with an older peer or one more socially experienced will enhance imaginative play. Children seek out familiar same-sex, same-age playmates.

Some children do not participate in sociodramatic play. There are many possible reasons for it and implications for the caregiver. Some children are more object-oriented than people-oriented, which may be their cognitive style (see Chapter 7). They learn through manipulating the physical environment and are convergent rather than divergent thinkers. Another related characteristic is fantasy-making disposition, which is positively linked with the ability to delay gratification and wait for turns (Johnson, et al., 1987). This child is frustrated by sociodramatic play, that increased aggressive play, that decreased acceptance by other children. It is a cycle of rejection that begins very early and may have negative effects on self-esteem.

It is well documented that children who are less aggressive are more readily accepted as playmates. The children who introduce wild animal themes and superheroes into dramatic play raise the level of aggressiveness of the play. Research has shown strong relationships between high television viewing and aggressiveness (Donnerstein, et al., 1994). Effects are also low imagination, more anxiety, and lower reading levels and school performance (Singer & Singer, 1990). These effects can be reduced if adults are mediators of the child's viewing. Talking about the difference between real and fantasy, and the possible results in real life if people did that, can help children gain self-control. Play themes from television are highly aggressive and antisocial, but television can teach prosocial behaviors with careful adult intervention.

Should superheroes be banned? There is much discussion and disagreement over this topic (see Slaby, et al., 1995; and Carlsson-Paige & Levin, 1990, in Resources). The observer can conduct ethnographic research about the effect of television superheroes on dramatic play through Anecdotal Recordings and Frequency Counts. There is no doubt that children use dramatic play to feel powerful (when they know they are not), feel grown up (when they know they are little), and do dangerous things (when they know they are not allowed). Sociodramatic play can provide a way for them to behave "beyond his average age, above his daily behavior; in play it is as though he were a head taller than himself" (Sutton-Smith in Berk & Winsler, 1995, p. 68).

Children more frequently play with same-sex playmates, with girls choosing family themes on everyday experiences whereas boys play physically active, superhero roles (Johnson, et al., 1987). Studies have been conducted to detect the roots of the differences, biological or cultural. It is the old nature vs. nurture question, with the ambiguous answer, "Both." There is no doubt that stereotypical play roles have been reinforced by parents, peers, television, storybooks, toy advertising, and

even by teachers. This happens overtly in comments like, "You girls might want to play with the new dolls we got for the housekeeping area." It may be covert by not providing dressup props for boys in the dramatic play area (not the housekeeping area). Observations of dramatic play roles, routines, and partners will give clues about the child's sex role identity. The role of the adult is also to broaden the child's exploration of play things and themes by providing a variety of opportunities.

Emotional. Children's emotions are displayed in dramatic play. Observers of young children have heard and seen the pretend crying of the "baby" or the shrill voice of fear as villains chase the good guys. The obvious enjoyment is seen when children are dressing up to go to the dance. However, Johnson and colleagues (1987) say, "There are little experimental data to back up the contention that play has an important role in emotional development" (p. 14). However, play therapy has been used extensively in the treatment of children's emotional disorders so the connection between dramatic play as a vehicle for expressing inward emotions is recognized. Johnson is emphasizing the lack of research in this area. Important events to the child, such as a new sibling, mommy going to work, moving, or major changes in the family, often are seen played out in the dramatic play themes. Exact conversations and gestures accompany the actions that help the child physically and mentally reenact what is troubling them inside. Recurring themes of going to the doctor, house on fire, spanking the baby all point to the emotional involvement of young children in dramatic play.

Emotional disturbances can be observed in children's dramatic play. Curry and Arnaud (1995, pp. 4–9) present three areas of children's play that may suggest an emotional need for intervention.

1. Thematic content: (a) a preoccupation with a single play theme, unchanging and rigid; (b) highly unusual play themes that may be traumatic events the child has witnessed; (c) play with explicit sexual content; or (d) excessive preoccupation with ordinary objects.
2. Style of play: (a) excessively rigid; (b) play in a style of a younger developmental stage; (c) inability to remove himself from the pretend role; or (d) unusual aggressiveness.
3. Social interactions in play: (a) isolated at a stage in the preschool years when sociodramatic play is at its peak; (b) cannot sustain play because of aggressiveness, disruptiveness, or social ineptness; (c) excessively imitative play; or (d) causes rejections.

IT HAPPENED TO ME:
Fan Fascination

A colleague conferred with me about a child who was preoccupied with fans. He watched the ceiling fan at home for long periods of time, his mother reported. At preschool he searched magazines and catalogs looking for pictures of fans. He carried pictures of them around in his pocket and talked about how things reminded him of fans. He was immature socially but linguistically advanced. These warning signals reminded me of this child with the fascination and aberration with fans. He was referred to a psychologist and worked with a play therapist.

Even very young children can have complicated and strange behavior. These can be clues of deeper difficulties or just a unique characteristic. Closer observation of the whole child can help make that determination.

Sociodramatic play, with its rules of varying complexity, calls for self-control of emotions and impulses. This does have the developmental effect of practicing in play what is required in real life. The private speech in fantasy play has a major role in the development of self-control. Children use it to regulate their own activity, such as, "I gotta be careful here. I'll pour carefully so I don't spill it" (Berk & Winsler, 1995).

Physical. The whole body using large and small muscles is involved in dramatic play. Large muscles are put into action when running away from the robbers and lifting heavy boards to construct a fort. Placing tiny horses in a row on a wobbly block wall or buttoning up opera gloves requires small muscle coordination, attention span, and patience.

IT HAPPENED TO ME
Thirty Buttons

I watched in amazement as one of the youngest children in the three-year-old class sat for about 20 minutes in the dramatic play area. She had put on a dress with fabric loops for buttonholes all the way down the front. There must have been 30 of them. She sat and buttoned every one. That was patience, long attention span, small muscle coordination, and one-to-one correspondence. A planned activity would never have taught her the lessons she learned that day. It was an observation full of details about her development.

An environment enriched with interesting props and possibilities expands dramatic play. When children are engaged in imaginative play, they do adapt their own props from whatever is available. Before that stage however, children first go through the stages of manipulation and exploration. They explored all the physical properties of objects first (Curry, 1992). Toddlers and threes require realistic props to complete their play theme. In *The Project Approach* (Katz & Chard, 1989), construction of models and displays that relate to real things in the children's lives are a significant part of the project.

Dramatic play incorporates the curriculum areas of art, language, science, math, and social studies. It helps develop interpersonal negotiations, physical coordination, language, and cognitive skills. Children ask their own questions, seek their own answers, and enhance all skill areas with the assistance of the teacher as a support.

Other Techniques for Observing Dramatic Play

Dramatic play can be captured very well through the use of Anecdotal Recording. Some delightful and insightful Anecdotal Recordings of dramatic play comprise the writings of Vivian Gussin Paley. Her book, *Boys and Girls: Superheroes in the Doll Corner* (1984) is a wonderful accompaniment to the discussions of this chapter. (See Chapter 3 for an excerpt and Resources for others.)

A Class List Log can be used for a quick check on who does and does not participate in fantasy play. This may be expanded into a Frequency Count over the course of a week or so, as children present a dramatic rendition of *Three Billy Goats Gruff* or some other story. Repeating the Class List Log or Frequency Count will indicate if more children are engaged in sociodramatic play as the year progresses.

Time samples will indicate if play is occurring in the dramatic play area. The observer may want to develop a code for the time sample, perhaps a "D" to designate dramatic play occurring in other areas. Under the climber or outdoors, an exciting cops and robbers theme may be acted out. In the block area, a city may be constructed in anticipation of an earthquake or a bombing. Children do play out the traumatic events of the news that are even more frightening than the cartoons they watch. While taking the time sample, if an event that is interesting or important occurs, the observer could turn the paper over and jot down some notes. Later these could be amplied into a more formal Anecdotal Recording for the class file or child's portfolio.

Developmental Checklists and Rating Scales often have one or more criterion for recording the presence, absence, or level of involvement of the child in dramatic play.

Beaty's (1994) Imagination Checklist includes the following items in a developmental progression:

Pretends by replaying familiar roles

Needs particular props to do pretend play

Assigns roles or takes assigned roles

May switch roles without warning

Uses language for creating and sustaining plot

Uses exciting, danger-packed themes

Takes on characteristics and actions related to role

Uses elaborate and creative themes, ideas and details (p. 337).

The Reflective Journal is a place to ponder the meaning of what is seen and heard during fantasy play, to wonder about its roots, and to explore possible actions in the future, Figure 11.5. Thought given to possible scenarios and responses may be considered *before* they occur, to be ready with comfortable, considered answers.

SPECIAL POPULATIONS AND SOCIODRAMATIC PLAY

It is not surprising that differences exist in the ways children approach dramatic play when they come from diverse backgrounds, cultures, and experiences, as well as varying levels of language,

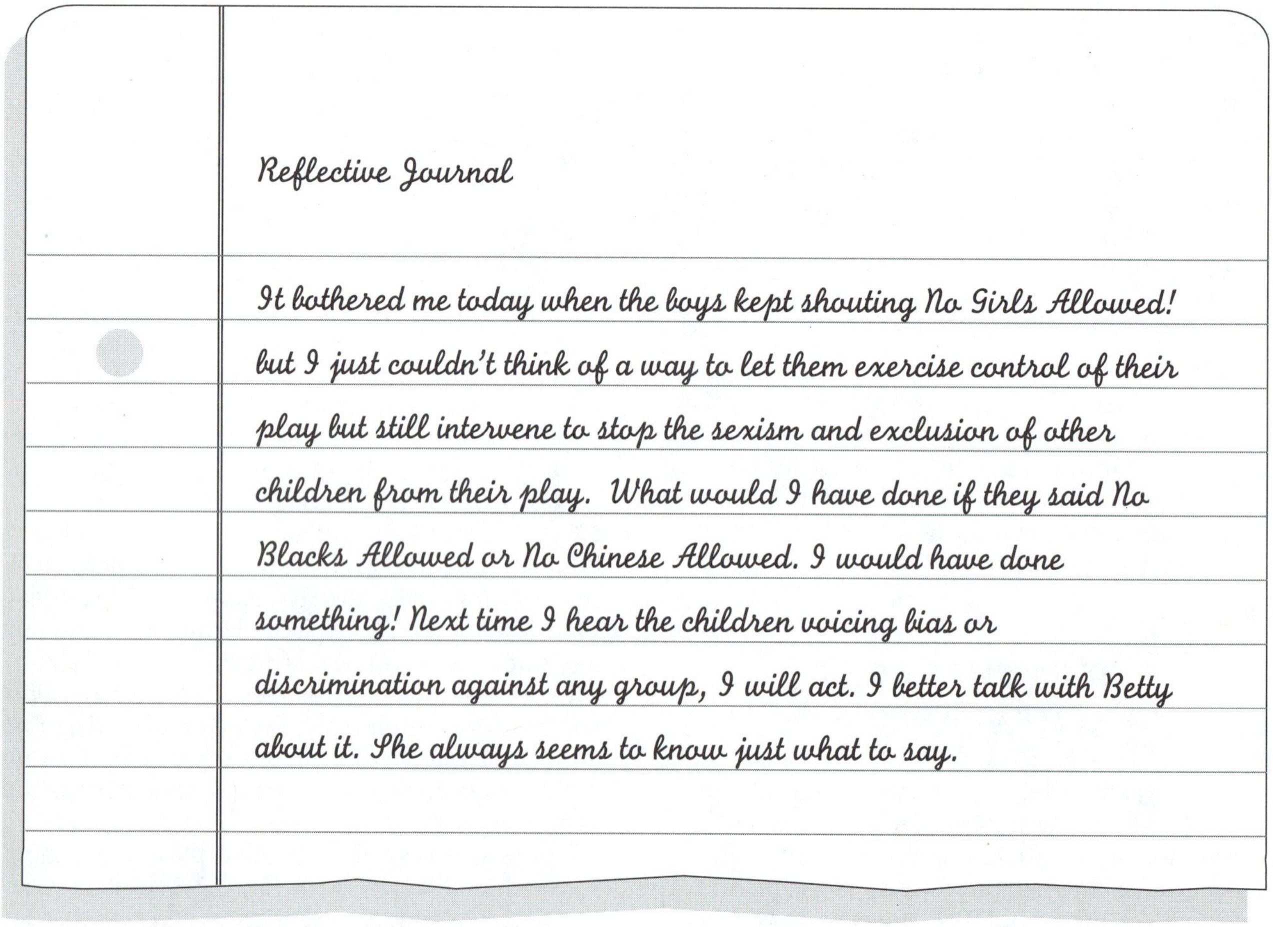

Reflective Journal

It bothered me today when the boys kept shouting No Girls Allowed! but I just couldn't think of a way to let them exercise control of their play but still intervene to stop the sexism and exclusion of other children from their play. What would I have done if they said No Blacks Allowed or No Chinese Allowed. I would have done something! Next time I hear the children voicing bias or discrimination against any group, I will act. I better talk with Betty about it. She always seems to know just what to say.

Figure 11.5 A Reflective Journal is a place to think about what has been observed and make plans for future actions.

cognitive, and emotional development. Some factors influence the play to such an extent that generalizations can be made that help the teacher reflect on appropriate teaching practices.

Socioeconomic Differences in Dramatic Play

Smilansky and Shefatya's (1990) observations of the play of economically deprived children give insight into the play of these children. It was more object-centered with the object determining the theme rather than the theme suggesting the object. The objects were used in a more rigid way and were possessed with determination. Verbal interactions were more functional for management and announcement of roles. They rarely took on the "voice" of the role they were playing. The language was more authoritative than democratic. They used less humor, more criticism, aggressiveness, and control in dealing with problems.

Cultural Differences in Dramatic Play

While developmental capacities have individual differences, it is widely held that most are universal. For example, children between two and three all over the world begin to talk. The social and cultural influences on development, attitudes, and dispositions are evident, however, they are even more obvious in dramatic play, especially in the social-emotional realm. Certain cultures do not value fantasy. Those children enter group situations without the desire or skills to interact in this way. Older Mexican-American siblings, however, made expert sociodramatic play partners. In some societies (Russian and East African), fantasy and imaginative play appear to be absent (Johnson, et al., 1987). It is difficult to draw conclusions from limited evidence. The observer should cultivate an awareness so expectations are tempered by the consideration of the many possible factors affecting the development.

Differing Abilities and Dramatic Play

Children with physical challenges participate in all kinds of play in the classroom, including dramatic play. The teacher's role supports a higher level of activity by modifications to the environment.

The adult interprets for the hearing impaired, gives sensory experiences to the visually impaired, and mediates for children with serious learning and behavior problems. The teacher looks for ways that the child with disabilities could participate.

The child with limited vision may need explanations about the nature of the play and suggestions of roles or actions she could contribute.

Children who are hearing impaired will use realistic props to join in the play but may need assistance when the play turns to transformational or representational props. The significance of a rope for a fire hose may not be understood. Children with physical disabilities can use their abilities to join in the play but may need the adult's help. Giving other children ideas about how to involve the child, creating roles for the child, and giving a prop to add to the play are ways that the adult can help (Karnes, 1992.) The application of private speech for children with self-regulatory problems like ADHD is being explored (Berk & Winsler, 1995).

IT HAPPENED TO ME: Empty Eyeglasses

One day in my optometrist's office I offhandedly asked if they ever had any eyeglass frames they could donate to the preschool. They called me in a few weeks with a wonderful collection! These were added to the dramatic play area and at once became favorite props for play. Most of all, they helped all the children relate to a child in the class who wore glasses. It prepared them for that possibility themselves in the future. Sometimes a serendipitous action becomes an important one.

HELPING PROFESSIONALS FOR PLAY CONCERNS

There may be children who exhibit no desire or attention to dramatic play experiences. This does not mean that these children are not creative but this is not an area that interests them. Young children are working out the differences between real and imaginary and become very arbitrary sometimes in only wanting to be involved in the real rather than the pretend, rejecting that as younger behavior. This is usually not a problem, just an observation that one can make from the child's play and interactions with the environment.

On the other hand, there occasionally are some children so caught up in dramatic play and the imaginary world that they lose touch with reality. The causes may be varied, from giftedness in the area of creativity, to escape from a traumatic real-world experience. The observer assesses the range of normal expected behavior, alert to excessive or compulsive behavior that may be a clue of a deeper problem. After observation, documentation, and discussion with the teaching team, the family is consulted for advice and insight. If a referral is made, it may be to one of the psychological professionals such as

psychologist—professional trained in human behavior

psychiatrist—physican specializing in social or emotional disorders

Week 11, Assignment A

MEDIA USE IN DRAMATIC PLAY FOR ALL

Get a signed audio/video/photo release from each child's parent. File the signed release in each child's program file with parent information forms and a copy in each child's portfolio. *If there is no release, or if the parent checked no, place a prominent notation on the file and inform all staff.* Use some alternate method for recording dramatic play or blocks.

Use some type of media to record each child's dramatic play. (Use a checklist to be sure you have recorded every child in the class.)

Audio Tape

Tape record conversations as children are involved in a dramatic play episode.

What to Do with It. Transcribe portions of the tape that are significant, noting that the tape is available in the class file. Place individual notes from transcription in each child's portfolio noting its presence on the overview sheet with the date and your name. Make comments in the appropriate developmental area that it documents, Figure 11.6.

Share what you have heard with parent and child if appropriate: "Mrs. Truax, today when I was observing Dionne's block play, the conversation was so interesting I tape recorded it. Would you like to take it home to listen? I wrote down some of the conversation for Dionne's portfolio on imagination."

"Gretchen, today when you were playing with the Play Doh, you were giving the directions to make spaghetti and singing a song about it. Remember when I turned on the tape recorder? Would you like to hear it? Where did you learn that song? Can you tell me about how your mother makes spaghetti? Maybe she'd bring her pasta machine to school some day and you and she could show us all how to do it."

Photographs

Take photographs of each child as they play, even if no dramatic play is observed. If these are groups playing together, take a sequence of shots for the number of children playing there. For example, if three children are building with blocks, take three pictures as the building progresses. It will not only show the sequence but also will give you a picture for each child's portfolio. Or, you can take one picture and have a number of prints made.

What to Do with It. In each child's portfolio place the photo, the date, and the situation, either on the back or mount the photo on a piece of paper. Make any comments about the child's level of play, conversations heard, interesting points, and questions the play brought up to you.

Note the presence of the photo under dramatic play (or relevant area) on the overview sheet, date, and your name.

Share with the parents and child, if appropriate. Show parents the photo. Perhaps have a bulletin board at first with all the photos displayed: "Children at Work." Discuss the situation of the photo and its significance. Tell the parent and

CREATIVE AND DRAMATIC PLAY		
Documentation	Recorder	Date
Photo Dram Play		*11/20*
Video		*12/22*
RR - Episode includes doctor's office	*MS*	*1/31*

Figure 11.6 Portfolio Overview Example

child it will be in the portfolio and will be given to them at the end of the year.

Videotape

Take a video of the children as they play. Try to get whole segments of play and as much conversation as you can. Include every child in the class in some way on the tape.

What to Do with It. Later that day, or as soon as possible, show the tape to the class. They love to see themselves. You could stop after each segment and ask the children involved to explain what they were doing. Invite the other children to ask questions or make suggestions on how the play could have been different. These discussions could be documented as further evidence of sociodramatic play or language practice.

Show the tape at a parent meeting or have it playing as parents arrive to pick up the children at the end of the day. File the tape in the class file, and add to it later in the year.

As you view the tape, you can use a Class List Log to check the children's appearance and activity on the tape and file that with the tape as a reference.

You can use the tape to analyze areas of development and make notes in the child's portfolio. Refer to the videotape of (date), or use the counter to indicate the position on the tape.

Week 11, Assignment B

RUNNING RECORD IN DRAMATIC PLAY/ BLOCKS OR FREEPLAY FOR GROUP B

Each day this week, select children from group B. Using a Running Record (see Chapter 4), gather a segment of regular play during dramatic play, block play, or free time. On the left column of a sheet of paper, record the child's name, date, your name, and time begun. Follow the child with your recording, telling accurately and descriptively where the child is, what action is taking place, and any conversation in which the child is participating. Just describe without commentary or inferences.

What to Do with It

Later in the day, in the right-hand column of the Running Record, make any comments, explanations, or evaluations of areas of development.

In each child's portfolio, note on the overview sheet the presence of this Record in the area that it most vividly documents, along with the date and your name.

Share the recordings or your observations with the parents and the child, if appropriate, such as: "Mr. Williamson, today when I was observing Jared in the block corner he was counting the floors of the building he made. When I was writing down what he was doing he looked over at me and said, 'Did you get that? I counted to ten.' And he had! He is such a character!" or "Taohou, today when I was writing down what you were working on at the puzzle table, I saw you could put together the Lion King puzzle with your eyes closed! How did you know where to put the pieces?"

File the recordings in the child's portfolio.

Week 11, Assignment C

REFLECTIVE JOURNAL

Respond to the following in your Reflective Journal, kept in a private file at home.

When I think about using media as an observation technique, I wonder about...

It is interesting to watch children in dramatic play. As a child I remember most pretending to be...

My fantasies today involve...

They call it "private speech" when young children do it. I call it "talking to myself." I notice myself doing it most when...

I wonder if it's because...

REFERENCES

American Psychological Association. (1990). Ethical principles of psychologists (amended June 2, 1989). *American Psychologist,* 390–395.

Beaty, J. (1994). *Observing development of the young child* (3rd ed.). New York: Merrill, an imprint of Macmillan Publishing Company.

Berk, L. E. (1994). Vygotsky's theory: The importance of make-believe play. *Young Children (50),* (1), 30–39.

Berk, L. E. & Winsler, A. (1995). *Scaffolding children's learning: Vygotsky and early childhood education.* Washington, DC: National Association for the Education of Young Children.

Carlsson-Paige, N. & Levin, D. (1990). *Who's calling the shots? How to respond effectively to children's war play and war toys.* Philadelphia: New Society Publishers.

Cherry, C. (1976). *Creative play for the developing child: Early childhood education through play.* Belmont, CA: Fearon Pitman Publishers.

Curry, N. (1992). Four- and five-year-olds: Intuitive, imaginative players. In V. Dimidjian, (Ed.), *Play's place in public education for young children.* Washington: National Education Association of the United States, pp. 37–48.

Curry, N. & Arnaud, S. (1995). Personality difficulties in preschool children as revealed through play themes and styles. *Young Children 50,* (4), 4–9.

Donnerstein, E., Slaby, R. G., & Eron, L. (1994). The mass media and young aggression. In L. D. Eron, J. H. Gentry, & P. Schlegel, (Eds.) *Reason to hope: A psychosocial persepctive on violence and youth.* Washington, DC: American Psychological Association.

Fein, G. G. & Kinney, P. (1994). He's a nice alligator: Observations on the effective organization of pretence. In A. Slad, & D. P. Wolf (Eds.). *Children at play: Clinical and developmental approaches to meaning and representation.* New York: Oxford University Press.

Herr, J. & Libby, Y. (1995). *Creative resources for the early childhood classroom.* Albany, NY: Delmar Publishers.

Holzberg, C. (1993). Roll 'Em: Camcorders & VCR's for education. *Electronic Learning, 88,* 12.

Isenberg, J. & Jalongo, M. (1993). *Creative expression and play in the early childhood curriculum.* New York: Merrill, an imprint of Macmillan Publishing Company.

Johnson, M. E., Christie, J. F., & Yawkey, T. D. (1987). *Play and early childhood development.* New York: Harper Collins Publishers.

Karnes, M. (1992). Dramatic play and children with special needs. *Pre-K Today, 7* (2), 72.

Katz, L. & Chard, S. (1989). *Engaging Children's Minds: The Project Approach.* Norwood, NJ: Ablex Publishing Corporation.

Negroponte, N. (1995). *Being digital.* New York: Alfred A. Knopf, Inc.

Peterson, R. & Felton-Collins, V. (1986). *The Piaget Handbook for Teachers and Parents.* New York: Teachers College Press.

Poor, F. (personal communication), December 26, 1995. Web site address: fpoor@PoorHouse.Lexington.Ma.US

Singer, D. G. & Singer, J. L. (1990). *The house of make-believe: Children's play and the developing imagination.* Cambridge, MA: Harvard University Press.

Slaby, R., Roedell, W., Arezzo, D., & Hendrix, K. (1995). *Early violence prevention: Tools for teachers of young children.* Washington: National Association for the Education of Young Children.

Smilansky, S. & Shefatya, L. (1990). *Facilitating play: A medium for promoting cognitive, socio-emotional and academic development in young children.* Gaithersburg, MD: Psychosocial & Educational Publications.

Wood, D., McMahon, L., & Cranstoun, Y. (1980). *Working with under fives.* Ypsilanti, MI: High/Scope.

RESOURCES

Carlsson-Paige, N. & Levin, D. (1990). *Who's calling the shots? How to respond effectively to children's war play and war toys.* Philadelphia: New Society Publishers.

Paley, V. G. (1984). *Boys and girls: Superheroes in the doll corner.* Chicago: University of Chicago Press.

Paley, V. G. (1988). *Bad guys don't have birthdays.* Chicago: University of Chicago Press.

Slaby, R., Roedell, W., Arezzo, D., & Hendrix, K. (1995). *Early violence prevention: Tools for teachers of young children.* Washington: National Association for the Education of Young Children.

Using Documentation for Child Abuse Suspicions and Looking at Self-Concept

IN THIS CHAPTER

✔ Using Documentation for Child Abuse Suspicions

✔ Topics in Observation: Dealing with Parents Suspected of Child Maltreatment

✔ Special Populations and Child Abuse

✔ Self-Concept and Self-Esteem

✔ Special Populations and Self-Esteem

✔ Helping Professionals for Child Abuse and Self-Esteem Concerns

USING DOCUMENTATION FOR CHILD ABUSE SUSPICIONS

Observing children in group settings is not always a pleasant experience. The observer of children has a grave responsibility to fulfill in recognizing and reporting signs of abuse or neglect. This section is one that everyone wishes would not be necessary but child abuse is a reality. There are people who hurt children physically, psychologically, or use children for sexual purposes.

Neglect is characterized by failure to provide for the child's basic needs, which include physical, medical, educational, and emotional. A form of neglect for infants and young children is organic failure to thrive, caused by physiological problems, or nonorganic, due to nourishment. **Physical abuse** includes any nonaccidental injury caused by the child's caregiver, intentional, or nonintentional. **Sexual abuse** includes a wide range of behavior, including exploitation through prostitution or pornography. **Emotional maltreatment** is psychological or emotional abuse through blaming, belittling, or rejecting a child.

As the teacher interacts with children, they win the child's trust. They have the opportunity to see and hear what children do and talk about the experiences they have had. They may be the one who prevents neglect or abuse from happening again. People who abuse children need help, and the child needs help. Not reporting suspected abuse allows it to continue.

Physical and Behavioral Indicators of Abuse

Teachers and child care workers must be familiar with the physical and behavioral indicators of abuse. Indicators may give very clear evidence of maltreatment, but they also may have other explanations. Some may result from the personality of the child, a new setting with new adults, poverty, different cultural values, accidents, or illnesses. Judgment must be used, but for the protection of the child it is better to report those suspicions.

Reasonable Cause to Suspect. The suspicion of child abuse or neglect grows from visual observations, verbal disclosures, or an accumulation of circumstances that build to a reasonable cause to suspect. This does not place the reporter in the position of investigator, interrogator, or prosecutor, but just giving an initial alert based on factual observations, Figure 12.1.

The child's appearance. For infants and preverbal children, abuse and maltreatment can be observed in the normal routines of being with the child. By the location and formation of bruises, cuts and inflammations, concerns are raised. Obvious wounds are usually met by a teacher's empathetic comments, such as "Ooo, that bruise looks sore," or interested questions of verbal children such as, "Why are you walking like that? Does something hurt?" The child's response may be a first-hand account of what happened, a **disclosure** statement.

The child's description or disclosure. The child may say, "My daddy twisted my arm," or "Uncle John hurt me in my goo goo." Comments like these always catch teachers by surprise but it is important that facial or verbal expressions not reveal the shock, revulsion, or disapproval of what has happened to this child, Figure 12.2. An appropriate response is, "Can you tell me what happened?" This expresses concern while gently probing for more details. These disclosures call for immediate action and documentation. Besharov (1990) in *Recognizing Child Abuse* stresses that once a mandated reporter has "reasonable cause," probing for all the details is not necessary. In fact, detailed probing may actually place the child in greater jeopardy. The questions should be asked only to answer the question in the reporter's mind: "Do I know enough to *suspect* that this injury or behavior could have been caused by abuse or neglect?" To probe further will inevitably compromise later interviews of the child by child protective authorities. When children must repeat their story to different adults, they may leave out information to protect a loved one. They may recant their story for fear of the consequences, or add untrue details to be more believed. This detailed interviewing is best left to the authorities. Besharov emphasizes, however, that if the child willingly offers and needs to talk about it, by all means be a ready *listener,* and then accurately document questions and comments by both the child and adult.

Beskharov recommends if the child willingly offers and needs to talk about it, by all means be a ready listener, (see figure 12.3 on page 240). Conduct the interview in private. Sit next to the child, not across the table or desk. Ask the child to clarify words or terms that you do not understand. Be supportive; the child is likely to be frightened about telling "family secrets." Stress that anything that happened was not the child's fault (p. 59).

Circumstantial evidence. Suspicious injuries may suggest child abuse or maltreatment. Children's explanations are often protective statements. Behavioral indications by themselves are not sufficient basis for a report, but in combination or continued appearance should be documented and discussed with a supervisor.

Recording Any Indicators of Maltreatment

The most appropriate method for recording episodes that document suspected abuse or maltreatment is the Anecdotal Record. It is effective for this information because the accounts

- are written shortly after the episode or event occurs, based on notes jotted at the time
- contain a detailed account, including date and time, people involved in the episode, actions, and exact conversations. This is especially important in situations in which a child reveals to a teacher that someone is hurting him or her. The questions and comments that the adult says must be accurately recorded also. This indicates that the child was not led or influenced in the description of the event
- contain separate comments by the recorder, such as opinions or questions, from the body of the recording

In addition to the narrative, diagrams and specific descriptions of size and nature of wounds should be made. Explanations or conjecture about their cause should be separate from the diagram.

Some states allow the taking of photographs by mandated reporters, but this should be confirmed in the recorder's state. In most cases, however, photographs taken by those other than the authorities are unnecessary and may be very inappropriate. Photographs by authorized persons are considered to be evidence and can be used as such only under controlled conditions. This is best left to child protection, law enforcement, or medical authorities. Further trauma may be added to the child by photographing the injuries. For many sexually abused children, being photographed may be a part of their history of abuse. In any event, photographs, should they be taken, must be turned over to the authorities immediately. *The accurate recording and prompt reporting of suspected child abuse and maltreatment cannot be stressed enough.*

Type of Abuse/ Maltreatment	Physical Indicators	Child Behavioral Indicators	Parental Behavioral Indicators
Physical Abuse	* unexplained or inadequately explained bruises, welts, burns, lacerations, abrasions or fractures. * frequent injuries that are "accidental" or "unexplained". * patterned, reflecting shape of article used to inflict injury (e.g., elec. cord, belt buckle). * bilateral (both sides of body) or on several different surfaces. * regularly appearing after absence, weekend, vacation, etc. * in various stages of healing. * human bite marks: <3cm. between canines.	* reports injury by parents. * exhibits behavioral extremes: aggressive, demanding, destructive or shy, withdrawn, compliant, passive. * frequently late or absent from school or comes too early and/or stays late. * wary of adult contacts. * seems frightened of parents. * wears long-sleeved or similar clothing to hide injuries. * afraid to go home or shows little distress at being separated from parents. * seeks affection from any adult.	* seems unconcerned about child. * takes an unusual amount of time to obtain medical care for the child. * offers an inadequate or inappropriate explanation for the child's injury. * gives different explanations for the same injury. * misuses drugs or alcohol. * disciplines the child too harshly considering the child's age or what he/she did wrong. * sees the child as bad or evil. * has history of abuse as a child. * attempts to conceal the child's injury. * takes the child to a different doctor or hospital for each injury.
Neglect	* frequently hungry, inappropriately dressed for the weather, and/or has poor hygiene. * consistently left alone or inadequately supervised for long periods of time or in dangerous circumstances. * often tired or listless. * needs medical/dental care. * has been abandoned. * being exposed to unsafe living conditions.	* frequently late or absent from school or comes too early and/or stays late. * begs or steals food. * constantly falls asleep in school. * exhibits delinquent behavior; used alcohol or drugs, engages in vandalism or sexual misconduct. * states there is no parent or caretaker. * excessive responsibility for younger siblings.	* misuses alcohol or drugs. * has disorganized, upsetting home life. * is apathetic, feels nothing will change. * is isolated from friends, relatives, neighbors. * has long-term, chronic illness. * cannot be found. * has history of neglect as a child.
Sexual Abuse	* somatic problems (ulcers, migraines, etc.). * has difficulty in walking or sitting. * has torn, stained, or bloody underclothing. * experiences pain or itching in genital area. * has venereal disease (especially in pre-teens). * is pregnant * weight gain/loss. * problems with hygiene.	* poor self-esteem, peer relationships. * is unwilling to participate in physical activities or change clothes for gym. * appears withdrawn, fantasy or infantile behavior, depressed or suicidal. * fear of physical contact. * is engaging in delinquent acts or runs away. * reports sexual assault by parent or caretaker. * change in affect or body language when particular adult is discussed. * sexually acting out/seductive; excessive sexual knowledge. * academic problems, difficulty concentrating.	* role reversal, blurred boundaries. * very protective, jealous, or controlling. * encourages child to engage in prostitution or sexual acts in the presence of caretaker. * misuses alcohol or other drugs. * older siblings leaving home at early age. * history of sexual abuse. * low self-esteem. * socially isolated. * incapacitated mother. * reunited with estranged parent.
Emotional Neglect	* habit disorders (sucking, biting, rocking, etc.) * eating disorders. * physically underdeveloped. * neurotic traits (sleep disorders, speech disorders, inhibition of play). * psychoneurotic reactions (hysteria, obsessions, compulsion, phobias, hypochondria).	* poor self-image. * exhibits behavioral extremes: aggressive, demanding, or compliant, shy, passive. * is overly adaptive, either inappropriately adult or infantile. * exhibits physical, mental or emotional developmental lags. * attempts suicide, self-destructive. * substance abuse. * poor social skills, low frustration intolerance, academic dysfunction.	* poor self-image. * treats children in the family unequally. * doesn't seem to care much about child's problems. * blames or belittles child. * is cold and rejecting. * withholds love. * unrealistic expectations. * substance abuse.

NOTE: Some behavioral indicators may be common to all children at one time. When indicators are noticeable in a sufficient number and strength to characterize a child's overall manner, they may indicate abuse or neglect.

Figure 12.1 Child Abuse and Maltreatment Indicators. (Courtesy of New York State Department of Social Services, 1995. *Child Protective Services, Mandated Reporter Manual.* Reprinted with permission.)

As responders it is critical that we be sensitive to issues of poverty and neglect, differing cultural expectations and values, and differing child rearing practices. The outline below should assist you in understanding the minimal standards of care to be expected as well as considerations of poverty, cultural influences, and differing practices.

GUIDELINES/MINIMAL STANDARDS OF CARE

	Expectations	Considerations
Supervision	* Young children are not left unattended. * Children are not left in the care of siblings who are too young to provide adequate care. * Children are not left with adult caregivers who are inadequate or unsafe.	* Did the parent/sitter abandon the children? * Are siblings, left to care for younger children, able and responsible? * Are there other child care options available to the parent(s)?
Clothing and Hygiene	* Children are dressed adequately and appropriately for the weather. * Babies and toddlers don't chronically suffer severe diaper rash, or other persistent skin disorders resulting from poor hygiene. * Children are not chronically dirty or unbathed.	* Is too small, clean clothing okay? * Has the child lost his/her winter coat? * It is "fashionable" from the child's point of view to wear sneakers even in the rain and snow? * Children playing in snow or outside find it difficult to stay dry and clean. * Are they bathed before they go to bed? Are they encouraged to "wash up" for meals?
Medical and Dental Care	* Children who are ill should be receiving proper medical care. * Children should be seen by the dentist and should have proper eye care.	* Are "free" clinics available? * Does the parent know where the clinic is? * Can they afford the appropriate, adequate medical, dental, and eye care?
Education	* Children should attend school on a regular basis. * Older children should not be kept at home to care for younger siblings.	* Are older children needed as interpreters by parents when they go to seek help or services from public and/or private agencies? * Are there ill children/adults home needing care?
Nutrition	* Children should have a sufficient quantity and good quality food. * Children should not continually complain of being hungry. * Severe developmental lags are sometimes indicators of poor nutrition.	* Be aware of poverty factors, as well as cultural factors in terms of what is considered a nutritious meal. * Does parent know how to use food stamps properly? * Does parent know what nutritious meals consist of? * Are children allergic to certain foods?
Adequate Shelter	* Housing should be structurally safe and free of exposed wiring. * There should be adequate heat. * The house should be clean and sanitary.	* Is the landlord/owner of the housing providing proper services?

Figure 12.1 (Continued.)

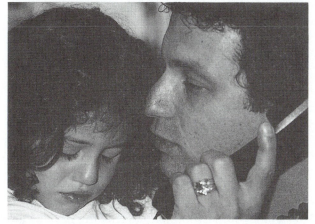

Figure 12.2 Teachers must give close attention to the child's physical appearance and explanations of bruises.

Next Steps

Immediate notification of the supervisor is the first step. Short, accurate notes made as soon as possible preserve vital details. The Hotline should be called immediately either by the supervisor or witness, depending on the policies and procedures already in place in the program. The local agency may be called to confer if indeed there is enough suspicion to file a Hotline report. The exception to this is if there is suspicion of sexual abuse or the life of the child is in danger. In that case, the law enforcement agency should be called *immediately*. If for some reason the supervisor does not make the call and the teacher has "reason to suspect" there has been possible abuse, then there is a legal and moral responsibility to make the call.

When Talking with the Child
DO:
- Make sure the ECE professional is someone the child knows and trusts.
- Conduct the discussion in a place that allows for privacy but is familiar to the child.
- Use only one or two ECE professionals.
- Sit next to the child at his/her level.
- Engage the child in a conversation but do not press the child to talk about the injuries if he/she does not want to.
- Ask the child to clarify words or terms that are not understood.
* Assure the child that he/she has done nothing wrong.
- _____
- _____

DO NOT:
- Suggest answers to the child.
- Probe or press for answers the child does not willingly offer.
- Force the child to remove clothing.
- Display horror, shock, or disapproval of the parent(s), child, or situation.
- Leave the child alone with a stranger.
- Ask "why" questions.
- _____
- _____

When Talking with the Parent(s)
DO:
- Select the person most appropriate to the situation.
- Conduct the discussion in private.
- Tell the parent(s) why the discussion is taking place.
- Be direct, honest, and professional.
- Reassure parent(s) of the program's support to them and to their child.
- Tell the parent(s) if a report was made or will be made.
- Advise the parent(s) of the program's legal and ethical responsibilities to report.
- _____
- _____

DO NOT:
- Try to prove the abuse or neglect; that is not an ECE professional's role.
- Display horror, anger, or disapproval of the parent(s), child, or situation.
- Pry into family matters unrelated to the specific situation.
- Place blame or make judgments about the parent(s) or child.
- _____
- _____

Figure 12.3 Tips for Talking With a Child or Parent. (Reprinted from *Caregivers of Young Children: Preventing and Responding to Child Maltreatment,* 1992, p. 24. U. S. Department of Health and Human Services.)

Legal Process of Reporting. Individual states vary in the definitions of child maltreatment but most include nonaccidental physical abuse, neglect, sexual abuse, and emotional (or mental) maltreatment by a person responsible for the child's welfare.

Exercise: According to the laws in your state, reportable child abuse is defined as what?

Every state has laws for reporting child abuse and a reporting number, many of which are 1-800, toll-free telephone calls. School personnel and day care and child care workers are **mandated reporters** by law in every state. A mandated reporter must report any "reasonable cause to suspect" a child has been maltreated. Not reporting suspected neglect or abuse could result in legal action. Reporters of suspected abuse are not responsible for proving the abuse, just to present the observable facts that led to the suspicions. If the report is **unfounded**—no evidence to prove it—the reporter is protected from civil action.

Exercise: Locate the Hotline or reporting number for child care workers in your state. Find the state and local agency and telephone number to whom you could ask questions. Write them on a separate sheet of paper.

    Reporting telephone number
    Agency and telephone number

When the Hotline or Law Enforcement Agency Is Called. The reporter will be asked to supply as much of the following information as possible. The lack of complete information *does not* prohibit a report from being made:

- the name and address of the child and his or her parents or legally responsible guardian
- the child's age, sex, and race
- the nature and extent of the child's injuries, abuse, or maltreatment (including any evidence of prior injuries, abuse, or maltreatment to the child or his or her siblings)
- the child's present location
- the name of the person or persons responsible for causing the injury, abuse, or maltreatment
- family composition; others residing in or at the home in regular intervals
- person making the report, where the person can be reached, and where the information was

obtained; names of other relevant school personnel who may provide critical information

- any action taken by the reporting source
- any additional information that may be helpful[1]

Though suspicions of abuse or neglect seem obvious by the very act of calling the Hotline, they must hear the reporter's concerns in those terms; "I believe this child to be abused or neglected because..." The report is strengthened if the reporter can

1. detail a pattern (not that a mother was overheard screaming at her child once, but this is how she interacts with her child routinely), *and*
2. state the impact on the child (e.g., behavioral signs, the child is doing poorly in school, and so on).

Needless to say, one would not wait for a pattern of injuries before alerting the authorities. If troublesome behavior by the parent and/or the child, though not reportable, has been observed, that information may be helpful to set a framework for the report to the Hotline. Documentation of these earlier concerns should be recorded in the style of an Anecdotal Recording and kept in a confidential file.

Once the call is made, the written Report of Suspected Child Abuse or Maltreatment should be completed and filed according to the directions in the state, Figure 12.4. A copy is kept in a confidential file, separate from the child's portfolio and separate from the class file, along with any written records referring to these suspicions. For the reporter's own use, a log should be kept of the time of the incident and the witness's exact response (writing anecdotal, reporting to supervisor, action taken). Additions to the log should be made as each step in the process occurs ("Made out written report, date," "answered questions by..."). This should be kept in the reporter's possession.

Do not discuss suspicions with the parents or the child. This is the one time when what was observed should not be discussed with parents or the child after the initial disclosure. The authorities should be allowed to take further action.

If the parent comes to school and asks who made the report, they should be referred to the supervisor. Parents should always be treated respectfully and tactfully. When they know a report has been made, they can be referred to the *Parent Handbook* where it states the policy of the program and the legal responsibility of mandated reporters. They are offered assistance to seek help and given referrals to agencies and support groups

in their area. The parents may be angry and abusive, but the child's safety is of the utmost consideration. Arguing and relating details to the parents are inappropriate actions. Supervisors may make a statement such as, "We have observed something that made us suspect the child may be abused and we have a legal obligation to report that suspicion. We have done what we think is best for the child. We stand ready to help in whatever way we can." That is all one needs to say, and all one should say, perhaps even *more* than one should say. It all depends on the circumstances.

SPECIAL POPULATIONS AND CHILD ABUSE

Child-rearing customs and practices are not standard between any two families, but even more varied because of racial, cultural, economic, and religious differences. Sometimes these come in conflict with the mainstream practices, and in the case of child abuse, with the legal system. This issue faces people who work with children and families. It is shocking to read child abuse statistics and think about the hurt each statistic represents.

Cultural Differences

Children of families of many cultures are participating in educational experiences. Sensitivity to cultures whose values and customs are different from one's own is an important trait in early childhood professionals. Child rearing has distinctive differences in various cultures concerning obedience, punishment, dependency, and eye contact. Open discussions about child rearing will help teachers gain an understanding of other cultures and ethnic groups. The responsibility of the teacher, however, is still to report child abuse and neglect as defined by the state regulations.

Different Abilities

Children with developmental disabilities are also victims of abuse, with some indications that it occurs at higher rates than in the regular population. They are often perceived as an "easy target" with limited defenses or protection. Observation of abuse is even more critical for children with disabilities because they may lack the verbal, physical, or mental skills to protect themselves or disclose what has been happening. The same criteria for signs of abuse are used for children with different abilities, physical, sexual, emotional, or neglect. Any questions that need to be asked

DSS-2221-A (REV. 9/91)

REPORT OF SUSPECTED
CHILD ABUSE OR MALTREATMENT

NEW YORK STATE   DEPARTMENT OF SOCIAL SERVICES

| ORAL RPT. DATE | STATE REGISTRY NO. | LOCAL REGISTRY NO. |
| TIME   AM PM | LOCAL CASE NO. | LOCAL AGENCY |

Subjects of Report

List all children in household, adults responsible for household, and alleged perpetrators.

Line No.	Last Name	First Name	M.I.	Aliases	Sex (M, F, Unk.)	Birthdate or Age — Mo.	Day	Yr.	Ethnic Code (* Over)	Susp. or Relation. Code (** Over)	Check (✓) if Alleged Perpetrator
1											
2											
3											
4											
5											
6											
7											

■ MORE

LIST ADDRESSES AND TELEPHONE NUMBERS:
HOUSEHOLD   TELEPHONE NO.

OTHERS
(Give Line Nos.)   TELEPHONE NO.

                                                                         TELEPHONE NO.

Basis of Suspicions

Alleged consequences or evidence of abuse or maltreatment - Give child(ren)'s line number(s). If all children, write "All".

_____ DOA/Fatality   _____ Child's Drug/Alcohol Use   _____ Educational Neglect
_____ Fractures   _____ Drug Withdrawal   _____ Emotional Neglect
_____ Subdural Hematoma, Internal Injuries _____ Lack of Medical Care   _____ Lack of Food, Clothing, Shelter
_____ Lacerations, Bruises, Welts   _____ Malnutrition, Failure to Thrive _____ Lack of Supervision
_____ Burns, Scalding   _____ Sexual Abuse   _____ Abandonment
_____ Excessive Corporal Punishment   _____ Other, specify :_____

State reasons for suspicion. Include the nature and extent of each child's injuries, abuse or maltreatment, any evidence of prior injuries, abuse or maltreatment to the child or his siblings and any evidence or suspicions of "Parental" behavior contributing to the problem.

(If known, give time and date of alleged incident):
Mo. Day Yr.
___|___|___   ■ PM
                Time _____ ■ AM

Sources of This Report

PERSON MAKING THIS REPORT		SOURCE OF THIS REPORT IF DIFFERENT	
NAME	TELEPHONE NO.	NAME	TELEPHONE NO.
ADDRESS		ADDRESS	
AGENCY/INSTITUTION		AGENCY/INSTITUTION	

Relationship (✓ for Reporter, X for Source)

■ Med. Exam./Coroner   ■ Physician   ■ Hospital Staff   ■ Law Enforcement ■ Neighbor   ■ Relative
■ Social Services   ■ Public Health ■ Mental Health   ■ School Staff   ■ Other (specify) _____

| For Use By Physicians Only | Medical Diagnosis on Child | Signature of Physician Who Examined/Treated Child X | Telephone No. |

Hospitalization Required: 0 ■ None   1 ■ Under One Week   2 ■ One - Two Weeks   3 ■ Over Two Weeks

Actions Taken or
About To Be Taken: 0 ■ Medical Exam   2 ■ X-Ray   4 ■ Removal/Keeping   6 ■ Not. Med. Exam./Coroner
                     1 ■ Photographs   3 ■ Hospitalization   5 ■ Returned Home   7 ■ Notified D.A.

| Signature of Person Making This Report   X | Title | Date Submitted Mo. Day Yr. |

Figure 12.4 New York State Child Abuse Report

TOPICS IN OBSERVATION: Dealing with Parents Suspected of Child Maltreatment

It needs to be said here that discussions with parents about their relationship and treatment of their child is an ongoing dialogue between teachers and families. That basic partnership relationship that has been emphasized throughout this text is never more important than in this section. Whether we feel the parents just do not know about good hygiene, appropriate discipline techniques or are deliberately hurting or neglecting their child to the point of placing them in danger, our position is the same. It is one of advocacy for the child and support and assistance to the family. Look again at the Ecological View of the Child from the Teacher's Viewpoint (Figure I.1). While viewing the child in the cold with no socks or boots, or with a nasty bruise the shape of an adult hand, think again of the surrounding factors. This is not to make excuses but to try to understand the context in which the family lives.

The difference between sympathy, feeling sorry for the child and family, and empathy is doing something about it. In cases where it seems that the child does not have the necessities for health and comfort, such as adequate clothing or food, the teacher's first response is not to report the family to the Hotline but to try to supply the need, if there truly is one. It takes all the tact and caring one can muster to determine if the child does not have a coat or just will not wear one. Then the next step may be some work with the family on parenting skills to help the parent take the responsibility for enforcing basic needs, Figure 12.5.

Even in cases in which reports must be made for the health and protection of the child, an

Figure 12.5 The partnership attitude of teacher and parent is never more important than when maltreatment is suspected.

attitude of empathy for the family still must prevail. The teacher tries not to see the parents as ogres or monsters but people who themselves are so needy or uninformed that these actions are really reactions to their own condition. The reporting then is not "tattling" but an assistance to the family to get the help they all need, as well as protecting the child from harm. This can be communicated again and again to the family but is even more evident by actions that support the family with physical acts of kindness, such as rides to appointments, a home-baked loaf of bread, or a phone call just to see how they are doing.

The teacher is an instrument of change in lives not only of the children in the class but their families. That is an awesome responsibility.

should be simple, concrete who, what, when, but *not* why. Drawings, dolls, or a sign interpreter may help the child express the details they want to disclose (Baladerian, 1993). Remember, the observer need not gather all the evidence. All that is needed for a report to try to protect the child is "reason to suspect." Child Protective Services personnel will take the next steps.

SELF-CONCEPT AND SELF-ESTEEM

Where does the development of **self-concept** begin? This book began the review of child development with attachment and separation. The circle is complete, coming back to that same important connection to self-concept and self-esteem. Whether it is parent and child, family and program, or new concepts and established schemata,

This section was prepared with the help of Jean Rose-Klein, Coordinator of the Broome County Child Abuse Council, Binghamton, NY.

relationships and connections are what it is all about. The development of healthy **self-esteem** is dependent on certain kinds of relationships. This chapter explores the contributing factors to the development of self-esteem, the stages of the development of a sense of self, and how it can be observed in the classroom. Parents and teachers are major influences on self-concept, with the goal of helping the child have high self-esteem based on a truthful vision of the self.

Self-concept resides in the cognitive, what one knows about oneself in many different areas. Physical appearance and ability is very important in American culture with millions spent on products, clothing, and exercise machines and clubs to improve that appearance. Sports figures are idols because they can jump, throw, catch, or move with outstanding coordination and skill. People measure themselves against others in appearance and physical ability.

Humans are social beings and crave approval, so interactions with other people profoundly affect how people perceive themselves. Connected to that social dimension is the emotional or affective side where feelings sometimes overrule what one knows to be true. One's ability to function mentally affects not only educational achievements but life's decision-making, possibly affecting economic status, which also has an effect on the perception of self. All of these parts contribute to one's self-perception, Figure 12.6.

Assessing these areas objectively is the self-concept, what one knows about oneself. It is not, however, simply a matter of assessing those areas. Another dimension enters in, the affective domain, the emotions. For example, a person may know their weight is in the range of normal on the charts (self-concept) but feel they are too heavy. They feel fat and not good about themselves (self-esteem). It may not be a true measurement but it is how the person perceives herself. It may be reflected from the appraisal of other people.

Exercise: Think about yourself in each of these areas, Figure 12.7. In the left column, write three words or phrases that you *know* about yourself in this category. In the right column, write three words or phrases about how you *feel* about yourself in this area.

Here is the tricky part, the dichotomy as Curry and Johnson (1990) call it, the division or two sides to the issue. They say, "Dichotomous thinking is also evident in the idea that good feelings about

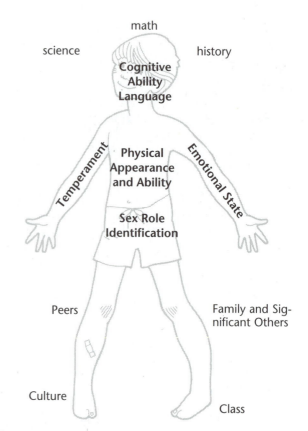

Figure 12.6 The Perception of the Whole Self

the self are always healthy, whereas bad self-feelings are to be avoided. But good feelings about the self can be self-deceptive and narcissistic (excessive pride)" (p. 4). For example, is it always desirable to have high self-esteem?

- High self-esteem about physical appearance is attained when a person finally diets down to 86 pounds?
- High self-esteem in sexual prowess when a man brags he has fathered 12 children by 12 different women?
- High self-esteem in cognitive ability because a person has memorized the phone book?
- High self-esteem in peer acceptance when a high school student gets a 20 on a math quiz because "Dumb is cool"?
- High self-esteem in economic status is proven by lighting a cigarette with a twenty-dollar bill?

Feeling good about oneself is only desirable when abilities are accurately assessed, not based on skewed thinking or misplaced values. For example, is low self-esteem always harmful?

- When low self-esteem about physical appearance prods millions of people into diets and exercise programs?

- When low self-esteem from a social encounter shames one into an apology for saying that unkind, hurtful remark?
- When low self-esteem over educational achievement motivates work on a high school equivalency diploma then on to a college degree?

Describe what you *know* you are like in these areas.	Describe what you *feel* you are like in these areas.
COGNITIVE	
Language	
History	
Math	
Science	
PHYSICAL	
Appearance	
Abilities	
Sex role	
SOCIAL	
Significant others, including family	
Peers	
Culture	
Socioeconomic status	
EMOTIONAL	
Temperament	
Emotional state	

Adapted from Shalveson in Owens (1993) and Lively (1991)

Figure 12.7 Self-Concept and Self-Esteem Worksheet

- When low self-esteem over computer phobia prompts a person to enroll in a computer workshop?
- When low self-esteem over cultural ignorance encourages one to attend a concert of multicultural music?

Low self-esteem based on low self-concept, knowing one's shortcomings or inadequacies, brings about action, then low self-esteem "can be constructive and energizing" (Curry & Johnson, 1990, p. 4). Low self-esteem, as a motivator, can raise self-concept and self-esteem.

Well-meaning people giving indiscriminate praise for the purpose of raising self-esteem can actually have the opposite effect. Insincerity, whether expressed to a child or adult, is not believed and tends to be dismissed. When one knows or feels the praise is undeserved it does not raise self-esteem. If the perception, or self-esteem, is higher than the actual ability, a false pride is present that may prevent future work on this area. This image of self is important to everyone for it directly affects the motivation to change and learn.

Exercise: Now look back at those words you wrote in the previous exercise. Where you see low self-esteem, let it be the motivator for a plan. Work to raise the competency, then the self-concept, then the self-esteem: self-improvement plan!

Development of Self-Esteem

Development, the progression from simple to complex over a period of time in sequential stages but at individual times, applies to both self-concept and self-esteem, Figure 12.8.

The First Year. The newborn infant is not aware of separateness from the environment. Actions are merely reflexes to stimuli. There is no recognition of self in the mirror, no recognition of people in his life. Between two and four months, the infant still has no concept of being separate. Now, however, needs are expressed in signals the family comes to understand. Coos and smiles appear as responses back to those people who are cooing and smiling. The child begins to reach toward that image seen in the mirror because it may be something to touch and handle. No, it is just something cold and flat that cannot be put in the mouth to be explored.

By the end of the first year, the knowledge of separateness is attained. The infant now knows he is separate from the people around him and the

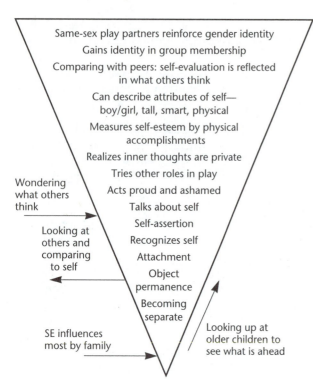

Same-sex play partners reinforce gender identity

Gains identity in group membership

Comparing with peers: self-evaluation is reflected in what others think

Can describe attributes of self— boy/girl, tall, smart, physical

Measures self-esteem by physical accomplishments

Realizes inner thoughts are private

Tries other roles in play

Acts proud and ashamed

Talks about self

Self-assertion

Recognizes self

Attachment

Object permanence

Becoming separate

Wondering what others think

Looking at others and comparing to self

SE influences most by family

Looking up at older children to see what is ahead

Figure 12.8 Self-Concept Development

physical environment. Important people still magically appear and disappear (object permanence). Attempts to keep them present with smiles and sounds work only temporarily. They go away, perhaps never to return. The new mobility of the one-year-old allows the child to go look for those disappearing objects. The knowledge is there that they exist somewhere. If the legs could only support the body, they could be found. The baby reaches for the baby in the mirror. When a toy is seen in the mirror, the baby reaches to the mirror to grab it. The long journey of individuation has begun, "the process by which the self or personal identity is developed and one's individual place in the social order is acquired" (Kostelnik, et al., 1993, p. 35).

During infancy and toddler ages, the child's self-concept is primarily influenced by the family and those closest to the child. Information is received about being "good," "cute," "lovable," "capable," "smart," and "accepted." This forms the child's ideas about identity and capability.

The Second Year. After walking is mastered, the toddler practices becoming more separate. They now take journeys away and come back, farther away, and back again. The toddler is checking each time that a return is possible if necessary. Trust is building that the person will be there when she needs her. Toward the second birthday, if a dot

is placed on the child's nose and shown in the mirror, the toddler reaches not to the mirror but to the nose to take it off. Ah, the emergence of self!

Words are multiplying and some important ones that show an increasing sense of self are "me," "mine," "me do it," "NO." The child displays great pride when attempts to do a task end in success. If efforts fail, the child expresses disappointment. If scolded, the child shows shame. Sometimes a tantrum erupts when the emotions are so strong they cannot be controlled. It may bring embarrassment or a feeling of unworthiness from those the child knows best. Everyone has witnessed or felt helpless when a child throws a tantrum if his wants are not fulfilled. The child is really helpless also, unable to control these strong emotions.

Older Preschoolers. In the preschool years, children talk about being a boy or a girl, how old they are, how big they are, and what toys they have. Toward kindergarten age, they begin to remember the dreams they had last night and they can talk about their thinking. They are beginning to realize their thoughts are part of a private self. No one else can see or know their thoughts unless they are revealed. They used to play with brooms to sweep and trucks to dump, then those brooms became horses and trucks were spaceships. Now they play with their friends in elaborate scenarios in which they leave themselves behind and become other people, talking with other people's words and voices and gestures, doing what grown-ups do. They constantly read their playmates faces to look for acceptance. The teacher's words are carefully weighed against what they know they really can do. They are beginning to worry about what others will think of them.

Confronted with many new tasks to try, encouragement and approval of the attempts bring pleasant feelings of competence. This gives motivation to try the next new challenge, expending effort with the confidence of past successes. Success brings more success and even risks at failure. The overall feeling of well-earned, high self-esteem will emerge.

Another child may try as well at all those new things, drawing a circle, tying his shoe, naming his colors. But he is reminded his circle is not round. His shoe does not stay tied. This color is red not green. His attempts at other tasks he is working on may not even be noticed. When he tries again, he feels anxiety because he does not really think he can do it. He could not do it before. Maybe he will not even try or he will try but not very hard, then he will not be disappointed when he cannot do it. He looks to see who is watching but no one is, so he does not even try. Someone comes along and says he did it perfectly and wonderfully but he knows they are wrong. Even when he tries and it works, he believes it was just an accident. He really did not cause it to work. The child's feeling of incompetence is reinforced by powerful adults, such as parents and teachers, that causes a decline in motivation, willingness to try or risk, and results in lowered self-esteem. This is the beginning of the cycle of failure many children experience in school.

The social comparisons of this age are limited to the child's estimation of performance, mainly physical. They have come so far and can now do so many tasks that they could not do in toddlerhood, still a strong memory. They compare themselves to those big seven-year-olds who can ride a two-wheeler. Because of the successes of the past, they have no doubt they will be able to do it. Social comparisons to older, more developed children only bring hope and confidence of coming accomplishments.

School-agers. Feedback from formal schooling will be about acceptance, competence, and moral worth, while often removing much of the power. New abilities may be heightened by new challenges or squashed by criticism and labeling. In this stage of Industry versus Inferiority, as Erikson (1950, 1968) called it, much of the self-esteem is dependent on school success. The child is moving into a new stage of cognitive development, Concrete Operations (Piaget, 1968). She is now in new social settings and more interested in the acceptance of friends than family. Most of the abilities in the physical realm will now be used more competitively in sports and in the writing tasks of school. All of these new opportunities can negatively or positively affect self-concept and self-esteem.

This is the age when comparisons to others and the internalization of what other people think is very important. Constant comparisons and competitiveness bring more reality to self-estimations than in the preschool years. The self-esteem is fragile with inside doubts of abilities and acceptance. Clubs, exclusive friendships, and put-downs of others stem from this quest to feel good about oneself.

Families and Schools That Build Self-Esteem

What makes the difference in children's self-esteem? Basic intellect? Innate ability? The family had more money? The family lived in the ghetto? It is all about acceptance. In Susan Harter's (in Lazaerson, 1984) social-learning analysis, she shows that when efforts and independence are praised, they produce internal rewards. This gives the feeling of competence and confidence that motivates greater efforts, more independence and higher self-esteem. The opposite is also true. Dependence is increased when efforts are criticized. It is accompanied by feelings of incompetency and a lack of control. Anxiety and doubt fail to motivate. Future efforts are then approached tentatively, expecting failure. External rewards and the approval of others, which is rarely forthcoming, increases dependency. Competency and self-esteem are lowered.

Harter's cycles make sense. The socialization of the family toward competency sets the course of the path. Owens (1993) reports that children with high self-esteem had mothers who were content with their role, were calm and poised with both parents accepting of others, and led active personal lives. The mothers gave reasons for behavior control and the fathers took away privileges rather than using punishment. They both used firm follow through, communicating commitment to the child's welfare, and a willingness to *listen* to the child's ideas.

. . . .

IT HAPPENED TO ME: Listen to What He Did Now

. . . .

Every day when Jason's mother would come to school, she had a horror story to relate of Jason's latest episode. He had deliberately poured grape juice on the white rug, painted the basement paneling with tar, and pulled up the neighbor's pumpkin patch. I tried to get her not to talk about these things in front of Jason and all the other parents and children, but each day she came with a new story of his escapades. One day as the children arrived I suggested they go check the incubator. "Oh no, you hatched chicks. Don't let Jason go near them. He'll kill them," she exclaimed. Well, you guessed it. Sometime during the free play time, Jason opened the incubator and squeezed a baby chick. Was this Jason's fault? He was just living up to expectations. It is sad that those expectations were not for kind acts, gentle touches, and controlled behavior. I often won[der what] happened to Jason. I wond[er what I] have done to try to chan[ge his] attitude.

. . . .

Children with low self-esteem had parents who were coercive, rejecting, and controlling by strict restrictions. They were overprotective or neglectful, either resulting in the child's feeling of incompetence (Owens, K., 1993, pp. 399–405). The family has a primary influence over the child's self-esteem.

Schools also have a major part to play in the building of a child's self-esteem. Children need to build a sense of competency, to have an environment with experiences that develop real skills in the cognitive, physical, social, and emotional realms. They need to feel they have the power to make things happen. Involvement in decision making, understanding clear and realistic expectations help children feel powerful. They thrive in a predictable environment where there are plenty of opportunities to make choices. Their opinions and ideas are accepted as worthy and the curriculum capitalizes on their strengths. Teachers give informative praise that gives specific reactions and focuses on what they know and do. Negative labels are avoided. The only labels are on the shelves. Children are seen as individuals. That sounds like the teachers *know* each child and their accomplishments. The teachers have watched closely to determine the level of development of each child and provided an environment where the child could have success. That is a place where a child could go to a portfolio with his name on it and look at a history of his work. He could even add to it or take something out. He knew it was about all the things he could do.

Figure 12.9 lists some questions adults can ask.

Self-Concept and Acceptance, Power, Morality, and Competence

Curry and Johnson (1990) present these four themes, revisited throughout life as each person seeks to define the self, Figure 12.10.

Acceptance. From the attachment of the infant to the desire for friendship, **acceptance** is the human quest. Young children desire to please adults and other children. They want to feel they are worthy of being heard. From the crawler tugging on dad's pant leg to the tattler telling of other children's misdeeds, self-concept and self-esteem involve acceptance.

Power. The infant is exercising **power** when he struggles away from the shirt being pulled over his head. The toddler is exercising power when she says, "No." The preschooler exercises power when he ws his bread into a gun shape to escape the "No

guns in school rule." The teenager exercises power. Adults exercise power through the vote, purchasing power, in any number of ways. It is all saying, "I can make things happen." That is part of self-concept,

- How do I ensure that each child is challenged just enough to succeed?
- How actively do children participate and take responsibility for their actions?
- How often do children experience safe but real consequences of their actions? How do children become more aware of relationships between cause and effect?
- How does the selection of materials (wide paint brushes, large sheets of paper) match children's growing capabilities?
- How do the equipment and furnishings (indoor and outdoor) contribute to children's independence?
- How often do children figure things out for themselves?
- What personal responsibility skills are taught by example or guided participation (conflict resolution, dressing, handwashing)?
- How well are children progressing in the ability to use words rather than actions to express feelings?

McCracken, J. P. (1995). Image-building: A hands-on developmental process. *Child Care Information Exchange, 104,* July/August, p. 55. Reprinted with permission.

Figure 12.9 Learning Environments Support Self-Understanding: Questions to Ask Ourselves. (Reprinted with permission. McCracken, J. P. *Image-Building: A Hands-on Developmental Process.* 1995. Child Care Information Exchange, PO Box 2890, Redmond, WA, 98073, 1-800-221-2864, Issue 104, July/August, p. 55.)

High Self-Esteem
Acceptance
Power
Morality
Competence

Low Self-Esteem
Isolation
Vulnerability
"Bad" Label
Dependent

Figure 12.10 Self-Esteem Factors

the knowledge that one has the ability to influence events rather than passively receive or observe them, resigned to accept their consequences.

Morality. Morality is the innate desire to be considered "good" rather than "bad," the recognition between right and wrong by society. Self-esteem is affected by knowing the expectations or the rules and following them. The rules may be social, like manners or certain behavior codes (such as quiet in the movies, or controlled rowdiness at a sports event). They may be legal (such as the speed limit or not stealing) or they may be religious in nature. Self-esteem is increased by following the rules or expectations. Those may even be contrary to the code of the majority of society, like the Code of Thieves, or a cult or terrorist group. No matter what, it gains acceptance, illustrates self-control, and represents a feeling of competence.

Competence. Satisfaction is the result of accomplishing a task by applying knowledge, skill, and energy and seeing the expected result. This **competence** raises the self-concept and self-esteem because it is the evaluation of the effort and positive feeling from the result. It gains acceptance, demonstrates power, and adds to moral worth.

These four aspects are threads that weave through all developmental areas as we observe children's behavior. Their influence affects self-concept and self-esteem.

Sex-Role Identity and Self-Esteem

At the moment of birth, the baby's gender is announced and the people around the baby begin to form the **sex role or gender identity,** Figure 12.11. In the first few days of life she receives a name. This distinguishes her sexual identity to the rest of the world. She is held more gently, sometimes covered with a certain color blanket and congratulations to her parents are sometimes tempered with resignation. She receives gifts that are soft and pastel-colored or toys that inspire nurturing actions instead of construction. She watches her mother to see what women are like and watches her father to see what men are like. Even at two, when she pretends to be grown up, she plays the role of mommy, not daddy. By three she tells people she is a girl, because she has long hair. She knows that someday she will be a woman, though until she is almost six, she may think she can still change her mind. When she looks at toy advertising, she sees that the girls are playing dolls or the boys are building with blocks. When she watches television, she sees that most of the powerful roles

Figure 12.11 Sex-role identity is affected by society.

are male. When she has boy playmates, they say, "You can't do this. You're a girl." Her grandma frowns when she climbs a tree and smiles when she pours the tea. She goes to preschool and the teacher says, "The girls can line up first because they're the quietest."

Children are **socialized,** taught the ways to behave in both overt and covert ways. Sexual identity begins with the physiology, the biological indicators of male or female. The view of one's own sexuality is gender identity, the socialized behaviors by parents, siblings, peers, significant other people, culture, and media, communicated by imitation, direct instruction, and reinforcement. Gender enters the subject of self-concept and self-esteem when it is examined by those four factors that Harter (1983) speaks of as lifelong issues:

- acceptance—Does she feel accepted as a girl, valued for her worth, not just because of her sex, or less because of it?
- Power and control—Has she been given autonomy, power over herself in making decisions, allowed to take risks?

- Moral virtue—Has she had opportunities to feel useful and "good," not guilty?
- Competence—Does she know about all the things she can do well, given opportunities to show her physical strength, logical mind, self-reliant behaviors?

These are much more at issue for girls than boys, so the choice of using "she" in this section was deliberate. Stereotyping female gender behavior, such as dependency and weakness, has prevented girls from feeling powerful and competent, sometimes in very subtle ways. Deaux (as cited in Markus, et al., 1990) found that girls were socialized to believe that effort brought success, while boys were led to believe it was ability. Thus, when failures came, girls explained it as lack of ability while boys attributed it to lack of effort. The implications of that theory profoundly affect girls low self-esteem. They will feel; "I just didn't have it" rather than, as the boys would, "I just didn't try hard enough." There is a very great difference.

Perceptions about the body leading to self-esteem can be affected in infancy and toddler stages during diapering. When adults use words like *dirty* or *nasty,* genital areas become associated with negative feelings. Children often engage in masturbation for a variety of reasons, most often because it is pleasurable. If the child perceives adults' reactions as negative, they can have an affect on how the child feels about his body, his sexuality, and total self-esteem. Children will also commonly engage in sex play, just as they play out other adult roles. In a similar way, the breadth of experiences will determine how much reality is incorporated into the play. Children often play out explicit television scenes in the preschool classroom or home playroom. Adult reactions to these simulations will also bring value judgments and affect self-concept and self-esteem about their play and ultimately their sexual identity.

Observing Self-Concept and Self-Esteem

All areas of human development contribute to self-concept and self-esteem. Observable behavior demonstrates what a person knows and can do, and the feeling about that knowledge or ability. Self-esteem has defied researchers' attempts to devise measurement instruments, especially for young children outside of the mainstream (Marshall, 1989, p. 44). Harter (1990, p. 90) found two main categories early childhood educators used to define the high self-esteem child:

1. Active displays of confidence, curiosity, initiative, and independence
2. Adaptive reaction to change or stress

Inferring high or low self-esteem from observing behavior can be highly biased. The indicators of self-esteem adapted from Samuels (1977) parallel the areas of development covered in the preceding chapters of this book:

- unafraid of a new situation
- independent, needs minimal help
- comfortable with physical activities, coordinated
- makes friends easily
- seems to be happy most of the time
- talks freely
- does not rely on others for directions
- experiments with new materials
- creative, imaginative, has own ideas
- participates in classroom activities
- cooperative and largely self-controlled
- trusts people even if they are newly acquainted

The underlying self-concept is observed while the observer has been assessing each child's developmental areas. The Self-Esteem Class List (in Appendix D) will be used in Assignment A to note these characteristics or behaviors.

Separation. How the child separates from the parent at the beginning of the school year or day depends on the self-concept. The child has the sense of belonging and trust in the adult. He feels so worthy of love and care that he is sure his parent would not think of not returning to reclaim this treasure.

Self-Care. The child who is secure in self-concept will feel capable and competent and want to do things independently. She will want to take care of physical needs and not depend on adults. This is observed in the self-care area of toileting, eating, and dressing. The children whose parents have given them instructions, let them try, and rewarded their attempts are more likely to be independent and do things for themselves.

Physical. Physical competence or ability instills pride, Figure 12.12. Climbing to the top of the climber and sliding down, riding the two-wheeler without training wheels, or printing a name can raise a child's self-esteem. The child may have the physical ability but doubts or lacks confidence in the ability. The resulting behavior is avoidance of the activity, need for assistance, or unsteadiness, resulting in a fall. All these behaviors only end in lowering self-esteem. The observer infers self-esteem while watching the physical skills and

Figure 12.12 I did it!

recording what the child accomplishes. The reactions when attempts are successful or unsuccessful give clues of self-esteem.

Social. Excessive withdrawal from social encounters is a sign the child may not feel worthy to be a friend. There may be other reasons, but self-concept is a strong determining factor in a child's social development. By observing children's interactions, the self-concept can be indicated. Self-esteem can be heightened when classroom activities promote prosocial behaviors.

Emotional. Self-esteem resides in the emotional realm. It is the feeling about the various competencies, the feeling about how capable one is compared to other people, the feeling about how acceptable one is as a playmate. This is observable in the demeanor of the child, the facial and verbal expressions that indicate the emotions inside. Children with good feelings about themselves will appear happy, while those who are uncertain of their competencies and worthiness will appear unhappy, sober, or expressionless. The inborn personality or temperament of the child enters here. Care must be

taken not to misinterpret a more quiet, introspective person as one with low self-esteem.

Speech and Language. When people are in stressful situations, new encounters where they feel uncertain, it is normal to be more quiet and reserved. They may not risk revealing the self by speaking. As one is more accustomed to a situation, one feels more free to speak and less concerned about the hearer's reactions or judgments. The child who freely talks to teachers, other children, the janitor, the bus driver, or the UPS delivery person is usually displaying a strong self-concept. "I am important enough for you to listen to what I have to say." Hearing a child constantly say "I can't" will give clues that the child is feeling incompetent and unwilling to risk, indicating low self-esteem.

This is an area in which children who are unsure of their language (especially nonmajority language speakers) are observed and often misjudged as having low self-esteem. Because they cannot or are unsure about their competencies in communication, they do not speak, even after they have learned many words. These children need to find other areas in the classroom in which to feel competent. Language attempts will not be so much of a risk to self-esteem.

Memory and Attention Span. Just as emotions govern self-esteem, cognitive abilities govern self-concept. The child is using the cognitive and memory abilities to observe other children's capabilities. She remembers past attempts and failures. Because so many adult-child conversations rely on closed questions like a constant quiz, "What color is your shirt?" "How many crackers are on your napkin?" "What shape is this puzzle piece?" children form an image very quickly of what they know and do not know in comparison to the adult's expectations. In creating an environment to build cognitive structures and positive self-esteem, opportunities should be presented for divergent thinking, exploring not reciting.

Literacy. School is a place of literacy. Watching the child's contact with the written word, whether it is in signs, books, or attempts at writing, can reveal self-concept. The child who has had the advantage of many opportunities with literacy will feel very comfortable in the literacy classroom. The child who has not will exhibit discomfort there, unable to listen and uninterested in stories. No connections are made between the sign in the block area and the sound. It is difficult for the child to find his name on the helper chart. Behavior observations will inform the watcher. What the child is *not* choosing is as revealing as what is chosen. Those areas and activities the child feels the least competent about will not be chosen.

Creativity. Whether it is wondering about what a magnet will pick up, using a variety of materials to glue a design on a piece of tile, or acting as the pilot on an airplane bound for Disney World, children can be observed exhibiting creativity. There may be a child who is unwilling to try the magnet. A pattern is needed for art projects. Dramatic play is avoided. This gives the observer clues about not just creativity but self-esteem. It takes comfort and confidence in oneself to venture away from the tray of metal pieces the teacher has put out and into the room to test out other materials. It takes boldness to try to glue a nail on end to a collage. It inspires others to announce to the passengers on the plane that she is about to have a baby. Creativity is being observed here as well as self-concept and self-esteem.

Adjustment to a New Setting. Because of that secure attachment with the parent, the child has the self-esteem to feel lovable. It makes the child feel capable enough to be comfortable in any setting after a nominal period. The child who learns self-control and follows the routines of the classroom shows confidence. Trust is exhibited that the teacher is a supporter, not an enemy. The child will feel secure enough to want to participate with the group. This gives the observer information, not just about the child's adjustment but about self-concept. Acceptable behavior is assumed and success is expected. This is observable behavior.

Is self-concept and self-esteem observable? Not of itself, but it appears that by watching the child interact with the environment peers and adults can make some substantial assumptions about self-concept and self-esteem.

Why Not Ask?

If a person wants the answer to a question, the most logical thing to do is ask someone who is most likely to know. Marshall (1989, p. 46) suggests some questions an observer might ask a child, probably above four years old, that would get first-person information concerning self-esteem:

"What can you tell me about yourself? Why is that important?"
"What can you tell me that is best about you?"
"What are you good at doing?"

Samuels (1977) suggests asking young children the question, "If you had a wish, what would it be?" The voice quality as well as the actual answer will give the observer information on which to infer the child's level of self-esteem. This is consistent with the principle of the child as the informant. By asking the child, they verbalize what they may have never thought of before. "What am I good at?" It is a strategy that Bev Bos promotes in her workshops on self-esteem.

SPECIAL POPULATIONS AND SELF-ESTEEM

It cannot be ignored that different ethnic, racial, and cultural values affect self-esteem. While the toddler's autonomy and the preschooler's independence may be a western value, other cultures may hold those same accomplishments with contempt for children in their families. Expectations of competence and styles of interpersonal relations vary between cultures. For example, praising a Middle Eastern boy's ability to clear his dishes and wash the table may not raise his self-esteem. The child who refuses to participate in a holiday event may not be antisocial but acting according to a religious tradition. Cultural differences affect behavior. They may be misinterpreted as a self-esteem issue. Conversely, expectations in the classroom may conflict with the positive self-concept and self-esteem of a child of a minority group.

Even ethnicity awareness can be identified in a developmental progression. At about three years old, a racial awareness begins and by six years old it is well ingrained (Derman-Sparks, 1989). Young children are in the throes of classification tasks. They are sorting by color and shape, looking for similarities and differences, and making matches of everything in their environment. It is only natural for them to look at each other and compare and contrast. They will notice racial cues, mainly color of skin and texture of hair. While they are classifying, they are also labeling objects. Parental and societal labels often have values attached, which the child also absorbs. Experiences and attitudes about groups that bear high or low self-esteem are transmitted. The young child absorbs all this as well.

Observation of racial awareness, especially when it is in the form of children's questions or negative comments, should be addressed right away. Derman-Sparks (1989) recommends:

- Do not ignore.
- Do not change the subject.
- Do not answer indirectly.

If you are uncomfortable, identify what gets in the way of your responding directly, matter-of-factly, and simply. (p. 33)

Disabilities and Self-Esteem

When disabilities interfere with a child's functioning while included in a regular classroom, self-concept and self-esteem issues arise, Figure 12.13. Peer relations are especially affected when hearing impairment impedes communication. Visual impairment depends on manual contact and results in less smiling. Physical impairments prevent active participation with other children. Mental retardation may reduce responsiveness or limit play options.

For these children, the self-concept and self-esteem issues are acceptance and the power to be independent and feel competent. Social comparisons of children with disabilities are more often not upward to other children but to children with more severe disabilities (Frey & Ruble, 1990, p. 184). That alleviates some of the criticism about inclusion's damaging effect on the special child's self-esteem.

It is the children with normal abilities in an inclusive classroom who become very aware of differences when that social measurement takes place. Observers may see children playing at being visually, hearing, or physically challenged, making up explanations for the disability and exhibiting fear (Kostelnik, et al., 1993). Every child should be recognized for their abilities, rather than the dis-

abilities, labels, or things they cannot do. This attitude or viewpoint will help all gain an understanding of differences not disabilities and give the acceptance that they all want. By recognizing the child's abilities and giving clear explanations of limitations, the other children will be made aware of opportunities to help, but the disabled child must have plenty of opportunity to do for himself what he can. It is that old "Never do for *any* child what he can do for himself" philosophy. It increases independence, raises competency levels, and ultimately results in positive self-esteem.

These are sensitive, yet vitally important, issues to young children's self-concept and self-esteem. They are challenging.

HELPING PROFESSIONALS FOR CHILD ABUSE AND SELF-ESTEEM CONCERNS

There are many agencies and professionals in most communities to prevent, investigate, advise, protect, and even punish child abuse. Researchers, psychologists, and sociologists are seeking causes and solutions.

Child Protective Services—This is a governmental agency that receives, investigates, and takes action on reports of child abuse or maltreatment. They are a resource for education for mandated reporters, available to answer individual questions and work as advocates for the protection of the child. They protect the confidentiality of all records dealing with the family.

Psychologists and psychiatrists—With specialized training in social and emotional disorders, these professionals work with children and families on issues concerning the causes and results of abuse and maltreatment but also issues dealing with self-esteem. Either may interfere with the child's functioning in the social realm. These professionals may serve as educational resources for parenting education for the prevention of child abuse or the development of healthy self-concepts and self-esteem.

Figure 12.13 Peer relations are even more important for the self-esteem of an exceptional child.

Week 12, Assignment A

CLASS LIST LOG ON SELF-ESTEEM FOR ALL

Copy the Self-Esteem Class List Log form found in Appendix D. Based on the past 11 weeks of observations, interpret the child's behaviors as they relate to self-concept and self-esteem. Make a note *for yourself*, marking *H* for high or *L* for low under each criteria.

What to Do with It

Because this is so subjective, *this is for your use only. Keep it in the class file, not in any child's portfolio.* This will be used for individualizing the curriculum and to guide you in your interactions with each child. Relate the ratings to the child's knowledge, skills, and behavior in each area to reflect on the reason for the rating. In areas of high self-

esteem, make sure the child has plenty of opportunities to exercise this skill and that the child knows that you know of their success. In areas of lower self-esteem, consider ways you can "scaffold." Your actions can fill in the gap for the child between present ability and next level. The child can then feel successful. Point out the "working on" skills to use the lower self-esteem areas as motivation. For example, the child who is not yet able to write his name: He can write the first letter. "That's a start, good *J*, Jamal, I'll write the rest of your name until you are ready to make the *a, m, a, l*." This shows acceptance of the child at this level of skill. It gives him the power to try or not. He is not labeled "bad" because he cannot write his name yet, but recognizes his competence in making the *J*.

Remember, acceptance, power, morality, and competence are the four components of self-esteem.

Week 12, Assignment B

ANECDOTAL RECORD TO OBSERVE SELF-IDENTITY FOR GROUP C

Select all the children from group C and each day write an Anecdotal Recording about how the child displays an aspect of Self-Identity, how the child sees him/herself or Self-Esteem, how the child feels about him/herself. Include all the details and exact quotes written on the left column of the paper. In the right column, make your comments or questions.

What to Do with It

Note the recording on the portfolio overview sheet with the date and your name, Figure 12.14.

Share the Anecdotal Recording with the child's parents or the child, if it is appropriate. For example: "Mrs. Quon, Tia has been working so hard at lacing her new boots and tying a bow. Today she did it! It made her so proud! She hated it when the other children were finished dressing for outside before she was and she had to ask for help. She is

SELF–IDENTITY Documentation	Recorder	Date
CL confident	*Ban*	*11/27*
CL "		*6/12*

Figure 12.14 Portfolio Overview Example

a very independent person," or "Alexia, I know you didn't like it when Robert called you a 'bad girl' when that whole pitcher of milk spilled. It hurt your feelings and made you cry. Remember when I told you we have a new cook. She didn't know which pitchers were for our class and not to fill the pitchers so full. It was just too much for you to handle, but not your fault. That is why it spilled, not because you wanted it to. Robert made a mistake and didn't know it was an accident."

File the Anecdotal Recording in the child's portfolio.

Week 12, Assignment C

REFLECTIVE JOURNAL

Copy this form, rate your own self-esteem and keep it in a private file at home.
Using the similar criteria from the child's self-esteem form, rate your own self-esteem:

❏ I am usually unafraid of new situations.

❏ I am independent, taking pride in doing things for myself.

❏ I am comfortable with physical activities, coordinated, feel all right about my appearance.

❏ I make friends easily.

❏ I feel happy most of the time.

❏ I talk freely in groups.

❏ I show initiative and do not rely on others for directions.

❏ I try new things.

❏ I am creative, imaginative, have ideas of my own.

❏ I participate in social activities.

❏ I am cooperative with coworkers.

❏ I talk comfortably to clerks, cab drivers, and servers.

From the preceding list, I think the thing that helps me most as I deal with children is...

I would like to change...

Some ways might be...

REFERENCES

Baladerian, N. J. (1993). *Abuse of children and youth with disabilities: A prevention and intervention guidebook for parents and other advocates.* Culver City, CA: Disability, Abuse, and Personal Rights Project.

Besharov, D. (1990). *Recognizing child abuse: A guide for the concerned.* New York: The Free Press.

Curry, N. & Johnson, C. (1990). *Beyond self-esteem: Developing a genuine sense of human value.* Washington: National Association for the Education of Young Children.

Derman-Sparks, L. (1989). *Anti-bias curriculum: Tools for empowering young children.* Washington, DC: National Association for the Education of Young Children.

Erikson, E. H. (1950). *Childhood and society.* New York: Norton.

Erikson, E. H. (1968). *Identity: Young and crisis.* New York: Norton.

Fischer, K., Lazerson, A. (1984). *Human development: From conception through adolescence.* New York: W. H. Freeman and Company.

Frey, K. S. & Ruble, D. N. (1990). Strategies for comparative evaluation: Maintaining a sense of competence across the life span. In R. J. Sternberg & J. Kolligan (Eds.), *Competence considered,* 167–189.

Greenberg, P. (1991). *Encouraging self-esteem and self-discipline in infants, toddlers and two year olds.* Washington: National Association for the Education of Young Children.

Harter, S. (1983). Developmental perspectives on the self-system. In E. M. Hetherington (Ed.) & P. H. Mussen (Series Ed.), *Handbook of child psychology: Vol. 4. Socialization, personality and social development* (4th ed.) (pp. 275–386). New York: Wiley.

Harter, S. (1990). Causes, correlates and the functional role of the global self-worth: A life-span perspective. In R. J. Sternberg & J. Kolligan (Eds.), *Competence considered,* 67–97.

King, E., Chipman, M., & Cruz-Janzen, M. (1994). *Educating young children in a diverse society.* Boston: Allyn and Bacon.

Koralek, K. (1992). *Caregivers of young children: preventing and responding to child maltreatment.* U. S. Department of Health and Human Services, National Center on Child Abuse and Neglect.

Kostelnik, M., Stein, L., Whiren, A., & Soderman, A. (1993). *Guiding children's social development.* Albany: Delmar Publishers.

Lively, V. E. & Lively, E. (1991). *Sexual development of young children.* Albany, NY: Delmar Publishers.

Markus, H, Cross, S., & Wurf, E. (1990). The role of the self-system in competence. In R. J. Sternberg & J. Kolligan (Eds.), *Competence considered,* 205–225.

Marshall, H. (1989). The development of self-concept. *Young Children, 44* (5) 44–51.

McCracken, J. P. (1995). Image-building: A hands-on developmental process. *Child Care Information Exchange, 104,* July/August, 48–55.

Owens, K. (1993). *The world of the child.* New York: Merrill, an imprint of Macmillan Publishing Company.

Piaget, J. (1968). *On the development of memory and identity.* Worcester, MA: Clark University Press.

Saifer, S. (1990). *Practical solutions.* St. Paul, MN: Redleaf Press.

Samuels, S. C. (1977). *Enhancing self-concept in early childhood: Theory and practice.* New York: Human Science Press.

RESOURCES

Baladerian, N. J. (1990). *Abuse of children and youth with disabilities: A prevention and intervention guidebook for parents and other advocates.* Culver City, CA: Disability, Abuse and Personal Rights Project.

Besharov, D. (1990). *Recognizing child abuse: a guide for the concerned.* New York: The Free Press.

Derman-Sparks, L. (1989). *Anti-bias curriculum: Tools for empowering young children.* Washington: National Association for the Education of Young Children.

King, E., Chipman, M., & Cruz-Jansen, M. (1994). *Educating young children in a diverse society.* Boston: Allyn and Bacon.

Koralek, K. (1992). *Caregivers of young children: preventing and responding to child maltreatment.* U.S. Department of Health and Human Services, National Center on Child Abuse and Neglect.

Kostelnik, M., Stein, L., Whiren, A., & Soderman, A. (1993). *Guiding children's social development.* Albany: Delmar Publishers.

Saifer, S. (1990). *Practical solutions.* St. Paul, MN: Redleaf Press.

CHAPTER 13

Using Program Assessments to Look at Children in Groups

IN THIS CHAPTER ···

✔ Assessing Early Childhood Programs

✔ Topics in Observation: Assessing the Environment—Pointing Back at You

✔ Looking at the Adjustment of the Child to the Program

✔ Special Populations in Group Settings

✔ Helping Professionals for Program Evaluation and Support

ASSESSING EARLY CHILDHOOD PROGRAMS

The child is enrolled in an early childhood group setting. It could be in a child care center of many types: for profit, nonprofit, employer supported, or religiously affiliated. It may be a part-day program called a preschool, nursery, nursery school, play group, or parent cooperative. Head Start programs serve thousands of three- and four-year-olds across the country, and in some places also serve infants and toddlers. Public and private schools provide educational experiences for children from kindergarten and up. Some schools also have programs for prekindergarten and some for infants and toddlers as well. Many school districts and outside agencies provide programs for children before and after school and on school holidays. There are many programs for children with special needs to receive early intervention in separate settings or included within regular classrooms. Some programs draw specific audiences, such as music, gymnastics, and dance schools. Whenever young children are in group settings outside their home, the program should be evaluated, by some agency, for its safety and appropriateness for children.

Each state has its own criteria and process for licensing or regulating the care and education of children in groups.

Exercise: Find out the regulatory agency for the program in which you work or are doing observations.

Child care—state licensing agency
School—state agency

Obtain a copy of the regulations and look for the method of program evaluation: yearly review or report, on-site visit, or accreditation.

Parents are the most important evaluators with the greatest risk, their own child. Parents have the right and responsibility to freely access the building in which their child is enrolled. They should ask questions and observe that the program meets their expectations and their child's needs. Parents should have a voice in evaluating the program, no matter what type it is. There are many parent surveys available that can be adapted to ask specific questions about the program. They typically include questions concerning parents' satisfaction with the facilities, program, and staff; communication; interactions between the child and staff; comfort with the policies and procedures; and ask for suggestions or recommendations.

Figure 13.1 is a sample parent survey from the *Child Care Information Exchange, 67,* (Parent Evaluation of Child Care Programs, 1989, p. 25).

The observation and recording method of this section is not focused on the child but on the program. Several program evaluation tools are presented to familiarize the reader with options available to assess the quality of the early childhood program.

A Setting Observation

Exercise: Let's take a trip to a child care center or school. You can think about one you have visited or make up one in your mind. No children need to be present. You will observe the setting to see what it tells you. Drive into the parking lot.

What do you see?/What could it mean?
(Record your answers on a separate sheet of paper.)

From the parking lot:

Sign for the program:

Playground:

Entranceway:

Inside a classroom:

Children's spaces:

Learning materials:

Displays:

Adult spaces:

Reactions to a Setting Observation. Without ever observing a program in action, much information is gathered, impressions formed, and judgments made. A program's purpose and practices are observed readily and interpreted from the environment. It is healthy to inspect one's own environment with a visitor's eye. It is also an exercise in professionalism to visit other programs. These bits of information are taken in by the senses and associated with information already stored. Reflection on possible meanings infer the values, philosophies, economic sponsorship, and even the housekeeping habits of the teacher. Some decisions for action can result.

"Oh, I can't wait to get back to my classroom and use that idea."

"I could really tell they emphasize…"
"I wonder what they did with that? I'll have to ask."
"I wonder how they provide for…?
"If that were my room, I would…"
"I certainly don't agree with… but they must have a different philosophy."
"I will not comment on… but I can talk about…"

Always as a professional courtesy, "I'll write a note and tell them how much I appreciated the visit and that I particularly liked…" Remember the evaluation principles: Look for the accomplishments not the deficits; specific praise raises self-esteem.

IT HAPPENED TO ME:
Where Is Everyone?

I was attending a meeting at the office of a child care director. I arrived on time and walked through the center without hearing a sound, an eerie feeling. What could that mean?

As I walked down the hall, I smelled, then saw vomit puddles ahead of me. I called out, "Anybody here?" A weak voice from the other end of the hall replied, "In here." It was from the bathroom where two staff people and one child were huddled over sinks. A volatile virus had struck and all other children and staff had been sent home, some sick, and the rest as a precaution. This little person and two staff were the last ones left but were sick as well. What a pitiful sight! I donned gloves and helped them clean up. The meeting had been cancelled since the director had gone home, too sick to think of calling me. Illness can strike quickly and powerfully when people are in group settings.

Program Assessments

Exercise: What do these things tell you?

Checkbook balance
Bathroom scale
Speedometer
Wristwatch
Windsock

Child's Class_____

Based on the experiences of my child and myself in this child care program, I am able to say that:

Yes No

❏ ❏ My child's teacher knows and cares about my child and responds to her/his individual needs.

❏ ❏ I feel comfortable and at ease leaving my child here each day.

❏ ❏ My child's teacher listens to me, respects me as a parent, and supports us as a family.

❏ ❏ I know who to go to with my concerns and feel confident that my concerns will be addressed respectfully and promptly.

❏ ❏ I am comfortable with the style and forms of limit setting used by the staff.

❏ ❏ The communication systems keep me well informed about what is happening in the program each day and what I need to know to plan.

❏ ❏ The atmosphere here is warm and nurturing.

❏ ❏ I feel welcome to visit any time I wish to do so.

❏ ❏ My child is happy and safe here.

❏ ❏ My child's growth and development have been supported and stimulated by her/his participation in this program.

❏ ❏ Staff know what they are doing and are enthusiastic about working here.

❏ ❏ The daily conversations and parent-teacher conferences sufficiently inform me of my child's progress.

❏ ❏ Center policies are clear, fair, and consistently enforced.

❏ ❏ The meals and snacks served are nutritious and varied.

❏ ❏ Tuition rates reflect the quality of service we receive.

❏ ❏ Outdoor spaces are thoughtfully designed and well maintained.

❏ ❏ Indoor spaces are clean and appealing and meet the needs of the children.

❏ ❏ Supplies and equipment are adequate and kept in good condition.

❏ ❏ The curriculum meets my child's needs and is fun for my child.

❏ ❏ I read the newsletters and messages sent home and posted for parents.

❏ ❏ My participation in the program is welcome—I have a variety of opportunities and choices about how to participate.

❏ ❏ Parent functions keep me informed and help me feel more comfortable in the program.

❏ ❏ I am comfortable recommending this program to friends and have done so.

Please take a few minutes to complete the following:

I could work better with the staff if…

The program could better meet my needs if…

A recent incident that made me feel good about the program was…

A recent incident that made m unhappy about the program was…

When my child talks about the center at home, she/he says…

I wish my child's teacher would…

My child's teacher has helped me most by…

Are there any other concerns, comments you wish to express at this time?

This form was developed by Exchange Press as a service to our readers. Please use it in your program. We have built on forms developed by several programs and wish to acknowledge: Early Learning, Champaign, IL; Home Day Care, Evanston, IL; The Lincroft Center for Children, Holmdel, NJ; School's Out? Child Care Center, Richmond, VA; Smokey Row Children's Center, Powell, OH; Steve Eberhardt, Wellness Child Care, Madison, NJ; Patricia Sheppard, Educational Environments, Eugene, OR; Alison Jacobs Ruiz, Live Oak Kid Care, Santa Cruz, CA; and Deborah Begner, Concord Children's Center, Concord, MA

Figure 13.1 Parent Evaluation of Child Care Program. (Reprinted with permission from *Child Care Information Exchange*, PO Box 2890, Redmond, WA 98073, 1-800-221–2864, Issue Number 67, June, 1989, pp. 25,26.)

Mirror
Bookmark
Diploma
Roadmap
Report Card

Yes, you guessed it. You are so clever. These are all measurements or visual indicators of important facts. Money, weight, speed, time, wind direction, hair check, last chapter read, course completed, roads travelled, evaluation—constant vigilance is part of life.

In *Week by Week,* many areas of child development have been examined for indicators of progress and possible delays. Programs need evaluation as well, for indicators of progress and warning signs of poor quality situations. **Program evaluation** can be informal, such as a staff discussion at the end of the year to recap the successes, the difficulties, and forecasts based on the past. Aspects of program quality can be measured with some of the same methods used to observe children's development, Figure 13.2.

An important measuring stick of a program's effectiveness is the growth and development of the children enrolled. Attendance figures give indicators of the health and safety procedures of the program. Young children in close surroundings do not share toys but they do share germs. Staff must give constant consideration to infection control. Children require nourishment to grow. If they are nourished developmentally, they will show progress. Portfolios measuring children's progress are one indication of an effective program. Another indicator is children's active involvement with the learning environment. Peeks into classrooms should show children busy working on a variety of activities with the adult's facilitating the learning. The rooms should be filled with children's voices, talking, and laughing, with a minimum of adult voices. Children can be surveyed to hear what they have to say about the school, the program, and the learning activities. Even very young children can tell what they like about their school or child care center and what they do not. Adults should listen.

Total Program Evaluations

There are many evaluation instruments available, some determined by the type of the program, others elected for use. All have evaluation as their basic premise, the assessment or measurement of aspects of the program, comparison with an

Child Observation Method	Program Observation
Developmental Checklists	Checklists: Safety Appropriate programming
Anecdotal Records	Teacher's stories
Frequency Counts	Teacher behaviors Use of slang Negative discipline
Time Samples	Assess learning center use Measure effect of adult presence in learning area
Interviews	Parent/Child surveys Parent/teacher conferences
Work Samples	Examples of teacher projects Bulletin boards Newsletters
Observation	Outside reviewers Licensing agents Accreditation validators

Figure 13.2 Observation Techniques for Program Evaluations

accepted standard of quality, and action implemented to bring the program into compliance or increased effectiveness.

Head Start—SAVI. Head Start programs evaluate themselves annually with the Self-Assessment Validation Instrument (SAVI) developed by the U. S. Department of Health and Human Services (revised 1979). This is a comprehensive checklist to measure national performance standards of Head Start components: education, health services, social services, and parent involvement. The assessment is conducted by a team, including community members and parents, with the involvement of policy committees or councils. All assessment participants attend a training meeting to ensure the process is followed. The criteria are assessed by following the guidance column that suggests how to gather the information to make the decision. In some cases, it is a direct observation or spot checks of random items. Some criteria are determined by interviewing staff, parents, or volunteers. Written policies and documents such as lesson plans and child records are reviewed also. The checklist ratings of compliance offer choices of *yes* or *no*. Codes are provided to give reasons for the No Compliance rating. This is made in the second phase by the delegate agency, which follows up on noncompliance items and forms the plan for improvement. The Regional Head Start Office reviews and validates the performance instrument.

High/Scope—PIP. High/Scope has developed a program evaluation tool for all early childhood settings, especially those implementing the High/Scope Curriculum. *The Program Implementation Profile (PIP) Administration Manual* (1989) includes thirty items divided into four sections considered in evaluating the appropriateness of early childhood programs: physical environment, daily routine, adult-child interaction, and adult-adult interaction. A rating scale of 1 through 5 is provided with criteria for 1, 3, and 5, and a space for notes. Items are rated from observation and additional sources such as the Record of Classroom Change. Proceedings from staff and parent meetings, planning forms, and interviews with administrators and personnel are included.

The *Manual* suggests potential uses for the PIP: as High/Scope registry assessment, as a training tool to illustrate "model" program or document progress, as ongoing monitoring for quality control, as in-service training, or for goal setting. It also suggests it be used for information and dissemination. It explains the meaning of developmentally appropriate programs or High/Scope curriculum to a variety of individuals, such as administrators, researchers, support staff, and parents, Figure 13.3.

Figure 13.3 Adults collaborate and plan for program improvements.

NAEYC Center Accreditation. The National Association for the Education of Young Children has an **accreditation** system for early childhood programs, the *Accreditation Criteria and Procedures of the National Academy of Early Childhood Programs, Revised Edition* (1991), which is the Academy's plan to improve the quality of care and education for young children in settings. Programs are eligible that serve a minimum of ten children from birth through age five in part- or full-day group programs. They have been in operation at least one year and meet the state's **license requirements** by the state or are exempt. The criteria measures interactions between staff and children and staff and parents. It also looks at the administration of the program, curriculum, physical environment, health safety, and nutrition. Staff needs are assessed by criterion for staff qualifications and development, staffing patterns, and program evaluation. It does this through a three-step process of self-study in which program personnel and parents conduct a self-study, indicating their rating of unmet, partially met, or fully met. This self-study is designed to indicate areas that need improvements; an improvement plan is implemented and ratings are changed. Every classroom staff person, the administrators, and parents have components of the entire criteria to assess. Once the self-study and improvements are complete, the administrator submits the program description to the Academy and applies for a validation visit. The Academy assigns a validator to observe in the classrooms and spot check the documentation of the administrator's report to validate or confirm that the ratings are accurate. That validation report is submitted to a three-person commission for the accreditation decision. Programs are not required to demonstrate 100 percent compliance. The accreditation is valid for three years, then the self-study and validation are repeated.

NCCA Program Accreditation. The National Child Care Association (NCAA) has developed the *National Early Childhood Program Accreditation (NEPA)*. It calls for the owner or director to assemble demographic information and lead a self-paced, self-study evaluation. Surveys are completed by staff and parents along with classroom observations. Improvements are made to the program based on the evaluations, and the program participates in an on-site verification visit by an assigned validator. The scored indicators and program profile are presented to the NEPA's National Accreditation Council for the accreditation decision. The accreditation is valid for three years. The accreditation system is entering the technological age with a new automated system, Automated Accreditation Indicator Systems (AAIS™).

Family Day Care Accreditation. The National Association for Family Day Care also has an accreditation system for family day care workers: the *National Association for Family Day Care Accreditation (NAFDA)*. These are caregivers who provide licensed or regulated care for other people's children in the provider's home for more than 18 months. It requires a provider self-evaluation with the assessment profile for family day care, parent questionnaires, a parent observation, and validator observation. This also is valid for three years.

Special Focus Instruments

There are some formal program assessment tools that can be used to evaluate one aspect of a program. This can be accomplished as a self-study, by the administration, or by a consultant. The advantage of a self-study is the staff considers quality criterion items, standards set by an outside source. These are less threatening and not taken as criticism or a pet peeve but as objective benchmarks against which to compare and consider their appropriateness for this particular situation.

When evaluations are done by the director or administrator, it gives them first-hand information about the program, recognizing the strengths of the program. It also may indicate areas that need attention, from which they can implement change. Often the staff has been aware of the situation and desiring change but were not in a position to affect the change themselves. Now that can happen. This type of evaluation can stress the staff and alienate them from administrators if the staff feels they are under scrutiny. Evaluation is only helpful if it focuses on strengths and plans build on those strengths not the deficits. They can be addressed in a cooperative way with group decision making more effectively than from edict or top-down proclamations.

Outside consultants may be enlisted to perform the assessment. This objective outside person can observe, evaluate, and make recommendations without the fear of recriminations from administrators or alienation from the staff. Issues that staff or administrators have been aware of can surface from an outside consultant and can be addressed easier than from within. Whatever the source of evaluation, the outcome should be to discover and proclaim the strengths of the program, and to recommend changes or next steps that are reasonable, attainable, and measurable. This is the same principle that is used in the child's developmental evaluation.

Here are a few program evaluations that may be used and a short description of each evaluation's use.

Early Childhood Environment Rating Scale (ECERS). The ECERS (Harms & Clifford, 1980) is a comprehensive Rating Scale to assess personal care routines, furnishings and displays, language reasoning experiences, fine and gross motor activities, creative activities, social development activities, and adult needs. Each is rated on a scale of 1 to 7 with quality points of 1, 3, 5, 7 described in detail. The Rating Scale format gives clear criteria, and a goal if a score of less than 7 is determined. The *Infant/Toddler Environment Rating Scale* (Harms, et al., 1990) follows the same format but is specific to younger age groups. Neither one of these rating scales specifically looks at curriculum. The *Family Day Care Rating Scale* (Harms & Clifford, 1989) and the *School-Age Care Environment Rating Scale* (Harms, et al., 1996) are two additional Rating Scales measuring environments for special settings.

Early Childhood Work Environment Survey. An assessment tool for anonymous staff response on coworker relations, supervisor support, decision-making influence, goal consensus, and the physical setting. It is designed for at least seven staff members who work more than 10 hours a week. The survey takes 20 minutes to complete and is submitted to the Project for computer processing. The results are returned as a profile, assuring anonymity. It is designed to inform directors of perceptions of staff and help improve overall morale and job satisfaction. It was developed by Dr. Paula Jorde Bloome, because of outreach by the Early Childhood Professional Development Project of National College of Education of National-Louis University, Evanston, Illinois.

Anti-Bias Curriculum. Derman-Sparks (1989) lists questions to be answered from videotaped classroom observations. Peers examine interactions between teachers and children that may subtly teach race, gender, racial, or disability biases. The whole book *Anti-Bias Curriculum: Tools for Empowering Young Children,* is a self-evaluative, consciousness-raising experience for the reader.

Playground Safety. Evaluation is more than assessment. It is making a change because of the assessment. Programs periodically should perform safety checks inside and outside using checklists such as the one completed in Chapter 3, found in Appendix D. Deteriorating equipment, overlooked hazards, and bad habits can be detected in these checklist formats for the protection of children's health and safety.

TOPICS IN OBSERVATION: Assessing the Environment—Pointing Back at You

When I tattled, my mother always said, "When you point your finger at someone else, three fingers are pointing back at yourself." That axiom has applications in observing children's development or lack of it. When we are careful observers, the attention is focused on the child, pointing at characteristics, skills, and behaviors. We tend to lay the source of the problem with the child. "Why is the child like that?" "Why can't she…?" "What's the matter with that child?"

The finger pointing up can be interpreted as "That's just the way those people are." Substantial elements of a child's development are genetically programmed. The adults in the child's life act as the observers of how that script is played out. However, the three fingers pointing backward are a reminder of the important role the adult plays, Figure 13.4. Rather than blaming the child or the genetic program,

Figure 13.4 When you point a finger at someone else, three fingers are pointing back at you.

some reflection may help. The influence of the adults in the child's life cannot be overlooked.

Repeatedly, the influence of the environment, in particular the early childhood setting, has been emphasized as a powerful force in each area of development. The role of the teacher is to provide, modify, enrich, support, supervise, and adapt that environment for each child. It begins with a knowledge of the child's physical development. How large are they? What do they need to be kept safe? What kind of equipment is needed for the routines and activities of the child while in this environment? That decision is based on the purpose and philosophies of the program. If it is a library story hour then one kind of equipment and materials is appropriate, whereas a gymnastics program may select different criteria.

The cognitive environment in a developmentally based program based will provide materials prompting children to ask questions. Answers are sought by following the child's level of thinking. Engaging or participating in the actual manipulation of real objects replaces one dimensional worksheets, watching an adult, or a video explanation of a principle. The adults in the environment support the exploration by asking open-ended questions, such as, "How do you think that happened?" or "Is there another way…?" "What would happen if…?"

The emotional environment of the early childhood setting provides for realistic expectations. Because young children are spillers, mops, paper towels, brooms, and dust pans are handy for clean up. Group experiences can be noisy and stressful for some children. A quiet, alone space is provided to watch the action or withdraw to rest and reduce the adrenalin flow. Because children are learners, approximations for a task are recognized and efforts are rewarded before full accomplishments are attained. Children are made to feel competent by being trusted with responsibility that matches their ability.

The social atmosphere of the environment is monitored constantly to promote cooperation rather than competition, sociability rather than sarcasm, and friendship rather than isolation. Small groups are encouraged to work and play together by the physical arrangement of the furnishings into small areas. Planned and spontaneous activities bring children physically close to one another. This helps them understand the rights and space needs of each person and the principle of cooperation. Whenever observing the child, give attention to the environment and note its possible influence on the child. If it is in a negative way, changes need to be made. That is the response of a responsible adult.

Assignments at the end of this chapter give the opportunity to assess the environment. The second assignment helps to assess the suitability to the needs of the child by observing the child's interactions with the group. A program may have a wonderful facility, the nicest equipment, materials, and supplies, but for some reason the child is not comfortable or learning there.

Advantages and Disadvantages of Formal Program Assessment

By using internal and external evaluation methods, programs measure and maintain the quality necessary for the safety, health, growth, and development of the children they serve. Other advantages include

- it ensures that the professionalism of the staff is monitored
- objective criteria is used to measure this program against others of the same type
- staff, administrators, and consultants have an objective instrument with which to measure
- evaluation has program improvement as its goal, not revocation of licensing or censure

The disadvantages of formal program assessment are

- there is usually a cost involved
- they are time-consuming
- occasionally, when the instrument does not fit the program, erroneous messages are given, which are not really helpful
- follow-up is necessary so that the assessment is like seeing a smudge on your face and not washing it off
- circumstances, such as economic or leadership, pose barriers to the implementation of evaluation findings

Pitfalls to Avoid

When considering a program evaluation, the disadvantages may be overcome by

- careful consideration of a good match of instrument to program ensures that the results will be helpful
- planning for the added cost not only of the evaluation process but the implementation helps it not be an exercise in futility
- knowledgeable, objective evaluators are key components to the success of the evaluation

LOOKING AT THE ADJUSTMENT OF THE CHILD TO THE PROGRAM

This section is not about measuring a child's development directly but about observing the child's **adjustment** and how the child is benefiting from the program. It ultimately does affect development. Many of the characteristics that have been discussed already as indicators of development are also indicators of appropriateness of a program for a child. These are reviewed along with the impact of group size, adult/child ratio, and program structure on the child's adjustment to the program, Figure 13.5.

Children may not, or possibly cannot, say, "I just love going to this program." There are behavioral signs that the child is emotionally, physically, socially, and cognitively comfortable there. Sometimes a program may not meet the needs of children. There may be a discontinuity between the child's home situation and the philosophy of the school. A child from a very structured home that stresses adult permission and obedience may have difficulty adjusting to a program that promotes independence and allows choices. A child from a small family with little contact with other children may find the large group setting a hard adjustment. The high energy of a colorful, noisy, busy center may be too much for a highly distractable child. Consideration should be given to the parents' values, the program's goals and the child's personality and experience.

Parents and staff watch for signs of that adjustment to judge if the program is meeting the needs of the child. The use of the portfolio to document the child's participation can give specific information on areas of development. Periodically, it is

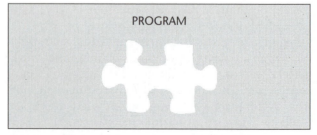

Figure 13.5 Does the program fit the child?

necessary to step back and view the whole child. Looking at the child's adjustment to the program does that. These indicators are for toddlers through early school age. Some require an advanced level, especially in language, but behavior can be interpreted even beyond language.

Behavioral Indicators of Comfort

The child gives behavioral indications of the suitability of the program for developmental needs. Some criterions may be answered with a "No" because the child is going through separation anxiety or another emotional upset. It is important for parents and staff to give attention to a child's discomfort. It is a form of communication. The program is appropriate when the child

- begins the day at the program without a fuss
- knows the schedule for the day and can anticipate what is coming next
- feels an affinity to the school and says things like, "My school," " My cubbie," "My teacher"
- has opportunities to play actively inside and outside every day
- talks freely at school (at maximum of language level)
- is able to make choices from sufficient equipment and materials
- is not exhibiting stress, such as crying or regressive behaviors
- has enough time to work at choice activities
- is warned of impending change in activities, and given opportunity to finish and clean up
- moves from one activity to the next comfortably
- does not have to wait before the next activity can begin
- does not have to receive step-by-step directions for activities but can explore materials independently
- is not forced to continue in an activity
- is able to watch or choose not to participate in an activity
- displays pride in the work brought home
- can relate what occurred at school when prompted specifically (Children need a reminder to trigger memory association.)
- talks about playing with other children in the group
- knows the teachers' names
- interacts with the teacher on a one-to-one basis several times during the day
- goes to the adult for assistance and comfort
- sleeps, eats, and toilets at school without difficulty

Parents and staff should work together to determine if the child is in the right placement where the child is receiving not just physical care but learns and feels acceptance and belonging.

Looking at the Program Through the Child's Eyes

At times any one or more of the previously listed indicators may be answered with a "No." That does not mean necessarily there is an adjustment problem. It may mean that the child is moving through a developmental phase, struggling with the change in thinking or feeling. It may mean there are personality differences between the child and a staff member. The child may feel threatened by an aggressive child in the group. There may be changes happening at home that are affecting the child at school. A child exhibiting such behaviors should be closely observed in an attempt to learn the cause. There are many factors that influence the child's adjustment to the program.

The Make Up of the Peer Group. Different activities depend on a certain number of people to be successful.

Exercise: How many people would you like in your group for the following activities?

Cheering your team at a football game:
Sleeping:
Changing a light bulb:
Taking a shower:
Talking on the phone:
Eating:
Riding in a car:
Birthing a child:
Numbering all the books in a library:
Playing a card game:

Some activities are solitary, or at least intimate. The space and action also determine the number of people who can participate in certain activities. The size of the task at hand, and the skill required, or the occasion, are also factors in group size. When thinking of young children in group settings, some of these same factors need to be considered.

More than 57 percent of children younger than five whose mothers were employed are cared for by nonrelatives. Thirty-two percent of those children are in center-based care while 25 percent are in family child care homes (Children's Defense Fund, 1995). Children are grouped together by different criteria in different programs. There are rationales, advantages, and disadvantages to each decision.

Chronological Age Groups. Most center-based child care and public schools group children by chronological age. Grouping children by age assumes that children who are in the same age range have similar needs and interests. This is usually the case, especially when curriculum is open-ended so that a range of developmental abilities can all find success. Individual differences, especially of exceptional children (those with disabilities or giftedness), and arbitrary age cutoffs sometimes make decisions about group placement difficult. At 15 months, a child might be advanced physically, walking steadily. She is interested in the wider environment of the young toddler room. Regulations or policies might prevent her advancement into the next group. The wobbly walker may be arbitrarily "promoted" to the young toddler room at 18 months. For a slow-to-walk infant, a room of two-year-olds is a fearsome place. Grouping of children by age has different criteria and functions for the child's interactions in the group setting.

Mixed-Age or Multi-Age Groups. **Mixed-age group** or heterogeneous grouping most resembles the family group with members of different ages, Figure 13.6. It gives young children the opportunity to observe, imitate, and learn from older ones. It gives older children occasions to practice nurturing skills, reteach learned skills, and feel competent. Most family child care settings have children of mixed-age groups since they usually care for siblings. In Kontos's review of group size, the average family day care group was from five to eight (1992, p. 60). Some centers have mixed-age groups or vertical grouping with the state regulating the size of the group and the adult-child ratio. Prosocial behaviors, such as help-giving, sharing, and turn-taking are elicited in the older children toward the younger ones. Older children can lead younger ones to higher levels of cognitive thinking by assisting in collaborative efforts as "experts." Evangelou (1989) recommends the consideration of the optimum age range and the proportion of older to younger children. The allocation of time to the mixed-age group and the curriculum and teaching strategies are crucial to the success of mixed-age grouping.

The Size of the Group. In a large study comparing children at home and in center-based day care, the size of the group and adult/child ratio mattered a great deal. "Children in classes with more children per caregiver made smaller gains in cognitive development, were less socially skilled with unfamiliar peers, and were less compliant. There are apparently some benefits of being in a class with low adult-child ratio; these children learn to curb their aggressive behavior" (Clark-Stewart, et al., 1994, p. 240). Family day care studies also indicate that as the group size increased, the interaction of adults with children decreased (Kontos, 1992). Even in elementary schools, an experiment in class size including 7,000 children kindergarten through third grade, showed students in classes of 15 raised math and reading standardized scores dramatically (Mosteller, 1995).

The various states have a wide range of children allowed in groups according to age. Figure 13.7 illustrates an interesting comparison from the Children's Defense Fund (1995).

Infants (Birth to 18 Months). It is common sense that the younger the child, the more care they require, so the size of the group should be smaller. Newborn infants need the care and attention from a few of the same people. It is critical that infants receive the required care. The National Day Care Study (Roupp, et al., 1979) found that children under two years needed a small group and low staff-infant ratios. It also found strong caregiver qualifications predicted positive outcomes. Infants should be cared for in groups no larger than eight with two adults, or in a group of three with one adult (Reynolds, 1990). The quality and frequency of adult-child interactions are the critical variables in infant care (Phillips, 1987). The interaction with adults provides for each infant's individual physical and emotional needs. This includes feeding, diapering, and holding. Infants of younger than eight months interact with the teacher while in close physical proximity to other infants. The space size requirements vary by state regulation, but 35 square feet per child is considered minimum.

Observations of the infant in the group setting would expect to see her looking at other infants,

Figure 13.6 There are advantages and disadvantages to multi-age groups.

**Maximum Number of Children Allowed Per Caretaker and
Maximum Group Size in Child Care Centers, By Age of Children**

	Child per Caretaker			Group Size		
	12 Months	2 Years	4 Years	12 Months	2 Years	4 Years
Alabama	6	8	20	6	8	20
Alaska	6	6	10	—	—	—
Arizona	5	10	15	—	—	—
Arkansas	6	9	15	—	—	—
California	4	12	12	—	—	—
Colorado	5	7	12	10	14	—
Connecticut	4	4	10	8	8	20
Delaware	7	10	15	—	—	—
District of Columbia	4	4	10	8	8	20
Florida	6	11	20	—	—	—
Georgia	8	10	18	18	20	36
Hawaii	5	8	16	12	—	—
Idaho	12	12	12	—	—	—
Illinois	4	8	10	12	16	20
Indiana	4	5	12	10	15	—
Iowa	4	6	12	—	—	—
Kansas	5	7	12	10	14	24
Kentucky	6	10	14	12	20	28
Louisiana	8	12	16	—	—	—
Maine	4	5	8	12	15	24
Maryland	3	6	10	6	12	20
Massachusetts	3	4	10	7	9	20
Michigan	4	4	12	—	—	—
Minnesota	4	7	10	8	14	20
Mississippi	9	12	16	10	14	20
Missouri	4	8	10	8	16	—
Montana	4	8	8	—	—	—
Nebraska	4	6	12	—	—	—
Nevada	6	8	13	—	—	—
New Hampshire	4	5	12	12	15	24
New Jersey	4	7	15	4	7	20
New Mexico	6	10	12	—	—	—
New York	4	5	8	8	10	16
North Carolina	7	12	20	14	24	—
North Dakota	4	5	10	—	—	—
Ohio	6	8	14	12	16	28
Oklahoma	6	8	15	12	16	30
Oregon	4	4	10	8	8	20
Pennsylvania	4	5	10	8	10	20
Rhode Island	4	6	10	8	12	20
South Carolina	7	7	14	—	—	—
South Dakota	5	5	10	20	20	20
Tennessee	7	8	15	14	16	20
Texas	6	13	20	14	35	35
Utah	7	7	15	8	14	25
Vermont	4	5	10	8	10	20
Virginia	4	10	12	—	—	—
Washington	7	7	10	14	14	20
West Virginia	4	8	12	—	—	—
Wisconsin	4	6	13	8	12	24
Wyoming	5	8	15	—	—	—
Recommended	3-5	4-6	8-10	6-12	8-12	16-20

Figure 13.7 Child Group Size and Ratio By State. (Reprinted with permission from *The State of America's Children Yearbook, 1995.* Washington, DC: Children's Defense Fund, 1995, p. 121.)

smiling and touching them. The adult monitors the physical contact, for the infant has no knowledge that their squeezes and hair pullings hurt. They also lack the self-control to keep from doing it. Other children are part of the world to be manipulated. Once infants become mobile by crawling, creeping, cruising, or walking, they approach other children with simple chase games and peek-a-boo. They enjoy little fingerplays and songs together and a book shared with another child on the lap of the adult. They begin to make vocal exchanges with each other, using vocal signals to invite attention or alert the teacher that they need to be removed from this stressful situation.

The babies' and toddlers' compliance with the adults' requests begin with realistic expectations for children's behavior. Some guidelines from Jennifer Birckmayer, Cornell University (1988) are

1. Have age-appropriate expectations for children's behavior.
2. Tell children what they can do.
3. Distraction is a good technique to use with very young children.
4. Change the environment instead of the behavior.
5. Offer choices only when you can accept child's decision.
6. Use words and actions to guide behavior.
7. Have a few, simple rules consistently enforced.
8. Recognize children's efforts.
9. Be a friend.
10. Be a good role model.

The teacher watches for developmental milestones that occur almost daily at this age and marks the developmental checklist the program is using. Daily contact sheets are used to document the amount of time and type of activities provided for the infant each day. A copy is kept in the child's file. It is desirable to send a copy home at the end of every day, Figure 13.8.

Toddlers (18 Months to 3 Years). The recommended ratio is five toddlers to one adult and a total group size of ten. This ensures the safety and exchanges with responsive adults needed for this age. Considerations for the toddler in a group setting begin with a safe, healthy environment. The emotional environment provides support, with places to withdraw. The toddler needs consistent teachers and adequate space and materials. He is still developing coordination and has limited social skills. The child is observed as he interacts with the materials, demonstrating his physical development. He can participate in small groups

for very short periods of time. This could include songs, fingerplays, and short story books. His play with other children is at the functional level, using toys in a repetitive manner but advancing to more make-believe play, simulating grown-up activities. He will pretend to drive a car, bake a cake, sweep the floor, especially when he sees the steering wheel, cake pans, or broom. Interactions with other children will be stormy because of limited language and the inability to take another's viewpoint. He wants the big ball of Play Doh, so he takes it. When the other player protests, there is little self-restraint in the responses.

Toddlers are fast moving, independent, yet needing much adult assistance with self-care skills. Observations include documentation of the child's ability to dress, eat, and the beginning interest in toileting. Socially, the child is taking an interest in other children but with little emotional control or awareness of the feelings of others. This leads to aggressiveness and the possibility for physical harm. The child is rapidly developing language skills but often uses biting as an expression of frustration or aggression.

Toddlers have learned the sequence of the events of the day and depend very heavily on its stability. Arrivals and departures are handled in a routine way that allows for a relaxed, unrushed atmosphere. They need programming that allows them mostly free-play activities from a wide range of choices, including outside play and soft, quiet areas. Sleep and rest time should be adaptable to individual schedules and needs, with some children needing frequent short naps, and others needing long afternoon naps. Eating times are social opportunities with self-care skills, food exploration, and casual conversation included.

Transitions between periods of play, sleeping, eating, and diapering or toileting should be natural and relaxed. Waiting time should be eliminated and children warned that the end of that phase of the day is coming to an end (Psaltis & Stonehouse, 1990). When these elements are included in the program, the child is observed as she follows routines, interacts with adults and children, and maximizes the learning environment, Figure 13.9.

Circle times for toddlers include songs, fingerplays, creative movement, and short books or storytelling. Participation should be optional. It can last as long or as short as they are interested. Guidelines for group behavior, including self-discipline, depend on a knowledge of child development to be realistic. The young child is egocentric, not able to put himself in someone else's place. The young child is impulsive without the ability to

INFANT DAILY CARE SHEET

Child's Name: _____

Today's Date: _____

PARENT INFORMATION

How did your child sleep last night?

Is there medication today?   _____

What is your child's feeding schedule?   _____

_____

Is there any other information?   _____

_____

CAREGIVER INFORMATION

NUTRITION

Bottles:

Snacks:

Lunch:

BATHROOMING

Time	Wet	BM

NAPPING

From _____ to _____

_____ to _____

_____ to _____

Some things we have observed today...

_____	Hand games	_____	Babbled	_____	Rolled
_____	Books	_____	Talked	_____	Crawled
_____	Ball play	_____	Giggled	_____	Stood
_____	Used toys	_____	Cuddled	_____	Danced
_____	Climbed	_____	Cried, but comforted when held		
_____	Outside	_____	Other		

Questions or comments for home:

Signed _____

Figure 13.8 Daily Contact Sheet for Infants and Toddlers. (Reprinted with permission from the BC Center, Broome Community College, Binghamton, NY.)

TODDLER DAILY CARE SHEET

Child's Name: _____

Today's Date: _____

PARENT INFORMATION

Is there medication today? _____

Is there any other information? _____

_____

CAREGIVER INFORMATION

NUTRITION

Snacks:

A.M.

P.M.

Lunch:

None   Some   Most   All

BATHROOMING

Time	Wet	BM

NAPPING

From _____ to _____

_____

Some of the things we observed today/special activities...

_____ Books   _____ Markers/Crayons   _____ Legos

_____ Climber   _____ Painted   Special activity of the day was:

_____ Play Doh   _____ Outside   _____

_____ Water table   _____ Movement   _____ Puzzles

_____ Housekeeping area   _____ Special games   _____ Music

Questions or comments for home:

Signed _____

Figure 13.8 Daily Contact Sheet for Infants and Toddlers. (Reprinted with permission from the BC Center, Broome Community College, Binghamton, NY.)

Figure 13.9 Toddlers need *small* groups.

control emotional urges. Language is not fully developed yet, with vocabulary centered on things rather than ideas and symbolic actions. It is not developed enough to present a rational point of view or to capably negotiate. The young child's experience in life has been limited and memory is still developing, so that does not help in self-control. Adults control the environment by placing matches where the child cannot reach them or by placing furniture where a child cannot use it to climb to forbidden objects in cupboards or on shelves. Adults' directions are clear and specific. They give warning of an impending change in activities. It is the child's desire to please adults yet develop autonomy. The two desires come into conflict. The payoff might be a reward or the absence of punishment. Adults may give direct instruction about expectations of behavior (Kostelnik, et al., 1993, p. 180):

- telling children what is right and what is wrong
- informing children of expected standards
- restricting certain behaviors
- advising children about how to meet the standards the group has set
- redirecting children's behavior
- providing children with information about how their actions affect themselves and others
- giving children information about how their behavior looks to others

Observing the toddler during play gives information about her concept of right and wrong. She might paint continually on the wall, even after being reminded to paint on paper. It is noted that her inner controls might be missing. She is not understanding the directions. The cause may be emotional in nature, seeking attention, or demonstrating an open defiance to rules.

When the child knows clearly what is expected, observing the child adhere to those expectations gives information about memory, cognitive, and emotional development. The child understands and can resist temptation to do what he wants to follow the standard. When adults set firm limits about what behavior is not allowed, children learn to comply, first from outside control, but eventually internalizing the standards. The adults role model and make suggestions about how the child can meet the standards, giving them choices. By providing children with alternate activities, the adult gives a way for the child to focus his own attention and energies in another direction. When the adult indicates what effect the actions have on others, the child is receiving instruction on cause and effect and the consequences of his actions. Giving the child an outside view of how the actions appear to others begins the movement away from egocentrism.

Preschoolers (Three- to Five-Year-Olds). A total group size of 15 to 20 is recommended, with younger children in the lower range. The recommended adult-child ratio is two adults for that size group. Developmentally appropriate practices (Bradekamp, 1987) recommend that the schedule of the day include long periods of uninterrupted involvement in a variety of areas, commonly called learning centers. These usually are set up for independent use to develop physical, cognitive, creative, and social skills. When integrated curriculum or the project approach is used, there is a thematic connection between learning center areas. Woven throughout the schedule are routines for eating, sleeping or resting, toileting, and outside play. Circle time for the whole group, meetings, plan/do/review groups (High/Scope), and small group gatherings may be included, depending on the curriculum model.

School Age. Children attending public school have been placed traditionally in grades by chronological age. The cut-off dates for school entrance may vary as much as six months. Some are in early summer and others are not until the end of the calendar year. There are many in between. This makes it difficult when children are moving from one school district or state to another. Attempts to place children in classes by developmental age have met with difficulties, Figure 13.10. There are different opinions on the criteria and validity of the instruments. Questions have been raised on screenings, such as the Gesell Preschool Readiness Test (1978).

Children of different ages and at different stages present either a dilemma or opportunity to the

Figure 13.10 Children come in all sizes, ages, and stages—the school's dilemma.

school, depending on the philosophy. Some schools have divided each class into smaller groups by ability. This is to teach lessons closer to the levels of development. Many oppose this early tracking or separating children by abilities. Whole group instruction is difficult when children are functioning at a wide range of abilities. This is addressed by the exploration of the curriculum and teaching practices calling for "developmentally appropriate" rather than "age appropriate" strategies.

Whole Group Times. A whole group time may occur at the beginning of the day as a transition between home and school. It welcomes the group and informs them of the choices of the day. It is sometimes held in the middle of the day, usually right before lunch. Then it serves as a transition to review the work done in the morning and to prepare for lunch and rest time and afternoon activities. At the end of the day, some programs have a whole group time to summarize the day, recalling the highlights, looking forward to tomorrow, and transitioning to home. Beaty (1992) points out that these whole group times help children feel a common bond, a sense of community. They can include singing, fingerplays, large motor games and musical games, and creative movement. Hohmann and Weikart (1995) say group times should *not* include rigid routines, competitive games, or teacher-led lessons. They recommend it be held in a spacious location, with a specific plan. The adult should have the materials prepared and draw children in with a transition activity. They begin right away, not waiting until every child is in place. The activity is then turned over to the children. The adult's role is to watch and listen while children are the leaders and to transition the group into the next experience. It is

a different vision from the traditional whole group time (p. 269).

Unscheduled class meetings may be called to address class announcements, class problems, or mistaken behaviors. Gartrell (1994) refers to Glasser's model (1969) of class meetings that build a sense of togetherness. The general rules are that anyone can talk, take turns, be honest, and be kind. Besides the opening, middle, and closing meetings, unscheduled meetings are called out of necessity for spontaneous discussion. Problem solving by the group is underlined by protection of the dignity of the people involved in the problem. The situation is described using "I" messages; solutions are brainstormed and a course of action is decided by the group. This promotes community responsibility and cooperation.

Questionable Value of Calendar and Show and Tell.

Exercise: Imagine you are sitting on the floor. The leader says, "Now let's recite the Dow Jones Averages. What was it yesterday? Which stocks sold the most shares? How much was bid for IBM? How much offered? Now say after me, Alco Standard Corp, Am Home Products, Apple Computer, AT&T, Bell Atlantic, Chase Manhattan. Now you know the top-selling stocks. Don't you?

- Do you *really* know them?
- How would you feel if you couldn't remember?
- What if you heard others around you saying them but you couldn't?

Think about this in relation to children reciting numbers from the calendar and days of the week that have no meaning to them.

There are many programs that include counting the days on the calendar and reciting the days of the week and months of the year. These are abstract principles, not readily understood by young children. This exercise is rote memorization without much value. The time could be better spent on other topics of relevant interest to the children. If counting is the purpose or objective of the group time, there should be concrete objects for the children to count. This is according to child development principles. The association of the numeral is symbolic of the quantity and beyond the level of this developmental stage.

Exercise: Now you are sitting on the rug and it is Show and Tell time. Mary brings a full-length mink coat out of her backpack. She puts it on and walks around but you are told not to touch it. You might get it dirty. Then Gabriel brings out a new shotgun his father just gave him. He is so proud of it but the teacher is horrified. "Put that away. We don't allow guns at school." Next, it is Katharine's turn. She has an hour-long video of her trip to the Mall of America. There are things all around you that you want to do but you have to sit there and watch it.

Would you

- touch Mary's coat anyway?
- feel disappointed and angry that you did not get to talk about your prized gift?
- wiggle, reach for a toy, pinch a neighbor, and not listen to Katharine's trip monologue?

Show and Tell has its champions who claim it raises the self-esteem of children to bring an object from home and talk about it. They point out the value also of speaking before the whole group. Show and Tell usually involves long waiting. The children become disinterested in someone else's object because they are egocentric. The pressure builds to show bigger and better toys. These reasons present contrary evidence of its worth. Many have attempted to resolve the difficulties of Show and Tell with creative alternatives, some of which may be successful. Again, a careful consideration should be given to the objectives of the program. This is because of the knowledge of what young children are like:

> They cannot wait and watch without touching.
> They learn best by doing.
> They have limited capacity to describe an object.
> They have sensitivity already to the "haves" and the "have nots."

Teaching practices should be based on what is known about how children learn and develop. Reconsideration of practices sometimes causes resistance and defensiveness in teachers. Calendar and Show and Tell are topics for reflection and reconsideration.

High/Scope Small Group Time. Without espousing any curriculum model, the small group time of High/Scope gives effective principles for any program's group time. Small group time is conducted in an intimate place. It is just the right size for a few children and the adult. The same adult and children hold group time every day in that place, where the adult initiates a learning activity with real materials. The children explore the materials, deciding what to do with them. The

adult helps the children carry out their plan if they need assistance. At the end she helps them recall what they did (Hohmann & Weikart, 1995).

Transitions. Even though a daily routine necessitates many changes, most humans are resistant to change.

Exercise: List on a separate sheet of paper all the changes in activities and places you have been today.

Some people have difficulty getting out of bed, out of pajamas and into clothes, or out of the house and off to work or school. Every change means an adjustment in body position, temperature, sometimes clothing, change in social contacts, and perhaps a change in behavior.

This is difficult for adults but even harder for children. They have no concept of time, minutes, hours, or days. They are stationed in the present. "I am doing this now and I want to continue doing it." They may be forced to change activities. There was not enough time to finish what they were doing. They are led to another activity that they are not so sure they can or want to do. They become stressed. This is the time when children act out, cry, or withdraw.

Transition times need planning with just as much consideration as the activities. Routine signals such as bells, music, gentle whispers, and simple games all give children a clue rather than a command that it is time to make a change. When the schedule of the day is consistent, they quickly come to anticipate and adjust to the changes, especially when they are pleasantly carried out. Steffen Saifer's *Practical Solutions to Practically Every Problem* (1990) gives some suggestions:

> Transition from eating: Move immediately to next activity, provide table toys while they are waiting, station a teacher at next activity, or have snack or the meal in small groups.

> Transition to outdoor time: A teacher is stationed inside and one outside so children do not have to wait. Involve the children in a song while getting ready and have children make outside play choices ahead of time.

> Transition to clean up: Label all shelves to ease replacement, have child-sized mops, brooms, handy clean-up materials for self-care of room. Make a game of cleanup. Make it cooperative, not competitive or punishment.

> Transition to going home: End the day looking at books or listening to music, a quiet activity, end the day with a hug or handshake (pp. 32, 33)

When adults consider the child's needs first, plans are made for the program, activities, and interactions to fit those needs. When adults then consider each child as an individual and adapt the plans for that particular child, then the program is truly individually appropriate. If the child is exhibiting adjustment problems, it very likely is the program at fault, not the child.

SPECIAL POPULATIONS IN GROUP SETTINGS

The fit of the program to the needs of the child is vitally important to every child, but for a child with special needs it is critical. *Mainstreaming, integration, inclusion,* and *least restricted environment* are all terms related to the legal-legislative postures as well as child advocates promoting normalizing educational settings for children with special needs. The benefits of regular early childhood settings for children with special needs are many:

- In regular placements, negative views of children with handicaps are reduced because they are not isolated.
- When children of all abilities are grouped together, tolerance and understanding increase.
- Through interactions with typical children, peers become the behavior and skill role models in a demanding environment.
- Early intervention is beneficial for most handicaps.
- Younger children accept others more readily than older children who may have learned to stigmatize those who are different from themselves.

Planning and consideration of many factors ensure a successful placement for children with special needs in regular classrooms. Cook and colleagues (1992) suggest some of the same points of consideration discussed earlier in this chapter:

- Developmental levels rather than age groupings—By placing children with special needs with younger children, it decreases the developmental differences.
- Ratio of integrated children in the group—Some have suggested that when only one or two children with special needs are integrated into a group, they still experience isolation. When more than one and up to one-third of the class is children with special needs, true

integration is more likely to be successful. The caveat here is dependent on the nature of the special needs, the training of the teacher, and supplemental classroom assistance available.
- Individualized learning experiences—The curriculum for all children should be based on their interests and their strengths. Building on what they can do and modifying the environment and activities so that each child finds success is the principle of developmentally appropriate curriculum for all children.
- Partnerships with parents—The parents of children with special needs must be advocates for their own child. They are involved in more educational decisions about their child than other parents and must monitor their child's progress closely. This places the relationship and communication between teacher and parents in a priority position.

The placement decisions for children with special needs must be carefully considered so their abilities are maximized and needs are met.

HELPING PROFESSIONALS FOR PROGRAM EVALUATION AND SUPPORT

Help can come from referring to experts or from other people who have had a similar experience.

Consultants—The humorous definition of a consultant is someone from more than one hundred miles away. A consultant is a specialist who is enlisted, and paid, for their advice. Programs who want an impartial, outside evaluation often contract with a consultant to provide that service.

Support groups—Groups with like concerns often informally or formally band together to discuss, seek answers, commiserate, and give advice to one another. They can become a legislative force for change or a united voice to raise the public's awareness regarding an issue. Many support groups have been formed of families with children who have a specific diagnosed disorder. The program should be aware of these in the local community to make them known to families in the program who may benefit from such an alliance.

Week 13, Assignment A

SETTING OBSERVATION

Visit an early childhood program using the Setting Observation Form found in Appendix D. (It can be your own program, but try to look with a visitor's eyes.) Make notes of what you observe. After the observation, reflect on the meaning, impressions, inferences, and judgments. Write about how you think the setting reveals the philosophy of the program, the personality and style of the staff, and how the setting may affect the children, parents, and people who work there.

What to Do with It

If this is your own center, write a plan for improvements based on your observation. File the Setting Observation in the class file and share your plan with other staff. Set a timeline and action plan for implementing improvements. You may want to share the plan with parents and children. For example, in the newsletter, "We've been taking a good look at our classrooms lately and have noticed many pieces of equipment are in need of repair. So we are inviting you to a painting party to help us spruce up and make our learning place more appealing. It won't be all work. Mr. Jones has consented to bring his three-piece band to play for us between 12 and 1 as we eat our lunch, graciously provided by the Wong's Family Restaurant. We hope you can come to help, or even if you just can come for lunch. Please return the reservation form or call the school to let us know how many paint brushes to have available and how many to expect for lunch. Bring the children; we have paint projects for all and the Baby Room will be staffed."

Week 13, Assignment B

CLASS LIST LOG GROUP PARTICIPATION FOR ALL

Use the Class List Log found in Appendix D and observe the class this week at times when the whole group is together. It may be meeting, circle, planning, lunch, then storytime. Make notes about each child's participation and how each appears to be adjusting to the program. You may also want to make a column for transitions and note the individual behaviors displayed during times of change between activities.

What to Do with It

Transfer any significant information to the child's portfolio overview sheet. Note each child's level of involvement. If a child appears to be having difficulty, make a plan to do a more detailed observation (Anecdotal Recording) to look closer for signs of difficulty in adjustment.

Share the results with the class, parents, or a particular child, if appropriate. For example, "Yesterday when I was making notes during Circle Time I saw some people really were interested and some people didn't want to be there. Let's talk about it and see what we can decide," or "I've been observing Latricia for several weeks now and I am concerned that she still does not appear comfortable when presented with the wide range of choices we have in the room. We have decided to narrow it down to two choices for her to get started. Perhaps at home you could give her choices between two shirts, or pants or a dress, or between two acceptable foods. These things will give her more experience and confidence in her own decision-making ability."

File the Class List Log in the class file.

Week 13, Assignment C

ANECDOTAL RECORDING OF GROUP INTERACTIONS FOR GROUP D

This week select all the children in group D. Watch them for any episodes or actions that particularly demonstrate the child's typical interactions with the group. When you see it, jot some notes and amplify into a full Anecdotal Recording, with as many details as possible about action and conversation. In the right column, write your comments, explanations, and questions.

GROUP INTERACTIONS		
Documentation	Recorder	Date
CL short circle time	MS	12/5
AR games with turns	BAN	12/21
CL comfortable leader	MS	6/9

Figure 13.11 Portfolio Overview Example

What to Do with It

In each child's portfolio, note the presence of the Anecdotal Recording on the overview sheet with your name and date, Figure 13.11.

Share your findings with parent or child if appropriate. For example, "I've been observing some children this week watching for signs of their adjustment or comfort with group activities. Donato fully participates and has an understanding of turn-taking, which is unusual for this age. He says you play games a lot at home. That has obviously helped him," or "Patrick, when I was watching you play 'Doggie, Doggie, Where's your Bone?' today, you kept getting angry when no one picked you. Maybe if you pretended to have the bone, like put your hands behind your back, they would think you had it. Maybe you could try that next time and see."

File the recording in each child's portfolio. If there are any followup recommendations or questions from the observation, be sure to make a note somewhere to remember to do it.

Week 13, Assignment D

REFLECTIVE JOURNAL

Respond to the following in your Reflective Journal, kept in a private file at home.

	This week when I took the "trip" I noticed...
	It really bothered me because...
	I am never going to...
	I'm worried about...
	Could it be...
	I need to remember to...
	The funniest thing that happened this week was...

REFERENCES

Beaty, J. (1992). *Preschool appropriate practices.* New York: Harcourt Brace Jovanovich.

Birckmayer, J. (1988). *Discipline for babies and toddlers.* Unpublished manuscript, Cornell University, Ithaca, NY.

Bradekamp, S. (Ed). (1987). *Developmentally appropriate practice in early childhood programs serving children from birth through age 8.* Washington, DC: National Association for the Education of Young Children.

Children's Defense Fund. (1995). *The state of America's children yearbook, 1995.* Washington, DC: Author.

Clark-Stewart, K., Gruber, C., & Fitzgerald, L. (1994). *Children at home and in day care.* Hillsdale, NJ: Lawrence Erlbaum Associates, Publishers.

Derman-Sparks, L. (1989). *Anti-bias curriculum: Tools for empowering young children.* Washington, DC: National Association for the Education of Young Children.

Evangelou, D. (1989). *Mixed-Age Groups in Early Childhood Education. ERIC Digest* ED308990 90.

Gartrell, D. (1994). *A guidance approach to discipline.* Albany: Delmar Publishers.

Gesell Institute of Human Development. (1978). *Preschool readiness test.* New Haven, CT: Author.

Glasser, W. (1969). Schools without failure. New York: Harper & Row.

Gordon, T. (1970). *Parent effectiveness training.* New York: P. H. Weyden.

Harms, T. & Clifford, R. M. (1980). *Early childhood environment rating scale (ECERS).* New York: Teachers College Press.

Harms, T. & Clifford, R. M. (1989). *Family day care rating scale (FDCRS).* New York: Teachers College Press.

Harms, T., Cryer, D. & Clifford, R. M. (1990). *Infant/toddler environment rating scale (ITERS).* New York: Teachers College Press.

Harms, T., Jacobs, E. V., & White, D. R. (1996). *School-age care environment rating scale (SACERS).* New York: Teachers College Press.

High/Scope Press. (1989). *Program implementation profile (PIP administration manual.* Ypsilanti, MI: High/Scope Educational Research Foundation.

Hohmann, M. & Weikart, D. (1995). Educating young children. Ypsilanti, MI: High/Scope Press.

Kontos, S. (1992). *Family day care: Out of the shadows into the limelight.* Washington, DC: National Association for the Education of Young Children.

Kostelnik, M., Stein, L., Whiren, A., & Soderman, A. (1993). *Guiding children's social development, second edition.* Albany: Delmar Publishers.

Mosteller, F. (1995). The Tennessee study of class size in *The future of children.* Cambridge, MA: American Academy of Arts and Sciences.

National Association for the Education of Young Children. (1991). *Accreditation criteria and procedures of the national academy of early childhood programs.* Washington, DC: Author.

Parent Evaluation of Child Care Programs. (1989, June). *Child Care Information Exchange, 67,* 25–26.

Phillips, D. (1987). *Quality in child care, what does research tell us?* Washington, DC: National Association for the Education of Young Children.

Psaltis, M. & Stonehouse, A. (1990). Toddler centered routines in A. Stonehouse (Ed.). *Trusting toddlers: Planning for one- to three-year-olds in child care centers.* St. Paul, MN: Toys 'n Things Press.

Reynolds, E. (1990). *Guiding young children: A child-centered approach.* Mountain View, CA: Mayfield Publishing Company.

Roupp, R., Travers, J., Glantz, F., & Coelen, C. (1979). *Children at the center: Final results of the national day care study.* Cambridge, MA: Abt Associates.

Saifer, S. (1990). *Practical solutions to practically every problem: The early childhood teacher's manual.* St. Paul, MN: Redleaf Press.

U. S. Department of Health and Human Services. (1979). *Head Start program performance standards: Self-assessment validation instrument.* Washington, DC: Office of Human Development Services, Administration for Children, Youth, and Families.

Using Portfolios to Conference with Parents and Looking at the Child's Interactions with Adults

IN THIS CHAPTER ....

✔ Using Portfolios to Conference with Parents

✔ Looking at the Child's Interactions with Adults

✔ Topics in Observation: Does the *Week by Week* System Meet NAEYC Guidelines for Assessment?

✔ Special Populations and Home and School Communications

✔ Helping Professionals for Home and School Communications

✔ Next Week

Observations have been accumulating in the portfolio. Their effective use in home and school communication is the topic of the final observation feature. "Good information is priceless but if we can't get to it, it's useless," someone said recently concerning the usefulness of becoming computer literate. It could be extended with another phrase, "and if we don't do something with it, it's foolish." That applies to all the information and documentation accumulated about the child. At the end of the year comes the question, "What to Do with It?" The future possession of the portfolio, the class file, and the Reflective Journal conclude this section.

Parents are the authorities on their own children. In group settings, children are shared with other people, teachers, who can provide a different perspective on the child. That is an awesome responsibility. Daily contacts with parents are the preferable mode of communicating the observations and assessments between home and school. Maximizing these opportunities is discussed. Sometimes written communication about the child is the vehicle of transferring

information. There are advantages and pitfalls to this mode of exchange. More formal written reports, such as progress reports and child studies, are sometimes warranted, so templates and advice for writing reports about the child are presented. Combining verbal and written reports in a parent conference is a unique time of sharing between home and school. More effective parent conferences occur with careful preparation and implementation. Guidance will be given for successful parent conferences. Occasionally, parent conferences of a distinct type are necessary, such as problem solving, parent questions, complaints, or an exit interview. Whenever parents and staff of a program have a discussion, there is great potential to benefit the child. That is the guiding beacon this section follows.

Children, entrusted to other adults in other settings, must adjust and adapt to other schedules, expectations, and ways of interacting. All have seen the difference in a child's behavior with the parents, then the grandparents. How well they know their allies! In this final section which looks at child development, this adjustment of the child to other adults is an important one, concluding the child development portion of this book.

A final assessment of the *Week by Week* plan ends this chapter and the book.

USING PORTFOLIOS TO CONFERENCE WITH PARENTS

Exercise: Using a separate sheet of paper, connect these dots alphabetically:

AB   C

D

A and B are the parents, and C is the child. Color that connection in as tightly as you see it. It will be darker and bolder for some, almost becoming one rectangular block. For some, A and B may be farther apart or one not even in the picture. For others, the line between AB and C may be a zig zag of volatile relationships. D is the teacher who comes into the lives of AB and C at some point. The connection of D to A and B is through C. The professional recognizes that role as connected but apart, a temporary one that supports both A, B, and C. The lines to D are erasable, because they are temporary but in an effort to positively affect the child, the teacher does all to establish communication lines to A and B, the parents. Those lines of communication may take many forms, a telephone line, written communication, now even electronics, but whatever form, the goal is to make it a solid, two-way communication to ultimately benefit the child.

Parent involvement does not have to be spaghetti suppers, fund raisers, or discipline classes (though all of those are worthwhile). Parent involvement, in its truest sense, is the knowledge parents have about their child while in the program. Involved parents are familiar with the goals of the program, its policies and procedures, and how those relate to their child. They also know what the child's day is like and how the child is functioning in the group setting. Confidence is built that the staff will keep them informed of important facts about their child.

The first step is a well-planned intake process, informing parents of the facts they need to know. From the program's personal contacts with the parents, parents will build trust in the program. Even if they may not understand all the program is about, they can tell these people care about them and their child. This trust is extended through various ways during the year, in daily contacts, written communications, progress reports, and parent conferences. Whatever the mode, these communications should be positive, descriptive, and personal, Figure 14.1.

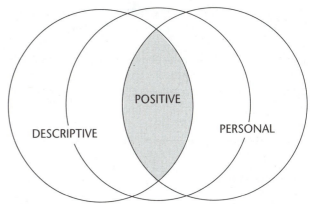

Figure 14.1 Parent-teacher communications must be positive, descriptive, and personal.

DAILY CONTACTS

Personal

The best way for contacts to be personal is if the staff and parents know each other. Through home visits, open house, parent visits to the classroom, phone calls, and notes, the staff establishes rapport with each parent. This is not to become friends, though that may happen, but to extend friendliness, courtesy, and partnership in a shared interest—the child. The teacher may have to make the effort again and again. It is like the persistent salesperson using different techniques to reach the customer. Many teachers react that it is their job to teach or care for the child, not the parent. They cannot adequately and single-handedly do that job without the parents' cooperation or at least acknowledgment of the role each plays.

Programs that have daily contact with parents who bring and pickup their children have wonderful opportunities. Each day tidbits of information about the child are casually shared by the parent. This gives background and breadth to what the teacher knows about the child to help interpret behavior and help the child develop. Sharing the tidbits of the day with parents at dismissal time gives insight to parents about the child's day, accomplishments, and attempts. This is an important, crucial part of the teacher's responsibility. The teacher establishes rapport with each parent, seeing them day in and day out. Getting to know them and their child should be a priority. Noticing the new hairstyle, or employment badge, or hurried look indicates to the parent they are recognized as human beings. The teacher sees them not just as the client, the tuition check writer, or Amber's daddy. Not all are suited to this task, so the person on the teaching team who is the most adept at personal contacts should be the "doorperson." That person provides a friendly welcoming face and attitude, a receptive ear, and tactful conversation.

Descriptive

It is a luxury to be able to greet parents at the end of the day and complete the circle by relating a bit of the child's day back to the parent. It gives the parent and child a springboard for later conversations about the day that may need a little nudge. A flood of talk springs forth when parents have a little seed to get the child started. The comments at the door also let the parent have an idea of not only what the child did but how they are doing. They make comparisons with other children, "Gee, all the children in Heather's class can put on their own boots. Maybe I better work with her to learn how," or "The teacher said Tamiche played for a long time with the Play Doh and she gave me a recipe to make it at home. Maybe that would occupy her while I fix dinner." Parenting education is occurring in subtle ways.

It is impossible to give daily detailed comments to every parent. Using the many communication modes, descriptive little vignettes like those in the assignments should be shared with parents often. Just as it is important to observe every child in the group, it is important to share information with every parent. It is easy to share those shining moments but for some children, remembering to turn the water off after they wash their hands is an accomplishment to be shared. It takes tact and practice to describe daily happenings accurately and without sarcasm. With practice it becomes natural. A little tip: The doorperson can keep a Class List Log in a private spot and jot down who received little "gems" at the door. After a few days a spot check will show that some children have not had any good news shared for a while. The teacher can make a conscious effort to observe and share a bit of information.

Positive

All comments shared informally, at the door or in other means, should be *positive* ones. At the end of the day a parent is tired. The child has long forgotten the mistaken behaviors. Other parents are

present. This is no time to bring out a litany of problems the child had that day. Those conflicts, whether with another child, the staff, or the materials, cannot be solved then so there is no need to talk about them. Staff who tell "bad news" at the end of the day are venting anger. They are displaying their ineptness at guiding the child's behavior. They seem to be expecting the parent to take action on something that happened at school. That seems like an unfair request. It could even be interpreted as laying blame on the parent for raising such a destructive, aggressive, unruly child. Teachers list "tattletale" at the top of the list of characteristics they do not like in children. Telling parents about a child's mistaken behaviors at the end of the day is in the same vein. No, the doorperson should only tell good news, Figure 14.2.

Looking at development is from the positive viewpoint. The baseline is, "What has the child accomplished so far?" Despite the level of development, it has been accomplished and can be shared as good news.

"Derek made it to the bathroom once today."
  Rather than: "Derek had three toilet accidents today."
"Cecilia used her blanket for comfort today but did let go of it to go down the slide."
  Rather than: "Cecilia whined most of the day and didn't play hardly at all."
"Roshann made an *R* today."
  Rather than: "He painted an *R* on the wall."

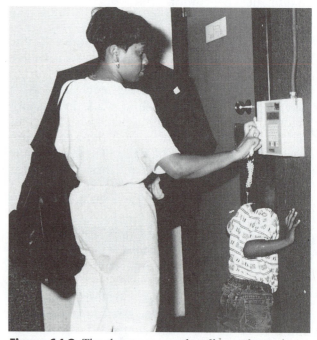

Figure 14.2 The doorperson only tells good news!

It may not be possible to relate "good news" stories to every parent at the end of every day, but they should receive frequent, descriptive positive messages. If parents pickup their children at the center, *every parent* and *every child* should be acknowledged as they leave. It also relieves those anxious moments when suddenly someone says, "I didn't see Serina leave." The doorperson can say, "I was at the door and Mrs. Bigelow was in a hurry so scooted in and out. I saw them leave." A system of signout also safeguards this possibly dangerous time of the day. The personal touch brings closure to the day for the child and reinforces the friendly relationship between the home and program.

Written Communication

Exercise: Number the following pieces of mail from 1 to 10 in the order you would open them.

___ Card-sized envelope with no return address
___ Credit card preapproval
___ Offer for a free water test
___ Newsletter from an organization
___ Advertisement for a new early childhood magazine
___ Letter from your grandmother
___ Letter from the IRS, stamped "Refund"
___ Telephone bill
___ Letter from the "love of your life"
___ Registered letter from a collection agency

A letter from a friend or someone highly regarded is opened expectantly. Those unsolicited pieces of mail are often not even read. Some mail brings apprehension and anxiety as it is opened, causing feelings of depression, anger, or uncertainty.

Written communications from the early childhood program should be closer to the beginning of the above list than the end. The same points about daily contacts could be made regarding written communications. They should be personal, descriptive, and positive.

Parent Handbook. Educational institutions, from playgroups to universities, have policies or sets of guidelines under which they operate. The people involved with those institutions need to know what those guidelines are to follow them. It is like knowing the rules when playing a game. Early childhood programs should state a clear mission or purpose, policies and procedures. The people participating in that program need to know the policies of enrollment, services, what they can expect from the program, and what their responsi-

bility is to it. This is usually done in a *Parent Handbook,* a guide with all the necessary information parents need to know. Often parents are too busy to read it or the guide book is too involved and intimidating. Efforts to make it user-friendly with indexes, graphics, and concise format have proven to be effective. Orientations where the most important details are presented verbally help the non-reader, the visual learner, and reinforces important elements. Home visits and individual conversations can clarify those points that parents need to know most. All of this is done with respect for the parents, with an attitude of partnership and consideration for the ultimate benefit of the child.

Newsletters. A periodic newsletter informing parents of current news helps with parent involvement. Descriptions of past events with short anecdotes from the children give the readers a sense of being there. This should be easy to do from the Anecdotal Recordings. Names of children and volunteers in a newsletter increases its readers' interest. Details parents need to know should be bold, concise, not imbedded in lines and lines of writing. Short daily or weekly plans in a calendar format will give the parents and child a conversation topic. Future events could be anticipated, "It says here that a bunny will visit today. Maybe you want to take a carrot to feed it?" Past events are remembered, "It says here that you had a bee hive and bee keeper visit your class. I didn't know that. Can you tell me about it?"

Positive encouragement for parents should be the theme of newsletter writing. It is a tough job. Parents are not interested in articles telling them they should be doing more, more, and more.

"Did you know that we have books to borrow so you don't have to make a trip to the library?"
Rather than: "You should read to your child 15 minutes every day. If you don't, they won't be good readers."

There are some commercial newsletters that are very well done that can be personalized by additional pages or by using only edited portions of them. The newsletter should be friendly in tone and fun to read, with short, informative articles. The print should be clear and readable with one-half as much white space as there is print. That means that drawings by the children, poems centered in columns, and graphics should comprise one-third of the space. These will catch the reader's eye and illustrate the text. It draws the reader's interest to an article a few paragraphs in length, Figure 14.3.

Happy Notes. In situations in which parents and teachers do not have daily contact, happy notes serve the purpose of comments made at the door. They can be written and tucked in a knapsack or handed to a parent with one-line, personal, descriptive, and positive comments about the

---

CONKLIN PRESCHOOL
JANUARY NEWSLETTER

January finds us winding down from the hectic pace of the holiday season. Here is a big "THANK YOU" to those of you who have given so much during the first months of school. Thanks for selling candy bars (the sale was a huge success), for driving on field trips, for those of you who supported Toys-for-Tots, for party food and most of all for your spirit. Without each one of you giving our holiday would have been less bright, how did we do so much?

LET'S PRETEND - Young children delight in pretending. It's a way of life for them. They grow emotionally, socially, and intellectually. It helps them make sense out of their world. It helps them make friends and feel good about themselves. Young children need more than space, equipment and time, they need you-your encouragement and participation. Pretending should be in all homes. Have you planned any "Let's pretend" days lately? It's fun!

SLEIGH RIDING

We have a winter wonderland right outside the preschool door and plan on spending a lot of time enjoying this. Each day we will go out the last 15 to 20 minutes to sleigh ride or shovel snow. The children must be dressed with boots, hats or hoods, mittens, and snowsuit or they will be unable to go outside. If you DO NOT want your child going out please come back 20 minutes early.

CANDY BARS

This years fund raiser is winding down, we've circulated almost 9,600 candy bars throughout the community. What an ambitious endeavor for our school, but the challenge was met and our goal reached! Money continues to be returned, so we are unable to calculate the recipients of the tuition prizes at this time. Winners will be posted on the bulletin board. A big "THANK YOU" to everyone who worked so hard selling candy.

ICE CASTLE

We are going to attempt to build a castle from ice. Get excited about this by filling empty 1/2 gallon milk cartons with water, add a few drops of food coloring, and put them outside to freeze. Be PATIENT, don't rush the blocks by putting them in the freezer, they'll just melt

outside. When they are completely frozen remove the cartons, bring them to school and watch the castle grow. The ingredients necessary for a beautiful castle are milk drinkers, cold weather and patience.

ADVISORY COUNCIL

The school year is half over and the Parent Advisory Council is well underway. Sharon and Connie, Co-presidents say, "Come and join us, we promise you'll have a good time." Kathy Lipsky, one of our preschool parents, will spend some time discussing home health hazards, what they are and how to prevent them. After eating the soup and bread, prepared by the hospitality committee, you're sure to feel the warmth that only comes from good food and good friends. We'll see you on January 18th at 12:00, childcare is provided.

PLEASE JOIN US!!

COUNTRY LINE DANCING
January 31st
7:00
Elks Club in Kirkwood Route 11
Meet us there or
at school at 6:45 to car pool.
$3 per person
Everyone is invited
They'll teach us to DANCE!

Figure 14.3 Newsletter Example. (Reprinted with permission. Conklin Preschool, Conklin, NY.)

child that day. Every recording assignment could bring out material from which to draw these comments. Finding the time to do these is a consideration. How about one a day? Does that seem manageable? If so, then use a class list and write one a day, focusing on one positive achievement or skill that child displayed today. See Chapter 1 for an example.

Technology. Electronic and technical innovations are changing the way people communicate.

Email. With email, it is possible to send electronic messages, electronic happy notes, to parents who are linked to computer messaging. The day's events or newsletter could be "mailed" to everyone in the class via the computer modem and a distribution list. Future inventions will modify the way people communicate.

Voice Mail. Parents with voice mail (answering machines) can receive short messages of good news from the program. That would be a good welcome home at the end of the day to hear the teacher's voice say, "Mr. and Mrs. Jones, listen to what James learned today. James, want to sing the Snowman song for Mommy and Daddy?" Answering machines at the school could provide reminders for the next day, little parenting tips, or songs by the children. Anyone who wants to call the program in the evening after hours would hear them and leave a message for the teacher "after the beep."

Traveling Journals. Many programs have made traveling journals that go back and forth between school and home. Some are notes written between the parent and the teacher. Several programs have a traveling journal in a tote bag with toys or art materials. In this preschool, families were asked to do something with Rags, a cute stuffed puppy, write about it, and send it back to school for the next child. The responses are delightful, showing parents' creativity, encouraging the child to draw or write as well. While they have the journal at home, they read the other entries and look at drawing and writing attempts. Here are a few that accompanied a stuffed dog Rags, along with a tape of the songs they would be singing for several weeks. Older children could write their own journal entries for their classmates and their families to read, Figure 14.4. A cassette recorder and a tape on which the teacher has recorded songs sung in school or a short review of projects in progress can inform parents of school events. Recordings by each child adding a bit to the tape have also been successful.

Positive, Descriptive, Personal Reports

Why is report card time so dreaded by parents, children, and teachers? It is a time of stress. The teacher is placing a value on the child's efforts that may come as a surprise to the parents, and sometimes even the child.

Exercise: Imagine going to the doctor for a routine physical examination. You feel fine but they run tests and now you are there for the results. What are you feeling?

There is always some apprehension that tests may reveal some unsuspected problem. If that is the case, there are various reactions. First of all, the patient wants to see the file and the test results to verify that there is no mistake. If the doctor will not show the actual test results, suspicions are raised. The diagnosis may be rejected because there were no previous indicators. The doctor must be wrong. The patient may want to wait a while or have the tests repeated to see if there is a change. A second opinion may be sought to decide exactly what the extent of the problem is and how to remedy it. These same apprehensions and reactions are common in parent-teacher interactions.

When there is an ongoing exchange of descriptive information from school to home, there are no surprises when progress reports or report cards are issued. When parents see the portfolio and know they have access to it, they develop trust that the information about the child is based on credible evidence not just guesses. How often do parents say, "She doesn't like my child so she gave him a failing mark." The work in the portfolio documents educational decisions. Even if they never look at the portfolio, when they understand what it is about, they have confidence they can look at it if they want. That knowledge brings trust. The Sunshine Law affords people the right to examine public records. It is only acted upon by a few, but gives everyone confidence to exercise it if the need or desire arises.

The same advice is extended about only positive notes sent home to parents. Rather than "telling" on the child, if there is a concern or problem, it is best addressed in person with both parties prepared for the topic. A "bad news note" is like receiving the medical test results in the mail, with no explanation. It leaves a knot of anxiety in the stomach. Most people would rush to the phone to have an explanation. That is exactly what parents do. They want to know more, usually calling with feelings of anxiety, anger, and frustration at the bad surprise.

Rags first day at my house was very pleasant. Rags took a nap with my brother Christopher. My brother helped me take care of Rags. Rags went with me to my Daddy's house and spent the night. Rags also went with me to the babysitter's house. I took Rags in my tent with me. I held Rags and hugged him the whole time he was with me. I had a great time with Rags. I even shared Rags with my brother.

Figure 14.4 Journals from home to school are a part of parent communication and involvement. (Reprinted with permission. Conklin Preschool, Conklin, NY.)

Exercise: Read the note in Figure 14.5 the parent of a second-grader received. How would it make you feel if you were the parent? What elements do you notice?

This is page 2 of what is at least a four-page note. She went on and on and on. If there were so many concerns, a conference could explain this so much better. Did you notice every comment is negative? Not one positive line! The teacher also is giving the parent a strong order "Please see to it…" Would a parent treasure this note or would the child feel encouraged to work

harder? You can be sure the parent called for an appointment.

Exercise: On a separate sheet of paper, write about a report card you remember as a child.

Many people still have report cards on which teachers wrote negative, sarcastic comments and made dire predictions that this person was doomed to fail. Thankfully, most of those people did not believe the teacher and went on to succeed and prove her wrong. Remember, what is written is permanent and could be misinterpreted. The teacher

---

PUPIL *Marcy Johnson*   GRADE *2*

Teacher Comment

She is also behind in the independent reading series in the classroom. She must get caught up in these areas as they are a mandatory part of Reading. She has been allowed to take a few books home to catch up. Please see to it that she works on these. She must learn to use her time wisely!

I am not pleased with Marcy's math grade this term. She must practice.

TEACHER: *Mrs. Marshfield*

Dear Parent:
You may keep this for your records. If you wish to reply to the above comment, then please use the reverse side of this sheet and return it in the envelope. You may call to make an appointment with the teacher.

Figure 14.5 Read this note and see how you would feel as a parent.

must exercise caution, even in happy notes, that words are not misconstrued or the comments questionable in meaning.

Exercise: Rewrite the following comments to be positive, descriptive, and personal.

"She usually shares with other children."
"Grady only will play with other children if he can have his own way."
"Stephanie can't write her name, zip her own coat, or tie her shoes."
"Lynn is always the mother giving orders when playing in the dramatic area."

The word *usually* is one to avoid when writing progress reports. It leaves so many questions about what happens at other times. That is an example of the care and caution in writing progress reports.

Progress Reports. Progress reports are just what the name implies. They are short reviews of development in written format. They give parents a glimpse of the child from another's perspective. They should be positive in tone. They are reporting progress. Unless there is some serious trauma, all children make progress over time. It definitely

is not at the same rate in each developmental area. It most likely is different from any other child. It is still progress, Figure 14.6. (This form also appears in Appendix D.).

A narrative progress report is a more complete report, following very closely the outline of the portfolio. Developmental checklists or charts supply the criteria. A short, descriptive sentence or two in each area is all that is required. An outline and progress at a glance can be included in the portfolio to aid in organizing your thoughts for writing.

It should be headed with the child's name, the date, the writer's full name, and the name of the program, Figure 14.7.

A Positive and Negative Example. Compare the tone and wording of the following Progress Reports.

These reports were written about the same child, telling the same information but giving a whole different tone. The first portrays the child as active and imaginative in the beginning stages of socialization. The second typifies the child as an airhead, not able to do many things that are expected. The second uses language such as one-to-one correspondence and cooperative play stage that is not understood by most parents so should be avoided.

PROGRESS AT A GLANCE   Child's Name _____

PERIOD 1:   Date_____   Recorder _____

Strengths _____

Areas still developing _____

_____

Educational plan to facilitate development _____

_____

_____

PERIOD 2:   Date_____   Recorder _____

Strengths _____

Areas still developing _____

_____

Educational plan to facilitate development _____

_____

_____

PERIOD 3:   Date_____   Recorder _____

Strengths _____

Areas still developing _____

_____

Educational plan to facilitate development _____

_____

_____

PERIOD 4:   Date_____   Recorder _____

Strengths _____

Areas still developing _____

_____

Educational plan to facilitate development _____

_____

_____

Figure 14.6 Progress at a Glance (form)

XYC CENTER
NICOLE LIND
November 29, 199X
Age: 4 yrs., 3 mo.
Sandra Richards, Teacher

ADJUSTMENT TO SCHOOL: Nicole had no difficulty from the first day of school. She hangs up her coat and is ready to participate.

SELF-HELP: She can unzip, zip with help. She can pour juice and cut food with ease. She handles the bathroom by herself. She participates in picking up the room.

PHYSICAL DEVELOPMENT: She runs with coordination, balances on one foot. She makes circles and lines with markers and cuts slashes with scissors.

SOCIAL: She plays primarily with two other girls but joins small groups in organized activities.

EMOTIONAL: She smiles a lot and allows herself to be comforted if she is hurt or tired.

SPEECH AND LANGUAGE: She can be understood and speaks freely to adults and other children.

MEMORY AND ATTENTION SPAN: She spends long times in dramatic play and active outdoor play. She knows the words to songs we sing and knows the sequence of the day's activities.

LITERACY: She knows how to look at a book right side up and turn pages. She listens to stories individually read.

MATH AND SCIENCE: She can count out loud to 10. She has a wide knowledge about hamster,s including their birth. She has several at home and has provided little ones for the class.

CREATIVE ARTS: She fills the page with color and notices lines and shapes in her art. She prefers easel painting to table art like collage, watercolors, or clay.

DRAMATIC PLAY: This is the area she chooses most frequently, dressing up, taking on a variety of roles, using her language in an imaginative way.

ADJUSTMENT TO SCHOOL: She seems happy here, comfortably follows the routine, and is making progress mainly in dramatic and physical play.

WORKING ON: Providing her with dramatic play props that require small hand muscle movement. We are beginning small group storybook reading time into the dramatic play area.

XYC CENTER
NICOLE LIND
November 29, 199X
Age: 4 yrs., 3 mo.
Sandra Richards, Teacher

ADJUSTMENT TO SCHOOL: Nicole is indifferent to parent leaving. Arrives in a whirl.

SELF-HELP: Can't zip her own coat. Serves self more food than she can finish. Licks the spoon. Needs reminding about washing hands after toileting.

PHYSICAL DEVELOPMENT: Runs and climbs. Cannot pedal bicycle yet. Scribbles. Still working on cutting.

SOCIAL: Parallel play stage, not cooperative.

EMOTIONAL: Happy most of the time, sometimes has bouts of silliness.

SPEECH AND LANGUAGE:.Talks a lot. Sometimes hard to understand.

MEMORY AND ATTENTION SPAN: Does not participate in whole group activities though she listens to the songs. Reminds teacher what should be happening next.

LITERACY: Not interested in story time yet.

MATH AND SCIENCE: Does not have one-to-one correspondence yet. Often lets hamsters loose in the classroom.

CREATIVE ARTS: Paints whole page one color then paints on lines and circles mixing the paint.

DRAMATIC PLAY: Habitual play area in a fantasy world. Makes up words and imaginary language.

ADJUSTMENT TO SCHOOL: She seems happy here as long as she gets to play in the dramatic area or outside. Those are her favorite things to do. Seems uninterested in learning materials or group times.

WORKING ON: Zipping, cutting, small manipulatives, language.

Figure 14.7 Progress Report Examples: Positive and Negative

Tips for Progress Reports. The following suggestions will aid in writing progress reports.

Short, concise descriptive statements
Positive
Child "can do"
Positive
No technical terms
Positive
Keep a copy in the portfolio and in the class file.

Case Studies. A comprehensive narrative of the child is called a **case study** or **child study.** It can be used as an end-of-the-year report. It can be sent with the parent as the child moves to another program or as a report to a referral agency, upon the written request of the parent.

A child study follows much the same format as the **progress report** but amplifies the information given in each area and references comments with the documentation. This reference is much in the way an author references information from another source. In this way, the reader can go to that source for further information, possibly as evidence of what the author said or to learn more about the subject. The reader may then draw a different conclusion from that source.

Figure 14.8 is a sample child study from the same child in Figure 14.7 at the end of the year.

The reader should feel acquainted with the child by reading the child study and reviewing the documentation. It is extensive because there are so many specific details, gathered week by week, on which to draw conclusions. The summaries of the child study are also *positive,* relating what the child can do. The documentation is there for proof of the inferences about the child's progress and development. An extensive child study may not be necessary for every child, especially if the child is remaining in the program, moving from one classroom to another. A series of progress reports may be sufficient.

Template for a Progress Report and Child Study. The mechanics of preparation of the Child Study are much the same as any term paper. (The progress report is shorter with only one or two main points under each topic, without references to documentation although they are present.)

1. Begin by calculating the child's age. The child's age is calculated in years and months at the time the report is written. In the life of a young child, much change takes place in a year so the difference between just three and almost four is very great. This poses a bit of a mathematical problem to report writers.

Exercise: Try these for practice:

a) The date is October, 1996. Joseph's birthdate is July, 1991. How old is he? (Simple.)

$$
\begin{array}{rr}
1996 & \text{10th month} \\
- \quad 1991 & - \quad \text{7th month} \\
\hline
5 \text{ years} & 3 \text{ months}
\end{array}
$$

b) The date is October, 1996. Martha's birthdate is November, 1992. How old is she? (Trickier.)

$$
\begin{array}{rr}
1996 & \text{10th month} \\
- \quad 1992 & - \quad \text{11th month}
\end{array}
$$

Oops! We have to borrow 12 months from 1995.

$$
\begin{array}{rr}
1995 & 22 \text{ months} \\
- \quad 1992 & - \quad 11 \text{ months} \\
\hline
3 \text{ years} & 11 \text{ months}
\end{array}
$$

Rule: When the child has not yet had a birthday in that year, you have to borrow 12 months from the current year to calculate the year and month age.

Try some:

Janice was born in August, 1993.
Frederick was born in February, 1992.
Natalie was born in October, 1992.

The correct answers will depend on the month and year you are reading and calculating this equation.

2. Next define the topic. Know about whom you are writing and focus on one child at a time.
3. Assemble the raw data, the research, and the reference material. Have the portfolio and notes in either chronological order or organized by developmental area.
4. Prepare an outline. Here it is:

Heading: Child's name, birthdate, name of program, name of reporter.
Family: Birth order, family make-up, contact with extended family, other caregivers, community contacts.
Physical: Appearance, size, build, ways of moving, health, attendance, large and small muscle development.
Social development: With adults—parents, caregivers, other adult helpers, teachers, visitors to the classroom. With children—stage of play, who the child's friends are, how the child interacts with other children, how the child solves problems with other children
Adjustment to school: Separation behavior, areas of interest, participation and avoidance, adjustment to school routines, ability

XYC CENTER	NICOLE LIND	June 14, 199X 4 yrs. 9 mo.

Reporter: Mary McGwinn, 4's Teacher

Nicole is the oldest of three children, all of whom attend the XYC Center. Nicole has been at the XYC Center since September and will be attending kindergarten at Brinker School in the fall. She lives with her family next door to her grandparents with whom she spends much time. She talks about them lovingly. She has many cousins and extended family that make up her social circle. She attends church weekly where she participates in a children's choir. She attends dance lessons on Saturdays and will be dancing in her first recital in a few weeks.

PHYSICAL DEVELOPMENT: She is of average height and weight and in good health as evidenced by her almost perfect attendance record (see attendance record). She was absent for one week with chicken pox and a day occasionally with slight fevers accompanying colds. Her interest in dancing and advanced body coordination skills work together to demonstrate agility and confidence in movement. Her writing and hand muscles for smaller tasks are developing. She can fringe paper with scissors and put together eight-piece puzzles (checklist: physical development). She can write her name in large letters progressing from just the first *N* to the whole name (samples 10/05/9X, 1/17/9X, 4/4/9X).

SOCIAL DEVELOPMENT: Nicole is comfortable with the staff at XYC seeking help mainly for comfort from falls (which are infrequent) or frustration with small muscle tasks. She has little confidence in her abilities and seeks adults to assist her (anecdotal record 11/1/9X, 3/17/9X). With adults holding the paper or providing her with encouragement, she can perform those tasks she tries. Nicole is called *friend* by many children in the class (photo of Nicole and friends taken 2/2/9X). She plays mostly with girls in the dramatic play area, dressing in the various theme props provided there. She had an especially long play sequence when the area was set up as an animal hospital (class video, running record 3/13/9X). Through this interest in dramatic play she has gained negotiation skills. Compare anecdotal record of 10/6/9X and 2/27/9X. She has moved from playing along side other children along the same theme to interacting and problem solving, assigning, and carrying out intricate play-acting roles, even putting on accents. This is demonstrated on the audio tape.

ADJUSTMENT TO SCHOOL: Nicole has adjusted to the routine of this center since she entered in September. She often goes down the hall "to see how the babies are doing," as she refers to her little sisters. She is welcomed by the teachers and allowed to spend time there, playing with the younger children. She has been observed in a protective, nurturing role captured in some photos (10/1/9X and 12/17/9X). She is comfortable with the routine, using free-play time to be involved in the dramatic play themes. She begins the day with painting since she often arrives before her friends. Her paintings have moved from experimentation with paint (9/29/9X) to more intricate designs (1/6/9X) and on to recognizable forms of people and animals (4/26/9X).

SELF-ACCEPTANCE: She acts independently in caring for her own needs in dressing, eating, and toileting (overview sheet). She independently chooses play areas, companions, and activities (time samples 10/21/9X, 2/03/9X). She exhibits a feeling of competence in physical activities, taking leadership roles 4/7/9X). She has a cheerful temperament. She displays no aggressiveness or antisocial behaviors (frequency counts 10/12/9X, 3/11/9X). She appears to be self-assertive in relations with others. She has a firm sense of self (interviews 11/2/9X, 2/17/9X).

COGNITIVE DEVELOPMENT: Nicole recognizes the letters in her name but not by themselves. She can count to 10 accurately and to 20 if assisted with the "teens." She knows the names of the colors, the names of the geometric shapes, and is beginning to add small numbers mentally (see interview 11/19/9X, 5/2/9X).

She has a wide knowledge of animal life, and a special interest in hamsters. She has raised several litters and provided several classmates with pets along with explicit directions on how to care for them (audio recording 3/22/9X). Her interest and ability in writing is at the beginning stages but her concern for the hamster's care prompted her to write a book. It told her friends how to care for hamsters. She dictated the book then illustrated it (sample, 12/12/9X). This was duplicated and given to each hamster owner. She felt this was a significant work. She talked about it on the tape (12/19/9X).

When listening to Nicole speak on the tape, some irregularities are noticed that are not apparent when talking to her casually (tape 9/29/9X). This was reviewed by her parents and pediatrician and a decision was made

CONTINUED

Figure 14.8 Child Study Example

to wait six months for these sounds to develop. Another tape on 04/6/9X showed those sounds were now present. This was reviewed by her parents and the pediatrician and confirmed. No further action was necessary.

CREATIVITY: Nicole's creativity is centered in the dramatic play realm. She can carry out a role imaginatively and encourage others to do so as well, displaying an advanced degree of concentration and social awareness (running record 1/29/9X). Her drawings are more realistic than her daily paintings, almost methodical in nature from one day to the next (samples 10/30/9X, 10/31/9X, 11/1/9X, 11/2/9X). She called it "practicing." She used scissors, collage, and clay in much the same way by experimenting with the same materials day after day then leaving them for months.

Nicole will enter kindergarten with strong social skills, confidence in her physical abilities, and the beginnings of literacy. Her adaptability to the group setting and helping adults should ensure that her school experience is a good one. She talks of school and all the things she will learn there. Once she saw the loft in the kindergarten rooms with extensive dramatic play areas, she was convinced that it was a good place.

I am happy to answer any questions about this review of Nicole's time at XYC Center. She is a joy to know.

Signed _____

Figure 14.8 Child Study Example (continued)

to follow directions, mistaken behaviors requiring guidance

Self-acceptance: Self-care skills, independence, level of self-esteem, emotional development, self-control, aggressiveness.

Cognitive development: What the child knows—numbers, alphabet, shapes, interest in books, language vocabulary, clarity of speech, what the child's attitude toward learning is.

Creativity: Child's use of imagination in art, movement, dramatic play, language.

Closing paragraph, personal best wishes.

Signature of writer, date of report.

5. Write a rough draft from the outline. Think about the child in relation to each of those topics and jot some notes.

6. Refer to sources to document statements. Look through the portfolio and find representative pieces to provide data. Note type of recording and dates.

7. Prepare final document. This is a document that will be preserved maybe for the life of the child. It represents the professionalism of the program and the integrity of the writer. It should be in complete, grammatically correct sentences. Type it, and check for spelling.

8. Proofread. Have a team member who knows the child (for confidentiality, not an outsider), read the document for content, grammar, and tone.

9. Produce the document. Type, or use a word processor, to print the final child study docu-

ment as perfectly as you can make it. This represents the reputation of the writer and the subject of the study.

10. Copy the document. The parents should receive the original either separate or with the portfolio. A copy should be kept in the class file. File parents' written request for a copy to be sent to a referral agent in the class file, along with the program's copy of the document.

These ten steps will become more automatic with experience in writing this type of report. If they are written for the whole class, the task can be divided just as the other observation assignments, with one-fourth of them done each week. The *Week by Week* plan gives you assignments to accomplish this several times a year. It will come easier.

What to Do with the Child Study. Once the child study is printed, two copies are made, one to be kept in the portfolio and one to go in the class file.

The child study belongs to the parents. It is best presented to them in a parent conference (see later section). In this way, each section can be discussed with even more personalized anecdotal remembrances shared with the parents. The child study could be mailed to the parents if a parent conference cannot be arranged. The risk is always present that the clarity of the message of writing is more obscure to the reader than the writer. The parents may misinterpret the wording of the child study. There should always be an opportunity for reply or challenge.

The child study may be included in the portfolio if it is to be given to the parents. With the parents' permission, the child study could be sent to the next program, school, or referral agent such as therapists or medical personnel. In that case, copies of the referenced documentation should be copied.

Parent Conferences

The parent conference's main purpose should be for a developmental overview of the child. The early childhood program may be the first contact the child and family has had with people outside the family. It is a serious responsibility to be allowed to get so intimately acquainted with their child. This conference is not just the teacher telling the parent but an exchange of information, a discussion, a sharing of points of view. The teacher is seeking the advice from the parent for the benefit of the child. With this attitude conveyed in word and behavior, the conference has a better chance at success. The progress reports and child study can be the reference. These should be held periodically throughout the year or any time at the request of the parent.

Much has been written giving advice about parent conferences. Their success is fragile depending on so many variables. Many preparations and precautions should be taken to guarantee an open, informative, positive exchange.

Tips for Parent Conferences. Parent conferences can be successful exchanges of information, socially satisfying and affirming for parent, teacher, and child. Here are some practical suggestions.

1. Be prepared. Have the progress report or child study complete with documentation in an organized system.
2. Make the conference times convenient for parents and provide child care if needed.
3. Prepare the environment by having comfortable chairs, at the same height, next to one another or at right angles with no table between.
4. Make sure the location is private so no one else can hear and there are no interruptions.
5. Begin with social exchange, greetings, small talk.
6. Open the portfolio and let parents know what it holds.
7. Make eye contact, lean forward, nod to their comments, listen.
8. Speak in understandable language.
9. Ask questions, ask for questions.
10. Summarize and make plans for further contact.

IT HAPPENED TO ME:
Excuse Me!

I was holding parent conferences midway through the year. They were scheduled every half hour, one after another. Between two conferences I had to leave the room. When I came back, the next parent was looking through all the portfolios I had arranged for the next conferences. I was dumbfounded. What nerve! I got her child's folder and said, "Excuse me! This must be the one you're looking for." My mind raced through what else I could say but I was so angry nothing positive came to mind so I went on with the conference. After all, it was about her child that we came together.

It taught me a lesson that I share with you. Keep all records secure. I did from that day onward.

Parent Conferences When a Problem Is Suspected. Positive stories are related at the door. Positive statements are printed in the newsletters. Positive progress reports and positive child studies are written. The question arises, "But when do you ever tell them the bad news?" "When do you tell them the truth?" "When do you tell them what the child is *really* like?" When? Only after a certain process has taken place should the teacher talk to the parent about a concern, Figure 14.9.

Documented Observations. If there is a concern for a child in a specific area or areas, it is critically important to gather data. This should be with the methods that are the least inferential, the most accurate. The Anecdotal Record meets that criteria. If possible, have another member of the teaching team also gather data.

Review Developmental Guidelines. The observers should read some basic information about developmental expectations and a clear understanding based on research.

Confer with the Team and Your Supervisor. The group should look at the data, review the research, and look again at the child. Theories should be explored, searching for possible causes or influences. Every attempt should be made to eliminate biases whatever their origin. When it is the consensus of the group that the parent should

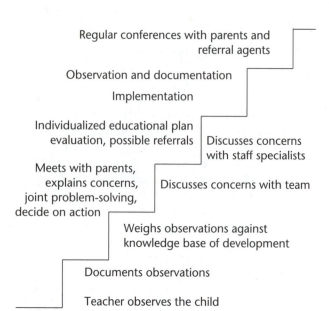

Figure 14.9 Steps in a Problem-Solving Parent Conference

be consulted, the team should decide the approach and who should be involved. Usually the classroom teacher alone is sufficient for the first step in this process. Discussion topics, possible scenarios, and options can be explored. Resources for referral should be researched and prepared for the parents beginning with the least alarming, usually beginning with a full physical evaluation.

Approach the Parents. In *private,* the teacher conveys concerns and a request for a conference to discuss those concerns. The teacher may ask for the parents to be thinking about the areas of concern or give the parents some reading material to think about before that meeting.

"We have been noticing and documenting... and wondering if you have noticed this at home? When would it be convenient to get together to discuss it?"

"We've been trying different things to help Robert with... but we need some suggestions from you. Can we stop by on our way home tomorrow or could you come by here?"

"The next time you take Lucy to the doctor you may want to ask about... Would you have time later on this afternoon to give me a call so we could talk about it? I really don't think it's serious but it has been nagging at me and I'd like to see what you think."

Try not to get into a discussion at this time. Set a time when possible. Be prepared to have the meeting within 24 hours, but it is best not to have it immediately. This gives the parents time to consider the questions and topic.

The Meeting. The meeting should begin with social pleasantries. It is a meeting of people who have common bonds, but this meeting needs to go on since the topic is serious. The basis for the concerns are presented, referring to documenting evidence. This evidence should be available if needed. Then the parents should have the opportunity to respond with their thoughts on the situation or topic. The teacher's role is to *listen.* The teacher must remember the parent is the authority on the child.

The Discussion. The meeting is conducted with attempts at clear communication and empathy. Possible solutions can be explored from moderate to drastic. The teacher should be prepared for strong reactions from the parents. These may be denial, projection of blame, fear, guilt, mourning or grief, withdrawal, rejection, and finally acceptance (Chinn, et al., 1978; and Chinn, 1984; in Berger, 1995).

The Decision. The parents and teacher come to a decision and to an agreement to carry out the next steps. Referral information should be available if the decision is to seek outside help. The progression is usually to begin with medical personnel to investigate or rule out physical causes. Other agencies may be referred to the parent, depending on the nature of the concern.

Follow Up. The program should make every effort to implement the plan the parents have made. It is the responsibility of the program to keep the parents informed of the actions taken and the results. If the parents are taking an action, they should be asked to keep the program informed.

Documentation. A record of the conference's main points and action planned and the follow-up should be kept in the school's file. It may be warranted to keep it in the confidential file rather than the class file, depending on the nature of the concerns.

Pitfalls to Avoid for a Successful Conference of Any Kind. Gestwicki (1992) lists the following pitfalls.

1. Avoid using technical terminology, such as *motor development* or Piagetian terminology.
2. Avoid the role of "expert." Remember the real expert on the child is the parent.
3. Avoid negative evaluations. Avoid using words such as *problem, behind, immature, never/can't, and hyperactive.*
4. Avoid unprofessional conversation
   - about other children, families, staff
   - personal topics: marital status, financial, lifestyle

- taking sides: between parents, between other staff, between this and other programs
5. Avoid giving advice, either requested or unsolicited. Instead, recommend books, or refer to other parents.
6. Avoid rushing into solutions. See this as a collaborative effort.

What to Do with the Documentation

"What to do with it" has become a common phrase to readers of this book, a point to consider with each piece of written documentation. Now it becomes the question regarding the whole portfolio of each child, the class file and the Reflective Journal, Figure 14.10.

The Portfolio. The program or school implementing a portfolio system should set a policy at that time. The parent has the right of access to the portfolio at all times. It remains the property of the school and it is the right of the school to decide when to give it to the parent or retain ownership. Any records retained by the school are to be kept confidential, with access only to the parents of a child to their own child's file. Child studies are retained as comprehensive overviews and are the property of the program not the teacher. They can be transferred to other agencies upon the written permission of the parent.

The portfolio could be transfered to the:

1. Parents. At the close of the year or upon leaving the program, the portfolio may be given to the child and family. For some these become precious mementos. They contain vast amounts of information about the child, along with samples of the child's work.
2. Next teacher within the school. If the child remains in the school or program, it could be passed on and added to by the next teacher. Because of the large volume of material, it may be sorted and reduced in size. The next teacher can refer to the portfolio to come to know the child through it. The teacher may decide not to read the portfolio and form independent viewpoints. That is the teacher's prerogative.
3. Next school. The parents may designate the portfolio be sent to the child's next school or program. Upon written authorization, that request is carried out.
4. Referral agent or helping professional. Parents may wish to release the portfolio, in writing, to medical or psychological personnel. Observations taken periodically through a multitude of techniques can be very valuable for diagnosis of disorders or disabilities.

What to Do with the Class Files. Again, the school policy is set for the retention of this file. It may be considered the property of the school and retained as a record of that class. It could be used for accountability of the teacher and the program. The class file may be the property of the teacher, kept as a record of the work done that year. The documentation in the class files is of the whole class rather than focused on individual children.

What to Do with the Reflective Journal. This, of course, is the property of the writer. It has been used for personal and professional reflection and represents the thoughts and feelings of the writer. From these thoughts may come insights and deeper understandings of self and the profession. This is what is referred to as action research. This process begins with observation, that kind of "child watching" that comes with the pictures the eyes take and the sounds the ears hear. Those register against what is known about child development.

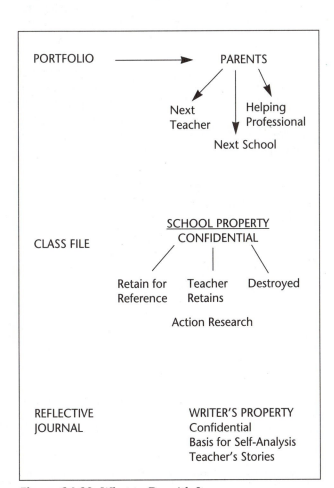

Figure 14.10 What to Do with It

The thinking about what matches and what clashes is the reflective process. This is frequently shared in an informal way.

Action research is a collaborative effort between observers. They get together to discuss the principles, new ideas, questions, and theories. They consider the difference between what is seen and what is known. The environment for this collaboration is of primary importance. It must be among people who trust one another, in an intimate group setting where each is free to speak. Time is provided for an unpressured discussion. It is possible that an article, a book, a video, or a report from one person's workshop could stimulate the discussion. Teachers relate experiences and try to make sense of the dilemma. They may decide to go away and experiment with different approaches and come back to report. The lessons learned from reflection and action research make meaningful reading for others, commonly called **teacher's stories,** interesting glimpses into the classroom and the teacher's reflections upon the meaning of the occurences. The Reflective Journals could be used as a basis for action research and teacher's stories. But the journal itself is a private document, for the writer's use alone, and should be protected for privacy.

LOOKING AT THE CHILD'S INTERACTIONS WITH ADULTS

When a child enters a child care program or school, it is the beginning of moving out into the world. The child begins to realize there are differences in people and their views on behavior. As the child gains self-control, adherence to the expectations for behavior is possible. The interactions with adults involve a guidance model by the adult, setting the boundaries, communicating realistic expectations, and helping facilitate the child's behavior to meet them. By looking at the child through this lens, the observer gets a glimpse of the child's development in all the other developmental areas.

The role of the teacher is different from that of the parent. As a professional, the child is technically the client to be kept at an emotional distance. That definition is foreign to the intensely personal relationship of child and teacher, but the objective detachment must be recognized. The teacher does not love the child as a parent does. Gartrell calls this feeling **unconditional positive regard** (Gartrell, 1994), "full acceptance of the child as a developing human being and member of the group" (p. 60). This is in accord with the positive view of the child's development. Observation assessment methods are used, not to catch children who are failing or to find their "weaknesses." Assessment methods measure individual levels of accomplishments and facilitate the next step in the progressive stage for each child.

How Observation and Recording Aids Child-Adult Interactions

The connection with child-adult interactions should be clear. As observations are made and documented, the adult interacts with the child. The child knows the adult is writing about what he is doing because the teacher tells him. She asks questions about his work and writes about it. Samples of his work are collected for the portfolio the teacher has shown him. He is interviewed, photographed, and audiotaped. As a result of observations, the adult knows the child from these interactions. The child knows the teacher's unconditional acceptance. She has not told him he is doing it wrong, but has just observed and written descriptions of what he is doing without judgment. In classrooms where children are treated and moved as a group, where the whole class does art or science or math or story activities, where the teacher's time is spent giving directions rather than interacting, the teacher does not know the individual child. When the curriculum is appropriate with the teacher as the facilitator in the learning, then positive interactions between child and adult occur, Figure 14.11.

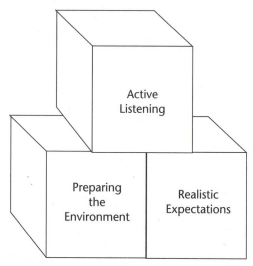

Figure 14.11 Building Blocks of the Teacher's Role in Child Guidance

The various recording techniques can be used to record the child-adult interactions as well:

- Class List Log—A quick survey of aspects of child-adult interactions can be made, probably from memory. Criterion items could be:

  Seeks the adult for comfort
  Behavior within state guidelines
  Guidance needed in situations of...
  Still gaining self-control in...

- Anecdotal or Running Records are ideal for capturing all the factual information of an incident showing the adult and child interacting.
- Frequency Count could measure how many times in a day or week the child needed adult intervention.
- Time Sampling could indicate the presence of the adult and the presence of the child, inferring relationships from contacts with the adult.
- Interviews give information about the nature of the relationship. The child's cooperativeness, comfort with the adult, and willingness to speak indicate a good relationship.
- Work Samples may demonstrate the child's feelings for the adult with love notes and letters, gifts of drawings and work (such as my spotted dog in Chapter 10).
- Checklists and rating scales may have criterion regarding adult-child interactions to observe and document. It is the inference of the observer with no details recorded.

Media, such as photographs and video, may capture the child and adult interactions. It is hoped that if it is to be preserved, they are positive interactions.

The documentation accumulated in the portfolio presents a view of the child from the staffs' eyes, with contributions from the child with work samples. Some ways to use the portfolio to communicate with parents and other individuals comprise this last section.

The Teacher's Role in Child Guidance

The adult takes the initiative to get acquainted with the child, recognizing the stages of stranger anxiety, differences in temperaments, and range of experiences the child has had with strangers outside the family. This was discussed in Chapter 1, with strategies for the staff member to begin the relationship with the child and family. It was repeated in discussions on attachment, social and emotional development, and self-concept and self-

esteem. The teacher uses different methods in preparing the classroom environment and in interacting with the child.

Preparing the Environment. This has been mentioned many times as the first step in planning curriculum. It is the active involvement of the child with her environment in which she constructs her own learning. The adult's role is to prepare that environment. It is also prepared with thought to help the children control their own behavior. The equipment and materials are organized, accessible, in good condition, varied, and sufficient for the numbers of children in the group. The space is divided into clearly defined areas from which to choose, with enough floor or table space to adequately use the materials. For example, blocks are organized on labeled shelves next to a carpeted surface, free from people walking through. Thus the builders can be comfortable, undisturbed, and not frustrated by constructions being tipped or knocked down. Blocks of time are needed so teachers are not interrupting play for their own purposes.

IT HAPPENED TO ME:
The Bare Room

A student teacher warned me of the room's lack of equipment in the setting where she was working. When I visited her, I saw she was not exaggerating. The children were jumping from the top of a play refrigerator, the only piece of equipment in the room besides a table and chairs and a shelf with ditto coloring sheets and crayons. She told me she was having a terrible time "controlling" their behavior, trying to keep them from climbing and jumping off the refrigerator. The story was that each time the children "misbehaved" the lead teacher took away a piece of equipment so they were down to the last piece. Children must play, so they used the refrigerator for the large muscle equipment they were missing. Needless to say, the lead teacher and director were not providing an appropriate environment, nor practicing positive guidance approaches. Behavior problems persist when teachers do not adequately prepare the environment.

Realistic Expectations. The observer has a knowledge base of child development against which to measure skills and behavior. When adults expect behaviors that are not appropriate, it is like expecting an infant to walk and punishing him when he does not. Adult's interactions with children must be based on developmental norms and appropriate practice principles so that children are not expected to behave in a way beyond their years or ability. That phrase, "Children can't wait" is so true in many ways. When that principle is understood, then the adult modifies his or her own behavior rather than struggle to make children do what they cannot do. For example, the teacher will not make all the children wait until everyone has washed their hands before they begin to eat.

The realistic expectations are stated in terms that children can understand, from the positive, what they can do rather than not do. When children hear, "Don't run," because of what is known about attention span, selective listening skills, and cognitive structures, young children get the opposite message, "Run." It is the word emphasized, heard last and loudest, without the child's knowledge of the negating feature of the word preceding it.

Active Listening. Another facet of adult-child interactions is listening to the child, listening not only to the words they say but how they are said, and using intuitive ears to really hear the intended meaning. **Active listening,** a strategy in Gordon's (1975) Parent Effectiveness Training, focuses on what the child is saying, listening actively, and responding to the feelings implied. In the development of emotions, children have strong feelings but lack the vocabulary to express them. They also think that others feel what they feel because they are egocentric. Marian Marion (1995) gives these active listening tips (p. 240):

- Listen carefully.
- Do not interrupt.
- Try to understand what the message means.
- Listen for what the child is feeling.
- Suspend judgment.
- Avoid preaching, giving advice, or trying to persuade the child to feel something else.
- Merely feed back your perception of the child's feelings.

The adult manages the environment, sets realistic stated expectations, and actively listens. Then the adult and child interactions can focus on more important topics, such as where butterflies go when it rains, or how this ball can stay on top of the cone collage base.

Adult Intervention of Problem Behavior

The adult role is first to keep children safe. Sometimes in the execution of that role for one child, interactions with another child strain relationships. A child starts throwing chairs, ripping other children's artwork, or yelling obscenities at another child. In the positive guidance model, children are not punished but guided to help control their own behavior and seek solutions and remedies for problems. Clare Cherry (1983) recommends:

- natural consequence: Other children tell her to stop or the adult points out the consequence.
  "When you…it hurts, makes them mad, makes them sad."
- logical consequence: Helps the child correct the action or approximates the desired behavior.
  "Place the chair next to the table so that people can use it for sitting," or "Get the tape and try to fix the drawings," or "Call her by her name."
- unrelated consequences: Outcomes by the adult are not related to the act.
  "At recess, you will have to stay inside."

The first two are considered consistent with positive guidance techniques. As a last resort, unrelated consequences are used. This is more like punishment and does not help the child learn to control her own behavior.

Possible Causes of Problem Behavior. The close observer and interpreter of children's behavior looks beyond misbehavior, and considers the consequences, in light of the child's individual situation. Again, it is the empathetic, reflective, professional looking at behavior indicators to seek reasons, causes, contributing factors before blaming the child for deliberately breaking rules. Reynolds (1990, p. 226) presents these possible causes of problem behavior:

- separation from parents
- lack of attention
- the home
- abuse
- alcoholism and drugs
- nutrition
- allergies and sensitivities
- parenting styles
- perfectionist parents
- divorce
- sibling rivalry
- power struggles
- heredity

Through observation and appropriate professional practice, the child in group settings can be assessed for physical and psychological safety. Nonpunitive, positive guidance techniques are used to help the child gain self-control. In this way, the teacher does not give up on any child and has a career of **liberation teaching** (Ginott in Gartrell, 1994, p. 295). The teacher sees the child as an individual, recognizing and respecting the cultural differences. Teachers work to help each child be a self-directed, competent, accepted, and moral individual.

SPECIAL POPULATIONS AND HOME AND SCHOOL COMMUNICATIONS

Children from Diverse Backgrounds

Communication is the key component to working in partnership with parents. Whether the parent speaks a language unknown to the teacher or lives in such a different lifestyle it is almost impossible to comprehend, it is the teacher's responsibility to find some common ground. That common ground is concern for the child and the desire to know and assist the child in development. When that is the motivation, interpreters, adaptions of schedules, overlooking lifestyles without judgments, all can be managed with creativity and conviction.

Children with Special Needs

Parents whose children have special needs must be advocates for their child. They want for their child what every other parent wants: an opportunity to learn and be treated equally. In the classroom, to some children to receive what they need, some interventions or modifications must be made. It takes an intense amount of understanding between parents and teachers to come to satisfactory arrangements that do not overburden the teacher or the program yet provide for the needs of every child in the group. This may mean adding extra adults who specifically help that child. It may mean the teacher modifies the environment and the routines for one particular child while meeting the needs of the rest as well. This can only be accomplished through open communication between parents and teachers, regularly sharing information, frustrations, and problem solving together. It can be done.

· ·

TOPICS IN OBSERVATION: Does the *Week By Week* Plan Meet NAEYC Guidelines for Assessment?

· ·

The National Association for the Education of Young Children (NAEYC) and the National Association of Early Childhood Specialists in State Departments of Education (NAECS/SDE) jointly developed guidelines to evaluate assessment practices. The *Week by Week* system should provide affirmative responses to *all* the questions (NAEYC, 1991, p. 34).

1. Is the assessment procedure based on the goals and objectives of the specific curriculum used in the program?

The *Week by Week* system guides the teacher to observe each child and plan curriculum to meet the goals and objective. It specifies no particular curriculum and can be adapted to meet the program's uniqueness.

2. Are the results of assessment used to benefit children, i.e., to plan for individual children, improve instruction, identify children's interest and needs, and individualize instruction, rather than label, track, or fail children?

The purpose of the *Week by Week* system is to provide vehicles for the teacher to *know* the child, to see the child as an individual, and take action based on that knowledge.

3. Does the assessment procedure address all domains of learning and development—social, emotional, physical, and cognitive—as well as children's feelings and dispositions toward learning?

The *Week by Week* system not only looks at all areas of development through observation assignments, but includes methods of observation that see the behavior of the child showing the affective approach to learning.

TOPICS IN OBSERVATION: continued

4. Does assessment provide useful information to teachers to help them do a better job?

Observations of each child using the *Week by Week* system help the teacher individualize the curriculum, measure the child's progress, and monitor her own teaching practices.

5. Does the assessment procedure rely on teachers' regular and periodic observations and recordkeeping of children's everyday activities and performance so that results reflect children's behavior over time?

Weekly assignments ensure that each child is observed regularly, during activities in the classroom, revisiting each developmental area at least three times during the year to measure progress.

6. Does the assessment procedure occur as part of the ongoing life of the classroom rather than in an artificial, contrived context?

All observation assignments in the *Week by Week* system are made while children are interacting with each other, the teacher, and the learning environment.

7. Is the assessment procedure performance-based, rather than only testing skills in isolation?

The observer using the *Week by Week* system observes the child in the normal routine of the classroom environment and activities.

8. Does the assessment rely on multiple sources of information about children, such as collections of their work, results of teacher interviews and dialogues as well as observations?

The *Week by Week* system collects children's work periodically in a portfolio. These include language samples, writing samples, creative work and electronic reproductions, such as audio or videotape and photography. At least seven different methods of recording are used to control bias and to meet the objectives for the observation. Interviews, both formal and informal, are included in the assignment plan.

9. Does the assessment procedure reflect individual, cultural, and linguistic diversity? Is it free of cultural, language, and gender biases?

Natural observation techniques recording raw data or objective criteria are basic to the *Week by Week* system. The observer's diversity awareness is heightened in discussions of Special Populations included in each chapter.

10. Do children appear comfortable and relaxed during assessment rather than tense or anxious?

Children are observed and assessed during their regular routine and interactions in the classroom where they are most comfortable. They become aware that observation is the role of the teacher using the *Week by Week* system.

11. Does the assessment procedure support parents' confidence in their children and their ability as parents rather than threaten or undermine parents' confidence?

Parents are made aware of the presence and purpose and their accessibility to the portfolio. Since the assessment is an ongoing, regular part of the classroom routine, there is no anxiety to parents or children. Their confidence in the *Week by Week* system is in their ability to look at the portfolio at any time.

12. Does the assessment examine children's strengths and capabilities rather than just their weaknesses or what they do not know?

The word *weakness* does not appear in the *Week by Week* system. It is continually emphasized that assessment of development is looking for the measure of accomplishment.

13. Is the teacher the primary assessor and are teachers adequately trained for this role?

The *Week by Week* system provides the teacher with detailed instructions to adequately use the observation methods. A review of child development principles ensures that each observer, regardless of role—teacher, assistant teacher, family worker, or volunteer—has realistic expectations for behavior and can recognize and classify behavior in appropriate categories.

14. Does the assessment procedure involve collaboration among teachers, children, administrators, and parents? Is information from parents used in planning

TOPICS IN OBSERVATION: continued

instruction and evaluating children's learning? Are parents informed about assessment information?

Teachers and all staff people in contact with the child may contribute to the portfolio and the assessment process. In the *Week by Week* system, teachers inform children of the purpose of their observations and invite children's comments on it. Administrators are involved in referrals and concerns about the child. They may read progress reports before they are sent home to be sure they reflect the policies and goals of the program.

The portfolio begins with the parents' information form about the child. This is used by the teachers to know the parents' goals for the child and helps to individualize the curriculum.

Parents are invited to read and contribute to the portfolio. They are continually reminded in the *Week by Week* system that the portfolio is a changing collection of documents open for their inspection and comment. Daily contacts concerning the observations are recommended. Regular progress reports are a part of the *Week by Week* system to keep parents informed of their child's progress.

15. Do children have an opportunity to reflect on and evaluate their own learning?

Throughout the year, using the *Week by Week* system, children are regularly interviewed about their own progress. They have knowledge of the portfolio at their learning level and have opportunities to see and contribute to it.

16. Are children assessed in supportive contexts to determine what they are capable of doing with assistance as well as what they can do independently?

The observation methods in the *Week by Week* system are implemented during the child's regular activities. The level of independence or need for assistance in performing at this level is noted in many of the observation methods and addressed specifically in some of them.

17. Is there a systematic procedure for collecting assessment data that facilitates its use in planning instruction and communicating with parents?

That is what the *Week by Week* system is, a collection plan to individualize curriculum and build a portfolio of documentation of development for all.

18. Is there a regular procedure for communicating the results of assessment to parents in meaningful language, rather than letter or number grades, that reports children's individual progress?

All through the *Week by Week* system, regular communication with parents concerning the assessment observations is stressed. A periodic narrative progress report briefly describes the child's accomplishments in each developmental area. These are presented to parents in parent conferences and become a part of the portfolio. A child study, covering the whole year is optional as an additional review of the assessment of the child.

It appears that the *Week by Week* system meets the NAEYC and NAECS/SDE guidelines. *Week by Week* assessments of every child's development, using a variety of observation techniques, and professional reflection, have been braided together. Together they make the whole strand stronger—the strand of professional practice.

HELPING PROFESSIONALS FOR HOME AND SCHOOL COMMUNICATIONS

Psychologists and social workers can help as intermediaries between schools, programs, and parents. They can assess an individual child's emotional state in relation to the adults in the program, how the program is meeting the child's particular needs, and help the parents deal with agencies with its own policies and procedures.

No matter what the circumstances of the family, the teacher's first responsibility is to provide for the needs of the child within the goals and objectives of the program. Working with families in a cooperative partnership helps accomplish those goals.

IT HAPPENED TO ME:
As I Wrote This Book

These are the "truisms" that have come to me in the process of working out this *Week by Week* plan:

Observations cannot be done occasionally because the novelty of being watched changes children's behavior. Children need to see the teacher writing about them every day.

Writing meaningful observations as they are occurring cannot happen in a teacher-directed classroom. The teacher is too busy.

Useful observations cannot be gathered the week before progress reports or parent conferences are due.

A fair assessment of the child cannot be gathered with any one recording instrument.

Every child deserves to be observed and recorded individually.

Observing and recording does no good if it does not change the teacher's practices or individualize the approach the teacher uses with each child.

Because some children in the class have reached a certain developmental level does not mean that others should be there too.

They have other strengths.

When we look at what the child cannot do, we fail to see all the child can do.

Pointing blame at others—the parents, the child, or the program—leaves three fingers pointing back at us. We must reflect on what we could do to make things better for the parent, the child, and the program.

Parents are the authorities of the child. They lend them to us and we pay them back with interest.

This organized plan comes from a person who is disorganized but enacts plans that get things done.

Teaching is not about transferring knowledge. It is about learning, and the one who learns the most is the teacher.

This book could never have been accomplished had I not set *Week by Week* goals for myself. On a calendar near my computer I plotted chapters, working back from deadlines, so that if I stayed on course I could meet the deadlines. It worked for me. It can work for you!

It is my sincere goal for each one using this plan to *know* the child. Because we know, we do. In that knowing, we will do what is right for that child.

Week 14, Assignment A

CLASS LIST LOG TO OBSERVE INTERACTION WITH ADULTS FOR ALL

Using a Class List Log form, found in Appendix D, jot notes on how each of the children relates to the adults in the classroom. Note behaviors such as cooperation, independence, preferences, reliance, and reaction to new people.

What to Do with It

On the portfolio overview, note the presence of the observation, and transfer a few words to give information about the child, Figure 14.12.

Share it with the parents or the child, if it is appropriate. For example, say privately to the parent, "Today when the firefighters came to school and taught the children 'Stop, Drop, and Roll,' Andrea asked if they were strangers. She was a little afraid of them, I believe. It's a hard one to explain and I know you are trying to protect her safety. It gave me the idea we might want to invite

INTERACTIONS WITH ADULTS		
Documentation	Recorder	Date
CL comfortable with staff quiet with sub	Ban	12/12
CL talkative, confident	MS	5/3

Figure 14.12 Portfolio Overview Example

Dr. Greene, the psychologist, to our Parent Night to talk about the topic. Would you like to make the phone call?" or "Ananiy, when I was watching you play outside I saw you ask Mr. Chapin to help Brett get his shoe unstuck from the fence. That was a brave thing you did to go for help and to think of Mr. Chapin, the janitor. I wrote it down so I would remember to talk to you about it. I'll bet Brett was glad."

File the Class List Log in the class file.

Week 14, Assignment B

CHECKLIST ON PHYSICAL DEVELOPMENT FOR ALL

Using the Checklists from Week 3, review each child's large and small muscle devlopment. You may use the same form, just use a different colored pen or write in the new date of this assessment.

What to Do with It

Note the date of the second observation on the physical development portion of the portfolio overview, and refile the checklist in the portfolio. If little progress has been observed, take a closer look to see if you can determine a reason. Try to interest the child in more activities that approximate the next criteron on the Checklist. If a serious lag appears, speak to your supervisor and then to the parents if it is warranted.

Week 14, Assignment C

PROGRESS REPORTS FOR GROUP D

Each day this week, take some time with the portfolios of each child in group D. Write a progress report following the suggestions in the chapter. Remember: Be positive, descriptive, and personal.

Heading
Family (optional for progress report)
Physical
Social
Adjustment to School
Self-Acceptance
Cognitive
Creativity
Closure

What to Do with It

Have a supervisor check the progress report. Make a copy to place in the portfolio and one in the class file. Go over the original with the parent in a parent conference if possible. If not, send it home with a note of explanation, such as:

> This year we are instituting a new system of portfolio collections of observations and the children's work. Now that we have been together more than three months, this is a review of your child's development from what we've seen. Please comment or ask questions. We value your information. After all, you know the child best.

NOTE: When you are using the *Week by Week* plan next year you may need to do progress reports earlier than 14 weeks into the school year. Here is a suggestion for earlier assignments.

Week 10: Progress reports for Group A
Week 11: Progress reports for Group B
Week 12: Progress reports for Group C
Week 13: Progress reports for Group D

Week 14, Assignment D

REFLECTIVE JOURNAL

Respond to the following in your Reflective Journal, kept in a private file at home.

The progress reports make me feel...

Parent conferences wouldn't be dreaded if...

I think I'd be ready for parent conferences when...

The gathering of documentation throughout this book has been a singular work from one source, you. In reality, the responsibility and fun of this should be shared among the teaching team. Reflection on the observations involves much personal thought, which is not shared, but can bring out some revelations that would be valuable as discussion topics. This sounds like a very worthwhile effort to do with the new knowledge you have gained in observation techniques and child development.

Try some of this action research with a few colleagues. Use the skills you have gained in reflection to then write a story of one of the processes. Others can gain from your exploration.

Maybe I'll try the action research idea. I'll invite...

My story would begin with...

NEXT WEEK

In Appendix A is the *Week by Week* Schedule so you can see the whole year's assignments.

In Appendix B you will find the assignments for the completion of the forty *Week by Week* observation plan. By taking one week at a time, a few children, and a different method, you can gather documentation in all developmental areas several times over the course of the year.

Appendix C is a spreadsheet of the developmental areas and children's groups so you can see how the plan revisits each area, and each child has five focused observations throughout the year.

Forms are included in Appendix D for you to duplicate.

REFERENCES

Berger, E. (1995). *Parents as partners in education: Families and schools working together.* Englewood Cliffs, NJ: Merrill, an imprint of Prentice Hall.

Cherry, C. (1983). *Please don't sit on the kids.* Fearon Teacher Aids, Simon & Schuster.

Gartrell, D. (1994). *A guidance approach to discipline.* Albany: Delmar Publishers.

Gestwicki, C. (1996). *Home, school, and community relations: A guide to working with parents.* Albany: Delmar Publishers.

Gordon, T. (1975). *P.E.T. Parent Effectiveness Training.* New York: Wyden.

Kostelnik, M. J., Stein, L. C., Whiren, A. P., & Soderman, A. K. (1993). *Guiding children's social development* (2nd ed.). Albany: Delmar Publishers.

Marion, M. (1995). *Guidance of young children* (4th ed.). Englewood Cliffs, NJ: Merrill, an imprint of Prentice Hall.

National Association for the Education of Young Children and The National Association of Early Childhood Specialists in State Departments of Education (NAEYC and NAECS/SDE). (1991). Guidelines for appropriate curriculum content and assessment in programs serving children ages 3 through 8. *Young Children, 46* (3), 21–38.

Reynolds, E. (1990). *Guiding young children: A child-centered approach.* Mountain View, CA: Mayfield Publishing Company.

RESOURCES

Portfolios

Grace, C. & Shores, E. F. (1991). *The portfolio and its use: Developmentally appropriate assessment of young children.* Little Rock, AR: Southern Early Childhood Association.

Adult-Child Interactions

Clare, C. (1983). *Please don't sit on the kids.* Fearon Teacher Aids, Simon & Schuster

Gartrell, D. (1994). *A guidance approach to discipline.* Albany: Delmar Publishers.

Marion, M. (1995). *Guidance of young children.* (4th ed.). Englewood Cliffs, NJ: Merrill, an imprint of Prentice Hall.

Reynolds, E. *Guiding young children: A child-centered approach.* (1990). Mountain View, CA: Mayfield Publishing Company.

APPENDIX

A

Week by Week: An Observation Plan for Portfolio Building

WEEK	METHOD	AREA	ON WHOM
1	Class List Log Work Samples Reflective Journal	Separation and Adjustment Art	All All Self
2	Anecdotal Record Class List Log Reflective Journal	Self-Care Self-Care	Group A All Self
3	Checklist Anecdotal Record Reflective Journal	Physical Development Physical Development	All Group B Self
4	Running Record Class List Log Reflective Journal	Social Development Social Play Stage	Group C All Self
5	Frequency Count Anecdotal Record Reflective Journal	Emotional Development Emotional Development	All Group D Self
6	Interview and Checklist Class List Log Reflective Journal	Speech and Language Speech and Language	Group A All Self
7	Time Sample Interview and Checklist Reflective Journal	Attention Span Speech and Language	All Group B Self
8	Task Experiments Checklist Interview and Checklist Reflective Journal	Cognitive Math and Science Speech Language	Choice All Group C Self
9	Rating Scale Interview and Checklist Reflective Journal	Literacy Speech and Language	All Group D Self

WEEK	METHOD	AREA	ON WHOM
10	Work Samples Anecdotal Record Progress Reports* Reflective Journal	Creative Creative Process	All Group A Group A Self
11	Media Running Record Progress Reports* Reflective Journal	Dramatic Play and Blocks Dramatic Play	All Group B Group B Self
12	Class List Log Anecdotal Record Progress Reports* Reflective Journal	Self-Esteem Self-Identity	All Group C Group C Self
13	Setting Observation Class List Log Anecdotal Record Progress Reports* Reflective Journal	Environment Group Interactions Group Interactions	Visit All Group D Group D Self
14	Class List Log Checklist Progress Reports Reflective Journal *See Week 14, Assignment C	Interactions with Adults Physical Development	All All Group D Self
15	Class List Log Running Record Reflective Journal	Social Stage of Play Self-Identity	All Group A Self
16	Frequency Count Running Record Reflective Journal	Emotional Development Emotional Development	All Group B Self
17	Checklist Time Sample Reflective Journal	Language Development Attention Span	All All Self
18	Running Record Checklist Reflective Journal	Free Play Cognitive	Group C All Self
19	Rating Scale Writing Samples Reflective Journal	Literacy	All All Self
20	Work Samples Anecdotal Record Reflective Journal	Creative Creative Process	All Group D Self

WEEK	METHOD	AREA	ON WHOM
21	Media Interview and Checklist Progress Reports Reflective Journal	Dramatic Play and Blocks Speech and Language	All Group A Group A Self
22	Class List Log Interview and Checklist Progress Reports Reflective Journal	Choices in Play Speech and Language	All Group B Group B Self
23	Class List Log Interview and Checklist Progress Reports Reflective Journal	Group Time Speech and Language	All Group C Group C Self
24	Time Sample Interview and Checklist Progress Reports Reflective Journal	Attention Span Speech and Language	All Group D Group D Self
25	Checklist Anecdotal Record Reflective Journal	Social Development Creative	All Group C Self
26	Class List Log Running Record Reflective Journal	Self-Care Free Play	All Group D Self
27	Frequency Count Anecdotal Record Reflective Journal	Emotional Development Emotional Development	All Group A Self
28	Class List Log Anecdotal Record Reflective Journal	Adjustment to Routines Literacy	All Group B Self
29	Time Sample Checklist Reflective Journal	Attention Span Cognitive	All All Self
30	Rating Scale Samples Reflective Journal	Literacy Writing	All All Self
31	Work Samples Anecdotal Record Reflective Journal	Creative Emotional Development	All Group C Self
32	Class List Log Anecdotal Record Reflective Journal	Interaction with Adults Self-Identity	All Group D Self

WEEK	METHOD	AREA	ON WHOM
33	Checklist Running Record Reflective Journal	Physical Free Play	All Group A Self
34	Checklist Anecdotal Record Reflective Journal	Social Development Social Development	All Group B Self
35	Frequency Count Interview and Checklist Reflective Journal	Emotional Development Speech and Language	All Group C Self
36	Class List Log Interview and Checklist Reflective Journal	Group Interactions Speech and Language	All Group D Self
37	Checklist Interview and Checklist Progress Report Reflective Journal	Cognitive Development Speech and Language	All Group A Group A Self
38	Rating Scales Interview and Checklist Progress Report Reflective Journal	Literacy Speech and Language	All Group B Group B Self
39	Class List Log Time Sample Progress Report Reflective Journal	Self-Identity Attention Span	All All Group C Self
40	Work Samples Progress Report Reflective Journal	Creative	All Group D Self

Weeks 15 through 40: Assignments

After the completion of Week 14 (the last chapter of this book) observation and recording should not stop. This is designed to be an ongoing assessment of each child in the class over a whole year, so each developmental area is revisited and recording methods are used again and again. Weeks 15 through 40 follow with assignments for observing all the developmental areas using the methods presented in this book. If the plan is followed, all areas will have several documentations and each child will have group and individual assessments added to the child's portfolio. Progress report assignments are included, but may be modified depending on the program policies and calendar. Of course, all assignment topics, methods, and focus children can be modified to meet the policies of the program and the needs of the child. It is important, however, that individual children are not singled out for observations, ignoring the rest of the class. Equality of observation is one of the basic principles of the *Week by Week* plan. See Appendix C for a summary of the developmental areas and child groups.

The forms you will need to complete these assignments are printed in Appendix D for you to use as masters to copy.

Week 15, Assignment A

CLASS LIST LOG ON SOCIAL STAGES OF PLAY FOR ALL

This week, use a Class List Log form to observe each child's stage of play. You may modify the form by drawing vertical lines to indicate the social play stages: onlooker, solitary, parallel, associative, and cooperative. Observe the children as they interact with each other. Place a check mark in the stage next to their name. If you can, indicate what type of play it is: functional (F), constructive (C), dramatic (D), or games with rules (G).

What to Do with It

At the end of the week, take the Class List Log and transfer the stage you observed onto the portfolio overview sheet with your name and date of the observation.

Share your observations with the parents and the child, if appropriate. For example: "I was watching to see the progress of the children's interactions with each other when I noticed Fatima and how much more social she is now than at the beginning of the school year. She comes in and joins in groups of children who are already playing. That's sometimes hard to do," or "Fatima, I saw how you went right over to the block area when you got here today and joined Manuel and Shawn in building the skyscraper. They liked the way you added the little people on the top floors. How many floors are in the apartment house where you live? Do you ride the elevator or walk up?"

File the Class List Log in the class file. If you notice children who have not progressed, plan some cooperative activities and think about modeling some social play strategies to get them started.

Week 15, Assignment B

RUNNING RECORD ON SELF-IDENTITY FOR GROUP A

Each day this week, observe one or more of the children in group A, selecting a segment of the day when you can write a Running Record of a typical block of time (5 to 10 minutes). Write on the left side of lined notebook paper. Remember to begin with the child's name, the date, and your name. Each day this week, observe and write on each child in group A.

What to Do with It

On the right column, note any indicators of the child's knowledge, skills, dispositions, or attitudes, and feelings of empowerment or autonomy that contribute to self-identity.

Share with parents and child, if appropriate. For example: "Mrs. Ramirez, today when I was observing Joseph, I saw him pouring his juice so carefully. When he put the pitcher down, he looked up with a great big smile and said, 'No dejes caev una gota!' ('I didn't spill a drop.') He was so proud of himself and felt the power of doing things for himself."

If further action is needed, make a note of it in the class file and follow through. Perhaps the child needs more encouragement or opportunities to feel successful.

Note the presence of the Running Record with the recorder's name and date on the overview sheet, and file the Record in each child's portfolio.

Week 15, Assignment C

REFLECTIVE JOURNAL

Respond to the following in your Reflective Journal, kept in a private file at home.

I feel I know more about. . . than all the other children. I think it is because. . .

I am still puzzled about. . .

As the children leave for the day, I think. . .

When I face a loss or a separation, it helps me to. . .

Week 16, Assignment A

FREQUENCY COUNT ON EMOTIONAL DEVELOPMENT FOR GROUPS A AND B, THEN C AND D

Early in the week, select groups A and B, and later in the week groups C and D. Observe the children during free choice time for 30 minutes looking for evidence of prosocial or antisocial behaviors. Make a mark each time one of these occurs next to the name of the child in the appropriate column. On another day, repeat the observation with children in groups C and D.

What to Do with It

Compare this Frequency Count to the one done in week 5. Do you see differences in the totals for the class? For individual children? Do you think the prosocial curriculum activities for ten weeks made a difference? If so, write a short summary and send your findings to the authors. They would love to hear it. Share it in your school's newsletter or in a happy gram to parents.

Explore strategies for individual children who may need help in controlling aggression or for the whole group in problem solving or developing prosocial behaviors. Make a plan, implement, and document the results, perhaps with another Frequency Count after implementation. If it did not make a difference, why not? Summarize the project, and file it in the class file.

Week 16, Assignment B

RUNNING RECORD ON EMOTIONAL DEVELOPMENT FOR GROUP B

On Monday, watch child 1 in group B. Select a segment of the day when you can write a Running Record of a typical block of time (5 to 10 minutes). Write on the left side of lined notebook paper. Remember to begin with the child's name, the date, and your name. Each day this week observe and write on each child in group B. Make notes in the right-hand column of how this sample recording portrays the child's emotional development. If any action is indicated to assist the child or follow up on some other interest or concern, note that also and follow up on it.

What to Do with It

In the child's portfolio overview, note that the Running Record is present in the portfolio with your name as the recorder and the date.

Share the recording with parents and the child, if appropriate. For example: "Farrah is making progress in leaving at the end of the day. I was observing her yesterday and noticed how that new plan we made worked. I'm glad you suggested having her put all her things in the totebag right after nap. That begins to get her prepared to go home and makes leaving much calmer" or "Marcus, when I was writing about your play today, I noticed that you were angry when Carlo took away the big truck you were on but you just told him you had it first in a big voice and he listened. That's so much better than hitting. Hitting hurts but your words let him know what you wanted."

Week 16, Assignment C

REFLECTIVE JOURNAL

Respond to the following in your Reflective Journal, kept in a private file at home.

When children are dependent on me, I feel...

The parent I feel the most comfortable with is...

    I think it's because...

The parent I feel the least comfortable with is...

    I think it's because...

Maybe if I...

This day would have been better if...

The funniest thing I heard a child say this week was...

Week 17, Assignment A

CHECKLIST ON LANGUAGE DEVELOPMENT

Review the Speech and Language Checklist in each child's portfolio and note any changes since the checklist in week 6 and the interviews in weeks 6, 7, 8, and 9. Use a different color pen to note any changes.

What to Do with It

Make a note on the portfolio overview sheet with your name and date. Note any changes and place in each child's portfolio. Share progress with parents or child, if appropriate. For example: "I was observing all the children's language this week and I noticed from my notes that Devon's speech is sounding clearer now. He is pronouncing /l/ and /th/, which he wasn't doing a few months ago. And he's using many more words," or "Shaquinta, where did you hear that great jump rope song you were singing outside? The sounds of the words were such great fun. Would you teach it to me and the class after lunch while we're waiting for the bus? Would you like to add it to your tape in your portfolio?

Week 17, Assignment B

TIME SAMPLE ON ATTENTION SPAN FOR ALL

Select a day this week during free play time without planned interruptions. Prepare the form from Appendix D with learning center areas that are open. Complete the Time Sample.

What to Do with It

Compare to Time Samples done previously (week 7). Later in the day, draw conclusions and write notes in the child's portfolio about each child's attention span, play preferences, social interactions, and the changes from the last recording. Note the presence of the recording on the overview chart and file it in the class file. If this Time Sample showed an unusual pattern or you have an explanation for why a certain thing happened, write that down as well. Your incidental observations are important too. For example: "There were a lot of children around the water table today because it is new.")

Discuss observations from the Time Sample with parents or child, if appropriate.

Use the Time Sample to guide curriculum decisions about individual children. For example: "Sara still isn't leaving the art area. I'll try to get her to decorate a bike to ride or encourage her to join her friend Becky in making a sign for the block area." Follow through and make a note of it.

Week 17, Assignment C

REFLECTIVE JOURNAL

Respond to the following in your Reflective Journal, kept in a private file at home.

From my observations, I have seen how physical development and self-esteem are connected when. . .

I think because of that I should. . .

The benefits to the children would be. . .

My own life could benefit from. . .

Week 18, Assignment A

RUNNING RECORD ON FREE PLAY FOR GROUP C

Select the children in group A and each day this week write a Running Record of a segment of play, recording as many details as possible about the action, interaction with other children, and exact quotes.

What to Do with It

On the right column of each recording, make any notes of interpretation, concern, and any explanation for what you saw. Make a note on each child's portfolio overview sheet in the section of development that this observation most illustrates. File in the child's portfolio.

Share your observation findings with the parents or the child, if appropriate. For example: "As I was writing about Laura's play in the dramatic area today, I noticed how she is beginning to use longer sentences and words like *when* and *because*. I didn't think she was doing that a few months ago. When I checked back in the language sample I had in her portfolio, it showed an earlier stage," or "Sammy, when I was watching you play today, I wrote down something you said but I didn't understand it. When you were riding trucks with Peter you told him, 'If you go too fast you'll get popped.' Can you explain what that meant?"

If a question arises from the Running Record, follow it up to help understand it better or plan to include a project in the curriculum to expand this theme.

Week 18, Assignment B

CHECKLIST ON COGNITIVE SKILLS FOR ALL

Using your program's checklist, review the cognitive criteria and assess each child's level. If your program is not using a developmental checklist, revisit the assessment done in week 8. Ask the children the same questions and note their level now. If there is little progress, first check the environment and the curriculum. Are math manipulatives and science explorative materials present? Do the teachers facilitate their use, change them frequently, include them in the integrated curriculum tying books, field trips, art, music, and motor activities together with science and math?

What to Do with It

Share your observations with parents and the child, if appropriate. Maybe a happy note would be appropriate:

In October (or when first check was made) your child _____

_____

could _____

_____

and now

_____

_____

_____ .

Hurray!

Week 18, Assignment C

REFLECTIVE JOURNAL

Respond to the following in your Reflective Journal, kept in a private file at home.

When I watch children play, I can't help but wonder. . .

When I talked to parents this week I. . .

I'm looking forward to. . .

In the ten weeks that have gone by since we last observed cognitive development, the changes that surprised me the most were. . .

The biggest gains were made by. . .

I think it is because. . .

Week 19, Assignment A

RATING SCALE IN LITERACY FOR ALL

Look again in each child's portfolio at the Rating Scale you did in week 9. Observe and mark the progress you have seen in each child's reading and writing. Make notes with a different color pen.

What to Do with It

On the overview sheet, note progress and the date. Refile the Rating Scales. If you noticed no progress in a child's literacy, make a note to yourself to look further at the child's other developmental areas and make some theories and a plan to follow through.

Share your observations with parents or the child, if appropriate For example: "In the last few months, Hassan has made amazing progress in his awareness of books. He wasn't interested at all when he first entered school and now they've become one of his favorite choice activities. He's really into the small group story time we have every day. Once a book is read, he can take it and tell it back almost word for word. Now I've heard him sounding out words on his own from the letters," or "Dominique, I noticed the story today was too long for you to sit through. Let's look through the books and find a shorter one to read tomorrow, maybe one about that dog Spot since you have a new puppy."

Week 19, Assignment B

SAMPLES IN WRITING FOR ALL

This week, try to collect samples of each child's writing. It could be asking them to sign in as they arrive (name writing). Suggest they go to the writing center or art area, and make a book about a topic you have been working on this week. Sitting with them while they do it will give you a close observation of how they approach the task. Write a few notes about it and attach it to the sample.

What to Do with It

Often children will not want to part with their work, so you may have to make a copy of it on the copier. If a copier is not available, old-fashioned carbon paper is inexpensive and may even be a novel way to get reluctant writers to try it. Be sure to leave it out for later experimentation.

File the sample and your notes attached in the child's portfolio, making a note under literacy that it is there with the date and your name.

Share writing sample observations with parents and the child, if appropriate. For example: "Today

when I was gathering some samples of the children's writing Jamal really went to town on his *J*s. He calls them fish hooks. They do go in every direction but that's normal for this age. He's still experimenting with the shape and will eventually get them turned around most of the time by the time he's five or six," or "Jennifer, you are working so hard at writing your name. It has many letters in it. See here in the middle, you have two that are the same, the *n*s. Jamal's name also starts with a *J* but it's shorter and has an *L* at the end instead of an *R* like yours."

Children at three, four, and five years old will exhibit a wide range of written literacy ability. If you notice a much lower level than expected in a child's written language, think about what could be the cause. If there is something that should be addressed, such as possible vision or motor difficulties, discuss it with your supervisor and then the parent about a possible follow up. Provide the parent with possible resources in finding out more about it.

Week 19, Assignment C

REFLECTIVE JOURNAL

Respond to the following in your Reflective Journal, kept in a private file at home.

I've been thinking about reading and writing since the last journal entry, and I think...

The most interesting thing I've read recently was...

It made me think about...

When I was gathering the writing samples, I realized...

Because of that, I think I'd better...

Week 20, Assignment A

CREATIVE WORK SAMPLES FOR ALL

This week, collect a sample of creative work from every child. Make comments on the Work Samples Checklist or the creative section of your program's checklist.

Note the presence of the work on the portfolio overview sheet with your name and the date. Note any changes in art stage from week 10. On a sticky note on the back of the work, write your observations as you watched the child create this work, measurement of the child's developmental progress, and any interesting points to be remembered.

What to Do with It

Share with the parents, "Today Mario made a square for the first time. That's a milestone we've been waiting for. Before they really have those shapes in mind and the ability to draw them, they will be experimenting with them. He's coming right along," or if the child is present, "Anthony spent so long on his painting today he decided he didn't even want snack, so he just worked right through snack time. Boy, Anthony, you must love painting. You're really an artist."

File the sample in the child's portfolio.

Week 20, Assignment B

ANECDOTAL RECORD IN THE CREATIVE PROCESS FOR GROUP D

This week, begin with the first child in group D and write an Anecdotal Record on each one of them, detailing some aspect of their creativity in art, music, dramatic play, and block building. Include the situation, the details of the action, and exact quotes on the left side of the paper. In the right column give any explanation, judgments, questions you wonder about, or indications of development that the action signifies.

What to Do with It

Note on the portfolio overview sheet that the Anecdotal Record is there with the date and your name.

Share your observations with the parents, or the child, if appropriate. For example: "Today when I was writing observations of the children's play, I saw that your Sylvia was involved in a really interesting play episode in our family center. She was obviously the working mother getting ready to go to work but one of the boys argued "No, you stay home. I go to work." You have been a role model of a working mother because she came back to him and told him, nose to nose, 'I can be a good mother, go to work and still cook dinner. Now get on the back of this motorcycle.' He did and away they went. Family of the year 2000!" or "Lonnie, when I was watching the block center today, I saw you building a huge tower. You stacked the blocks across then stood one block in each of the four corners and came up with another story. You kept that pattern up until you couldn't reach any farther then you got a chair and carefully stood on it to make a few more stories. I took a picture of it so we can add it to our album. What would you like me to write in the book as the title of your building? 'You can write, "Here's Lonnie's tallest building he ever built."' That's a good description. I'll write it here with my notes so I'll remember. You write your name on this paper and we'll put it next to the building so everyone will know who built it.

File the photo and the child's dictation in the child's portfolio.

Week 20, Assignment C

REFLECTIVE JOURNAL

Respond to the following in your Reflective Journal, kept in a private file at home.

Now that I've been watching the children's creations more closely, I see...

I think that has changed my teaching approach so that now I...

I wonder, though, about...

Week 21, Assignment A

MEDIA DRAMATIC PLAY FREE PLAY FOR ALL

Make sure there are parent releases from all parents. (Note especially the children's files who have entered the program since week 11.) *If there is no release, or if the parent checked NO, place a prominent notation on the file and inform all staff.* Use some alternate method for recording dramatic play.

On all children this week, use some method of media for recording a segment of play that shows the child's imagination. It may be dramatic play, blocks, sand, manipulatives, or art.

Audio Tape Recording

Perhaps there is a child who loves to sing favorite songs or make up songs. Tape that on their language tape started in week 9. Perhaps ask a child to tell the tape recorder about the art work as it is being created or the process of making a collage or a Lego construction. A child may want to record a story about the building that is just finished. These make excellent language and imagination samples.

What to Do with It

Note the presence of the tape recording on the overview sheet with the date and your name. Make a note from what you have observed in the area of development it most accurately documents.

Share the recording with the parents and the child, if appropriate. For example: "When I was talking with Colleen today, she told me about the poem you taught her. It was so beautiful, I had her recite it on the tape that I'm collecting of each child talking. It's in her portfolio. If you want to listen to it sometime I could send it home," or "Marcella, while you were playing with Heather today in the sand I had the tape recorder nearby. It recorded how you were taking turns at using that scoop. That was a friendly thing to do. Would you like to hear it? It's in your portfolio."

Photographs

Take some pictures this week as the children play. Have them developed and have each child dictate a story or tape record one to tell about what they were doing.

What to Do with It

Make a bulletin board display of the children's photos and comments for the children to look at. Or place them in a photo album for the book area. Make a note in each child's file of an observation based on the photograph or their comments. Note it on the overview sheet in the corresponding developmental area.

Invite the parents to look at the photo display, especially their child's.

Videotape

Take a video of children as they play. Try to get whole segments of play and as much conversation as you can. Include every child in the class in some way on the tape.

What to Do with It

Later that day or soon, show the tape to the class. Show the segment that was recorded earlier. Invite a discussion about what was different then and now. Perhaps make a chart, "Tape 1" and "Tape 2," as they dictate the differences. These discussions could be documented as further evidence of sociodramatic play or language practice.

Share the tape with parents at a parent meeting or have it playing at the entrance as they bring or pick up the children. File it in the class file after you have made any notes to add to each child's file in the area the tape documents. Note its existence on the portfolio overview sheet.

Week 21, Assignment B

INTERVIEW AND CHECKLIST FOR GROUP A

Refer to the guidelines and Speech and Language Checklist in Chapter 6.

Select each child in group A to interview each day this week. If possible, tape record the interview as well as make written notes (literacy role model) as you speak with each child.

Afterward, analyze the interview for what it reveals about the child's knowledge, emotional state, social development, and speech and language, using the Speech and Language Checklist.

What to Do with It

Enter a summary, the recorder's name, and the date on the portfolio overview sheet.

Compare to the Interviews done on each child earlier in the year. If a significant lag appears, discuss it with your supervisor to confirm it, then with the parent. Have available a list of resources to refer the parent to where a speech and language evaluation may be obtained.

Share with the parents and child something of interest that came from the interview. For example: "I was talking with Jane and noticed how the orthodontics have moved her teeth. Her speech has improved from when she first got them. She has adjusted well, hasn't she?" or "When we made the tape recording of our talk today, I learned how much you knew about iguanas. Maybe someday you could bring one to school. We could play the tape you made and show the storybook that goes with it."

Is any follow-up needed?

Week 21, Assignment C

PROGRESS REPORTS FOR GROUP A

Follow the format from Chapter 14. Each day this week take some time with the portfolios of the children in group A. Remember: Be positive, descriptive, and personal.

Heading
Family (optional for progress report)
Physical
Social
Adjustment to school
Self-acceptance
Cognitive
Creativity
Closure

What to Do with It

Have a supervisor check the progress reports. Make copies. Place one in the portfolio and one in the class file. Go over the original with the parent in a parent conference if possible.

Week 21, Assignment D

REFLECTIVE JOURNAL

Respond to the following in your Reflective Journal, kept in a private file at home.

When I listened to children more closely this week, I found. . .

My work on my own language habit is. . .

The funniest thing I heard a child say this week was. . .

The scariest thing I heard a child say this week was. . .

Week 22, Assignment A

CLASS LIST LOG ON CHOICES IN BLOCKS AND DRAMATIC PLAY FOR ALL

Use the Class List Log from Appendix D during free play this week, and note the choices that each child makes in the areas of creative and dramatic play.

What to Do with It

On each child's portfolio overview, note the child's free play choices from the Class List Log and the date observed. File the Class List Log in the class file.

Use this information to individualize curriculum, building on the child's interests by providing additional props, books, and follow-up activities to enrich the play. This also can be used to interest the child in areas not frequently chosen. For example, a child who always plays with blocks but seldom uses small muscles for writing could be encouraged to trace blocks or draw block buildings. A child who always chooses dramatic play could be provided with literacy materials to encourage writing interest.

Share observations with the parents and the child, if appropriate. For example: "Today when I was watching Sergi I saw he spent a long time with the hammer and nails. Tomorrow I'm putting some small mallets out with the clay to see if he can become interested in an area he has not yet tried."

Week 22, Assignment B

INTERVIEW AND CHECKLIST FOR GROUP B

Refer to the guidelines and Speech and Language Checklist in Chapter 6.

Select the children in group B to interview each day this week. If possible, tape record the interview as well as make written notes (literacy role model) as you speak with each child.

Afterward, analyze the Interview for what it reveals about the child's knowledge, emotional state, social development, and speech and language, using the Speech and Language Checklist.

What to Do with It

Enter a summary, the recorder's name, and date on the portfolio overview sheet.

Compare to the Interviews done on each child earlier in the year. If a significant lag appears, discuss it with your supervisor to confirm it, then with the parent. Have available a list of resources to refer the parent to where a speech and language evaluation may be obtained. Is any follow-up needed?

Week 22, Assignment C

PROGRESS REPORTS FOR GROUP B

Follow the format from Chapter 14. Each day this week take some time with the portfolios of the children in group B. Remember: Be positive, descriptive, and personal.

Heading
Family (optional for progress report)
Physical
Social
Adjustment to school
Self-acceptance
Cognitive
Creativity
Closure

What to Do with It

Have a supervisor check the progress reports. Make copies. Place one in the portfolio and one in the class file. Go over the original with the parent in a parent conference if possible.

Week 22, Assignment D

REFLECTIVE JOURNAL

Respond to the following in your Reflective Journal, kept in a private file at home.

Is this year half over already?!

Or does it still have. . . months to go?

What's my attitude?

Why do I feel this way?

Look at the class list and sort the children into two lists using any criteria you want.

List #1	List #2

Week 23, Assignment A

CLASS LIST LOG ON GROUP TIME FOR ALL

Some time this week during a time when the group is all engaged in the same activity—eating, outside time, or circle time—use the Class List Log to write a few words about each child's involvement.

What to Do with It

By this time in the year, children should be displaying signs of comfort and active participation. If you notice a child not participating, look closely at their behavior and draw conclusions. It may be they are new, just learning the language, or are indicating some need. Decide on a follow-up action, such as speaking to other staff about the child.

Write any important information on the overview sheet of each child's portfolio, along with the date and your name.

Share with the parent or the child. For example: "Today when I was watching all the children playing the game Loobey Lou I noticed that Roxanne knows her left from right. That is really unusual for children this age," or "Krissy, today when we were sitting at the lunch table I was making some notes so I wouldn't forget to ask some people some questions. I wanted to ask you about never sitting at Brigette's table. I saw you move your name tag to the other table when you saw Lizette put yours at Brigette's table. Let's talk about Brigette. Does it scare you when she makes those noises because she can't talk yet. Did you know she can only talk when she uses that machine? Later today would you like to see how it works?"

File the Class List Log in the class file.

Week 23, Assignment B

INTERVIEW AND CHECKLIST FOR GROUP C

Select the children in group C to interview each day this week. If possible, tape record an informal conversation or structured Interview as well as make written notes as you speak with each child. Add this interview to the tape begun in week 6.

Informal Interview

If you wish, record a conversation you have with the child about the child's play, an event, or an explanation of a piece of art or construction.

Structured Interview

Two- and three-year-olds:
What's your name?
How old are you?
Go get the book. (receptive)
Say, "I want the ball."
What's this?
What's this sound? (make a toy sound without the child seeing it)

Show a mirror. Who is that?
What's his name?

Four- and five-year-olds:
What's your name? What's your last name?
Look around the room and tell me what you see.
What makes you happy? sad? mad?
What do you like to do best when you aren't at school?
Can you tell me about a dream you've had?
Do you remember what we talked about the last time we did this?
Do you know any jokes?

What to Do with It

Afterward, analyze the interview for what it reveals about the child's knowledge, emotional state, social development, and speech and language.

Refer to the Speech and Language Checklist done in week 6. Make any notations of progress the child has made since then.

On the overview sheet, note the addition to the tape and any comments about the child's speech and language or other areas revealed in the conversation.

Share the observation with parents or the child if appropriate. For example: "I was listening in particular today to Adi speak then I played back the tape I had made many weeks ago. I couldn't believe the difference. His sentences are so much longer and he's using lots of new words. I can tell he just loves having his grandmother here. He talks about her a lot and all the things they do together. He seems so happy," or "April, that was such fun talking with you on the tape recorder. That joke about the chicken crossing the road was one I hadn't heard before. You'll have to tell Bernardo that one. He's really into jokes right now."

File the tape in each child's portfolio.

Week 23, Assignment C

PROGRESS REPORT FOR GROUP C

Write a progress report on children in group C. You have spent individual time with them this week in the interview and have a portfolio of past observations as documentation. Follow the format:

Heading
Family (optional for progress report)
Physical
Social
Adjustment to school
Self-acceptance
Cognitive
Creativity
Closure

What to Do with It

Give the report to each child's parents individually and privately if possible. Briefly go over the highlights and offer them the opportunity to look through the portfolio some time when they are at school. Ask for them to read it and jot down any questions or comments they may have about it.

Keep a report in the child's portfolio and one in the class file.

Week 23, Assignment D

REFLECTIVE JOURNAL

Respond to the following in your Reflective Journal, kept in a private file at home.

	I'm still thinking about last week when...
	My body is telling me...
	Write about an emergency situation you faced and how you reacted.
	Draw a doodle that represents how you feel about your job.

Week 24, Assignment A

TIME SAMPLE ON ATTENTION SPAN FOR ALL

Select a day this week during free play time without planned interruptions. Prepare the form from Appendix D with learning center areas that are open. Complete the Time Sample.

What to Do with It

Compare to Time Samples done previously (week 7 and week 13). Later in the day, draw conclusions and write notes in the child's portfolio about each child's attention span, play preferences, social interactions, and the changes from the last recording. Note the presence of the recording on the overview chart and file it in the class file.

Share with the child's parents how the attention span has lengthened or play choices have changed. Be specific from your notes, showing you are a careful observer and you know their child. Indicate how you plan to use this information to individualize the curriculum. For example: "Edna is staying longer in the story area, taking an interest in looking at books, even when she is the only one there. I think it really helped when we got some books that have flaps to open and wheels to turn. She always has her hands in motion so these books appeal to her," or "Lucienne, I was watching where everyone was playing yesterday and I saw that you stayed for a long time watching the fish. I wonder if you would look through this catalog from the pet store and see what fish we could buy that would cost less than $5. Here's the calculator. Maybe you could get Paulette to help you. She knows how to use it."

Week 24, Assignment B

INTERVIEW/CHECKLIST FOR GROUP D

Select the children in group D to interview each day this week. If possible, tape record an informal conversation or structured Interview as well as make written notes as you speak with each child. Add this Interview to the tape begun in week 7.

What to Do with It

Afterward, analyze the Interview for what it reveals about the child's knowledge, emotional state, social development, and speech and language.

Refer to the Speech and Language Checklist done in week 6. Make any notations of progress the child has made since then.

On the overview sheet, note the addition to the tape and any comments about the child's speech and language or other areas revealed in the conversation.

Share the observation with parents or the child, if appropriate. For example: "I listened closely to a tape recorded conversation you and Alexia taped at home. I heard the dysfluent speech you were concerned about but it really is common for four-year-olds. Let's talk again in a month and try not to pressure her to talk. Maybe you should mention it to the pediatrician" or "Lorraine, that story you told on the tape recorder about the big dog was really scary. When you see that dog loose from its leash next time, be sure to stay away. Do you want to tell you mom that story or should she listen to the tape? You decide."

File the tape in each child's portfolio.

Week 24, Assignment C

PROGRESS REPORT FOR GROUP D

Follow the format from Chapter 14. Each day this week take some time with the portfolios of the children in group D. Remember: Be positive, descriptive, and personal.

Heading
Family (optional for progress report)
Physical
Social
Adjustment to school
Self-acceptance
Cognitive
Creativity
Closure

What to Do with It

Have a supervisor check the progress report. Make a copy to place in the portfolio, and one to place in the class file. Go over the original with the parent in a parent conference if possible.

Week 24, Assignment D

REFLECTIVE JOURNAL

Respond to the following in your Reflective Journal, kept in a private file at home.

I'm really seeing their imagination and creativity developing. I wonder what other things I can do to spark it. Maybe if I . . .

The school year is more than half over (or is it less than half to go?) How do I feel about it?

This media thing is . . .

After all these many weeks I still don't feel like I know . . .

Why don't they . . .

Week 25, Assignment A

CHECKLIST FOR SOCIAL DEVELOPMENT

If your program is using a developmental checklist with a social area, rate each child's social development by that criteria this week or use some of the questions from Chapter 4 from the Social Skills Checklist.

What to Do with It

Note the presence of the recording on the portfolio overview sheet. Think about the meaning of what you have seen and how it relates to the child's developmental progress.

Share your observations with parents and the child, if appropriate. For example: "This week when I was watching to see how the children's social skills are coming along, I noticed how Henning is now branching out in his friendships. I think he's picking up more English words and that helps," or "Deidre, I saw you waiting your turn when the children were jumping rope and holding Melagro's sweater. That's what friends do."

Make a note if further action is indicated and follow through with some individual curriculum planning.

Week 25, Assignment B

ANECDOTAL ON CREATIVITY FOR GROUP C

Observe each of the children in group C this week for an incident that displays an aspect of creativity. Selecting one child a day, record an anecdote with as many details as you can about how the child approached creative media, dramatic play, block building, music, or some other aspect of play. Write a factual account of the incident so the reader has the feel of being there, along with exact quotes of what was said. In the right-hand column, jot down your comments, your interpretation of the incident, and any change in development this incident shows compared to past recordings.

What to Do with It

Note the presence of the recording on the overview sheet with the date and your name.

Share the anecdote with parents or the child, if appropriate. For example: "I've been writing inci-

dents as the children play, and today while I was watching Edward I saw a really curious thing. He has been drawing very detailed drawings of houses with doors and windows and trees and swing sets but today when he started to draw a house he started to cry and get very upset. He took a crayon and scribbled all over the page and said 'I hate this house. I hate this house.' I thought maybe he is still holding in the death of his grandpa. He hasn't talked about it at all. Are you seeing any signs of stress like this? Let's make an appointment to talk about it soon. I'd like to discuss what we can do at school to help," or "That sure was an interesting collage you made today with all the buttons piled on top of one another. I was watching you count them and put them all in rows. It looked like you were making stairs with them. Here's my notes where I drew the pattern you were gluing. Does that look like what you were doing? Did I get it right?"

File the recording in each child's portfolio.

Week 25, Assignment C

REFLECTIVE JOURNAL

Respond to the following in your Reflective Journal, kept in a private file at home.

I was surprised to see the Anecdotal Recording show that. . .

I think I'll try to. . .

I'm getting to know...a lot better and that helps because. . .

The child who seems to have less friends than all the others is. . .

I think it's because. . .

I'll try to. . .

Week 26, Assignment A

CLASS LIST LOG ON SELF-CARE FOR ALL

Using the Class List Log from Appendix D, make notes this week about each child's eating, toileting, dressing, personal hygiene, sleeping, and classroom self-care. Review checklist items for the age of the children in your group from Chapter 2, and observe, noting the degree of self-care in each of those areas.

What to Do with It

Look back in the class file at the Class List Log done in week 2. On each child's portfolio overview sheet, note the date of the Class List Log and self-care observed and change from that time, along with your name.

Share your observations with parents and the child, if appropriate. For example: "Over the course of the year, Steven has progressed so far in the ability to care for his own needs in the classroom. This not only shows he is growing more independent but has had a great effect on his self-esteem. He is so proud of all he can now do for himself, like zip, tie, pour, and even help others."

File the Class List Log in the class file.

Week 26, Assignment B

RUNNING RECORD ON FREE PLAY FOR GROUP D

This week during free play time, select each child from group D and write a Running Record. Observe and write for 5 to 10 minutes, preserving a specimen of each child's typical behavior. Later in the day, make notes in the right-hand column about the observation, what questions it raises, if this is usual or unusual behavior, and what this incident reveals about the child's development.

What to Do with It

On the portfolio overview sheet, make a few notes in the developmental area in which the recording is most revealing and the presence of the full recording with your name and date.

Share any interesting information with parents or the child, if appropriate. For example: "When I was observing Brenden today, he said the funniest thing..." or "You really made me laugh when you told that funny story about your shoe getting stuck in the mud. I wrote it down for your portfolio. If you want me to read it to you sometime I will."

File the recording in the child's portfolio.

Week 26, Assignment C

REFLECTIVE JOURNAL

Respond to the following in your Reflective Journal, kept in a private file at home.

I feel like I know. . .   very well but not. . .

I wonder if it's because. . .

I think I need to know more about. . .

Maybe if I. . .

It really hurt me when. . .   said. . .

I think it's because. . .

Week 27, Assignment A

FREQUENCY COUNT ON EMOTIONAL DEVELOPMENT FOR GROUPS A AND B, THEN GROUPS C AND D

Prepare the Frequency Count form from Appendix D. Early in the week, select children in groups A and B and observe during free choice time for 30 minutes. Look for evidence of prosocial or antisocial behaviors. Make a mark next to the name of the child in the appropriate column each time one of these occurs. On another day, repeat the observation with children in groups C and D.

What to Do With It

Compare your findings with week 5 and week 16. What changes do you see? What do you think are the causes? The children are half a year older from the first observation. Can you see that in their emotional control?

Make notes in each child's portfolio and file the Frequency Count form and your answers to the preceding questions in the class file.

Share your positive findings and the observation with parents and the child, if appropriate. For example: "I was observing the class today and found that overall there are 50 percent less aggressive acts than at the start of the year. We've really been working on encouraging prosocial behaviors and it appears to be working."

For those children still having difficulty with emotional control, make a special plan for them and carry it out, documenting the results.

Week 27, Assignment B

ANECDOTAL RECORDING ON EMOTIONAL DEVELOPMENT FOR GROUP A

Select each of the children in group A. On Monday, observe child 1; Tuesday, child 3, and so on. Observe for incidents that give information about emotional development, such as the child displaying joy, happiness, anger, aggression, and fear. Make notes and by the end of the day write an Anecdotal Record about the incident with as many details as possible on the right column of a sheet of paper. On the left side, comment on the significance of the incident, if it was usual or unusual, and possible contributing factors.

What to Do with It

In the child's portfolio, jot a few summary words, that the Anecdotal Recording is being included, the date, and your name.

Share your observations with parents and the child, if appropriate. For example: "When Tara began school here she cried very easily, with transition times between routines in the day especially upsetting to her. She now knows the routines and is even able to handle the unexpected. I hadn't realized what a change had taken place until I was filing the latest observation in her portfolio and reread some of the previous ones. When you get a chance, stop by and curl up in the parent room and read them. They're better than a Danielle Steele novel," or "Grayson, do you remember how afraid you were whenever we had a fire drill and had to practice how quickly we could leave the building. Now you just stop what you're doing, and help the other children get to the door. How did that change happen?" Grayson replied, "I guess I just growed up."

File in each child's portfolio.

If a strategy to help the child cope with emotions is indicated, discuss it with the parents or the supervisor to decide on a course of action. Follow through.

Week 27, Assignment C

REFLECTIVE JOURNAL

Respond to the following in your Reflective Journal, kept in a private file at home.

I felt so happy when I saw. . .

I'm wondering why the curriculum doesn't seem to meet. . .

needs. Could it be. . .

I might try. . .

It was so funny when. . .

Week 28, Assignment A

CLASS LIST LOG ON ARRIVALS AND DEPARTURES AND ADJUSTMENT TO SCHOOL FOR ALL

Using the Class List Log from Appendix D, make notes about each child's arrivals and departures and adjustments to school this week.

What to Do with It

Compare your observations to the Class List Logs done on week 1 and week 13. Draw conclusions about what the comparison indicates.

Make notes in each child's portfolio from your observation. This would be a good comparison to add to the end-of-the-year report.

Share your observations with the parents or the child, if appropriate. For example: "I was observing as the children left the center this week and noticed how much more organized Marco is now. He methodically gathers all his things together and gets them all into his backpack without any help. He's showing his independence and anticipating what is coming next. His memory is so much longer and he knows it. He even said, "I don't forget like I did when I was little," or "Brienne, when I was watching all the children arrive on the bus today I noticed you were waiting for Stephanie. It takes her longer because of her crutches. I'm sure it pleased her to have you wait for her so she wouldn't be lonely. She sure moves fast on those computer keys though. I saw how she showed you how to load and start that new program. I guess you two make a good pair."

File in the class file.

Week 28, Assignment B

ANECDOTAL RECORD IN LITERACY FOR GROUP B

This week, select the children from group B to observe, watching for aspects of literacy such as book interest and handling, writing interest and ability, and reading ability (logos, words in context, phonics). Write an Anecdotal Record on each child that illustrates literacy. In the right-hand column, note the meaning, comments, and questions you have about this anecdote.

What to Do with It

Compare these observations with the Literacy Rating Scales done in week 9 and week 19. Note the child's progress on the portfolio overview sheet, referring to the Anecdotal Record, the date, and your name. Decide how you can build on what the child can now do to encourage further development. Plan individual curriculum to accomplish this goal.

Share your observations with parents and the child, if appropriate. For example: "I was watching Lynette as she picked up a book. She looked at it and immediately turned it right side up and began to turn pages from the front to the back, one at a time. That's a milestone for a toddler. I wrote about it for her portfolio," or "Donato, I saw you playing restaurant, pretending to be the waiter. You wrote down people's orders. Could I have their order papers, after they pay their checks, of course? I'd like to include your writing with this writing I did about your play."

File the recordings in each child's portfolio.

Week 28, Assignment C

REFLECTIVE JOURNAL

Respond to the following in your Reflective Journal, kept in a private file at home.

The ten things that are the most valuable to me are. . .

Dealing with. . . is the most difficult thing I had to face this week because. . .

I am achieving. . .

Next week I will. . .

Week 29, Assignment A

TIME SAMPLE ON ATTENTION SPAN FOR ALL

Select a day this week during a normal free play time without planned interruptions. Prepare the Time Sample form from Appendix D with learning center areas down the left margin. Record where each of the children choose to be and with whom, at five-minute intervals for half an hour.

What to Do with It

Compare to the Time Sample done previously (weeks 7, 17, and 24). Later in the day, draw conclusions and write notes in the child's portfolio about each child's attention span, play preferences, social interactions, and the changes from the last recording. Note the recording on the overview chart, and file it in the class file. Write on it any general statements that would help a reader understand what the Time Sample illustrated.

Discuss with parents or the child, if appropriate. For example: "When I was making notes in the portfolio about attention span I noticed that Huye is playing a lot more with other children as he learns more English words. Here's a new children's book with names of things that might help too," or "When I was watching the class play today I noticed that you really didn't play with anyone else, you just went to places where no other children were playing. This must have been one of those days when you just wanted to be by yourself. Is that the way you were feeling?"

Use the Time Sample to check if a learning center needs to be renewed by the addition of some different materials. If a particular area seems to be the place where a lot of pushing and pulling take place, evaluate if the area has enough materials for the children who are there or if there is something about its arrangement that causes children to infringe on each other's space.

Week 29, Assignment B

CHECKLIST ON COGNITIVE SKILLS FOR ALL

Refer to the cognitive portion of your program's developmental checklist. Mark the criteria in this section on each child in the class by observing as they work.

What to Do with It

Share the progress with the parents and the child, if appropriate. For example: "Today Anjanette was playing with these tubes and placed them in order according to size perfectly. That shows her mathematical ability," or "Julien, the last time we played this game with the colored bears you had trouble with the color names. This time you knew every one! How'd you remember them this time?"

If you see little or no progress since the last review of the criteria, do a closer observation, making anecdotal notes. Use the child's interests to introduce the concepts that are yet to be developed.

File the checklist in each child's portfolio.

Week 29, Assignment C

REFLECTIVE JOURNAL

Respond to the following in your Reflective Journal, kept in a private file at home.

As we get closer to the end of the year with only a few weeks left, I really wish I had . . .

I'll be glad that. . .

In thinking more about math and science, I believe. . .

I have the longest attention span when I am. . .

Week 30, Assignment A

RATING SCALE ON LITERACY FOR ALL

Revisit the Literacy Rating Scale in each child's portfolio. Note the progress and date the observation. Write a short summary on the back of the page about what you've seen over the course of the months and the reasons you think caused the change.

What to Do with It

Refile the Rating Scale in the portfolio after making a notation on the overview sheet, with the date and your name.

Share it with the parents and the child, if appropriate. For example: "Well, look at this. I was observing Emilie today and I saw her pick up a new book from the library and pick out many words she knew by sounding them out. At the beginning of the year, she was still learning the alphabet. Isn't it amazing how they learn to read? All those books you borrow every week and read to her have really helped," or "How did you know it was Jamal's turn to water the plants and Jennifer's turn to feed the guinea pig? Here's a list of all the children's names in the class. Can you read them all? I think you can. What a surprise."

Week 30, Assignment B

SAMPLES ON WRITING FOR ALL

This week, collect more samples of each child's writing and knowledge of print. You could have them dictate a letter to a sick class member or a thank-you to a recent visitor. From their dictation, you can talk about the writing. If they are to the level of writing themselves, provide interesting paper or tools to encourage their writing, perhaps a pen that writes gold, or print their name with a pencil pressing into a foam meat tray. (Make a copy for the file.) They can then use a paint brayer to make prints of their writing. It will be backwards so warn them and show them how to read it in a mirror. Sitting with them while they work will give you a close observation of how they approach the task. It also is an opportunity for individual time together. Write a few notes about it and attach it to the sample.

What to Do with It

Compare the writing sample to that done in week 19. See the progress each one has made and make a note of it on the portfolio overview sheet. File the sample in the child's portfolio.

Share it with the parents and the child, if appropriate. For example: "When I was observing and making notes on Matthew's interest in books, I saw that he really pays attention more closely to the story in group time when he sits right up close and often pushes other children and says, 'I can't see.' And when he was writing, he bends right down close to the paper. Have you noticed if he might have trouble seeing other things, like when he's playing with Legos or watching television? A vision check next time you go to the doctor might be a good idea. We also have a pediatric eye specialist who will do a free vision screening for children in our program. Here's her number if you want to follow it up before then," or "K-E-N-D-R-A is one way to write your name in big letters. We call those capitals. Here's another way that also says K-e-n-d-r-a. The capital or big letter is the first letter, then the rest are small letters or lower-case letters. They both spell Kendra and mean you. Do you think that's why you couldn't find your name at the lunch table? How about if we write it in capitals on one side and upper- and lower-case letters on the other so you can always know it's your name."

Week 30, Assignment C

REFLECTIVE JOURNAL

Respond to the following in your Reflective Journal, kept in a private file at home.

I have the right to...

If I were to compare myself to an animal, I am most like a...
because...

My teaching style has been most influenced by...

If I were going to advise a brand new teacher, the most helpful
piece of advice would be...

Week 31, Assignment A

WORK SAMPLES ON CREATIVITY FOR ALL

This week, try to collect a sample of each child's creative work. It may be a painting, drawing, collage, clay, or blocks that could be sketched or photographed. It is possible the child may decorate one panel of the portfolio file folder.

What to Do with It

Compare the work to that done in week 10 and week 20. Note the progress from what you know about the stages in children's creative development.

Share the observations with the parents and the child, if appropriate. For example: "Alexis is really advancing in her ability to represent her thoughts in pictures. She worked diligently on a drawing of your house. I would have recognized it driving down the street from her details of the dormers, the bushes, and the letter *S* on the chimney. She had it all there. That is unusual for a child her age," or "Tom, you made so many little balls from the clay that you used it all up. Are you planning what to do next?"

File the work samples in the child's portfolio, dated, and with any comments attached to the back of the work with a sticky note.

Week 31, Assignment B

ANECDOTAL RECORD ON EMOTIONAL DEVELOPMENT FOR GROUP C

Select all the children in group C and watch this week for events or episodes that give information to amplify what you know about the child's emotional development. Make notes and write it down as soon as possible. In the left column, relate the episode in factual terms, describing the participants, the actions, and the exact words spoken. In the right-hand column write your explanations, inferences, and questions raised from what you saw and heard.

What to Do with It

Note the Anecdotal Recording on each child's overview sheet in the developmental area it describes.

Share it with the parents and the child, if appropriate. For example: "Today when I was observing April she asked Mrs. Martinez to write down the words to a story. She told this long, involved tale about a boy going on a trip, forgetting his suitcase, losing his ticket, and getting lost in the airport. I hope she wasn't relating your husband's latest business trip. She has quite an imagination but it sounded so real and she appeared quite disturbed about it," or "Robert, you really know a lot about farms. Today when I was watching you build with the farm set we borrowed from the other class, you told all the builders about how the milk goes into a big tank and how the truck comes to pump it out and what they do with the milk at the creamery. Then I remembered, your grand dad used to work there. Did he take you there with him so you could watch what happens to the milk in those big steel tanks? You and he were such good buddies. I think playing with this set helps you remember how it was before he died."

File the Anecdotal Recording in the child's portfolio.

Week 31, Assignment C

REFLECTIVE JOURNAL

Respond to the following in your Reflective Journal, kept in a private file at home.

The last time I cried was when. . .

I would never cry if . . .   was around because. . .

I think crying is. . .

Thinking about crying helps me to. . .

Maybe I'll talk with. . .   about. . .

Week 32, Assignment A

CLASS LIST LOG ON INTERACTIONS WITH ADULTS FOR ALL

Using the Class List Log from Appendix D, make notes this week about each child's reaction and interactions with adults in the classroom, other teachers, staff, and visitors. Ask another person to watch each child's reaction to you.

What to Do with It

Transfer your notes to each child's portfolio overview sheet with the date and your name.

Share your observations with the parents or the child, if appropriate. For example: "This week when I was watching Deidre, I saw how she has really made friends with our practicum student Rosa. She loves to touch Rosa's long, braided hair and she looks so closely at Rosa's dark eyes then at her own blue ones in the mirror. They say at two years old children begin to have racial awareness. I believe that's what she is doing. She's really making those observations and taking it all in. Rosa is very understanding and patient with her."

"Luo, today I saw you sitting in Mrs. Wilkins lap listening to a story. Here's the book *The Foot Book*. You can take it home and read it to your little brother."

File the Class List Log in the class file.

Week 32, Assignment B

ANECDOTAL RECORDING ON SELF-IDENTITY FOR GROUP D

Select all the children in group D, and this week observe them as they work in the classroom for signs of how they perceive or feel about themselves. Review Chapter 12 for some of the indicators. Make notes as incidents happen that give you clues about each child's self-identity. Later that day, amplify them with as many details and descriptions as you can, writing them down the left column of a sheet of paper. In the right-hand column, write your judgments, comments, theories, concerns, or questions.

What to Do with It

On each child's portfolio overview sheet, note the presence of the Anecdotal Record, the date, and your name as recorder. If a child's actions indicate a negative self-identity, make a plan for that child to feel competent and powerful. Implement the plan and revisit the subject with more notes in the portfolio.

Share positive anecdotes with parents. You may decide the negative ones would not be helpful to be placed in the portfolio. For example: "Mrs. Jamieson, Jerimiah has such a 'can do' attitude. He is never afraid to try a new thing or to say he can't do something. Whatever you did to instill that quality in him has surely benefitted him. He has plenty of friends, is developing in all areas right on track, and seems happy most of the time. Other parents would love to know your secret," or "Marinka, here's a flashlight. You could go over to the block corner and shine it on the buildings like the sun or the moon. I'm sure they will let you be the shiner or will trade a builder's job for the flashlight. Let's see what will happen."

File the Anecdotal Records in each child's portfolio.

Week 32, Assignment C

REFLECTIVE JOURNAL

Respond to the following in your Reflective Journal, kept in a private file at home.

My body is telling me. . .

My mind is telling me. . .

My better sense is telling me. . .

I think I'll listen to my. . .   and. . .

Week 33, Assignment A

CHECKLIST ON PHYSICAL DEVELOPMENT FOR ALL

Revisit the checklist on physical development from week 3 and week 14. Using the same form with a different color pen, mark the checklist.

What to Do with It

Enter a summary, your name, and the date on the portfolio overview sheet. Note the changes and place in each child's portfolio.

Share accomplishments and progress with the parents and the child, if appropriate. For example:

"Gretchen can throw and catch a ball, walk the balance beam, and even jump rope. Those are difficult tasks for a three-year-old. Where does she get all that coordination?" or "Christopher, I know you want to climb to the top of the climber and jump off but I can't catch you. When your body tells you it's safe to jump, you will be able to jump without help. For now, climb to step number three and jump from there. That's where you are able to feel safe."

Make note if further action is indicated.

Week 33, Assignment B

RUNNING RECORD ON FREE PLAY FOR GROUP A

Select all the children in group A and each day this week write a Running Record of a segment of play, recording as many details as possible about the action, interaction with other children, and exact quotes.

What to Do with It

On the right column of each recording, make any notes of interpretation, concern, and any explanation for what you saw. Make a note on each child's portfolio overview sheet in the section of development that this observation most illustrates. File in the child's portfolio.

Share observation findings with the parents or the child, if appropriate. For example: "While I was watching Toby at the manipulative area today,

I noticed him building a very intricate Lego building. He said he was building the 'monument' and when I asked him about it he told all about your trip to Washington, about staying in the hotel, riding the elevator to the top floor to see the city lights, and going to see the long, black wall with names on it of dead Viet Nam soldiers. He included so many details. What a memory," or "While I was watching you play today and writing about it for your portfolio I could tell you remembered all about the house we built in school back in the fall. I heard you talking into the tape recorder and telling the story from the pictures that we took and you told them all in a row, what happened first, then what happened next. How did you remember all that?"

Record answers to conversations like this at the end of the Running Record to amplify the record.

Week 33, Assignment C

REFLECTIVE JOURNAL

Respond to the following in your Reflective Journal, kept in a private file at home.

When I'm on playground duty, the hardest part is. . .

My dream playground would look like this. (Draw or sketch if you'd like.). . .

The child who seems to have the most difficulty with physical development is. . .

I think it's because. . .

Maybe I could. . .

What smudges appeared on my glass this week? (Look back at the frame of reference.)

Week 34, Assignment A

CHECKLIST ON SOCIAL DEVELOPMENT FOR ALL

Two months have passed since the last Class List Log on social development. This week, do another, and compare it to the ones done in weeks 4, 15, and 25. Take one of your Class List Log forms from Appendix D and draw six vertical lines, designating the columns left to right: unoccupied, onlooker, solitary, parallel, associative, and cooperative. This week during free play time, observe the children as they interact. See if the children have progressed from one level to another or are playing at a more sophisticated level.

What to Do with It

At the end of the day, take the Class List Log and transfer the stage you observed onto the portfolio overview sheet with your name and the date of the observation.

Share with the parents and the child, if appropriate. For example: "Today, Shaun stayed near Sergey all day. A friendship seems to be growing there," or "Kerry, I was making notes today and I saw how you talked with Jessica. I didn't know you knew so many words in sign language."

Make a note if further action is indicated.

Week 34, Assignment B

ANECDOTAL RECORDING ON SOCIAL DEVELOPMENT FOR GROUP B

Select all the children in group B. Watch for an episode that tells about this child's social development. Write it as it is happening or jot notes and write the whole episode up by the end of the day while it's fresh in your memory. Record on the left column of lined paper, capturing as many details as possible about where the episode is taking place and who is involved. The selected child is the focus, so be sure to record actions and words carefully to be descriptive. The reader should have the feeling of seeing it through your eyes.

In the right column make your comments, give reasons, indicate if this is usual or unusual behavior, and what you think made the child act in this way. Block out the names of the other children involved unless there is a reason to leave them revealed. This episode may also give a glimpse into the actions of another child. Then you can copy this Anecdotal Recording, blot out this child's name, and file it in the other child's folder with appropriate comments.

What to Do with It

Note the presence of the Anecdotal Record on the child's portfolio overview sheet under social development.

Share with the parents and the child, if appropriate. For example: "He loved playing Uno today and took turns and kept track of other people's turns. Good thinking."

Make note if further action is indicated.

Week 34, Assignment C

REFLECTIVE JOURNAL

Respond to the following in your Reflective Journal, kept in a private file at home.

I never would have thought that. . .   and. . .   would become friends. I wonder if it's because. . .

I think. . .   would have friends if he or she didn't. . .

Next year I'm going to. . .   to help facilitate friendships.

My best friend is. . .

We are friends because. . .

I am a good friend to. . .   because . . .

Week 35, Assignment A

FREQUENCY COUNT ON EMOTIONAL DEVELOPMENT FOR ALL

Early in the week, observe children in groups A and B during free choice time for 30 minutes. Look for evidence of prosocial or antisocial behaviors. Make a mark next to the name of the child in the appropriate column each time one of these occurs. On another day, repeat the observation with children in groups C and D.

What to Do with It

Compare this Frequency Count to the ones done in weeks 5, 16, and 27. Do you see differences in the totals for the class? for individual children? Do you think the prosocial curriculum activities for ten weeks made a difference? If so, write a short summary and send your findings to the authors. They would love to hear it. Share it in your school's newsletter or in a happy gram to parents.

If it did not make a difference, why not? Summarize the project and file it in the class file.

Week 35, Assignment B

INTERVIEW AND CHECKLIST ON SPEECH AND LANGUAGE FOR GROUP C

Select each of the children in group C to interview each day this week. If possible, tape record the interview as well as make written notes (literacy role model) as you speak with each child.

What to Do with It

Analyze the Interview for what it reveals about the child's knowledge, emotional state, social development, and speech and language, using the Speech and Language Checklist (Week 6, Assignment B). You may use the same sheet, but mark it with a different color pen.

Share with the parents and the child, if appropriate. For example: "Today when I was talking with Mohammed he told me about your vacation to the 'One Thousand Islands.' I'm glad I had the tape recorder on. You can listen to it some time. It is really interesting," or "Oksana, today when we were playing that game with the tape recorder I was so surprised you knew your whole name, address, and phone number. How do you remember all that?"

File the tape and notes with the checklist in each child's portfolio.

Week 35, Assignment C

REFLECTIVE JOURNAL

Respond to the following in your Reflective Journal, kept in a private file at home.

I just love to hear. . .

I really need to get started. . .

The observations this week made me think more about. . .

Week 36, Assignment A

CLASS LIST LOG ON GROUP INTERACTION FOR ALL

During group time (small group or whole group, depending on your class's age, your program schedule, and philosophy) do a Class List Log jotting down how each child functions in the group situation.

What to Do with It

On each child's overview sheet under group, make a few notes and reference it to the Class List Log done on (date). File the Class List Log in the class file.

Share with the parents or the child, if appropriate, any observation that they might like to hear about the child's group participation. For example: "Today when I was making some notes about each child's functioning in story time, I noticed Devon was intently listening to the story *When I Was Young in the Mountains*, singing and tapping his feet to the folk musician we had as a guest, and he even danced the Virginia Reel. I believe that is the most involved I've seen him this year. He's come a long way in his attention span and ability to participate in group things. That will help him a lot next year in kindergarten," or "Shequinta, today I was watching you and the other children making hand shadows with Kristy's grandpa. I noticed how well you waited until it was your turn to make your shadow. That was a *long* wait. When you got your turn you did that butterfly he had been showing everyone. The wait must have given you time to watch how to do it so when it was your turn you already knew. Some people learn a lot by watching. I guess you're one of those people. Keep those eyes open and you'll learn a lot."

Week 36, Assignment B

INTERVIEW AND CHECKLIST ON SPEECH AND LANGUAGE FOR GROUP D

Select each of the children in group D to interview each day this week. If possible, tape record the Interview as well as make written notes (literacy role model) as you speak with each child.

What to Do with It

Analyze the Interview for what it reveals about the child's knowledge, emotional state, social development, and speech and language, using the Speech and Language Checklist (Week 6, Assignment B). You may use the same sheet, but mark it with a different-colored pen.

Share your observations with the parents and the child, if appropriate.

Refile the tape and the Speech and Language Checklist in the child's portfolio. Note any concerns and follow up with a more formal screening or speech and language evaluation if concerns persist.

Week 36, Assignment C

REFLECTIVE JOURNAL

Respond to the following in your Reflective Journal, kept in a private file at home.

The highlight of the week was. . .

The "low light" this week was. . .

Here's a drawing of what I do best. . .

Here's the story. . .

Week 37, Assignment A

CHECKLIST ON COGNITIVE DEVELOPMENT FOR ALL

Using the cognitive portion of the developmental checklist your program uses, assess each child by the criteria listed there. Update the checklist and see the changes since weeks 18 and 29. As the children play, watch for signs of mathematical concepts, such as counting or one-to-one correspondence; physics, such as recognition of geometric shapes, puzzle problem solving, or changes in the physical environment.

What to Do with It

Share the observations of progress with the parents in the upcoming progress reports. Give parents specific examples of how the child is exhibiting cognitive development as she interacts with the environment.

File the checklist in the portfolio.

Week 37, Assignment B

INTERVIEW AND CHECKLIST ON SPEECH AND LANGUAGE FOR GROUP A

Select each of the children in group A to interview each day this week. If possible, tape record the Interview as well as make written notes (literacy role model) as you speak with each child.

What to Do with It

Analyze the Interview for what it reveals about the child's knowledge, emotional state, social development, and speech and languages using the Speech and Language Checklist (Week 6, Assignment B). You may use the same sheet but mark it with a different-colored pen.

Share your observations with the parents and the child, if appropriate. For example: "Audrey has an amazing memory for songs and poems and stories. She just has to hear them once and can say them right back. When you get a chance, take the tape into the parent room and spend some time listening to the conversation we had about what happened to the snowman. It's hilarious," or "Manuel, when you are at home you speak Spanish but at school you speak English. Do you know how you keep them separate?"

Refile the tape and the checklist in each child's portfolio.

Week 37, Assignment C

PROGRESS REPORT FOR GROUP A

Review all the documentation in the portfolios of the children in group A. Note each developmental area and the progress made in 37 weeks in each of the areas. List what the child has accomplished in each area. Remember: Be positive, descriptive, and personal.

Heading
Family (optional for Progress Report)
Physical
Social
Adjustment to school
Self-acceptance
Cognitive
Creativity
Closure

What to Do with It

Have a supervisor check the progress report. Make a copy to place in the portfolio and one to place in the class file. Go over the original with the parent in a parent conference if possible. Determine what is to be done with the portfolio at the conclusion of the year.

Week 37, Assignment D

REFLECTIVE JOURNAL

Respond to the following in your Reflective Journal, kept in a private file at home.

More than anything I want. . .

My teaching has changed this week the most in the area of. . .

I think it is because. . .

I was really embarrassed when. . .

This week I thought a lot about. . .

Week 38, Assignment A

RATING SCALES ON LITERACY DEVELOPMENT FOR ALL

Use the Rating Scales from Appendix D for literacy development or the literacy section of your program's developmental checklist. Rate each child's interest and abilities to read and write. Make one final entry on the Rating Scales or checklist in a different color.

What to Do with It

Use the Rating Scales as documentation to your comments in progress reports concerning literacy, reading, and writing, at whatever level the child is.

Refile the Rating Scales in the child's portfolio.

Week 38, Assignment B

INTERVIEW AND CHECKLIST ON SPEECH AND LANGUAGE FOR GROUP B

Select each of the children in group B to interview each day this week. If possible, tape record the Interview as well as make written notes (literacy role model) as you speak with each child.

What to Do with It

Analyze the Interview for what it reveals about the child's knowledge, emotional state, social development, and speech and language, using the Speech and Language Checklist (Week 6, Assignment B). You may use the same sheet, but mark it with a different-colored pen.

Share your observations with the parents and the child, if appropriate. For example: "Harriet has been using a lot of baby talk lately. I know this has been a difficult time for her while your mother is sick and you have to spend so much time caring for her. Maybe this is just her way of saying she wants to be cared for like a baby too. Are there any tasks that you could do together or caring things she could do for grandma to be a part of her care? Maybe you could talk to Mrs. Jimenez. She just went through a similar situation," or "Cassidy, I was listening to you and your friends at the snack table when you said Jimmy was the same color as the gingerbread man. You are right, he is just that shade of brown. Can you find some colors in the room that match your skin?"

Refile the tape and language checklist in each child's portfolio. Follow up on any concerns that came out of the Interview.

Week 38, Assignment C

PROGRESS REPORT FOR GROUP B

Review all the documentation in the portfolios of the children in group B. Note each developmental area and the progress made in 38 weeks in each of the areas. List what the child has accomplished in each area. Remember: Be positive, descriptive, and personal.

Heading
Family (optional for progress report)
Physical
Social
Adjustment to school

Self-acceptance
Cognitive
Creativity
Closure

What to Do with It

Have a supervisor check the progress report. Make a copy to place in the portfolio and one to place in the class file. Go over the original with the parent in a parent conference if possible. Determine what is to be done with the portfolio at the conclusion of the year.

Week 38, Assignment D

REFLECTIVE JOURNAL

Respond to the following in your Reflective Journal, kept in a private file at home.

I think my favorite creative activity this year was. . .

The reason I liked it so well was. . .

When I was in school, art. . .

I now think. . .

Next year I'd like to try more. . .

Week 39, Assignment A

CLASS LIST LOG ON SELF-IDENTITY FOR ALL

Using the Class List Log for self-identity from Appendix D, based on how well you know the child, place a rating on each child's self-identity in the areas listed on the Class List Log.

What to Do with It

Compare this to the Class List Log done in week 12. Think about each child and what is con-tributing to the child's high or low self-esteem. At this point in the year there is nothing to be done but to use this information and experience to help the next group of children in your class. Self-iden-tity is influenced directly by the feeling of compe-tence, knowledge, power, and acceptance. Vow to do all you can next year to help each child experi-ence those attributes.

File this in the class file. Since it is so subjective, it is not made a part of the child's portfolio.

Week 39, Assignment B

TIME SAMPLE ON ATTENTION SPAN FOR ALL

Use the Time Sample form from Appendix D with free choice areas down the left column. For at least one-half hour of free play time, list every five minutes where each child is in the classroom.

What to Do with It

Compare the Time Sample with those done in Weeks 7, 17, 24, and 29. Draw conclusions about each child's attention span, area of interest, closest playmates, and areas avoided. Use the Time Sample to make summaries and recommendations on the final progress reports.

File in each child's portfolio.

Week 39, Assignment C

PROGRESS REPORT FOR GROUP C

Review all the documentation in the portfolios of the children in group C. Note each develop-mental area and the progress made in 39 weeks in each of the areas. List what the child has accom-plished in each area. Remember: Be positive, descriptive, and personal.

Heading
Family (optional for progress report)
Physical
Social
Adjustment to school

Self-acceptance
Cognitive
Creativity
Closure

What to Do with It

Have a supervisor check the progress report. Make a copy to place in the portfolio and one to place in the class file. Go over the original with the parent in a parent conference if possible. Determine what is to be done with the portfolio at the conclusion of the year.

Week 39, Assignment D

REFLECTIVE JOURNAL

Respond to the following in your Reflective Journal, kept in a private file at home.

I won't send it, but I'd like to write a letter to _____'s

parents and tell them. . .

(If you wish, actually write the letter then tear it up in little

pieces.)

I just don't understand why. . .

Maybe it's because. . .

or it could be. . .

I loved my job this week when. . .

I hated my job this week when. . .

Week 40, Assignment A

WORK SAMPLES ON CREATIVITY FOR ALL

This week, try to collect a final sample of work from every child. Make comments on the Work Samples Checklist or the creative portion of your program's checklist.

Note on the portfolio overview sheet that work is present with a few notes, the date, and your name.

What to Do with It

On the Work Sample Checklist form note the significance of the work and what it demonstrates about the change in the child's development since week 10.

Share the observation with the parents or the child, if appropriate. For example: "Here is the drawing Rana did in the fall and here is how she is drawing now. See the details she's now including in her self-portrait: eyelashes, earrings, and pupils in the eyes. We placed a mirror on the drawing table and encouraged the children to look closely at themselves as they drew. It shows not only an advance in physical drawing skills but cognitive skills as well. A scrapbook of her drawings from her first scribbles is a wonderful treasure as she gets older. I'm going to put that suggestion in the newsletter next month if it's okay with you that I give you credit for the idea," or "Uri, look at this. This is the drawing you did on the cover of your portfolio where I keep all my notes. And this is the one you did this week. Look how different they are. You said when you were drawing it that, 'Now I know how to draw.' Why do you think that is? How did you learn it?"

File in the child's portfolio.

Week 40, Assignment B

PROGRESS REPORT FOR GROUP D

Review all the documentation in the portfolios of the children in group D. Note each developmental area and the progress made in 40 weeks in each of the areas. List what the child has accomplished in each area. Remember: Be positive, descriptive, and personal.

Heading
Family (optional for progress report)
Physical
Social
Adjustment to school
Self-acceptance
Cognitive
Creativity
Closure

What to Do with It

Have your supervisor check the progress reports. Make a copy to place in the portfolio and one to place in the class file. Go over the original with the parent in a parent conference if possible. Determine what is to be done with the portfolio at the conclusion of the year.

Week 40, Assignment C

REFLECTIVE JOURNAL

Respond to the following in your Reflective Journal, kept in a private file at home.

In this last Reflective Journal entry for these assignments, I would just like to say. . .

My favorite story from this year is. . .

I will always remember. . .   because. . .

My personal progress report would read. . .

Draw a map here of the journey you have taken this year, the mountaintops and the valleys. On the back of the paper, make a dotted line for your map of the future, setting your goals to achieve, watching for pitfalls and barriers, building bridges and hurdling high to reach your goals.

Week 40, Assignment D

FINAL REPORTS

A final report is an excellent way to look back over the year. Reflect on the accomplishments, the difficulties, and their resolutions. Ponder the still unanswered questions and projections for the future. Begin planning for next year now while ideas and resolutions are fresh in your mind. An outline is suggested here to help organize your thoughts:

- When I began the year...
- The year's highest accomplishments were...
- The children who made the greatest gains were...
- The disappointments were...
- If I knew then what I know now I would have...
- Next year I want to remember to...

What to Do with It

When the year comes to a close (that is at different times for everyone), distribute files as program policy dictates:

Portfolios—to parents, next teacher, or next program

Class File—to teacher's file, director or administrator, program file

Refective Journal—teacher's private property to keep or destroy

Summary of Assignments by Developmental Areas

The *Week by Week* plan is designed to

- use a variety of recording methods
- revisit developmental areas over the course of a 40-week school year
- equally focus on individual children who have been arbitrarily assigned to a group A, B, C, or D. (See the note preceding the assignments in Chapter 2.)

The pages that follow classify the assignments by developmental area and children's groups to demonstrate the equality of the plan.

The abbreviations that are used are

CL	Class List Log
AR	Anecdotal Recording
CK	Checklist
RR	Running Record
FC	Frequency Count
I	Interview
TS	Time Sample
WS	Work Sample
M	Media
PR	Progress Report

The number following the letters indicates the week of the assignment. The square around the recording indicates individual focused observations.

	ARRIVALS AND DEPARTURES ADJUSTMENT	SELF-CARE	PHYSICAL DEVELOPMENT	SOCIAL DEVELOPMENT	EMOTIONAL DEVELOPMENT	SPEECH AND LANGUAGE	MEMORY AND ATTENTION SPAN	COGNITIVE/ MATH AND SCIENCE
	CHAPTER 1	CHAPTER 2	CHAPTER 3	CHAPTER 4	CHAPTER 5	CHAPTER 6	CHAPTER 7	CHAPTER 8
GROUP A	CL1	AR2	CK3	CL4	FC5	1, CK6	TS7	CK8
	CL22	CL2	CK14	CL15	FC16	CL6	TS17	CK18
	CL28	CL26	CK33	CK25	FC27	CK17	TS24	CK29
	RR33			CK34	AR27	1, CK21	TS29	CK37
					FC35	1, CK37	TS39	
GROUP B	CL1	CL2	CK3	CL4	FC5	CL6	TS7	CK8
	CL22	CL26	AR3	CL15	FC16	1, CK7	TS17	CK18
	CL28		CK14	CK25	RR16	CK17	TS24	CK29
			CK33	CK34	FC27	1, CK22	TS29	CK37
				AR34	FC35	1, CK38	TS39	
GROUP C	CL1	CL2	CK3	RR4	FC5	CL6	TS7	CK8
	RR18	CL26	CK14	CL4	FC16	1, CK8	TS17	CK18
	CL22		CK33	CL15	FC27	CK17	TS24	CK29
	CL28			CK25	AR31	1, CK23	TS29	CK37
				CK34	FC35	1, CK35	TS39	
GROUP D	CL1	CL2	CK3	CL4	FC5	CL6	TS7	CK8
	CL22	CL26	CK14	CL15	AR5	1, CK9	TS17	CK18
	RR26		CK33	CK25	FC16	CK17	TS24	CK29
	CL28			CK34	FC27	1, CK24	TS29	CK37
					FC35	1, CK36	TS39	

	LITERACY	CREATIVE ARTS	CREATIVE DR. PLAY BLOCKS	SELF-IDENTITY	GROUP INTERACTIONS	INTERACTIONS WITH ADULTS	PROGRESS REPORTS
	CHAPTER 9	CHAPTER 10	CHAPTER 11	CHAPTER 12	CHAPTER 13	CHAPTER 14	1
GROUP A	RS9 RS19 WS19 RS30 WS30 RS38	WS1 WS10 AR10 WS20 WS31 WS40	M11 M21	CL12 RR15 CL39	CL13 CL23 CL36	CL14 CL32	PR10 PR21 PR37
GROUP B	RS9 RS19 WS19 AR28 RS30 RS38	WS1 WS10 WS20 WS31 WS40	M11 RR11 M21	CL12 CL39	CL13 CL23 CL36	CL14 CL32	PR11 PR22 PR38
GROUP C	RS9 RS19 WS19 RS30 WS30 RS38	WS1 WS10 WS20 AR25 WS31 WS40	M11 M21	CL12 AR12 CL39	CL13 CL23 CL36	CL14 CL32	PR12 PR23 PR39
GROUP D	RS9 RS19 WS19 RS30 WS30 RS38	WS1 WS10 WS20 AR20 WS31 WS40	M11 M21	CL12 AR32 CL39	CL13 AR13 CL23 CL36	CL14 CL32	PR13 (PR14*) PR24 PR40

Observation Forms

CLASS LIST LOG   Date _____

Observing _____   Recorder _____

_____

_____

_____

_____

_____

_____

_____

_____

_____

_____

_____

_____

_____

CLASS LIST LOG   Date _____

Observing _____   Recorder _____

_____

_____

_____

_____

_____

_____

_____

_____

_____

_____

_____

_____

_____

PORTFOLIO OVERVIEW SHEET

NAME _____   BIRTH DATE _____

SEPARATIONS AND ADJUSTMENT

Documentation	Recorder	Date

SELF-CARE

Documentation	Recorder	Date

PHYSICAL DEVELOPMENT

Documentation	Recorder	Date

SOCIAL DEVELOPMENT

Documentation	Recorder	Date

EMOTIONAL DEVELOPMENT

Documentation	Recorder	Date

SPEECH AND LANGUAGE

Documentation	Recorder	Date

MEMORY AND ATTENTION SPAN

Documentation	Recorder	Date

COGNITIVE DEVELOPMENT

Documentation	Recorder	Date

LITERACY DEVELOPMENT

Documentation	Recorder	Date

CREATIVITY— ART AND BLOCKS

Documentation	Recorder	Date

CREATIVE—DRAMATIC PLAY

Documentation	Recorder	Date

SELF-IDENTITY

Documentation	Recorder	Date

GROUP INTERACTIONS

Documentation	Recorder	Date

INTERACTIONS WITH ADULTS

Documentation	Recorder	Date

OTHER DOCUMENTATION

PHYSICAL DEVELOPMENT CHECKLIST
(The Frost-Wortham Developmental Checklist)
Gross and Fine Motor

_____ Colored Pen   Date _____

_____ Colored Pen   Date _____

_____ Colored Pen   Date _____

Motor Development: Preschool (Gross Movement)

Level III (approx. age 3)	Introduced	Progress	Mastery
1. Catches a ball with both hands against the chest	❏	❏	❏
2. Rides a tricycle	❏	❏	❏
3. Hops on both feet several times without assistance	❏	❏	❏
4. Throws a ball five feet with accuracy	❏	❏	❏
5. Climbs up a slide and comes down	❏	❏	❏
6. Climbs by alternating feet and holding on to a handrail	❏	❏	❏
7. Stands on one foot and balances briefly	❏	❏	❏
8. Pushes a loaded wheelbarrow	❏	❏	❏
9. Runs freely with little stumbling or falling	❏	❏	❏
10. Builds a tower with nine or ten blocks	❏	❏	❏

Level IV (approx. age 4)	Introduced	Progress	Mastery
1. Balances on one foot	❏	❏	❏
2. Walks a straight line forward and backward	❏	❏	❏
3. Walks a balance beam	❏	❏	❏
4. Climbs steps with alternate feet without support	❏	❏	❏
5. Climbs on a jungle gym	❏	❏	❏
6. Skips haltingly	❏	❏	❏
7. Throws, catches, and bounces a large ball	❏	❏	❏
8. Stacks blocks vertically and horizontally	❏	❏	❏
9. Creates recognizable block structures	❏	❏	❏
10. Rides a tricycle with speed and skill	❏	❏	❏

Level V (approx. age 5)	Introduced	Progress	Mastery
1. Catches and throws a small ball	❏	❏	❏
2. Bounces and catches a small ball	❏	❏	❏
3. Skips on either foot	❏	❏	❏
4. Skips rope	❏	❏	❏
5. Hops on one foot	❏	❏	❏
6. Creates Tinkertoy and block structures	❏	❏	❏
7. Hammers and saws with some skill	❏	❏	❏
8. Walks a balance beam forward and backward	❏	❏	❏
9. Descends stairs by alternating feet			

CONTINUED

PHYSICAL DEVELOPMENT CHECKLIST (continued)

Motor Development: Preschool (Fine Movement)

Level III (approx. age 3)	Introduced	Progress	Mastery
1. Places small pegs in pegboards	❑	❑	❑
2. Holds a paintbrush or pencil with the whole hand	❑	❑	❑
3. Eats with a spoon	❑	❑	❑
4. Buttons large buttons on his or her own clothes	❑	❑	❑
5. Puts on coat unassisted	❑	❑	❑
6. Strings bead with ease	❑	❑	❑
7. Hammers a pound toy with accuracy	❑	❑	❑
8. Works a three- or four-piece puzzle	❑	❑	❑

Level IV (approx. age 4)	Introduced	Progress	Mastery
1. Pounds and rolls clay	❑	❑	❑
2. Puts together a five-piece puzzle	❑	❑	❑
3. Forms a pegboard design	❑	❑	❑
4. Cuts with scissors haltingly and pastes	❑	❑	❑
5. Eats with a fork correctly	❑	❑	❑
6. Holds a cup with one hand	❑	❑	❑
7. Puts a coat on a hanger or hook	❑	❑	❑
8. Manipulates large crayons and brushes	❑	❑	❑
9. Buttons and zips zippers haltingly			

Level V (approx. age 5)	Introduced	Progress	Mastery
1. Cuts and pastes creative designs	❑	❑	❑
2. Forms a variety of pegboard designs	❑	❑	❑
3. Buttons buttons, zips zippers, and ties shoes	❑	❑	❑
4. Creates recognizable objects with clay	❑	❑	❑
5. Uses the toilet independently	❑	❑	❑
6. Eats independently with a knife and fork	❑	❑	❑
7. Dresses and undresses independently	❑	❑	❑
8. Holds and manipulates pencils, crayons, and brushes of various sizes	❑	❑	❑
9. Combs and brushes hair	❑	❑	❑
10. Works a twelve-piece puzzle	❑	❑	❑

FREQUENCY COUNT

Date _____ Recorder _____

Make a tally mark in the column next to the child's name each time you observe a behavior which you would classify as prosocial or antisocial.

CHILD'S NAME	PROSOCIAL Helping, sharing, hugging, calling another child by a kind name	ANTISOCIAL Hurting, hoarding, bad-name calling, rejecting another child
TOTALS		

SPEECH AND LANGUAGE CHECKLIST

Child _____ Date _____
_____

Sounds: Underline the ones that you hear. Circle if there is difficulty.
_____

p, w, h, m, n, (usually by 3 years)

b, k, g, d, y (usually by 4 years)

f, ng, t, r, l (usually by 6 years)

ch, sh, j, s, z, v, th, zh, br, tr (clear by 7-8 years)

_____

Language: Underline the ones that are present. Circle it there seems to be difficulty.
_____

Correct word order (by 2½)

Uses pronouns (by 2 ½)

Gives name (by 3)

Uses plurals, some prepositions (by 3)

Tells day's schedule in sequence (by 4)

Can tell an imaginative story about a picture (by 4)

Speaks in adultlike sentences (by 4)

_____

Note Language Behaviors:
_____

Turn taking–displays understanding of conversational shift

Communication signals

　　　eye contact

　　　facial expression

　　　gestures

　　　tone of voice

_____

Meaning: What did the conversation tell you about the child? _____
_____
_____
_____
_____
_____
_____
_____
_____

(Adapted from Machado, J. M. [1990] and Breyen & Gallagher [1983])

TIME SAMPLE

Class _____ Date _____ Recorder _____

TIMES (at 5-minute intervals)

LEARNING CENTERS

MATH AND SCIENCE CHECKLIST

Name _____ Birth Date _____

_____

Dates of Observations _____

_____ _____ _____   Can sort objects by color

_____ _____ _____   Can name colors: red, blue, yellow, green, orange, purple, white, black, brown

_____ _____ _____   Can name positions: first, middle, last

_____ _____ _____   Can sort objects by size: smallest, medium, largest

_____ _____ _____   Can sort objects by shape: circle, square, triangle, rectangle

_____ _____ _____   Can name shapes: circle, square, triangle, rectangle

_____ _____ _____   Can count by rote to _____ .

_____ _____ _____   Can count _____ objects accurately: 2, 5, 7, 10, more

_____ _____ _____   Can name number before and after: 3, 8, 11

_____ _____ _____   Can mentally subtract (Put out 5 objects. If I took one, how many would be left?)

_____ _____ _____   Can predict pattern ABABAB (Line up blocks, red, blue, red, blue, red, blue: Which one goes next?)

_____ _____ _____   Can locate: ear, foot, elbow, knee, forehead, wrist

_____ _____ _____   Can name when pointed to: ear, foot, elbow, knee, forehead, wrist

_____ _____ _____   Can repeat two, three, four digits (Say four. "Four." Say two, nine. "Two, nine." Say six, one, eight. "Six, one, eight.")

_____ _____ _____   Where does milk come from? cow, store, carton, other

_____ _____ _____   What's in the sky at night? moon, stars, clouds, other

LITERACY RATING SCALE

Child's Name _____

INTEREST IN BOOKS

No interest, avoids	Only if adult-initiated	Brings books to adult to read	Looks at books as self-initiated activity

LISTENING TO BOOKS

Wiggly, no attention	Intermittent attention	Listens in one-on-one situation	Listens as part of a group, tuning out distractions

INVOLVEMENT WITH BOOKS BEING READ

Little or no response	Emotional response, laugh, frown	Comments, asks questions	Joins in during reading

HANDLING BOOKS

No voluntary touching	Rough handling	Exploratory manipulation	Books as favorite toys

CONCEPT OF BOOK FORMAT

No idea of front/back, up/down	Holds book right side up but skips pages	Demonstrates front/back concept	Looks at pages left to right

CONCEPT OF STORY BOOK

Labels pictures	Retells story in sequence from pictures	Accurately repeats some story lines	Points to print while accurately retelling from pictures

PRINT IN THE ENVIRONMENT

Notices signs, labels	Asks, "What's that say?"	Reads signs, labels out of context	"Writes" signs to label constructions

BEGINNING READING

Recognizes own name	Recognizes letters in name in other words	Reads simple words	Sounds out letters in unfamiliar words

CONTINUED

LITERACY RATING SCALE (continued)

MANIPULATION OF WRITING TOOLS

Fist hold	High hold on pencil	Adult grip, little control	Adult grip, good control

COMMUNICATION THROUGH WRITING

Communicates ideas through drawing	Will dictate on request	Initiates dictation	Draws and writes words

BEGINNING WRITING

Scribbles, no reference to writing	Named scribbles "Says my name"	Single letters, random	Writes name

WRITING IN PLAY

No reference to writing	Asks for signs, words to be written	Asks for adult to spell words	Sounds out words and writes on own

WORK SAMPLES CHECKLIST

Child's Name_____ Dates _____

_____

COMMENTS

Separation
❑ Separates from adult to do creative work alone
❑ Works independently without requiring adult presence or direction

Self-Care
❑ Independently selects materials
❑ Makes preparations to work (Example: Puts on a smock)
❑ Uses materials independently
❑ Cleans up spills, messes
❑ Writes name on work
❑ Places finished product in proper place
❑ Washes and dries hands if necessary
❑ Replaces materials to storage place

Physical Development
❑ Controls whole body movement during work
❑ Controls small muscles to hold tool
❑ Controls tool to form desired product
❑ Draws, prints, paints, pastes
❑ Squeezes glue bottle
❑ Picks up collage materials
❑ Manipulates clay or Play Doh
❑ Cuts with scissors
❑ Controls body to stay within the space (on the paper, building on a rug, clay on table)

Social Skills
❑ Represents important people in life and work
❑ Desires and can work near other children
❑ Shares materials and supplies
❑ Engages in positive commentary on other children's work
❑ Works cooperatively on a joint project

Emotional Development
❑ Uses art work to express emotions of happiness, anger, fear
❑ Verbalizes feelings about work
❑ Enjoys manipulation and creation
❑ Controls emotions of frustration when work meets difficulties
❑ Uses the media as a stress release, pounding clay, tearing paper, painting

Speech and Language Development
❑ Names scribbles, buildings, creations
❑ Talks about work using vocabulary connected with art materials and design
❑ Uses language to describe process, intent, and satisfaction with product
❑ Vocabulary reflects knowledge of shapes (circle, square, triangle, rectangle, lines)

CONTINUED

WORK SAMPLES CHECKLIST (continued)

COMMENTS

Memory and Attention Span
❑ Includes details in art from memories of experiences
❑ Focuses attention on project to produce a finished work
❑ Tunes out distractions of simultaneous play, talk, and work
❑ Gives attention and makes connections between designs, colors, patterns in environment, and own work

Math and Science
❑ Includes numerals and quantity in work
❑ Shows one-to-one correspondence in work designs
❑ Shows perceptual awareness of color, space, form
❑ Explores cause and effect and experimentation with variables in art media
   (Example: Sees differences in paint when water and sand are added)
❑ Observes similarities and differences, forming theories and testing them out by manipulating the medium
❑ Working with clay or liquid—displays knowledge of the concept of conservation
   (volume stays the same even though form changes—ball flattened is the same amount)

Literacy
❑ Includes alphabet letters in art work
❑ Recognizes the difference between drawing and writing
❑ Uses creative products as symbols of ideas
❑ Work illustrates or connects with stories
❑ Gives attention to art in story books and knows the difference between text and illustrations

Creativity
❑ Uses materials in a novel way, displaying flexibility in seeing new possibilities in materials
❑ Explores all facets of the medium
❑ Draws from experiences to create representations
❑ Incorporates creativity into other areas of play, constructing with blocks, drawing and constructing in
   dramatic play, forming designs in sand and other medium
❑ Demonstrates creativity in secondary awareness (seeing, hearing, touching, smelling, tasting)

Self-Identity
❑ Displays risk-free attitude in work
❑ Reveals self in content of work
❑ Work shows a sense of identity and individuality
❑ Expresses satisfaction in art work, confident self-esteem
❑ Portrays self, family, world in creative work
❑ Work demonstrates child's sex-role identification
❑ Work shows child moving from egocentric view of self to an awareness of self as part of larger society
❑ Indicates favorite art medium (singular), media (plural)

Group Time Behaviors
❑ Participates in cooperative and collaborative work

Interaction with Adults
❑ Involves adults in art work as (facilitator, participator, director)

SELF-ESTEEM CLASS LIST LOG

Date _____   Recorder _____

Consider each child's self-esteem in each of the categories. Write an *H* for high or an *L* for low.
For teacher's use only.

Child's Name	Unafraid of a new situation	Independent, needs minimal help	Comfortable with physical activities, coordinated	Makes friends easily	Seems to be happy most of the time	Talks freely	Does not rely on others for directions	Experiments with new materials	Creative, imaginative, has ideas of his own	Participates in classroom group activities	Cooperative and largely controlled	Trusts teacher even though they are strangers

SETTING OBSERVATION

Name of Center _____   Date of Visit _____

Address _____

_____

Phone _____

Type of Program: ❑ Day Care   ❑ Nursery School   ❑ Kindergarten

Age of children in classroom described below: _____

Number present: _____

1. Describe the building (location, type of building, other uses). _____

_____

_____

_____

2. Describe the entry to the building (signs, decorations, security). _____

_____

_____

_____

3. Classroom
    Draw a floor plan in the space below, indicating room arrangement, furniture, shelves, learning centers, carpeted areas, sink, doorways, windows, and so on. Be as detailed and close to scale as possible.

CONTINUED

SETTING OBSERVATION (continued)

4. List and describe other areas used by class (gym, kitchen bathrooms). _____
   _____
   _____
   _____

5. At the conclusion of visiting this setting, write a paragraph about the "feeling" of this center. What attitudes, values, friendliness, safety, or enrichment did you experience while there? How do you think this environment affects the children, their parents, and the staff who work there?

   _____
   _____
   _____
   _____
   _____
   _____
   _____
   _____
   _____

6. Complete the following chart on learning centers. Make detailed lists of the following.

Learning Center	Equipment and Furnishings	Materials

PROGRESS AT A GLANCE   Child's Name _____

PERIOD 1:   Date_____   Recorder _____

Strengths _____

Areas still developing _____

_____

Educational plan to facilitate development _____

_____

_____

PERIOD 2:   Date_____   Recorder _____

Strengths _____

Areas still developing _____

_____

Educational plan to facilitate development _____

_____

_____

PERIOD 3:   Date_____   Recorder _____

Strengths _____

Areas still developing _____

_____

Educational plan to facilitate development _____

_____

_____

PERIOD 4:   Date_____   Recorder _____

Strengths _____

Areas still developing _____

_____

Educational plan to facilitate development _____

_____

_____

Glossary..

The number following each definition refers to the chapter in which the term is discussed first.

acceptance—the feeling of being loved and appreciated, contributes to self-esteem (12)

accommodation—takes in new information, balances with previous knowledge, and adjusts response (7)

accreditation—voluntary submission to a standard through a review process, usually consisting of a self-study and verification (13)

action research—informal collection of information about a child or children, nonstandardized (6)

active listening— technique for clarifying the message and the feelings(14)

ADD, ADHD—attention deficit disorders, professionally diagnosed impairments that affect attention span and cause impulsivity and distractibility (7)

adjustment—ability of a child to socially and emotionally adapt (13)

aggression—actions that injure people, things, or emotions (5)

anecdotal recording—factual narrative of an incident (2)

animism—Preoperational child believes natural world is ruled by willful intent like humans (7)

articulation—the sounds of speech (6)

artificialism—Preoperational child believes that humans create and influence nature (7)

assessment—process of observing, recording, and documenting a child's actions, skills, and behaviors (I)

assimilation—information received that adjusts previously related information (7)

association—information received that matches previously related information (7)

associative play—play that is similar, in the same theme but still with each player playing individually (4)

attachment—the emotional bond that infants show to a person (usually the mother) with whom they have had a stable, trusting relationship (1)

audio recorder—device that makes a taped reproduction of sound (11)

autonomy—the process of governing oneself (2)

bias—preconceived attitudes that may affect objectivity, either positively or negatively (3)

case study (child study)— a comprehensive written overview of the child; it may be documented by written evidence and the child's work (14)

centration—focus of attention on one attribute, ignoring other variables (7)

cephalocaudal—sequence of the development of muscle control from head to toe (3)

checklist—a method of documenting the presence or absence of a skill or behavior in a developmental sequence (3)

Class List Log—method of gathering a specific piece of information on every child in the group (1)

classification—matching or grouping similar data (7)

closed method—the recorder makes a judgment from observation and records it with a check, slash, few words. Raw data is not available for the reader (3)

closed question—one expected answer, like a test (6)

cognitive—knowing, thinking, reasoning, and remembering (8)

competence—the feeling of capability, independence, and autonomy, contributes to self-esteem (12)

Concrete Operational Stage—period of development (seven to eleven years old), using logic and reasoning; mental actions are still related to "concrete" objects (7)

conservation—understanding that volume or measurability of objects remains the same if nothing is added or subtracted, but the form is changed (7)

constructive play—manipulating objects, such as blocks, to create a physical product (4)

contextualized literacy—ability to read words when other clues are present, such as cereal names, restaurants, and traffic signs (9)

convergent thinking—the ability to arrive at a single answer, more difficult for young children with still-developing classifying, listening, and attending skills (10)

cooperative play—play where players are in the same theme and working toward a common goal (4)

coping mechanism—strategy for overcoming uncomfortable circumstances (1)

coping skills—strategies to overcome emotional traumas (5)

core emotions—basic emotions present at birth from which other emotions evolve (5)

development—change that takes place in a predictable sequence, from simple to complex, but at a different pace for individual people (2)

diagnostic interview—conversations designed to yield developmental information about a child (6)

diary—journal; a style of recounting past events including feelings these events arouse (1)

disclosure—a statement that indicates the speaker has been a victim of abuse or maltreatment (12)

disequilibrium—cognitive conflict when new information does not associate or match previous data (7)

displacement—turning angry feelings away from the source of the anger (5)

divergent thinking—ability to think of a wide range of possibilities, associated with creativity and giftedness (10)

dramatic play—symbolic play, pretend (4)

dyslexia— an impairment of the ability to read (9)

Ebonics—nonstandard English spoken by some (6)

egocentric—the cognitive stage in which the child is not able to take another's point of view (4)

egocentrism—preoperational child's inability to understand that others do not share his or her perspective (7)

emergent literacy—continuous process of becoming a reader and writer (9)

emotional maltreatment—psychological damage from blaming, belittling, or rejecting a child (12)

evaluation—comparison of information gathered against a standard or set of criteria (I)

experiments—repetition of a process to test a theory (8)

expressive language—messages that are communicated through words and gestures (6)

failure to thrive—developmental delays caused by physical or emotional factors (5)

frame of reference—individual point of view influenced by many factors (3)

frequency count—recording method to measure how often a specified event occurs (5)

functional play—manipulation of objects with no particular goal other than to examine and practice repetitive motions (4)

games with rules—play where players take turns and act according to a mutually understood standard (4)

gender—general term for the biological differences in the two sexes, male and female (12)

good-bye rituals—established routines to help the child with separation (1)

growth—quantitative change that can be measured in numbers (3)

holographic—one-word sentences that have meaning (6)

inference—conclusion; judgment; explanation (2)

informal interview—spontaneous conversations between adult and child that yield information (6)

inter-rater reliability—two or more raters use the same instrument on the same child to control bias (9)

invented spelling—phonetic spelling with a letter for each sound (9)

invulnerable child—child who escapes from childhood psychological trauma without harm (5)

language—the meaning of the words and gestures that are communicated (6)

large muscle (gross motor)—muscles used in moving the body from one place to another (3)

learning disabilities—an interference with the ability to process written communication (9)

least restrictive environment—legal term referring to the educational placement of exceptional children in regular settings to the maximum extent possible (3)

liberation teaching—theory that the teacher does not give up on any child by seeking to meet the child's needs (14)

license requirements—required standards, usually set by the individual states (13)

logico-mathematical knowledge—understanding principles of the nature of matter by reasoning rather than intuition or appearances (7)

mandala—universal symbol combining circle and intersecting lines (10)

mandated reporters—those individuals who by law must report suspicions of child abuse to specified agencies (12)

matching—recognizing the similarities of an attribute of an object (7)

medium (singular), **media** (plural)—art material(s) (10)

mixed-age groups—also known as heterogeneous, multi-age, vertical, ungraded, nongraded, and family grouping; groups of children not separated by chronological age (13)

morality—characteristic of making choices based on a set of standards set by social group (12)

morphemes—smallest unit of language, words (6)

multiple intelligences—individual ways of processing information (7)

neglect—the withholding of basic survival needs: food, water, shelter, clothing, medical care; constitutes maltreatment (12)

nonrepresentational—young child's drawing a symbol of mental image; not able to "represent" a recognizable symbol; difficult to draw what they are thinking (10)

norm—standard against which others are measured (7)

object permanence—the cognitive understanding that objects and persons continue to exist even out of sight (4)

objective—detached, impersonal, unprejudiced, data-only recordings (1)

observing—watching children to know more about their development (I)

one-to-one correspondence—ability to count objects accurately by assigning one number to each object (7)

onlooker play—watch others play; may talk or ask questions (4)

open method—recording method that preserves the raw data; only records actions and words so separate conclusions can be drawn (2)

open question—no single, correct answers, creative answers (6)

ordinal numbers—indicating the order or succession such as first, second, or third (8)

overgeneralizations—early stage in grammar construction where child adds "s" to all words for plural and "ed" to all words for past tense. (6)

parallel play—play that is near, maybe even doing the same actions or using the same equipment or toys but not interacting (4)

phonemes—basic unit of sound in spoken language (6)

physical abuse—any nonaccidental physical injury caused by the child's caretaker (12)

physical knowledge—knowledge about the general properties of the physical world: gravity, motion, and nature (7)

portfolio—a systematic collection of documentation about the child's development (I)

power—the ability to control one's actions and destiny, rather than depending on outside agents (12)

precocity—exceptional early development in cognitive or creative ability (10)

preschematic—stage in drawing development before the child has attained the motoric and cognitive abilities to draw recognizable symbols (10)

program evaluation—the process of examining all the components of a program to measure effectiveness and quality (13)

progress report—a periodic written overview of short-term goals the child has achieved(14)

proximodistal—development of muscle control from center of body to extremities (3)

quality points—milestones or measurement intervals on a rating scale (9)

rating scale—measuring a specific behavior, skill, or attribute by choosing from three or more descriptors (9)

receptive language—that which is heard, taken in (6)

record—documentation of an event, may be written, audio or video recorded, photographed (6)

recording—a system or method of writing down what has been observed (I)

reflection—thoughtful consideration of past events for analysis (1)

reflective journal—a private, written record in which to express feelings; not a part of child's record, but property of the writer (1)

reflex—automatic muscular movement (3)

reflexes—muscle reactions to stimuli, not controlled by intent (4)

reliability—quality of tests that will produce a similar score by the same individual on the same test (7)

reversibility—Concrete Operational child understands that any change can be mentally reversed, for example, think of an ice cube as water (7)

rote counting—counting by memory, may be inaccurate or out of sequence (7)

Running Records—detailed accounts of a segment of time focused and recording all behaviors and quotes during that time (4)

schema—symbol in art that is repeated over and over representing a real object (10)

schematic—stage in which symbolic representations go through modifications as child develops cognitively (10)

screening—a test given to a broad population to indicate possibilities that are evaluated further (7)

scribbling—experiments with drawing media, can be uncontrolled or controlled (doodling) (10)

selective method—the recording instrument dictates what is to be observed (9)

self-care—ability to eat, toilet, dress, keep clean and keep safe (2)

self-concept—the qualities one attributes to one's self, self-identity (12)

self-esteem—the valuing of that knowledge based on self and social comparisons (12)

Sensorimotor Stage—stage from birth to age two when the child "takes in" information mainly by sensory means and gains differentiation of self from the environment (7)

separation anxiety—distress when a parent leaves an infant's presence, beginning at 8 or 9 months and usually disappearing at about 24 months (1)

seriation—the ability to order objects by some standard rule, height, weight, shade, or tone (7)

sexrole (or genter) identity—socialized preference of behavior identified with one gender or the other (12)

sexual abuse—sexually explicit conduct with a minor (12)

stranger anxiety—distress when approached by an unfamiliar person, beginning at 7 to 9 months and ending around one year

small muscle (fine motor)—muscles that control hands and fingers (3)

social conventional knowledge—information gathered from influential adults about general rules of conduct acceptable to that group (7)

socialized—behavior learned to adapt to the expectations of the social group (12)

sociodramatic play—fantasy play episode with others involved (11)

solitary play—play that is focused on objects or movements, not involved with others (4)

speech—the sounds produced to make words, phonemes (6)

standardized tests—scores are measured against the norm group that has taken the test (7)

stranger anxiety—distress when approached by an unfamiliar person, beginning at 7 to 9 months and ending around one year (1)

structured interview—planned conversations to find out specific information about a child (6)

subjective—influenced by state of mind, point of view, inferential, interpreting the meaning, or cause of an event (1)

syntax—order of words in a sentence that give them meaning; grammar (6)

tadpole man—beginning drawings of humans with lines protruding from circles (10)

teacher's stories—the relating of classroom experiences to child development or professional practice principles; may be related orally or in written form (14)

telegraphic—few-word sentences that have meaning (6)

time sample—method of recording where children are by choice at a certain time, measuring attention span and interests (7)

transitions—period between activities, time periods, or programs; may be problematic without planning (13)

unconditional positive regard—feelings a teacher should have for a student (14)

unfounded—child abuse reports that upon investigation lack evidence for criminal or civil charges (12)

unoccupied play—not interested in play, wanders around room (4)

valid—describes quality of a test that measures what it proposes to measure (7)

video recorder—device that makes a taped reproduction of image and sound (11)

zone of proximal development—behavioral levels that can be approximated with assistance (5)

Index ....